THE 50s THE STORY OF A DECADE

EVERY HOUR
PEOPLE
BUY AT
BON
TWO TROU
BOND
MAXWELL

THE 50s
THE STORY OF A DECADE

THE NEW YORKER

Edited by Henry Finder
Introduction by David Remnick

RANDOM HOUSE
NEW YORK

Published in the United States by Random House, an imprint and division of Random House LLC, a Penguin Random House Company, New York.

Random House and the House colophon are registered trademarks of Penguin Random House LLC.

All pieces in this collection were originally published in *The New Yorker.*

The publication dates are given at the beginning or end of each piece.

LIBRARY OF CONGRESS CATALOGING-IN-PUBLICATION DATA
The 50s: the story of a decade / The New Yorker; edited by Henry Finder;
introduction by David Remnick.
pages cm
ISBN 978-0-679-64481-1
eBook ISBN 978-0-679-64482-8
1. United States—Civilization—1945– 2. Nineteen fifties. I. Finder, Henry, editor. II. New Yorker (New York, N.Y.: 1925) III. Title: Fifties.
E169.12.A187 2015
973.92—dc23 2015030067

Printed in the United States of America on acid-free paper

randomhousebooks.com

246897531

FIRST EDITION

Book design by Simon M. Sullivan

CONTENTS

PART THREE · SHIFTING GROUNDS

PART FOUR · FAR-FLUNG

PART FIVE · TAKES

CHARACTERS

COMPUTERS

CURIOUS DEVELOPMENTS

PART SIX · THE CRITICS

A Note by Adam Gopnik 453

BOOKS

THE CURRENT CINEMA

THE THEATRE

TELEVISION

ART & ARCHITECTURE

MUSIC

PART SEVEN · POETRY

PART EIGHT · FICTION

INTRODUCTION

THE NEW YORKER IN THE FIFTIES

David Remnick

JUST THE OTHER day, feeling a ripple of melancholy after cleaning out desk drawers and stacking books into orange moving crates, I wandered into the office next to mine. After ninety years in a micropocket of midtown bordered by Times Square and Bryant Park, *The New Yorker* was heading to new quarters, at the southern tip of Manhattan.

My colleague Pamela Maffei McCarthy greeted me at her door and, with a sly smile, pressed on me four fat folders. "You're going to want to look at these," she said.

As deputy editor, Pam may have accumulated more files than anyone else in our offices, so I suspected that she was attempting a wily offloading maneuver, sticking me with a papery hillock of old expense reports. No backsies! But, after I took the files to my desk and started to sort through the delicate onionskin pages, I realized that this was treasure—hundreds of editing memos written by Harold Ross, who founded *The New Yorker,* in 1925, and ran it for a generation. The memos were dated 1950 and 1951, his last two years alive.

Ross was suffering from lung cancer and other painful maladies in those final years, but his eccentric, unstoppable obsessiveness, his unembarrassed habit of questioning every matter of grammar, usage, and fact, no matter how niggling, seemed undiminished. Encountering "Bird of Passage," a short story by a pup writer named Roger Angell, Ross riddled the query pages with numbered points of contention, a spray of editorial buckshot. A few pellets:

I was told recently that banks stay open until 4 o'clock.

Do people say *executive,* i.e., use it in conversation. It's pretty much of a writer's word.

It is my recollection that most hotels have uncarpeted marble or floors that look like marble.

Reading John Cheever's short story "Clancy in the Tower of Babel," Ross responds, "One technical point in this piece bothers me. Cheever has Clancy, his elevator man Clancy, around the building early in the morning and late of the evening. . . . I think under union rules, which govern these things, elevator men gain the day shift by seniority." He senses that a reporting piece from Berlin by Joseph Wechsberg is overly sympathetic: "I still think it is too soon for us to go pro-German."

And, as he considers an essay by Lionel Trilling, you can practically hear the sigh of a man who set out to create a "comic weekly" surrendering to the demands of a graver sensibility: "I suppose there's no other way of doing this, but it always bothers me when a reviewer writes as if he's talking the book over with someone who has already read it, and knows what's on p. 236."

In those days, Ross had to spend many days in the hospital. He was quick to disappointment and exasperation, and yet he had a successor in mind, an editor as seemingly recessive in manner as he had been aggressive and incandescent. William Shawn, a shy newspaperman from Chicago, worked in the early thirties for Ross as an "idea man." Ben Yagoda writes in *About Town,* an excellent history of the magazine, that on Shawn's first two days on the job he conceived ideas for ten Talk pieces, including the "Jac Mac Famous School of Acrobatics"; pigeon farms on Manhattan rooftops; a rat exterminator on Riker's Island; and George Selkirk, the talented, if not quite immortal, outfielder whose destiny it was to replace Babe Ruth in right for the Yankees. Shawn made his mark as an editor by directing the magazine's coverage of the Second World War. Ross came to think of him as indispensable. As he wrote to Kay Boyle, in 1949, "I can't do anything with Shawn away, for the future is in his head." When Ross died in December 1951, Raoul Fleischmann, the magazine's owner, appointed Shawn. He remained in the job for the next thirty-five years.

In his attention to detail and his urge to clarity, Shawn resembled

Ross. Yagoda relates how Shawn sent a memo to Matthew Josephson telling him that his Profile of William Knudsen, a leader of the automobile industry, was "a stunning piece of historical reporting." Then he wrote that he was appending "a few questions." There were 178.

But Shawn, who took over the magazine in January 1952, was a distinctly different personality. Shawn assumed for himself far more authority than Ross, who was prepared to delegate a greater amount to his various deputies, or "Jesuses." Shawn was also quiet, subtle, secretive, elliptical, and, to some, quite strange. He was a variety of genius who enjoyed funny writing as well as serious fiction, supported completely the individual artists and writers on a profoundly variegated staff, and expressed his myriad curiosities about the world by sending writers out to explore its many corners. J. D. Salinger called him "the most unreasonably modest of born great artist-editors." Beneath the modesty, however, was a steely tactical will. Harold Brodkey suggested that Shawn combined the qualities of Napoléon Bonaparte and Saint Francis of Assisi.

Shawn was also working in radically different circumstances than Ross. In the early years of the magazine, Ross was often at odds with ownership and battling over questions of principle and money. As with most fledgling editorial enterprises, the central concern was existence itself. Would the thing survive? *The New Yorker* almost closed its doors more than once. I have on my wall a rueful letter from Fleischmann informing a business-side colleague that he was shutting the magazine down. It is dated May 1925—three months after the debut issue. There were many such moments of despair and rescue. But the magazine found its financial footing, and, by the early fifties, it was in happy synch with the postwar consumer boom. Educated middle- and upper-middle-class readers seemed to want what *The New Yorker* was providing, and advertisers identified the magazine as uniquely suited to reaching those free-spending readers.

With that kind of security, and with so many editorial columns to fill, Shawn could think expansively about the magazine. He could build on the deepening ambitions of the forties with the plump resources of the fifties. If he wanted reporting from the newly independent country of Ghana, the big East-West summit in Geneva, or the Bandung Conference, in Indonesia, he did not consult the ledger books; he sent a writer. In fact, the sheer proliferation of advertising demanded that Shawn scramble in search of more and more editorial matter. This, he found, had an inevitable drag on quality. There is, in this world, after all, only so much talent at a given time—only so much good writing. At a certain point, he found it necessary to limit the pages in a weekly issue to 248—as fat as a phone book in some towns. In his tenure as editor, Shawn made innumerable hires, tried out countless freelancers, and ran long, multipart series—some forgettable, some central to the literary and journalistic history of mid-century America. His relationship to advertising was distinguished mainly by the ads he found too distasteful to accept. A manufacturer of bathroom fixtures once told me that his ads for bathtubs and sinks had been rejected, because, as Shawn told him, "They are in the bathroom, which means they are next to the, well, you know . . ."

Decorum was important to Shawn, even though the world was changing. Rachel MacKenzie, a fiction editor, rejected Philip Roth's forty-thousand-word novella "Goodbye, Columbus" less because of its length—the magazine had just run J. D. Salinger's fifty-thousand-word "Zooey"—but, rather, because, as MacKenzie wrote, "taste would rule out here much of what is essential to the narrative." The magazine accepted Roth's "Defender of the Faith" but not his more frenetic story "Eli, the Fanatic." "We all agree that there are remarkable things in the story," MacKenzie wrote to Roth's agent, "but we feel that it keeps sliding off into caricature and farce and that in the end it falls between realism and didactic modern fable, the emotional thread breaking and the lesson taking over."

Shawn was also wary of the Beats, perhaps the most lasting school of literary outrage in the fifties. When the fiction editor Katharine White rejected the author of *On the Road*, she wrote, "We read with a great deal of interest John Kerouac's 'Go, Go, Go,' and it makes us hope that he will have other short stories to send us. . . . We hope that Mr. Kerouac will try something for us that is not about this particular group of wild kids." Similarly, the magazine, which was alive to the work of young poets like James Merrill, Adrienne Rich, and Sylvia Plath, was not a home for "Howl" or "Kaddish." Jane Kramer would write a marvelous multipart Profile of Allen Ginsberg, but not until the late sixties.

Critics like Seymour Krim worried that *The New Yorker*, which had exhibited so much bite in its first few decades, was now getting complacent and reserved in middle age. But no magazine can be a completist omnibus of the cultural or political moment, and this one never aspired to be one. History will inevitably find it wanting in some way or another. A reader looking in the fifties archives for a Profile of Chuck Berry will be disappointed. The coverage of jazz did not prove worthy of the form until Shawn gave Whitney Balliett a jazz column, in 1957, by which time rock and roll was under way. Shawn's magazine was much more in the groove of its time with other arts, as some of the pieces here make thrillingly evident: Lillian Ross's irresistible Hemingway Profile, Winthrop Sargeant's Profiles of Richard Avedon and Marianne Moore, Berton Roueché's piece on Jackson Pollock, Truman Capote's barbed portrait of a youngish Marlon Brando, Thomas Whiteside's Profile of Pat Weaver, the executive-maestro of NBC.

One of the lasting triumphs of cultural reporting for the magazine in the fifties was Lillian Ross's five-part series about John Huston, Hollywood, and the making of a mediocre adaptation of Stephen Crane's *The Red Badge of Courage*. Ross had joined the magazine during the war, one of a small number of women who found a place there when so many men were in the service. Having obtained unfettered access to Huston, the cast, the set, and the relevant executives, Ross painted a dramatic, detailed, and wicked portrait of all the ambitions and compromises that go into even a failed and ephemeral production. Ross's prose is direct, and unembellished, but the simplicity is deceptive. The influence of the work was significant. Norman Mailer, when discussing *The Executioner's Song,* credited Ross as a pioneer in nonfiction.

Political and foreign reporting had become a great deal more serious during the Second World War, and there was no going back to the wide-eyed, we-are-confused-little-men fripperies of the bygone world. Reading the best of it here, you get an uncanny sense of writers coming to grips with issues and maps that are with us today. A. J. Liebling in Gaza and Janet Flanner in Algeria confront the emerging Middle East; Joseph Wechsberg in Berlin and Emily Hahn in China draw the fault lines of the Cold War. Bernard Taper's travels with Thurgood Marshall, in his days with the NAACP, is an early look at the civil-rights movement. And Richard Rovere, a Communist who, as a result of the Molotov-Ribbentrop Pact of 1939, had become an anti-Communist liberal, covered Washington as an outsider living in Rhinebeck, New York. His running portrayal of the malign phenomenon of Joseph McCarthy was some of the most impressive political coverage that the magazine had yet produced.

Harold Ross liked to pose as anti-intellectual—he famously declared himself unsure whether Moby Dick was "the man or the whale." Shawn was without any such ambivalence toward intellectual ambition. One of the first writers he hired was Dwight Macdonald, who had been an editor at *Partisan Review*. Macdonald was capable of both outrageously witty criticism—as when he dissects Mortimer Adler's Great Books set—and vivid, sympathetic political reporting, as with his Profile of the Catholic social activist Dorothy Day.

The postwar fifties had a certain technological utopianism about them—not unlike our current era—and the magazine was notably alive to this. Shawn was wary of modern gadgetry (he would not ride in an elevator without an attendant), but that did not quash his curiosity. There are pieces here on the whizbangery of push-button phones, videotape, home freezers, the "perceptron simulator," data processing, and, with real depth, the dawning of the Computer Age.

Finally, Shawn had a sharp eye for that essential component of any institution that wishes to develop: new talent with new things to say. The fifties saw the rise of one such talent in particular, John Updike, who, for the next fifty-five years, was an unfailingly prolific and versatile contributor to *The New Yorker.* His fine-grained prose was there from the start, and, with time, his sharp-eyed intelligence alighted on seemingly every surface, subject, and subtext. Updike was, out of the box, an American writer of the first rank. He was profoundly at home at *The New Yorker* and, at the same time, able to expand the boundaries of its readers' tastes. He could *seem* tweedy and suburban—a modern, golf-playing squire—and yet, as a critic, he introduced to the magazine's readers an array of modernists and postmodernists, along with writing from countries far beyond the Anglo-American boundaries; as a writer of fiction, he was not a revolutionary, but his short stories make up a vast social, political, and erotic history of postwar America, or at least some precincts of it.

One of the more persistent myths of the magazine came up in those Ross-era files—the putative tyranny of its stylistic prejudices. Roald Dahl, whose story "Taste" is published here, wrote to one of Ross's editors that he was in a "howling fury" because of the outrageous and peremptory changes reflected in a set of proofs that had just arrived in the mail. "You have sprinkled commas about all over the pages as though you were putting raisins in a plum-pudding," Dahl wrote. "*I* know what commas I want. *I* know what phrases I wish to use. It is my story. I wrote it." And yet, as any reader will see, even in the fifties, before the arrival of experimentalists like Donald Barthelme and Max Frisch, writers in possession of a real voice did not lose it, despite the magazine's at times persnickety ministrations. Nabokov, Welty, Flanner, Ross, Liebling,

Mitchell, Capote, Thurber, Updike—they are utterly themselves, their preferences and hesitations as distinct as can be.

Now we've moved downtown to the end of Manhattan island and into the tallest skyscraper in the city. From our floor, there is an astonishing view of the harbor that used to be Joe Mitchell's beat. At a certain point, certainly by the fifties, Joe told editors and friends that the city was changing—changing so profoundly that he no longer saw it as his own and, gradually, he wrote more about the past, about his interior New York, about the memories that carved through the present like initials gouged in old tabletops. This is often what happens. Young men and women arrive and it is their work to describe the world that is becoming. That's the way it is now.

PART ONE

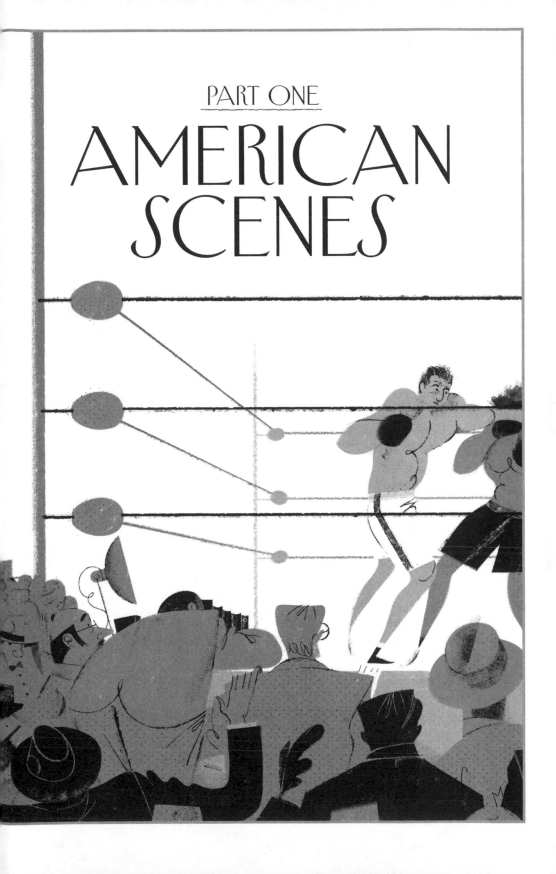

AMERICAN SCENES

A NOTE BY ELIZABETH KOLBERT

"THE FIFTIES WERE captured in black and white, most often by still photographers," the journalist David Halberstam once observed. By contrast, the sixties (and every subsequent decade) were "caught in living color on tape or film." The shift in film stock has produced—or maybe just confirmed—a perceptual bias. In our cultural shorthand, the fifties were a time of innocence, when Americans trusted their leaders, let their kids play in the street, attended church regularly, and had time to read weekly magazines.

Like all such formulas, this one is, at best, half accurate. After the Second World War, many Americans doubtless did feel the need for calm and stability. But change came, anyway—exciting, disruptive, and even radioactive. If the fifties were *Leave It to Beaver,* they were also *Lolita*. They were "Be-Bop-A-Lula" *and* the Montgomery bus boycott, Chevy Bel Airs *and* Sputnik, the opening of Disneyland *and* the invention of the H-bomb. The pieces about the American scene that follow reflect the decade's dividedness. Taken together, they suggest a country in which little is changing and everything is.

In 1950, it was possible to go to the Sunset Appliance Store, in Rego Park, Queens, and, if the stars were aligned, be shown a twelve-inch TV by Jackie Robinson. "We" did this one afternoon and watched Robinson sell a set to a "short man in a heavy overcoat." It may have been a stunt of salesmanship, but the authors of "Success," John Graham and Rex Lardner, play along, and, even when Robinson is hawking TVs, his modesty and essential decency come through. Besides stealing bases, he has, it turns out, a knack for moving merchandise.

"Mr. Hunter's Grave" is a classic Joseph Mitchell portrait of a marginalized New Yorker. In this case, his subject, George Hunter, lives, quite literally, on the edge of the city, in southwestern Staten Island. Eighty-seven, he is the son of a former slave and grew up in a community of black oystermen known as Sandy Ground. By the time Mitchell visits, the world of Sandy Ground is disappearing. The water has become too polluted for oyster farming and the village is all but abandoned. Mitchell and Hunter have a long, rambling conversation about revival meetings, about the two wives and the son Hunter has buried, about baking cakes, and about Revelation. Then they go to look at the community's overgrown graveyard. The piece is carried by the rhythms of Hunter's voice and by his dignity as death approaches.

"Ahab and Nemesis," by A. J. Liebling, like Mitchell a stalwart of *The New Yorker* since the 1930s, and "The Cherubs Are Rumbling," by Walter Bernstein, best known as a screenwriter who was blacklisted during the McCarthy era, are both reflections on violence. Liebling's is the lighthearted sort. His piece chronicles the heavyweight bout between Rocky Marciano and Archie Moore, and, in true Liebling style, it is filled with punchy lines and witty allusions, some of which land and some of which don't. Bernstein is more somber. His subject is a gang of "delinquents," the Cherubs, who are involved in a turf war with a rival Brooklyn gang called the Stompers. A well-meaning gym teacher, Vincent Riccio, is trying to keep the boys out of jail.

"Everybody thinks all you're good for is breaking heads," Riccio tells the Cherubs. "I know different—although I know you're pretty good at breaking heads, too." Sixty years later, the toughs no longer seem very tough. They hang out in a candy store. They have nicknames like Johnny Meatball. They wield switchblades and issue threats that seem cribbed from the movies they've seen: "Shut up a minute, or I'll bust you right in the mouth!"

"Fallout," by Daniel Lang, tells the story of an H-bomb code-named Shrimp. Shrimp was detonated by the United States on Bikini Atoll on March 1, 1954, and, as Lang observes, it was "the shot that made the world fallout-conscious."

Calculations performed at Los Alamos had predicted Shrimp would have a yield of five megatons. Instead the yield turned out to be three times as great. The firing crew was stationed in a concrete bunker on Enyu, an island twenty miles from the test site. A few seconds after the blast, the bunker started to shake, one of the men later recalled, as if "it was resting on a bowl of jelly." The explosion pulverized billions of pounds of coral reef and seafloor; much of this debris was sucked into the atmosphere by the rising fireball. When the radioactive dust settled, some of it fell on a Japanese fishing vessel, inaptly named the *Lucky*

Dragon, and some floated down on the residents of Rongelap, a tiny speck in the Marshall Islands. The crew members of the *Lucky Dragon* arrived back at port nauseated, feverish, and covered with blisters. The Rongelap Islanders suffered radiation burns and their hair fell out.

The title of "Fallout" refers both to the radioactive dust and to the awkward situation it created for the U.S. government. Lang's piece appeared more than a year after the "shot," and the Atomic Energy Commission was still trying to allay public fears. The AEC's scientists pooh-poohed the burns and the hair loss and treated the Rongelap Islanders' forced evacuation as a sort of extended vacation. Lang seems, in large part, to accept the official line; for instance, he notes that the exiled Rongelapers have "been shown their first Wild West motion pictures, which they think are terrific." But doubt creeps in, anyway. The Second World War is a decade in the past, the Gulf of Tonkin Resolution a decade into the future, and Lang, in 1955, seems to be positioned, uncomfortably, in the middle. Reading "Fallout," you sense a writer holding back, and the world rushing forward.

SUCCESS

John Graham and Rex Lardner

JANUARY 7, 1950 (ON JACKIE ROBINSON, TV SALESMAN)

ON LEARNING THAT Jackie Robinson, the Brooklyn Dodgers' second baseman, is spending Monday, Wednesday, and Friday evenings each week as a television-set salesman in the Sunset Appliance Store in Rego Park, Queens, we hurried over to the place to see how he is making out. From a talk we had with Joseph Rudnick, president of Sunset, just before Robinson appeared, we learned that he is making out fine. Rudnick, a small, alert-looking man, graying at the temples, whom we found in an office on a balcony at the rear of the store, informed us that the accomplished young man had been working there, on a salary-and-commission basis, for five weeks, and that if he liked, he could work there forever, the year around. "Business booming like wildfire since Jackie came," Rudnick told us, looking down at a throng milling about among television sets, washing machines, and refrigerators. "Sports fans flocking in here," he said with satisfaction. "Young persons, curious about the National League's Most Valuable Player and one of the best base-stealers since Max Carey. Jackie signs baseballs for them and explains about the double steal. Since he's been here, he's sold sets to Joe Louis and Sugar Ray Robinson, among others. The newsreel people shot him selling a set to a customer. He's a natural salesman, with a natural modesty that appeals to buyers. The salesman wrapped up in himself makes a very small package. Campanella, Hodges, and Barney dropped by to wish him luck. Campanella's his roomy. There's Jackie now! With his business agent." Robinson and a bigger, more strapping man with a florid face were making their way along the floor, the big man in the lead. "He'll be right up," Rudnick said. "Hangs his coat here. One other thing we do," he went on, "when a bar buys a television set, we send Gene Stanlee over to the bar—the wrestler. Mr. America."

Robinson and his manager for radio and television appearances came up, and we were introduced, learning that the latter's name is Harry Solow. "Jackie don't have to lay awake nights worrying about his condition, bucking that mob three times a week," Solow said. Rudnick told us that Solow also manages Joe Franklin and Symphony Sid, and Solow explained that they are radio personalities. "Jackie's all lined up for his own radio program," he continued. "He's mostly interested in boys' work, though. Spends all his spare time at the Harlem Y.M.C.A." "How I keep in shape is playing games with kids," Robinson said in a well-modulated voice. "When I quit baseball, I intend to give it full time." We learned that the Robinsons have a television set with a sixteen-inch screen and that their only child, three-year-old Jackie, Jr., likes Howdy Doody, Mr. I. Magination, and Farmer Gray better than anything else on video. As Robinson was about to go down to the main floor, it occurred to us to ask him if he'd developed any special sales technique. He looked surprised and replied that he didn't think so. "If a customer is going to buy a set, he's going to buy it," he said philosophically. "You can't twist his arm." "On the other hand," Rudnick observed, "the right angle for a salesman is the try-angle."

We bade Rudnick and Solow goodbye and followed Robinson downstairs. A short man in a heavy overcoat got him first. He wanted to see a twelve-inch set. "There's a bunch of them in the basement," Robinson told him. "All playing at once." He led the man down to the basement. We followed. It was quite dark there, but we could make out rows and rows of sets and see customers being herded from one model to another by spirited salesmen. Robinson conducted his man to a twelve-inch set, turned it on, adjusted the picture, and in rather a shout, to get his voice above the hubbub of the amplifiers, named the price and outlined the guarantee. "I like it!" the man hollered. "Could my wife work it—all those knobs?" "A child could work it," said Robinson, and it was a deal.

FROM

FALLOUT

Daniel Lang

JULY 16, 1955 (ON RADIOACTIVE DEBRIS)

FALLOUT, THE RADIOACTIVE debris that accumulates in the upper atmosphere following the detonation of a nuclear bomb and sooner or later comes to earth, often many hundreds, and even thousands, of miles from the scene of the explosion, is usually less visible than the soot that settles on Manhattan every day at the rate of a ton to every square mile. The particles of dust that constitute most fallout look like any other dust, cannot be smelled, felt, or tasted, and descend and land soundlessly. As a general rule, fallout can be detected only by instruments—notably, of course, by the Geiger counter but also by such less celebrated devices as the scintillation counter and the ion chamber. Scientists checking on the density of fallout frequently differ in their interpretations of their findings, but there is clearly no room for disagreement about one thing: This dry rain of tainted matter increases the degree of radiation in any locality it visits. The point of conflict among the experts, as I have come to realize while looking into the problems presented by fallout, is over the danger, if any, of the increase, and this at present seems to be more a matter of opinion than of scientific determination. It appears indisputable, however, that no community need be apprehensive over a slight rise in the level of radiation (as commonly used, the word is synonymous with radioactivity), for in normally rainy weather certain radioactive natural gases that almost everywhere are constantly emanating from the ground do not diffuse as readily as they do at other times, and so increase the amount of radiation in the immediate vicinity, occasionally as much as 400 percent—a phenomenon that has been commonplace all over the world since long before anyone ever heard of fallout and has been definitely proved to be harmless.

Fallout varies greatly in intensity, depending, in part, upon the amount of energy released—or, to use the technical term, "yielded"—by the bombs that create it. This nation's high-yielding bombs are tried out over remote islands in the Pacific and its low-yielding models over the Atomic Energy Commission's Nevada Proving Ground. Early in 1951, the A.E.C. became sufficiently impressed by the fallout that its low-yielding bombs were precipitating on widespread portions of this country to set up a nationwide system of observation stations for monitoring fluctuations in the density of radiation. The system now has eighty-nine stations, and not one of them, whether near the test area or thousands of miles away from it, has ever failed to report a rise in radiation following a "shot," which is the A.E.C. people's term for the setting off of a bomb. Seemingly satisfied by the reports from these stations, Lewis L. Strauss, the chairman of the A.E.C., issued a statement last February declaring that as far as the Nevada experiments were concerned, "the hazard [of dangerously radioactive fallout] has been successfully confined to the controlled area of the Test Site." A month later, however, two scientists at the University of Colorado were reported by the newspapers as having asserted that fallout over their state had reached a point where it could no longer be ignored by those concerned with public safety. The Governor of Colorado, a former United States senator who served on the Joint Committee on Atomic Energy while he was in Washington, responded to this by calling the scientists' warning "phony" and saying that they ought to be arrested. The clamor quieted down when the president of the university issued a statement to the effect that the two scientists had qualified their warning by saying that the fallout would be dangerous if its radioactivity was maintained at the peaks it occasionally reached.

The Colorado ruckus was only one, and by no means the first, of a number of public warnings and bickerings over the issue of fallout. In 1953, the chairman of the Physics Department of the University of Utah, in Salt Lake City, in a state bordering on Nevada, expressed the belief that Americans' capacity for tolerating radiation was being sapped by fallout, and that same year five sheep ranchers in Cedar City, Utah, some two hundred miles from the Proving Ground, sued the government for damages, claiming that fallout had been fatal to approximately a thousand of their animals. The A.E.C. investigated and found no evidence to support the contention that the death of the sheep had been caused by fallout. The case of the sheep ranchers, which is still pending, brought back memories of the explosion of the first atomic bomb, on July 16, 1945, in New Mexico, which, among many other things, inflicted burns on a nearby herd of cattle and caused the animals' hair to turn gray. (The cattle were presently sent to Oak Ridge, Tennessee, where they and, more recently, their progeny have been studied ever since by members of the faculty of the University of Tennessee School of Agriculture, who are endeavoring to determine the long-range effects of overexposure to radiation.) Fallout from that first explosion in New Mexico also contaminated cornstalks in Indiana that were later converted into strawboard to make packing cartons; some of these found their way to Rochester, New York, where the Eastman Kodak people innocently used them to ship out a supply of film, which is exceptionally sensitive to radiation. The film was ruinously fogged. It is now standard practice for the A.E.C. to forewarn photographic-supply companies of impending test blasts, so that they can take certain well-established protective measures against possible fallout, but so far nobody has come up with any similar measures to alert the owners of cornstalks.

Others who appreciate advance notice of forthcoming shots include archeologists, who, if they failed to allow for fallout, might be off by several centuries in calculating the age of ancient relics on the basis of how much carbon 14—a radioactive isotope that is present in a constant amount in all living things and disintegrates at a known rate after death—they still contain. Uranium prospectors, too, like to be warned ahead of time; back in the days before the far-reaching effects of the tests were understood, more than one prospector was momentarily led to believe that he had at last come upon a bonanza when his Geiger counter set up a wild clicking in response to fallout.

The manner in which a bomb is detonated also strongly affects the intensity of its fallout. If the bomb is exploded at a high altitude—high enough, that is, so that the mass of luminescent gas known as the fireball, from which rises the now all too familiar mushroom, does not touch the earth's surface—its radioactivity has nothing to condense with except whatever dust it encounters in the air and the vaporized bomb casing. In such instances—and all shots of any consequence within the continental limits of the United States are of this kind—the dust and vapors, swept upward by the blast to an altitude of possibly forty thousand feet, are carried away on the strong winds of that altitude, which, owing to the earth's rotation, are generally westerly, and may remain aloft for months. By the time the dust particles finally settle, they may well have travelled clear around the globe, becoming so thoroughly scattered and having so thoroughly dissipated their radioactivity in the atmosphere that they are presumed to be harmless. The higher the explosion the better, from the point of view of the eventual effects of its fallout, for the descent of the dust particles is apt to be hastened if they happen into a formation of rain clouds, which they are not likely to encounter until they have drifted down to within twenty thousand feet of the earth.

A surface or near-surface shot—the sort the United States restricts to the Pacific area—is something else again; indeed, radiologically speaking, it is an extremely dangerous proposition. Immediately after such a shot, the bomb's fireball (the biggest one yet reported measured from three to four miles in diameter) sucks up millions of tons of material from the surface of the earth—rocks, sand, vegetation, water—as it rises, almost with the speed of sound. Moving up through the stem of the mushroom to its head, this hideously contaminated, or "hot," material also soars up into the stratosphere, where it too is eventually blown away by the wind. But, unlike the radioactive dust of a high-altitude shot, much of this debris is far too heavy to be blown around the world. The winds that beneficently carry the dust of high-altitude shots such great distances blow the fallout from a ground-level shot only far enough away from the testing area to make it a menace. The debris falls rapidly while still intensely radioactive, polluting to a probably lethal degree what the A.E.C. has described as a "comparatively localized" area. Just outside the comparatively localized area, however, lies a much larger one that is definitely jeopardized by the fallout from a ground shot, for during the first few hours after the explosion some of the lighter fragments of debris spread out over thousands of square miles. Given reliable meteorological information, scientists can predict the size and general course of this fallout with a fair amount of accuracy, but, owing to the different weights of the bits and pieces that constitute the mass, and the erratic nature of the winds in the upper regions, they can't do much more than that. For whatever comfort it might afford people who fear the fallout from surface shots, Dr. Willard F. Libby, a commissioner of the A.E.C., a while ago ventured a guess that in the event of a thermonuclear attack on the United States the enemy would set off "a large fraction" of its bombs high above the earth, since the blast and heat damage of aerial explosions is tactically superior to that of ground blasts. "In other words, the fallout problem might be minimized by the enemy's attempt to maximize the blast and thermal effects," Dr. Libby said.

• • •

The fireball of a very large thermonuclear bomb that was set off on March 1st of last year on a coral island in a lagoon at Bikini Atoll touched the surface of the earth. This was the shot that made the world fallout-conscious, and it earned its sorry distinction not only by dangerously contaminating seven thousand square miles of land and sea—an area somewhat larger than Connecticut and Rhode Island together—but by injuring people who were nearly a hundred miles away from the site. The Commission naturally felt deep chagrin at this outcome of the blast, especially since it had gone to great pains to make sure that no lives would be endangered. Weeks before the bomb was detonated, the Commission saw to it that marine and aviation navigational publications printed announcements of the forthcoming test and gave their readers explicit information about the boundaries of a thirty-thousand-square-mile danger zone that had been decided upon. For days prior to the blast, aircraft crisscrossed the zone and the waters adjacent to it to warn away shipping. A meteorological study of the whole region was made, in which special attention was paid to the behavior of winds at all relevant altitudes. "The area for which meteorological data had to be compiled and analyzed was far greater than just that thirty-thousand-square-mile danger zone," an official of the A.E.C. said later. "In fact, it was greater than that of the United States, and we had only eight or ten observation stations to cover it." In its report of the shot and of what went wrong with it, the A.E.C. made the mildly consolatory point that without the knowledge derived from the test "we would have been in ignorance of the extent of the effects of radioactive fallout and, therefore . . . much more vulnerable to the dangers from fallout in the event an enemy should resort to radiological warfare against us." In addition to the unanticipated lessons it learned about the vagaries of fallout during the March 1st test, the Commission collected some grim testimony as to its potency, expressed in terms of roentgens—one of the units in which radiation is measured. Having previously established that a person exposed to a total accumulation of four hundred and fifty roentgens in the arbitrarily set period of thirty-six hours stands only a 50 percent chance of surviving, the Commission found that during the first thirty-six hours after the March 1st blast, anyone on Bikini, ten miles down-wind from the explosion, would have been exposed to five thousand roentgens, and even if he had had sufficient warning to get to Rongelap Atoll, a hundred miles to the east, the roentgen count against him in at least one section of that tiny island would still have been twenty-three hundred.

The March 1st bomb went off shortly before four in the morning, announcing itself with a blinding flash over a broad expanse of the Pacific. The islet that had served as its platform abruptly disintegrated into pulverized coral, which was swept up into the stratosphere, and it was there that things began to go wrong. As the particles of coral gathered like a pendulous cloud in the sky—this was one time when fallout was all too plainly visible—the wind, which had been counted on to blow them to the northeast, unexpectedly veered a few degrees and began to drive them due east. Natives of the Marshall Islands, Americans participating in the test, and Japanese fishermen—all of them outside the official danger zone, which extended some fifty miles east of Bikini—were now directly in the path of the fallout, which, as it billowed toward them, assumed the shape of a monstrous cigar, two hundred and twenty miles long and up to forty miles wide.

A total of two hundred and thirty-six Marshall Islanders, all residents of the atolls of Rongelap and Utirik, were evacuated as hastily as possible by destroyer to Kwajalein. There only those from Rongelap—seventy-four of them, constituting the island's total population—were found to have been seriously exposed. (Happily, none had been in the twenty-three-hundred-roentgen section of the atoll.) All the Rongelapians were suffering from radiation burns of the scalp or neck—the most sensitive parts of the body that are usually exposed—and all had ingested, as the nuclear people put it, small amounts of fallout-blighted foods or beverages; the hair of thirty-nine of them had dropped out in patches. Five Navy doctors reported to the convention of the American Medical Association in Atlantic City last month that the children of Rongelap had lost more hair than their elders and that the counts of the children's white blood cells, which fight infection and which are always affected by serious exposure to radiation, had dropped to lower levels. According to the A.E.C., the islanders' burns are now healed, hair has grown back on their bald patches, and they all appear to be in good physical shape. They have not yet been taken back to their island, because it is still contaminated, but have been moved to Majuro Atoll, where, the Commission says, they are temporarily occupying "buildings built for them . . . of a new and improved type, better adapted to the comfort and the needs of the people than the usual type of island houses." There they have been shown their first Wild West motion pictures, which they think are terrific. There, too, they are being studied by American physicians. Now and then, one of the doctors makes a stab at trying to explain radiation to the Rongelapians, but without much success. As a rule, the attempt quickly turns into a party of some sort. "You start talking to a couple of the islanders, and pretty soon the whole population has gathered around you, smiling and beaming and ready for some kind of fun," an A.E.C. physician who was assigned to Majuro for a while told me. "They're an extremely friendly people, which I suppose, considering the circumstances, is just as well."

The Americans who were threatened by the fallout—thirty-one members of the Army, Navy, and Air Force—were on Rongerik Atoll when the wind shifted. They, too, were evacuated to Kwajalein, where they were examined by American physicians, and from there they were sent on to Tripler General Hospital, in Hawaii, for further examination. None of them was found to have been seriously affected and none has shown any aftereffects.

The Japanese in the path of the fallout were, as the whole world presently came to know, the twenty-three members of the crew of the Lucky Dragon, a hundred-ton trawler engaged in fishing for tuna. On the morning of the big blast, the vessel, which the warning aircraft had somehow missed, was about ninety miles east of Bikini, some forty miles outside the official danger zone, when several members of the crew who happened to be on deck saw a white flash tinged with red far away on the pre-dawn horizon. Seven or eight minutes later, they heard a loud explosion. In about three hours, a fine white dust of radioactive coral particles began to fall on the superstructure of the Lucky Dragon; it was so dense, one of the crew later reported, that it was faintly audible as it landed on the deck. The strange downpour continued until about noon, and by the time it let up, the dust had covered the boat, the men, and their catch like a white sheet; it lay so thick on the deck that the men left footprints when they walked on it. The fishermen had no idea what all this meant, but it was something that they had never experienced before, and plainly something weird, and it made them so uneasy that they hauled in their lines that same day and headed for their home port of Yaizu. As a matter of good seamanship, they washed down their vessel, and this probably saved the lives of a good many of them. The voyage home took thirteen days, during which a number of the men filled bottles with the odd dust to keep as souvenirs, and the whole crew, it was subsequently estimated by Japanese scientists, was exposed to the baleful assault of between two hundred and five hundred roentgens. By the time the Lucky Dragon reached Yaizu, on March 14th, practically every one of the fishermen was ridden with nausea, blisters, lesions, fever, conjunctivitis, abdominal pains, and other symptoms of overexposure to radiation.

Americans who were in Japan in the days that followed the cruise of the Lucky Dragon had some difficult moments in their relations with the people there, but, in retrospect, most of them agree that the Japanese, tragically aware as they already were of the effects of a nuclear explosion, reacted to the incident pretty much the way the citizens of any other country might have. The Japanese were angry, anxious, and voluble. As soon as word of the peculiar condition of the Lucky Dragon's mariners reached knowledgeable authorities, the fishermen—or at least those who could be rounded up at once—were hustled off to Tokyo and hospitalized. A few days elapsed before the last of the twenty-three was accounted for, in the course of which a couple of them were picked up as they were bicycling through the streets of Yaizu, each with a grossly radioactive dried shark fin from the boat lashed to his back mudguard. Japanese scientists, wearing protective gauze masks and rubber gloves, trooped aboard the Lucky Dragon, where they found some samples of radioactive coral ash still on the bridge and carried off the tuna that had not yet been sold. When they debarked, their masks were radioactive, which gave them good reason to believe that the crew had suffered serious internal injuries.

Back in the laboratory, analysis of various items taken from the trawler, including some tuna that were still waiting for a buyer, revealed the presence of two telltale radioactive elements common to all fallout—radioiodine and radiostrontium, both of which the body can ingest or inhale. Radioiodine tends to single out and damage the cells of the thyroid gland; radiostrontium has a special affinity for the bones and, if enough of it works its way into them, may produce cancer. Word went out to the public-health authorities to confiscate the tuna that had got to the market, but it was discovered that fishmongers in the Osaka Prefecture had already sold parts of them to about a hundred customers. (Fortunately for the customers, the fish were dead at the time of the blast, so only their skin, according to the Japanese scientists, was affected and this had been removed before eating.)

American radiation specialists in Japan offered their fullest cooperation, but their Japanese counterparts, while always personally cordial, indicated that they would prefer to handle the situation themselves. American physicians were not allowed near the fishermen, although they might have been able to make some helpful therapeutic suggestions. But even if there had not been this atmosphere of professional coolness, it is unlikely that the widespread resentment that boiled up in Japan over what had befallen the crew of the Lucky Dragon could have been avoided. And, as time passed, more or less extraneous events seemed to conspire to add heat to the resentment. On March 19th, the A.E.C., in preparing for two more shots on Bikini, announced that the danger zone would be expanded—a step that some Japanese appeared to feel was rather belated. Nor did the shots themselves, which came less than a month after the return of the Lucky Dragon, act as a precisely soothing influence upon the population. At about the same time, a rainstorm over the Atsumi Peninsula blurred the glass panes of several greenhouses with a peculiar substance that a researcher at the Nagoya Technical Research Institute said was dust infused with artificially induced radioactivity, and presently a professor at Kagoshima University asserted that he had found some local vegetables, milk, and drinking water to have been mildly affected by another "radioactive rain."

In late summer, a thirty-nine-year-old member of the Lucky Dragon's crew, Aikichi Kuboyama, who was suffering from hepatitis, took a turn for the worse, and his case became a primary national concern. Buddhist priests prayed for his life. Hospital bulletins reporting his condition were more prominently displayed in the press than most news of international importance, and they were broadcast hourly over the radio. Kuboyama died on September 23rd (all his fellow-crewmen have survived and seem to be recovering) and his death took on political implications of the first magnitude. The Japanese Foreign Minister and other dignitaries crowded into the hospital to pay their last respects to the fisherman, and the American Ambassador in Tokyo sent a letter of condolence to the Japanese Foreign Ministry and a check for a million yen (about $2,800) to Kuboyama's widow "as a token of the deep sympathy felt by the Government and people of the United States." A Japanese Minister of State called publicly on the United States to show "more sincerity" by increasing the amount of money—a million dollars—that had already been offered to his government as compensation for the injuries to the crew and for the loss to the nation's fishing industry. (The United States eventually paid two million dollars in reparations.) Japanese labor organizations, newspapers, leading citizens, and public opinion in general, impressed by the indiscriminating nature of fallout, called for an end to thermonuclear-bomb tests anywhere, by any country. As the national temper rose, only one incident occurred that somewhat mitigated the wave of anti-American feeling, and this, ironically, was a disaster of greater proportions, even if not of greater significance, than that of the Lucky Dragon—the drowning of more than twelve hundred persons, including about eighty Americans, when a ferryboat capsized in northern Japan just a few days after Kuboyama died. "The Japanese were quite sympathetic," an A.E.C. man who was in Japan at the time told me. "The accident seemed to clear the atmosphere a little by reminding them that Americans can also die."

• • •

The Japanese are not the only ones who have demanded that no more thermonuclear bombs be tested. Their views have been echoed by some highly articulate authorities in the United States as well as by various qualified critics in other countries. One of the latter—Dr. Frederick Soddy, a British winner of a Nobel Prize for studies in the chemistry of radioactive substances and the origin and nature of isotopes—has warned of the dangers of "fouling the air with radioactivity." In particular, much concern has been expressed over the hereditary effects of increased radioactivity on the genes of the human race. Estimating that seventy-five hydrogen bombs exploded at intervals over a period of thirty years will double the natural amount of radiation in the world, Joseph Rotblat, Professor of Physics at the Medical College of St. Bartholomew's Hospital, in London, has written, "Rough as this estimate may be, it certainly shows that we are sailing much closer to the wind than many of us thought. . . . It is no longer a question of two nations, or groups of nations, devastating each other, but of all the future generations of *all* nations, who will forever pay, through disease, malformation, and mental disability, for our folly."

In this country, the Federation of American Scientists has urged that the United Nations "obtain and evaluate scientific opinion on the biological and genetic effects of radiation on human beings," and last April, Senator Frederick G. Payne, of Maine, introduced a resolution calling on the President to instruct our chief delegate to the United Nations to propose such a study. Apparently, the President did so, for at the tenth-anniversary meeting of the U.N. in San Francisco three weeks ago,

Henry Cabot Lodge suggested that all member nations pool their research on fallout to allay "unjustified fears." The National Academy of Sciences, this country's most distinguished scientific body, has, with the help of the Rockefeller Foundation, embarked on an exhaustive survey of the problem. Dr. Linus Pauling, a Nobel Prize–winning chemist at the California Institute of Technology, noting that radioactive rains have fallen in Japan and Germany as a result of the tests, has suggested that these may have started "a new cycle" of leukemia. And Dr. James R. Arnold, an associate professor at the Institute for Nuclear Studies of the University of Chicago, has come forward with the proposal that in the future the A.E.C. conduct all its thermonuclear tests within the continental limits of the United States. "It may be objected that the number of casualties would very likely be increased," he wrote in the *Bulletin of the Atomic Scientists* last November. "This is true, but they would be American citizens. A nation which feels itself in danger has some right to ask certain of its citizens to run special risks on behalf of all. This is the principle behind compulsory military service. Even though the Japanese are our allies and the Marshallese our wards, we have no such right with them, in a world which holds to the idea of national sovereignty. Americans who were hurt would doubtless be properly indemnified. All the same, the taxpayer would benefit greatly, since the lowering of costs of the test operation would pay for any probable casualty list many times over."

In the face of all this outcry, the A.E.C., which possesses more information about fallout than any other agency—or individual—steadfastly maintains that the tests have not got out of hand. The Commission contends that in the ten years since this country started testing nuclear weapons—to be followed presently, of course, by the Soviet Union and Great Britain—not more than one-tenth of a roentgen has been added to the amount of radiation normally absorbed by each individual in the United States. This is the equivalent of what a patient is subjected to in a single chest X-ray, and as for its genetic effects, it is only one one-hundredth of the normal radiation to which most men and women have always been exposed up to and through their reproductive lifetimes. "Most of the categorical predictions of adverse genetic effects are about as reasonable as claiming that meteors from outer space are a major threat to highway safety," Dr. John C. Bugher, Director of the A.E.C.'s Division of Biology and Medicine, assured me.

The A.E.C. considers the amounts of radioiodine and radiostrontium that have fallen in this country insignificant insofar as their immediate effect upon the population is concerned. In view of the fact that these elements, absorbed in the soil, may become part of plant tissues that are either eaten by human beings or eaten by grazing animals that, in turn, provide food for man, the Commission, by means of roving teams and experimental farms, carries on a series of year-round checkups on the radioactivity in many localities all over the nation. Radioiodine has been found in the thyroids of cattle and sheep grazing near the Nevada Proving Ground; the thyroids of living human beings cannot be tested for small amounts of radioiodine, but urine analyses of persons living in the same area have indicated that they have been less severely affected than the livestock, showing only a minute fraction of the amount of radioiodine that would cause damage. As for radiostrontium, Dr. Bugher estimates that the amount now present in the United States would have to be multiplied by a million before an increase in the frequency of bone cancer would be perceptible. On the other hand, Dr. Bugher revealed some months ago in an address before the seventh annual Industrial Health Conference, held in Houston, Texas, that laboratory experiments conducted on animals have demonstrated that one of the possible effects of overexposure to radiation is a shortening of life expectancy. "This phenomenon does not result from any specific cause of death but apparently from a general acceleration of the aging process," he said, adding wryly that human beings have yet to experience the distinction between a condition that does not cause death but shortens life.

However sound the A.E.C.'s position may be, the commissioners are finding it hard to win quite a number of worried citizens over to it. "One of our big difficulties is a popular tendency to confuse close-in fallout with distant fallout," an A.E.C. radiation expert told me. "When people in the United States read about the hundreds of roentgens that hit those Japanese fishermen, they think it's sheer luck the same thing hasn't happened to them, and figure maybe the next shot will be their turn."

Another thing that handicaps the A.E.C. in its efforts to present its case is the fact that the very word "radiation" evokes dread in the public mind. "On wet days, we get anxious phone calls from men and women who want to know if the rain is bringing fallout down on them," a man in the A.E.C.'s New York office told me. "That's a perfectly rational question, but then they suddenly break down completely—crying and carrying on about what's going to become of the world." It may be, he suggested, that radiation's bad name goes all the way back to the famous case of the girls who, working in a New Jersey factory during the First World War, painted watch dials with radium, tipping their brushes with their tongues, and years later began dying, one by one, from overexposure.

The big point the A.E.C. is trying to put across is that it's the cumulative exposure that counts, and not the mere presence of radiation. Air, water, and soil emit radiation under normal conditions; so do the cosmic rays that are constantly assaulting the earth from outer space. For that matter, man himself is radioactive, since his body contains potassium 40, carbon 14, and radium 226—all radioactive isotopes. "The world is radioactive," Commissioner Libby stated in an address he delivered last December at the Conference of Mayors, in Washington. "It always has been and always will be." And Merril Eisenbud, Director of the A.E.C.'s Health and Safety Laboratory, points out that since the very beginning of life, radioactivity has been one of the principal factors in the furtherance of evolution, causing changes, or mutations, in the genes of living organisms and so bringing man to his present stage of development, whatever one's opinion of that stage may be. "Without radioactivity, we'd have less to think about today," Eisenbud told me—a statement with which even the Commission's harshest critics would hardly quarrel. "Without it, perhaps we'd all still be slime in the primeval swamp."

• • •

But in these times, as the A.E.C. knows all too well, the subject of mutations is a touchy one. Many people find it much easier to contemplate—in theory, at least—the possible destruction of the world while they themselves are still inhabiting it than to reflect that their descendants, centuries hence, may inherit genes that were impaired by the current tests. There are sound scientific reasons for apprehension over radiation's effect on genes. Radiation, the A.E.C. believes, causes from 10 to 20 percent of all mutations, and about 99 percent of all mutations result either in prenatal death or in sterility or some other functional disability; what the public knows as "monsters" and scientists call "lethal mutants" are nearly always stillborn. In those rare instances where mutations are beneficial to an organism, the law of natural selection dictates that the new form survive at the expense of weaklings or the parent form. In any society, the frequency of mutations depends largely on the total amount of radiation that its members' reproductive organs are subjected to before parenthood, and not on the intensity of exposure on any particular occasion.

Dr. E. L. Green, the A.E.C.'s geneticist, starting with the premise that for every billion genes (about one hundred thousand people) five thousand mutations turn up, estimates that exposure to the extra tenth of a roentgen introduced by the nuclear tests will mean an additional ten to twenty mutations among each hundred thousand of the population. The field of genetics is still a mass of unsolved riddles, but the authorities are generally agreed that if and when the tenth-of-a-roentgen mutations start showing up, it will be difficult to single them out as the direct results of nuclear explosions.

According to Professor H. J. Muller, a Nobel Prize–winning geneticist, "each detrimental mutation, even though small in effect and lost to view in the jumble of a heterogeneous population, tends to continue from generation to generation and to hamper successive descendants, until at last it happens to tip the scales against one of its possessors, and that line of descent then dies out in consequence of the inherited disability." In a speech before the National Academy of Sciences this spring, Muller condemned prominent publicists of the government, including physicians, who have claimed that the bombing of Hiroshima and Nagasaki will have no harmful effect on the future populations of those cities and, indeed, may even improve them. He also cited the A.E.C.'s favorite analogy of the chest X-ray, but he gave it a somewhat different twist; in genetics, he implied, the reproductive organs are really rather more important than the chest. Muller pointed out that the additional radiation to which Americans are being exposed because of the bomb tests must be considered in terms not of the individual but of the whole population; that is, one-tenth of a roentgen multiplied by 160,000,000, or 16,000,000 roentgens. Muller noted that this means that the United States may expect about as many mutations to result from the current nuclear tests, wherever held, as he anticipates will turn up in Hiroshima, since the 160,000 survivors in that city were exposed to an average of one hundred roentgens. In both instances, he said, the number of mutations caused by the artificial increase of radiation to date will probably someday amount to around eighty thousand—or from two and a half to five times as many as Dr. Green predicts—and in the end, several times that many lives will be adversely affected. Still, Muller went on, in view of the total number of people involved during the scores of generations in which the mutations will be occurring, it is unlikely that the population as a whole will be undermined, and he recommended that before calling for a ban on all future tests, thought be given to what the alternative damage might be if the tests were discontinued. In a way, he said, the case was similar to that of people who visit their doctors regularly for X-ray examinations as a precautionary measure against serious illness even though a Public Health Service survey has shown that every year the average person receives much more radiation from this source than from the nuclear tests. "Have we no right to expect individual sacrifices when the stakes are democracy and intellectual freedom themselves?" Muller asked rhetorically. To this, any person now alive would appear to be obliged to give a stoutly affirmative answer, but the question also, of course, raises the nagging dilemma of the propriety of attempting to speak for those who are yet to be born into a world the nature of which no one can predict.

There are those who believe that some of the A.E.C. scientists might, if they were not restrained by loyalty to that agency, be just as vocal as their present adversaries in expressing anxiety over the dangers of fall-out. However that may be, it is unlikely that the scientists on either side of the fence are enjoying their wrangling. "It's no fun, this constantly being cast in the role of villain," an A.E.C. man told me. "Some people apparently think that from our point of view it's all a great big game, and that we're just blowing up bombs for the hell of it. They seem to forget entirely that their country is mixed up in an international situation that makes these tests necessary. Is it a crime to try to hold our lead in this miserable race for superior weapons, in view of what might well happen to all of us if we should lag behind?"

To many laymen who have come to expect scientists to be starkly objective in their approach to technical problems and whose schooling pretty much encouraged the belief that there is always only one right answer to any question concerning science, the current disagreement among the authorities is both exasperating and baffling, if not actually frightening. Part of the trouble is, of course, that in this instance the question is not purely scientific but is also a matter of ethics, statesmanship, and clairvoyance—three notoriously treacherous quagmires for theorists. Moreover, so much about the workings of genetics remains obscure that, as the A.E.C. has gently observed, "there is still a wide range for admissible opinion" on the subject, and many scientists feel that there is an equally wide range when it comes to the more immediate effects of radiation. In other words, even if there *is* only one right answer to any question concerning science, those who are critical of the A.E.C.'s seeming complacency feel that until more is known about the awesome mysteries involved there should be no attempt to give any answer at all. Such critics might be said to belong to the play-it-safe school of thought. And to them the A.E.C. may justifiably reply, "Yes, but which is the safe way to play it?"

AHAB AND NEMESIS

A. J. Liebling

OCTOBER 8, 1955 (ON ROCKY MARCIANO VS. ARCHIE MOORE)

BACK IN 1922, the late Heywood Broun, who is not remembered primarily as a boxing writer, wrote a durable account of a combat between the late Benny Leonard and the late Rocky Kansas for the lightweight championship of the world. Leonard was the greatest practitioner of the era, Kansas just a rough, optimistic fellow. In the early rounds, Kansas messed Leonard about, and Broun was profoundly disturbed. A radical in politics, he was a conservative in the arts, and Kansas made him think of Gertrude Stein, *les Six,* and nonrepresentational painting, all of them novelties that irritated him.

"With the opening gong, Rocky Kansas tore into Leonard," he wrote. "He was gauche and inaccurate, but terribly persistent." The classic verities prevailed, however. After a few rounds, during which Broun continued to yearn for a return to a culture with fixed values, he was enabled to record: "The young child of nature who was challenging for the championship dropped his guard, and Leonard hooked a powerful and entirely orthodox blow to the conventional point of the jaw. Down went Rocky Kansas. His past life flashed before him during the nine seconds in which he remained on the floor, and he wished that he had been more faithful as a child in heeding the advice of his boxing teacher. After all, the old masters did know something. There is still a kick in style, and tradition carries a nasty wallop."

I have often thought of Broun's words in the three years since Rocky Marciano, the reigning heavyweight champion, scaled the fistic summits, as they say in *Journal-Americanese,* by beating a sly, powerful quadragenarian colored man named Jersey Joe Walcott. The current

Rocky is gauche and inaccurate, but besides being persistent he is a dreadfully severe hitter with either hand. The predominative nature of this asset has been well stated by Pierce Egan, the Edward Gibbon and Sir Thomas Malory of the old London prize ring, who was less preoccupied than Broun with ultimate implications. Writing in 1821 of a "milling cove" named Bill Neat, the Bristol Butcher, Egan said, "He possesses a requisite above all the art that *teaching* can achieve for any boxer; namely, *one hit* from his right hand, given in proper distance, can gain a victory; but three of them are positively enough to dispose of a giant." This is true not only of Marciano's right hand but of his left hand, too—provided he doesn't miss the giant entirely. Egan doubted the advisability of changing Neat's style, and he would have approved of Marciano's. The champion has an apparently unlimited absorptive capacity for percussion (Egan would have called him an "insatiable glutton") and inexhaustible energy ("a prime bottom fighter"). "Shifting," or moving to the side, and "milling in retreat," or moving back, are innovations of the late eighteenth century that Rocky's advisers have carefully kept from his knowledge, lest they spoil his natural prehistoric style. Egan excused these tactics only in boxers of feeble constitution. I imagine Broun would have had a hard time fitting Marciano anywhere into his frame of reference.

Archie Moore, the light-heavyweight champion of the world, who hibernates in San Diego, California, and estivates in Toledo, Ohio, is a Brounian rather than an Eganite in his thinking about style, but he naturally has to do more than think about it. Since the rise of Marciano, Moore, a cerebral and hyper-experienced light-colored pugilist who has been active since 1936, has suffered the pangs of a supreme exponent of *bel canto* who sees himself crowded out of the opera house by a guy who can only shout. As a sequel to a favorable review I wrote of one of his infrequent New York appearances a year ago, when his fee was restricted to a measly five figures, I received a sad little note signed "The most unappreciated fighter in the world, Archie Moore." A fellow who has as much style as Moore tends to overestimate the intellect—he develops the kind of Faustian mind that will throw itself against the problem of perpetual motion, or of how to pick horses first, second, third, *and* fourth in every race. Archie's note made it plain to me that he was honing his harpoon for the White Whale.

When, during some recent peregrinations in Europe, I read newspaper items about Moore's decisioning a large, playful porpoise of a Cuban heavyweight named Nino Valdes and scoop-netting a minnow like Bobo Olson, the middleweight champion, for practice, I thought of him as a lonely Ahab, rehearsing to buck Herman Melville, Pierce Egan, and the betting odds. I did not think that he could bring it off, but I wanted to be there when he tried. What would *Moby Dick* be if Ahab had succeeded? Just another fish story. The thing that is eternally diverting is the struggle of man against history—or what Albert Camus, who used to be an amateur middleweight, has called the Myth of Sisyphus. (Camus would have been a great man to cover the fight, but none of the syndicates thought of it.) When I heard that the boys had been made for September 20th, at the Yankee Stadium, I shortened my stay abroad in order not to miss the Encounter of the Two Heroes, as Egan would have styled the rendezvous.

• • •

In London on the night of September 13th, a week before the date set for the Encounter, I tried to get my eye in for fight-watching by attending a bout at the White City greyhound track between Valdes, who had been imported for the occasion, and the British Empire heavyweight champion, Don Cockell, a fat man whose gift for public suffering has enlisted the sympathy of a sentimental people. Since Valdes had gone fifteen rounds with Moore in Las Vegas the previous May, and Cockell had excruciated for nine rounds before being knocked out by Marciano in San Francisco in the same month, the bout offered a dim opportunity for establishing what racing people call a "line" between Moore and Marciano. I didn't get much of an optical workout, because Valdes disposed of Cockell in three rounds. It was evident that Moore and Marciano had not been fighting the same class of people this season.

This was the only fight I ever attended in a steady rainstorm. It had begun in the middle of the afternoon, and while there was a canopy over the ring, the spectators were as wet as speckled trout. "The weather, it is well known, has no terrors to the admirers of Pugilism and Life," Egan once wrote, and on his old stamping ground this still holds true. As I took my seat in a rock pool that had collected in the hollow of my chair, a South African giant named Ewart Potgieter, whose weight had been announced as twenty-two stone ten, was ignoring the doctrine of Apartheid by leaning on a Jamaican colored man who weighed a mere sixteen stone, and by the time I had transposed these statistics to three hundred and eighteen pounds and two hundred and twenty-four pounds, respectively, the exhausted Jamaican had acquiesced in resegregation and retired. The giant had not struck a blow, properly speaking, but had shoved downward a number of times, like a man trying to close an over-filled trunk.

The main bout proved an even less gruelling contest. Valdes, eager to get out of the chill, struck Cockell more vindictively than is his wont, and after a few gestures invocative of commiseration the fat man settled in one corner of the ring as heavily as suet pudding upon the unaccustomed gastric system. He had received what Egan would have called a "ribber" and a "nobber," and when he arose it was seen that the latter had raised a cut on his forehead. At the end of the third round, his manager withdrew him from competition. It was not an inspiring occasion, but after the armistice eight or nine shivering Cubans appeared in the runway behind the press section and jumped up and down to register emotion and restore circulation. *"Ahora Marciano!"* they yelled. "Now for Marciano!" Instead of being grateful for the distraction, the other spectators took a poor view of it. "Sit down, you chaps!" one of them cried. "We want to see the next do!" They were still parked out there in the rain when I tottered into the Shepherd's Bush underground station and collapsed, sneezing, on a train that eventually disgorged me at Oxford Circus, with just enough time left to buy a revivifying draught before eleven o'clock, when the pubs closed. How the mugs I left behind cured themselves I never knew. They had to do it on Bovril.

• • •

Because I had engagements that kept me in England until a few days before the Encounter, I had no opportunity to visit the training camps of the rival American Heroes. I knew all the members of both factions, however, and I could imagine what they were thinking. In the plane on the way home, I tried to envision the rival patterns of ratiocination. I could be sure that Marciano, a kind, quiet, imperturbable fellow, would plan to go after Moore and make him fight continuously until he tired enough to become an accessible target. After that, he would expect concussion to accentuate exhaustion and exhaustion to facilitate concussion, until Moore came away from his consciousness, like everybody else Rocky had ever fought. He would try to remember to minimize damage to himself in the beginning, while there was still snap in Moore's arms, because Moore is a sharp puncher. (Like Bill Neat of old, Marciano hits at his opponent's arms when he cannot hit past them. "In one instance, the arm of Oliver [a Neat adversary] received so paralyzing a shock in stopping the blow that it appeared almost useless," Egan once wrote.) Charlie Goldman, Marciano's hand-chipped tactical adviser, would have instructed him in some rudimentary maneuver to throw Moore's first shots off, I felt sure, but after a few minutes Rocky would forget it, or Archie would figure it out. But there would always be Freddie Brown, the "cut man," in the champion's corner to repair superficial damage. One reason Goldman is a great teacher is that he doesn't try to teach a boxer more than he can learn. What he has taught Rocky in the four years since I first saw him fight is to shorten the arc of most of his blows without losing power thereby, and always to follow one hard blow with another—"for insurance"—delivered with the other hand, instead of recoiling to watch the victim fall. The champion has also gained confidence and presence of mind; he has a good fighting head, which is not the same thing as being a good mechanical practitioner. "A *boxer* requires a *nob* as well as a *statesman* does a head, coolness and calculation being essential to *second* his efforts," Egan wrote, and the old historiographer was never more correct. Rocky is thirty-one, not in the first flush of youth for a boxer, but Moore is only a few days short of thirty-nine, so age promised to be in the champion's favor if he kept pressing.

Moore's strategic problem, I reflected on the plane, offered more choices and, as a corollary, infinitely more chances for error. It was possible, but not probable, that jabbing and defensive skill would carry him through fifteen rounds, even on those old legs, but I knew that the mere notion of such a *gambade* would revolt Moore. He is not what Egan would have called a shy fighter. Besides, would Ahab have been content merely to go the distance with the White Whale? I felt sure that Archie planned to knock the champion out, so that he could sign his next batch of letters "The most appreciated and deeply opulent fighter in the world." I surmised that this project would prove a mistake, like Mr. Churchill's attempt to take Gallipoli in 1915, but it would be the kind of mistake that would look good in his memoirs. The basis of what I rightly anticipated would prove a miscalculation went back to Archie's academic background. As a young fighter of conventional tutelage, he must have heard his preceptors say hundreds of times, "They will all go if you hit them right." If a fighter did not believe that, he would be in the position of a Euclidian without faith in the hundred-and-eighty-degree triangle. Moore's strategy, therefore, would be based on working Marciano into a position where he could hit him right. He would not go in and slug with him, because that would be wasteful, distasteful, and injudicious, but he might try to cut him up, in an effort to slow him down so he could hit him right, or else try to hit him right and then cut him up. The puzzle he reserved for me—and Marciano—was the tactic by which he would attempt to attain his strategic objective. In the formation of his views, I believed, Moore would be handicapped, rather than aided, by his active, skeptical mind. One of the odd things about Marciano is that he isn't terribly big. It is hard for a man like Moore, just under six feet tall and weighing about a hundred and eighty pounds, to imagine that a man approximately the same size can be immeasurably stronger than he is. This is particularly true when, like the light-heavyweight champion, he has spent his whole professional life contending with boxers—some of them considerably bigger—whose strength has proved so near his own that he could move their arms and bodies by cunning pressures. The old classicist would consequently refuse to believe what he was up against.

• • •

The light-heavyweight limit is a hundred and seventy-five pounds, and Moore can get down to that when he must, in order to defend his title, but in a heavyweight match each Hero is allowed to weigh whatever he pleases. I was back in time to attend the weighing-in ceremonies, held in the lobby of Madison Square Garden at noon on the day set for the Encounter, and learned that Moore weighed 188 and Marciano 188¼—a lack of disparity that figured to encourage the rationalist's illusions. I also learned that, in contrast to Jack Solomons, the London promoter who held the Valdes-Cockell match in the rain, the International Boxing Club, which was promoting the Encounter, had decided to postpone it for twenty-four hours, although the weather was clear. The decision was based on apprehension of Hurricane Ione, which, although apparently veering away from New York, might come around again like a lazy left hook and drop in on the point of the Stadium's jaw late in the evening. Nothing like that happened, but the postponement brought the town's theatres and bars another evening of good business from the out-of-town fight trade, such as they always get on the eve of a memorable Encounter. ("Not a bed could be had at any of the villages at an early hour on the preceding evening; and Uxbridge was crowded beyond all former precedent," Egan wrote of the night before Neat beat Oliver.) There was no doubt that the fight had caught the public imagination, ever sensitive to a meeting between Hubris and Nemesis, as the boys on the quarterlies would say, and the bookies were laying 18–5 on Nemesis, according to the boys on the dailies, who always seem to hear. (A friend of mine up from Maryland with a whim and a five-dollar bill couldn't get ten against it in ordinary barroom money anywhere, although he wanted Ahab.)

The enormous—by recent precedent—advance sale of tickets had so elated the I.B.C. that it had decided to replace the usual card of bad preliminary fights with some not worth watching at all, so there was less distraction than usual as we awaited the appearance of the Heroes on the fateful evening. The press seats had been so closely juxtaposed that I could fit in only sidewise between two colleagues—the extra compression having been caused by the injection of a prewar number of movie stars and politicos. The tight quarters were an advantage, in a way, since they facilitated my conversation with Peter Wilson, an English prize-ring correspondent, who happened to be in the row behind me. I had last seen Mr. Wilson at White City the week before, at a time when the water level had already reached his shredded-Latakia mustache. I had feared that he had drowned at ringside, but when I saw him at the Stadium, he assured me that by buttoning the collar of his mackintosh tightly over his nostrils he had been able to make the garment serve as a diving lung, and so survive. Like all British fight writers when they are relieved of the duty of watching British fighters, he was in a holiday mood, and we chatted happily. There is something about the approach of a good fight that renders the spirit insensitive to annoyance; it is only when the amateur of the Sweet Science has some doubts as to how good the main bout will turn out to be that he is avid for the satisfaction to be had from the preliminaries. This is because after the evening is over, he may have only a good supporting fight to remember. There were no such doubts—even in the minds of the mugs who had paid for their seats—on the evening of September 21st.

At about ten-thirty, the champion and his faction entered the ring. It is not customary for the champion to come in first, but Marciano has never been a stickler for protocol. He is a humble, kindly fellow, who even now will approach an acquaintance on the street and say bashfully, "Remember me? I'm Rocky Marciano." The champion doesn't mind waiting five or ten minutes to give anybody a punch in the nose. In any case, once launched from his dressing room under the grandstand, he could not have arrested his progress to the ring, because he had about forty policemen pushing behind him, and three more clearing a path in front of him. Marciano, tucked in behind the third cop like a football ballcarrier behind his interference, had to run or be trampled to death. Wrapped in a heavy blue bathrobe and with a blue monk's cowl pulled over his head, he climbed the steps to the ring with the cumbrous agility of a medieval executioner ascending the scaffold. Under the hood, he seemed to be trying to look serious. He has an intellectual appreciation of the anxieties of a champion, but he has a hard time forgetting how strong he is; while he remembers that, he can't worry as much as he knows a champion should. His attendants—quick, battered little Goldman; Al Weill, the stout, excitable manager, always stricken just before the bell with the suspicion that he may have made a bad match; Al Columbo, the boyhood friend from Brockton, Massachusetts, which is Rocky's home town—are all as familiar to the crowd as he is.

Ahab's party arrived in the ring a minute or so later, and Charlie Johnston, his manager—a calm sparrow-hawk of a man, as old and wise in the game as Weill—went over to watch Goldman put on the champion's gloves. Freddie Brown, the surgical specialist, went to Moore's corner to watch *his* gloves being put on. Moore wore a splendid black silk robe with a gold lamé collar and belt. He sports a full mustache above an imperial, and his hair, sleeked down under pomade when he opens operations, invariably rises during the contest, as it gets water sloshed on it between rounds and the lacquer washes off, until it is standing up like the top of a shaving brush. Seated in his corner in the shadow of his personal trainer, a brown man called Cheerful Norman, who weighs two hundred and thirty-five pounds, Moore looked like an old Japanese print I have of a *Shogun Engaged in Strategic Contemplation in the Midst of War.* The third member of his group was Bertie Briscoe, a rough, chipper little trainer, whose more usual charge is Sandy Saddler, the featherweight champion—also a Johnston fighter. Mr. Moore's features in repose rather resemble those of Orson Welles, and he was reposing with intensity.

The procession of other fighters and former fighters to be introduced was longer than usual. The full galaxy was on hand, including Jack Dempsey, Gene Tunney, and Joe Louis, the *têtes de cuvée* of former-champion society; ordinary former heavyweight champions, like Max Baer and Jim Braddock, slipped through the ropes practically unnoticed. After all the celebrities had been in and out of the ring, an odd dwarf, advertising something or other—possibly himself—was lifted into the ring by an accomplice and ran across it before he could be shooed out.

The referee, a large, craggy, oldish man named Harry Kessler, who, unlike some of his better-known colleagues, is not an ex-fighter, called the men to the center of the ring. This was his moment; he had the microphone. "Now Archie and Rocky, I want a nice, clean fight," he said, and I heard a peal of silvery laughter behind me from Mr. Wilson, who had seen both of them fight before. "Protect yourself at all times," Mr. Kessler cautioned them unnecessarily. When the principals shook hands, I could see Mr. Moore's eyebrows rising like storm clouds over the Sea of Azov. His whiskers bristled and his eyes glowed like dark coals as he scrunched his eyebrows down again and enveloped the Whale with the Look, which was intended to dominate his will power. Mr. Wilson and I were sitting behind Marciano's corner, and as the champion came back to it I observed his expression, to determine what effect the Look had had upon him. More than ever, he resembled a Great Dane who has heard the word "bone."

A moment later the bell rang and the Heroes came out for the first round. Marciano, training in the sun for weeks, had tanned to a slightly deeper tint than Moore's old ivory, and Moore, at 188, looked, if anything, bigger and more muscular than Marciano; much of champion's weight is in his legs, and his shoulders slope. Marciano advanced, but Moore didn't go far away. As usual, he stood up nicely, his arms close to his body and his feet not too far apart, ready to go anywhere but not without a reason—the picture of a powerful, decisive intellect unfettered by preconceptions. Marciano, pulling his left arm back from the shoulder, flung a left hook. He missed, but not by enough to discourage him, and then walked in and hooked again. All through the round, he threw those hooks, and some of them grazed Moore's whiskers; one even hit him on the side of the head. Moore didn't try much offensively; he held a couple of times when Marciano worked in close.

Marciano came back to his corner as he always does, unimpassioned. He hadn't expected to catch Moore with those left hooks anyway, I imagine; all he had wanted was to move him around. Moore went to his corner inscrutable. They came out for the second, and Marciano went after him in brisker fashion. In the first round, he had been throwing the left hook, missing with it, and then throwing a right and missing with that, too. In the second, he tried a variation—throwing a right and then pulling a shoulder back to throw the left. It appeared for a moment to have Moore confused, as a matador might be confused by a bull who walked in on his hind legs. Marciano landed a couple of those awkward hooks, but not squarely. He backed Moore over toward the side of the ring farthest from me, and then Moore knocked him down.

Some of the reporters, describing the blow in the morning papers, called it a "sneak punch," which is journalese for one the reporter didn't see but technically means a lead thrown before the other man has warmed up or while he is musing about the gate receipts. This had been no lead, and although I certainly hadn't seen Moore throw the punch, I knew that it had landed inside the arc of Marciano's left hook. ("Marciano missed with the right, trun the left, and Moore stepped inside it," my private eye, a trainer named Whitey Bimstein, said next day, confirming my diagnosis, and the film of the fight bore both of us out.) So Ahab had his harpoon in the Whale. He had hit him right if ever I saw a boxer hit right, with a classic brevity and conciseness. Marciano stayed down for two seconds. I do not know what took place in Mr. Moore's breast when he saw him get up. He may have felt, for the moment, like Don Giovanni when the Commendatore's statue grabbed at him—startled because he thought he had killed the guy already—or like Ahab when he saw the Whale take down Fedallah, harpoons and all. Anyway, he hesitated a couple of seconds, and that was reasonable. A man who took nine to come up after a punch like that would be doing well, and the correct tactic would be to go straight in and finish him. But a fellow who came up on two was so strong he would bear investigation.

After that, Moore did go in, but not in a crazy way. He hit Marciano some good, hard, classic shots, and inevitably Marciano, a trader, hit him a few devastating swipes, which slowed him. When the round ended, the edge of Moore's speed was gone, and he knew that he would have to set a new and completely different trap, with diminished resources. After being knocked down, Marciano had stopped throwing that patterned right-and-left combination; he has a good nob. "He never trun it again in the fight," Whitey said next day, but I differ. He threw it in the fifth, and again Moore hit him a peach of a right inside it, but the steam was gone; this time Ahab couldn't even stagger him. Anyway, there was Moore at the end of the second, dragging his shattered faith in the unities and humanities back to his corner. He had hit a guy right, and the guy hadn't gone. But there is no geezer in Moore, any more than there was in the master of the Pequod.

Both came out for the third very gay, as Egan would have said. Marciano had been hit and cut, so he felt acclimated, and Moore was so mad at himself for not having knocked Marciano out that he almost displayed animosity toward him. He may have thought that perhaps he had not hit Marciano *just* right; the true artist is always prone to self-reproach. He would try again. A minute's attention from his squires had raised his spirits and slaked down his hair. At this point, Marciano set about him. He waddled in, hurling his fists with a sublime disregard of probabilities, content to hit an elbow, a biceps, a shoulder, the top of a head—the last supposed to be the least profitable target in the business, since, as every beginner learns, "the head is the hardest part of the human body," and a boxer will only break his hands on it. Many boxers make the systematic presentation of the cranium part of their defensive scheme. The crowd, basically anti-intellectual, screamed encouragement. There was Moore, riding punches, picking them off, slipping them, rolling with them, ducking them, coming gracefully out of his defensive efforts with sharp, patterned blows—and just about holding this parody even on points. His face, emerging at instants from under the storm of arms—his own and Rocky's—looked like that of a swimming walrus. When the round ended, I could see that he was thinking deeply. Marciano came back to his corner at a kind of suppressed dogtrot. He didn't have a worry in the world.

It was in the fourth, though, that I think Sisyphus began to get the idea he couldn't roll back the Rock. Marciano pushed him against the ropes and swung at him for what seemed a full minute without ever landing a punch that a boxer with Moore's background would consider a credit to his workmanship. He kept them coming so fast, though, that Moore tired just getting out of their way. One newspaper account I saw said that at this point Moore "swayed uncertainly," but his motions were about as uncertain as Margot Fonteyn's, or Arthur Rubinstein's. He is the most premeditated and best-synchronized swayer in his profession. After the bell rang for the end of the round, the champion hit him a right for good measure—he usually manages to have something on the way all the time—and then pulled back to disclaim any uncouth intention. Moore, no man to be conned, hit him a corker of a punch in return, when he wasn't expecting it. It was a gesture of moral reprobation and also a punch that would give any normal man something to think about between rounds. It was a good thing Moore couldn't see Marciano's face as he came back to his corner, though, because the champion was laughing.

The fifth was a successful round for Moore, and I had him ahead on points that far in the fight. But it took no expert to know where the strength lay. There was even a moment in the round when Moore set himself against the ropes and encouraged Marciano to swing at him, in the hope the champion would swing himself tired. It was a confession that he himself was too tired to do much hitting.

In the sixth, Marciano knocked Moore down twice—once, early in the round, for four seconds, and once, late in the round, for eight seconds, with Moore getting up just before the bell rang. In the seventh, after that near approach to obliteration, the embattled intellect put up its finest stand. Marciano piled out of his corner to finish Moore, and the stylist made him miss so often that it looked, for a fleeting moment, as if the champion were indeed punching himself arm-weary. In fact, Moore began to beat him to the punch. It was Moore's round, certainly, but an old-timer I talked to later averred that one of the body blows Marciano landed in that round was the hardest of the fight.

It was the eighth that ended the competitive phase of the fight. They fought all the way, and in the last third of the round the champion simply overflowed Archie. He knocked him down with a right six seconds before the bell, and I don't think Moore could have got up by ten if the round had lasted that long. The fight by then reminded me of something that Sam Langford, one of the most profound thinkers—and, according to all accounts, one of the greatest doers—of the prize ring, once said to me: "Whatever that other man want to do, don't let him do it." Merely by moving in all the time and punching continually, Marciano achieves the same strategic effect that Langford gained by finesse. It is impossible to think, or to impose your thought, if you have to keep on avoiding punches.

Moore's "game," as old Egan would have called his courage, was beyond reproach. He came out proudly for the ninth, and stood and fought back with all he had, but Marciano slugged him down, and he was counted out with his left arm hooked over the middle rope as he turned to rise. It was a crushing defeat for the higher faculties and a lesson in intellectual humility, but he had made a hell of a fight.

• • •

The fight was no sooner over than hundreds of unsavory young yokels with New England accents began a kind of mountain-goat immigration from the bleachers to ringside. They leaped from chair to chair and, after they reached the press section, from typewriter shelf to typewriter shelf and, I hope, from movie star to movie star. "Rocky!" they yelled. "Brockton!" Two of them, as dismal a pair of civic ambassadors as I have seen since I worked on the Providence *Journal & Evening Bulletin,* stood on Wilson's typewriter and yelled "Providence!" After the fighters and the hick delinquents had gone away, I made my way out to Jerome Avenue, where the crowd milled, impenetrable, under the elevated structure. Skirting it as well as I could, I made my way uptown toward 167th Street, the station north of the Stadium.

By boarding a train at 167th Street, you can get a seat before it reaches 161st, which is the Stadium station, and then, if you don't mind people standing on your feet, continue downtown. At least you don't have to fight to get on. If you are not in a great hurry, however (and why should you be at eleven-thirty or twelve on a fight night?), the best plan of all is to walk up to 167th and have a beer in a saloon, or a cup of tea in the 167th Street Cafeteria, and wait until the whole mess clears away. By that time, you may even get a taxi. After this particular fight, I chose the cafeteria, being in a contemplative rather than a convivial mood. The place is of a genre you would expect to find nearer Carnegie Hall, with blond woodwork, and modern functional furniture imported from Italy—an appropriate background for the evaluation of an aesthetic experience. I got my tea and a smoked-salmon sandwich on a soft onion roll at the counter, and made my way to a table, where I found myself between two young policemen who were talking about why Walt Disney has never attempted a screen version of Kafka's *Metamorphosis.* As I did not feel qualified to join in that one, I got out my copy of the official program of the fights and began to read the high-class feature articles as I munched my sandwich.

One reminded me that I had seen the first boxing show ever held in Yankee Stadium—on May 12, 1923. I had forgotten that it *was* the first show, and even that 1923 was the year the Stadium opened. In my true youth, the Yankees used to share the Polo Grounds with the Giants, and I had forgotten that, too, because I never cared much about baseball, although, come to think of it, I used to see the Yankees play occasionally in the nineteen-teens, and should have remembered. I remembered the boxing show itself very well, though. It happened during the spring of my second suspension from college, and I paid five dollars for a high-grandstand seat. The program merely said that it had been "an all-star heavyweight bill promoted by Tex Rickard for the Hearst Milk Fund," but I found that I could still remember every man and every bout on the card. One of the main events was between old Jess Willard, the former heavyweight champion of the world, who had lost the title to Jack Dempsey in 1919, and a young heavyweight named Floyd Johnson. Willard had been coaxed from retirement to make a comeback because there was such a dearth of heavyweight material that Rickard thought he could still get by, but as I remember the old fellow, he couldn't fight a lick. He had a fair left jab and a right uppercut that a fellow had to walk into to get hurt by, and he was big and soft. Johnson was a mauler worse than Rex Layne, and the old man knocked him out. The other main event, *ex aequo,* had Luis Angel Firpo opposing a fellow named Jack McAuliffe II, from Detroit, who had had only fifteen fights and had never beaten anybody, and had a glass jaw. The two winners, of whose identity there was infinitesimal preliminary doubt, were to fight each other for the right to meet the great Jack Dempsey. Firpo was so crude that Marciano would be a Fancy Dan in comparison. He could hit with only one hand—his right—he hadn't the faintest idea of what to do in close, and he never cared much for the business anyway. He knocked McAuliffe out, of course, and then, in a later "elimination" bout, stopped poor old Willard. He subsequently became a legend by going one and a half sensational rounds with Dempsey, in a time that is now represented to us as the golden age of American pugilism.

I reflected with satisfaction that old Ahab Moore could have whipped all four principals on that card within fifteen rounds, and that while Dempsey may have been a great champion, he had less to beat than Marciano. I felt the satisfaction because it proved that the world isn't going backward, if you can just stay young enough to remember what it was really like when you were really young.

MR. HUNTER'S GRAVE

Joseph Mitchell

SEPTEMBER 22, 1956 (ON A STATEN ISLAND CEMETERY)

When things get too much for me, I put a wild-flower book and a couple of sandwiches in my pockets and go down to the South Shore of Staten Island and wander around awhile in one of the old cemeteries down there. I go to the cemetery of the Woodrow Methodist Church on Woodrow Road in the Woodrow community, or to the cemetery of St. Luke's Episcopal Church on the Arthur Kill Road in the Rossville community, or to one on the Arthur Kill Road on the outskirts of Rossville that isn't used any longer and is known as the old Rossville burying ground. The South Shore is the most rural part of the island, and all of these cemeteries are bordered on at least two sides by woods. Scrub trees grow on some of the graves, and weeds and wild flowers grow on many of them. Here and there, in order to see the design on a gravestone, it is necessary to pull aside a tangle of vines. The older gravestones are made of slate, brownstone, and marble, and the designs on them—death's-heads, angels, hourglasses, hands pointing upward, recumbent lambs, anchors, lilies, weeping willows, and roses on broken stems—are beautifully carved. The names on the gravestones are mainly Dutch, such as Winant, Housman, Woglom, Decker, and Van Name, or Huguenot, such as Dissosway, Seguine, De Hart, Manee, and Sharrott, or English, such as Ross, Drake, Bush, Cole, and Clay. All of the old South Shore farming and oyster-planting families are represented, and members of half a dozen generations of some families lie side by side. In St. Luke's cemetery there is a huge old apple tree that drops a sprinkling of small, wormy, lopsided apples on the graves beneath it every September, and in the Woodrow Methodist cemetery there is a patch of wild strawberries. Invariably, for some reason I don't know and don't want to know, after I have spent an hour or so in one of these cemeteries, looking at gravestone designs and reading inscriptions and identifying wild flowers and scaring rabbits out of the weeds and reflecting on the end that awaits me and awaits us all, my spirits lift, I become quite cheerful, and then I go for a long walk. Sometimes I walk along the Arthur Kill, the tidal creek that separates Staten Island from New Jersey; to old-time Staten Islanders, this is "the inside shore." Sometimes I go over on the ocean side, and walk along Raritan Bay; this is "the outside shore." The interior of the South Shore is crisscrossed with back roads, and sometimes I walk along one of them, leaving it now and then to explore an old field or a swamp or a stretch of woods or a clay pit or an abandoned farmhouse.

The back road that I know best is Bloomingdale Road. It is an old oyster-shell road that has been thinly paved with asphalt; the asphalt is cracked and pocked and rutted. It starts at the Arthur Kill, just below Rossville, runs inland for two and a half miles, gently uphill most of the way, and ends at Amboy Road in the Pleasant Plains community. In times past, it was lined with small farms that grew vegetables, berries, and fruit for Washington Market. During the depression, some of the farmers got discouraged and quit. Then, during the war, acid fumes from the stacks of smelting plants on the New Jersey side of the kill began to drift across and ruin crops, and others got discouraged and quit. Only three farms are left, and one of these is a goat farm. Many of the old fields have been taken over by sassafras, gray birch, blackjack oak, sumac, and other wasteland trees, and by reed grass, blue-bent grass, and poison ivy. In several fields, in the midst of this growth, are old woodpecker-ringed apple and pear trees, the remnants of orchards. I have great admiration for one of these trees, a pear of some old-fashioned variety whose name none of the remaining farmers can remember, and every time I go up Bloomingdale Road I jump a ditch and pick my way through a thicket of poison ivy and visit it. Its trunk is hollow and its bark is matted with lichens and it has only three live limbs, but in favorable years it still brings forth a few pears.

In the space of less than a quarter of a mile, midway in its length, Bloomingdale Road is joined at right angles by three other back roads—Woodrow Road, Clay Pit Road, and Sharrott's Road. Around the junctions of these roads, and on lanes leading off them, is a community that was something of a mystery to me until quite recently. It is a Negro community, and it consists of forty or fifty Southern-looking frame dwellings and a frame church. The church is painted white, and it has purple, green, and amber windowpanes. A sign over the door says, "AFRICAN METHODIST EPISCOPAL ZION." On one side of the church steps is a mock-orange bush, and on the other side is a Southern dooryard plant called Spanish bayonet, a kind of yucca. Five cedar trees grow in the churchyard. The majority of the dwellings appear to be between fifty and a hundred years old. Some are long and narrow, with a chimney at each end and a low porch across the front, and some are big and rambling, with wings and ells and lean-tos and front porches and side porches. Good pine lumber and good plain carpentry went into them, and it is obvious that attempts have been made to keep them up. Nevertheless, all but a few are beginning to look dilapidated. Some of the roofs sag, and banisters are missing on some of the porches, and a good many rotted-out clapboards have been replaced with new boards that don't match, or with strips of tin. The odd thing about the community is it usually has an empty look, as if everybody had locked up and gone off somewhere. In the summer, I have occasionally seen an old man or an old woman sitting on a porch, and I have occasionally seen children playing in a back yard, but I have seldom seen any young or middle-aged men or women around, and I have often walked through the main part of the community, the part that is on Bloomingdale Road, without seeing a single soul.

For years, I kept intending to find out something about this community, and one afternoon several weeks ago, in St. Luke's cemetery in Rossville, an opportunity to do so presented itself.

I had been in the cemetery a couple of hours and was getting ready to leave when a weed caught my eye. It was a stringy weed, about a foot high, and it had small, lanceolate leaves and tiny white flowers and tiny seed pods, and it was growing on the grave of Rachel Dissosway, who died on April 7, 1802, "in the 27th Yr of her Age." I consulted my wild-flower book, and came to the conclusion that it was either peppergrass (*Lepidium virginicum*) or shepherd's-purse (*Capsella bursa-pastoris*), and squatted down to take a closer look at it. "One of the characteristics of peppergrass," the wild-flower book said, "is that its seed pods are as hot as pepper when chewed." I deliberated on this for a minute or two, and then curiosity got the better of me and I stripped off some of the seed pods and started to put them in my mouth, and at just that moment I heard footsteps on the cemetery path and looked up and saw a man approaching, a middle-aged man in a black suit and a clerical collar. He came over to the grave and looked down at me.

"What in the world are you doing?" he asked.

I tossed the seed pods on the grave and got to my feet. "I'm studying wild flowers, I guess you might call it," I said. I introduced myself, and we shook hands, and he said that he was the rector of St. Luke's and that his name was Raymond E. Brock.

"I was trying to decide if the weed on this grave is peppergrass or shepherd's-purse," I said.

Mr. Brock glanced at the weed. "Peppergrass," he said. "A very common weed in some parts of Staten Island."

"To tell you the truth," I said, "I like to look at wild flowers, and I've been studying them off and on for years, but I don't know much about them. I'm only just beginning to be able to identify them. It's mostly an excuse to get out and wander around."

"I've seen you from a distance several times wandering around over here in the cemetery," Mr. Brock said.

"I hope you don't mind," I said. "In New York City, the best places to look for wild flowers are old cemeteries and old churchyards."

"Oh, yes," said Mr. Brock, "I'm aware of that. In fact, I'll give you a tip. Are you familiar with the Negro community over on Bloomingdale Road?"

I said that I had walked through it many times, and had often wondered about it.

"The name of it is Sandy Ground," said Mr. Brock, "and it's a relic of the old Staten Island oyster-planting business. It was founded back before the Civil War by some free Negroes who came up here from the Eastern Shore of Maryland to work on the Staten Island oyster beds, and it used to be a flourishing community, a garden spot. Most of the people who live there now are descendants of the original free-Negro families, and most of them are related to each other by blood or marriage. Quite a few live in houses that were built by their grandfathers or great-grandfathers. On the outskirts of Sandy Ground, there's a dirt lane running off Bloomingdale Road that's called Crabtree Avenue, and down near the end of this lane is an old cemetery. It covers an acre and a half, maybe two acres, and it's owned by the African Methodist church in Sandy Ground, and the Sandy Ground families have been burying in it for a hundred years. In recent generations, the Sandy Grounders have had a tendency to kind of let things slip, and one of the things they've let slip is the cemetery. They haven't cleaned it off for years and years, and it's choked with weeds and scrub. Most of the gravestones are hidden. It's surrounded by woods and old fields, and you can't always tell where the cemetery ends and the woods begin. Part of it is sandy and part of it is loamy, part of it is dry and part of it is damp, some of it is shady and some of it gets the sun all day, and I'm pretty sure you can find just about every wild flower that grows on the South Shore somewhere in it. Not to speak of shrubs and herbs and ferns and vines. If I were you, I'd take a look at it."

A man carrying a long-handled shovel in one hand and a short-handled shovel in the other came into the cemetery and started up the main path. Mr. Brock waved at him, and called out. "Here I am, Joe. Stay where you are. I'll be with you in a minute." The man dropped his shovels. "That's Mr. Damato, our gravedigger," said Mr. Brock. "We're having a burial in here tomorrow, and I came over to show him where to dig the grave. You'll have to excuse me now. If you do decide to visit the cemetery in Sandy Ground, you should ask for permission. They might not want strangers wandering around in it. The man to speak to is Mr. George H. Hunter. He's chairman of the board of trustees of the African Methodist church. I know Mr. Hunter. He's eighty-seven years old, and he's one of those strong, self-contained old men you don't see much any more. He was a hard worker, and he retired only a few years ago, and he's fairly well-to-do. He's a widower, and he lives by himself and does his own cooking. He's got quite a reputation as a cook. His church used to put on clambakes to raise money, and they were such good clambakes they attracted people from all over this part of Staten Island, and he always had charge of them. On some matters, such as drinking and smoking, he's very disapproving and strict and stern, but he doesn't feel that way about eating; he approves of eating. He's a great Bible reader. He's read the Bible from cover to cover, time and time again. His health is good, and his memory is unusually good. He remembers the golden age of the oyster business on the South Shore, and he remembers its decline and fall, and he can look at any old field or tumble-down house between Rossville and Tottenville and tell you who owns it now and who owned it fifty years ago, and he knows who the people were who are buried out in the Sandy Ground cemetery—how they lived and how they died, how much they left, and how their children turned out. Not that he'll necessarily tell you what he knows, or even a small part of it. If you can get him to go to the cemetery with you, ask him the local names of the weeds and wild flowers. He can tell you. His house is on Bloomingdale Road, right across from the church. It's the house with the lightning rods on it. Or you could call him on the phone. He's in the book."

I thanked Mr. Brock, and went straightway to a filling station on the Arthur Kill Road and telephoned Mr. Hunter. I told him I wanted to visit the Sandy Ground cemetery and look for wild flowers in it. "Go right ahead," he said. "Nobody'll stop you." I told him I also wanted to talk to him about Sandy Ground. "I can't see you today," he said. "I'm just leaving the house. An old lady I know is sick in bed, and I made her a lemon-meringue pie, and I'm going over and take it to her. Sit with her awhile. See if I can't cheer her up. You'll have to make it some other time, and you'd better make it soon. That cemetery is a disgrace, but it isn't going to be that way much longer. The board of trustees had a contractor look it over and make us a price how much he'd charge to go in there with a bulldozer and tear all that mess out by the roots. Clean it up good, and build us a road all the way through, with a turn-around at the farther end. The way it is now, there's a road in there, but it's a narrow little road and it only goes halfway in, and sometimes the pallbearers have to carry the coffin quite a distance from the hearse to the grave. Also, it comes to a dead end, and the hearse has to back out, and if the driver isn't careful he's liable to back into a gravestone, or run against the bushes and briars and scratch up the paint on his hearse. As I said, a disgrace. The price the contractor made us was pretty steep, but we put it up to the congregation, and if he's willing to let us pay a reasonable amount down and the balance in installments, I think we're going ahead with it. Are you busy this coming Saturday afternoon?" I said that I didn't expect to be. "All right," he said, "I tell you what you do. If it's a nice day, come on down, and I'll walk over to the cemetery with you. Come around one o'clock. I've got some things to attend to Saturday morning, and I ought to be through by then."

• • •

Saturday turned out to be nice and sunny, and I went across on the ferry and took the Tottenville bus and got off in Rossville and walked up Bloomingdale Road to Sandy Ground. Remembering Mr. Brock's instructions, I looked for a house with lightning rods on it, and I had no trouble finding it. Mr. Hunter's house is fully equipped with lightning rods, the tips of which are ornamented with glass balls and metal arrows.

It is a trim, square, shingle-sided, two-story-and-attic house. It has a front porch and a back porch, both screened. The front porch is shaded by a rambler rose growing on a trellis. I knocked on the frame of the screen door, and a bespectacled, elderly Negro man appeared in the hall. He had on a chef's apron, and his sleeves were rolled up. He was slightly below medium height, and lean and bald. Except for a wide, humorous mouth, his face was austere and a little forbidding, and his eyes were sad. I opened the door and asked, "Are you Mr. Hunter?" "Yes, yes, yes," he said. "Come on in, and close the door. Don't stand there and let the flies in. I hate flies. I despise them. I can't endure them." I followed him down the hall, past the parlor, past the dining room, and into the kitchen. There were three cake layers and a bowl of chocolate icing on the kitchen table.

"Sit down and make yourself at home," he said. "Let me put the icing on this cake, and then we'll walk over to the cemetery. Icing or frosting. I never knew which was right. I looked up icing in the dictionary one day, and it said 'Frosting for a cake.' So I looked up frosting, and it said 'Icing for a cake.' 'Ha!' I said. 'The dictionary man don't know, either.' The preacher at our church is a part-time preacher, and he doesn't live in Sandy Ground. He lives in Asbury Park, and runs a tailor shop during the week, and drives over here on Sundays. Reverend J. C. Ramsey, a Southern man, comes from Wadesboro, North Carolina. Most Sundays, he and his wife take Sunday dinner with me, and I always try to have something nice for them. After dinner, we sit around the table and drink Postum and discuss the Bible, and that's something I do enjoy. We discuss the prophecies in the Bible, and the warnings, and the promises—the promises of eternal life. And we discuss what I call the mysterious verses, the ones that if you could just understand them they might explain everything—why we're put here, why we're taken away—but they go down too deep; you study them over and over, and you go down as deep as you can, and you still don't touch bottom. 'Do you remember that verse in Revelation,' I say to Reverend Ramsey, 'where it says such and such?' And we discuss that awhile. And then he says to me, 'Do you remember that verse in Second Thessalonians, where it says so and so?' And we discuss that awhile. This Sunday, in addition to the preacher and his wife, I've got some other company coming. A gospel chorus from down South is going to sing at the church Sunday morning, a group of men and women from in and around Norfolk, Virginia, that call themselves the Union Gospel Chorus. They sing old hymns. Reverend Ramsey heard about them, and got into some correspondence with them. There's seven of them, and they're coming up on the bus today, and they'll spend the night in Asbury Park, and tomorrow, after they sing, they're coming to my house for Sunday dinner. That'll be ten for dinner, including the preacher and his wife and me, and that's nothing. I have twenty to dinner sometimes, like at Thanksgiving, and do it all myself, and it doesn't bother me a bit. I'm going to give them chicken fricassee and dumplings for the main course. Soon as I finish this cake, I'll take you in the dining room and show you what else I'm going to give them. Did you have your lunch?"

"I had a sandwich and some coffee on the ferryboat coming over," I said.

"Now, you know, I like to do that," Mr. Hunter said. "I never go cross on the ferryboat without I step up to the lunch counter and buy a little something—a sandwich, or a piece of raisin cake. And then I sit by the window and eat it, and look at the tugboats go by, and the big boats, and the sea gulls, and the Statue of Liberty. Oh, my! It's such a pleasure to eat on a boat. Years and years ago, I was cook on a boat. When I was growing up in Sandy Ground, the mothers taught the boys to cook the same as the girls. The way they looked at it—you never know, it might come in handy. My mother was an unusually good cook, and she taught me the fundamentals, and I was just naturally good at it, and when I was seventeen or eighteen there was a fleet of fishing boats on Staten Island that went to Montauk and up around there and fished the codfish grounds, and I got a job cooking on one of them. It was a small boat, only five in the crew, and the galley was just big enough for two pots and a pan and a stirring spoon and me. I was clumsy at first. Reach for something with my right hand and knock it over with my left elbow. After awhile, though, I got so good the captain of the biggest boat in the fleet heard about my cooking and tried to hire me away, but the men on my boat said if I left they'd leave, and my captain had been good to me, so I stayed. I was a fishing-boat cook for a year and a half, and then I quit and took up a different line of work altogether. I'll be through with this cake in just a minute. I make my icing thicker than most people do, and I put more on. Frosting. Speaking of wild flowers, do you know pokeweed when you see it?"

"Yes," I said.

"Did you ever eat it?"

"No," I said. "Isn't it supposed to be poisonous?"

"It's the root that's poisonous, the root and the berries. In the spring, when it first comes up, the young shoots above the root are good to eat. They taste like asparagus. The old women in Sandy Ground used to believe in eating pokeweed shoots, the old Southern women. They said it renewed your blood. My mother believed it. Every spring, she used to send me out in the woods to pick pokeweed shoots. And I believe it. So every spring, if I think about it, I go pick some and cook them. It's not that I like them so much—in fact, they give me gas—but they remind me of the days gone by, they remind me of my mother. Now, away down here in the woods in this part of Staten Island, you might think you were fifteen miles on the other side of nowhere, but just a little ways up Arthur Kill Road, up near Arden Avenue, there's a bend in the road where you can sometimes see the tops of the skyscrapers in New York. Just the tallest skyscrapers, and just the tops of them. It has to be an extremely clear day. Even then, you might be able to see them one moment and the next moment they're gone. Right beside this bend in the road there's a little swamp, and the edge of this swamp is the best place I know to pick pokeweed. I went up there one morning this spring to pick some, but we had a late spring, if you remember, and the pokeweed hadn't come up. The fiddleheads were up, and golden club, and spring beauty, and skunk cabbage, and bluets, but no pokeweed. So I was looking here and looking there, and not noticing where I was stepping, and I made a misstep, and the next thing I knew I was up to my knees in mud. I floundered around in the mud a minute, getting my bearings, and then I happened to raise my head and look up, and suddenly I saw, away off in the distance, miles and miles away, the tops of the skyscrapers in New York shining in the morning sun. I wasn't expecting it, and it was amazing. It was like a vision in the Bible."

Mr. Hunter smoothed the icing on top of the cake with a table knife, and stepped back and looked at it. "Well," he said, "I guess that does it." He placed a cover on the cake, and took off his apron. "I better wash my hands," he said. "If you want to see something pretty, step in the dining room and look on the sideboard." There was a walnut sideboard in the dining room, and it had been polished until it glinted. On it were two lemon-meringue pies, two coconut-custard pies, a pound cake, a marble cake, and a devil's-food cake. "Four pies and four cakes, counting the one

I just finished," Mr. Hunter called out. "I made them all this morning. I also got some corn muffins put away, to eat with the chicken fricassee. That ought to hold them." Above the dining-room table, hanging from the ceiling, was an old-fashioned lampshade. It was as big as a parasol, and made of pink silk, and fringed and tasselled. On one wall, in a row, were three religious placards. They were printed in ornamental type, and they had floral borders. The first said "JESUS NEVER FAILS." The second said "NOT MY WILL BUT THINE BE DONE." The third said "THE HOUR IS COMING IN WHICH ALL THAT ARE IN THE GRAVES SHALL HEAR HIS VOICE, AND SHALL COME FORTH; THEY THAT HAVE DONE GOOD, UNTO THE RESURRECTION OF LIFE; AND THEY THAT HAVE DONE EVIL, UNTO THE RESURRECTION OF DAMNATION." On another wall was a framed certificate stating that George Henry Hunter was a life member of St. John's Lodge No. 29 of the Most Worshipful Prince Hall Grand Lodge of Free and Accepted Masons. While I was looking at this, Mr. Hunter came into the room. "I'm proud of that," he said. "There's several Negro Mason organizations, but Prince Hall is the biggest, and I've been a member since 1906. I joined the Masons the same year I built this house. Did you notice my floors?" I looked down. The floor boards were wide and made of some kind of honey-colored wood, and they were waxed and polished. "Virgin spruce," he said. "Six inches wide. Tongue and groove. Built to last. In my time, that was the idea, but in this day and time, that's not the idea. They've got more things nowadays—things, things, things; kitchen stoves you could put in the parlor just to look at, refrigerators so big they're all out of reason, cars that reach from here to Rossville—but they aren't built to last, they're built to wear out. And that's the way the people want it. It's immaterial to them how long a thing lasts. In fact, if it don't wear out quick enough, they beat it and bang it and kick it and jump up and down on it, so they can get a new one. Most of what you buy nowadays, the outside is everything, the inside don't matter. Like those tomatoes you buy at the store, and they look so nice and shiny and red, and half the time, when you get them home and slice them, all that's inside is mush, red mush. And the people are the same. You hardly ever see a son any more as good as his father. Oh, he might be taller and stronger and thicker in the shoulders, playing games at school and all, but he can't stand as much. If he tried to lift and pull the way the men of my generation used to lift and pull, he'd be ruptured by noon, they'd be making arrangements to operate. How'd I get started talking this way? I'm tired, that's why. I been on my feet all morning, and I better sit down a few minutes." He took a tablecloth from a drawer of the sideboard and shook it out and laid it gently over the cakes and pies. "Let's go on the back porch," he said.

• • •

There were two wicker rocking chairs on the back porch, and we sat down. Mr. Hunter yawned and closed his eyes and slowly lowered his chin to his chest. I looked at his back yard, in which there were several rows of sweet potatoes, a row of tomatoes, a weeping willow, and a feeding table for birds. Mr. Hunter dozed for about five minutes, and then some blue jays flew into the yard, shrieking, and they aroused him. He sat up, pressing his elbows against the chair, and followed the jays with his eyes as they swooped and swirled about the yard. When they flew away, he laughed. "I enjoy birds," he said. "I enjoy their colors. I enjoy the noise they make, and the commotion. Even blue jays. Most mornings, I get up real early and go out in the yard and scatter bread crumbs and sunflower seeds on the feeding table, and then I sit up here on the porch and watch. Oh, it's nice out here in the early morning! Everything is so fresh. As my mother used to say, 'Every morning, the world anew.' Some mornings, I see a dozen different kinds of birds. There were redbirds all over the yard this morning, and a surprising number of brown thrashers and red-winged blackbirds. I see a good many I don't recognize; I do wish I knew their names. Every so often, a pair of pheasants land on the feeding table. Some of the old fields around here are full of them. I was picking some tomatoes the other day, and a pair of pheasants scuttled out from under the tomato bushes and flew up right in my face. Whoosh! Up goes the cock bird. A second later—whoosh! Up goes the hen bird. One of her wings brushed against me. I had my mind on something else, or I could've caught her. I better not get on the subject of birds, or I'll talk your ears off. You said on the phone you wanted to know something about Sandy Ground. What do you want to know? How it began?"

"Yes, sir," I said.

"Oysters!" said Mr. Hunter. "That's how it began." There was a fly swatter on the floor beside Mr. Hunter's chair, and a few feet in front of his chair was an old kitchen table with a chipped enamel top. He suddenly reached down and grabbed the swatter and stood up and took a step toward the table, on which a fly had lit. His shadow fell on the fly, and the fly flew away. Mr. Hunter stared wildly into space for several moments, looking for the fly and muttering angrily, and then he sat back down, still holding the swatter.

"It's hard to believe nowadays, the water's so dirty," he continued, "but up until about the year 1800 there were tremendous big beds of natural-growth oysters all around Staten Island—in the Lower Bay, in the Arthur Kill, in the Kill van Kull. Some of the richest beds of oysters in the entire country were out in the lower part of the Lower Bay, the part known as Raritan Bay. Most of them were on shoals, under ten to twenty feet of water. They were supposed to be public beds, open to anybody, but they were mainly worked by Staten Islanders, and the Staten Islanders considered they owned them. Between 1800 and 1820, all but the very deepest of these beds gradually petered out. They had been raked and scraped until they weren't worth working any more. But the Staten Islanders didn't give up. What they did, they began to bring immature oysters from other localities and put them on the best of the old beds and leave them there until they reached market size, which took from one to four years, all according to how mature the oysters were to begin with. Then they'd rake them up, or tong them up, and load them on boats, and send them up the bay to the wholesalers in New York. They took great pains with these oysters. They cleaned the empty shells and bottom trash off the beds that they put them on, and they spread them out as evenly as possible. Handled this way, oysters grew faster than they did all scrouged together on natural beds. Also, they grew more uniform in size and shape. Also, they had a better flavor. Also, they brought higher prices, premium prices. The center of the business was the little town of Prince's Bay, over on the outside shore. There's not much to Prince's Bay now, but it used to be one of the busiest oyster ports on the Atlantic Coast.

"At first, the Staten Islanders used sloops and bought their seed stock close by, in bays in New Jersey and Long Island, but the business grew very fast, and in a few years a good many of them were using schooners that could hold five thousand bushels and were making regular trips to Maryland and Virginia. Some went into inlets along the ocean side of the Eastern Shore, and some went into Chesapeake Bay. They bought from local oystermen who worked natural beds in the public domain, and they usually had to visit a whole string of little ports and landings before they got a load. At that time, there were quite a few free Negroes among the oystermen on the Eastern Shore, especially in Worcester

County, Maryland, on the upper part of Chincoteague Bay, and the Staten Island captains occasionally hired gangs of them to make the trip North and help distribute the oysters on the beds. Now and then, a few would stay behind on Staten Island for a season or two and work on empty beds, cleaning them off and getting them ready for new seed stock. Late in the 1830s or early in the 1840s, a number of these men left their homes in and around Snow Hill, Maryland, the county seat of Worcester County, and came up to Staten Island to live. They brought their families, and they settled over here in the Sandy Ground section. The land was cheap in Sandy Ground, and it was in easy walking distance of Prince's Bay, and a couple of Negro families were already living over here, a family named Jackson and a family named Henry. The records of our church go back to 1850, and they show the names of most of the original men from Snow Hill. Three of them were Purnells—Isaac Purnell, George Purnell, and Littleton Purnell. Two were Lambdens, spelled L-a-m-b-d-e-n, only their descendants changed the spelling to L-a-n-d-i-n—Landin. One was a Robbins, and one was a Bishop, and one was a Henman. The Robbins family died out or moved away many years ago, but Purnells, Landins, Bishops, and Henmans still live in Sandy Ground. They've always been the main Sandy Ground families. There's a man from Sandy Ground who works for a trucking concern in New York, drives trailer trucks, and he's driven through Maryland many times, and stopped in Snow Hill, and he says there's still people down there with these names, plenty of them, white and Negro. Especially Purnells and Bishops. Every second person you run into in Snow Hill, just about, he says, is either a Purnell or a Bishop, and there's one little crossroad town near Snow Hill that's named Bishop and another one that's named Bishopville. Through the years, other Negro families came to Sandy Ground and settled down and intermarried with the families from Snow Hill. Some came from the South, but the majority came from New York and New Jersey and other places in the North. Such as the Harris family, the Mangin family, the Fish family, the Williams family, the Finney family, and the Roach family."

All of a sudden, Mr. Hunter leaned forward in his chair as far as he could go and brought the fly swatter down on the table. This time, he killed the fly.

"I wasn't born in Sandy Ground myself," he continued. "I came here when I was a boy. My mother and my stepfather brought me here. Two or three of the original men from Snow Hill were still around then, and

I knew them. They were old, old men. As a matter of fact, they were about as old as I am now. And the widows of several others were still around. Two of those old widows lived near us, and they used to come to see my mother and sit by the kitchen range and talk and talk, and I used to like to listen to them. The main thing they talked about was the early days in Sandy Ground—how poor everybody had been, and how hard everybody had had to work, the men and the women. The men all worked by the day for the white oystermen in Prince's Bay. They went out in skiffs and anchored over the beds and stood up in the skiffs from sunup to sundown, raking oysters off the bottom with big old claw-toothed rakes that were made of iron and weighed fourteen pounds and had handles on them twenty-four feet long. The women all washed. They washed for white women in Prince's Bay and Rossville and Tottenville. And there wasn't a real house in the whole of Sandy Ground. Most of the families lived in one-room shacks with lean-tos for the children. In the summer, they ate what they grew in their gardens. In the winter, they ate oysters until they couldn't stand the sight of them.

"When I came here, early in the 1880s that had all changed. By that time, Sandy Ground was really quite a prosperous little place. Most of the men were still breaking their backs raking oysters by the day, but several of them had saved their money and worked up to where they owned and operated pretty good-sized oyster sloops and didn't take orders from anybody. Old Mr. Dawson Landin was the first to own a sloop. He owned a forty-footer named the Pacific. He was the richest man in the settlement, and he took the lead in everything. Still and all, people liked him and looked up to him; most of us called him Uncle Daws. His brother, Robert Landin, owned a thirty-footer named the Independence, and Mr. Robert's son-in-law, Francis Henry, also owned a thirty-footer. His was named the Fannie Ferne. And a few others owned sloops. There were still some places here and there in the Arthur Kill and the Kill van Kull where you could rake up natural-growth seed oysters if you spliced two rake handles together and went down deep enough, and that's what these men did. They sold the seed to the white oystermen, and they made out all right. In those days, the oyster business used oak baskets by the thousands, and some of the Sandy Ground men had got to be good basket-makers. They went into the woods around here and cut white-oak saplings and split them into strips and soaked the strips in water and wove them into bushel baskets that would last for years. Also, several of the men had become blacksmiths. They made oyster rakes and repaired them, and did all kinds of ironwork for the boats. One of those men was Mr. William Bishop, and his son, Joe Bishop, still runs a blacksmith shop over on Woodrow Road. It's the last real old-time blacksmith shop left on the island.

"The population of Sandy Ground was bigger then than it is now, and the houses were newer and nicer-looking. Every family owned the house they lived in, and a little bit of land. Not much—an acre and a half, two acres, three acres. I guess Uncle Daws had the most, and he only had three and three-quarter acres. But what they had, they made every inch of it count. They raised a few pigs and chickens, and kept a cow, and had some fruit trees and grapevines, and planted a garden. They planted a lot of Southern stuff, such as butter beans and okra and sweet potatoes and mustard greens and collards and Jerusalem artichokes. There were flowers in every yard, and rosebushes, and the old women exchanged seeds and bulbs and cuttings with each other. Back then, this was a big strawberry section. The soil in Sandy Ground is ideal for strawberries. All the white farmers along Bloomingdale Road grew them, and the people in Sandy Ground took it up; you can grow a lot of strawberries on an acre. In those days, a river steamer left New Brunswick, New Jersey, every morning, and came down the Raritan River and entered the Arthur Kill and made stops at Rossville and five or six other little towns on the kill, and then went on up to the city and docked at the foot of Barclay Street, right across from Washington Market. And early every morning during strawberry season the people would box up their strawberries and take them down to Rossville and put them on the steamer and send them off to market. They'd lay a couple of grape leaves on top of each box, and that would bring out the beauty of the berries, the green against the red. Staten Island strawberries had the reputation of being unusually good, the best on the market, and they brought fancy prices. Most of them went to the big New York hotels. Some of the families in Sandy Ground, strawberries were about as important to them as oysters. And every family put up a lot of stuff, not only garden stuff, but wild stuff—wild-grape jelly, and wild-plum jelly, and huckleberries. If it was a good huckleberry year, they'd put up enough huckleberries to make deep-dish pies all winter. And when they killed their hogs, they made link sausages and liver pudding and lard. Some of the old women even made soap. People looked after things in those days. They patched and mended and made do, and they kept their yards clean, and they burned their trash. And they taught their children how to conduct themselves. And they held their heads up; they were as good as anybody, and better than some. And they got along with each other; they knew each other's peculiarities and took them into consideration. Of course, this was an oyster town, and there was always an element that drank and carried on and didn't have any more moderation than the cats up the alley, but the great majority were good Christians who walked in the way of the Lord, and loved Him, and trusted Him, and kept His commandments. Everything in Sandy Ground revolved around the church. Every summer, we put up a tent in the churchyard and held a big camp meeting, a revival. We owned the tent. We could get three or four hundred people under it, sitting on sawhorse benches. We'd have visiting preachers, famous old-time African Methodist preachers, and they'd preach every night for a week. We'd invite the white oystermen to come and bring their families, and a lot of them would. Everybody was welcome. And once a year, to raise money for church upkeep, we'd put on an ox roast, what they call a barbecue nowadays. A Southern man named Steve Davis would do the roasting. There were tricks to it that only he knew. He'd dig a pit in the churchyard, and then a little off to one side he'd burn a pile of hickory logs until he had a big bed of red-hot coals, and then he'd fill the pit about half full of coals, and then he'd set some iron rods across the pit, and then he'd lay a couple of sides of beef on the rods and let them roast. Every now and then, he'd shovel some more coals into the pit, and then he'd turn the sides of beef and baste them with pepper sauce, or whatever it was he had in that bottle of his, and the beef would drip and sputter and sizzle, and the smoke from the hickory coals would flavor it to perfection. People all over the South Shore would set aside that day and come to the African Methodist ox roast. All the big oyster captains in Prince's Bay would come. Captain Phil De Waters would come, and Captain Abraham Manee and Captain William Haughwout and Captain Peter Polworth and good old Captain George Newbury, and a dozen others. And we'd eat and laugh and joke with each other over who could hold the most.

"All through the eighties, and all through the nineties, and right on up to around 1910, that's the way it was in Sandy Ground. Then the water went bad. The oystermen had known for a long time that the water in the Lower Bay was getting dirty, and they used to talk about it, and worry about it, but they didn't have any idea how bad it was until around 1910, when reports began to circulate that cases of typhoid fever had been traced to the eating of Staten Island oysters. The oyster wholesalers in New York were the unseen powers in the Staten Island oyster business;

they advanced the money to build boats and buy Southern seed stock. When the typhoid talk got started, most of them decided they didn't want to risk their money any more, and the business went into a decline, and then, in 1916, the Department of Health stepped in and condemned the beds, and that was that. The men in Sandy Ground had to scratch around and look for something else to do, and it wasn't easy. Mr. George Ed Henman got a job working on a garbage wagon for the city, and Mr. James McCoy became the janitor of a public school, and Mr. Jacob Finney went to work as a porter on Ellis Island, and one did this and one did that. A lot of the life went out of the settlement, and a kind of don't-care attitude set in. The church was especially hard hit. Many of the young men and women moved away, and several whole families, and the membership went down. The men who owned oyster sloops had been the main support of the church, and they began to give dimes where they used to give dollars. Steve Davis died, and it turned out nobody else knew how to roast an ox, so we had to give up the ox roasts. For some years, we put on clambakes instead, and then clams got too expensive, and we had to give up the clambakes.

"The way it is now, Sandy Ground is just a ghost of its former self. There's a disproportionate number of old people. A good many of the big old rambling houses that used to be full of children, there's only old men and old women living in them now. And you hardly ever see them. People don't sit on their porches in Sandy Ground as much as they used to, even old people, and they don't do much visiting. They sit inside, and keep to themselves, and listen to the radio or look at television. Also, in most of the families in Sandy Ground where the husband and wife are young or middle-aged, both of them go off to work. If there's children, a grandmother or an old aunt or some other relative stays home and looks after them. And they have to travel good long distances to get to their work. The women mainly work in hospitals, such as Sea View, the big t.b. hospital way up in the middle of the island, and I hate to think of the time they put in riding those rattly old Staten Island buses and standing at bus stops in all kinds of weather. The men mainly work in construction, or in factories across the kill in New Jersey. You hear their cars starting up early in the morning, and you hear them coming in late at night. They make eighty, ninety, a hundred a week, and they take all the overtime work they can get; they have to, to pay for those big cars and refrigerators and television sets. Whenever something new comes out, if one family gets one, the others can't rest until they get one too. And the only thing they pay cash for is candy bars. For all I know, they even buy them on the installment plan. It'll all end in a mess one of these days. The church has gone way down. People say come Sunday they're just too tired to stir. Most of the time, only a handful of the old reliables show up for Sunday-morning services, and we've completely given up Sunday-evening services. Oh, sometimes a wedding or a funeral will draw a crowd. As far as gardens, nobody in Sandy Ground plants a garden any more beyond some old woman might set out a few tomato plants and half the time she forgets about them and lets them wilt. As far as wild stuff, there's plenty of huckleberries in the woods around here, high-bush and low-bush, and oceans of blackberries, and I even know where there's some beach plums, but do you think anybody bothers with them? Oh, no!"

. . .

Mr. Hunter stood up. "I've rested long enough," he said. "Let's go on over to the cemetery." He went down the back steps, and I followed him. He looked under the porch and brought out a grub hoe and handed it to me. "We may need this," he said. "You take it, if you don't mind, and go on around to the front of the house. I'll go back inside and lock up, and I'll meet you out front in just a minute."

I went around to the front, and looked at the roses on the trellised bush beside the porch. They were lush pink roses. It was a hot afternoon, and when Mr. Hunter came out, I was surprised to see that he had put on a jacket, and a double-breasted jacket at that. He had also put on a black necktie and a black felt hat. They were undoubtedly his Sunday clothes, and he looked stiff and solemn in them.

"I was admiring your rosebush," I said.

"It does all right," said Mr. Hunter. "It's an old bush. When it was getting a start, I buried bones from the table around the roots of it, the way the old Southern women used to do. Bones are the best fertilizer in the world for rosebushes." He took the hoe and put it across his shoulder, and we started up Bloomingdale Road. We walked in the road; there are no sidewalks in Sandy Ground.

A little way up the road, we overtook an old man hobbling along on a cane. He and Mr. Hunter spoke to each other, and Mr. Hunter introduced him to me. "This is Mr. William E. Brown," Mr. Hunter said. "He's one of the old Sandy Ground oystermen. He's in his eighties, but he's younger than me. How are you, Mr. Brown?"

"I'm just hanging by a thread," said Mr. Brown.

"Is it as bad as that?" asked Mr. Hunter.

"Oh, I'm all right," said Mr. Brown, "only for this numbness in my legs, and I've got cataracts and can't half see, and I had a dentist make me a set of teeth and he says they fit, but they don't, they slip, and I had double pneumonia last winter and the doctor gave me some drugs that addled me. And I'm still addled."

"This is the first I've seen you in quite a while," said Mr. Hunter.

"I stay to myself," said Mr. Brown. "I was never one to go to people's houses. They talk and talk, and you listen, you bound to listen, and half of it ain't true, and the next time they tell it, they say you said it."

"Well, nice to see you, Mr. Brown," said Mr. Hunter.

"Nice to see you, Mr. Hunter," said Mr. Brown. "Where you going?"

"Just taking a walk over to the cemetery," said Mr. Hunter.

"Well, you won't get in any trouble over there," said Mr. Brown.

We resumed our walk.

"Mr. Brown came to Sandy Ground when he was a boy, the same as I did," Mr. Hunter said. "He was born in Brooklyn, but his people were from the South."

"Were you born in the South, Mr. Hunter?" I asked.

"No, I wasn't," he said.

His face became grave, and we walked past three or four houses before he said any more.

"I wasn't," he finally said. "My mother was. To tell you the truth, my mother was born in slavery. Her name was Martha, Martha Jennings, and she was born in 1849. Jennings was the name of the man who owned her. He was a big farmer in the Shenandoah Valley in Virginia. He also owned my mother's mother, but he sold her when my mother was five years old, and my mother never saw or heard of her again. Her name was Hettie. We couldn't ever get much out of my mother about slavery days. She didn't like to talk about it, and she didn't like for us to talk about it. 'Let the dead bury the dead,' she used to say. Just before the Civil War, when my mother was eleven or twelve, the wife of the man who owned her went to Alexandria, Virginia, to spend the summer, and she took my mother along to attend to her children. Somehow or other, my mother got in with some people in Alexandria who helped her run away. Some anti-slavery people. She never said so in so many words, but I guess they put her on the Underground Railroad. Anyway, she wound up in what's now Ossining, New York, only then it was called the village of Sing

Sing, and by and by she married my father. His name was Henry Hunter, and he was a hired man on an apple farm just outside Sing Sing. She had fifteen children by him, but only three—me, my brother William, and a girl named Hettie—lived past the age of fourteen; most of them died when they were babies. My father died around 1879, 1880, somewhere in there. A few months after he died, a man named Ephraim Purnell rented a room in our house. Purnell was an oysterman from Sandy Ground. He was a son of old man Littleton Purnell, one of the original men from Snow Hill. He had got into some trouble in Prince's Bay connected with stealing, and had been sent to Sing Sing Prison. After he served out his sentence, he decided he'd see if he could get a job in Sing Sing village and live there. My mother tried to help him, and ended up marrying him. He couldn't get a job up there, nobody would have him, so he brought my mother and me and William and Hettie down here to Sandy Ground and he went back to oystering."

We turned off Bloomingdale Road and entered Crabtree Avenue, which is a narrow dirt road lined on one side with sassafras trees and on the other with a straggly privet hedge.

"I didn't like my stepfather," Mr. Hunter continued. "I not only didn't like him, I despised him. He was a drunkard, a sot, and he mistreated my mother. From the time we landed in Sandy Ground, as small as I was, my main object in life was to support myself. I didn't want him supporting me. And I didn't want to go into the oyster business, because he was in it. I worked for a farmer down the road a few years—one of the Sharrotts that Sharrott's Road is named for. Then I cooked on a fishing boat. Then I became a hod carrier. Then something got into me, and I began to drink. I turned into a sot myself. After I had been drinking several years, I was standing in a grocery store in Rossville one day, and I saw my mother walk past outside on the street. I just caught a glimpse of her face through the store window as she walked past, and she didn't know anybody was looking at her, and she had a horrible hopeless look on her face. A week or so later, I knocked off work in the middle of the day and bought a bottle of whiskey, the way I sometimes did, and I went out in the woods between Rossville and Sandy Ground and sat down on a rock, and I was about as low in my mind as a man can be; I knew what whiskey was doing to me, and yet I couldn't stop drinking it. I tore the stamp off the bottle and pulled out the cork, and got ready to take a drink, and then I remembered the look on my mother's face, and a peculiar thing happened. The best way I can explain it, my gorge rose. I got mad at myself, and I got mad at the world. Instead of taking a drink, I poured the whiskey on the ground and smashed the bottle on the rock, and stood up and walked out of the woods. And I never drank another drop. I wanted to many a time, many and many a time, but I tightened my jaw against myself, and I stood it off. When I look back, I don't know how I did it, but I stood it off, I stood it off."

We walked on in silence for a few minutes, and then Mr. Hunter said, "Ah, well!"

"From being a hod carrier, I became a bricklayer," he continued, "but that wasn't as good as it sounds; bricklayers didn't make much in those days. And in 1896, when I was twenty-seven, I got married to my first wife. Her name was Celia Ann Finney, and she was the daughter of Mr. Jacob Finney, one of the oystermen. She was considered the prettiest girl in Sandy Ground, and the situation I was in, she had turned down a well-to-do young oysterman to marry me, a fellow with a sloop, and I knew everybody thought she had made a big mistake and would live to regret it, and I vowed and determined I was going to give her more than he could've given her. I was a good bricklayer, and I was especially good at arching and vaulting, and when a contractor or a boss mason had a cesspool to be built, he usually put me to work on it. We didn't have sewers down in this part of Staten Island, and still don't, and there were plenty of cesspools to be built. So, in 1899 I borrowed some money and went into business for myself, the business of building and cleaning cesspools. I made it my lifework. And I made good money, for around here. I built a good house for my wife, and I dressed her in the latest styles. I went up to New York once and bought her a dress for Easter that cost one hundred and six dollars; the six dollars was for alterations. And one Christmas I bought her a sealskin coat. And I bought pretty hats for her—velvet hats, straw hats, hats with feathers, hats with birds, hats with veils. And she appreciated everything I bought for her. 'Oh, George,' she'd say, 'you've gone too far this time. You've got to take it back.' 'Take it back, nothing!' I'd say. When Victrolas came out, I bought her the biggest one in the store. And I think I can safely say we set the best table in Sandy Ground. I lived in peace and harmony with her for thirty-two years, and they were the best years of my life. She died in 1928. Cancer. Two years later I married a widow named Mrs. Edith S. Cook. She died in 1938. They told me it was tumors, but it was cancer."

We came to a break in the privet hedge. Through the break I saw the white shapes of gravestones half-hidden in vines and scrub, and realized that we were at the entrance to the cemetery. "Here we are," said Mr. Hunter. He stopped, and leaned on the handle of the hoe, and continued to talk.

"I had one son by my first wife," he said. "We named him William Francis Hunter, and we called him Billy. When he grew up, Billy went into the business with me. I never urged him to, but he seemed to want to, it was his decision, and I remember how proud I was the first time I put it in the telephone book—George H. Hunter & Son. Billy did the best he could, I guess, but things never worked out right for him. He got married, but he lived apart from his wife, and he drank. When he first began to drink, I remembered my own troubles along that line, and I tried not to see it. I just looked the other way, and hoped and prayed he'd get hold of himself, but there came a time I couldn't look the other way any more. I asked him to stop, and I begged him to stop, and I did all I could, went to doctors for advice, tried this, tried that, but he wouldn't stop. It wasn't exactly he wouldn't stop, he couldn't stop. A few years ago, his stomach began to bother him. He thought he had an ulcer, and he started drinking more than ever, said whiskey dulled the pain. I finally got him to go to the hospital, and it wasn't any ulcer, it was cancer."

Mr. Hunter took a wallet from his hip pocket. It was a large, old-fashioned wallet, the kind that fastens with a strap slipped through a loop. He opened it and brought out a folded white silk ribbon.

"Billy died last summer," he continued. "After I had made the funeral arrangements, I went to the florist in Tottenville and ordered a floral wreath and picked out a nice wreath-ribbon to go on it. The florist knew me, and he knew Billy, and he made a very pretty wreath. The Sunday after Billy was buried, I walked over here to the cemetery to look at his grave, and the flowers on the wreath were all wilted and dead, but the ribbon was as pretty as ever, and I couldn't bear to let it lay out in the rain and rot, so I took it off and saved it." He unfolded the ribbon and held it up. Across it, in gold letters, were two words. "BELOVED SON," they said.

. . .

Mr. Hunter refolded the ribbon and returned it to his wallet. Then he put the hoe back on his shoulder, and we entered the cemetery. A little road went halfway into the cemetery, and a number of paths branched off from it, and both the road and the paths were hip-deep in broom sedge. Here and there in the sedge were patches of Queen Anne's lace and a weed that I didn't recognize. I pointed it out to Mr. Hunter.

"What is that weed in among the broom sedge and the Queen Anne's lace?" I asked.

"We call it red root around here," he said, "and what you call broom sedge we call beard grass, and what you call Queen Anne's lace we call wild carrot."

We started up the road, but Mr. Hunter almost immediately turned in to one of the paths and stopped in front of a tall marble gravestone, around which several kinds of vines and climbing plants were intertwined. I counted them, and there were exactly ten kinds—cat brier, trumpet creeper, wild hop, blackberry, morning glory, climbing false buckwheat, partridgeberry, fox grape, poison ivy, and one that I couldn't identify, nor could Mr. Hunter. "This is Uncle Daws Landin's grave," Mr. Hunter said. "I'm going to chop down some of this mess, so we can read the dates on his stone." He lifted the hoe high in the air and brought it down with great vigor, and I got out of his way. I went back into the road, and looked around me. The older graves were covered with trees and shrubs. Sassafras and honey locust and wild black cherry were the tallest, and they were predominant, and beneath them were chokeberry, bayberry, sumac, Hercules' club, spice bush, sheep laurel, hawthorn, and witch hazel. A scattering of the newer graves were fairly clean, but most of them were thickly covered with weeds and wild flowers and ferns. There were easily a hundred kinds. Among those that I could identify were milkweed, knotweed, ragweed, Jimson weed, pavement weed, chickweed, joe-pye weed, wood aster, lamb's-quarters, plantain, catchfly, Jerusalem oak, bedstraw, goldenrod, cocklebur, chicory, butter-and-eggs, thistle, dandelion, selfheal, Mexican tea, stinging nettle, bouncing Bet, mullein, touch-me-not, partridge pea, beggar's-lice, sandspur, wild garlic, wild mustard, wild geranium, may apple, old-field cinquefoil, cinnamon fern, New York fern, lady fern, and maidenhair fern. Some of the graves had rusty iron-pipe fences around them. Many were unmarked, but were outlined with sea shells or bricks or round stones painted white or flowerpots turned upside down. Several had field stones at the head and foot. Several had wooden stakes at the head and foot. Several had Spanish bayonets growing on them. The Spanish bayonets were in full bloom, and insects were buzzing around their white, waxy, fleshy, bell-shaped, pendulous blossoms.

"Hey, there!" Mr. Hunter called out. "I've got it so we can see to read it now." I went back up the path, and we stood among the wrecked vines and looked at the inscription on the stone. It read:

DAWSON LANDIN
DEC. 18, 1828
FEB. 21, 1899
ASLEEP IN JESUS

"I remember him well," said Mr. Hunter. "He was a smart old man and a good old man, big and stout, very religious, passed the plate in church, chewed tobacco, took the New York *Herald,* wore a captain's cap, wore suspenders *and* a belt, had a peach orchard. I even remember the kind of peach he had in his orchard. It was a freestone peach, a late bearer, and the name of it was Stump the World."

We walked a few steps up the path, and came to a smaller gravestone. The inscription on it read:

SUSAN A. WALKER
MAR. 10, 1855
MAR. 25, 1912
A FAITHFUL FRIEND

"Born in March, died in March," said Mr. Hunter. "I don't know what that means, 'A Faithful Friend.' It might mean she was a faithful friend, only that hardly seems the proper thing to pick out and mention on a gravestone, or it might mean a faithful friend put up the stone. Susan Walker was one of Uncle Daws Landin's daughters, and she was a good Christian woman. She did more for the church than any other woman in the history of Sandy Ground. Now, that's strange. I don't remember a thing about Uncle Daws Landin's funeral, and he must've had a big one, but I remember Susan Walker's funeral very well. There used to be a white man named Charlie Bogardus who ran a store at the corner of Woodrow Road and Bloomingdale Road, a general store, and he also had an icehouse, and he was also an undertaker. He was the undertaker for most of the country people around here, and he got some of the Rossville business and some of the Pleasant Plains business. He had a handsome old horse-drawn hearse. It had windows on both sides, so you could see the coffin, and it had silver fittings. Bogardus handled Susan Walker's funeral. I can still remember his two big black hearse-horses drawing the hearse up Bloomingdale Road, stepping just as slow, the way they were trained to do, and turning in to Crabtree Avenue, and proceeding on down to the cemetery. The horses had black plumes on their harnesses. Funerals were much sadder when they had horse-drawn hearses. Charlie Bogardus had a son named Charlie Junior, and Charlie Junior had a son named Willie, and when automobile hearses started coming in, Willie mounted the old hearse on an automobile chassis. It didn't look fish, fowl, or fox, but the Bogarduses kept on using it until they finally gave up the store and the icehouse and the undertaking business and moved away."

We left Susan Walker's grave and returned to the road and entered another path and stopped before one of the newer graves. The inscription on its stone read:

FREDERICK ROACH
1891–1955
REST IN PEACE

"Freddie Roach was a taxi-driver," Mr. Hunter said. "He drove a taxi in Pleasant Plains for many years. He was Mrs. Addie Roach's son, and she made her home with him. After he died, she moved in with one of her daughters. Mrs. Addie Roach is the oldest woman in Sandy Ground. She's the widow of Reverend Lewis Roach, who was an oysterman and a part-time preacher, and she's ninety-two years old. When I first came to Sandy Ground, she was still in her teens, and she was a nice, bright, pretty girl. I've known her all these years, and I think the world of her. Every now and then, I make her a lemon-meringue pie and take it to her, and sit with her awhile. There's a white man in Prince's Bay who's a year or so older than Mrs. Roach. He's ninety-three, and he'll soon be ninety-four. His name is Mr. George E. Sprague, and he comes from a prominent old South Shore family, and I believe he's the last of the old Prince's Bay oyster captains. I hadn't seen him for several years until just the other day I was over in Prince's Bay, and I was going past his house on Amboy Road, and I saw him sitting on the porch. I went up and spoke to him, and we talked awhile, and when I was leaving he said, 'Is Mrs. Addie Roach still alive over in Sandy Ground?' 'She is,' I said. 'That is,' I said, 'she's alive as you or I.' 'Well,' he said, 'Mrs. Roach and I go way back. When she was a young woman, her mother used to wash for my mother, and she used to come along sometimes and help, and she was such a cheerful, pretty person my mother always said it made the day nicer when she came, and that was over seventy years ago.' 'That wasn't her mother that washed for your mother and she came along to help,' I said. 'That was her husband's mother. That was old Mrs. Matilda Roach.' 'Is that so?' said Mr. Sprague. 'I always thought it was her mother. Well,' he said, 'when you see her, tell her I asked for her.'"

We stepped back into the road, and walked slowly up it.

"Several men from Sandy Ground fought in the Civil War," Mr. Hunter said, "and one of them was Samuel Fish. That's his grave over there with the ant hill on it. He got a little pension. Down at the end of this row are some Bishop graves, Bishops and Mangins, and there's Purnells in the next row, and there's Henmans in those big plots over there. This is James McCoy's grave. He came from Norfolk, Virginia. He had six fingers on his right hand. Those graves over there all grown up in cockleburs are Jackson graves, Jacksons and Henrys and Landins. Most of the people lying in here were related to each other, some by blood, some by marriage, some close, some distant. If you started in at the gate and ran an imaginary line all the way through, showing who was related to who, the line would zigzag all over the cemetery. Do you see that row of big expensive stones standing up over there? They're all Cooleys. The Cooleys were free-Negro oystermen from Gloucester County, Virginia, and they came to Staten Island around the same time as the people from Snow Hill. They lived in Tottenville, but they belonged to the church in Sandy Ground. They were quite well-to-do. One of them, Joel Cooley, owned a forty-foot sloop. When the oyster beds were condemned, he retired on his savings and raised dahlias. He was a member of the Staten Island Horticultural Society, and his dahlias won medals at flower shows in Madison Square Garden. I've heard it said he was the first man on Staten Island to raise figs, and now there's fig bushes in back yards from one end of the island to the other. Joel Cooley had a brother named Obed Cooley who was very smart in school, and the Cooleys got together and sent him to college. They sent him to the University of Michigan, and he became a doctor. He practiced in Lexington, Kentucky, and he died in 1937, and he left a hundred thousand dollars. There used to be a lot of those old-fashioned names around here, Bible names. There was a Joel and an Obed and an Eben in the Cooley family, and there was an Ishmael and an Isaac and an Israel in the Purnell family. Speaking of names, come over here and look at this stone."

We stopped before a stone whose inscription read:

THOMAS WILLIAMS
AL MAJOR
1862–1928

"There used to be a rich old family down here named the Butlers," Mr. Hunter said. "They were old, old Staten Islanders, and they had a big estate over on the outside shore, between Prince's Bay and Tottenville, that they called Butler Manor. They even had a private race track. The last of the Butlers was Mr. Elmer T. Butler. Now, this fellow Thomas Williams was a Sandy Ground man who quit the oyster business and went to work for Mr. Elmer T. Butler. He worked for him many years, worked on the grounds, and Mr. Butler thought a lot of him. For some reason I never understood, Mr. Butler called him Al Major, a kind of nickname. And pretty soon everybody called him Al Major. In fact, as time went on and he got older, young people coming up took it for granted Al Major was his real name and called him Mr. Major. When he died, Mr. Butler buried him. And when he ordered the gravestone, he told the monument company to put both names on it, so there wouldn't be any confusion. Of course, in a few years he'll pass out of people's memory under both names—Thomas Williams, Al Major, it'll all be the same. To tell you the truth, I'm no great believer in gravestones. To a large extent, I think they come under the heading of what the old preacher called vanity—'vanity of vanities, all is vanity'—and by the old preacher I mean Ecclesiastes. There's stones in here that've only been up forty or fifty years, and you can't read a thing it says on them, and what difference does it make? God keeps His eye on those that are dead and buried the same as He does on those that are alive and walking. When the time comes the dead are raised, He won't need any directions where they're lying. Their bones may be turned to dust, and weeds may be growing out of their dust, but they aren't lost. He knows where they are; He knows the exact whereabouts of every speck of dust of every one of them. Stones rot the same as bones rot, and nothing endures but the spirit."

Mr. Hunter turned and looked back over the rows of graves.

"It's a small cemetery," he said, "and we've been burying in it a long time, and it's getting crowded, and there's generations yet to come, and it worries me. Since I'm the chairman of the board of trustees, I'm in charge of selling graves in here, graves and plots, and I always try to encourage families to bury two to a grave. That's perfectly legal, and a good many cemeteries are doing it nowadays. All the law says, it specifies that the top of the box containing the coffin shall be at least three feet below the level of the ground. To speak plainly, you dig the grave eight feet down, instead of six feet down, and that leaves room to lay a second coffin on top of the first. Let's go to the end of this path, and I'll show you my plot."

Mr. Hunter's plot was in the last row, next to the woods. There were only a few weeds on it. It was the cleanest plot in the cemetery.

"My mother's buried in the first grave," he said. "I never put up a stone for her. My first wife's father, Jacob Finney, is buried in this one, and I didn't put up a stone for him, either. He didn't own a grave, so we buried him in our plot. My son Billy is buried in this grave. And this is my first wife's grave. I put up a stone for her."

The stone was small and plain, and the inscription on it read:

HUNTER
1877 CELIA 1928

"I should've had her full name put on it—Celia Ann," Mr. Hunter said. "She was a little woman, and she had a low voice. She had the prettiest little hands; she wore size five-and-a-half gloves. She was little, but you'd be surprised at the work she done. Now, my second wife is buried over here, and I put up a stone for her, too. And I had my name carved on it, along with hers."

This stone was the same size and shape as the other, and the inscription on it read:

HUNTER
1877 EDITH 1938
1869 GEORGE

"It was my plan to be buried in the same grave with my second wife," Mr. Hunter said. "When she died, I was sick in bed, and the doctor wouldn't let me get up, even to go to the funeral, and I couldn't attend to things the way I wanted to. At that time, we had a gravedigger here named John Henman. He was an old man, an old oysterman. He's dead now himself. I called John Henman to my bedside, and I specifically told him to dig the grave eight feet down. I told him I wanted to be buried in the same grave. 'Go eight feet down,' I said to him, 'and that'll leave room for me, when the time comes.' And he promised to do so. And when I got well, and was up and about again, I ordered this stone and had it put up. Below my wife's name and dates I had them put my name and my birth year. When it came time, all they'd have to put on it would be my death year, and everything would be in order. Well, one day about a year later I was talking to John Henman, and something told me he hadn't done what he had promised to do, so I had another man come over here and sound the grave with a metal rod, and just as I had suspected, John Henman had crossed me up; he had only gone six feet down. He was a contrary old man, and set in his ways, and he had done the way he wanted, not the way I wanted. He had always dug graves six feet down, and he couldn't change. That didn't please me at all. It outraged me. So, I've got my name on the stone on this grave, and it'll look like I'm buried in this grave."

He took two long steps, and stood on the next grave in the plot.

"Instead of which," he said, "I'll be buried over here in this grave."

He stooped down, and pulled up a weed. Then he stood up, and shook the dirt off the roots of the weed, and tossed it aside.

"Ah, well," he said, "it won't make any difference."

FROM

THE CHERUBS ARE RUMBLING

Walter Bernstein

SEPTEMBER 21, 1957 (ON JUVENILE GANGS)

ONE SATURDAY NIGHT a few weeks ago, I attended a dance at a Y.M.C.A. in Brooklyn given by the Cherubs, a street gang with about thirty-five members, all between the ages of fourteen and seventeen. The Cherubs are not good boys. They regard the police as their natural enemies, and most policemen who have come to know them reciprocate this attitude—with some justification. The Cherubs fight other gangs, using knives, baseball bats, and guns; they have been known to steal; they occasionally commit rape, though usually of the statutory kind; many of them are truants; a few of them take dope; and while they fear the law, they do not admire or respect it. The prospect that the Cherubs, if left to themselves, will grow into model citizens is not at all bright. Their normal activity, though organized, is rarely social, and for this reason I was interested to learn that they were about to give an organized social dance. I heard about it from a friend of mine named Vincent Riccio, who knows the Cherubs well. He lives in their neighborhood and teaches physical education at Manual Training High School, in South Brooklyn, where some of them are reluctant students. Before becoming a teacher, in 1955, Riccio spent five years as a street-club worker for the New York City Youth Board, an agency dealing with problems of juvenile delinquency. His job was to go into a neighborhood that had a street gang known for particularly vicious habits, try to win the confidence of its members, and then, if possible, guide them in the direction of healthier pursuits. He is generally considered to have been the most successful street-club worker the Youth Board has ever had. "In his day, the Youth Board in Brooklyn *was* Riccio," a present Youth Board worker told me. Riccio has almost total empathy with young people—especially the delinquent kind—and they trust him. He speaks their language without patronizing them. Like most of the delinquents he has worked with, he comes from a rough, semi-slum background; his parents were immigrant Italians, and they had twenty-one children, six of whom have survived. As a boy, he did his share of gang fighting and thievery, though he claims to have been interested in stealing food rather than money. His specialty was looting the Mrs. Wagner pie trucks. His youthful experiences have convinced him that, except for the relatively rare psychotic cases, no delinquents are beyond help—that all are responsive to anyone they feel really cares for them. Riccio cares very deeply; he may even care too much. He had good reasons for switching to teaching as a career—among other things, he had a family to support—but he has a strong sense of guilt about having quit the Youth Board, and feels that it was a betrayal of the boys he had been working with.

For all practical purposes, Riccio hasn't quit. He has a name among the young people in his part of Brooklyn, and they are still likely to come to him for help with their problems, seeking him out either at home or at the school. He takes pride in this, and does what he can for them. He was particularly enthusiastic about the Cherubs' dance—as I could see when he asked if I'd like to attend it with him—because one of the gangs he had worked with when he was employed by the Youth Board was the forerunner of the Cherubs. That gang was also called the Cherubs, while the gang now known as the Cherubs was called the Cherub Midgets. Today, although a few of Riccio's former charges are in jail, most of them are respectable young men, gainfully employed and, in some cases, married. They are no longer bound together in a gang, but, Riccio explained, they take a collective avuncular interest in the current lot. In fact, they had helped organize the dance, and some of them were to act as chaperons. "They're trying to steer the kids straight," he said. "Show them they can get status by doing something besides breaking heads."

• • •

Riccio had asked me to meet him in front of the Y.M.C.A. at about nine o'clock on the night of the dance, and when I arrived he was already there, looking like an American Indian in a Brooks Brothers suit. A swarthy, handsome man of thirty-eight, he has a sharply angular face, with a prominent hooked nose and high cheekbones. He is not tall but he is very broad; his neck is so thick that his head seems small for his body, and his muscular development is awesome. He used to be a weight lifter, and still has a tendency to approach people as though they were bar bells. Whenever I shake hands with him, I have an uneasy feeling that I will find myself being raised slowly to the level of his chest and then, with a jerk and press, lifted effortlessly over his head. Actually, Riccio's handshake, like that of many strong men, is soft and polite. He is essentially a polite man, anxious to please, and he has a quick, warm smile and a trust in people that might seem naïve in a less experienced person. I shook hands with him warily, then followed him inside the building and into an elevator. "The kids were lucky to get this place," he said as the door slid closed. "The last club dance held here broke up in a riot." We got out at the fourth floor and walked into a solid mass of music. It roared at us like water from a burst dam, and the elevator man hastily closed his door and plunged down again before he was flooded. A table stood by the elevator door. Seated importantly behind it was a boy of about sixteen, with long black hair carefully combed back in the style known as a ducktail and wearing a wide-shouldered double-breasted blue suit. He was a good-looking boy, with regular features, and he had an innocent look that did not seem quite genuine. His face lit up when he saw Riccio.

"Man, look who's here!" he said. "It's Rick!"

Riccio smiled and walked over to the table.

"Man, where you been keeping yourself?" the boy asked.

"You come to school once in a while, Benny, you'd know," Riccio said. He introduced me as his friend, and I felt for my wallet to pay the admission fee of a dollar that was announced on a piece of paper tacked to the table.

Benny reached across and put his hand on mine. "You're a friend of Rick's," he said reprovingly.

Riccio asked Benny how the dance was going. "Man, it's *crazy*!" the boy replied. "We got two hundred people here. We got Red Hook, Gowanus, the Tigers, the Dragons." He counted them on his fingers. "We got the Gremlins. We got a pack from Sands Street. We even got a couple of the Stompers."

"I thought the Stompers and Red Hook were rumbling," Riccio said.

"They called it off," Benny said. "The cops were busting them all over the place. They were getting *killed*." He laughed. "Man, the law busted more heads than they did."

"Well, I'm glad it's off," Riccio said. "Whatever the reason, it's better off than on. Nobody gets hurt that way."

"It'll be on again," Benny said. "You don't have to worry about *that.* Soon as the cops lay off, they'll swing again."

Leaving Benny, we went through a door into the room where the dance was being held. I was astonished to see that all the music came from four boys, about fifteen years old, who were seated on a bandstand at one end of the room. They were small but they looked fierce. They were playing trumpet, guitar, piano, and drums, and the room rocked to their efforts. It was a large room, gaily decorated with balloons and strips of crêpe paper. Tables and chairs ringed a dance floor that was crowded with teen-age boys and girls—including a few Negroes and Puerto Ricans—all wearing the same wise, sharp city expression. The usual complement of stags, most of them dressed in windbreakers or athletic jackets, stood self-consciously on the sidelines, pretending indifference.

I followed Riccio over to one corner, where two boys were selling sandwiches and soft drinks through an opening in the wall. Business appeared to be outstripping their ability to make change. As we came up, one of them bellowed to a customer, "Shut up a minute, or I'll bust you right in the mouth!" Watching all this tolerantly were two husky young men—in their early twenties, I guessed—who greeted Riccio with delight. He introduced them to me as Cherub alumni, who were helping chaperon the dance. One was called Louie, and the other, who limped, was called Gimpy. We stood watching the dancers, who were doing the cha-cha. He seemed pleased with what he saw. "Notice the Negro kids and the Puerto Ricans?" he said. "Two years ago, they wouldn't have dared come here. They'd have had their heads broken. Now when a club throws a dance any kid in the neighborhood can come—provided he can pay for a ticket." A pretty little girl of about twelve danced by with a tall boy. "She's Ellie Hanlon," Riccio told me, nodding in her direction. "Her older brother was a Cherub—Tommy Hanlon. He was on narcotics, and I could never get him off. I was just starting to reach him when I left the Youth Board. Two weeks later, he was dead from an overdose. Seventeen years old." Riccio had told me about Tommy Hanlon once before, and I had suspected that, in some way, he felt responsible for the boy's death.

Benny, the boy who had been collecting admissions, pushed his way through the crowd to us, his eyes wide with excitement. "Hey, Louie!" he said. "The Gremlins are smoking pot in the toilet."

"Excuse me," Louie said, and hurried away to deal with the pot, or marijuana, smokers.

"Them stinking Gremlins!" Benny said. "They're going to ruin our dance. We ought to bust their heads for them."

"Then you'd really ruin your dance," Riccio told him. "I thought you guys were smart. You start bopping, they'll throw you right out of here."

"Well, them Gremlins better not ruin our dance," Benny said.

I asked Riccio if many of the boys he knew smoked marijuana. He said that he guessed quite a few of them did, and added that he was more concerned about those who were on heroin. One trouble, he explained, is that dope pushers flock to neighborhoods where two gangs are at war, knowing they will find buyers among members of the gangs who are so keyed up that they welcome any kind of relaxation or who are just plain afraid. "You take a kid who's scared to fight," Riccio said. "He may start taking narcotics because he knows the rest of the gang won't want him around when he's on dope. He'd be considered too undependable in a fight. So that way he can get out of it." He paused, and then added, "You find pushers around after a fight, too, when the kids are let down but still looking for kicks." Riccio nodded toward a boy across the floor and said, "See that kid? He's on dope." The boy was standing against a wall, staring vacantly at the dancers, his face fixed in a gentle, faraway smile. Every few seconds, he would wipe his nose with the back of his hand.

"Man, that Jo-Jo!" Benny said. "He's stoned *all* the time."

"What's he on—horse?" Riccio asked, meaning heroin.

"Who knows with that creep?" Benny said.

I asked Benny if any special kind of boy went in for dope.

"The creeps," he said. "You know, the goofballs." He searched for a word. "The *weak* kids. Like Jo-Jo. There ain't nothing the guys can't do to him. Last week, we took his pants off and made him run right in the middle of the street without them."

"You wouldn't do that to Dutch," Riccio said.

"Man, Dutch *kicked* the habit," Benny said. "We told the guy he didn't kick the habit, he was out of the crew. We were *through* with him. So he kicked it. Cold turkey."

Louie returned, and Riccio asked him what he had done about the offending Gremlins. Louie said he had chased them the hell out of the men's room.

I kept watching Jo-Jo. He never once moved from his position. The music beat against him, but his mind seemed to be on his own music, played softly and in very slow motion, and only for him.

As the dance continued, Louie and Gimpy and several other chaperons policed the room with unobtrusive menace, and there was no further trouble; everyone seemed to be having a good time. At eleven-thirty, Riccio said to me, "Now is when you sweat it out." He explained that the last half hour of a gang dance is apt to be tricky. Boys who have smuggled in liquor suddenly find themselves drunk; disputes break out over which boy is going to leave with which girl; many of the boys simply don't want to go home. But that evening the crucial minutes passed and it appeared that all was going well.

. . .

A few minutes before midnight, the musicians played their last set, and proudly packed their instruments. The trumpet player took off his sombrero, and I saw that he already had the pale and sunken face of a jazz musician. As the crowd thinned out, Riccio said, with some relief, "It turned out O.K." We waited until the room was almost empty, and then walked to the doorway. Benny was standing at the entrance of a makeshift checkroom near the elevator. "Good dance, Ben," Riccio said. "You guys did a fine job." Benny grinned with pleasure.

Just then, a boy came out of the checkroom. He seemed to be agitated. Riccio said, "Hi ya, Mickey," but the boy paid no attention to him, and said to Benny, "I want my raincoat. I checked it here, it ain't here."

"Man, you checked it, it's here," Benny said.

"It ain't here," Mickey repeated. Benny sighed and went into the checkroom, and Mickey turned to Riccio. He was a small boy with a great mop of black hair that shook when he talked. "I paid eighteen bucks for that raincoat," he said. "You can wear it inside and out."

"You'll get it back," Riccio said.

"It's a Crawford," Mickey said.

Benny came out of the checkroom and said, "Somebody must have took it by mistake. We'll get it back for you tomorrow."

"I don't want it tomorrow," Mickey said.

"Man, you'll get it tomorrow," Benny said patiently.

"I want my raincoat," Mickey said, his voice rising. Some of the boys who had been waiting for the elevator came over to see what was happening.

"You're making too much noise," Benny said. "I don't want you making so much noise, man. You'll ruin the *dance*."

"There ain't no more dance," Mickey said. "The dance is over. I want my raincoat."

More boys were crowding around, trying to quiet Mickey, but he was adamant. Finally, Riccio pulled Benny aside and whispered in his ear. Benny nodded, and called to Mickey, in a conciliatory tone, "Listen, Mick, we don't find the raincoat tomorrow, we'll *give* you the eighteen bucks."

"Where the hell have you got eighteen bucks?" Mickey asked suspiciously.

"From what we made on the dance," Benny told him. "You can buy a whole new coat, man. O.K.? You satisfied? You'll shut up now and go home?"

"I don't want the eighteen bucks," Mickey said.

"Oh, the hell with him," one of the other boys said, and turned away.

"I want my raincoat," Mickey said. "It's a Crawford."

"You can buy another Crawford!" Benny shouted at him, suddenly enraged. "What are you—some kind of a wise guy? You trying to put on an act just because Rick's here? What do you think you are—some kind of a wheel?"

"I want my raincoat," Mickey said.

"And I don't want you cursing in here!" Benny shouted. "You're in the Y.M.C.A.!"

"Who's cursing?" Mickey asked.

"Don't *curse*," Benny said grimly, and walked away. The other boys stood about uncertainly, not knowing what to do next. In a moment, the elevator arrived, and Riccio asked the operator to wait. He went over to Mickey and spoke a few soothing words to him, then came back, and the two of us got into the elevator. Two boys from the crowd got in with us.

"What do you think of that creep, Rick?" one of them asked.

"Well, it's his coat," Riccio said. "He's got a right to want it back."

"I think he stole the coat in the first place," the boy said as the elevator reached the ground floor.

Riccio and I walked through the lobby, already dimmed for the night, and out into the street, where we saw Louie and Gimpy getting into a car. They offered us a lift, but Riccio said he had brought his own car, so they waved and drove off. At that instant, a couple of boys dashed out of the building, looked wildly around, and then dashed back in. "Now what?" Riccio said.

We followed them in, and found perhaps a dozen boys bunched near the entrance. I could see Mickey in the middle, red-faced and angry and talking loudly. Benny, who was standing on the edge of the group, told us, "Now he says one of the Stompers took his coat. Man, he's *weird*!" He waved at Mickey in disgust and went outside.

Riccio pushed his way into the center of the crowd and separated Mickey from several boys who were arguing with him heatedly. A few of these wore jackets with the name "Stompers" stitched across the back. "Come on, now," Riccio said to Mickey. "We got to get out of here."

"He says we robbed his lousy coat, Mr. Riccio," one of the Stompers said.

"It's a Crawford!" Mickey yelled at him.

"The coat was probably taken by mistake," Riccio said calmly. "You'll get it back tomorrow, Mickey. If you don't get it back, you'll get the money and you can buy a new one. You had a good time, didn't you?" He was speaking to all of them now, his arm around Mickey's shoulder as he guided the boy gently toward the door. "You ought to be proud, running such a dance. You want to spoil it now? Hey?"

Mickey was about to say something when a boy burst in through the door, shouting, "Hey, Benny and one of the Stompers are having it out!"

Everyone rushed for the door. When I got outside, I saw Benny and another boy swinging desperately at each other on the sidewalk. Benny hit the boy on the cheek, the boy fell against a car, and Benny moved in and swung again. The boy went into a clinch, and the two of them wrestled against the car. I heard a click near me and turned to see one of the Stompers holding a switch-blade knife in his hand, but before he or any of the other boys could join in, Riccio was down the steps and between the fighters, holding them apart. The boy with the knife turned suddenly and went back into the building, and then I saw what he must have seen—a policeman walking slowly across the street toward us. Riccio saw him, too. "Cut out!" he said, in a low voice, talking to the whole crowd. "Here comes the law! Cut out!" He pushed the fighters farther apart as two of the Stompers ranged themselves alongside Benny's opponent. "Beat it!" Riccio said, in the same low voice. "You want to end up in the can? Cut out!" The Stompers turned and started to walk away, but the rest of the boys continued to stand around the steps of the Y. The policeman, now at the curb, looked curiously at Riccio and Benny, and then at the boys. Everyone appeared casual, but the air was heavy with tension. The policeman hesitated a moment, and then went on down the block.

"All right," Riccio said, with a tone of finality.

"He started to rank me," Benny said, meaning that the Stomper had been taunting him.

"Now, forget it," Riccio told him. "You want a ride home?"

Benny shook his head. "I'll grab a bus," he said, looking up the street, where the Stompers could still be seen walking away. Then he turned back to Riccio and said defiantly, "Man, what did you *want* me to do? Punk out?" He straightened his jacket, ran his fingers through his hair, and set off across the street with several other Cherubs. We watched them until they got to the corner. The other Cherubs kept walking straight ahead, but Benny turned down the side street. "You see how it can start?" Riccio said. "One minute they're having a dance, and the next minute they're having a war."

We went down the block to where Riccio's car was parked. I got in beside him, and he drove to the corner, where he stopped for a red light. I found that my hands were shaking. The light changed, but Riccio did not move. "I got a feeling," he said reflectively. "If you don't mind, I want to go back for a minute." He drove around the block until we were in front of the Y again, and then he turned the corner where Benny had left the others. And there was Benny, caught in the glare of our headlights, held down on his knees in the middle of the street by two boys while a third boy savagely hit his bowed head. The headlights fixed the scene like a movie gone suddenly too real—Benny kneeling there and the boy's arm rising and falling—and then Riccio had slammed on the brakes and we were out of the car, running toward them. By the time we reached Benny, the other boys were gone, lost in the dark; all that was left was the echo of their footsteps as they ran off into the night, and then there was not even that—no sound at all except the soft, steady ticking of the motor in Riccio's car. Benny was getting slowly to his feet. "You O.K.?" Riccio asked, helping him up. Benny nodded, and rubbed his neck. "I figured something like this," Riccio said to me, and then, turning back to Benny, he asked, "You sure you're all right? Maybe we ought to stop by the hospital."

"Man, I'm all right," Benny said. "They didn't hit me hard."

After looking the boy over, Riccio took him by the arm and led him back to the car, and the three of us got into the front seat. We drove in silence to a housing project near the waterfront, where Benny got out, still without speaking. We watched him enter one of the buildings, and then Riccio drove me to a subway station. "Now you know about these kids," he said as we shook hands. "They can blow up while you're looking at them." Riding home, I kept thinking of Benny as he had knelt there in the street, his head bent as though in prayer.

• • •

One afternoon a few weeks later, I got a telephone call from Riccio. "I thought you might be interested," he said. "The Cherubs are rumbling. They just put Jerry Larkin, from the Stompers, in the hospital. Caught him out of his neighborhood and left him for dead. He'll be all right, but they beat him up pretty bad. I think they worked him over with one of those iron tire chains." He said that there was now a full-scale war between the Cherubs and the Stompers, and that he had been talking with members of both gangs, trying to get them to call it off. Then he told me he was going to try to mediate again that night, and asked if I would like to go along. I said I would, and we arranged to meet at his house at seven o'clock.

We got into Riccio's car, and he started to drive slowly through the neighborhood. "We ought to find some of the Stompers hanging around these corners," he said. At first, no boys were to be seen. The part of Brooklyn we were riding through was not quite a slum. The streets were lined with old and ugly brownstones, but they seemed in good repair. The whole effect was dispirited, rather than poor; it was a neighborhood without cheer. As night fell, the houses retreated gradually into shadow, but they lost none of their ugliness. The street lamps came on, casting pools of dirty-yellow light. "The Stompers used to have a Youth Board worker assigned to them," Riccio said. "But he was pulled off the job and sent up to the Bronx when all that trouble broke up there. I guess these kids won't get another worker until they kill somebody." He said this without rancor, but I knew he felt strongly that the best times to do any real good with a gang are before it starts fighting and after it stops.

Ahead of us, a boy appeared from around a corner and walked rapidly in our direction. "One of the Stompers," Riccio said, and drew over to the curb. He called out to the boy, and when the latter paid no attention, he called louder. "Hey, Eddie, it's me! Riccio!" The boy stopped and looked at us warily, and then, reassured, came over to the car. His face was bruised and he had a lump under his left eye. "What happened?" Riccio asked. "You get jumped?"

"The cops busted me," Eddie said. He was about fifteen, and he was wearing a leather jacket with spangles on the cuffs that glittered in the light from a street lamp. His hair was blond and wavy and long. "They just let me out of the God-damned station house," he added.

"Why'd they pick you up?" Riccio asked.

"For nothing!" Eddie said indignantly. "We was just standing around, and they picked us all up. We wasn't doing a thing." He paused, but Riccio asked where the other Stompers were now, and Eddie replied that he thought they were hanging around a nearby grammar school. "But not me," he said. "I'm going home."

"Good idea," Riccio said.

"I got to get my gun out of the house," Eddie said. "I don't want them coming around and finding it."

"Why don't you give it to me?" Riccio said.

"No, sir," Eddie said. "I paid three bucks for that piece. I'm going to leave it over at my uncle's house. Maybe I'll see you later." He waved and walked off.

I asked Riccio how teen-agers could buy guns for three dollars, or any amount. He shrugged wearily and told me that salesmen of second-hand weapons periodically canvass sections where gangs are known to be active. A good revolver, he said, costs about ten dollars, but an inferior one can be bought for considerably less.

In a minute or two, the grammar school loomed up before us in the darkness with a solid, medieval look, and we saw a group of boys lounging under a street light—hands in pockets, feet apart, and, as they talked, moving about in a street-corner pattern as firmly fixed as that of the solar system. Riccio parked the car, and we got out and walked over to them. They froze instantly. Then one of them said, "It's Rick," and they relaxed. Riccio introduced me, and I shook hands with each of them; their handshakes were limp, like those of prizefighters.

Riccio suggested that they all go into the school, where they could talk more comfortably, and led the way inside. Walking down a corridor, he asked the Stompers about Jerry, the boy who had been beaten up. They said he would be out of the hospital in a couple of days. "They thought he had a fractured skull," Ralphie said, "but all he had was noises in the head."

"I was with him when it happened," one of the other boys said. "There were four of them Cherubs in a car—Benny and that Bruno and two other guys."

"That Bruno ain't right in the head," another boy said.

"I got away because I was wearing sneakers," the first boy said. "That

Bruno came after me with that chain, I went right through the sound barrier."

• • •

Riccio pushed open a pair of swinging doors that led into the school gymnasium, and as I followed him in the dank, sweaty smell hit me like an old enemy; I had gone to a school like this and hated every minute of it. The windows were the same kind I remembered—screened with wire netting, ostensibly as protection against flying Indian clubs but actually, I still believe, to keep the pupils from escaping. Out on the floor, several boys were being taught basketball by a tall young man in a sweatsuit. Riccio went over to talk with him, and, returning, indicated some benches in a corner. "He says we can sit over there," he said. We moved over to the corner, where Riccio sat down on a bench while the boys grouped themselves around him, some on benches and others squatting on the floor and gazing up at him.

"All right," Riccio said. "What are you guys going to do? Is it on or off?"

The boys looked at Ralphie, who seemed to be the leader. "We ain't going to call it off," he said.

"They started it," one of the others said.

"They japped us," a third boy said, meaning that the Cherubs had taken them by surprise. "You want we should let them get away with that?"

"All right," Riccio said. "So they jap you, they put Jerry in the hospital. Now you jap them, maybe you put Bruno in the hospital."

"I catch that Bruno, I put him in the cemetery," Ralphie said.

"So then the cops come down on you," Riccio went on. "They bust the hell out of you. How many of you are on probation?" Two of the boys raised their hands. "This time they'll send you away. You won't get off so easy this time. Is that what you want?" The boys were silent. "O.K.," Riccio said. "You're for keeping it on. That's your decision, that's what you want. O.K. Just remember what it means. You can't relax for a minute. The cops are looking to bust you. The neighborhood thinks you're no good, because you're making trouble for everybody. You can't step out of the neighborhood, because you'll get jumped. You got to walk around with eyes in the back of your head. If that's what you want, O.K. That's your decision. That's how you want things to be for yourself. Only, just remember how it's going to be."

Riccio paused and looked around him. No one said anything. Then he started on a new tack. "Suppose the Cherubs call it off," he said. "Would you call it off if they do?"

"They want to call it off?" a boy asked.

"Suppose they do," Riccio said.

There was another silence. The basketball instructor took a hook shot, and I watched the ball arc in the air and swish through the net without touching the rim. The room echoed with the quickening bounce of the ball as one of the players dribbled it away.

"We ain't going to call it off," Ralphie said. "They started it. We went to their lousy dance and we didn't make no trouble, and they said we stole their lousy coat. Then they jumped Jerry, and that Bruno gave him that chain job."

"They say you guys jumped Benny after the dance," Riccio told them.

"He started it," one of the boys said.

"Don't you see?" Riccio said. "No matter who started what, you keep it up, all it means is trouble. It means some of you guys are going to get sent away. You think I want to see that happen? Man, it hurts me when one of you guys get sent away."

"We ain't calling it off," Ralphie said.

"Suppose they want to call it off," Riccio said.

"They're punks," Ralphie said. He stood up, and the others stood up and ranged themselves behind him. They looked like a gang now, with their captain out in front to lead them. Riccio sat where he was, looking up at one face after another.

"Just because they had a dance," Ralphie said. "You know what? We were going to have a dance, too. And not in that lousy Y.M.C.A. In the American *Legion*."

"Why didn't you?" Riccio asked.

"They took away our worker," one of the other boys said. "They wouldn't give us the American Legion hall unless we had a worker."

"You'll get the worker back," Riccio told them. "He'll come back in a week or two, and then you can have your dance."

"He said he was coming back last week," Ralphie said bitterly.

"I'll tell you what," Riccio said. "I'll talk to the people down at the Legion. Maybe if they know I'm working with you, they'll give you the hall."

"We were going to have an *eight*-piece band," one of the boys said.

"I'll see what I can do," Riccio said. "But you know how it is when it gets around that you're swinging with another crew. You'll have trouble getting the hall. And even if you do, who wants to come to a dance when there might be trouble? The girls won't want to come—they'll be too scared."

"You sure the Cherubs said they want to call it off?" a boy asked.

"I'm going over there right now," Riccio said.

• • •

We drove past the housing project where Benny lived. "The Cherubs hang out in that candy store down the block," Riccio said. He pulled up in front of the shop, which I could see was crowded with youngsters, and said, "Wait here while I take a look." He went inside, came out again, and got back in the car, saying, "The Cherubs aren't here yet, so we'll wait." We both settled back and made ourselves comfortable. It was only nine-thirty, but the neighborhood was deserted. The candy store was the only shop in sight that was open, and ours was the only car parked on the dark street. Above and behind the tops of the brownstones rose the great bulk of the housing project, like some kind of municipal mausoleum, but dotted here and there with lights as evidence that life persisted inside. Two boys came down the street and were about to enter the candy store when Riccio called out, "Hey, Benny!" They turned and walked over to the car, and Riccio said, "Get in. It's too jammed in there." They slid into the back seat, and Riccio, turning to face them, said to me "You know Ben, don't you?" and introduced me to the other boy—Bruno, the one who had used the tire chain on Jerry. He was very thin, and had enormous eyes. "I've just been over with the Stompers," Riccio said, without preamble. "I think they'll call it off if you'll call it off."

"We won't call it off," Bruno said.

"Not even if they do?" Riccio asked.

"Man, they *ruined* our dance," Benny said.

"Nobody ruined your dance," Riccio said. "Your dance was a big success. You had one of the best dances around here." He went on to give them the same arguments he had given the Stompers. They listened restlessly, shifting in their seats and looking everywhere but at him. "Well, how about it?" Riccio said, finally.

"We call it off, what else are we going to do?" Bruno asked.

"There's other things to do besides breaking heads," Riccio said, and then I jumped as the car shook from a violent bang against its left side and the head of a policeman suddenly appeared in the window next to the driver's seat.

"Out of the car!" the policeman said. "All of you! Out!"

"Boy, you scared me, Officer," Riccio said.

"Get out of the car!" the policeman repeated. *"Now!"*

"We're not doing anything wrong," Riccio said. "We're just sitting here talking."

"Get out of that car!" the policeman said, and with that we found ourselves staring at a gun, which he was pointing straight at Riccio's head. It looked as big as a cannon.

"Jesus, Rick, get out of the car!" Bruno whispered from the back seat. "I'm on probation. I don't want to fight with the law."

"I'm getting out," Riccio said. He opened the door on his side and the policeman stepped back, but not quickly enough. The door hit his hand and knocked the gun to the pavement.

"Oh, Christ!" Benny said. "Now he'll kill us all!"

I shut my eyes, then opened them. The policeman had dived to the ground and recovered his gun. "O.K.—all of you," he said tightly. He motioned with his gun, and we all got out of the car and stood beside Riccio. "Face the car and lean against it with your hands on the top," the policeman said. We did, and he ran his free hand down the sides of our clothes, searching for weapons. Finding none, he said, "O.K., turn around." We turned around, and he said to Riccio, "This your car?" Riccio nodded, and the policeman asked for his license and registration. Riccio handed them over, and the policeman peered at them and then went around to compare the number on the car's license plates with the one on the registration. When he saw that the numbers matched, he said to Riccio, "Open the trunk." Riccio opened the trunk, and the policeman looked inside. Then he closed the trunk.

"Satisfied?" Riccio asked.

"Shut up," said the policeman.

"We didn't do anything," Riccio said. "What right have you got subjecting us to all this humiliation?"

"I'll crack this thing over your head," the policeman said, but his voice now betrayed a lack of conviction. "You're pretty old to be hanging around with kids. What the hell do you do?"

"I'm a teacher at Manual Training High School," Riccio told him.

"Well, why didn't you say so?" the policeman said. He put the gun back in his holster, and Benny exhaled slowly. "How the hell am I supposed to know who you are?" the policeman went on. "It's a suspicious neighborhood."

"That's no reason to treat everybody in it like criminals," Riccio said.

"Here," the policeman said, handing Riccio his license and registration. He seemed glad to get rid of them. Riccio and the rest of us climbed back into the car. "You see some guys in a car with some kids, how the hell are you supposed to know?" the policeman asked.

Riccio started to answer, but Benny, from the back seat, broke in, "Hey, Rick, let's cut out of here, man. I got to get *home*."

"Sure, Ben," Riccio said over his shoulder, and then drove off, leaving the policeman standing in the street. As soon as we were well away, the boys started talking excitedly.

"Man!" Benny said. "You could of got your head kicked in!"

"Did you see that gun?" Bruno said. "A thirty-eight. He could of blowed you right apart with that gun!"

"Man, I thought we were *gone*!" Benny said. "And we weren't even doing anything!"

The idea of their innocence at the time appealed to the boys, and they discussed it at some length. They both got out at the housing project, still talking. "I'm setting something up with you and the Stompers," Riccio said. "Just two or three guys from each side to straighten this thing out. All right?"

"Did you think that cop was going to shoot you, Rick?" Bruno asked.

"He was just jumpy," Riccio said. "Now, look. I'll get a place for us to meet, and we'll sit down and talk this thing out. O.K.?"

"Man, I thought we were *all* going to be busted," Benny said. "And for *nothing*!"

They drifted away from the car, laughing, and Riccio let them go. "I'll be in touch with you, Ben," he called. Benny waved back at us, and we watched them as they disappeared into the depths of the project.

I asked Riccio if he was always that tough with policemen, and he looked surprised. "I wasn't trying to be tough," he said. "That guy's job is hard enough—why should I make it any harder? I was making a point for the kids. I always tell them, when you're right, fight it to the hilt. I thought we were right, so I had to practice what I preach. Otherwise, how will they believe me on anything?"

Riccio invited me to go home with him for coffee, but I said I'd better be getting along, so he drove me to the subway. As I got out, he said, "I'm going to try to get them together this week. If I do, I'll let you know." We said good night, and I went down the subway stairs. On the way home, I bought a newspaper and read about a boy in the Bronx who had been stabbed to death in a gang fight.

• • •

I did not hear from Riccio again that week. The following week, I called him one night at about ten o'clock. His wife answered the phone, and said he was out somewhere in the neighborhood. She sounded upset. "It used to be like this when he was working for the Youth Board," she said. "He'd go out, and I'd never know when he was coming back. Three in the morning, maybe, he'd come back, and then the phone would ring and he'd go right out again. I told him he'd get so he wouldn't recognize his own children."

The next day, Riccio called me. He sounded discouraged. "They had another rumble," he said. "The Stompers came down to the housing project and broke a few heads. I got there too late." Fortunately, he added, it hadn't been too bad. A few shots had been fired, but without hitting anyone, and although a Cherub had been slashed down one arm with a knife, the wound wasn't serious, and nobody else had been even that badly hurt. Riccio told me he was going out again that night, and I could hear his wife say something in the background. He muffled the phone and spoke to her, and then he said to me, almost apologetically, "I've got to go out. They don't have a worker, or anything. The newspapers have raised such a fuss that the Youth Board's got its workers running around in circles, and it hasn't enough of them to do the job anyway, even when things are quiet. If somebody doesn't work with these kids, they'll end up killing each other." Then he told me he still had hopes of a mediation meeting, and would let me know what developed. Ten days later, my telephone rang shortly before dinner, and it was Riccio again, his voice now full of hope. He said that he knew it was very short notice, but if I still wanted to be in on the mediation session, I should meet him at eight o'clock in a building at an address he gave me. "I got it all set up at last," he concluded.

By the time I reached the building—a one-room wooden structure in an alley—it was five minutes after eight. Riccio was already there, together with three Cherubs—Benny and Bruno and a boy he introduced to me as Johnny Meatball.

"I was just waiting until you got here," Riccio said. "Now I'll go get the Stompers." He went out, leaving me with the three boys. The room had a fireplace at one end, and was furnished with a wooden table and several long wooden benches. It was hard for me to believe that I was in the heart of Brooklyn, until I read some of the expressions scrawled on the walls. I asked Benny who ordinarily used the place, and he replied, "Man, you know. Them Boy Scouts."

Bruno said he had gone to a Boy Scout meeting once, because he liked the uniforms, but had never gone back, because the Scoutmaster was a creep. "He wanted we should all sleep outside on the ground," Bruno said. "You know—in the woods, with the bears. Who needs that?" This led to a discussion of the perils of outdoor life, based mostly on information derived from jungle movies.

It was a desultory discussion, however. The boys were restless, and every few minutes Benny would open the door and look out into the alley. Finally, Bruno said, "The hell with them. Let's cut out."

"I'm down for that," Johnny Meatball said.

"They ain't coming," Bruno said. "They're too chicken."

"I give them fifteen minutes," Benny said.

All three became quiet then. I tried to get them to talk, as a way of keeping them there, but they weren't interested. Just before the fifteen minutes was up, the door opened and Riccio walked in, followed by two Stompers—Ralphie and Eddie, the boy we had met going home to hide his gun. They held back when they saw the Cherubs, but Riccio urged them in and closed the door behind them. Though the Cherubs had bunched together, looking tense and ready to fight, Riccio appeared to pay no attention, and said cheerfully, "I went to the wrong corner. Ralphie and Eddie, here, were waiting on the next one down the street." He pulled the table to the center of the room. "You guys know each other," he said to the five boys. Then he pulled a bench up to each side of the table and a third bench across one end. He sat down on this one, and motioned to me to sit beside him. The boys sat down slowly, one by one—the Cherubs on one side and the Stompers on the other.

"There you are," Riccio said when everybody was seated. "Just like the U.N. First, I want to thank you guys for coming here. I think you're doing a great thing. It takes a lot of guts to do what you guys are doing. I want you to know that I'm proud of you." He smiled at them. "Everybody thinks all you're good for is breaking heads. I know different—although I know you're pretty good at breaking heads, too." A couple of the boys smiled back at this, and all of them seemed to relax a little. "All right," Riccio went on. "What are we going to do about this war? You each got a beef against the other. Well, what's the beef? Let's talk about it."

There was a long silence. The boys sat motionless, staring at the table or at the walls beyond. Riccio sat as still as any of them. They sat that way for at least three minutes, and then Bruno stood up and said, "Ah, let's cut out of here."

"Man, sit down," Benny said. He spoke calmly, but his voice carried authority. Bruno looked down at him and he looked up at Bruno, and Bruno sat down. Benny then turned to the two Stompers across the table. "You tried to ruin our dance," he said.

"Your guy said we stole his lousy coat," Ralphie said.

"You jumped Benny on the street," Johnny Meatball said. "Three of you guys."

"He started a fight," Ralphie said.

"Man, that was a *fair* one!" Benny said.

"You started it," Ralphie said.

"There was just the *two* of us," Benny said.

"You were beating the hell out of him," Ralphie said. "What did you want us to do—let you get away with it?"

The logic of this seemed to strike the Cherubs as irrefutable, and there was another silence. Then Eddie said, "You beat up two of our little kids."

"Not *us,*" Benny said. "We never beat up no little kids."

"The kids told us some Cherubs caught them coming home from the store and beat them up," Eddie said.

"Man, we wouldn't beat up *kids,*" Benny said.

"You got that wrong," Johnny Meatball said, backing Benny up.

"Those kids were just trying to be wheels," Bruno said.

The Cherubs were so positive in their denial of this accusation that the Stompers appeared willing to take their word for it.

There was another pause. Riccio sat back, watching the boys. They were now leaning across the table, the two sides confronting each other at close quarters.

"Remember that time at the Paramount?" Ralphie asked. "When me and Eddie was there with two girls?"

"Those were *girls*?" Bruno said.

"Shut up," Benny said.

Ralphie then said to Benny, "Remember we ran into eight of your crew? You ranked us in front of the girls. We had to punk out because there was so many of you."

"You want we should stay out of the *Paramount*?" Benny asked incredulously.

"It wasn't right," Ralphie said. "Not in front of the girls. Not when you knew we'd have to punk out."

After thinking this over, Benny nodded slowly, acknowledging the justice of the argument.

Ralphie pressed his advantage. "And you been hanging out in our territory," he said, naming a street corner.

"Man, that ain't your territory," Benny said. "That's *our* territory."

"That ain't your territory," Ralphie said. "We got that territory from the Dragons, and that's our territory."

The argument over the street corner grew hotter, and after a while Riccio broke it up by rapping on the table with his knuckles and saying, "I got a suggestion—why don't both sides give up the territory?" He pointed out that the corner had nothing to recommend it, being undesirable for recreation and difficult to defend. After debating about that for a minute or two, both sides agreed to relinquish their claim to the corner. Riccio had what he wanted now; I could feel it. The boys had lost the sharp edge of their hostility. Their vehemence became largely rhetorical; they were even beginning to laugh about assaults each side had made on the other.

"Hey, Ralphie," Bruno said. "You're a lucky guy, you know that? I took a shot at you the other night and missed you clean."

"You took a *shot* at me?" Ralphie asked.

Bruno nodded. "The night you came down to the project. I was waiting with a thirty-two, and you came down the street and I took a shot at you."

"I didn't even hear it," Ralphie said.

"There was a lot of noise," Bruno said. "I was right across the street from you."

"You must be a lousy shot," Eddie said.

"It was dark out," Bruno said.

"You know, you could have killed him," Riccio told Bruno.

"I wasn't looking to kill him," Bruno said.

The other boys proceeded to kid Bruno about his marksmanship—all except Ralphie, who had become subdued. After a few minutes, Riccio looked at his watch and said, "Hey, it's ten o'clock. We got to get out of here before they close the place." He stood up, stretched, and said casually, "I'm glad you guys are calling it off. You're doing the smart thing. You get a lot of credit for what you're doing."

"You took a shot at me?" Ralphie said again to Bruno.

"What's past is past," Riccio said. "There's no reason you can't get along from now on without breaking heads. If something comes up, you do what you've been doing tonight. Mediate. Get together and talk it over. Believe me, it's a lot easier than breaking heads."

"What if we can't get together?" Bruno asked. "Suppose they do something, and they say they didn't do it and we say they did it?"

"Then you have a fair one," Eddie told him. "We put out our guy and you put out your guy. We settle it that way. That's O.K., ain't it, Rick?"

"It's better not to do any bopping at all," Riccio said.

"I mean, it ain't wrong," Eddie said. "It ain't making any trouble."

"Suppose we have a fair one and our guy gets beat?" Bruno asked.

"Man, you don't put out a guy who's *going* to get beat," Benny said.

The boys were on their feet now, all mixed together. A stranger might have taken them for a single group of boys engaged in rough but friendly conversation. "Listen, we got to break this up," Riccio said. He told them again how proud he was of them, and then he advised the Cherubs and the Stompers to leave separately. "Some cop sees the five of you walking down the street, he'll pull you all in," he said. So the three Cherubs left first, with Benny in the lead. They said goodbye very formally, shaking hands first with Riccio, then with me, and then, after a little hesitation, with the two Stompers. When they had gone, Ralphie sat down again on his bench. "That crazy Bruno," he said. "He took a shot at me."

A few minutes later, the Stompers stood up to go. Riccio said he would be around to see them and help them plan their dance. They thanked him and left. Riccio looked around the room. "I used to come here when I was a kid," he told me. "I got my name carved on the wall somewhere." He looked for it for a moment, without success, and then said, "Well, we might as well run along."

• • •

We went outside and got into Riccio's car. "Evelyn said if it wasn't too late, she'd have coffee and cake for us," Riccio told me, and I said that would be fine. He drove to his house and, after parking, leaned back in the seat and lit a cigarette. "I want to slow down a little before I go upstairs," he said. We sat there quietly for a few minutes. I could hear the whistles of ships down in the harbor. "Benny and Ralphie," Riccio said finally. "Those are the two to concentrate on. Maybe Eddie, too. But that Bruno—I don't know how far you could get with him. He's a disturbed kid. But you have to try. You have to try to reach him. That's the whole trick—reaching them. If I could have reached Tommy Hanlon, he wouldn't be dead now. I was just starting to reach him when he died. The last real talk we had, he told me he was scared to get a job. He'd quit school very early, and he couldn't read or write very well. He was scared if he got a job they'd make him do arithmetic and he'd look stupid. He was scared that they might send him over to Manhattan on the subway and he wouldn't be able to read the station signs. He'd never been out of Brooklyn. This was a kid there wasn't anything anti-social he hadn't done. Short of murder, there wasn't a thing. He broke into stores, he broke into cars, he molested girls. And, of course, he was on narcotics. I tell you, I used to look at this kid and think, How the hell can you defend a kid like this to society? And I'd think, How the hell can I help him? What can I do? This is too much. At the same time, he was such a nice-looking kid. I mean, he had a very nice face. Never mind what came out of his mouth—he had the dirtiest tongue I ever heard on a kid. But I worked with him, and he was starting to come around. He was starting to trust me. I don't think he'd ever trusted anybody in his whole life. I was his father. I was his mother. I was his best friend, his father confessor. I was all the things this kid had never had. And he was starting to move a little. The gang ran a dance, and he volunteered for the sandwich committee. You know what that meant? The kid was participating socially for the first time in his whole life. And he worked twice as hard at it as anybody else. I was starting to reach him. And then I quit the Youth Board."

Riccio fell silent again. "I had to quit the Youth Board," he said presently. "I had a wife and two kids, and I wasn't making enough to support them. I was spending more time with these kids than with my own. So I quit. The day I quit, I went down the street to tell the kids. They were in the candy store and Tommy Hanlon was with them, and he looked at me and said, 'What did you quit for?' I told him I had to, and tried to explain why. 'You know, I'm on the stuff again,' he said. And I said, 'Yes, Tommy, I heard you are, and I'm very sorry.' And he said, 'What do I do now?' And I said, 'Tommy, I'll always be around. We can still talk. You can still come and see me.' Then some other kid called me over to talk to him, and when I looked around Tommy was gone. Two weeks later, he was dead."

Riccio paused, this time for a long while. His cigarette had gone out, and he looked at it blankly and threw it out the window. "I know," he said. "The kid destroyed himself. He was a disturbed kid. If he wasn't disturbed, he wouldn't have been on narcotics in the first place. I went to the funeral and I looked in the casket and saw him laying there in a suit, with a decent haircut and his face all washed—and looking like a little old man. And I watched that kid's father getting drunk with that kid laying there in the casket. And I wanted to get up there at the funeral and, everybody who was there, I wanted to shout at them, 'You're the people who caused it! All you big adults! All you wise guys on street corners that feel sorry for the kid! Now you throw away your money on flowers!' I wanted to grab them by the throat."

He paused again, and then said, his voice low, "We hear about a soldier, a normal guy, who goes through all the tortures of war and all this brainwashing—takes everything they throw at him—and comes home a hero. Well, here was a kid that had everything thrown at him, too. Only, he was all mixed up, and still he took everything anybody could throw at him for seventeen years, and that was all he could take, so he collapsed and died."

Riccio abruptly pushed the car door open and got out. I got out on my side, and we went into the house together. Mrs. Riccio was both surprised and relieved to have her husband back so early. She asked if things had gone well, and Riccio assured her that things had gone very well. She went into the kitchen to make the coffee, and Riccio and I watched a quiz program on television until she came back. The three of us chatted awhile over our coffee and cake, and then, just before saying good night, I asked Riccio if Mickey had ever found the coat he lost at the dance. Riccio said that he hadn't but that the Cherubs had given him the eighteen dollars and he had bought a new one.

Riccio called me a few days later to tell me that the Cherubs and the Stompers were observing their armistice but that the enmity between Ralphie and Bruno had become so pronounced that they had decided to settle it with a fair one. Both gangs had gone to Prospect Park one night to watch the two of them have it out. A squad car had happened along, and the policemen had run the whole bunch of them in. Riccio was on his way to court to see what he could do for the boys.

PART TWO

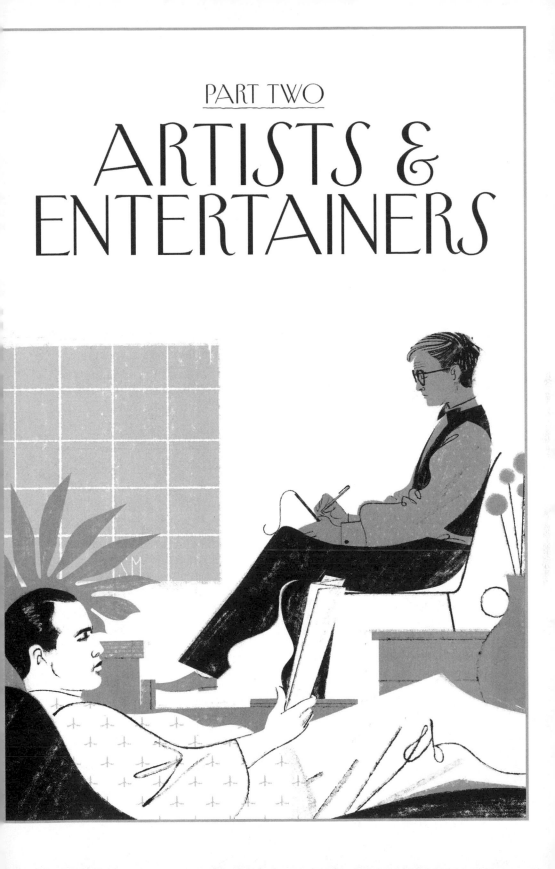

ARTISTS & ENTERTAINERS

A NOTE BY REBECCA MEAD

In May 1958, Dr. Marion E. Kenworthy, the newly elected president of the American Psychoanalytic Association, and professor emeritus of psychiatry at Columbia University, reported that her profession was in fine health and undergoing rapid growth: there were eight hundred practitioners in the United States, with a thousand more in training. "People joke about psychiatrists because they are afraid of psychiatrists," the *Times* quoted Dr. Kenworthy as saying, though whether she was smiling or not as she made this remark went unreported.

It wasn't until 1980 that the magazine profiled a psychoanalyst—in the person of the pseudonymous Aaron Green, vivisected by Janet Malcolm—but by the fifties there was a good chance that the subjects of profiles might be undergoing, or have undergone, psychoanalysis themselves, particularly if they were in the fields of arts and entertainment. Richard Avedon, profiled here by Winthrop Sargeant, the magazine's classical-music critic, speaks of his own possible unconscious hostility to masculine photographic subjects as offhandedly as if he were telling Sargeant about snarls in the crosstown traffic. It's possible that Marlon Brando might have opened up to Truman Capote without having been in analysis first: Capote was a singularly cunning pseudo confidant, who worked without the use of potentially inhibiting tools such as a notebook. (Today's fact-checkers would be in armed revolt.) But whether, without having been analyzed, Brando would have offered Capote a considered account of his mother's alcoholism and its effect upon his own psychological development—as he did, to his almost instantaneous regret—remains open to question. It seems certain that, without analysis, Brando would not have given Capote the devastating opportunity to show him musing about his own exquisite sensitivity, with consummately unaware self-involvement.

Even if profile subjects in the fifties sometimes came preshrunk, the magazine's tone was, as it had hitherto been, generally unpsychological. *New Yorker* Profiles do not tend to analyze their subjects, even in a cultural climate of analysis. Rather, a Profile is composed of laboriously accreted detail, lightly passed off as intuitive observation, and presented with a mildly ironical flourish and the withholding of explicit judgment. (Winthrop Sargeant notes that Richard Avedon once dispatched a newspaper reporter to interview his psychiatrist—an anecdote that tells the reader far more about Avedon than anything Sargeant could have learned from the psychiatrist in question.) One evolution in form from Profiles of earlier decades, however, is the increasing tendency of the reporter to feature his or her encounters with the subject as part of the story. While Janet Flanner wrote mini-biographies from which she was absent—you might not be able to tell from her Profiles whether or not she'd actually met her subject—writers like Capote and Lillian Ross, an excerpt of whose profile of John Huston is included here, organized their pieces around scenes, directly observed, and did not worry if they themselves were occasionally in the picture. This was a method that, at the time, was surprising and new, even if today it has sometimes been degraded into cliché: "I'm sitting in the lobby of the Chateau Marmont, waiting for celebrity X to arrive."

The five pieces included here are precursors of the contemporary celebrity profile—a genre that today is often characterized by a high seriousness of purpose, sometimes even, on occasion, in *The New Yorker*. (Such high seriousness may be an unconscious defensiveness against a fear of triviality, as a reporter undergoing psychoanalysis might acknowledge, were there any such reporters left.) That was not the *New Yorker* manner in the fifties. Philip Hamburger, in his lovely Profile of Oscar Hammerstein II, does not declare *South Pacific* and *Show Boat* and *Oklahoma* classics; instead, he lets it be known, in circular fashion, that they have been called classics so many times that they might categorically be described as such. Similarly, Winthrop Sargeant does not announce Marianne Moore to be America's greatest living poet, or one of them, after visiting her in her finely observed kitchen on Cumberland Street, in Fort Greene, Brooklyn. Instead, he states in varying forms that she is considered to be so by authorities whose opinion counts for something, among them T. S. Eliot and W. H. Auden.

This lightness of tone—authority wielded through authority surrendered—is a signature of *The New Yorker*. It's a fantastically comfortable garment to have inherited: put it on while writing, I find, and everything comes more easily and happily. Much has changed for the reporter, however, in the decades since these pieces were written. If Hollywood publicists today make every effort to circumscribe the access of a reporter to an actor, they are doing so in part because of the legacy of Capote—who, having been denied access to Brando, flew to Japan, showed up outside his hotel room one evening, and gained it anyway. Capote's structural conceit—to tell the whole story of Brando within the time frame of a few hours' conversation—is an exemplary case of turning a journalistic limitation into a writer's strength. (No waiting in the lobby of the Chateau Marmont for him.) Meanwhile, few film directors are likely now to call up a reporter, announce that their studio doesn't want them to make the movie they want to make, and say, Hey kid, come on over and I'll tell you all about it, and you can write all about it—as John Huston did to Lillian Ross at the outset of making *The Red Badge of Courage*.

Kid! Being patronized by her unwitting subjects turned out to be Ross's reportorial superpower for decades, while her piece about Huston's movie became *Picture,* a book-length, genre-inventing account of art meeting commerce on Huston's ranch in the San Fernando Valley. Like all the authors of these masterly profiles, Ross waited and watched and waited some more, and delivered what she learned without recourse to interpretation, saying all the more by doing so. "I said I would," Ross writes, of her response to Huston's invitation—a sentence that sums up the culture reporter's deceptively simple calling, then and now.

THE PERFECT GLOW

Philip Hamburger

MAY 12, 1951 (ON OSCAR HAMMERSTEIN II)

OSCAR HAMMERSTEIN II, the lyricist, librettist, and producer, went to the theatre for the first time when he was four years old. He considers the preceding years of his life a total loss. Now a robustly successful showman of fifty-five, Hammerstein recalls his initial glimpse of the mysteries and enticements of the stage with the mixed clarity and fuzziness of the possessed. For the better part of a year, he had been badgering his father, William, or Willie, Hammerstein, to take him downtown from the Hammerstein home, near Mount Morris Park, to see a show. Willie Hammerstein was firmly opposed to the notion. Oscar, he said, should stay home and play with his velocipede. Willie spoke with more than parental authority. He was managing Hammerstein's Victoria Theatre, at Forty-second Street and Seventh Avenue, for *his* father, Oscar Hammerstein I, and he had turned it into the leading variety house of its day. There was no business like show business, Willie conceded, but he was dead set against any offspring of his getting a taste of it. Oscar persisted, however, and one afternoon, in a moment of weakness, Willie succumbed. He took Oscar, by means of a series of trolley cars, to the Victoria to see a matinee performance of a vaudeville show. When Oscar and his father walked into the lobby of the Victoria, his grandfather, a short, squat, determined-looking man with a goatee, was standing beside the box office, scanning the line of ticket buyers. He was wearing a black silk top hat and a black jacket. He had a cigar in his mouth. Willie took Oscar II over to say hello. Oscar I glanced down at him, shook his head two or three times, made an odd clucking sound, and turned away. "I don't know what the old man had on his mind," Oscar II said recently. "I don't know whether he meant 'What's my grandson doing down here?' or 'What a silly-looking boy' or 'Good God, here's another generation of Hammersteins inside a theatre.'"

In any event, within a matter of minutes, Oscar II was alone in a box overlooking the stage. The auditorium was crowded. As the house lights were lowered, a hush came over the audience. The orchestra began to play, and the curtain went up. Oscar broke out in a cold sweat. His legs trembled. His stomach quivered. His excitement was so acute that he could barely see what was happening onstage. Actually, nothing much *was* happening. Several young ladies were posed around a large, tangled fish net. A bright, golden haze filled the stage. The girls, it seemed, were drying the net. One of them, disengaging herself from the others, stepped to the footlights and sang what he remembers as:

"Oh, I am a water maiden,
I live on the water,
A fisherman's daughter."

Oscar was transported. The mist before his eyes was like a London fog. After the maidens performed a short dance, other acts came on, but Oscar recalls nothing more until intermission, when his father fetched him from the box and said, "Now we'll go backstage." He was led down some narrow stairs, through a dark doorway, and up a few steps; he then found himself backstage, and face to face with a large cage. The cage was occupied by a lion. The lion was prowling up and down, and did not look especially happy. As Oscar was watching it, the cage began to roll toward him. He was too stunned to move. The lion let out a roar, and Oscar was snatched to safety by a stagehand. Other stagehands rushed forward to stop the cage. Oscar felt that he just might get sick to his stomach, and asked his father to take him home. When he reached home, his mother put him to bed. He slept for fourteen hours, and when he awoke, he announced that the theatre would be his lifework.

Hammerstein has spectacularly stuck to his word. He has been associated with more notable musicals than any other showman in the history of the American theatre. He has either written the book and lyrics or collaborated on the book and lyrics for some forty musicals, including *Rose-Marie, The Desert Song, Sunny, Show Boat, Oklahoma!, Carousel, Al-*

legro, South Pacific, and *The King and I.* Of these, at least three—*Show Boat, Oklahoma!*, and *South Pacific*—have been called classics of the American musical stage so many times and in so many places that today they can categorically be described as classics of the American musical stage. *South Pacific* and *The King and I,* two shows on which he collaborated with Richard Rodgers, the composer and producer, are now playing across from each other, on Forty-fourth Street, and neither one has had an empty seat since it opened. Together, the two shows gross more than a hundred thousand dollars a week. Hammerstein has written the words to almost a thousand songs, including "Ol' Man River," "Who?," "Oh, What a Beautiful Mornin'!," "People Will Say We're in Love," "Some Enchanted Evening," "We Kiss in a Shadow," and "The Last Time I Saw Paris." His songs are distinguished by such lucid wording, such unabashed sentimentality, such a gentle, even noble, view of life, and such an attachment to love, home, small children, his native country, nature, and dreams come true that he has been called the Bobbie Burns of the American musical stage. He has been called this so many times and in so many places that today he can categorically be described as the Bobbie Burns of the American musical stage. Since Hammerstein became professionally associated with the theatre, more than thirty years ago, he has earned more than five million dollars—royalties, profits as a producer, and receipts from the sale of sheet music and phonograph records—and he now enjoys an income that ranges exuberantly between a half and two-thirds of a million dollars a year, before taxes. (The government permits him to keep approximately one dollar out of every seven.) Not the least phenomenal aspect of his career is the affectionate regard in which he is held by his fellow-showmen. By and large, whenever a producer or writer on Broadway has a hit, other producers or writers turn up the collars of their coats and wander off alone, to drink quietly. When a venture with which Hammerstein is connected is pronounced successful by the press and the public, his competitors often appear as exhilarated as they would be if they owned the property themselves. "The only trouble with Oscar," a fellow-producer said not long ago, after the opening of *The King and I,* "is there's no trouble with Oscar. You have to love the fellow. He works hard, he's true-blue to his friends, he never speaks harshly to an actor, he's modest, he drinks sparingly, he keeps out of the niteries, he's in bed by midnight, he doesn't fool around with dames, he has no visible quirks, he's got a sense of humor, and he's talented. He doesn't sound human; he sounds like a stuffed shirt. Hell, he's the most human man I know."

• • •

Invisible as his quirks may be, Hammerstein is a major eccentric. "I am in love with a wonderful theatre," he often says. It is one of the monumental love affairs of history. He cannot enter a theatre without experiencing that acute aesthetic dizziness reported by travellers when they gaze for the first time upon the Taj Mahal. Hammerstein is six feet one and a half inches tall, weighs slightly less than two hundred pounds, and has the broad, hunched shoulders, the long, easy gait, and the ready, comforting, it's-going-to-be-all-right-fellows smile of a popular football coach, but passing through a stage door makes him feel weak and helpless. The sight of a bare stage illuminated by a single glaring rehearsal light sends sharp pains up and down his back. These sensations are nothing compared to the exquisite paralysis that comes over him when he stands at the rear of a packed theatre and observes an audience enjoying one of his own shows. Outwardly, he is calm, even indifferent, on such an occasion. Standing quietly, with his arms resting on the rail, he could easily be mistaken for a theatre manager. The only hint that the Furies are raging within is a slight droop at the corners of his mouth, which gives him the look of a man who fears, as Hammerstein feared at the Victoria when he was four, that he might any moment get sick to his stomach. Often, while one of his songs is being sung, he walks swiftly into the empty lobby and bursts into tears. Hammerstein has listened to "The Surrey with the Fringe on Top" at least five hundred times, but every time he has been reduced to weeping. "It's so beautiful that it makes a man want to cry," he explains.

Hammerstein's overpowering devotion to the theatre includes not only an intense appreciation of his own lyrics but an equally intense appreciation of the music composed for them by his partner, Richard Rodgers. Rodgers is sometimes able to sit down at a piano and turn out a hit tune in a few minutes. His head is filled with an extraordinary collection of whistleable airs that require only a set of lyrics to bring them out into the open. Hammerstein is a slow and tortured writer. He often labors for weeks to produce a refrain of fifty words or so. He worked for five weeks, for example, over the lyrics of "Hello, Young Lovers!," in *The King and I,* and finally threw all his previous efforts aside and wrote the song, in a frenzy of creation, in two days. Once he has completed the lyrics for a song, he is spiritually and physically exhausted. As a result, he is exceedingly attached to what he writes, and when he listens to the words he has a tendency to recall the suffering he underwent while putting them together. Hammerstein is a tolerant man, but his tolerance stops short of letting anyone tamper with so much as a word of his lyrics. Some years ago, a radio singer, not quite sure of "Oh, What a Beautiful Mornin'!," inadvertently substituted "An' a li'l ol' willer is laughin' at me" for "An' a ol' weepin' willer is laughin' at me." Hammerstein was tuned to the program, his eyes full of tears. Shocked by the alteration, he switched off the radio, and swore that *that* particular singer would have a pretty hard time ever getting into one of *his* shows.

Although Hammerstein is sentimental about the theatre, his affection has a pragmatic base. "Oscar is a very careful dreamer," one of his oldest friends says. In Oscar's estimation, the public is the final judge of what is and what is not a work of art, and he has small patience with the experimental theatre. The test of a good play, for Hammerstein, is the length of the line at the box office on a rainy morning. "With my shows," he says, "I don't want to wake up in the morning and have to worry about whether or not the weather will affect the size of the house." In spite of his firm faith in the judgment of audiences, Hammerstein has been engaged for years in a strange personal struggle with them. "It's a matter of love and hate," he explains. He has evolved a method of evaluating an audience's reactions to a show, which he uses during the out-of-town tryouts of his productions. He stands at the rear rail and observes the backs of the heads of the audience. He believes he can pretty well figure out what is going on inside the heads. "There's a silent criticism felt by all actors, and everybody else who knows the theatre," he says, "but my method goes beyond that. And I don't pay any attention to coughs, either. They don't mean a thing. But if the heads are motionless, we're O.K. If they move either up or down or from side to side, we're in trouble. If people start rustling through the programs, we're in *real* trouble." Hammerstein does not confine his researches to the backs of heads. He often goes into a box and peers down at the faces of the audience. If the customers are enjoying a show, he feels, an indefinable glow comes over their faces. "I can't describe it, I just know it when I see it," he says. He may concentrate on one face and, crouched low in the box, await the arrival of the glow. If, instead of the glow, the face reveals dislike or, what is even worse in Hammerstein's opinion, no expression at all, the muscles of his stomach become even tighter. "There are faces that rise to haunt me," he says. "Years ago, a man sat in the third row in a tryout in Trenton, a big, fat, red-faced, snorey fellow, everybody around him laughing and laughing, and he just sat there, no expression, no nothing. I remember every line of that face. I would recognize him anywhere. My dislike is still quite active. I remember, too, a young woman once in Baltimore. What a glow! The perfect glow! A lovely, sweet face, responsive to everything!"

Hammerstein feels that the severest test of how a show is working out comes the moment the first-act curtain falls. Just before this moment, Hammerstein leans forward and cups a hand to one ear, then stiffens like a bird dog. "If that curtain drops and there is silence followed by silence—oh, we're in trouble!" he says. "If that curtain falls and there is silence followed swiftly by an excited buzz of conversation, a sort of ground swell of buzzy talk, we're probably safe." After only a minute or two of such listening, he rushes into the lobby. There, head down, he mixes in with the crowd. "I concentrate on a man and woman who spy another man and woman they know," he says. "If one pair approaches the other and says a few quick words about the play, and then there's general conversation about the play, we're O.K. If they merely say, 'Pretty good first act. When are you and Mary coming over for bridge?,' we're in *real* trouble!" Hammerstein slips back into the theatre after the intermission and again is on the alert for the glow. He thinks that the glow is even more important during the second act. "If they glow when they get back into their seats," he says, "the chances are that the glow is permanent and we have 'em for good." Hammerstein feels that the glow induced by *Oklahoma!* may never be duplicated within his lifetime, or anybody else's. "People returned to their seats for the second act and the glow was like the light from a thousand lanterns," he says. "You could *feel* the glow, it was that bright."

Hammerstein has put all his adult years into inducing the glow. In what is perhaps his second most glowing triumph, *South Pacific,* the glow begins to spread across the faces of the audience soon after the curtain is up. Hammerstein has given a good deal of thought to the effect that *South Pacific* exerts upon audiences, and he is sure that he has pinned down some of the reasons for its phenomenal success, and glow. "The curtain rises," he recently told a friend, "and we are on an island in the Pacific with luxuriant foliage. A native boy and girl are singing a little song in French. The audience says, 'What's this?' Then, before they have even settled in their seats—bang!—you're off to the races with a complication. The hero and heroine come onstage—the curtain has been up a bare few minutes—and an honest approach to a love story has been placed before you. There is Emile de Becque, fifty-odd, a planter, cultured, a Frenchman, and a highly romantic figure. There is Nellie Forbush, in her twenties, American, fresh, young, beautiful, a nurse. Two people who have nothing whatsoever in common are in love. No lecherous stuff, you understand. Emile de Becque *loves* Nellie Forbush. There is nothing underhanded about it. She is ashamed to admit her love—afraid, really, for fear of its not being reciprocated. It's too good to be true, it's unbelievable. They express their love and we have the audience in a death grip; we jump on them, we beat them up. Then, suddenly—bang!—the scene changes and there's a fat old thing, a native woman, selling grass skirts. That's Bloody Mary, and she is unlike anything the audience has ever seen before. The change of pace is terrific. The audience is still in the death grip! They're caught, they're helpless, they can't breathe. We never let go!"

• • •

Hammerstein is a gentle person, with a genuine affection for his fellowman, and he takes extreme pains in his writing to avoid hurting anybody's feelings. While working on *The King and I,* he was acutely and almost constantly fearful that he might, in some way or other, offend the people of Siam, whose King is the King of the title. "I did not want to tread on any Oriental toes," he said recently. "I had to be careful about gags about the huge number of wives in the royal family. You know, I think we are crude in the West compared to the East. What was required was the Eastern sense of dignity and pageantry—and none of this business of girls dressed in Oriental costumes dancing out onto the stage and singing 'ching-a-ling-a-ling-ling' with their fingers in the air." For the most part, during the construction of a book for a musical, Hammerstein does not attempt to pry too deeply into any of the subtle and complex aspects of human relationships. He is content to stay close to what he considers the fundamentals—love, jealousy, death, and so on. A great many observers of his career regard this simplified attitude toward life as evidence of almost surpassing wisdom. "Oscar has pinned down the verities," a friend of his says. "He knows precisely what audiences want, their saturation point on any one emotion, and he gives them just that and no more. It's uncanny, it's wizardry." To another group of observers, equally fond of Hammerstein, the limitations of his plots indicate the boundaries of his experience. "Oscar has a beautiful and unsullied view of life," a man who has known him since childhood declares. "He's an anomaly in this ugly world. He believes that love conquers all, that virtue triumphs, and that dreams come true."

While he is working on lyrics, Hammerstein relies almost entirely upon flights of fancy, even when he is dealing with what would appear to be matters of fact. He does not feel that research adds materially to the value of his lyrics, so he rarely dips into a reference work. On the few occasions when he has undertaken research, it has been of an uncomplicated nature, and he early discovered that it raised more questions than it settled. While writing *Carousel,* he decided to compose a lyric about a clambake. He had never been to a clambake, but he had heard of them, and they sounded like fun. He found himself putting down the words "This was a real nice clambake," and they sounded like real nice words. He felt that in the second stanza he should describe the clambake in detail, and he tried to recall clambakes he had heard of or read of. He wrote about codfish chowder "cooked in iron kettles, onions floatin' on the top, curlin' up in petals," ribbons of salt pork, and so on, and he felt certain that he was on safe clambake ground. He was aware that lobsters often turn up at clambakes, but when he began to think about the lobsters, he ran into a snag. He assumed that they "sizzled and crackled and sputtered a song, fitten fer an angels' choir. Fitten fer an angels', fitten fer an angels', fitten fer an angels' choir!," but a pang of conscience struck him when he came to describing what happened to the lobsters after they were pulled out of the fire. He wrote, "We slit 'em down the front." Then he wrote, "We slit 'em down the back." Then he began to wonder just where in hell you do slit a lobster. He dropped in one day at an obscure sea-food restaurant and asked the chef there how he slit his lobsters. The man said down the back, and Hammerstein wrote it that way, adding, in the flush of creation, "and peppered 'em good, and doused 'em in melted butter." After *Carousel* opened, a disconcerting number of complaints poured in to Hammerstein. "HOW DARE YOU SAY THAT LOBSTERS EMPLOYED IN CLAMBAKE BE SPLIT DOWN BACK?" one telegram read. "ANY FOOL KNOWS LOBSTERS SPLIT DOWN FRONT. THAT WAS NO CLAMBAKE." "Shame on you for lack of facts re lobster split," read a sample letter. Hammerstein decided that thenceforth he would trust his intuitions. Since that unfortunate experience, he has done little research, but he did make an effort to gather background for *South Pacific* by glancing at some maps of the Pacific area and speaking to several people who had been out there during the war.

• • •

A man's lyrics, Hammerstein feels, are a reflection of his attitude toward life. "I couldn't write a sophisticated or sharp lyric, or something terribly, terribly clever, like some lyric writers," he once told a friend. "I couldn't, because I don't see things that way. To me, one of the most beautiful and expressive lyrics of all time is Irving Berlin's simple 'All alone, by the telephone.' Examine those words. Think about them. They tell an entire story. Nothing more needs to be said. You see the picture, complete and whole. All alone by the telephone—the girl jilted perhaps, lonely, unhappy, waiting for the phone to ring. I envy those who can write tricky words, but they are a different sort of man." Hammerstein feels, too, that if his lyrics display a certain simplicity and wholesomeness, it is largely because he tries to live a simple and wholesome life. His habits are a source of wonder along Broadway, and many of his colleagues regard the regularity of his life as dangerously close to heresy. "The fellow breaks all the rules," a producer said to a colleague in Lindy's early one morning. "Why, he's home now, sleeping like a baby. Isn't that horrible?" Hammerstein has a real dislike of night life, and he rarely turns up at night clubs. He does his best to avoid large parties, too, and when he is persuaded to attend one, he departs quietly about midnight. He sleeps a full eight hours each night, eats a large hot breakfast, works until one, eats a large hot lunch, works all afternoon, eats a large hot supper, and then, unless he goes to the theatre (he makes a point of seeing practically every show that comes to New York), pokes around in his study, either watching television or reading. He owns an imposing five-story house on East Sixty-third Street and an eighty-acre Bucks County farm near Doylestown, Pennsylvania, eighty-five miles from New York. In both town house and farmhouse, he has large, impressively furnished studies, and he spends a great deal of time in them, sometimes, for days at a stretch, emerging only to eat and sleep. Hammerstein's family life is a warm and affectionate one. He is married to the former Dorothy Blanchard, an attractive, red-headed woman who was understudy to Beatrice Lillie in *Charlot's Revue of 1924*. It is the second marriage for each of them, and each has two children by the previous marriage. The Hammersteins also have a twenty-year-old son, James, who works for Leland Hayward, the producer and agent.

When working on his lyrics, Hammerstein prefers to be on his farm. He is convinced that the muse has little chance of flowering among the fleshpots of New York. When he begins to write, he broods, and when he broods, he becomes unapproachable and sullen. He writes standing up, and in one corner of his Bucks County study there is a high writing desk, like a lectern. For hours at a time, clasping and unclasping his hands behind his back, he paces up and down the study, occasionally stopping before the desk to jot down a word or two on a sheet of yellow foolscap. The countryside around Doylestown nourishes his spirit, he claims, and he often walks along the roads, alone and brooding, his head down almost inside his coat collar. "Oscar meditating on a country road looks like something out of Thomas Hardy on a heath," a friend of his said not long ago. On rainy days when he feels the need for communion with nature, he tramps back and forth on the porch of his house. As soon as he hits upon a line for a lyric, he sets it to a dummy tune of his own and sings it to Mrs. Hammerstein. "Oscar's dummy tunes are so terrible they make you want to cry," she has declared, "but he has perfect rhythm."

Until he worked with Joshua Logan on the book of *South Pacific,* Hammerstein wrote his dialogue in longhand. Logan, a man who cannot utter a simple "Thank you" without making it sound like a second-act dénouement, had long been addicted to recording dialogue on a dictaphone. Hammerstein ridiculed the notion, but Logan persuaded him to speak a few of Emile de Becque's lines in *South Pacific* into his machine. "In peacetime, the boat from America comes once a month," said Hammerstein tentatively. "The ladies—the wives of the planters—often go to Australia during the hot months. It can get very hot here." Hammerstein listened to the playback and was somewhat bowled over by his performance. Throughout the writing of the book, all of which was done at the Hammerstein farm, the two men used Logan's dictaphone. They would speak several lines, passing the mouthpiece back and forth, and then listen with deep appreciation to their work. The writing of *South Pacific* accomplished another change in Hammerstein's habits. Logan is a nocturnal animal, and he does some of his best work during what are known as the small hours. He suffers from a chronic inability to fall asleep until nearly dawn, the time of day Hammerstein is usually leaping out of bed, ready for a day's work. The two men compromised by working until two in the morning. Hammerstein then retired, yawning. Logan went upstairs and alternately read poetry and took hot baths until four or five. He slept until noon, when he and Hammerstein would start revising a typed transcript of their dialogue of the previous evening. By the time this began, Hammerstein would have been up for hours, pacing his study, writing lyrics. "It was a real sacrifice for Oscar, working past midnight," Logan has told a friend. "I am very grateful."

In recent years, Hammerstein is convinced, books and lyrics have come into their own, and their contribution to a musical show is no longer taken for granted. Writing about his early days in show business, in an introduction to a collection of his lyrics, Hammerstein said, "The librettist was a kind of stable boy. If the race was won, he was seldom mentioned. If the race was lost, he was blamed for giving the horse the wrong feed." These days, he feels, words are as important as music, and the score of a musical comedy will not be successful if the lyrics lack interest, do not advance the plot, or are not carefully integrated with the music. In fact, Rodgers and Hammerstein have developed a new popular art form that is neither musical comedy nor opera but something in between. The most common question put to Hammerstein by people he meets is whether the words or the music come first. Hammerstein is a reasonable man, and doesn't mind answering the question, weary as he is of it. Until he began collaborating with Richard Rodgers, Hammerstein wrote his lyrics after the composer had written the music, but today, as a rule, his lyrics are done first. He considers this a sensible arrangement, far more favorable to the writing of good lyrics. Most scores, however, are done the other way. The music-first method, Hammerstein thinks, developed from the fact that during the first years of the century a good many musical shows were imported from the Continent, notably from Vienna, so that the American lyric writers had to fit their lines to the music. Some of the foreign composers subsequently were themselves imported to the United States. Lyric writers working with them discovered that if the words were written before the music, they sounded weird, and were sometimes completely unsingable, because of the composers' unfamiliarity with English. Hammerstein believes, too, that the rise of jazz and the fondness for dancing placed the emphasis on the music of a song, and that the lot of the lyricist was made easier if he performed his stint after the music had been composed.

Uppermost in Hammerstein's mind while he is writing a lyric is the larynx of the performer who will have to stand on a stage and sing the thing. "The larynxes of singers are limited," he has remarked. He tries to provide convenient breathing places in his lyrics, and to avoid climaxes in which a singer will be straining at a word that closes the larynx. "A word like 'sweet' would be a very bad word on which to sing a high note," he says. "The 'e' sound closes the larynx, and the singer cannot let go with his full voice. Furthermore, the 't' ending the word is a hard consonant, which would cut the singer off and thwart his and the composer's desire to sustain the note." Hammerstein worries a good deal about closed larynxes, and he is inclined to brood morbidly over the times he has permitted his affection for a word to outweigh his concern over a closed larynx. For example, he often berates himself for ending the refrain of "What's the Use of Wond'rin'?," in *Carousel,* with "You're his girl and he's your feller, And all the rest is talk." He feels that if he were to write this song again, his last line would go something like "And that's all you need to know." "The singer could have hit the 'o' vowel and held it as long as she wanted to, eventually pulling applause," he says. The song was not a distinguished success as sheet music or on records, and Hammerstein is convinced that the word "talk," which closed the singer's larynx at the finish, was responsible for this. The majority of his last lines are, he feels, forceful larynx-openers, conducive to applause-pulling, such as "Oh, what a beautiful day!," "Once you have found her, never let her go!," "Ol' man river, he jes keeps rollin' along," and "Bali Ha'i, Bali Ha'i, Bali Ha'i."

Hammerstein recalls with painful poignancy the problems he faced during the creation of certain lyrics. To a person who does not write lyrics, many of his dilemmas might seem elementary, but to Hammerstein they represent heroic struggles with the muse. "The problem of a duet for the lovers in *Oklahoma!* seemed insurmountable," he says. His leading characters—Curly, the cowboy, and Laurey, the young girl—are very much attracted to each other, but Laurey, who is shy, tries to hide her feelings. Curly does not like her attitude, and assumes a fairly belligerent one of his own. Instead of expressing their love, they take to bickering and squabbling. Since both Hammerstein and Rodgers wished to maintain the atmosphere of crackle and snap until at least the second act, it was impossible for Hammerstein to write a simple song in which Curly and Laurey said, out loud and with their larynxes open, "I love you." Hammerstein talked his dilemma over with Rodgers at great length. Together they hit upon the solution of having the two young people caution each other against demonstrating any warmth, since this might be construed by outsiders as an expression of affection. "People Will Say We're in Love" was the successful result. Hammerstein had another problem when he collaborated with Rodgers on the musical film *State Fair.* In the story, a young girl has the blues, for no particular reason, since her family is about to treat her to a visit to a state fair. Hammerstein wanted a song for her mood—it was time for a song, anyway—and it occurred to him, while he was pondering, that her melancholy condition bore a resemblance to spring fever. This thought made Hammerstein even more melancholy than the girl, since state fairs are held in the fall, not the spring. "I toyed with the notion of having her say, in effect, it's autumn but I have spring fever, so it might as well be spring," Hammerstein has said. He casually mentioned this possible solution to Rodgers. "That's it!" cried Rodgers. "All my doubts were gone," Hammerstein says. "I had a partner behind me." Out of this came the well-known "It Might as Well Be Spring."

Hammerstein thinks that one reason for his success as a lyricist is that his vocabulary is not enormous. A huge vocabulary, he is convinced, hampers a lyric writer; it might persuade him to substitute "fantasy," "reverie," "nothingness," "chimera," "figment," or even "air-drawn dagger" for the simple word "dream." He has discovered that a lyric writer seems always to have a supply of the word "dream" on hand, much as a housewife keeps salt in the house. Before composing the lyrics for *South Pacific,* he decided that he would avoid "dream." He felt that it had been turning up too often in his lyrics. When he had finished the *South Pacific* lyrics, he found that "dream" appeared with frightening regularity. "Bali Ha'i" speaks of "Your own special hopes, your own special dreams." "Some Enchanted Evening" says, "Then fly to her side, and make her your own, or all through your life you may dream all alone" and "The sound of her laughter will sing in your dreams." "Happy Talk" declares that "You gotta have a dream; if you don't have a dream, how you gonna have a dream come true? If you don't talk happy an' you never had a dream, den you'll never have a dream come true." Even one of the songs withdrawn from *South Pacific* during the pre-Broadway tryout said, "The sky is a bright canary yellow . . . you will dream about the view." Hammerstein lost his dream of the view but retained the view itself—the bright canary-yellow sky in "A Cockeyed Optimist."

The word "dream" has worried Hammerstein in more ways than one. Not only has it turned up uninvited in his lyrics but its meaning, he feels, is not precisely clear to him. He is certain that he has never written a word in which he did not believe, which did not spring from the heart, and he is therefore disturbed by the fact that he and the word "dream" don't entirely understand each other. "The most important ingredient of a good song is sincerity," he has often remarked. "Let the song be yours and yours alone." He can put down such words as "love," "ain't," "feelin'," "rain," "yes," "forget," "home," "blue," "bird," "star," "believe," "arms," "nice," "little," "moon," "trees," "kiss," "sky," "dame," "beautiful," "baby," again and again, and he has been doing so for thirty years, and his only concern is whether they belong in a lyric, or at that particular point in a lyric. These words do not trouble him at all. The word "love" poses no problems for him, and he has no qualms about using it all the time. He will write down "I'm in love, I'm in love, I'm in love, I'm in love, I'm in love with a wonderful guy" or "Dat's love! Dat's love! Dat's love! Dat's love!" without hesitation. He will even dwell upon the idea—"Love is quite a simple thing, and nothing so bewildering, no matter what the poets sing, in words and phrases lyrical. Birds find bliss in every tree, and fishes kiss beneath the sea, so when love comes to you and me, it really ain't no miracle"—eat a large supper, sleep eight hours, and rise the next morning to write another lyric about love. But the word "dream" perplexes him, even though he once went so far into dreamland in "Music in the Air" as to write, "There's a dream beyond a dream beyond a dream beyond a dream." It first made a real nuisance of itself seventeen years ago, while he was working with Sigmund Romberg on a motion picture. Romberg had turned out a waltz tune, and Hammerstein took it home to compose the lyrics. The moment he finished looking over the music, the first line, which he also thought would make a good title, popped into his head: "When I grow too old to dream." A moment later, a second line miraculously popped into his head, below the first: "I'll have you to remember." "I have it!" he recalls crying out loud. "'When I grow too old to dream, I'll have you to remember.'" Suddenly, and for perhaps the first time in his life, he was afflicted with a curious sensation that something was wrong with his words. He realized that he didn't understand what he had written. He remembers that he said to himself, "Too old for what kind of dreams? As a matter of fact, when you're old, aren't you likely to dream more than at any other time in your life, don't you look back and dream about the past?" For three weeks, he struggled with other words, but he kept returning to the original ones. "I loved to sing it to myself, alone in my study," he says. He decided to stick to these lines, and the song became a big hit, but its triumph shook Hammerstein deeply, since innumerable colleagues asked—and ask to this day—what the words meant. Before writing "When I grow too old to dream, I'll have you to remember," Hammerstein had religiously believed in simple, unambiguous lyrics. If he wanted to ask, "Why do I love you? Why do you love me?," he went ahead and asked it. Here, however, was a mysterious, perhaps meaningless combination of words, and they were commercially successful. The more Hammerstein brooded over the lyric, the more he felt that he had stumbled onto something bigger than himself. A year or so ago, still brooding, he brought the matter up in the introduction to his collection of lyrics. "Gertrude Stein has, of course, this unspecific approach to the use of words," he wrote, "and Edith Sitwell, in her group of songs entitled *Façade,* has made a deliberate attempt to write words with special emphasis on sound and very little attention to meaning or clarity. I do not believe that the future of good lyric writing lies in this direction, but my experience with 'When I grow too old to dream' forces me to admit that there is something in the idea. It belongs with the general flight from literalism in all art expression—notably painting—which characterizes the creative works of this century."

FROM

THROW THE LITTLE OLD LADY DOWN THE STAIRS!

Lillian Ross

MAY 24, 1952 (ON JOHN HUSTON AND THE MAKING OF *THE RED BADGE OF COURAGE*)

THE MAKING OF the Metro-Goldwyn-Mayer movie *The Red Badge of Courage,* based on the Stephen Crane novel about the Civil War, was preceded by routine disclosures about its production plans from Louella Parsons ("John Huston is writing a screen treatment of Stephen Crane's classic, *The Red Badge of Courage,* as a possibility for an M-G-M picture."); from Hedda Hopper ("Metro has an option on *The Red Badge of Courage* and John Huston's working up a budget for it. But there's no green light yet."); and from *Variety* ("Pre-production work on *Red Badge of Courage* commenced at Metro with thesp-tests for top roles in drama."), and it was preceded, in the spring of 1950, by a routine visit by John Huston, who is both a screen writer and a director, to New York, the headquarters of Loew's, Inc., the company that produces and distributes M-G-M pictures. On the occasion of his visit, I decided to follow the history of that particular movie from beginning to end, in order to learn whatever I might learn about the American motion-picture industry.

Huston, at forty-three, was one of the most admired, rebellious, and shadowy figures in the world of motion pictures. I had seen him a year before, when he came here to accept an award of a trip around the world for his film contributions to world unity. He had talked of an idea he had for making a motion picture about the nature of the world while he was going around it. Then he had flown back to Hollywood, and to the demands of his employers, Metro-Goldwyn-Mayer, and had made *The Asphalt Jungle,* a picture about a band of criminals engaged in pursuits that Huston described somewhere in the dialogue of the movie as "a left-handed form of human endeavor." Now, on this visit, shortly after the sudden death, in Hollywood, of his father, Walter Huston, he telephoned me from his Waldorf Tower suite and said he was having a terrible time trying to make *The Red Badge of Courage.* Louis B. Mayer and most of the other top executives at M-G-M, he said, were opposed to the entire project. "You know something?" he said, over the telephone. He has a theatrical way of inflecting his voice that can give a commonplace query a rich and melodramatic intensity. "They don't want me to make this picture. And I want to make this picture." He made the most of every syllable, so that it seemed at that moment to lie under his patent and have some special urgency. "Come on over, kid, and I'll tell you all about the hassle," he said.

• • •

The door of Huston's suite was opened by a conservatively attired young man with a round face and pink cheeks. He introduced himself as Arthur Fellows. "John is in the next room getting dressed," he said. "Imagine getting a layout like this all to yourself! That's the way the big studios do things." He nodded with approval at the Waldorf's trappings. "Not that I care for the big studios," he said. "I believe in being independent. I work for David Selznick. I've worked for David for fifteen years. David is independent. I look at the picture business as a career. Same as banking, or medicine, or law. You've got to learn it from the ground up. I learned it from the ground up with David. I was an assistant director on *Duel in the Sun*. I directed the scene of the fight between two horses. Right now, I'm here temporarily on publicity and promotion. David—" He broke off as Huston strode into the room. Huston made his entrance in the manner of an actor who is determined to win the immediate attention of his audience.

"Hel-lo, kid," Huston said as we shook hands. He took a step back, then put his hands in his trouser pockets and leaned forward intently. "Well!" he said. He made the word expand into a major pronouncement.

Huston is a lean, rangy man, two inches over six feet tall, with long arms and long hands, long legs and long feet. He has thick black hair, which had been slicked down with water, but some of the front strands fell raffishly over his forehead. He has a deeply creased, leathery face, high cheekbones, and slanting, reddish-brown eyes. His ears are flattened against the sides of his head, and the bridge of his nose is bashed in. His eyes looked watchful, and yet strangely empty of all feeling, in weird contrast to the heartiness of his manner. He took his hands out of his pockets and yanked at his hair. "Well!" he said, again as though he were making a major pronouncement. He turned to Fellows. "Art, order some Martinis, will you, kid?"

Huston sat down on the arm of a chair, fixed a long brown cigarette in one corner of his mouth, took a kitchen match from his trouser pocket, and scraped the head of the match into flame with his thumbnail. He lit the cigarette and drew deeply on it, half closing his eyes against the smoke, which seemed to make them slant still more. Then he rested his elbows on his knees, holding the cigarette to his mouth with two long fingers of one hand, and looked out the window. The sun had gone down and the light coming into the suite, high in the Tower, was beginning to dull. Huston looked as though he might be waiting—having set up a Huston scene—for the cameras to roll. But, as I gradually grew to realize, life was not imitating art, Huston was not imitating himself, when he set up such a scene; on the contrary, the style of the Huston pictures, Huston being one of the few Hollywood directors who manage to leave their personal mark on the films they make, was the style of the man. In appearance, in gestures, in manner of speech, in the selection of the people and objects he surrounded himself with, and in the way he composed them into individual "shots" (the abrupt closeup of the thumbnail scraping the head of a kitchen match) and then arranged his shots into dramatic sequence, he was simply the raw material of his own art; that is, the man whose personality left its imprint, unmistakably, on what had come to be known as a Huston picture.

"I just love the light at this time of the day," Huston said as Fellows returned from the phone. "Art, don't you just love the light at this time of the day?"

Fellows said it was all right.

Huston gave a chuckle. "Well, now," he said, "here I am, spending the studio's money on this trip, and I don't even know whether I'm going to make the picture I'm here for. I'm auditioning actors at the Loew's office and talking production up there and doing all the publicity things they tell me to do. I've got the *Red Badge* script O.K.'d, and I'm going down South to pick locations for the picture, but nothing is moving. We can't make this picture unless we have six hundred Confederate uniforms and six hundred Union uniforms. And the studio is just not making those uniforms for us. I'm beginning to think they don't *want* the picture!"

"It's an offbeat picture," Fellows said politely. "The public wants pictures like *Ma and Pa Kettle*. I say make pictures the public wants. Over here," he said to a waiter who had entered with a tray holding six Martinis in champagne glasses. "No getting away from it, John," Fellows went on, handing Huston a drink. "Biggest box-office draws are pictures catering to the intelligence of the twelve-year-old."

People underestimated the intelligence of the twelve-year-old, Huston said. He said he had an adopted son in his early teens, a Mexican-Indian orphan, Pablo, whom he had found while making *Treasure of Sierra Madre* in Mexico a few years ago, and his boy had excellent taste in pictures. "Why, my boy Pablo reads Shakespeare," he said. "Do you read Shakespeare, Art?"

"Television, John," said Fellows. "The junk they go for on television."

Huston asked him vaguely what the talk was in New York about television.

Television was booming, Fellows said, and all the actors, singers, dancers, directors, producers, and writers who hadn't been able to get work in Hollywood were going into television in New York. On the other hand, all the actors, singers, dancers, directors, producers, and writers who had gone into television in New York were starving and wanted to go back to Hollywood. "Nobody really knows what's happening," said Fellows. "All I know is television can never do what pictures can do."

"We'll just make pictures and release them on television, that's all. The hell with television," Huston said. "Do you kids want the lights on?" The room was murky. It made a fine tableau, Huston said. Fellows and I agreed that it was pleasant with the lights off. There was a brief silence. Huston moved like a shadow to a chair opposite mine and lit another brown cigarette, the quick glow from the match lighting up his face. "Been to the races out here, Art?" he asked.

A few times, Fellows said, but David Selznick had been keeping him so busy he hadn't had much time for horses.

"The ponies have me broke all the time," Huston said. "You know, I can't write a check for five hundred dollars. I am always broke. I can't even take an ordinary vacation. But there's nothing I'd rather spend my money on than a horse, especially when the horse is one of my own.

There's nothing like breeding and raising a horse of your own. I've got four horses racing under my colors right now, and in a couple of years I'll have more, even if I have to go into hock to support them. All I want is one good winner of my own. Everybody I know is conspiring to take my horses away from me. Someday I'll have one good winner, and then I'll be able to say, 'Well, you bastards, this is what it was all about!' "

Financial problems, Huston said, had prevented him from taking the trip around the world. Although his M-G-M salary was four thousand dollars a week while he was making a picture, he had had to get the company to advance him a hundred and fifty thousand dollars, which he was paying off in installments. He was bound by his contract to make at least one picture a year for the next three years for M-G-M. He was a partner in an independent company, Horizon Pictures, which he had started a couple of years before with a man named Sam Spiegel, whom he had met in the early thirties in London. Huston had directed one picture, *We Were Strangers,* for Horizon, but it had lost money. He was scheduled to direct another—*The African Queen,* based on the novel by C. S. Forester—as soon as he had completed *The Red Badge of Courage* for M-G-M. Huston said he thought *The African Queen* would make money, and if it did, he could then make some pictures on his own that he wanted to make as much as he did *The Red Badge of Courage.* The reason L. B. Mayer and the other M-G-M executives did not think that *The Red Badge of Courage* could be a commercial success, Huston said, was that it had no standard plot, no romance, and no leading female characters, and, if Huston had his way in casting it, would have no stars. It was simply the story of a youth who ran away from his first battle in the Civil War, and then returned to the front and distinguished himself by performing several heroic acts. Huston, like Stephen Crane, wanted to show something of the emotions of men in war, and the ironically thin line between cowardice and heroism. A few months earlier, Huston and an M-G-M producer named Gottfried Reinhardt, the son of the late Max Reinhardt, had suggested to Dore Schary, the studio's vice-president in charge of production, that they make the picture.

"Dore loved the idea," Huston said. "And Dore said he would read the novel." A couple of weeks later, Schary had asked Huston to write a screen treatment—a rough outline for the detailed script. "I did my treatment in four days," Huston said. "I was going down to Mexico to get married, so I took my secretary along and dictated part of it on the plane going down, got married, dictated some more after the ceremony, and dictated the rest on the plane trip back." Schary approved the treatment, and the cost of making the picture was estimated at a million and a half dollars. Huston wrote the screenplay in five weeks, and Schary approved it. "Then the strangest things began to happen," Huston said. "Dore is called vice-president in charge of production. L.B. is called vice-president in charge of the studio. Nobody knows which is boss." His voice rose dramatically. "We were told Dore had to O.K. everything. We got his O.K., but nothing moved. And we know that L.B. hates the idea of making this picture." His voice sank to a confidential whisper. "He just hates it!"

For the role of the Youth, Huston said, he wanted twenty-six-year-old Audie Murphy, the most-decorated hero of the Second World War, whose film career had been limited to minor roles. Huston said he was having some difficulty persuading both Schary and Reinhardt to let Murphy have the part. "They'd rather have a star," he said indignantly. "They just don't see Audie the way I do. This little, gentle-eyed creature. Why, in the war he'd literally go out of his way to find Germans to kill. He's a gentle little killer."

"Another Martini?" Fellows asked.

"I hate stars," Huston said, exchanging his empty glass for a full one. "They're not actors. I've been around actors all my life, and I like them, and yet I never had an actor as a friend. Except Dad. And Dad never thought of himself as an actor. But the best actor I ever worked with was Dad. All I had to tell Dad about his part of the old man in *Treasure* was to talk fast. Just talk fast." Huston talked rapidly, in a startling and accurate imitation of his father. "A man who talks fast never listens to himself. Dad talked like this. Man talking fast is an honest man. Dad was a man who never tried to sell anybody anything."

It was now quite dark in the room. We sat in the darkness for a while without talking, and then Huston got up and went over to the light switch. He asked if we were ready for light, and then snapped the switch. He was revealed in the sudden yellow brightness, standing motionless, a look of bewilderment on his face. "I hate this scene," he said. "Let's go out and get something to eat."

• • •

Five weeks later, Huston was back at the Waldorf, in the same suite. When he telephoned me this time, he sounded cheerful. During his absence, *The Asphalt Jungle* had opened in New York and had been reviewed enthusiastically, but he didn't mention that; what he felt good about was that he had just bought a new filly from Calumet Farms. When I went over to see him that evening, he was alone in his suite. Two days before, he had found a superb location for *The Red Badge of Courage* outside Nashville.

When Huston had returned to the studio after his Eastern trip, he told me, he had found that no preparations at all were under way for *The Red Badge of Courage*. "Those uniforms just weren't being made!" he said with amazement. "I went to see L.B. and L.B. told me he had no faith in the picture. He didn't believe it would make money. Gottfried and I went to see Dore. We found Dore at home, sick in bed. The moment we entered, he said, 'Boys, we'll make this picture!' Maybe it was Nick Schenck who gave Dore the go-ahead sign. Anyway, that night Dore wrote a letter to L.B. and said in the letter he thought M-G-M ought to make the picture. And the next morning L.B. called us in and talked for six hours about why this picture would not make any money. You know, I like L.B. He said that Dore was a wonderful boy, that he loved Dore like his own son. And he said that he could not deny a boy who wrote that kind of letter to him. And when we came out of L.B.'s office, the studio was bubbling, and the uniforms were being made!" Huston chortled. He and Reinhardt had found a marvellous actor named Royal Dano to play the part of the Tattered Man, he said, and Dano had that singular quality that makes for greatness on the screen. Charlie Chaplin and Greta Garbo have that quality, he said. "The screen exaggerates and magnifies whatever it is that a great actor has," he said. "It's almost as though greatness is a matter of quality rather than ability. Dad had it. He had that something people felt in him. You sense it every time you're near it. You see it in Audie Murphy's eyes. It's like a great horse. You go past his stall and you can feel the vibration in there. You can feel it. So I'm going to make the picture, kid. I'm going to direct it on horseback. I've always wanted to direct a picture on horseback."

The expenses at the Nashville site, he said, would be less than at the one he had originally hoped to get, in Leesburg, Virginia, and its terrain lent itself perfectly to the kind of photography he wanted—a sharply contrasting black-and-white approximating the texture and atmosphere of the Brady photographs of the Civil War.

"Tell you what," Huston said, in his amazed tone. "I'm going to show you how we make a picture! And then you come out to Hollywood and you can see everything that happens to the picture out there! And you can meet Gottfried! And Dore! And L.B.! And everybody! And you can meet my horses! Will you do it?"

I said I would.

• • •

Several weeks later, Huston telephoned again, this time from California. He was going to start making *The Red Badge of Courage* in a month, and the location was not going to be in Tennessee, after all, but on his own ranch, in the San Fernando Valley. He didn't sound too happy about it. "You'd better get out here for the fireworks," he said. "We're going to have the Civil War right here on the Coast."

• • •

When I arrived on the West Coast, Huston set about arranging for me to meet everybody who had anything to do with *The Red Badge of Courage.* The day I met Gottfried Reinhardt, the thirty-nine-year-old producer of *The Red Badge of Courage,* he was sitting in his office at the Metro-Goldwyn-Mayer studio, in Culver City, studying the estimated budget for the picture. It would be the fifteen-hundred-and-twelfth picture to be put into production since Metro-Goldwyn-Mayer was founded, on May 24, 1924. The mimeographed booklet containing the estimate was stamped "Production No. 1512." (The estimate, I learned later on, informed Reinhardt that the picture would be allotted nine rehearsal days and thirty-four production days; the footage of the finished film was expected to come to 7,865 feet; the total cost was expected to be $1,434,789.)

Reinhardt is a paunchy man with a thick mane of wavy brown hair; in his cocoa-brown silk shantung suit, he looked like a Teddy bear. There was a cigar in his mouth and an expression of profound cynicism on his face. A heavy gold key chain hung in a deep loop from under his coat to a trouser pocket. He speaks with a German accent but without harshness, and his words come out pleasantly, in an even, regretful-sounding way. "We promised Dore we would make our picture for one million five or under, and that we would make it in about thirty days," he said, sitting down at his desk again. He put a hand on the estimate and sighed heavily. "The producer's job is to save time and money." He bobbed his head as he talked. A strand of hair fell over his face. He replaced it and puffed at his cigar in a kind of restrained frenzy. Then he removed the cigar and, bobbing his head again, said, "When you tell people you have made a picture, they do not ask, 'Is it a good picture?' They ask, 'How many days?'" He tapped the ash from his cigar tenderly into a tray and gave another heavy sigh.

Reinhardt, who was born in Berlin, arrived in the United States in 1932, at the age of nineteen, for a visit. He had been over here a few months when Hitler came to power in Germany, and he decided to stay. Ernst Lubitsch, who had worked with the elder Reinhardt in Europe, offered Gottfried a job, without pay, at Paramount, as his assistant on a film version of Noël Coward's *Design for Living,* starring Fredric March, Miriam Hopkins, and Gary Cooper. In the fall of 1933, Reinhardt moved to Metro, as a hundred-and-fifty-dollar-a-week assistant to Walter Wanger, then a producer at that studio. Not long afterward, Wanger left and Reinhardt was made assistant to Bernard Hyman, who was considered a right-hand man of Irving Thalberg. Reinhardt became first a film writer (*The Great Waltz*) and then, in 1940, a producer (*Comrade X,* with Clark Gable and Hedy Lamarr; *Rage in Heaven,* with Ingrid Bergman and Robert Montgomery; *Two-Faced Woman,* with Greta Garbo, the last picture she appeared in). In 1942, he went into the Army. He worked on Signal Corps films for four years, and then returned to Metro and produced pictures featuring some of the studio's most popular stars, including Clark Gable and Lana Turner.

At Metro-Goldwyn-Mayer, Gottfried Reinhardt had witnessed a succession of struggles for power among the executives at the studio. He had learned many lessons simply by watching these battles, he told me. "M-G-M is like a medieval monarchy," he said. "Palace revolutions all the time." He leaned back in his swivel chair. "L.B. is the King. Dore is the Prime Minister. Benny Thau, an old Mayer man, is the Foreign Minister, and makes all the important deals for the studio, like the loan-outs of big stars. L. K. Sidney, one vice-president, is the Minister of the Interior, and Edgar J. Mannix, another vice-president, is Lord Privy Seal, or, sometimes, Minister without Portfolio. And John and I are loyal subjects." He bobbed his head and gave a cynical laugh. "Our King is not without power. I found, with *The Red Badge of Courage,* that you need the King's blessing if you want to make a picture. I have the King's blessing, but it has been given with large reservations." He looked at me over his cigar. "Our picture must be a commercial success," he said flatly. "And it must be a *great* picture."

• • •

The maze of paths followed by all the individuals at M-G-M who work together to make a motion picture led inexorably to the office of Louis B. Mayer, and I found him there one day, behind a series of doors, talking to Arthur Freed, a producer of musicals for the studio. Mayer's office was about half as large as the lounge of the Music Hall, and he sat behind a huge cream-colored desk overlooking a vast expanse of peach-colored carpet. The walls of the office were panelled in cream-colored leather, and there was a cream-colored bar, a cream-colored fireplace with cream-colored fire irons, cream-colored leather chairs and couches, and a cream-colored grand piano. Behind Mayer's desk stood an American flag and a marble statue of the M-G-M lion. The desk was covered with four cream-colored telephones, a prayer book, several photographs of lions, a tintype of Mayer's mother, and a statuette of the Republican Party's elephant. The big desk hid most of Mayer, but I could see his powerful shoulders, decked in navy blue, and a gay, polka-dot bow tie that almost touched his chin. His large head seems set upon the shoulders, without an intervening neck. His hair is thick and snow-white, his face is ruddy, and his eyes, behind glasses with amber-colored frames, stared with a sort of fierce blankness at Freed, who was showing him a report on the box-office receipts of his latest musical, then playing at the Radio City Music Hall.

"Great! I saw it!" Mayer said, sweeping Freed back with his arm. "I said to you the picture would be a wonderful hit. In here!" he cried, poking his index finger at his chest. "It wins the audience in here!" He lifted his snowy head and looked at the cream-colored wall before him as though he were watching the Music Hall screen. "Entertainment!" he cried, transfixed by what he seemed to see on that screen, and he made the face of a man who was emotionally stirred by what he was watching. "It's good enough for you and I and the box office," he said, turning back to Freed. "Not for the smart alecks. It's not good enough any more," he went on, whining coyly, in imitation of someone saying that winning the heart of the audience was not good enough. He pounded a commanding fist on his desk and looked at me. "Let me tell you something!" he said. "Prizes! Awards! Ribbons! We had two pictures here. An Andy Hardy picture, with little Mickey Rooney, and *Ninotchka,* with Greta Garbo. *Ninotchka* got the prizes. *Blue* ribbons! *Purple* ribbons! Nine bells and seven stars! Which picture made the money? *Andy Hardy* made the money. Why? Because it won praise from the heart. No ribbons!"

"Hah!" Mr. Freed said.

"Twenty-six years with the studio!" Mayer went on. "They used to listen to me. Never would Irving Thalberg make a picture I was opposed to. I had a worship for that boy. He worked. Now they want cocktail parties and their names in the papers. Irving listened to me. Never satisfied with his own work. That was Irving. Years later, after Irving passed away, they still listened. They make an Andy Hardy picture." He turned his powerful shoulders toward me. "Andy's mother is dying, and they make the picture showing Andy standing outside the door. *Standing*. I told them, 'Don't you know that an American boy like that will get down on his hands and knees and *pray*?' They listened. They brought Mickey Rooney down on his hands and knees." Mayer leaped from his chair and crouched on the peach-colored carpet and showed how Andy Hardy had prayed. "The biggest thing in the picture!" He got up and returned to his chair. "Not good enough," he said, whining coyly again. "Don't show the good, wholesome, American mother in the home. Kind. Sweet. Sacrifices. Love." Mayer paused and by his expression demonstrated, in turn, maternal kindness, sweetness, sacrifice, and love, and then glared at Freed and me. "No!" he cried. "Knock the mother on the jaw!" He gave himself an uppercut to the chin. "Throw the little old lady down the stairs!" He threw himself in the direction of the American flag. "Throw the mother's good, homemade chicken soup in the mother's face!" He threw an imaginary plate of soup in Freed's face. "*Step* on the mother! *Kick* her! That is *art*, they say. Art!" He raised and lowered his white eyebrows, wiggled his shoulders like a hula dancer, and moved his hands in a mysterious pattern in the air. "Art!" he repeated, and gave an angry growl.

"You said it," said Freed.

"*Andy Hardy*! I saw the picture and the tears were in my eyes," Mayer said. "I'm not ashamed. I'll see it again. Every time, I'll cry."

"In musicals, we don't have any of those phony artistic pretensions," Freed said.

Mayer gave no sign that he had heard Freed. "Between you and I and the lamppost," he said, straightening his bow tie, "the smart alecks around here don't know the difference between the heart and the gutter. They don't want to listen to you. Marie Dressler! Who thought you could take a fat old lady and make her a star? I did it. And Wally Beery. And Lionel Barrymore." He leaned back in his chair, one hand tucked into his shirt, his eyes squinting, his voice turning into the querulous rasp of Dr. Gillespie informing Dr. Kildare of his diagnosis of the disease. Then, resuming his natural manner, he said, "The audience knows. Look at the receipts. Give the audience what they want? No. Not *good* enough." He paused.

"Thoreau said most of us lead lives of quiet desperation," Freed said quickly. "Pictures should make you feel better, not worse."

Again Mayer did not seem to hear. "*The Red Badge of Courage,*" he said. "A million and a half. Maybe more. What for? There's no story. I was against it. They wanted to make it. I don't say no. John Huston. He was going to do *Quo Vadis.* What he wanted to do to the picture! No heart. His idea was he'd throw the Christians to the lions. That's all. I begged him to change his ideas. I got down on my hands and knees to him. I sang 'Mammy' to him. I showed him the meaning of heart. I crawled to him on hands and knees. 'Ma-a-ammy!' With tears. No! No heart! He *thanked* me for taking him off the picture. Now he wants *The Red Badge of Courage.* Dore Schary wants it. All right. I'll watch. I don't say no, but I wouldn't make that picture with Sam *Gold*wyn's money."

. . .

The administrative headquarters for the M-G-M studio is a U-shaped white concrete building identified, in metal letters, as the Irving Thalberg Building. The steps leading to the Thalberg Building, between broad, shrub-bordered lawns, are wide and smooth, and they shone whitely under the midsummer sun, as cool and as stately as the steps to the Capitol in Washington, as I headed for them one morning. A taxi drew over to the curb and jerked to a halt. The door opened and Huston leaped out. He plunged a hand into a trouser pocket, handed the driver a wadded bill, and rushed toward the steps. He had stayed in town the night before, he said, at one of his three places—a small house in Beverly Hills he rented from Paulette Goddard—and he had expected his secretary to telephone him and wake him up. She had not telephoned, and he had overslept. He seemed angry and tense. "Audie's waiting for me," he said irritably.

We went into a large reception room with gray-checkered linoleum on the floor, and Huston strode across it, nodding to a young man seated at a semicircular desk between two doors. "Good morning, Mr. Huston," the young man said brightly. At once, the catches on both doors started clicking, and Huston opened the one on the right. I hurried after him, down a linoleum-floored corridor, whose cream-colored walls were lined with cream-colored doors. On each door was a slot holding a white card with a name printed on it. At the end of the corridor, we turned to the right, down another corridor, and at the end of *that* we came to a door with his name on it, engraved in black letters on a brass plate. Huston opened it, and a young lady with curly black hair, seated at a desk facing the door, looked up as we came in. Huston turned immediately to a bench adjoining the entrance. Audie Murphy was sitting on it. He stood up.

"Hello, Audie. How are you, Audie?" Huston said gently, as though speaking to a frightened child. The two men shook hands. "Well, we made it, kid," Huston said, and forced an outburst of ho-ho-hos.

Murphy gave him a wan smile and said nothing. A slight young man with a small, freckled face, long, wavy reddish-brown hair, and large, cool gray eyes, he was wearing tan twill frontier riding pants, a matching shirt, open at the collar, and Western boots with pointed toes and high heels.

"Come in, Audie," Huston said, opening the door to an inner office.

"Good morning," the secretary behind him said. "Publicity wants to know what do you do when you hit a snag in writing a script?"

"Tell publicity I'm not here," Huston said in a tone of cold reproach. Then, his voice gentle again, he said, "Come in, Audie."

Huston's office had oak-panelled walls, a blue carpet, and three windows reaching from the ceiling to the floor. There was a long mahogany desk at one end of the room, and at the opposite end, facing it, was a blue leather couch. Several blue leather armchairs were scattered around the office.

"Sit down, guys," Huston said, and himself sat down behind the desk, in a swivel chair with a blue leather seat. "Well," he said, clenching his hands and resting his chin on them. He swung from side to side in his chair a few times, then leaned back and put his feet on the desk on top of a stack of papers.

Murphy sat down in an armchair facing one of the windows and ran a forefinger across his lower lip. "I've got a sore lip," he said. "'Bout six this morning, I went riding on my colt. I went riding without my hat, and the sun burned my lip all up." He spoke with a delicate plaintiveness, in the nasal, twangy drawl of a Texan.

"I've got the same thing, kid," Huston said, pursing his lips. "Tell you what, Audie. Bring your colt out to my ranch. You can have your colt right there with you, any time you want to ride while we're making the picture."

Murphy fingered his sore lip, as if trying to determine whether Huston's pleasant offer did anything for his affliction. Apparently it didn't, so he looked sadly out the window.

"We'll do a lot of riding together, kid," Huston said. "That's good riding country there in the hills, you know."

Murphy made a small, sighing noise of assent.

"I want you to hear this, Audie," Huston said, nervously unfolding a sheet of paper he had taken from his jacket. "Some new lines I just wrote for the script." He read several lines, then laughed appreciatively.

Murphy made another small noise of assent.

Huston continued to laugh, but his eyes, fastened on Murphy, were sombre. He seemed baffled and worried by Murphy's unresponsiveness, because usually actors were quick to respond to him. He took his feet down from his desk and picked up a slip of blue paper one heel had been resting on. "Inter-office Communication," he read aloud, and glanced quickly at Murphy to get his attention. "To Messrs. Gottfried Reinhardt, John Huston . . . SUBJECT: Hair for RED BADGE OF COURAGE Production. As per discussion this morning, we are proceeding with the manufacture of: 50 Hook-on Beards at $3.50 each, 100 Crepe wool Mustaches at 50c each, 100 Crepe wool Falls at $2.50 each—for Production No. 1512—RED BADGE OF COURAGE. These will be manufactured in the Makeup Department."

Huston stopped reading, looked at Murphy, and saw that he had already lost his attention. "Well, now," Huston said, "let's go get some breakfast. I haven't had any breakfast yet."

The door opened, and a stoop-shouldered young man with enormous, eager-looking eyes came in. He was introduced as Albert Band, Huston's assistant. Huston moved toward the door.

"Where you going?" Band asked, blinking his eyes. His eyelashes descended over his eyes like two dust mops.

"Breakfast," said Huston.

Band said that he had had his breakfast, but he would come along and watch Huston have his.

We went out a side door to the studio gates, where a policeman in a stone hut looked carefully at each of us as we filed through. "Mr. Huston," he said.

"Good morning," Huston said, giving full weight to each syllable.

We went down a narrow street between low, gray-painted buildings of wood or stucco, which had shingles identifying them as "Men's Wardrobe," "International Department," "Casting Office," "Accounting

Department," and "Danger 2300 Volts." Farther along the street were the sound stages, gray, hangarlike buildings. We passed a number of costumed actors and actresses, and people in casual summer dress who exchanged nods with Huston and looked piercingly at Murphy, Band, and me.

A portly gentleman in a gray pinstriped suit stopped Huston and shook hands with him. "Congratulate me," he said. "My picture opens next week in New York."

"Music Hall?" Huston asked.

"I have news for you," the man said in a dry tone. "Dore Schary personally produces a picture, *it* gets into the Music Hall. *I* got Loew's State."

• • •

Back in the Thalberg Building, Huston invited Murphy and me to see a number of test shots he had made on his ranch for *The Red Badge of Courage*. He had seen the tests and, with Reinhardt and Schary, had made the final decisions on the leading players in the cast. In addition to Audie Murphy as the Youth, there would be Bill Mauldin as the Loud Soldier, John Dierkes as the Tall Soldier, and Royal Dano as the Tattered Man. We trooped downstairs to a carpeted lounge in the basement and went into a projection room that contained two rows of heavy, deep leather armchairs. Beside the arm of one of the center chairs was a board holding a telephone and a mechanism called a "fader," which controls the volume of sound. The first shot showed the Youth, who had returned to his regiment after running away from battle, having his head bandaged by his friend, the Loud Soldier. Mauldin, dressed in Union blue, his ears protruding horizontally from under a kepi, said as he bound a kerchief around Murphy's head, "Yeh look like th' devil, but I bet yeh feel better."

In the audience, Murphy said in a loud whisper, "I was biting my cheek so hard trying to keep from laughing."

"Yes, Audie," said Huston.

The next scene showed Murphy carrying a gun and urging some soldiers behind him to come on. "Let's show them Rebs what we're made of!" Murphy called fiercely, on the screen. "Come on! All we got to do is cross this here field! Who's with me? Come on! Come on!" Murphy advanced, and Huston's voice came on the sound track, laughing and saying, "Very good."

"I was biting my cheek so hard my whole cheek was sore," Murphy said.

"Yes, Audie," Huston said.

Next there was a scene between Murphy and the Tall Soldier, played by John Dierkes. The Tall Soldier died, his breath rasping and then ceasing, and his hair blowing long and wild. The Youth wept.

The lights came on. "We're going to be just fine," Huston said.

Back in his office, where we found Band waiting for us, Huston, taking another cigarette, said that Dierkes would be just wonderful in the picture.

"Just great," said Band.

Murphy was back in his armchair, staring out the window as though lost in a distant dream. Huston gave him a sharp glance, then sighed and put his long legs up on the desk. "Well, now, Audie, we're going to have such fun making this picture on my ranch!" he said. "Let me tell you kids all about the ranch." There was a compelling promise in his tone. He waited while Murphy shifted his gaze from the window to him. Huston deliberately took his time. He drew on his cigarette, and blew the smoke away. He began by telling us that he had four hundred and eighty acres—rolling fields, pasture, a brook, and hills harboring mountain lions and jaguars. He had paddocks and stables for his horses, a pen for eight Weimaraner puppies, doghouses for the Weimaraner parents and three other dogs (including a white German shepherd named Paulette, after Paulette Goddard), and a three-room shack for himself, his adopted son Pablo, and a young man named Eduardo, who managed the ranch. Huston's wife, the former Ricki Soma, and their infant son lived at Malibu Beach, and Huston commuted between the two establishments. At the ranch, Huston had a cowboy named Dusty, and, with a good deal of laughter, he described Dusty's gaunt and leathery face and his big, black ten-gallon hat. "Oh, God!" he said, with a shake of his head, "Dusty wants to be in the picture." He coughed out a series of jovial ho-ho-hos. Murphy, who had given him a quiet smile, developed the smile into hollow-sounding laughter. Huston seemed satisfied that he had finally got a response out of Murphy.

The door opened and Reinhardt stood there, an expression of cynical bewilderment on his face, a large cigar between his lips.

"Come in, Gottfried," said Huston.

"Hello, Mr. Reinhardt," Murphy said, standing up.

Reinhardt took a few steps forward, bobbing his head paternally at everyone. "There's going to be trouble, John," he said, in a tone of dry, flat amiability. He chewed his cigar around to a corner of his mouth to let the words out. "The production office thought the river for the picture was a stream. In the script, it says, 'The regiment crosses a *stream*.' Now they want to know what you mean you need hundreds of men to cross the Sacramento *River*?" He bobbed his head again.

"Ho! Ho!" Huston said, crossing his legs on top of his desk. Murphy sat down again. Band paced the carpet in front of Huston's desk.

"Trouble!" Reinhardt said.

"Well, now, Gottfried, you and I are used to trouble on this picture," Huston said. He put a brown cigarette in his mouth. Band held a kitchen match to it. Huston cocked his head over the flame and gave Murphy a wry smile. "They're afraid the soldiers will get their little tootsies wet," he said, with a titter.

Murphy smiled sadly. Band laughed and batted his eyes first at Huston, then at Reinhardt.

"Now, *Albert* wouldn't be afraid to cross the river, would you, Albert?" Huston asked.

Murphy smiled.

"I have news for you," Band said. "I'm *going* to cross it. You promised me I could have a part in this picture."

Reinhardt laughed, the upper part of his body bouncing energetically. As Band continued pacing in front of Huston's desk, Reinhardt fell in ahead of him, and the two men paced together. Reinhardt's gold key chain looped into his trouser pocket flopped noisily as he paced. "Everybody in Hollywood wants to be something he is not," he said as Huston watched him over the tips of his shoes. "Albert is not satisfied to be your assistant. He wants to be an actor. The writers want to be directors. The producers want to be writers. The actors want to be producers. The wives want to be painters. Nobody is satisfied. Everybody is frustrated. Nobody is happy." He sighed, and sat down heavily in a chair facing Murphy. "I am a man who likes to see people happy," he muttered through his cigar.

The door opened, and John Dierkes entered. "Hi, John! Hi, everybody," he said cheerfully, in a rasping drawl. He had a thick shock of stringy orange hair. "Hi, sport!" he said to Murphy. "Hedda sure likes you, sport. Didja see what she said about you today?"

"Did you let your hair grow?" Reinhardt asked him.

"Sure did, Gottfried," said Dierkes. "It's been growin' and growin' for weeks." He sat down, clasped his hands between his knees, and beamed at Murphy. "You learnin' your lines, sport?" he asked.

Huston recrossed his legs impatiently and said that he had just seen Dierkes' screen test. "You look like an ugly bastard," Huston said. "You're the only man I know who is uglier than I am."

Dierkes dropped his long chin in an amiable smile. "That's what you said the first time we met, John," he said. "In London. I was in the Red Cross and you were sure spiffy in your major's uniform. 1943."

"I was on my way to Italy," Huston said. "That's when we made *The Battle of San Pietro.*"

Reinhardt turned to Murphy. "Did you ever see the picture *K-Rations and How to Chew Them*?" he asked in a loud voice. He tilted his cigar to a sharp angle and pointed a finger at himself. "Mine," he said.

"England was just wonderful in the war," Huston said. "You always wanted to stay up all night. You never wanted to go to sleep."

Reinhardt said, "I'll bet I'm the only producer who ever had Albert Einstein as an actor." Attention now focussed on him. He said that he had been making an Army film called *Know Your Enemy—Germany,* the beginning of which showed some notable German refugees. "Anthony Veiller, a screen writer who was my major, told me to tell Einstein to comb his hair before we photographed him. I said, 'Would *you* tell Einstein to comb his hair?' He said no. So we photographed Einstein with his hair not combed." Reinhardt bounced merrily in his chair and laughed.

"God, those English bootmakers!" Huston said. "The love and affection they lavish on their boots! Whenever I go to London, I head straight for Maxwell and order boots made."

Reinhardt got up and went to the door, saying that in the afternoon there was going to be a conference of the key members of the crew assigned to the picture. The cost of making a picture depended largely on the time it took, he observed. The director and his actors might work together only three hours of an eight-hour day; the balance of the time would be spent waiting for scenes to be prepared. Reinhardt wanted to discuss what he called the leapfrog method, which meant having an assistant director line up shots in advance, so that Huston could move from one scene to another without delay. "We bring this picture in early, we will be real heroes," Reinhardt said.

"Don't worry, Gottfried," Huston said.

"I will see you later?" Reinhardt asked.

"I'll be there, Gottfried. Don't worry," Huston said.

• • •

Since most of the film was to be shot about thirty miles from Hollywood, on Huston's ranch, in the San Fernando Valley, Huston arranged to look over the terrain one day with Reinhardt and the production crew. I arrived at the ranch about eleven o'clock in the morning, and a few minutes later the crew drove up in a large black limousine. Huston came out of his ranchhouse to greet us, dressed in a red-and-green checked cap, a pink T shirt, tan riding pants flapping out at the sides, tan leggings, tan suspenders, and heavy maroon shoes that reached to his ankles. Included in the crew were the cameraman, Harold Rosson, a short, stocky, gum-chewing, middle-aged man with a sharp face; the unit manager, Lee Katz, a heavyset man in his late thirties, with thin blond fuzz on his head, a brisk, officious manner, and a perpetual ingratiating smile; the leapfrog director, Andrew Marton, whom the others addressed as Bundy, a serious, pedantic Hungarian-American with a heavy accent and a nervous, solicitous manner, whose job it would be to arrange things so that Huston would not have to wait between scenes; the art director, Hans Peters, a stiff, formal German with cropped hair, who also had a heavy accent; another assistant director, Reggie Callow, a harassed-looking man with a large red face, a bowl-shaped midriff, and the gravelly voice of a buck sergeant; and the technical adviser, Colonel Paul Davidson, a retired Army officer with a mustache, dark glasses, and a soldierly bearing. All were carrying copies of the script.

Shortly after we arrived, Reinhardt and Band drove up in a gray Cadillac convertible with the top down. Reinhardt had a navy-blue beret on his head and a cigar in his mouth. He came over and pumped Huston's hand. "Happy birthday, John," he said.

"Oh, yes. I almost forgot," Huston said. "Well, gentlemen, let's get started."

Everybody was wearing rough clothes except Reinhardt, who wore neat gabardine slacks of bright blue and a soft shirt of lighter blue. Band had on Russian Cossack boots, into which were tucked ragged cotton pants. Marton wore dungarees and a khaki bush jacket, which, he said, he had brought from Africa, where he had recently worked as co-director of *King Solomon's Mines.* Colonel Davidson wore Army fatigues.

Dusty, the Huston-ranch cowboy who wanted to play in the picture, stood around while the crew got organized. He went into the stables and returned leading a large black horse, saddled and bridled. Huston mounted it, and then Dusty brought out a white-and-brown cow pony.

"I'll ride Papoose, pal," Rosson said to Huston, and heaved himself aboard the cow pony.

"He was once married to Jean Harlow," Band said to Colonel Davidson, pointing to Rosson.

"Let's go, gentlemen!" Huston called, waving everybody on. He walked his horse slowly down the road.

"John can really set a saddle," Dusty said, watching him go.

Rosson started after Huston. Reinhardt and Band followed in the Cadillac. The rest of us, in the limousine, brought up the rear of the cavalcade.

Marton peered out the window at Rosson, rocking along on the cow pony. "He used to be married to Jean Harlow," he said thoughtfully. "Reggie, what do we do first?"

Callow said that they were going to stop at the location for the scene showing the Youth's regiment on the march, to determine how many men would be needed to give the effect of an army on the march. It was Scene 37. All the script had to say about it was "MEDIUM LONG SHOT—A ROAD—THE ARMY ON THE MARCH—DUSK."

"The mathematics of this discussion is important," Callow said.

Katz, whose primary job was to serve as a liaison man between the crew and the studio production office, was sitting up front. He turned around and said, smiling, "Mathematics means money."

"Everything is such a production," said Marton. "Why can't they just turn Johnny loose with the camera?"

Colonel Davidson, who was sitting in a jump seat next to Peters, cleared his throat.

"What, what?" Katz said to him.

"Warm today," the Colonel said, clearing his throat again.

"Nothing," Marton said. "In Africa, we had a hundred and fifty degrees in the shade."

"That so?" said the Colonel.

Katz turned around again. There were beads of perspiration on his forehead and in the fuzz on his head. "You boys are going to have a time climbing these hills today," he said cheerily. "Hot, hot."

Peters said, without moving his head, "Very warm."

"It's going to be a tough war," Callow said.

. . .

The road for the MEDIUM LONG SHOT was a dirt one curving around a hill and running through sunburned fields. A large oak tree at the foot of the hill cast a shadow over the road. Huston and Rosson sat on their horses near the top of the hill, waiting for the rest of the party to struggle up to them through dry, prickly grass. Reinhardt was carrying a sixteen-millimetre movie camera. A hawk flew overhead, and Reinhardt stopped, halfway up the hill, and trained his camera on it. "I like to take pictures of birds," he said. When everyone had reached Huston and was standing around him, Huston pointed to the bend in the road.

"The Army comes around there," he said commandingly. He paused and patted the neck of his horse. "Colonel," he said.

"Yes, sir!" Colonel Davidson said, coming to attention.

"Colonel, how far apart will we put the fours?" Huston asked.

"About an arm's length, sir," said the Colonel.

"Get away from my script!" Callow said to Huston's horse, who was attempting to eat it.

Huston gave Callow a reproachful look and patted the horse's neck. "Never mind, baby," he said.

"Gentlemen," Rosson said, "keep in mind we must not have these Western mountains in what was primarily an Eastern war." He dismounted and gave the reins of his pony to Band, who clambered clumsily into the saddle. The pony started turning in circles.

"It's only me, little baby," Band said to it.

"Albert!" Huston said. Band got off the pony, and it calmed down.

"Gentlemen," Huston said. "The range finder, please."

Marton handed him a cone-shaped tube with a rectangular window at the wide end. It would determine the kind of lens that would be needed for the shot. Huston looked at the road through the finder for a long time. "A slow, uneven march," he said dramatically. "The Union colonel and his aide are leading the march on horseback. Looks wonderful, just wonderful. Take a look, Hal." He handed the finder to Rosson, who looked at the road through it.

"Great, pal!" Rosson said, chewing his gum with quick, rabbitlike chomps.

"Doesn't it look like a Brady, kid?" Huston said to Rosson.

"Great, pal," said Rosson.

The two men discussed where the camera would be set up, how the shot of the column of soldiers would be composed, when the shot would be taken (in the early morning, when the light on the troops would be coming from the back). They also discussed the fact that the scene, like most of the others in the picture, would be photographed as if from the point of view of the Youth. Then they got to talking about how many men would be needed for the scene.

"How about four hundred and fifty?" said Katz.

"Eight hundred," Huston said immediately.

"Maybe we could do with six hundred and fifty," Reinhardt said, giving Huston a knowing glance.

Katz said that the column would be spaced out with horses and caissons, and that they could get away with less than six hundred and fifty infantrymen.

Huston gave Colonel Davidson a sly glance and winked.

The Colonel quickly cleared his throat and said, "Sir, to be militarily correct we ought to have a thousand infantry."

"God!" Reinhardt said.

"Never, never," Katz said.

"Make the picture in Africa," Marton said. "Extras cost eighteen cents a day in Africa."

"That's exactly fifteen dollars and thirty-eight cents less than an extra costs here," Callow said. "We could change it to the Boer War."

"Is it to be six hundred and fifty, gentlemen?" Huston said impatiently.

"If that's the way you want it," Katz said. "Anything I can do you for."

• • •

We went from one site to another, trudging up and down hills and breaking paths through heavy underbrush. The afternoon sun was hot, and the faces of the crew were grimy and wet, and their clothes were dusty and sprinkled with burs and prickly foxtails. Only Reinhardt seemed unaffected by his exertions. His blue slacks were still creased, and a fresh cigar was in his mouth as he stood beside Huston examining the site for a scene—to be shot some afternoon—that would show the Youth coming upon a line of wounded men, who would be moving down a path on a slope. Huston and Reinhardt looked at a grassy slope that led down to a road and a patch of trees. The distance from the top of the slope to the road was two hundred and seventy yards, Callow told Huston and Reinhardt. The three men estimated that they would need a hundred extras to make an impressive line of wounded men.

Huston looked through the finder at the slope. "The Youth sees a long line of wounded staggering down," he said, in a low voice.

"We've got to have something for these men to do in the *morning*," Katz said. "We can't have a hundred extras on the payroll and have them stand around with nothing to do for half a day."

Huston lowered the finder. "Let's just put the figures down as required for each shot, without reference to any other shot," he said coldly.

Katz smiled and threw up his hands.

"And if we find we need twenty-five more men—" Huston began.

"I will appeal to Mr. Reinhardt," Katz said.

"You have great powers of persuasion," said Huston.

Reinhardt bobbed his head and laughed, looking at his director with admiration.

Callow sat by the side of the path, laboriously pulling foxtails out of his socks. "I'm stabbed all over," he said. "I fought the Civil War once before, when I was assistant director on *Gone with the Wind*. It was never this rough, and *Wind* was the best Western ever made."

Reinhardt was aiming his camera at a small silver-and-red airplane flying low overhead.

"That's no bird; that's Clarence Brown," said Band.

"Clarence is up there looking for gold," Marton said.

"There is a great story about Clarence Brown," Reinhardt said. "A friend says to him, 'What do you want with all that money, Clarence? You can't take it with you.' 'You can't?' Clarence says. 'Then I'm not going.'" Band and Marton agreed that it was a great story, and Reinhardt looked pleased with himself.

Katz was saying that the first battle scene would have four hundred infantrymen, fifty cavalrymen, and four complete teams of artillerymen and horses, making a total of four hundred and seventy-four men and a hundred and six horses.

"More people than we ever had in *Wind*," Callow said.

Huston, now on his horse, leaned forward in the saddle and rested the side of his face against the neck of the horse.

"We accomplished a lot today," Reinhardt said.

Huston said, with great conviction, "It looks just swell, Gottfried, just wonderful."

"It must bc a grcat picture," Reinhardt said.

"Great," Band said.

Huston wheeled his horse and started across the slope at a canter. He approached a log on top of a mound of earth, spurred his horse, and made a smooth jump. Reinhardt trained his camera on Huston until he disappeared around a wooded knoll.

HUMILITY, CONCENTRATION, AND GUSTO

Winthrop Sargeant

FEBRUARY 16, 1957 (ON MARIANNE MOORE)

Among people who like to feel that they know just how things stand, Marianne Craig Moore is regarded, variously, as America's greatest living woman poet, or as one of America's greatest living poets, or even as America's greatest living poet—three views that combine to establish her squarely as a literary monument, handily labelled for ready reference. There may be some doubt in the minds of those who are not well up on modern verse about just how these titles have been arrived at, but there is no doubt that they are supported by an overwhelming assortment of prizes, memberships in societies of immortals, and honorary Litt. D.s that Miss Moore has collected over nearly half a century of writing verse, and by many qualified authorities, among them a number of distinguished fellow-poets, such as W. H. Auden, who has gallantly confessed to plundering her work for technical ideas, and T. S. Eliot, who has stated that in his opinion "her poems form part of the small body of durable poetry written in our time." There are, however, other ways of looking at Miss Moore. A large public that has never opened any of the books responsible for her fame has been led by articles about her in big-circulation family magazines to see her as a quaint and rather stylish spinster who, at the age of sixty-nine, lives in a cluttered apartment in Brooklyn and writes poems about animals—a picture that is essentially accurate, if considerably oversimplified. To some of the more complicated types who frequent literary teas and cocktail parties in

Manhattan, Miss Moore is a quite outrageous chatterbox and intellectual comedienne; to others, more fondly disposed toward her, she is a gentle lioness of formidable glamour, capable of non-stop conversational monologues, richly interspersed with observations on life and letters, which they feel should be treasured for their outspokenness and originality. At gatherings of this kind, her meticulous and all but breakneck manner of expressing herself—mirroring a mind in which wisdom and innocence are curiously combined—often produces a flow of imagery and anecdote whose quality leads some of her admirers to contend that she not only writes but talks literature.

And there is still another Miss Moore—the one known to her neighbors in the fairly nondescript area surrounding her modest five-room, fifth-floor apartment on Cumberland Street, in the Fort Greene Park section of Brooklyn. To her neighbors she is, and has been for many years, a familiar and affectionately regarded figure as—dressed with a conservative smartness that often includes a skimmer or a tricorne hat, armed with a shopping basket, and exuding an air of invincible energy and cheerfulness—she passes the time of day with her grocer or her vegetable man. Along Cumberland Street, her claim to distinction rests not so much on her writing or on her drawing-room wit as on certain aspects of her conduct and bearing that mark her, in the eyes of people she has daily dealings with, as a great lady who represents the genteel traditions of a noble and nearly forgotten era. "For my money, they don't come any finer than Miss Moore," says Henry Burfeindt, one of the clerks at the Oxlord Delicatessen, a couple of blocks from her apartment. "She gave me one of her books—and she autographed it. It says 'To Henry' in the front of it. One of these days I'm going to lay in the sun and read it." And Mike Moscarella, who runs a shoe-repair shop at the corner of Carlton Street and De Kalb Avenue, a block and a half away, says, "She don't dress modern. She makes friends easy, and she's a real home lady. Very interesting to talk to, too. She likes to talk about scenery and flowers." Among another group of her Brooklyn acquaintances—the parishioners of the nearby Lafayette Avenue Presbyterian Church—Miss Moore is revered for still different virtues, of a sort not often associated with poets nowadays. She regularly attends services at the church, and invariably says grace before meals. Moreover, she strictly avoids alcohol, tobacco, and even coffee. So highly is she thought of by the church authorities that on several occasions they have asked her to write a special benediction to be delivered at church dinners on Thanksgiving or some other ceremonial day, but this she has so far declined to do. "I don't believe in substituting conscious expression for spontaneous devotion," she says.

. . .

These diverse facets of Miss Moore's public personality suggest that the individual embodying them is a phenomenon of some complexity. Since poetry—and contemporary poetry in particular—is one of the most personal of the arts, and since connoisseurs long familiar with Miss Moore and her verse believe that her poems are works of self-portraiture to an even greater extent than those of most poets, it is natural to look for clues to the essential character of this phenomenon in the half-dozen volumes of verse that, except for a book of essays and some translations, constitute her life work to date. The poems in these volumes are instantly striking for the exquisite care with which they have been put together; Miss Moore sets down her metaphors and images in neat, precise patterns, using schemes of metre and rhyme that are at once as intricate and as clearly defined as needlepoint embroidery, and even the typographic schemes of her printed verses are fastidiously original. A good example of this last is a fragment from "In Distrust of Merits," one of the few poems she has written on subjects of major social significance:

> There never was a war that was
>   not inward; I must
> fight till I have conquered in myself what
> causes war, but I would not believe it.
>   I inwardly did nothing.
>   O Iscariotlike crime!
>   Beauty is everlasting
>   and dust is for a time.

In general, her poems reveal an intense preoccupation with often microscopic visual detail and an extraordinary joy in the contemplation of such minutiae as the sheen of sea shells, the tendrils of plants, and the legs and wings of insects. While Miss Moore's scrupulous descriptions of her abundant observations would hardly constitute poetry in themselves, she has a flair for symbolism that gives them meaning, making each small object the protagonist of an engrossing drama—a drama that, as often as not, points a moral of some sort. The sequence in which the visual images swiftly appear and vanish is not so much a matter of logic as it is of kaleidoscopic association, and the agility with which Miss Moore jumps from one association to the next is such that even the most diligent reader sometimes loses his way in attempting to follow her—a drawback that she tries to minimize by including a series of explanatory notes at the end of each volume. A reader who, with or without the notes, is able to keep pace with Miss Moore finds himself being led through an aggregation of sensations and perceptions that are similar in effect to a collage or a mosaic, and are highlighted by epigrams and descriptive phrases memorable for the particularly vivid insight they give into one truth or another.

In "The Labours of Hercules," a poem about poetry, Miss Moore has written "that one detects creative power by its capacity to conquer one's detachment, that while it may have more elasticity than logic, it knows where it is going"—an eminently logical assertion and a justification of the elastic, or intuitive, method that characterizes most of her writing. A great deal of the charm of her work lies in the originality of her point of view; somehow she is able to describe things as if they were being seen for the first time by a mind without preconceptions. This faculty, similar to that of a child or a primitive, enables her to avoid clichés of thought and expression; her poetry contains no second-hand ideas, except when she openly borrows from other writers, in which case she takes pains to make that fact clear by using quotation marks—a sort of code, informing the knowing reader that he will find the source listed back among the notes. She seems, indeed, to be perpetually and delightedly poised on the frontier of fresh experience—a narrow and perilous region where she can lean neither on learning nor on generalized principles. Miss Moore is, of course, neither a child nor a primitive but an urbane and educated woman, and her position on this frontier—as consciously maintained as that of a tightrope walker—demands an air of ingenuousness that is patently calculated artifice but nevertheless a most appealing one.

Much of Miss Moore's poetry takes the form of slyly satirical criticism—criticism of art, of literature, of human behavior—expressed in economical, tightly packed phrases, and in this criticism she shows herself to be something of a stickler for what she considers propriety. Of alcohol, that traditional midwife of the poet, she states uncompromisingly, "The wine cellar? No. It accomplishes nothing and makes the soul heavy." (Since these lines and the quotations immediately following have been taken out of context, they are reproduced here without regard for the typographical niceties of their author's versification.) In discussing literature, she writes, "Originality is in any case a byproduct of sincerity," and she taunts the French by describing them as a people "in whose products mystery of construction diverts one from what was originally one's object—substance at the core." She dislikes "authorities whose hopes are shaped by mercenaries" and "writers entrapped by teatime fame and commuters' comforts." She deplores the abnormal perfection of roses, assuring them that "your thorns are the best part of you." Her attitude toward her art is sometimes rather thorny itself, as when she observes, "Reading [poetry] . . . with a perfect contempt for it, one discovers in it after all, a place for the genuine." As a believer in good taste, she favors reticence: "The deepest feeling always shows itself in silence; not in silence, but restraint." Objective little notations like these seem to indicate an extremely reflective and slightly acid mind that abhors excess and prefers detached observation to participation, and this impression is reinforced by the rather striking fact that Miss Moore's verse is almost devoid of anything approaching passionate warmth toward her fellow-man; indeed, her fellow-man very seldom appears in it at all. Her love is expended instead on a still-life or a landscape world inhabited by plants and animals that are usually small and very self-sufficient. Yet she is apt to regard this world pessimistically; the environment in which her little animals play out their dramas is nearly always a threatening one. The odds are against them, even though, often covered with protective armor, they make their dwellings in snug holes and have admirable qualities of adaptability and strong powers of survival. They appear as symbols of virtues that Miss Moore repeatedly extolls—courage, patience, firmness, loyalty, integrity, good sense, modesty, persistence, and independence. Like many another poet, Miss Moore celebrates what philosophers have called the *élan vital,* but she celebrates it with restraint, and its most impressive victories in her poetry are achieved by the small living things she portrays as holding their own against the hostile surroundings of nature, as in "Nevertheless":

> The weak overcomes its
> menace, the strong over-
> comes itself. What is there
>
> like fortitude! What sap
> went through that little thread
> to make the cherry red!

Miss Moore's associative process of thought, which leads her discursively through her world of menaced and courageous creatures and often winds up with a pronouncement on human behavior, is well illustrated by a poem called "Snakes, Mongooses, Snake-Charmers and the Like." This starts off with a tribute to the mongoose's claws, passes on to images evoking the austerity of India and then to snakes and tortoises and chameleons, and finally poses the question of why the snake was invented. Typically, the answer is oblique, and ends with an aphorism:

> We do not know; the only positive thing about it is its shape;
> but why protest?
> The passion for setting people right is in itself an afflictive
> disease.
> Distaste which takes no credit to itself is best.

• • •

The connoisseurs who regard Miss Moore's poems almost literally as self-portraits are convinced that all those tiny beleaguered organisms surviving in adversity by means of fortitude, intelligence, and patience represent Miss Moore herself, and, moreover, that her manner of expression is as revealing as her subject matter. These judgments would appear to be sound, since a reader of Miss Moore's verse who had never met its author or heard anything about her would be justified in concluding that she was a rather remote and isolated individual, a meditative soliloquist, a fascinated observer of life, a digressive but deliberately elegant thinker, a stoic, a moralist, and something of a frontierswoman in the realm of sensation, capable of extracting enormous drama from the slightest experiences and impressions—and all this is pretty much confirmed by the poet's habits and the environment she has chosen for herself. Although her various obligations in the roles of monument, lioness, neighborhood *grande dame,* and pillar of the church involve her in a great deal of what she terms "dashing around," Miss Moore feels and responds to the creative person's need for privacy. Between her forays into the outer world, she lives alone, cooking her own meals at such times as she remembers to eat at all, corresponding with her numerous friends, and inviting the mood of "humility, concentration, and gusto" that she says is conducive to the difficult task of writing verse. She has likened herself during such intervals to "a cat in a basket with the lid on," "a badger under a hedge of poison ivy," and "a rat in a cheese"—similes that not only relate characteristically to animal life but convey a sense of snugness that is plainly very congenial to her.

Miss Moore's apartment is the apotheosis of snugness; indeed, it is snug almost to the point of restricting free movement, owing to a vast collection of miscellaneous objects she has amassed over the years. "I suppose my life is made happier by hoarding these things," Miss Moore says apologetically, and a visitor is likely to suspect that she attaches great sentimental value to everything around her. In addition to the furniture (comfortably old-fashioned and not in itself obtrusive), the hoard includes a tremendous array of books, in which the Bible and the Book of Common Prayer rub bindings with Latin classics and volumes on science, history, and travel—all of them painstakingly dusted and kept either in crowded bookcases or in upended apple boxes that line the narrow hallways. It includes a walrus tusk from the Greely Expedition to the Arctic in 1881, countless porcelain and ivory likenesses of tigers and elephants, and a mass of bric-a-brac in less readily identifiable shapes. And it includes paintings, drawings, and etchings, as well as pictures that Miss Moore has cut from magazines and framed—a display whose sheer square footage threatens to overflow the limited wall space that is not occupied by bookcases. Some of these mural ornaments are so faded that only the sharpest eye can make out what they are supposed to represent; others, more distinct, are works of purely personal interest, executed by friends (a stiff and naïve painting of a flower by E. E. Cummings, for example), or prints by artists of long ago (William Blake, for example). The subjects of the whole informal gallery are preponderantly animals—elephants, kangaroos, alligators, chickens, mice, hermit crabs, and very nearly all the rest. "Our ancestors!" Miss Moore explains, joyously embracing the entire display with a wave of the hand. Occasionally, though, the encroaching multitude of her possessions drives her to the verge of impatience. "I never want to own anything any more," she told a visitor not long ago. "No more shells and feathers! People present you with things they think may suggest an idea for a poem, but there simply aren't enough alcoves and embrasures to put them all in." Miss Moore does not usually remain in this mood for long, however, and she has never been able to bring herself to discard any of her remarkable accretion. Even in her most exasperated moments, the mere mention of some old coin or bit of porcelain in her collection will prompt her to dig it out and show it off with undisguised affection.

In contrast to the rest of the apartment, Miss Moore's kitchen has an air of practicality about it that suggests another side of her nature. A few pots and pans suffice for her culinary needs. "Cook and sew enough of the time and you feel degraded," she says. "I cook only the essentials—meat and potatoes. I've never baked a pie." On the kitchen table stands a Mason jar containing carrot juice, to which Miss Moore repairs for sustenance between meals, replenishing her supply from time to time with the help of a vegetable-juicer. "Carrot juice increases vigor," she says. The austerity of her kitchen is relieved only by a singular tool rack, of her own design and construction, in which she keeps various convenient implements—a plane, an auger, a pair of tin-cutting shears, a pair of pliers, two axes, a jar opener, a pair of scissors, and a gimlet, to name a few—all mounted in their proper places with a feeling for order that would do credit to the curator of a museum. The variety of these utensils not only bespeaks Miss Moore's prowess as a domestic craftsman but adds to the impression that her apartment is a thoroughly self-sufficient refuge—that its occupant, when hidden away in it, is as independent of the world at large as a barnacle in its shell.

• • •

As a consequence of Miss Moore's literary eminence, she does not remain hidden away as much as she perhaps would like to. Her apartment has become a place of pilgrimage for editors, publishers, critics, poets, artists, and other admiring folk, who gladly undertake the trip across the river in order to pay their respects. While Miss Moore does not encourage wholesale invasions of her privacy, she is nevertheless gratified by an occasional visit and deeply appreciative of the effort people make in journeying all the way to what is for most of them a previously unexplored region of Brooklyn. By way of demonstrating this appreciation, she keeps a large supply of subway tokens on hand, and invariably urges guests from Manhattan to dip into it and so spare themselves the trouble of having to stop and buy one in the station before heading back under the East River. Sometimes her offer of a token is accepted casually, but sometimes it is accepted only after quite a show of reluctance, and once in a while it is flatly refused. There are those who suspect that Miss Moore likes to study the varied reactions to her considerate little gesture, and she is reported to have once admitted as much to a friend. "I know they don't need it, and they know that I know they don't need it, but I like to see what happens," she is supposed to have said. "The most interesting people take it without making a fuss." Questioned about this recently, Miss Moore denied ever having said any such thing. "Why, I would be incapable of testing a person in that way!" she exclaimed. But then she added, "Still, I do prize people a little more highly if they don't make a big thing of it."

When guests arrive at the apartment, Miss Moore serves them tea, which she brews unostentatiously but with great care, seeing to it that her Chinese teapot is properly warmed beforehand and putting it in an upholstered basket when the tea is ready for pouring. During this ceremony, she moves about swiftly among the treasures in her living room in an easy, athletic fashion not generally associated with women of her age, and her manner, which in privacy resembles that of a preoccupied librarian, is transformed into that of a piquant and highly animated actress. The transformation is a very striking one. Her cheeks redden, she smiles slyly, and she becomes Marianne Moore the public personality, with all the challenges to wit and originality that this implies. She seems to grow appreciably taller. Her face, topped by a braid of gray hair wrapped around her head and held in place by a large celluloid hairpin, assumes an expression of girlish enthusiasm sharpened by occasional gleams of mockery, and she talks softly but very volubly, with a slightly flat drawl that may reflect her Midwestern origins.

Miss Moore's conversation is remarkable for its diversity, and for a certain recklessness that is likely to lead her, by a sequence of crowding and tumbling associations, into fields far removed from her starting point. For instance, while she has a high opinion of tea, she is aware that some of her guests may prefer something stronger, and therefore keeps on hand a bottle of Harvey's Shooting Sherry. There is a hunting scene on the label, and on occasion this has served as a springboard for one of her dizzying monologues. At an afternoon gathering in her apartment a couple of months ago, the label led her to a consideration of other labels (though she might just as easily have veered in the direction of rabbits or quail), and this, in turn, led her to comment on grocery-store stocks, specifically on the stocks of the S. S. Pierce store, in Boston. "Very discriminating grocers," she went on. "Even if they do carry cigars and wine and cosmetics along with their cheese, jam, cakes, soups, and all kinds of crackers. I can't abide dilutions or mixtures, but I like candy. If I drank whiskey, I would drink it straight. I have a lethal grudge against people who try to make me drink coffee. My friend Mrs. Church grinds her own coffee from French and American beans. Her husband's grandfather was a chemical inventor who invented a brand of bicarbonate of soda. His wife is a Bavarian. Mrs. Church, I mean. She had a house at Ville-d'Avray with a big cedar of Lebanon and a dog named Tiquot. They had a gardener who also drove the car. They wouldn't have begonias on the place. They did have a few geraniums, though. Mr. Church was a close friend of Wallace Stevens, who wrote *The Necessary Angel.* He reprinted an anecdote about Goethe wearing black woollen stockings on a packet boat. I like Goethe. My favorite language is German. I like the periodic structure of the sentences. 'And Shakespeare inspires me, too. He has so many good quotations. And Dante. He has a few, too.' That's from Ruth Draper. At Monroe Wheeler's once, we played a game called 'Who would you rather be except Shakespeare?' I wouldn't mind being La Fontaine, or Voltaire. Or Montaigne? No. I wouldn't be Montaigne—too sombre. I have always loved the vernacular. It spites me that I can't write fiction. And that book of essays I wrote. I let myself loose to do my utmost, and now they make me uneasy. The critics didn't care a great deal for them, but their reviews weren't really vipish. Those readings of my verse I made for the phonograph—well, they're here forever, like the wheat in the pyramids. I'm fond of Bach and Pachelbel and Stravinsky. I'm also fond of drums and trumpets—snare drums. If I find that a man plays the trumpet I am immediately interested. . . ."

The torrent of impressions and observations continues unstintingly. Miss Moore's listeners, in forming an opinion of it, tend to fall into two groups—those who delightedly occupy themselves in smelting out a memorable simile or adjective, and those who complain that it requires an enormous amount of strenuous concentration to make any sense at all of what she is saying. On the afternoon when S. S. Pierce received its pat on the back, one of the guests finally reached the point of exhaustion, and exclaimed, "Marianne, don't jump around so in your conversation!"

Miss Moore paused, turned pityingly toward the heretic, and replied with spirit, "It isn't jumping around. It's all connected." Then she was off again.

On another recent occasion, a bewildered guest interrupted Miss Moore to ask, "Do you realize where you started this digression?"

Miss Moore drew herself up and, smiling a bit austerely, said, "Wasn't it Aristotle who observed that 'the ability to see a connection between apparently incongruous things is the sign of a poet'?" Then she looked worried. "Or was it the 'mark' of a poet?" she said. "I hate people who can't quote things correctly, and then I go and make all kinds of mistakes myself. Was it the 'mark' of a poet or the 'sign' of a poet?" Another listener remarked that since the line was a translation anyhow, either word ought to be acceptable. But this was not enough for Miss Moore. By the following morning, she had tracked down the passage to its source and begun busily telephoning her guests to make elaborate apologies and give them the accurate version. "The sentence actually reads, 'It is the mark of a poet to see a connection between apparently incongruous things,'" she told one of them breathlessly. "I feel as degraded as a worm at the bottom of an umbrella stand. But I'm so relieved to have got it right at last."

Some of Miss Moore's friends interpret this reverence for scholarly exactitude, so at odds with her headlong habits of conversation, as one of a whole set of attitudes that are related to her conception of morals and propriety. She is as scrupulous in her regard for good form as the heroine of a Jane Austen novel, and there is about her a suggestion of both the Puritan woman and the Prussian knight. She dislikes seeing women apply makeup in public, and she herself, whether in public or alone, has an odd distaste for looking in a mirror, possibly—although she isn't really sure why—because she has a deep-seated feeling that the act is too frivolous. This is not to imply that she is in any way frumpy; on the contrary, while she disapproves of luxurious living in the broad sense, she has a fondness for certain luxuries, especially that of dressing well, and she is under no illusion that a woman can be well dressed on a cut-rate basis. "A friend of mine once told me that I could find the equivalent of Saks Fifth Avenue clothes on Fourteenth Street," she said not long ago. "I don't believe it. Besides, I don't like to get bargains, because I don't feel comfortable exploiting a store." The flow of Miss Moore's thought, whether written or spoken, is interspersed with allusions indicating a deep respect for romantic ideals of behavior—ideals involving monasticism, gallantry, and soldierliness. Despite an inveterate hatred of war, she thinks highly of the military life. "It means a great deal to me to know that there are in the world a few real enemies of enslavement and that some of them are generals—General Eisenhower, General MacArthur, and General de Tassigny," she told an interviewer in 1951. And, for all the indirectness of her own mental habits, she greatly reveres directness and workaday logic in others. "I like the writing of precise scientific thinkers," she says. "Lots of these scientists don't stand forth as littérateurs, but I find their devotion to fact very stimulating. They are much more competent than I am, particularly where precision is concerned." She prizes the works of chroniclers like Gibbon, and among her favorite authors are Julius Caesar and Xenophon. "Xenophon has wonderful qualities of restraint and latent satire," she says. "He loved horses, and he believed that a good cavalry officer should be religious."

Not one to confine her admiration for living organisms to those on the lower rungs of the evolutionary ladder, Miss Moore goes along with Xenophon in loving horses. Her most daring encounter with them—and possibly with any of the creatures of which she writes—occurred in 1952. She had become so interested in the race horse Tom Fool after reading about him in Arthur Daley's sports column in the *Times* that she wrote a poem in his honor ("Tom Fool is 'a handy horse,' with a chiselled foot . . ."), which appeared in *The New Yorker.* When her milliner, a lady with something of a weakness for the track, heard about the poem, she offered to take Miss Moore to the races at Jamaica, and Miss Moore accepted. She had never been to a race track before and (except for a staged visit with a magazine photographer) she has not been to one since. The experience was, therefore, unique, and, compared to most of her experiences, it was an extremely turbulent one. The two women visited the paddock, where Tom Fool was being saddled, and Miss Moore decided on the spot to risk fifty cents on him. "I've never seen a horse so limber," she says. On learning that two dollars is the minimum bet, she took the plunge at the two-dollar window, fearlessly going all out on a win-or-nothing basis. Tom Fool came in second. "That cured me of betting," Miss Moore says emphatically. As for her surroundings at the track, she had some reservations. "It certainly is a *tough* place, although I tried to look at the best side of it," she said later. "I've never seen so much liquor in my life. And the people in the stands don't seem happy even when they win." The afternoon was cold and the last race was late, and on the way back Miss Moore complained of chills, so her companion took her to her own house, where she broiled her a steak and gave her some brandy to warm her up. Miss Moore accepted the latter only as a prudent medicament, but it added one more fillip to an adventure that struck her as having its decidedly rakish aspects. "I learned my lesson never to become a race-track habitué," she has since told friends, and they have little fear that she will. When Jock Whitney, the horse's owner, read her poem about Tom Fool, he asked to buy the original manuscript. Miss Moore was willing to give it to him but not to sell it to him. "I thought it wouldn't be exactly fitting to be paid twice for the same poem," she says.

• • •

Although Miss Moore has a number of very good friends who share her interests, and several hundred acquaintances who are more or less celebrated for their accomplishments in the arts, her closest attachment is to a person of a wholly different outlook. This is her brother, Captain John Warner Moore, who is a retired chaplain of the United States Navy and currently the chaplain of the Gunnery School, a prep school for boys in Washington, Connecticut. While Miss Moore's affection for her brother is naturally attributable in large measure to their blood relationship, it appears to be intensified by the circumstance that he is a man both of staunch religious faith and of staunch military habits—two qualities that his sister, of course, greatly admires. The Captain is a tall, spare, white-haired gentleman, some seventeen months older than Miss Moore, who combines an erect bearing with a fatherly manner in such a way as to give an impression of dignity, dependability, and kindliness. Like his sister, he speaks with a slight Midwestern drawl, and he also resembles her in certain facial and other physical features, and in his patrician air of old-fashioned self-respect. In his time, Captain Moore, who is married and the father of four children, was a small-boat sailing champion in the Navy, winning several titles in the Pacific and officiating as one of the coaches of the Navy team that competed against Germany at Kiel in 1937. While his mental processes are, as might be expected, quite unlike his sister's—his thoughts tend to run on a logical track rather than by free and headlong association—and it is evident that he would be much more at home on the deck of a cruiser than in a Manhattan poetry salon, he is extremely proud of the eminence she has attained in the literary world. And Miss Moore, in turn, believes that in at least one way he is her literary superior. "My brother is much better at an essay than I am," she observed recently. "But he doesn't get time to write much. He's too busy with his work at the school."

Miss Moore and her brother are drawn still nearer to each other by a strong personal tie they share—a deep devotion to the memory of their mother, who died ten years ago. It would be difficult to imagine a closer family relationship than the one that existed between Mrs. Moore and her two children. A devout Presbyterian who also had a high opinion of the Quakers, she combined her religious feeling with definite literary leanings by saying a different grace—newly minted by her and often in poetic form—before every meal; as her son has recalled, "She had faith in the providence and goodness of God, and matters of honor were more important to her than food." She was a vigorous fighter for causes she believed in, and these, when she was in her prime, ranged from woman suffrage to crusading against cruelty to animals; in the first instance, she marched in parades, and in the second she stopped in the street to remonstrate with drivers who were mistreating their horses. People who were acquainted with Mrs. Moore differ widely in their recollections of the sort of woman she was; some remember her as a frighteningly intellectual person and a tremendous talker, while others remember her as demure, tenderly attentive, and gentle, though possessed of a strong will and easily outraged by any offense against her notion of correct behavior. In general, however, both sides agree that she was small, quite pretty, distinctly Irish in appearance, and rather witty. ("Knowing the mother, it was easy to see where Marianne's sense of humor came from," a friend of the family remarked recently.) And almost everyone qualified to judge believes that as a mentor and critic she could with justice claim part of the credit for her daughter's success. Probably the person best qualified to judge is Miss Moore herself, and she readily admits that she often made changes in her poetry to please her mother, and sometimes incorporated figures of speech her mother suggested. For years, mother and daughter were almost inseparable, enjoying a spiritual and mental intimacy so profound that some of their friends came to think of the two women as a single personality. A good many of the mementos in the Brooklyn apartment are closely connected with Mrs. Moore in the mind of her daughter, who further keeps her memory alive by observing little household procedures of which she approved, such as using a Pyrex pot, rather than a kettle, to boil water for tea, "because Mother said you couldn't air a kettle properly, and she wouldn't have one around."

Neither Miss Moore nor her brother ever knew their father, who was a construction engineer and a member of an old New England family that settled in Ohio immediately after the Revolution, but some of his forebears—among them Clement Moore, the author of "A Visit from St. Nicholas"—showed literary proclivities or exhibited other traits of character that a genealogical theorist might consider significant in explaining Miss Moore's development. Her paternal grandfather, for example, was a well-to-do river pilot and shipowner in Portsmouth, Ohio, who, in addition to taking a great interest in birds and cats, was bookishly inclined and owned an enormous collection of morocco-bound volumes; he finally gave it to the Carnegie Library of Portsmouth, retaining only a set of the Encyclopædia Britannica, which he methodically read through in his declining years, starting with the letter "A." His brother, also a pilot

(Captain Bixby, celebrated in Mark Twain's *Life on the Mississippi*, learned the ways of the river from him), had such a tender regard for insects that he wouldn't allow flypaper in his house and had a long record of fishing drowning flies out of the river.

It is not recorded that Miss Moore's father, John Milton Moore, had any similar side interests. Shortly after the Civil War, his father and uncle pooled their resources and opened a foundry in Portsmouth to manufacture boilers and other fittings for steamboats, and it was there that he learned his trade. In 1885, he married Mary Warner, the daughter of the Reverend John Riddle Warner, who was a Scotch-Irish Presbyterian minister then preaching in Kirkwood, Missouri. John Moore, being something of a visionary, was obsessed with the idea of building a smokeless furnace, and not long after his marriage he took his wife to Newton, Massachusetts, where, against the advice of his father and uncle, he put up a factory of his own for that purpose. The venture failed, and the resultant financial worries so preyed on his mind that he suffered a breakdown, from which he never recovered. The Reverend Mr. Warner, a widower, fetched his daughter back to Kirkwood, together with an infant son she had borne while in Massachusetts, and she moved in with him as his housekeeper—an arrangement that was soon briefly suspended by the arrival of her second child, Marianne, on November 15, 1887. The marriage was, in effect, terminated; her shattered husband returned to Portsmouth, where his parents took him under their care, while she continued to keep house for her father until he died, in 1894.

After staying briefly with relatives in Pittsburgh to get her bearings and plan her future, Mrs. Moore was persuaded by a friend to move to Carlisle, Pennsylvania, where she rented a house and settled down to raise her children, living on a small inheritance from her father. She became known to the community as a cultured and intelligent woman, and when, in 1900, an English teacher was needed at Carlisle's Metzger Institute, a school for girls that has since become a part of Dickinson College, she was offered—and accepted—the job. Even so, the little family was often in financial difficulties, but Mrs. Moore was a woman of indomitable vigor and optimism, and she managed so well that she was once able to take her children on a vacation trip to Florida and contrived to send them to college after they had graduated from the local high school. The son chose Yale and his sister Bryn Mawr, where—curiously, since for years she had been carefully instructed in literature by her mother—she was unable to meet the requirements for taking the advanced courses in English she had been looking forward to. "I was interested in the English and foreign-language courses, but I was too young, too immature for them, so most of my time was spent in the biology laboratory," Miss Moore recalled the other day. She did quite a bit of extracurricular writing, however, including some verse for *Tipyn O'Bob,* the college monthly literary magazine. Of these poems Miss Moore observes today, "A few of them were of some interest metrically, but in general they were tentative and ephemeral."

After graduating from Bryn Mawr, in 1909, Miss Moore took a secretarial course at the Carlisle Commercial College, and this enabled her to get a job as an instructor in typing, shorthand, and bookkeeping at the Carlisle Indian School, where one of her pupils was the famous Indian athlete Jim Thorpe. Not surprisingly, she found the subjects she taught uninspiring. "I was half good," she has since said. "I could fix typewriters, but rapid calculating and bookkeeping were just too much for me. It was a necessary financial adventure, and I would have much preferred to sit by the fire and read." In 1914, her brother was ordained, and two years later he was called to the Ogden Memorial Presbyterian Church, in Chatham, New Jersey. His post included a manse, so his mother and sister quit their jobs and went to Chatham to keep house for him. Theirs was indeed a tightly knit little family.

When the United States entered the First World War, the Reverend Mr. Moore gave up his parish in Chatham and joined the Navy, leaving his mother and sister more or less on their own. Three years before, Miss Moore had paid her first visit to New York, spending six days here and living at a Y.W.C.A. on Lexington Avenue, and those six days were enough to convince her that New York was where she ultimately wanted to live. Now, with her brother in the Navy, she was able to persuade her mother to move here, and in 1918 they rented a basement apartment on St. Luke's Place, in Greenwich Village, where they remained eleven years. The Reverend Mr. Moore stayed on in the Navy after the war, and in 1929 was stationed at the Brooklyn Navy Yard. That year, his mother caught pneumonia as a result (so he thought) of the draughtiness of the basement apartment, and he resolved to find quarters for her and his sister that would be both more salubrious and closer to his post. The quarters he found were in the apartment house in Brooklyn that Miss Moore still occupies—about three blocks from the Navy Yard.

• • •

For a while after settling in New York, Miss Moore worked as a private tutor and as a secretary in a girl's school. She spent a great deal of her spare time in her neighborhood branch of the Public Library, at Seventh Avenue South and St. Luke's Place—so much of it, in fact, that the authorities there, impressed by her interest, presently gave her a job. "I was not very good at library work," she recalls. "But, after all, it was not my field." Her field, of course, as she was becoming increasingly aware, was poetry. In April, 1915, when she was living in Carlisle, the *Egoist,* a London periodical specializing in imagist verse, published "To the Soul of Progress," her first poem to reach more than a campus audience; the person who supplied the improbable link between Carlisle and London was the poet Hilda Doolittle, a classmate of Miss Moore's at Bryn Mawr, who had married Richard Aldington, one of the editors of the *Egoist.* Almost coincidentally—a month later, in fact—Harriet Monroe's Chicago magazine *Poetry* published five of Miss Moore's poems. In 1921, under the imprint of the Egoist Press, Miss Doolittle and the then Mrs. Robert McAlmon ("H.D." and "Bryher") at their own expense brought out a small volume of poems of hers that had appeared in the *Egoist.* Three years later, Miss Moore assembled a number of the poems that had been printed here or in England, and they made up what proved to be her first important book. Entitled *Observations,* it immediately won the 1924 Dial Award, as a distinguished contribution to American literature, and this brought her not only a welcome two thousand dollars but considerable prestige. (The previous winner was T. S. Eliot, and subsequent winners included E. E. Cummings, William Carlos Williams, and Ezra Pound.) Moreover, it led Miss Moore into a long association with the *Dial,* a magazine that in the twenties held a unique position in the van of the nation's progressive literary and artistic life. Miss Moore began by writing verse and book reviews for the publication; then she became its acting editor, and, in 1926, its editor-in-chief.

Looking back, Miss Moore remembers the *Dial* as "an elysium for people who were really interested in quality," and, like many others who have memories of its beautifully printed pages, she cannot restrain a feeling of nostalgia for the era of intellectual exuberance that the magazine represented. The drab conformity of Marxist thought that later paralyzed the minds of so many writers in Europe and the United States had yet to make itself felt, and the great tide of mechanized mass communication and mass entertainment that has since threatened to swamp the minds of thinking individuals was still far off. "Those were the days when, as Robert Herring has said, things were opening out, not closing in," Miss Moore wrote in 1940, in a memoir describing her connection with the magazine. "There was for us of the staff a constant atmosphere of excited triumph—interiorly, whatever the impression outside; and from editor and publisher a natural firework of little parenthetic wit too good to print—implying that afflatus is not chary of surplus." The *Dial* was concerned neither with politics nor with theories of social progress but purely with the arts of writing, painting, and music, and its index of contributors was crowded with names that guaranteed the quality of which Miss Moore wrote in her memoir—Thomas Mann, Ortega y Gasset, Paul Morand, Maxim Gorky, Ezra Pound, T. S. Eliot, D. H. Lawrence, W. B. Yeats, Roger Fry, Robert Morss Lovett, Paul Valéry, Ford Madox Ford, Gilbert Seldes, William Carlos Williams, Wallace Stevens, and Kenneth Burke among them. The magazine also contained colored reproductions of paintings by an extraordinary number of artists who were then fairly new to this country, including Picasso, Seurat, di Chirico, Brancusi, Lachaise, Kuniyoshi, Sheeler, Marin, Stuart Davis, Max Weber, and Wyndham Lewis.

In the middle of all this intellectual ferment sat Miss Moore, fastidiously reading and editing manuscripts. The offices of the *Dial* were in a three-story brick building on West Thirteenth Street that had brownstone steps leading up to the front door, carpeted staircases, and rooms with fireplaces and white mantelpieces. "There was the recurrent flower-crier in summer, with his slowly moving wagon of pansies, fuchsias, geraniums, petunias, ageratum," Miss Moore recalled in her memoir. "Or a man with strawberries for sale; or a certain fishman with his pushcart-scales, and staccato refrain so unvaryingly imperative, summer or winter, that Kenneth Burke's bit of parenthetic humour comes back to me almost as an epic, 'I think if he stopped to sell a fish my heart would skip a beat.'" As an editor in these pleasant surroundings, Miss Moore is reputed to have worked with tact, taste, and vast enthusiasm. Once, when a visitor to her office asked her if she didn't ever grow weary of reading manuscripts, she replied, "To me, it's a revel."

Miss Moore's revelry, however, left her almost no time to write verse. She had even less time after 1926, when Scofield Thayer, a founding editor of the magazine and one of its two leading backers, fell ill and had to retire. Three years later, the *Dial*'s other important backer—Dr. James Sibley Watson, a wealthy physician originally from Rochester—decided to return home, where, with the assistance of the Eastman Kodak Company, he could indulge his powerful interest in photography. (He made several medical motion-picture documentaries, and is now head of the Radiology Department of the University of Rochester's School of Medicine and Dentistry.) With two-thirds of the magazine's principals departed, Miss Moore had no compunction about becoming the final third and returning to poetry, and in 1929 the *Dial* folded.

Since then, Miss Moore has done no professional editing, although she devotes a lot of time to such related activities as book reviewing and giving young poets advice about their manuscripts; as a critic, she shows a tendency to be appreciative rather than caustic. She has also done a number of translations, most notably a monumental English version, undertaken at the suggestion of W. H. Auden and published in 1954, of *The Fables of La Fontaine,* which in sheer bulk far outweighs all her books of poetry. She toiled over the *Fables* for something like nine years, and the project caused her much anxiety. "I worked practically all the time," she says. "I'd wake up at six and get right to work, and I'd keep at it all day and all evening, except for an occasional brief stop to eat, or maybe I'd have to go to the market and buy a few odds and ends. Then back to the job again. I did the whole thing over completely four times." Miss Moore's revisions of her own revisions would alone have been sufficient to keep her publishers in a state of anxiety equal to her own, but those unhappy gentlemen soon found that their headaches did not end there, for she worried not only about the literary quality of the forthcoming book but about details of its typography, paper, and binding—about almost everything, in fact, except the remuneration she was to receive for her labors. Of that, she was characteristically oblivious; when it comes to money, her attitude always seems to be that her publishers are doing her a great favor in printing her work, and all she asks is that they make a handsome job of it. The opinions of the critics who reviewed Miss Moore's version of the *Fables* were mixed—it can hardly be denied that in spots the text reads a great deal more like Moore than like La Fontaine—but the literary workmanship involved received general acclaim, and one reviewer declared that the work was among the most ambitious projects ever attempted by a modern poet.

• • •

Miss Moore doubts whether anything could induce her to tackle another task like the *Fables.* She now contents herself with writing poems and book reviews and carrying on her voluminous correspondence with friends. Her neighbors are aware that creative work—mysterious but important—is going on in their midst, and parents on her block have cautioned their children to play quietly in the street at times when she is believed to be writing. As she emerges from her apartment house, bound for market or for the subway station to catch a train to Manhattan, sidewalk passersby are likely to inquire respectfully, "How's the writing going, Miss Moore?," to which she usually replies, "Very slow, very slow." Inspired by her example, several of her neighbors have taken to writing poetry themselves, and they frequently ask her for her opinion of their efforts. While she does not always find it easy in such cases to maintain her appreciative approach to criticism, she has thus far avoided the caustic alternative so adroitly that Cumberland Street is fast becoming one of the nation's most thriving hotbeds of amateur prosody.

Placid though others might find most of Miss Moore's sorties into the world beyond her apartment, she embarks upon each of them in a spirit of adventure, and in her highly volatile mind each of them is charged with terrific drama. Her capacity for stepping up the voltage of ordinary experience is so great that the most commonplace happening or encounter becomes for her a major emotional event. Passing this smiling, delicate-looking elderly lady on her way down the street with her market basket or handbag, only an extraordinarily perceptive person would suspect that a heroic odyssey was in progress and that her impending purchase of a bunch of radishes or a box of crackers would provide her with enough vivid impressions to occupy her thinking for half a day. The primary source of all this internal excitement is Miss Moore's wildly gymnastic self-starting imagination, but once it swings into action it is liberally fed by the combined resources of her singular gift for observing even the smallest components of an object and her uncanny ability to remember everything she has observed. A friend of hers still speaks wonderingly of the time, a couple of years ago, when he left her outside while he went into a drugstore to make a short telephone call; after he had rejoined her and they were continuing on their way, he recalls, she casually described in minute detail more than fifty miscellaneous items she had noticed in the shop window. Some of Miss Moore's most rewarding adventures are trips to museums. "I get so excited in them that before long I can't see anything," she says. To overcome this difficulty, she has developed the habit of concentrating on a single exhibit and firmly ignoring the rest; a few minutes spent in this way gives her all the stimulation she needs to make the expedition profitable, as the associations of what she has seen begin to multiply in her mind by geometric progression. Another place that Miss Moore heads for when she feels in need of excitement is the Brooklyn Institute of Arts and Sciences, where she sits beguiled during illustrated lectures on fungi, lichens, snakes, and other flora and fauna, large and small.

A few of the adventures that Miss Moore fervently refers to from time to time have been more nearly in line with what most people would consider adventuresome—learning to drive an automobile (in Brookline, Massachusetts, four years ago) and playing tennis (on the public courts in Fort Greene Park). Of her tennis she says "I'm not so very good at it, but I'm very reliable. I have a bad backhand and I try to make up for it by roaring around the ball." By ordinary standards, her most strenuous adventure in a long time was a trip she made to Bermuda last winter to visit some people she knew there. Not only did her ship, to her apprehensive delight, run into a storm on the return voyage ("So reckless!") but when she reached New York the customs people kept her waiting interminably while they went through her luggage, which contained some liquor she had brought back to give to friends here, and then there was another long wait—"in not exactly a porte-cochere but a kind of barn"—until she could get a taxi. Whether or not the lack of a porte-cochere was responsible, Miss Moore came down with what she calls a case of pneumonia and what her friends call "Marianne's psychosomatic flu"—a malady that frequently lays her low and that appears to affect her disposition far more seriously than her physical condition. "It depresses me as well as incommodes me," she says. "It's dire! And all that penicillin and other things in bottles! It's like the forcible feeding of an important reptile."

When alone at home, Miss Moore does not spend all her time writing. She is an earnest water-colorist and draftsman as well as a poet, specializing in meticulously realistic reproductions of landscapes, flowers, and insects, which reveal the same love of delicate organisms, if not the same expertness of craftsmanship, that is evident in her verse; guests at her apartment occasionally get the feeling that she takes greater pride in her pictures than in her poems. In view of Miss Moore's obvious devotion to small living things, visitors from time to time express surprise that there is not a single animal or plant in her apartment, but she has a ready answer for them. "If you keep pets or flowers, you are a slave to them," she says.

• • •

Unlike many people who have exchanged material gain for the pleasures of contemplative peace and quiet, Miss Moore bears no ill will toward the world of business, finance, and technological progress. On the contrary, she regards it as an interesting and worth-while world, and gladly concedes that some of its activities are quite possibly even more interesting and worth while than the writing of verse. For example, she seldom mentions a magazine without commenting on its advertising, which in a number of instances she rates a good bit higher than the editorial matter it accompanies. She has a way of deprecating romantic notions about her profession, and she has no patience whatever with the tradition of starving for the sake of art. A few months ago, a young and unknown poet called on her with a letter of introduction from a friend, and soon made it apparent that he was deeply depressed because no one seemed to care much one way or the other about his verse. Miss Moore asked if he had a family to support, and he replied that he had a wife and two children. "Well, then," said Miss Moore with finality, "you had better give up writing and get into something where you can earn a proper living."

The respect Miss Moore shows for the practical and prosaic approach to life stands out in such striking contrast to the workings of her own high-flying, fanciful mind that it raises the question of just where in the scheme of things she places both her esoteric art and her bright and elusive contributions to it. It is a question that even Miss Moore herself is unable to answer precisely, but on the basis of her writings, her offhand remarks, and her reactions to various situations it seems safe to say that she looks upon poetry with a mixture of love and petulance. She has often commented on it disparagingly, as in the opening line of her poem unequivocally entitled "Poetry," which reads, "I, too, dislike it: there are things that are important beyond all this fiddle," and elsewhere she has conveyed the same definite impression that, notwithstanding her lifelong dedication to the art, she thinks of it as a luxury—or, at any rate, a nonessential—when weighed against the really serious aspects of life. Among her friends is one who likens her to a daring performer on a flying trapeze, hugely enjoying her own acrobatics but reassuring herself every now and then by glancing down at a safety net that is sturdily supported by Gibbon, Julius Caesar, Xenophon, the Presbyterian Church, and a handful of male contemporaries, military and scientific, who are accustomed to think—as she conspicuously is not—in what she approvingly calls "a straight line." In this view, Miss Moore, soaring and pirouetting above the world of reality, assumes the role of a charmingly quixotic intellectual flirt, seeming, both as a poet and as a personality, to tease those who put their faith in humdrum logic but at the same time to regard them with admiration and a certain coquettish timidity. Any attempt to discern in this spectacle so much as a trace of a consistent philosophy can lead only to bafflement, but few philosophers, after all, have been good poets.

THE DUKE IN HIS DOMAIN

Truman Capote

NOVEMBER 9, 1957 (ON MARLON BRANDO IN KYOTO)

Most Japanese girls giggle. The little maid on the fourth floor of the Miyako Hotel, in Kyoto, was no exception. Hilarity, and attempts to suppress it, pinked her cheeks (unlike the Chinese, the Japanese complexion more often than not has considerable color), shook her plump peony-and-pansy-kimonoed figure. There seemed to be no particular reason for this merriment; the Japanese giggle operates without apparent motivation. I'd merely asked to be directed toward a certain room. "You come see Marron?" she gasped, showing, like so many of her fellow-countrymen, an array of gold teeth. Then, with the tiny, pigeon-toed skating steps that the wearing of a kimono necessitates, she led me through a labyrinth of corridors, promising, "I knock you Marron." The "l" sound does not exist in Japanese, and by "Marron" the maid meant Marlon—Marlon Brando, the American actor, who was at that time in Kyoto doing location work for the Warner Brothers–William Goetz motion-picture version of James Michener's novel *Sayonara*.

My guide tapped at Brando's door, shrieked "Marron!," and fled away along the corridor, her kimono sleeves fluttering like the wings of a parakeet. The door was opened by another doll-delicate Miyako maid, who at once succumbed to her own fit of quaint hysteria. From an inner room, Brando called, "What is it, honey?" But the girl, her eyes squeezed shut with mirth and her fat little hands jammed into her mouth, like a bawling baby's, was incapable of reply. "Hey, honey, what *is* it?" Brando again inquired, and appeared in the doorway. "Oh, hi," he said when he saw me. "It's seven, huh?" We'd made a seven-o'clock date for dinner; I was nearly twenty minutes late. "Well, take off your shoes and come on in.

I'm just finishing up here. And, hey, honey," he told the maid, "bring us some ice." Then, looking after the girl as she scurried off, he cocked his hands on his hips and, grinning, declared, "They kill me. They really kill me. The kids, too. Don't you think they're wonderful, don't you love them—Japanese kids?"

The Miyako, where about half of the *Sayonara* company was staying, is the most prominent of the so-called Western-style hotels in Kyoto; the majority of its rooms are furnished with sturdy, if commonplace and cumbersome, European chairs and tables, beds and couches. But, for the convenience of Japanese guests who prefer their own mode of décor while desiring the prestige of staying at the Miyako, or of those foreign travellers who yearn after authentic atmosphere yet are disinclined to endure the unheated rigors of a real Japanese inn, the Miyako maintains some suites decorated in the traditional manner, and it was in one of these that Brando had chosen to settle himself. His quarters consisted of two rooms, a bath, and a glassed-in sun porch. Without the overlying and underlying clutter of Brando's personal belongings, the rooms would have been textbook illustrations of the Japanese penchant for an ostentatious barrenness. The floors were covered with tawny *tatami* matting, with a discreet scattering of raw-silk pillows; a scroll depicting swimming golden carp hung in an alcove, and beneath it, on a stand, sat a vase filled with tall lilies and red leaves, arranged just so. The larger of the two rooms—the inner one—which the occupant was using as a sort of business office where he also dined and slept, contained a long, low lacquer table and a sleeping pallet. In these rooms, the divergent concepts of Japanese and Western decoration—the one seeking to impress by a lack of display, an absence of possession-exhibiting, the other intent on precisely the reverse—could both be observed, for Brando seemed unwilling to make use of the apartment's storage space, concealed behind sliding paper doors. All that he owned seemed to be out in the open. Shirts, ready for the laundry; socks, too; shoes and sweaters and jackets and hats and ties, flung around like the costume of a dismantled scarecrow. And cameras, a typewriter, a tape recorder, an electric heater that performed with stifling competence. Here, there, pieces of partly nibbled fruit; a box of the famous Japanese strawberries, each berry the size of an egg. And books, a deep-thought cascade, among which one saw Colin Wilson's *The Outsider* and various works on Buddhist prayer, Zen meditation, Yogi breathing, and Hindu mysticism, but no fiction, for Brando reads none. He has never, he professes, opened a novel since April 3,

1924, the day he was born, in Omaha, Nebraska. But while he may not care to read fiction, he does desire to write it, and the long lacquer table was loaded with overfilled ashtrays and piled pages of his most recent creative effort, which happens to be a film script entitled "A Burst of Vermilion."

In fact, Brando had evidently been working on his story at the moment of my arrival. As I entered the room, a subdued-looking, youngish man, whom I shall call Murray, and who had previously been pointed out to me as "the fellow that's helping Marlon with his writing," was squatted on the matting fumbling through the manuscript of "A Burst of Vermilion." Weighing some pages on his hand, he said, "Tell ya, Mar, s'pose I go over this down in my room, and maybe we'll get together again—say, around ten-thirty?"

Brando scowled, as though unsympathetic to the idea of resuming their endeavors later in the evening. Having been slightly ill, as I learned later, he had spent the day in his room, and now seemed restive. "What's this?" he asked, pointing to a couple of oblong packages among the literary remains on the lacquer table.

Murray shrugged. The maid had delivered them; that was all he knew. "People are always sending Mar presents," he told me. "Lots of times we don't know who sent them. True, Mar?"

"Yeah," said Brando, beginning to rip open the gifts, which, like most Japanese packages—even mundane purchases from very ordinary shops—were beautifully wrapped. One contained candy, the other white rice cakes, which proved cement-hard, though they looked like puffs of cloud. There was no card in either package to identify the donor. "Every time you turn around, some Japanese is giving you a present. They're crazy about giving presents," Brando observed. Athletically crunching a rice cake, he passed the boxes to Murray and me.

Murray shook his head; he was intent on obtaining Brando's promise to meet with him again at ten-thirty. "Give me a ring around then," Brando said, finally. "We'll see what's happening."

Murray, as I knew, was only one member of what some of the *Sayonara* company referred to as "Brando's gang." Aside from the literary assistant, the gang consisted of Marlon Brando, Sr., who acts as his son's business manager; a pretty, dark-haired secretary, Miss Levin; and Brando's private makeup man. The travel expenses of this entourage, and all its living expenses while on location, were allowed for in the actor's contract with Warner Brothers. Legend to the contrary, film studios are not usually so lenient financially. A Warner man to whom I talked later explained the tolerance shown Brando by saying, "Ordinarily we wouldn't put up with it. All the demands he makes. Except—well this picture just *had* to have a big star. Your star—that's the only thing that really counts at the box office."

Among the company were some who felt that the social protection supplied by Brando's inner circle was preventing them from "getting to know the guy" as well as they would have liked. Brando had been in Japan for more than a month, and during that time he had shown himself on the set as a slouchingly dignified, amiable-seeming young man who was always ready to cooperate with, and even encourage, his co-workers—the actors particularly—yet by and large was not socially available, preferring, during the tedious lulls between scenes, to sit alone reading philosophy or scribbling in a schoolboy notebook. After the day's work, instead of accepting his colleagues' invitations to join a group for drinks, a plate of raw fish in a restaurant, and a prowl through the old geisha quarter of Kyoto, instead of contributing to the one-big-family, houseparty bonhomie that picture-making on location theoretically generates, he usually returned to his hotel and stayed there. Since the most fervent of movie-star fans are the people who themselves work in the film industry, Brando was a subject of immense interest within the ranks of the *Sayonara* group, and the more so because his attitude of friendly remoteness produced, in the face of such curiosity, such wistful frustrations. Even the film's director, Joshua Logan, was impelled to say, after working with Brando for two weeks, "Marlon's the most exciting person I've met since Garbo. A genius. But I don't know what he's like. I don't know anything about him."

• • •

The maid had reentered the star's room, and Murray, on his way out, almost tripped over the train of her kimono. She put down a bowl of ice and, with a glow, a giggle, an elation that made her little feet, hooflike in their split-toed white socks, lift and lower like a prancing pony's, announced, "Appapie! Tonight on menu appapie."

Brando groaned. "Apple pie. That's all I need." He stretched out on the floor and unbuckled his belt, which dug too deeply into the swell of his stomach. "I'm supposed to be on a diet. But the only things I want to eat are apple pie and stuff like that." Six weeks earlier, in California, Logan had told him he must trim off ten pounds for his role in *Sayonara,* and before arriving in Kyoto he had managed to get rid of seven. Since reaching Japan, however, abetted not only by American-type apple pie but by the Japanese cuisine, with its delicious emphasis on the sweetened, the starchy, the fried, he'd regained, then doubled this poundage. Now, loosening his belt still more and thoughtfully massaging his midriff, he scanned the menu, which offered, in English, a wide choice of Western-style dishes, and, after reminding himself "I've *got* to lose weight," ordered soup, beefsteak with French-fried potatoes, three supplementary vegetables, a side dish of spaghetti, rolls and butter, a bottle of *sake,* salad, and cheese and crackers.

"And appapie, Marron?"

He sighed. "With ice cream, honey."

Though Brando is not a teetotaller, his appetite is more frugal when it comes to alcohol. While we were awaiting the dinner, which was to be served to us in the room, he supplied me with a large vodka on the rocks and poured himself the merest courtesy sip. Resuming his position on the floor, he lolled his head against a pillow, drooped his eyelids, then shut them. It was as though he'd dozed off into a disturbing dream; his eyelids twitched, and when he spoke, his voice—an unemotional voice, in a way cultivated and genteel, yet surprisingly adolescent, a voice with a probing, asking, boyish quality—seemed to come from sleepy distances.

"The last eight, nine years of my life have been a mess," he said. "Maybe the last two have been a little better. Less rolling in the trough of the wave. Have you ever been analyzed? I was afraid of it at first. Afraid it might destroy the impulses that made me creative, an artist. A sensitive person receives fifty impressions where somebody else may only get seven. Sensitive people are so vulnerable; they're so easily brutalized and hurt just because they *are* sensitive. The more sensitive you are, the more certain you are to be brutalized, develop scabs. Never evolve. Never allow yourself to feel anything, because you always feel too much. Analysis helps. It helped me. But still, the last eight, nine years I've been pretty mixed up, a mess pretty much. . . ."

• • •

The voice went on, as though speaking to hear itself, an effect Brando's speech often has, for, like many persons who are intensely self-absorbed, he is something of a monologuist—a fact that he recognizes and for which he offers his own explanation. "People around me never say anything," he says. "They just seem to want to hear what I have to say. That's why I do all the talking." Watching him now, with his eyes closed, his unlined face white under an overhead light, I felt as if the moment of my initial encounter with him were being recreated. The year of that meeting was 1947; it was a winter afternoon in New York, when I had occasion to attend a rehearsal of Tennessee Williams' *A Streetcar Named Desire,* in which Brando was to play the role of Stanley Kowalski. It was this role that first brought him general recognition, although among the New York theatre's cognoscenti he had already attracted attention, through his student work with the drama coach Stella Adler and a few Broadway appearances—one in a play by Maxwell Anderson, *Truckline Café,* and another as Marchbanks opposite Katharine Cornell's Candida—in which he showed an ability that had been much praised and discussed. Elia Kazan, the director of *A Streetcar Named Desire,* said at that time, and has recently repeated, "Marlon is just the best actor in the world." But ten years ago, on the remembered afternoon, he was still relatively unknown; at least, I hadn't a clue to who he might be when, arriving too early at the *Streetcar* rehearsal, I found the auditorium deserted and a brawny young man stretched out atop a table on the stage under the gloomy glare of work lights, solidly asleep. Because he was wearing a white T shirt and denim trousers, because of his squat gymnasium physique—the weight-lifter's arms, the Charles Atlas chest (though an opened *Basic Writings of Sigmund Freud* was resting on it)—I took him for a stagehand. Or did until I looked closely at his face. It was as if a stranger's head had been attached to the brawny body, as in certain counterfeit photographs. For this face was so very untough, superimposing, as it did, an almost angelic refinement and gentleness upon hard-jawed good looks: taut skin, a broad, high forehead, wide-apart eyes, an aquiline nose, full lips with a relaxed, sensual expression. Not the least suggestion of Williams' unpoetic Kowalski. It was therefore rather an experience to observe, later that afternoon, with what chameleon ease Brando acquired the character's cruel and gaudy colors, how superbly, like a guileful salamander, he slithered into the part, how his own persona evaporated—just as, in this Kyoto hotel room ten years afterward, my 1947 memory of Brando receded, disappeared into his 1957 self. And the present Brando, the one lounging there on the *tatami* and lazily puffing filtered cigarettes as he talked and talked, was, of course, a different person—bound to be. His body was thicker; his forehead was higher, for his hair was thinner; he was richer (from the producers of *Sayonara* he could expect a salary of three hundred thousand dollars, plus a percentage of the picture's earnings); and he'd become, as one journalist put it, "the Valentino of the bop generation"—turned into such a world celebrity that when he went out in public here in Japan, he deemed it wise to hide his face not only by wearing dark glasses but by donning a surgeon's gauze mask as well. (The latter bit of disguise is not so *outré* in Japan as it may sound, since numerous Asians wear such masks, on the theory that they prevent the spreading of germs.) Those were some of the alterations a decade had made. There were others. His eyes had changed. Although their *caffè-espresso* color was the same, the shyness, any traces of real vulnerability that they had formerly held, had left them; now he looked at people with assurance, and with what can only be called a pitying expression, as though he dwelt in spheres of enlightenment where they, to his regret, did not. (The reactions of the people subjected to this gaze of constant commiseration range from that of a young actress who avowed that "Marlon is really a very *spiritual* person, wise and very sincere; you can see it in his eyes" to that of a Brando acquaintance who said, "The way he looks at you, like he was so damn sorry for you—doesn't it make you want to cut your throat?") Nevertheless, the subtly tender character of his face had been preserved. Or almost. For in the years between he'd had an accident that gave his face a more conventionally masculine aspect. It was just that his nose had been broken. And, maneuvering a word in edgewise, I asked, "How did you break your nose?"

". . . by which I don't mean that I'm *always* unhappy. I remember one April I was in Sicily. A hot day, and flowers everywhere. I like flowers, the ones that smell. Gardenias. Anyway, it was April and I was in Sicily, and I went off by myself. Lay down in this field of flowers. Went to sleep. That made me happy. I was happy *then*. What? You say something?"

"I was wondering how you broke your nose."

He rubbed his nose and grinned, as though remembering an experience as happy as the Sicilian nap. "That was a long time ago. I did it boxing. It was when I was in *Streetcar*. We, some of the guys backstage and me—we used to go down to the boiler room in the theatre and horse around, mix it up. One night, I was mixing it up with this guy and—crack! So I put on my coat and walked around to the nearest hospital—it was off Broadway somewhere. My nose was really busted. They had to give me an anesthetic to set it, and put me to bed. Not that I was sorry. *Streetcar* had been running about a year and I was sick of it. But my nose healed pretty quick, and I guess I would've been back in the show practically right away if I hadn't done what I did to Irene Selznick." His grin broadened as he mentioned Mrs. Selznick, who had been the producer of the Williams play. "There is one shrewd lady, Irene Selznick. When she wants something, she wants it. And she wanted me back in the play. But when I heard she was coming to the hospital, I went to work with bandages and iodine and mercurochrome, and—Christ!—when she walked in the door, I looked like my head had been cut off. At the least. And *sounded* as though I were dying. 'Oh, Marlon,' she said, 'you poor, *poor* boy!' And I said, 'Don't you worry about anything, Irene. I'll he back in the show tonight!' And she said, 'Don't you dare! We can manage without you for—for—well, a *few* days more.' 'No, no,' I said. 'I'm O.K. I want to work. Tell them I'll be back tonight.' So she said, 'You're in no condition, you poor darling. I *forbid* you to come to the theatre.' So I stayed in the hospital and had myself a ball." (Mrs. Selznick, recalling the incident recently, said, "They didn't set his nose properly at all. Suddenly his face was quite different. Kind of tough. For months afterward, I kept telling him, 'But they've *ruined* your face. You must have your nose broken again and reset.' Luckily for him, he didn't listen to me. Because I honestly think that broken nose made his fortune as far as the movies go. It gave him sex appeal. He was too beautiful before.")

Brando made his first trip to the Coast in 1949, when he went out there to play the leading role in *The Men,* a picture dealing with paraplegic war veterans. He was accused, at the time, of uncouth social conduct, and criticized for his black-leather-jacket taste in attire, his choice of motorcycles instead of Jaguars, and his preference for obscure secretaries rather than movie starlets; moreover, Hollywood columnists studded their copy with hostile comments concerning his attitude toward the film business, which he himself summed up soon after he entered it by saying, "The only reason I'm here is that I don't yet have the moral courage to turn down the money." In interviews, he repeatedly stated that becoming "simply a movie actor" was the thing furthest from his thoughts. "I may do a picture now and then," he said on one occasion, "but mostly I intend to work on the stage." However, he followed *The Men,* which was more of a *succès d'estime* than a commercial triumph, by recreating Kowalski in the screen treatment of *A Streetcar Named Desire,* and this role, as it had done on Broadway, established him as a star. (Defined practically, a movie star is any performer who can account for a box-office profit regardless of the quality of the enterprise in which he appears; the breed is so scarce that there are fewer than ten actors today who qualify for the title. Brando is one of them; as a box-office draw, male division, he is perhaps outranked only by William Holden.) In the course of the last five years, he has played a Mexican revolutionary (*Viva Zapata!*), Mark Antony (*Julius Caesar*), and a motorcycle-mad juvenile delinquent (*The Wild One*); earned an Academy Award in the role of a dockyard thug (*On the Waterfront*); impersonated Napoleon (*Désirée*); sung and danced his way through the part of an adult delinquent (*Guys and Dolls*); and taken the part of the Okinawan interpreter in *The Teahouse of the August Moon,* which, like *Sayonara,* his tenth picture, was partly shot on location in Japan. But he has never, except for a brief period in summer stock, returned to the stage. "Why should I?" he asked with apathy when I remarked on this. "The movies have a greater potential. They can be a factor for good. For moral development. At least some can—the kind of movies I want to do." He paused, seemed to listen, as though his statement had been tape-recorded and he were now playing it back. Possibly the sound of it dissatisfied him; at any rate, his jaw started working, as if he were biting down on an unpleasant mouthful. He looked off into space suddenly and demanded, "What's so hot about New York? What's so hot about working for Cheryl Crawford and Robert Whitehead?" Miss Crawford and Whitehead are two of New York's most prominent theatrical producers, neither of whom has had occasion to employ Brando. "Anyway, what would I be in?" he continued. "There aren't any parts for me."

Stack them, and the playscripts offered him in any given season by hopeful Broadway managements might very well rise to a height exceeding the actor's own. Tennessee Williams wanted him for the male lead in each of his last five plays, and the most recent of these, *Orpheus Descending,* which was pending production at the time of our talk, had been written expressly as a co-starring vehicle for Brando and the Italian actress Anna Magnani. "I can explain very easily why I didn't do *Orpheus,*" Brando said. "There are beautiful things in it, some of Tennessee's best writing, and the Magnani part is great; she stands for something, you can understand her—and she would wipe me off the stage. The character I was supposed to play, this boy, this Val, he never takes a stand. I didn't really know what he was for or against. Well, you can't act a vacuum. And I told Tennessee. So he kept trying. He rewrote it for me, maybe a couple of times. But—" He shrugged. "Well, I had no intention of walking out on any stage with Magnani. Not in that part. They'd have had to mop me up." Brando mused a moment, and added, "I think—in fact, I'm sure—Tennessee has made a fixed association between me and Kowalski. I mean, we're friends and he knows that as a person I am just the opposite of Kowalski, who was everything I'm against—totally insensitive, crude, cruel. But still Tennessee's image of me is confused with the fact that I played that part. So I don't know if he could write for me in a different color range. The only reason I did *Guys and Dolls* was to work in a lighter color—yellow. Before that, the brightest color I'd played was red. From red down. Brown. Gray. Black." He crumpled an empty cigarette package and bounced it in his hand like a ball. "There aren't any parts for me on the stage. Nobody writes them. Go on. Tell me a part I could do."

In the absence of vehicles by worthy contemporaries, might he not favor the work of older hands? Several responsible persons who appeared with him in the film had admired his reading of Mark Antony in *Julius Caesar,* and thought him equipped, provided the will was there, to essay many of the Mount Everest roles in stage literature—even, possibly, Oedipus.

Brando received reminders of this praise blankly—or, rather, he seemed to be indulging his not-listening habit. But, sensing silence again, he dissolved it: "Of course, movies *date* so quickly. I saw *Streetcar* the other day and it was already an old-fashioned picture. Still, movies do have the greatest potential. You can say important things to a lot of people. About discrimination and hatred and prejudice. I want to make pictures that explore the themes current in the world today. In terms of entertainment. That's why I've started my own independent production company." He reached out affectionately to finger "A Burst of Vermilion," which will be the first script filmed by Pennebaker Productions—the independent company he has formed.

And did "A Burst of Vermilion" satisfy him as a basis for the kind of lofty aims he proposed?

He mumbled something. Then he mumbled something else. Asked to speak more clearly, he said, "It's a Western."

He was unable to restrain a smile, which expanded into laughter. He rolled on the floor and roared. "Christ, the only thing is, will I ever be able to look my friends in the face again?" Sobering somewhat, he said, "Seriously, though, the first picture *has* to make money. Otherwise, there won't be another. I'm nearly broke. No, no kidding. I spent a year and two hundred thousand dollars of my own money trying to get some writer to come up with a decent script. Which used my ideas. The last one, it was so terrible I said I can do it better myself. I'm going to direct it, too."

Produced by, directed by, written by, and starring. Charlie Chaplin has managed this, and gone it one better by composing his own scores. But professionals of wide experience—Orson Welles, for one—have caved in under a lesser number of chores than Brando planned to assume. However, he has a ready answer to my suggestion that he might be loading the cart with more than the donkey could haul. "Take producing," he said. "What does a producer do except cast? I know as much about casting as anyone does, and that's all producing is. Casting." In the trade, one would be hard put to find anyone who concurred in this opinion. A good producer, in addition to doing the casting—that is, assembling the writer, the director, the actors, the technical crew, and the other components of his team—must be a diplomat of the emotions, smoothing and soothing, and, above all, must be a skilled mechanic when it comes to dollar-and-cents machinery. "But seriously," said Brando, now excessively sober, "'Burst' *isn't* just cowboys-and-Indians stuff. It's about this Mexican boy—hatred and discrimination. What happens to a community when those things exist."

Sayonara, too, has moments when it purports to attack race prejudice, telling, as it does, the tale of an American jet pilot who falls in love with a Japanese music-hall dancer, much to the dismay of his Air Force superiors, and also to the dismay of her employers, though the latter's objection is not the racial unsuitability of her beau but simply that she has a beau at all, for she is a member of an all-girl opera company—based on a real-life counterpart, the Takarazuka Company—whose management promotes a legend that offstage its hundreds of girls lead a conventlike existence, unsullied by male presences of any creed or color. Michener's novel concludes with the lovers forlornly bidding each other *sayonara,* a word meaning farewell. In the film version, however, the word, and consequently the title, has lost significance; here the fadeout reveals the twain of East and West so closely met that they are on their way to a matrimonial bureau. At a press conference that Brando conducted upon his Tokyo arrival, he informed some sixty reporters that he had contracted to do this story because "it strikes very precisely at prejudices that serve to limit our progress toward a peaceful world. Underneath the romance, it attacks prejudices that exist on the part of the Japanese as well as on our part," and also he was doing the film because it would give him the "invaluable opportunity" of working with Joshua Logan, who could teach him "what to do and what not to do."

But time had passed. And now Brando said, with a snort, "Oh, *Sayonara,* I love it! This wondrous hearts-and-flowers nonsense that was supposed to be a serious picture about Japan. So what difference does it make? I'm just doing it for the money anyway. Money to put in the kick for my own company." He pulled at his lip reflectively and snorted again. "Back in California, I sat through twenty-two hours of script conferences. Logan said to me, 'We welcome any suggestions you have, Marlon. Any changes you want to make, you just make them. If there's something you don't like—why, rewrite it, Marlon, write it your own way.'" Brando's friends boast that he can imitate anybody after fifteen minutes' observation; to judge by the eerie excellence with which he mimicked Logan's vaguely Southern voice, his sad-eyed, beaming, aquiver-with-enthusiasm manner, they are hardly exaggerating. "*Rewrite?* Man, I rewrote the whole damn script. And now out of that they're going to use maybe eight lines." Another snort. "I give up. I'm going to walk through the part, and that's that. Sometimes I think nobody knows the difference anyway. For the first few days on the set, I tried to act. But then I made an experiment. In this scene, I tried to do everything wrong I could think of. Grimaced and rolled my eyes, put in all kind of gestures and expressions that had no relation to the part I'm supposed to be playing. What did Logan say? He just said, 'It's wonderful. Print it!'"

A phrase that often occurs in Brando's conversation, "I only mean forty percent of what I say," is probably applicable here. Logan, a stage and film director of widely recognized and munificently rewarded accomplishments (*Mister Roberts, South Pacific, Picnic*), is a man balanced on enthusiasm, as a bird is balanced on air. A creative person's need to believe in the value of what he is creating is axiomatic; Logan's belief in whatever project he is engaged in approaches euphoric faith, protecting him, as it seems designed to do, from the nibbling nuisance of self-doubt. The joy he took in everything connected with *Sayonara,* a film he had been preparing for two years, was so nearly flawless that it did not permit him to conceive that his star's enthusiasm might not equal his own. Far from it. "Marlon," he occasionally announced, "says he's never been as happy with a company as he is with us." And "I've never worked with such an exciting, inventive actor. So pliable. He takes direction beautifully, and yet he always has something to add. He's made up this Southern accent for the part; I never would have thought of it myself, but, well, it's exactly right—it's perfection." Nevertheless, by the night I had dinner in Brando's hotel room Logan had begun to be aware that there was something lacking in his rapport with Brando. He attributed it to the fact that at this juncture, when most of the scenes being filmed concentrated on Japanese background (street crowds, views, spectacles) rather than actors, he had not yet worked with Brando on material that put either of them to much of a test. "That'll come when we get back to California," he said. "The interior stuff, the dramatic scenes. Brando's going to be great—we'll get along fine."

• • •

There was another reason for Logan's inability, at that point, to give his principal player the kind of attention that might have established closer harmony: he was in serious disharmony with the very Japanese elements that had contributed most to his decision to make the picture. Long infatuated with the Japanese theatre, Logan had counted heavily on interlacing *Sayonara* with authentic sequences taken from the classic Kabuki theatre, the masked Nō dramas, the Bunraku puppet plays; they were to be, so to say, the highbrow-lights of the film. And to this end Logan, along with William Goetz, the producer, had been in negotiation for over a year with Shochiku, the gigantic film company that controls a major part of Japan's live theatrical activities. The ruler of the Shochiku empire is a small, unsmiling eminence in his eighties, known as Mr. Otani; he has a *prénom,* Takejiro, but there are few men alive on such familiar terms that they would presume to use it. The son of a butcher (and therefore, in Japan's Buddhist society, a member of the outcast group), Otani, together with a brother now dead, founded Shochiku and nurtured it to the point where, for the last four years, its payroll has been the biggest of any single company in Japan. A tycoon to rival Kokichi Mikimoto, the late cultured-pearl potentate, Otani casts a cloaklike shadow over the entire Japanese entertainment industry; in addition to having monopolistic control of the classic theatre, he owns the country's most extensive chain of movie houses and music halls, produces many films, and has a hand in radio and television. From Otani's vantage point, any transactions with the Messrs. Logan and Goetz must have looked like very small *sake.* However, he was at first in sympathy with their project, largely because he was impressed by the fervor of Logan's veneration for Kabuki, Nō, and Bunraku, the three unquestionably genuine gems in the old man's crown, and the ones closest to his heart. (According to some specialists, these ancient arts owe their continued health mainly to his generosity.) But Otani is not all philanthropist; when Shochiku's negotiations with the *Sayonara* management were supposedly concluded, the former had given the latter, for a handsome price, franchise to photograph scenes in Tokyo's famed Kabuki Theatre, and, for a still handsomer honorarium, permission to make free use of the Kabuki troupe, the Nō plays and players, and the Bunraku puppeteers. Shochiku had also agreed to the participation of its own all-girl opera company—a necessary factor in the production of the film, since the Takarazuka troupe depicted in the novel had deeply resented Michener's "libel" and refused any cooperation whatever. Logan, leaving for Japan, was so elated he could have flown there under his own power. "Otani's given us carte blanche, and this is going to be it, the real thing," he said. "None of that fake Kabuki, that second-rate stuff, but the real thing—something that's never been put in a picture before." And was not destined to be; for, across the wide Pacific Logan and his associates had a personal Pearl Harbor awaiting them. Otani is seldom seen; he usually appears in the person of bland assistants, and as Logan and Goetz disembarked from their plane, a group of these informed the film-makers that Shochiku had made an error in its financial reckoning; the bill was now much higher than the initial estimate. Producer Goetz objected. Otani, certain that he held the stronger cards (after all, here were these Hollywood people in Japan, accompanied by an expensive cast, an expensive crew, and expensive equipment), replied by raising the tab still more. Whereupon Goetz, himself a businessman as tough as tortoise shell, ended the negotiations and told his director they would have to make up their own Kabuki, Nō, Bunraku, and all-girl opera company from among unattached, free-lancing artists.

Meanwhile, the Tokyo press was publicizing the contretemps. Several papers, the *Japan Times* among them, implied that Shochiku was to be censured for having "acted in bad faith"; others taking a pro-Shochiku, or perhaps simply an anti-*Sayonara,* line, expressed themselves as delighted that the Americans would not have the opportunity to "degrade our finest artistic traditions" by representing them in a film version of "a vulgar novel that is in no way a compliment to the Japanese people." The papers antagonistic to the *Sayonara* project especially relished reporting the fact that Logan had cast a Mexican actor, Ricardo Montalban, in the part of a ranking Kabuki performer (Kabuki is traditionally an all-male enterprise; the grander, more difficult roles are those of women, played by female impersonators, and Montalban's assignment was to portray one such) and then had had the "effrontery" to try and hire a genuine Kabuki star to substitute for Montalban in the dance sequences, which, one Japanese writer remarked, was much the same as "asking Ethel Barrymore to be a stand-in." All in all, the local press was touchily interested in what was taking place down in Kyoto—the city, two hundred and thirty miles south of Tokyo, in which, because of its plethora of historic temples, its photogenic blue hills and misty lakes, and its carefully preserved old-Japan atmosphere, with elegant geisha quarter and paper-lantern-lighted streets, the *Sayonara* staff had decided to take most of their location shots. And, all in all, down in Kyoto the company was encountering as many difficulties as its ill-wishers could have hoped for. In particular, the Americans were finding it a problem to muster nationals willing to appear in their film—an interesting phenomenon, considering how desirous the average Japanese is of having himself photographed. True, the movie-makers had rounded up a ragbag-picking of Nō players and puppeteers not under contract to Shochiku, but they were having the devil's own time assembling a presentable all-girl opera company. (These peculiarly Japanese institutions resemble a sort of single-sex, innocent-minded Folies-Bergère; oddly, few men attend their performances, the audiences being, on the whole, as all-girl as the cast.) In the hope of bridging this gap, the *Sayonara* management had distributed posters advertising a contest to select "the one hundred most beautiful girls in Japan." The affair, for which they expected a big turnout, was scheduled to take place at two o'clock on a Thursday afternoon in the lobby of the Kyoto Hotel. But there were no winners, because there were no contestants; none showed up. Producer Goetz, one of the disappointed judges, resorted next, and with some success, to the expedient of luring ladies out of Kyoto's cabarets and bars. Kyoto—or, for that matter, any Japanese city—is a barfly's Valhalla. Proportionately, the number of premises purveying strong liquor is higher than in New York, and the diversity of these saloons—which range from cozy bamboo closets accommodating four customers to many-storied, neon-hued temples of fun featuring, in accordance with the Japanese aptitude for imitation, cha-cha bands and rock 'n' rollers and hillbilly quartets and *chanteuses existentialistes* and Oriental vocalists who sing Cole Porter songs with American Negro accents—is extraordinary. But however low or however de-luxe the establishment may be, one thing remains the same: there is always on hand a pride of hostesses to cajole and temper the clientele. Great numbers of these sleekly coifed, smartly costumed, relentlessly festive *jolies jeunes filles* sit sipping Parfaits d'Amour (a syrupy violet-colored cocktail currently fashionable in these surroundings) while performing the duties of a poor man's geisha girl; that is, lightening the spirits, without necessarily corrupting the morals, of weary married men and tense, anxious-to-be-amused bachelors. It is not unusual to see four to a customer. But when the *Sayonara* officials began to try to corral them, they had to contend with the circumstance that nightworkers, such as they were dealing with, have no taste for the early rising that picture-making demands. To acquire their talents, and see that the ladies were on the set at the proper hour, certain of the film's personnel did everything but distribute engagement rings.

Still another annoyance for the makers of *Sayonara* involved the United States Air Force, whose cooperation was vital, but which, though it had previously promised help, now had fits of shilly-shallying, because it gravely objected to one of the basic elements of the plot—that during the Korean War some American Air Force men who married Japanese were shipped home. This, the Air Force complained, may have been the *practice*, but it was not official Pentagon policy. Given the choice of cutting out the offending premise, and thereby removing a sizable section of the script's entrails, or permitting it to remain, and thereby forfeiting Air Force aid, Logan selected surgery.

Then, there was the problem of Miss Miiko Taka, who had been cast as the Takarazuka dancer capable of arousing Air Force Officer Brando's passion. Having first tried to obtain Audrey Hepburn for the part, and found that Miss Hepburn thought not, Logan had started looking for an "unknown," and had come up with Miss Taka, poised, pleasant, an unassuming, quietly attractive nisei, innocent of acting experience, who stepped out of a clerking job with a Los Angeles travel bureau into what she called "this Cinderella fantasy." Although her acting abilities—as well as those of another *Sayonara* principal, Red Buttons, an ex–burlesque, ex–television jokester, who, like Miss Taka, had had meagre dramatic training—were apparently causing her director some concern, Logan, admirably undaunted, cheerful despite all, was heard to say, "We'll get away with it. As much as possible, I'll just keep their faces straight and their mouths shut. Anyway, Brando, he's going to be so great *he'll* give us what we need." But, as for giving, "I give up," Brando repeated. "I'm going to give up. I'm going to sit back. Enjoy Japan."

. . .

At that moment, in the Miyako, Brando was presented with something Japanese to enjoy: an emissary of the hotel management, who, bowing and beaming and soaping his hands, came into the room saying "Ah, Missa Marron Brando—" and was silent, tongue-tied by the awkwardness of his errand. He'd come to reclaim the "gift" packages of candy and rice cakes that Brando had already opened and avidly sampled. "Ah, Missa Marron Brando, it is a missake. They were meant for derivery in another room. Aporogies! Aporogies!" Laughing, Brando handed the boxes over. The eyes of the emissary, observing the plundered contents, grew grave, though his smile lingered—indeed, became fixed. Here was a predicament to challenge the rightly renowned Japanese politesse. "Ah," he breathed, a solution limbering his smile, "since you rike them very much, you muss keep one box." He handed the rice cakes back. "And they"—apparently the rightful owner—"can have the other. So, now everyone is preased."

It was just as well that he left the rice cakes, for dinner was taking a long while to simmer in the kitchen. When it arrived, I was replying to some inquiries Brando had made about an acquaintance of mine, a young American disciple of Buddhism who for five years had been leading a contemplative, if not entirely unworldly, life in a settlement inside the gates of Kyoto's Nishi-Honganji Temple. The notion of a person's retiring from the world to lead a spiritual existence—an Oriental one, at that—made Brando's face become still, in a dreaming way. He listened with surprising attention to what I could tell him about the young man's present life, and was puzzled—chagrined, really—that it was not all, or at all, a matter of withdrawal, of silence and prayer-sore knees. On the contrary, behind Nishi-Honganji's walls my Buddhist friend occupied three snug, sunny rooms brimming with books and phonograph records; along with attending to his prayers and performing the tea ceremony, he was quite capable of mixing a Martini; he had two servants, and a Chevrolet, in which he often conveyed himself to the local cinemas. And, speaking of that, he had read that Marlon Brando was in town, and longed to meet him. Brando was little amused. The puritan streak in him, which has some width, had been touched; his conception of the truly devout could not encompass anyone as *du monde* as the young man I'd described. "It's like the other day on the set," he said. "We were working in a temple, and one of the monks came over and asked me for an autographed picture. Now, *what* would a monk want with my autograph? A picture of me?"

He stared questioningly at his scattered books, so many of which dealt with mystical subjects. At his first Tokyo press conference, he had told the journalists that he was glad to be back in Japan, because it gave him another chance to "investigate the influence of Buddhism on Japanese thought, the determining cultural factor." The reading matter on display offered proof that he was adhering to this scholarly, if somewhat obscure, program. "What I'd like to do," he presently said, "I'd like to talk to someone who *knows* about these things. Because—" But the explanation was deferred until the maid, who just then skated in balancing vast platters, had set the lacquer table and we had knelt on cushions at either end of it.

"Because," he resumed, wiping his hands on a small steamed towel, the usual preface to any meal served in Japan, "I've seriously considered—I've very *seriously* thought about—throwing the whole thing up. This business of being a successful actor. What's the point, if it doesn't evolve into anything? All right, you're a success. At last you're *accepted*, you're welcome everywhere. But that's it, that's all there is to it, it doesn't lead anywhere. You're just sitting on a pile of candy gathering thick layers of—of *crust*." He rubbed his chin with the towel, as though removing stale makeup. "Too much success can ruin you as surely as too much failure." Lowering his eyes, he looked without appetite at the food that the maid, to an accompaniment of constant giggles, was distributing on the plates. "Of course," he said hesitantly, as if he were slowly turning over a coin to study the side that seemed to be shinier, "you can't *always* be a failure. Not and survive. Van Gogh! There's an example of what can happen when a person never receives any recognition. You stop relating; it puts you outside. But I guess success does that, too. You know, it took me a long time before I was aware that that's what I was—a big success. I was so absorbed in myself, my own problems, I never looked around, took account. I used to walk in New York, miles and miles, walk in the streets late at night, and never *see* anything. I was never sure about acting, whether that was what I really wanted to do; I'm still not. Then, when I was in *Streetcar*, and it had been running a couple of months, one night—dimly, dimly—I began to hear this roar. It was like I'd been asleep, and I woke up here sitting on a pile of candy."

Before Brando achieved this sugary perch, he had known the vicissitudes of any unconnected, unfinanced, only partly educated (he has never received a high-school diploma, having been expelled before graduation from Shattuck Military Academy, in Faribault, Minnesota, an institution he refers to as "the asylum") young man who arrives in New York from more rural parts—in his case, Libertyville, Illinois. Living alone in furnished rooms, or sharing underfurnished apartments, he had spent his first city years fluctuating between acting classes and a fly-by-night enrollment in Social Security; Best's once had him on its payroll as an elevator boy. A friend of his, who saw a lot of him in those pre-candy days, corroborates to some extent the rather somnambulistic portrait Brando paints of himself. "He was a brooder, all right," the friend has said. "He seemed to have a built-in hideaway room and was always rushing off to it to worry over himself, and gloat, too, like a miser with his gold. But it wasn't all Gloomsville. When he wanted to, he could rocket right out of himself. He had a wild, kid kind of fun thing. Once, he was living in an old brownstone on Fifty-second Street, near where some of the jazz joints are. He used to go up on the roof and fill paper bags with water and throw them down at the stiffs coming out of the clubs. He had a sign on the wall of his room that said, 'You Ain't Livin' If You Don't Know It.' Yeah, there was always something jumping in that apartment—Marlon playing the bongos, records going, people around, kids from the Actors' Studio, and a lot of down-and-outers he'd picked up. And he could be sweet. He was the least opportunistic person I've ever known. He never gave a damn about anybody who could help him; you might say he went out of his way to avoid them. Sure, part of that—the kind of people he didn't like and the kind he did, both—stemmed from his insecurities, his inferiority feelings. Very few of his friends were his equals—anybody he'd have to *compete* with, if you know what I mean. Mostly they were strays, idolizers, characters who were dependent on him one way or another. The same with the girls he took out. Plain sort of somebody's-secretary-type girls—nice enough but nothing that's going to start a stampede of competitors." (The last-mentioned preference of Brando's was true of him as an adolescent, too, or so his grandmother has said. As she put it, "Marlon always picked on the cross-eyed girls.")

The maid poured *sake* into thimble-size cups, and withdrew. Connoisseurs of this palely pungent rice wine pretend they can discern variations in taste and quality in over fifty brands. But to the novice all *sake* seems to have been brewed in the same vat—a toddy, pleasant at first, cloying afterward, and not likely to echo in your head unless it is devoured by the quart, a habit many of Japan's *bons vivants* have adopted. Brando ignored the *sake* and went straight for his filet. The steak was excellent; Japanese take a just pride in the quality of their beef. The spaghetti, a dish that is very popular in Japan, was not; nor was the rest—the conglomeration of peas, potatoes, beans. Granted that the menu was a queer one, it is on the whole a mistake to order Western-style food in Japan, yet there arise those moments when one retches at the thought of more raw fish, sukiyaki, and rice with seaweed, when, however temptingly they may be prepared and however prettily presented, the unaccustomed stomach revolts at the prospect of eel broth and fried bees and pickled snake and octopus arms.

As we ate, Brando returned to the possibility of renouncing his movie-star status for the satisfactions of a life that "led somewhere." He decided to compromise. "Well, when I get back to Hollywood, what I *will* do, I'll fire my secretary and move into a smaller house," he said. He sighed with relief, as though he'd already cast off old encumbrances and entered upon the simplicities of his new situation. Embroidering on its charms, he said, "I won't have a cook or maid. Just a cleaning woman who comes in twice a week. But"—he frowned, squinted, as if something were blurring the bliss he envisioned—"wherever the house is, it has to have a *fence.* On account of the people with pencils. You don't know what it's like. The people with pencils. I need a fence to keep them out. I suppose there's nothing I can do about the telephone."

"Telephone?"

"It's tapped. Mine is."

"Tapped? Really? By whom?"

He chewed his steak, mumbled. He seemed reluctant to say, yet certain it was so. "When I talk to my friends, we speak French. Or else a kind of bop lingo we made up."

Suddenly, sounds came through the ceiling from the room above us—footfalls, muffled voices like the noise of water flowing through a pipe. "Sh-h-h!" whispered Brando, listening intently, his gaze alerted upward. "Keep your voice down. *They* can hear everything." They, it appeared, were his fellow-actor Red Buttons and Buttons' wife, who occupied the suite overhead. "This place is made of paper," he continued, in tiptoe tones, and with the absorbed countenance of a child lost in a very earnest game—an expression that half explained his secretiveness, the looking-over-his-shoulder, coded-bop-for-telephones facet of his personality that occasionally causes conversation with him to assume a conspiratorial quality, as though one were discussing subversive topics in perilous political territory. Brando said nothing; I said nothing. Nor did Mr. and Mrs. Buttons—not anything distinguishable. During the siege of silence, my host located a letter buried among the dinner plates, and read it while he ate, like a gentleman perusing his breakfast newspaper. Presently, remembering me, he remarked, "From a friend of mine. He's making a documentary, the life of James Dean. He wants me to do the narration. I think I might." He tossed the letter aside and pulled his apple pie, topped with a melting scoop of vanilla ice cream, toward him. "Maybe not, though. I get excited about something, but it never lasts more than seven minutes. Seven minutes exactly. That's my limit. I never know why I get up in the morning." Finishing his pie, he gazed speculatively at my portion; I passed it to him. "But I'm really considering this Dean thing. It could be important."

James Dean, the young motion-picture actor killed in a car accident in 1955, was promoted throughout his phosphorescent career as the All-American "mixed-up kid," the symbol of misunderstood hot-rodding youth with a switch-blade approach to life's little problems. When he died, an expensive film in which he had starred, *Giant,* had yet to be released, and the picture's press agents, seeking to offset any ill effects that Dean's demise might have on the commercial prospects of their product, succeeded by "glamorizing" the tragedy, and, in ironic consequence, created a Dean legend of rather necrophilic appeal. Though Brando was seven years older than Dean, and professionally more secure, the two actors came to be associated in the collective movie-fan mind. Many critics reviewing Dean's first film, *East of Eden,* remarked on the well-nigh plagiaristic resemblance between his acting mannerisms and Brando's. Off-screen, too, Dean appeared to be practicing the sincerest form of flattery; like Brando, he tore around on motorcycles, played bongo drums, dressed the role of rowdy, spouted an intellectual rigmarole, cultivated a cranky, colorful newspaper personality that mingled, to a skillfully potent degree, plain bad boy and sensitive sphinx.

"No, Dean was never a friend of mine," said Brando, in response to a question that he seemed surprised to have been asked. "That's not why I may do the narration job. I hardly knew him. But he had an *idée fixe* about me. Whatever I did he did. He was always trying to get close to me. He used to call up." Brando lifted an imaginary telephone, put it to his ear with a cunning, eavesdropper's smile. "I'd listen to him talking to the answering service, asking for me, leaving messages. But I never spoke up. I never called him back. No, when I—"

The scene was interrupted by the ringing of a real telephone. "Yeah?" he said, picking it up. "Speaking. From where? . . . Manila? . . . Well, I don't know anybody in Manila. Tell them I'm not here. No, when I finally met Dean," he said, hanging up, "it was at a party. Where he was throwing himself around, acting the madman. So I spoke to him. I took him aside and asked him didn't he know he was sick? That he needed help?" The memory evoked an intensified version of Brando's familiar look of enlightened compassion. "He listened to me. He knew he was sick. I gave him the name of an analyst, and he went. And at least his *work* improved. Toward the end, I think he was beginning to find his own way as an actor. But this glorifying of Dean is all wrong. That's why I believe the documentary could be important. To show he wasn't a hero; show what he really was—just a lost boy trying to find himself. That ought to be done, and I'd like to do it—maybe as a kind of expiation for some of my own sins. Like making *The Wild One*." He was referring to the strange film in which he was presented as the Führer of a tribe of Fascistlike delinquents. "But. Who knows? Seven minutes is my limit."

From Dean the conversation turned to other actors, and I asked which ones, specifically, Brando respected. He pondered; though his lips shaped several names, he seemed to have second thoughts about pronouncing them. I suggested a few candidates—Laurence Olivier, John Gielgud, Montgomery Clift, Gérard Philipe, Jean-Louis Barrault. "Yes," he said, at last coming alive, "Philipe is a good actor. So is Barrault. Christ, what a wonderful picture that was *Les Enfants du Paradis*! Maybe the best movie ever made. You know, that's the only time I ever fell in love with an actress, somebody on the screen. I was mad about Arletty." The Parisian star Arletty is well remembered by international audiences for the witty, womanly allure she brought to the heroine's part in Barrault's celebrated film. "I mean, I was really in *love* with her. My first trip to Paris, the thing I did right away, I asked to meet Arletty. I went to see her as though I were going to a shrine. My ideal woman. Wow!" He slapped the table. "Was that a mistake, was that a disillusionment! She was a tough article."

The maid came to clear the table; *en passant,* she gave Brando's shoulder a sisterly pat, rewarding him, I took it, for the cleaned-off sparkle of his plates. He again collapsed on the floor, stuffing a pillow under his head. "I'll tell you," he said, "Spencer Tracy is the kind of actor I like to watch. The way he holds back, *holds* back—then darts in to make his point, darts back. Tracy, Muni, Cary Grant. They know what they're doing. You can learn something from them."

Brando began to weave his fingers in the air, as though hoping that gestures would describe what he could not precisely articulate. "Acting is such a tenuous thing," he said. "A fragile, shy thing that a sensitive director can help lure out of you. Now, in movie-acting the important, the *sensitive* moment comes around the third take of a scene; by then you just need a whisper from the director to crystallize it for you. Gadge"—he was using Elia Kazan's nickname—"can usually do it. He's wonderful with actors."

Another actor, I suppose, would have understood at once what Brando was saying, but I found him difficult to follow. "It's what happens inside you on the third take," he said, with a careful emphasis that did not lessen my incomprehension. One of the most memorable film scenes Brando has played occurs in the Kazan-directed *On the Waterfront;* it is the car-ride scene in which Rod Steiger, as the racketeering brother, confesses he is leading Brando into a death trap. I asked if he could use the episode as an example, and tell me how his theory of the "sensitive moment" applied to it.

"Yes. Well, no. Well, let's see." He puckered his eyes, made a humming noise. "That was a seven-take scene, and I didn't like the way it was written. Lot of dissension going on there. I was fed up with the whole picture. All the location stuff was in New Jersey, and it was the dead of winter—the cold, Christ! And I was having problems at the time. Woman trouble. That scene. Let me see. There were seven takes because Rod Steiger couldn't stop crying. He's one of those actors loves to cry. We kept doing it over and over. But I can't remember just when, just how it crystallized itself for me. The first time I saw *Waterfront,* in a projection room with Gadge, I thought it was so terrible I walked out without even speaking to him."

A month earlier, a friend of Brando's had told me, "Marlon always turns against whatever he's working on. Some element of it. Either the script or the director or somebody in the cast. Not always because of anything very rational—just because it seems to comfort him to be dissatisfied, let off steam about something. It's part of his pattern. Take *Sayonara.* A dollar gets you ten he'll develop a hoss on it somewhere along the line. A hoss on Logan, maybe. Maybe against Japan—the whole damn country. He loves Japan *now*. But with Marlon you never know from one minute to the next."

I was wondering whether I might mention this supposed "pattern" to Brando, ask if he considered it a valid observation about himself. But it was as though he had anticipated the question. "I ought to keep my mouth shut," he said. "Around here, around *Sayonara,* I've let a few people know the way I feel. But I don't always feel the same way two days running."

. . .

It was ten-thirty, and Murray called on the dot.

"I went out to dinner with the girls," he told Brando, his telephone voice so audible that I could hear it, too; it spoke above a blend of dance-band rumble and barroom roar. Obviously he was patronizing not one of the more traditional, cat-quiet Kyoto restaurants but, rather, a place where the customers wore shoes. "We're just finishing. How about it? You through?"

Brando looked at me thoughtfully, and I, in turn, at my coat. But he said, "We're still yakking. Call me back in an hour."

"O.K. Well . . . O.K. Listen. Miiko's here. She wants to know did you get the flowers she sent you?"

Brando's eyes lazily rolled toward the glassed-in sun porch, where a bowl of asters was centered on a round bamboo table. "Uh-huh. Tell her thanks very much."

"Tell her yourself. She's right here."

"No! Hey, wait a minute! Christ, *that's* not how you do it." But the protest came too late. Murray had already put down the phone, and Brando, reiterating "*That's* not how you do it," blushed and squirmed like an embarrassed boy.

The next voice to emanate from the receiver belonged to his *Sayonara* leading lady, Miss Miiko Taka. She asked about his health.

"Better, thanks. I ate the bad end of an oyster, that's all. Miiko? . . . Miiko, that was very *sweet* of you to send me the flowers. They're beautiful. I'm looking at them right now. Asters," he continued, as though shyly venturing a line of verse, "are my favorite flowers. . . ."

I retired to the sun porch, leaving Brando and Miss Taka to conduct their conversation in stricter seclusion. Below the windows, the hotel garden, with its ultra-simple and *soigné* arrangements of rock and tree, floated in the mists that crawl off Kyoto's waterways—for it is a watery city, crisscrossed with shallow rivers and cascading canals, dotted with pools as still as coiled snakes and mirthful little waterfalls that sound like Japanese girls giggling. Once the imperial capital and now the country's cultural museum, such an aesthetic treasure house that American bombers let it go unmolested during the war, Kyoto is surrounded by water, too; beyond the city's containing hills, thin roads run like causeways across the reflecting silver of flooded rice fields. That evening, despite the gliding mists, the blue encircling hills were discernible against the night, for the upper air had purity; a sky was there, stars were in it, and a scrap of moon. Some portions of the town could be seen. Nearest was a neighborhood of curving roofs. The dark façades of aristocratic houses fashioned from silky wood yet austere, northern, as secret-looking as any stone Siena palace. How brilliant they made the street lamps appear, and the doorway lanterns casting keen kimono colors—pink and orange, lemon and red. Farther away was a modern flatness—wide avenues and neon, a skyscraper of raw concrete that seemed less enduring, more perishable, than the papery dwellings stooping around it.

Brando completed his call. Approaching the sun porch, he looked at me looking at the view. He said, "Have you been to Nara? Pretty interesting."

I had, and yes, it was. "Ancient, old-time Nara," as a local cicerone unfailingly referred to it, is an hour's drive from Kyoto—a postcard town set in a show-place park. Here is the apotheosis of the Japanese genius for hypnotizing nature into unnatural behavior. The great shrine-infested park is a green salon where sheep graze, and herds of tame deer wander under trim pine trees and, like Venetian pigeons, gladly pose with honeymooning couples; where children yank the beards of unretaliating goats; where old men wearing black capes with mink collars squat on the shores of lotus-quilted lakes and, by clapping their hands, summon swarms of fish, speckled and scarlet carp, fat, thick as trout, who allow their snouts to be tickled, then gobble the crumbs that the old men sprinkle. That this serpentless Eden should strongly appeal to Brando was a bit surprising. With his liberal taste for the off-trail and not-overly-trammelled, one might have thought he would be unresponsive to so ruly, subjugated a landscape. Then, as though apropos of Nara, he said, "Well, I'd like to be married. I want to have children." It was not, perhaps, the non sequitur it seemed; the gentle safety of Nara just could, by the association of ideas, suggest marriage, a family.

"You've got to have love," he said. "There's no other reason for living.

Men are no different from mice. They're born to perform the same function. Procreate." ("Marlon," to quote his friend Elia Kazan, "is one of the gentlest people I've ever known. Possibly the gentlest." Kazan's remark had meaning when one observed Brando in the company of children. As far as he was concerned, Japan's youngest generation—lovely, lively, cherry-cheeked kids with bowlegs and bristling bangs—was always welcome to lark around the *Sayonara* sets. He was good with the children, at ease, playful, appreciative; he seemed, indeed, their emotional contemporary, a co-conspirator. Moreover, the condoling expression, the slight look of dispensing charitable compassion, peculiar to his contemplation of some adults was absent from his eyes when he looked at a child.)

Touching Miss Taka's floral offering, he went on, "What other reason is there for living? Except love? That has been my main trouble. My inability to love anyone." He turned back into the lighted room, stood there as though hunting something—a cigarette? He picked up a pack. Empty. He slapped at the pockets of trousers and jackets lying here and there. Brando's wardrobe no longer smacks of the street gang; as a dresser, he has graduated, or gone back, into an earlier style of outlaw chic, that of the prohibition sharpie—black snap-brim hats, striped suits, and sombre-hued George Raft shirts with pastel ties. Cigarettes were found; inhaling, he slumped on the pallet bed. Beads of sweat ringed his mouth. The electric heater hummed. The room was tropical; one could have grown orchids. Overhead, Mr. and Mrs. Buttons were again bumping about, but Brando appeared to have lost interest in them. He was smoking, thinking. Then, picking up the stitch of his thought, he said, "I can't. Love anyone. I can't trust anyone enough to give myself to them. But I'm ready. I want it. And I may, I'm almost on the point, I've really got to . . ." His eyes narrowed, but his tone, far from being intense, was indifferent, dully objective, as though he were discussing some character in a play—a part he was weary of portraying yet was trapped in by contract. "Because—well, what else is there? That's all it's all about. To love somebody."

(At this time, Brando was, of course, a bachelor, who had, upon occasion, indulged in engagements of a quasi-official character—once to an aspiring authoress and actress, by name Miss Blossom Plumb, and again, with more public attention, to Mlle. Josanne Mariani-Bérenger, a French fisherman's daughter. But in neither instance were banns ever posted. One day last month, however, in a sudden and somewhat secret ceremony at Eagle Rock, California, Brando was married to a dark, sari-swathed young minor actress who called herself Anna Kashfi. According to conflicting press reports, either she was a Darjeeling-born Buddhist of the purest Indian parentage or she was the Calcutta-born daughter of an English couple named O'Callaghan, now living in Wales. Brando has not yet done anything to clear up the mystery.)

"Anyway, I have *friends*. No. No, I don't," he said, verbally shadow-boxing. "Oh, sure I do," he decided, smoothing the sweat on his upper lip. "I have a great many friends. Some I don't hold out on. I let them know what's happening. You have to trust somebody. Well, not all the way. There's nobody I rely on to tell *me* what to do."

I asked if that included professional advisers. For instance, it was my understanding that Brando very much depended on the guidance of Jay Kanter, a young man on the staff of the Music Corporation of America, which is the agency that represents him. "Oh, Jay," Brando said now. "Jay does what I tell *him* to. I'm alone like that."

The telephone sounded. An hour seemed to have passed, for it was Murray again. "Yeah, still yakking," Brando told him. "Look, let *me* call *you*. . . . Oh, in an hour or so. You be back in your room? . . . O.K."

He hung up, and said, "Nice guy. He wants to be a director—eventually. I was saying something, though. We were talking about friends. Do you know how I make a friend?" He leaned a little toward me, as though he had an amusing secret to impart. "I go about it very gently. I circle around and around. I circle. Then, gradually, I come nearer. Then I reach out and touch them—ah, so gently . . ." His fingers stretched forward like insect feelers and grazed my arm. "Then," he said, one eye half shut, the other, à la Rasputin, mesmerically wide and shining, "I draw back. Wait awhile. Make them wonder. At just the right moment, I move in again. Touch them. Circle." Now his hand, broad and blunt-fingered, travelled in a rotating pattern, as though it held a rope with which he was binding an invisible presence. "They don't know what's happening. Before they realize it, they're all entangled, involved. I have them. And suddenly, sometimes, I'm all *they* have. A lot of them, you see, are people who don't fit anywhere; they're not accepted, they've been hurt, crippled one way or another. But I want to help them, and they can focus on me; I'm the duke. Sort of the duke of my domain."

(A past tenant on the ducal preserve, describing its seigneur and his subjects, has said, "It's as though Marlon lived in a house where the doors are never locked. When he lived in New York the door always *was* open. Anybody could come in, whether Marlon was there or not, and everybody did. You'd arrive and there would be ten, fifteen characters wandering around. It was strange, because nobody seemed to really know anybody else. They were just there, like people in a bus station. Some type asleep in a chair. People reading the tabs. A girl dancing by herself. Or painting her toenails. A comedian trying out his night-club act. Off in a corner, there'd be a chess game going. And drums—bang, boom, bang, boom. But there was never any drinking—nothing like that. Once in a while somebody would say, 'Let's go down to the corner for an ice-cream soda.' Now, in all this Marlon was the common denominator, the only connecting link. He'd move around the room drawing individuals aside and talking to them alone. If you've noticed, Marlon can't, *won't,* talk to two people, simultaneously. He'll never take part in a *group* conversation. It always has to be a cozy tête-à-tête—one person at a time. Which is necessary, I suppose if you use the same kind of charm on everyone. But even when you know that's what he's doing, it doesn't matter. Because when *your* turn comes, he makes you feel you're the only person in the room. In the world. Makes you feel that you're under his protection and that your troubles and moods concern him deeply. You have to believe it; more than anyone I've known, he radiates *sincerity.* Afterward, you may ask yourself, 'Is it an act?' If so, what's the point? What have you got to give him? Nothing except—and this *is* the point—affection. Affection that lends him authority over you. I sometimes think Marlon is like an orphan who later on in life tries to compensate by becoming the kindly head of a huge orphanage. But even outside this institution he wants everybody to love him." Although there exist a score of witnesses who might well contradict the last opinion, Brando himself is credited with having once informed an interviewer, "I can walk into a room where there are a hundred people—if there is *one* person in that room who doesn't like me, I know it and have to get out." As a footnote, it should be added that within the clique over which Brando presides he is esteemed as an intellectual father, as well as an emotional big brother. The person who probably knows him best, the comedian Wally Cox, declares him to be "a creative philosopher, a very deep thinker," and adds, "He's a real liberating force for his friends.")

. . .

Brando yawned; it had got to be a quarter past one. In less than five hours he would have to be showered, shaved, breakfasted, on the set, ready for a makeup man to paint his pale face the mulatto tint that Technicolor requires.

"Let's have another cigarette," he said as I made a move to put on my coat.

"Don't you think you should go sleep?"

"That just means getting up. Most mornings, I don't know why I do. I can't face it." He looked at the telephone, as though remembering his promise to call Murray. "Anyway, I may work later on. You want something to drink?"

Outside, the stars had darkened and it had started to drizzle, so the prospect of a nightcap was pleasing, especially if I should have to return on foot to my own hotel, which was a mile distant from the Miyako. I poured some vodka; Brando declined to join me. However, he subsequently reached for my glass, sipped from it, set it down between us, and suddenly said, in an offhand way that nonetheless conveyed feeling, "My mother. She broke apart like a piece of porcelain."

I had often heard friends of Brando's say, "Marlon worshipped his mother." But prior to 1947, and the premiere of *A Streetcar Named Desire,* few, perhaps none, of the young actor's circle had met either of his parents; they knew nothing of his background except what he chose to tell them. "Marlon always gave a very colorful picture of home life back in Illinois," one of his acquaintances told me. "When we heard that his family were coming to New York for the opening of *Streetcar,* everybody was very curious. We didn't know what to expect. On opening night, Irene Selznick gave a big party at '21.' Marlon came with his mother and father. Well, you can't imagine two more attractive people. Tall, handsome, charming as they could be. What impressed me—I think it amazed everyone—was Marlon's attitude toward them. In their presence, he wasn't the lad we knew. He was a model son. Reticent, respectful, very polite, considerate in every way."

Born in Omaha, Nebraska, where his father was a salesman of limestone products, Brando, the family's third child and only son, was soon taken to live in Libertyville, Illinois. There the Brandos settled down in a rambling house in a countrified neighborhood; at least, there was enough country around the house to allow the Brandos to keep geese and hens and rabbits, a horse, a Great Dane, twenty-eight cats, and a cow. Milking the cow was the daily chore that belonged to Bud, as Marlon was then nicknamed. Bud seems to have been an extroverted and competitive boy. Everyone who came within range of him was at once forced into some variety of contest: Who can eat fastest? Hold his breath longest? Tell the tallest tale? Bud was rebellious, too; rain or shine, he ran away from home every Sunday. But he and his two sisters, Frances and Jocelyn, were devotedly close to their mother. Many years later, Stella Adler, Brando's former drama coach, described Mrs. Brando, who died in 1954, as "a very beautiful, a heavenly, lost, girlish creature." Always, wherever she lived, Mrs. Brando had played leads in the productions of local dramatic societies, and always she had longed for a more brightly footlighted world than her surroundings provided. These yearnings inspired her children. Frances took to painting; Jocelyn, who is at present a professional actress, interested herself in the theatre. Bud, too, had inherited his mother's theatrical inclinations, but at seventeen he announced a wish to study for the ministry. (Then, as now, Brando searched for a belief. As one Brando disciple once summed it up, "He needs to find something in life, something in himself, that is permanently true, and he needs to lay down his life for it. For such an intense personality, nothing less than that will do.") Talked out of his clerical ambitions, expelled from school, rejected for military service in 1942 because of a trick knee, Brando packed up and came to New York. Whereupon Bud, the plump, towheaded, unhappy adolescent, exits, and the man-sized and very gifted Marlon emerges.

Brando has not forgotten Bud. When he speaks of the boy he was, the boy seems to inhabit him, as if time had done little to separate the man from the hurt, desiring child. "My father was indifferent to me," he said. "Nothing I could do interested him, or pleased him. I've accepted that now. We're friends now. We get along." Over the past ten years, the elder Brando has supervised his son's financial affairs; in addition to Pennebaker Productions, of which Mr. Brando, Sr., is an employee, they have been associated in a number of ventures, including a Nebraska grain-and-cattle ranch, in which a large percentage of the younger Brando's earnings was invested. "But my mother was everything to me. A whole world. I tried so hard. I used to come home from school . . ." He hesitated, as though waiting for me to picture him: Bud, books under his arm, scuffling his way along an afternoon street. "There wouldn't be anybody home. Nothing in the icebox." More lantern slides: empty rooms, a kitchen. "Then the telephone would ring. Somebody calling from some bar. And they'd say, 'We've got a lady down here. You better come get her.'" Suddenly, Brando was silent. In silence the picture faded, or, rather, became fixed: Bud at the telephone. At last, the image moved again, leaped forward in time. Bud is eighteen, and: "I thought if she loved me enough, trusted me enough, I thought, then we can be together, in New York; we'll live together and I'll take care of her. Once, later on, that really happened. She left my father and came to live with me. In New York, when I was in a play. I tried so hard. But my love wasn't enough. She couldn't care enough. She went back. And one day"—the flatness of his voice grew flatter, yet the emotional pitch ascended until one could discern like a sound within a sound, a wounded bewilderment—"I didn't care any more. She was there. In a room. Holding on to me. And I let her fall. Because I couldn't take it any more—watch her breaking apart, in front of me, like a piece of porcelain. I stepped right over her. I walked right out. I was indifferent. Since then, I've been indifferent."

The telephone was signalling. Its racket seemed to rouse him from a daze; he stared about, as though he'd wakened in an unknown room, then smiled wryly, then whispered, "Damn, damn, damn," as his hand lurched toward the telephone. "Sorry," he told Murray. "I was just going to call you. . . . No, he's leaving now. But look, man, let's call it off tonight. It's after one. It's nearly two o'clock. . . . Yeah. . . . Sure thing. Tomorrow."

Meanwhile, I'd put on my overcoat, and was waiting to say good night. He walked me to the door, where I put on my shoes. "Well, *sayonara*," he mockingly bade me. "Tell them at the desk to get you a taxi." Then, as I walked down the corridor, he called, "And listen! Don't pay too much attention to what I say. I don't always feel the same way."

• • •

In a sense, this was not my last sight of him that evening. Downstairs, the Miyako's lobby was deserted. There was no one at the desk, nor, outside, were there any taxis in view. Even at high noon, the fancy crochet of Kyoto's streets had played me tricks; still, I set off through the marrow-chilling drizzle in what I hoped was a homeward direction. I'd never before been abroad so late in the city. It was quite a contrast to daytime, when the central parts of the town, caroused by crowds of fiesta massiveness, jangle like the inside of a *pachinko* parlor, or to early evening—Kyoto's most exotic hours, for then, like night flowers, lanterns wreathe the side streets, and resplendent geishas, with their white ceramic faces and their teal looping lacquered wigs strewn with silver bells, their hobbled wiggle-walk, hurry among the shadows toward meticulously tasteful revelries. But at two in the morning these exquisite grotesques are gone, the cabarets are shuttered; only cats remained to keep me company, and drunks and red-light ladies, the inevitable old beggar-bundles in doorways, and, briefly, a ragged street musician who followed me playing on a flute a medieval music. I had trudged far more than a mile when, at last, one of a hundred alleys led to familiar ground—the main-street district of department stores and cinemas. It was then that I saw Brando. Sixty feet tall, with a head as huge as the greatest Buddha's, there he was, in comic-paper colors, on a sign above a theatre that advertised *The Teahouse of the August Moon*. Rather Buddhalike, too, was his pose, for he was depicted in a squatting position, a serene smile on a face that glistened in the rain and the light of a street lamp. A deity, yes; but, more than that, really, just a young man sitting on a pile of candy.

A WOMAN ENTERING A TAXI IN THE RAIN

Winthrop Sargeant

NOVEMBER 8, 1958 (ON RICHARD AVEDON)

To PEOPLE WHO are only casually interested in such matters, fashion is a bewildering phenomenon. It has been denounced as "spinach" and "a racket for selling clothes." It constitutes, as nearly everybody knows, the third-largest industry in the country, and it is responsible for the existence of a considerable publishing business. Its interest in rapid obsolescence is transparent, and its aesthetic standards—as those who have recently been exposed to the sack, the trapeze, and the balloon will agree—are apt to shift quickly from the classic to the downright bizarre. It has attracted the attention of psychiatrists, some of whom have traced its lineage directly to the Marquis de Sade and maintain sombrely that it is largely the product of male designers suffering from a pathological fear of women and seeking to render them harmless by making them look grotesque. The doctors' theory may very well be sound, but it leaves unexplained the fact that the women who are the victims of this curious assault on feminine charm seem to cherish their martyrdom and submit to those who impose it on them like lionesses under the lash of the tamer. The probable answer is that women don't care about the motives of their dictators. What they are after is elegance—a quality, undefinable in terms of logic, that is quite distinct from allure. Many women possess allure almost from the cradle, but elegance is the product of deliberate art, rather than of nature; superficially, it seems to have little relation to sexual attraction—but only superficially. The outward manifestations of elegance change more or less violently from year to year, causing the masculine mind to pursue a cycle that leads from surprise to horror, from horror to resignation, from resignation to apprehension over what is coming next, and so back again to surprise, but at least elegance attracts attention, as spectacular martyrdom always does, and attention, as the late José Ortega y Gasset has pointed out, is an indispensable prelude to love. Thus, however roundabout the route, elegance does appear to have a sexual object in the end. It also takes on, in the minds of its devotees, the character of a religious ritual whose Olympus is Paris and whose principal scriptures are *Vogue* and *Harper's Bazaar.* Not long ago, Mrs. Diana Vreeland, the fashion editor of the latter publication, summed up a major part of its scriptural doctrine when she remarked, "One cannot live by bread alone. One needs *élan*, chinchillas, jewels, and the touch of a master designer, to whom a woman is not just a woman but an illusion."

Since the time of Charles Dana Gibson, the propagation of the illusion has rested largely in the hands of the fashion photographer, a specialist who today is the religion's principal evangelist. For many years, this specialist entered so wholeheartedly into the advancement of the cult that he depicted the illusion pretty much as it existed in the mind's eye of the designer, and the result was that fashion photography, as an art, tended to show a certain Byzantine aloofness from human concerns. The gaunt, skinny, praying-mantis model—an image calculated to frighten most males out of their wits—was a caricature of her sex, a fierce, denying goddess. Presumably she sold the clothes that she wore, for that was her expensive purpose, but her chic was exclusively that of the limited world of high fashion, where any suggestion of womanliness was banished as vulgar. She was as vivacious as a marble statue and as appealing as a mummy—an overt symbol of the death that all good fashion designers, according to the psychiatrists, unconsciously wish to visit on womankind.

About twelve years ago, this approach to fashion photography began to be subtly undermined by a sprightly and ingenious photographer for *Harper's Bazaar* named Richard Avedon. As far as he was concerned, the statues and mummies went out the window. The model became pretty, rather than austerely aloof. She laughed, danced, skated, gambolled among herds of elephants, sang in the rain, ran breathlessly down the Champs-Elysées, smiled and sipped cognac at café tables, and otherwise gave evidence of being human. Whether she thereby sold more clothes is open to question. But the new trend certainly brightened the page of

Harper's Bazaar, and Avedon was widely conceded to have reached a previously unattained artistic level in fashion photography. A good deal of this accomplishment can be attributed to his imagination and resourcefulness in handling a camera, but some of it undoubtedly stems from the fact that his primary interest is not in fashion but in women.

The Avedon photograph—or, more broadly, the Avedon photographic style—has by now become a lively contribution to the visual poetry of sophisticated urban life. Nearly everybody is familiar with it, for it has long since overflowed the pages of *Harper's Bazaar* and influenced the advertising in most of the slick-paper periodicals. It has been imitated by other photographers, but the imitations have seldom approached the animation of the originals; in any case, as soon as the imitators have mastered at least the surface elements of one of Avedon's innovations, he has always popped up with some entirely new departure, for he has never been one to stand still. The world he depicts is an artificial one; his polished and rather romantic art flatly contradicts the bromide that the camera never lies. Avedon's camera unquestionably lies, but it does so in such a poetic and ingratiating manner that the photographic fiction it produces has become a sort of folklore of the world in which fashionable elegance counts. The characters in this fiction are women of unbelievable beauty and grace, moving about in an environment that exists largely in the imagination. This is a composite of mists, glowing lights, the moods of nocturnal revellers, nostalgic memories of bars and gaming tables and theatres, and such ephemeral minutiae as the feeling of enchantment at the sight of a taxi in the rain whose door is opened to receive a suave and mysterious beauty, or the moment of gaiety when some lovely girl decides to throw dignity aside, or the magical second in which the casual motions of a beautiful woman are observed secretly across a restaurant table—all fragments of a metropolitan fairyland, glimpsed by ordinary mortals only at times of heightened illusion.

Technically, Avedon's work shows little reverence for the ideals of sharpness and accuracy that are still the goal of most commercial photographers. Not being concerned with realism, Avedon sometimes deliberately reproduces the imperfections of elementary photography in order to create pictures that have an unrehearsed and improvised—almost accidental—air about them. His camera often invades a penumbral region in which the blur—for years regarded by professionals as the mark of the bungler—is used as a means of poetic evocation. His control of various kinds of blur—blurred backgrounds, blurred lighting, blurred movement by the model—has added a new dimension to what used to be an extremely literal art. The Avedon blur has, in fact, become a sort of colophon. He is not the only photographer who has intentionally produced the fuzzy effects that are the continual humiliation of the amateur, but he has been more consistent and resourceful than most. As might be imagined, the Avedon blur calls for a lot more ingenuity and technical mastery than are required for pictures that are merely clear, since it involves, among other things, determining just how much blurriness is desirable for the job at hand, and then capturing precisely that amount on the negative, working out contrasts between blurriness and sharpness in a single picture, and deciding intuitively when to blur and when not to blur.

For not all Avedon photographs are blurred, nor can blurriness even be said to be the basis of his craftsmanship. In many of his pictures, everything has been eliminated but the model, who stands out in sharp outline against an absolutely blank white background; moreover, his portraits are notable for an almost microscopic delineation of human character that reveals a stark concentration on personality. The key to Avedon's art is to be found not in his technical devices, which he invents and discards with restless rapidity, but in his preoccupation with the looks, mannerisms, and gestures of human beings, whom he appears to regard as actors performing in dramas of his own invention. In fashion photography, the human beings are, of course, beautiful women, and as seen through his camera lens they actually do take on the semblance of leading ladies on the stage. They may, in passing, also make the clothes they are wearing seem desirable, but what principally attracts the eye is the spirited way they seem to be participating in a psychological situation. The woman inside the clothes may look joyous, wistful, lonely, arrogant, bored, expectant, surprised, annoyed—she may even weep, though weeping models have not been particularly popular with the editors of *Harper's Bazaar*—but in no case does her display of emotion betray any sign of affectation. On the contrary, she invariably seems to have been caught unawares by the camera at some evanescent moment, and everything about her expression and bearing suggests a drama beginning long before and concluding long after the click of the shutter. It is this power to induce the conviction that one is witnessing a crucial instant in the emotional life of the subject, and to stimulate curiosity as to what brought it about and what will ensue, that gives the Avedon photograph its peculiar distinction—that of being not so much a picture of a well-dressed beautiful woman as a revelatory glimpse of a feminine psyche confronted with a situation involving action or passion.

Any inquiry into the nature of Avedon's singular talent as a photographic dramatist leads, naturally, beyond the sphere of mere dexterity with a camera to a consideration of the photographer's own personality. So slim (five feet seven and a half; a hundred and twenty-five pounds) as to give a deceptive appearance of fragility, he is a rather handsome, black-haired, dark-eyed, and, at thirty-five, still boyish-looking man—fastidious, but with no trace of self-consciousness in his manner, and endowed with an acute sensitivity to his surroundings and the people in them. Toward women—especially toward those who happen to be his models—he is courtly and attentive, and his understanding of their potentialities and foibles is comparable to that of a veteran casting director. When the model pleases him, he is so laudatory that she may well come to believe she is the embodiment of his ideal of a leading lady. In his studio—a surgically tidy suite of seven rooms on the top floor of a two-story taxpayer on East Forty-ninth Street, adjoining Manny Wolf's Chop House—he usually works in his shirtsleeves and a pair of tight-fitting Edwardian slacks, hopping about like an undergraduate stage manager and bossing a staff of half a dozen secretaries and laboratory assistants without ever losing his temper or using an even remotely dictatorial tone. The studio is constantly throbbing with activity—props being constructed, whole stage sets being erected, complex lighting systems being laid out—and the transient fauna on the premises may include not only the models but a flock of doves or a pack of greyhounds. One cold day last winter, a portable swimming pool was installed in the place, from which a young lady emerged, dripping, to face the camera for a series of bathing-cap shots while Avedon thoughtfully provided her with restorative draughts of brandy.

No matter how frenzied the bustle, though, Avedon is never too hurried to spend half an hour (at a cost to him of perhaps sixty dollars in model's fees) sitting serenely with a distressed model on a couch in the studio, discussing whatever it is that is troubling her. A model is likely to arise from one of Avedon's cultivated pep talks with the idea that she really is lovely, and that, instead of merely posing, she is gloriously holding the center of an imaginary stage, free to act as her own dramatic impulses dictate. In this frame of mind she will very probably reveal the instinctive individual charm that may be expected of any beautiful girl when given her head in an aura of masculine admiration. When, presently, she finds herself facing the camera, the theatrical atmosphere is heightened not only by Avedon's cries of delight and his occasional bantering comments, which are designed to bring about changes of mood and expression, but also by a nearby hi-fi set, playing music carefully tailored to the model's personality and preferences. This musical accompaniment is important. Suzy Parker, Avedon's current favorite model, for example, gets a big lift from listening to Lena Horne and to "Witchcraft" as sung by Frank Sinatra. "She needs this sort of thing," Avedon explains. "One kind of music or another brings out the best in all of them."

• • •

As a leading prophet of the mystique of the elegant and beautiful woman, Avedon has achieved considerable worldly success—to the extent of something like a quarter of a million dollars a year. Since, even today, *Harper's Bazaar* pays him only a few hundred dollars for a full-page picture, it is plain that most of his income is derived from other sources. These are the numerous arrangements he has with advertisers, under which he celebrates such disparate products as Revlon lipstick and Pabst beer. He seldom permits his name to be used in connection with his advertising work, and he takes great care to distinguish between it and what he calls his "creative" work, which, since 1945, has appeared almost exclusively in *Harper's Bazaar,* and always with a credit line. Avedon's rise to eminence in his profession has been more in the nature of suddenly and effortlessly attaining a plateau than of painfully climbing to a peak of success, for he arrived pretty much where he is today when he was only twenty-two. He was born on May 15, 1923, in Manhattan, the descendant of a Jewish family that had migrated here from Russia two generations before. His father, who for many years was co-owner of a women's-wear department store called Avedon's Fifth Avenue, had a strong regard for the practical, and was determined to make his son appreciate the importance of being economically independent, a theme that he emphasized by repeated admonitions that if young Richard didn't look out, he would join the army of illiterates and end up as a taxi-driver. To impress him further with the value of money, he gave the boy a weekly allowance of five cents, in pennies, payable on presentation of a budget allocating every cent of it. When Richard was twelve, or thereabouts, his father illustrated a lecture on the perils of drink by giving him a bottle of wine, which the youngster immediately polished off and which induced, first, a spirited impersonation of Fred Astaire and, later, a monumental hangover. To the best of Avedon's recollection, he was seventeen when he left home, determined to make his way by himself and not wind up as a taxi-driver. Simultaneously, he quit De Witt Clinton High School, without graduating; except for some extension courses in literature at Columbia later on, that was the end of his formal education.

The plateau came in sight when Avedon got his first job—as an errand boy for a small photographic concern at Fifty-seventh Street and Sixth Avenue—but he did not recognize it, for his ambition just then was to become a poet. He reverently studied the works of Sandburg, Yeats, Jeffers, MacLeish, and T. S. Eliot, and wrote a great many poems himself, some of which were published in the *Journal-American* and in H. I. Phillips' column in the New York *Sun*, bringing him both a modicum of fame and—at twenty-five cents a line—an addition to his income. His published works show a certain tendency toward repetition. Having made Phillips' column with the couplet

> City snow, like sodden cotton,
> Is obviously good for notton,

Avedon, not a man to waste a poetic image, a few months later used it again in this quatrain:

> Summer heat, like sodden cotton,
> Is obviously good for notton,
> And being quite candid,
> I just can't standid.

The cause of poetry was set back by the Second World War, because in 1942 Avedon enlisted in the Merchant Marine.

During the days when his father was interested in women's wear, Avedon had often found copies of fashion magazines lying about the house, and had even kept a scrapbook of photographs from them that he liked. At the time, he had not the slightest idea that he might someday become a photographer himself, but he was an admirer of good fashion and theatre photography, and of the pictures by Cecil Beaton, Edward Steichen, Martin Munkacsi, and Anton Bruehl that were then appearing in *Harper's Bazaar, Vogue,* and *Vanity Fair.* When he enlisted in the Merchant Marine, his father gave him a Rolleiflex camera as a going-away present, and, almost haphazardly, Avedon applied for a job in the service's photography branch, perhaps feeling that as long as he had a camera, he might as well go in for photography. He was assigned to a group that spent most of its time on land, at Sheepshead Bay, and though he went briefly to sea a couple of times to take pictures of wrecks, most of his work consisted in turning out identification photographs of Merchant Marine personnel. On the side, and in his spare moments, he amused himself by making pictures of a more ambitious sort, some of which contained the first traces of the Avedon blur. One of these was a portrait of two brothers; the brother in the foreground was in sharp detail, and the brother in the background was out of focus, merely a suggestion of a looming presence. Avedon's extracurricular blurry photographs were, of course, of no interest to the Merchant Marine, but he saw something in them that excited him, and in 1944, as soon as he was demobilized, he presented himself at Bonwit Teller, still in uniform, and asked to be allowed to photograph some clothes free of charge. Fashion photography at the time was by no means a difficult field to break into. Apart from a few star performers like Louise Dahl-Wolfe, George Hoyningen-Huene, and Toni Frissell, it was peopled by some of the most commonplace hacks to be found in the photographic profession. Avedon was, and is, voluble and persuasive. He was given some clothes by the store, and, hiring Bijou Barrington (then the most expensive model in New York) with money he had saved from his Merchant Marine pay, he photographed them—unblurred. Bonwit liked the pictures, put them up in the store elevators, and gave him some other jobs. A year later, Avedon made up a portfolio of his best Bonwit work, added his Merchant Marine brothers for luck, and went around to *Harper's Bazaar*. At the time, the magazine's art director was Alexey Brodovitch, a dedicated romantic, a balletomane, and himself a dabbler in fanciful, poetically misty photography. He riffled through Avedon's fashion shots, discarded them, and picked up the two brothers. That one interested him; he liked the blur. Accordingly, Avedon was hired, despite certain initial misgivings that Brodovitch had about the young man's prowess as a technician, and assigned, in the beginning, to the section of the magazine known as *Junior Bazaar*. "His first photographs for us were technically very bad," Brodovitch recalls. "But they were not snapshots. It has always been the shock-surprise element in his work that makes it something special. He has an amazing capacity for spotting the unusual and exciting qualities in each subject he photographs. Those first pictures of his had freshness and individuality, and they showed enthusiasm and a willingness to take chances." Before long, the chances that Avedon took as an upstart photographer—and the graver chances that Brodovitch took in publishing his pictures—started paying off. In the thirteen years that Avedon has been at *Harper's Bazaar*, working most of the time under Brodovitch's benign and exquisitely perceptive eye, he has been permitted the full exercise of his imaginative talent, even—or perhaps especially—when that talent has led him far from the conventions of fashion-magazine photography. He has found *Harper's Bazaar* a gallery in which to exhibit his most distinctive, not to say his most eccentric, gifts, and, notwithstanding the relatively trifling effect nowadays of its payments on his bank account, he still looks upon it as an unequalled showcase for an aspirant to artistic prestige.

A sense of this high-fashion prestige also affects that peculiar world inhabited by photographers' models. The legion of photogenic beauties who make a living for the most part by ornamenting ads for soap and refrigerators regard an appearance in the pages of *Harper's Bazaar* or *Vogue* much as a singer regards an appearance at the Metropolitan Opera House. These magazines do not pay the models they hire anything like what can be earned in the advertising business. But they bestow on them a standing that is dearer than gold and that has the practical advantage of enhancing their market value no end in the profane environs of Madison Avenue, where, like Avedon, they make their financial killings. To become a *Harper's Bazaar* or *Vogue* fashion model is to reach the peak of a crowded and highly competitive profession, a peak from which various promised lands—the theatre, the movies, marriage to a polo player—may be more or less confidently contemplated. The situation is one that has made Avedon a great power in the modelling business.

In justice to Avedon, it should be said that he exercises his power with becoming humility and concern for the standards of his profession. Although he can make a model the toast of the advertising business almost overnight—and has, in fact, repeatedly done so—his motives on such occasions have been predominantly aesthetic and have always reflected the exigencies of his approach to photography. He chooses his models not only for their beauty but for certain dramatic qualities of personality that he recognizes as suited to his particular theatrical needs. Now and then, he has detected just the right combination after only the briefest encounter with a stranger in some public place; he made one such discovery among the passengers in an elevator at De Pinna, and another while getting out of a cab in the East Fifties. But this doesn't happen often. As a rule, Avedon selects his leading ladies from the ranks of established professionals. Once he has become interested in a girl, he sticks to her with the fidelity of a reigning diva's impresario—applauding her triumphs, developing her most striking characteristics, and observing by the hour her personality quirks and her mannerisms, both when she is moving about and when she is in repose. Avedon, of course, has no lien on the services of a particular model; she can be hired by any photographer willing to pay her fee. Furthermore, in any given period of time he is likely to work with several models. But there is always one who, in his mind, is "his" model—the one on whom his creative thinking is centered, and on whom he can depend for complete projection of his ideas. Naturally, these girls change—in fashion, constancy is death—but Avedon tends to remain faithful to each one for a long time; when he finally feels obliged to let her go, he suffers intense pangs of regret. Several years ago, he felt so unhappy after dismissing a model that he continued to photograph her, trying to catch the sad, wistful essence of a woman forsaken in love. The mood was quite real, since there was little possibility that the model would ever again achieve the renown she had enjoyed while working for Avedon. But the photographs were not all he had hoped they might be, and in the end, with a sigh, he gave up.

• • •

Not surprisingly, the loyalty and admiration that Avedon extends to whoever is "his" model at any given time has led some of his associates to speculate on the nature of the relationship. The situation is complicated by the fact that early in his career on *Harper's Bazaar* he was married to a model—Dorcas Nowell, a beautiful young thing known professionally as Doe Avedon. Nothing pleased him more than to dress her up to the nines and show her off in public. The couple were divorced after five years, however. In retrospect, some of Avedon's friends are inclined to believe that he thought of her mainly as a lovely creation of his camera eye. Later, after consulting a psychiatrist, Avedon was quoted as saying, "I have to be a little bit in love with my models"—doubtless a true statement if "love" is taken to mean, in large measure, an emotion induced by professional delight at successfully recording the personality and charm of the woman in question on film. Pressed, not long ago, for an explanation of where he stands in this matter, Avedon thought sombrely for a while and then replied, "It's like the feeling you have for kittens or puppies." In any case, the issue is believed never to have ruffled the placidity of Avedon's life with his second wife, Evvie, a highly intelligent woman, totally dissociated from the fashion world, whom he married in 1951. Avedon himself has described models in general as "a group of underdeveloped, frightened, insecure women, most of whom have been thought ugly as children—too tall and too skinny. They are all subject to trauma where their looks are concerned. You have to make them *feel* beautiful." After the breakup of his first marriage, Avedon went through a long course of psychoanalysis, following which both his art and his relation to women seemed to change. Before, as a friend has remarked, he had a tendency to confuse women in general with elegant, idealized images of the species—a confusion that was evident in his early fashion photographs. Afterward, a preoccupation with the human being underneath the dress and makeup began to manifest itself immediately. Miss Parker recently expressed her admiration for him as an individual by stating simply, "He's the most wonderful man in the business, because he realizes that models are not just coat hangers."

Avedon's first widely celebrated model was Dorian Leigh, a woman of somewhat subtle beauty, who became the most famous model of her time. Of all the pictures Avedon took of her, the best known was undoubtedly the one used by the Revlon nail-polish people for their Fire and Ice ad, in which she was shown standing majestically in a jewelled gown and a red cape with the fingers of one hand splayed before her face. Miss Leigh was Avedon's reigning model from 1948 to 1951, and he wistfully remembers her as the loveliest and most versatile subject he has ever had before his camera. In the end, however, she fell in love with a wealthy, car-racing Spanish nobleman, gave up modelling, and later went into business for herself, as head of a model agency in Paris. Miss Leigh was followed by a dark-haired, formidably exotic-looking Irish-American girl named Dorothy Horan, who assumed for professional purposes the name Dovima—"Do" for "Dorothy," "vi" for "victory," and "ma" for her ma, to whom she was attached. Dovima, who worked for Avedon from 1951 to 1955, was a devout Catholic and—in rather startling contrast to her aspect in the pages of *Harper's Bazaar*, which strongly hinted that she was in the same league with Cleopatra and Salammbô—a homebody. On her trips with Avedon to make photographs on location, she was generally accompanied by a husband and invariably by an armful of comic books. Under Avedon's supervision, she became a face and figure known throughout the world of fashion and advertising, and an image capable of disturbing masculine dreams as well as selling clothes and lipstick. She was, like all Avedon models, an instinctive actress, and entered into the business of building up a fictitious public personality as a *femme fatale* with a fervor that was both disarming and wholly at odds with her extremely conventional notions of conduct. To dramatize Dovima, Avedon photographed her posing in the midst of a herd of wild-eyed elephants; he took her—and her husband and a trunkload of comic books—to Paris, where she impersonated the ultimate in sophisticated elegance for his camera; noting that she bore a resemblance to the famous bust of the Egyptian Queen Nefertiti, he carted her to Egypt, where she posed for him in front of the Sphinx. Dovima was so overcome by the grandeur of her Egyptian role that she underwent a mystical experience.

"He is speaking to me," she said softly, pointing to the Sphinx. "He is saying, 'Dovima . . .' "

"How interesting that he should know your name," remarked Avedon, trying, as always, to sound vitally attentive and inspiriting.

"He is saying, 'Dovima, you belong here,' " concluded Dovima, with an air of slight annoyance at the interruption.

When she returned to the United States, a friend inquired how she had liked Africa.

"I didn't get to Africa," she said. "But I was in Egypt."

"But Egypt *is* in Africa," the friend pointed out.

"It is?" Dovima said. "Good Lord, if I'd known I was going to *Africa,* I'd have charged double."

Dovima was succeeded by Sunny Harnett, a rather racy-looking blonde who "resembled the ideal of the luxury-drenched woman of the world, with money to throw away," as Mrs. Vreeland has described her, adding, "She wore chinchilla and diamonds as carelessly as if they really belonged to her, and Dick had a way of making her believe that they did." Avedon saw Miss Harnett as the epitome of sophistication; among the many dramas in which she played the leading lady, perhaps the most triumphant was set in the Casino at Le Touquet, where Avedon photographed her draped with reckless dignity over the gaming tables, looking stunningly world-weary and dangerous. After a year, Miss Harnett was, in turn, succeeded by Dorian Leigh's younger sister, Suzy Parker, a lanky, high-spirited model whose spectacular looks and sparkling manner, besides earning her the opportunity to adorn fashion pictures and ads for Pabst beer, have recently made her a Hollywood movie star. "There is nothing to modelling," Miss Parker has been quoted as saying. "All you do is shut off your mind and go to work." Actually, Miss Parker does nothing of the sort. An intelligent girl and an amateur photographer herself, she is quick to visualize the dramatic ideas that Avedon works out for her, and often makes valuable suggestions of her own. Certainly no one has ever held a glass of beer aloft with more instinctive grace or with an expression of more intellectual appreciation than Miss Parker, who continually awes and delights Avedon by the endless variety of moods and movements, most of them ranging from the playful to the hilarious, that her face and body present to his camera. She recalls one instance when Avedon took a rather peremptory attitude toward her (she had protested that she looked awful that day, and he said, "It doesn't matter how you look—it is *I* who make you beautiful") but on the whole their relationship seems to be as cozy as that of a devoted brother and sister. It is conceivable that Miss Parker will shortly give up modelling to concentrate on her movie career. But so far, in spite of her Hollywood commitments, she has managed to keep working at the profession that gave her her start and in which, as the unequalled diva of the moment, she earns a hundred and twenty dollars an hour (and double that after five o'clock).

• • •

Avedon has lately had more than his accustomed share of public attention, owing to a movie called *Funny Face,* which was supposedly based on his life as a fashion photographer, and to a Bachrach advertisement that shows a camera portrait of him, wearing an immaculate business suit and looking every inch the executive, together with the message "When Richard Avedon, great fashion photographer, wants portraits for his personal use he comes to Bachrach." Both these tributes are to some extent misleading. *Funny Face,* a musical starring Fred Astaire and Audrey Hepburn, deals with a love affair between a fashion photographer and his model, and contains many photographic devices and techniques drawn from Avedon's work—blurs, blank white backgrounds, and so on, including Dovima, Miss Harnett, and Miss Parker—but it is far afield when it comes to questions of fact. The film was made in Hollywood and Paris, and Avedon himself went both places, at a fee of ten thousand dollars, to serve as "visual consultant." The Bachrach ad is misleading simply because, in real life, Avedon has hardly ever been seen in anything more formal than shirtsleeves, and has certainly never been taken for any sort of tycoon.

Formality is, in fact, just about the last quality that comes to mind in connection with Avedon. He may be, as many people suspect, fundamentally shrewd and calculating in his professional life, but, whether he is working or not, his manner is that of an eager youth, intensely preoccupied with those offhand, intimate forms of human communication that have been of such value to him in lulling his models into a mood of relaxed spontaneity. "I am always stimulated by people," he says. "Almost never by ideas." His candor about himself is so great, and so unabashedly exhibitionistic, that once, after being interviewed by a young lady from a newspaper, he sent her around to talk with his psychiatrist, to make sure that she had the whole story. He leads what might be called a functional existence, in that he chooses the way of maximum ease, casting aside the useless baggage of display by which many men seek to impress others. Until the recent growth of his studio into what shows promise of becoming a major industrial enterprise, Avedon, unlike most successful magazine photographers, always insisted on doing his own developing and printing, since some of the effects he has made his name on involve the laboratory as crucially as the lens. He has now turned the laboratory work over to a technician named Frank Finocchio, who has worked with him so long and so closely that, once he has been shown what is desired, his eye can be trusted to react like a replica of Avedon's own.

In Paris, where Avedon and Louise Dahl-Wolfe take turns at the frantic job of photographing the semiannual collections of the big dressmaking houses for *Harper's Bazaar,* he relies on a minimum, or a maximum, of equipment—at times using a Rolleiflex for an entire collection, and at other times renting generator trucks to illuminate Paris for blocks, and police to hold back the crowds. He is noted for his tireless industry on these expeditions, rising long before dawn and keeping at it until late at night, either laboring over actual pictures or experimenting with new schemes to give a novel twist to what, owing to the coverage by the daily press, will be a familiar story by the time his photographs appear. Over the years, there have been many tales about his troubles with capricious models in Paris (they made up a good deal of the plot of *Funny Face*), and most of them are true. Models *do* get lost and have to be tracked down through the mazes of boulevard night life; they *do* occasionally fall into the Seine; they *do* sometimes elope with wealthy playboys; and Dovima *did* nearly topple from the Eiffel Tower in an access of dramatic fervor. But for Avedon, crises of this kind are a desirable part of the theatrical background that he considers vital to his work. His leading lady must always be involved in a drama of some sort, and if fate fails to provide a real one, Avedon thinks one up. He often creates in his mind an entire scenario suggested by a model's appearance. She may be a waif lost in a big and sinful city, or a titled lady pursued in Hispano-Suizas by gentlemen flourishing emeralds, or an inconsolably bored woman of the world whose heart can no longer be touched—and so on. Avedon models play scene after scene from these scripts, and sometimes help out by actually living an extra scene or two. The result is extraordinary for its realism—not the kind of realism found in most photography but the kind found in the theatre.

• • •

It might be imagined that Avedon's surroundings, which shift from the *haut monde* of Paris to the no less *haut* world of the well-dressed American woman, would have made him into a wide-ranging man-about-town. But this is not the case. While he knows his way around the cocktail-party circuit, he has little use for the milieu except professionally, and the scenes of life there as revealed in his photographs are, to a large extent, the product of his imagination. He abhors night clubs, and attends large social functions seldom and reluctantly. In addition to his pictorial reporting on fashions for *Harper's Bazaar,* he supplies the magazine with a steady stream of portraits of well-known people. On one side of his work, he is always meeting people whose names keep popping up in the gossip columns; on the other side, people whose names appear in the news and society columns. But his intimate friends are comparatively few, consisting generally of old cronies whose friendship he values even though no newspaper desk has ever heard of them. A man who rarely drinks and never smokes, Avedon lives quietly with his wife and their five-year-old son, Johnny, in a six-room apartment on Park Avenue, less than a five-minute taxi ride from his studio—quietly, that is, when Johnny, who attends the Dalton School, is not romping with a large, floppy dog named Bunky. There is nothing self-consciously aesthetic, or even especially distinctive, about the décor of the apartment, a comfortably furnished one decorated by Mrs. Avedon in conventional competition with the usual hi-fi and television sets. Mrs. Avedon, a native of

Springfield, Massachusetts, is an attractive blonde, though by no means a spectacular glamour girl in the Avedon photographic tradition. (She has never permitted her husband to take a picture of her.) While even the authorities at *Harper's Bazaar* have praised her instinctive taste in dress on formal occasions, she cares nothing about fashion, and loves to wander about the house without shoes or stockings and to dispense, rather pointedly, with the artificial glamour that plays such a conspicuous role in Avedon's professional life. Like her husband, she is difficult to pry away from domestic privacy for big social functions; she enjoys talking seriously with persons who interest her—but preferably a few at a time—and she is quite content to spend entire evenings at home alone or with her husband. "My wife dislikes all our friends equally," Avedon once remarked, softening the exaggeration with a smile.

Mrs. Avedon is very canny at sizing up people, and has good taste in books, music, and photography, including her husband's, which she is perfectly ready to comment on, favorably or not, to him or to others. She is very proud of his standing in his field, goes along unobtrusively on all his Paris expeditions, and talks over each new project with him before he sets to work on it. Friends of the couple also credit her with having given the Avedon ménage much of its stability by providing a tranquil refuge for her husband, one of those dedicated men whose work is the principal—almost the exclusive—end of existence. Often working late into the night or getting up before dawn to hop in a taxi and hurry to his studio, Avedon spends nearly all his waking hours planning photographs or taking photographs or worrying about photographs. He is a distinctly urban type, to whom the thought of living in the country is appalling—as it is to his wife. Asked not long ago if he had ever considered buying a country place, he looked startled and said, "What on earth would I do with one? It would take me hours to get to my studio, and I would probably never see my wife." The Avedons don't own a car, because it would be a nuisance in the city and they have no desire to drive anywhere else. To both of them, the countryside—meaning the rural areas of the Temperate Zone northeast—is a bore, and they prefer to look at it, if at all, from the veranda of a hotel. They are not so critical, however, about the landscape in Jamaica, where they go every winter for a vacation; apparently, they find the tropical vistas, while not precisely urban, a little easier to take.

Though Avedon is far from desultory in bargaining with his advertising clients, he claims that his interest in money is not worldly but based solely on his concept of it as a tribute to his prestige. He appears to view his fairly princely income with some surprise. "Why, you know, I sometimes get almost as much as Picasso for a picture," he mused recently—and this comparison of his financial success with that of an artist, rather than, say, that of a banker or an industrialist, is highly typical of his way of thinking. Like most men with a generous surplus of cash, Avedon invests in various stocks and bonds, and for advice about them he often calls on his friend Cleveland Amory, who is not only a writer but a methodical student of the market. Amory, however, is likely to be dismayed by the use that Avedon makes of his advice. Not long ago, he advised Avedon to take a cautious flyer in a certain oil stock. Avedon bought the stock, all right, and it went up even beyond Amory's expectations, but when they next met, Avedon had forgotten all about Amory's advice. "I just *knew* it would go up," he said. "I wouldn't have thought of buying any until I consulted an astrologer, and he said that my horoscope predicted good luck in oil."

• • •

Shortly after Avedon went to work for *Harper's Bazaar,* the editors of *Life* asked him to do a series of pictures of New York. Avedon accepted the assignment eagerly, since it seemed to promise another sudden rise in prestige, but he soon discovered that the project involved work of a kind he was not instinctively fitted for, and he never completed it. "The trouble was that when I got out into the street, I just couldn't do it," he says. "I didn't like invading the privacy of perfect strangers. It seemed such an aggressive thing to do. Also, I have to control what I shoot, and I found that I couldn't control Times Square." The place where he could control what he wanted to shoot was, of course, his studio. "I began trying to create an out-of-focus world—a heightened reality, better than real, that suggests, rather than tells you," he has explained. "Maybe the fact that I'm myopic had something to do with it. When I take off my glasses, especially on rainy nights, I get a far more beautiful view of the world than twenty-twenty people get. I wanted to reproduce this more poetic image that I was privately enjoying." During Avedon's first five years as a commercial photographer, many potential advertising clients shied away from him, because they were afraid he would portray their products bathed in an impenetrable mass of fog. But *Harper's Bazaar* had steadfast faith in him. "They even ran a picture I took of the Hope Diamond in which you couldn't see the facets," he recalls. "What you got was the *il-*

lusion of the diamond—the feeling a woman would have while wearing it." Some Avedon admirers date the turning point in his style from a celebrated photograph he made for *Harper's Bazaar* in 1950, in which Dorian Leigh was shown bursting into laughter while throwing her arms around the winner of a French bicycle race. The picture created a sensation in the profession, since embracing sports heroes and laughing had not previously been thought suitable activities for fashion models, and the extent of its influence soon became clear as models began to appear everywhere embracing bicycle riders, matadors, coachmen, and Lord knows what else, in a state of hilarity. Next, Avedon, again a good jump ahead of the pack, started photographing models with handsome young men posing as their husbands, and then—most revolutionary of all—models wheeling children in perambulators or, to make the family scene complete, dangling them in baskets gaily held by the father, too. The theme of domesticity also caught on, and has since been furthered in the philosophy of "togetherness" so relentlessly propagated by the editors of *McCall's*. Avedon, though, restless as ever, already regards this accent on love and the home as an outworn fad, and is casting about for something to supersede it. "Everyone in the ads is loving everyone else," he says dourly. "Perhaps it's time for a shift to privacy."

As far as Avedon's work is concerned, there will undoubtedly be a shift of some sort, and then another and another, for he has a horror of formulas. "He never brings the same mental attitude to the same problem twice, and in fashion photography, where a certain amount of repetition is taken for granted, this is a trait that amounts to genius," a *Harper's Bazaar* editor observed a while ago. It is also a trait that Avedon deliberately cultivates. Even when his gift of improvisation fails him, he refuses to fall back on routine procedures; at least once, he has given up photography altogether for as long as six months, simply because he felt that his pictures were becoming monotonous. Notwithstanding the elaborate dramatic scenarios he invents for his models, he seldom knows just what scene in them he is going to photograph until he arrives at his studio. If nothing unexpected strikes him and he feels that he can't lay hands on a completely original idea, he is more than likely to abandon the project. One of his few theories about photography is that if it does not provide a lot of fun for both him and his model, it is not worth bothering with, because his work will become static, methodical, and dull.

Perhaps the *Harper's Bazaar* portraits that Avedon takes of celebrated people constitute his most valid claim to consideration as a serious artist. They, too, have an improvised look, and no two of them are alike in pose or treatment. Here, Avedon is under no obligation to make his subjects look elegant, and some of the portraits are almost caricatures—photographic impressions that probe for every psychological weakness and theatrical affectation in the sitter's character. Curiously, Avedon has never had much success in attempting to photograph specimens of heroic masculinity, such as Montgomery Clift or Marlon Brando. "I suppose it is because of unconscious hostility on my part, or possibly a sense of rivalry," he says, with his customary frankness in passing along the findings of his psychiatrist. On the other hand, the ravaged face of the late Humphrey Bogart stirred him to such pity that he achieved a truly memorable portrait, one that conveys an almost pathological sense of fear. In his portrait work, Avedon appears to be inspired mainly by subjects in whom he can find qualities that excite his compassion—advanced age, physical debility, ugliness, or the pathos often underlying the surface insouciance of professional comedians or inveterate poseurs. Avedon portraits in *Harper's Bazaar* have shown Frank Lloyd Wright carelessly and arrogantly wearing a day's growth of beard, Truman Capote apparently impersonating St. Anthony, Elsa Maxwell in bed with a telephone and a pet skunk, and a head of Charles Laughton so enlarged that it looks like something seen through a microscope. None of Avedon's subjects seem to resent this kind of treatment; most of them move in circles, both here and in Europe, where being selected to sit for one of his *Harper's Bazaar* portraits ranks as an accolade.

From time to time, people watching Avedon's smooth day-to-day performance on his secure and tranquil plateau are inclined to wonder where he can go from here. He is still a young man, and one whose restless imagination and inventiveness might be expected to urge him on to the exploration of other branches of photography. His wife, for instance, believes that he ought to devote more attention to realistic reporting, in the manner of Henri Cartier-Bresson. He has already, in the case of *Funny Face,* flirted with the movies, and a year or so ago he directed a television show starring Judy Garland. During the first four minutes of this production, Miss Garland carried on in stark splendor against a standard Avedon blank white background—a scene that *Variety* praised as an entirely new development in television—but in general the show was less enthusiastically received, and Avedon soon returned to his own snug studio, happy to be back where he could work as an individual and control the elements of his art. The answer to the question of where he goes from here may be "Nowhere." He may already *be* there—if by "there" is meant a state of exuberant, tumbling transition between one photographic inspiration and the next.

PART THREE

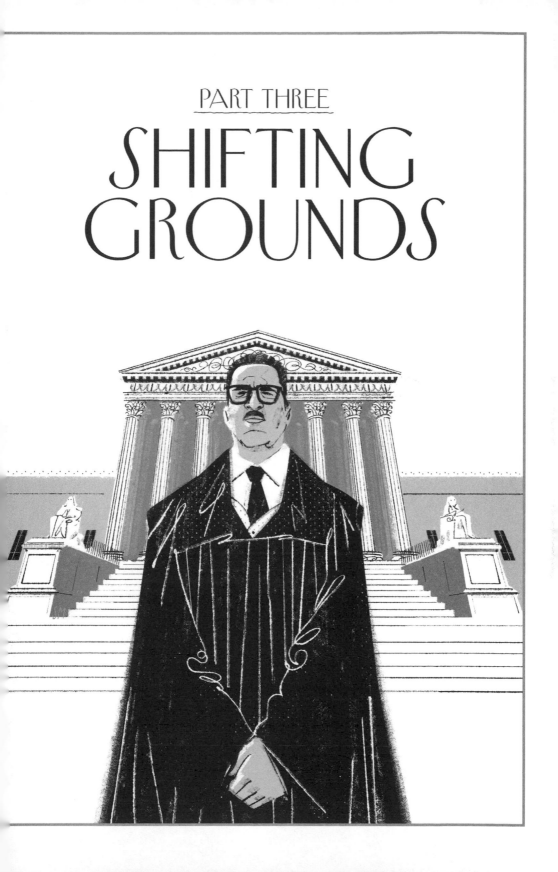

SHIFTING GROUNDS

A NOTE BY JILL LEPORE

IT WAS A jumpy time. "Said Mr. A to Mr. B, 'I doubt the loyalty of C,'" E. B. White wrote in "The ABC of Security," in 1953, the year Julius and Ethel Rosenberg were executed as Soviet spies, and Joseph McCarthy, blustering about subversion and perversion, began holding hearings on security risks in the U.S. Army and the federal government. Un-American activities, atomic bombs, blacklists, loyalty tests: everyone was rattled. The anti-anti-Communists were uneasy, the anti-anti-anti-Communists uneasier. "The first actually means men who are against men who are against Communists, and the second, when you unravel it, means men who are against men who are against men who are against Communists," James Thurber explained helpfully. Neither was to be confused with an ex-ex-Communist, "a man who may have ceased to be a man who may have ceased to be a Communist," or, when you pare that down, a man who may have ceased to be a man. This gobbledygook must have seemed at the time to be on everyone's lips, but, in retrospect, some of it came, one way or another, from the National Security Agency, the postwar, top-secret counter-counter-intelligence agency formed in 1952, although not many people knew about it: its existence was classified. All the same, already, the word "security" and the catchphrase "national security" were degenerating into meaninglessness. "In politics," Thurber wrote, "'security' itself has come to mean 'insecurity.'" It wasn't so much gibberish (which is how Mencken would have described it), or bunk (a Harold Ross-ism), or doublespeak (in the Orwellian sense), as it was an atomic-era epidemic of overclassification.

The year 1955, when Thurber wrote "The Psychosemanticist Will See You Now," was also the year of Ginsberg's "Howl": the "yacketayakking screaming vomiting whispering facts and memories and anecdotes and eyeball kicks and shocks." A lot of magazine writing from the decade aims at being hip, if not hip to the howl, hip to the lingo about the lingo:

to be unbewildered. In a Profile of Dorothy Day, Dwight Macdonald described the Catholic Worker movement this way: "Politically, the Catholic Workers are hard to classify. They are for the poor and against the rich, so the capitalists call them Communists; they believe in private property and don't believe in class struggle, so the Communists call them capitalists; and they are hostile to war and to the State, so both capitalists and Communists consider them crackpots."

No one wants to be labeled. But the trick of writing during an epidemic of overclassification, wishing to be heard above the howl, is to say something that holds its meaning—to say something certain—without appearing to be a crackpot. That's what drew Macdonald, the critic, to Day, the believer: her conviction. Not her religious faith, per se, but her belief in the moral idea "that it is possible even today to live in peace and brotherhood." Say what he would about Day, devotion set Macdonald back on his heels. "The Catholic Workers are religious in a way that is hard for most people even to understand, let alone sympathize with," Macdonald wrote. "They practice their faith on Mondays, Tuesdays, Wednesdays, Thursdays, Fridays, and Saturdays, as well as Sundays." The jab at Sunday churchgoers is misplaced: those "most people" are Macdonald. He knew Day wasn't a crackpot; still, he wasn't sure what she was. He didn't find her serenity consoling; he found it discomfiting.

Bernard Taper had something of the same flustered, deeply admiring response to Thurgood Marshall when he flew with him from New York to Atlanta in the winter of 1956, to attend a meeting of the NAACP. "He is a tall, vigorous man of forty-seven, with a long face, a long, hooked nose above a black mustache, and heavy-lidded but very watchful eyes," Taper wrote about the man who had argued *Brown v. Board of Education*, in 1954. Two years later, Marshall was serving as the NAACP's special counsel. On the flight, Taper orders a Scotch and soda; Marshall, observing Lent with an amused abstemiousness, drinks a cup of coffee. Taper expects Marshall to be furious and impatient and terrified he'll be killed; he isn't. Instead, Marshall, lighting one cigarette after another, is mainly worried that smoking won't be allowed at the upcoming meeting. Taper: "Of all the worries that might beset a Negro leader setting out for Georgia, this was one I had not anticipated." At the meeting in Atlanta, Taper watches as delegates from every state report on the state of school desegregation. "West Virginia was doing extremely well," he wrote. "The news from Arkansas, Kentucky, and Texas was rather less encouraging." In the face of this, Taper is only more awed by Marshall's faith:

"The concreteness, the calm, the serene feeling of assurance that the law would eventually prevail—these I had definitely not expected." Taper thought Marshall would be edgier, angrier. How could he be so cool?

Accounting for the challenge to segregation and the rise of the national-security state hadn't exactly been in the brief of Harold Ross's *New Yorker*. "I guess *The New Yorker* hangs on, but it is a hell of a different magazine from the one I went to work for in the twenties," E. B. White wrote in 1950, the year *The New Yorker* celebrated its twenty-fifth anniversary. "Ross worries about this constantly but always ends with the remark: 'Ah Jesus Christ it's still worth 20 cents.'" But long before Ross's death, in 1951—beginning, really, with the war in Europe—the magazine had been covering politics and the world. Richard Rovere started writing his Letter from Washington in 1948. The idea had come from William Shawn, who told Rovere not to write like a reporter. "I should not, he said, think of myself as being in competition with *Time* or *Newsweek* or the dailies; they were in the news business, and we were not," Rovere later explained. "My job in Washington was not to 'report' on the White House or anything else—except in the way that a reviewer might 'report' on a book."

Rovere wrote as an outsider. He didn't live in Washington. He lived in upstate New York, with his wife and three kids. Every few weeks, he'd take the sleeper to D.C. and stay for a day or two. Like Thurber, blowing his stack over the "classificatory degradationists" who talked, unendingly, about creeping Socialists, ritualistic liberals, massive retaliationists, agonized reappraisalists, and unorthodox thinkers, Rovere knew his left from his right, but he didn't have much use for political taxonomy. He'd always wanted to study eighteenth-century English literature; he liked farce. "Lack of excitement and inspiration is, of course, the general rule at political conventions, and more often than not any enthusiasm manifested is contrived and bogus," Rovere wrote from the Democratic Convention in Chicago in 1956. "Still, there is more to politics than rhetoric and stage management," he wrote from the Republican Convention, later that summer, in San Francisco, "and the key political fact about the gathering now breaking up is that it has made Richard M. Nixon the symbol, if not the center, of authority in the Republican Party." The reward, reading Rovere, is appreciating the acuity with which he could see, past the swagger, what was genuinely at stake. "People have been bothered by Nixon without being able to say precisely why," he wrote. Then, there's his evenhandedness. The civil-rights planks on both 1956 party platforms, he explained, "scarcely go beyond acknowledging that the Founding Fathers saddled us with the United States Supreme Court and that we are obliged to honor its decisions—though not necessarily today or tomorrow."

Tomorrow came soon enough. In the fall of 1957, Rovere took the sleeper to Washington again, after Eisenhower sent troops from the 101st Airborne Division to Little Rock, where the governor had deployed the National Guard to prevent nine black children from attending a city high school. "He doubtless reckoned, as almost everyone here reckons, that it was a mite better to uphold the courts with bayonets than not to uphold the courts at all," Rovere wrote about the president. Still, "there is a taint on justice whenever it has to be enforced at the point of a gun."

There's an interregnum, in the middle of Taper's Thurgood Marshall piece, during a break in the meeting when most of the delegates go to get dinner at "the Negro Y.M.C.A." It was snowing when Taper and Marshall left New York. In Atlanta, it is hot. Taper goes for a long walk, into a white neighborhood, and ends up eating a sandwich and drinking a beer at a restaurant. In a pretty park across the street, white children are playing in the grass. Time passes. "The sky was pink now, and I started back," Taper wrote. "It was dark by the time I reached the church."

It got darker. Taper had asked Marshall what the NAACP would do if it kept winning in the courts but losing on the streets. "I don't know what we'd do," Marshall answered. "It would be anarchy. It would be the end of the country." Who wouldn't be jumpy?

FROM

THE FOOLISH THINGS OF THE WORLD

Dwight Macdonald

OCTOBER 4/11, 1952 (ON DOROTHY DAY)

MANY PEOPLE THINK that Dorothy Day is a saint and that she will someday be canonized. In 1933, with the late Peter Maurin, a French-born itinerant preacher, who has been affectionately described as "an apostle on the bum" and who advocated "a Utopian Christian communism," she founded the Catholic Worker movement, and, despite her best efforts to the contrary, she still dominates it. She is a rangy woman of fifty-five whose thick gray hair is braided tightly around her small, well-shaped head. High cheekbones and slanting eyes give her a Slavic look, although her ancestry is Scotch-Irish. Her face—patient, gentle, and understanding—might suggest a passive temperament were it not for her wide, mobile mouth and the expression of her eyes, which is at times dreamily remote, at times as naïvely expectant as a young girl's, but always alive. She smiles a good deal when she talks, and she often makes little jokes about herself and her movement. "We Catholics talk about the saints and martyrs, but I've heard it said that the Catholic Workers are made up of the saints, and the martyrs who are willing to live with the saints," she said once. Her own patron saint, after whom she named her only child, is the gay and impetuous Teresa of Avila, who used to pray, "May God deliver me from surly saints." In her sensible shoes and drab, well-worn clothes, Miss Day looks like an elderly schoolteacher or librarian; she has the typical air of mild authority and of being no longer surprised at anything children or book-borrowers may do. She also looks like a grandmother, which she is, for her daughter now has five children. Upon first meeting her, most people who are familiar with her career are surprised to find that, far from being dynamic, she is quiet and almost diffident. Although she has been speaking in public for years, her platform manner is retiring and hesitant, and she makes not even a stab at rhetorical effect. She has no "presence" at all, but in spite of that, or perhaps because of it, she is impressive to meet or hear, communicating a moral force compounded of openness, sincerity, earnestness, and deprecatory humor. She has lived with intellectuals all her adult life, from the time when, at the age of nineteen, she established herself in Greenwich Village society as a writer for radical publications, but she is not one herself. She is more a feeler and a doer than a thinker. Not that she does not constantly deal with ideas, and often most fruitfully, but her mind works by free association rather than logic, and her writings and public talks—"speeches" would hardly be the right word—are as haphazardly put together as her clothes. Her temperament combines mystical feeling and practicality in a way not common in the everyday world but not uncommon in the annals of hagiography.

The physical manifestations of the movement that Miss Day and Maurin founded nineteen years ago consist of the *Catholic Worker,* a monthly paper with an anti-capitalist, anti-Communist viewpoint and a circulation of fifty-eight thousand, together with fifteen so-called Houses of Hospitality, in New York and other cities, here and abroad, and eight communal farms, scattered around the country—a total of twenty-three centers where the homeless are sheltered, the hungry are fed, and the ragged are clothed. New York is the headquarters of the movement, offering benign advice and encouragement to the centers elsewhere but, with the exception of two nearby farms, exercising no direct control over them. The whole organization is operated by perhaps a hundred men and women who give all or most of their time to it without pay, living cheerfully in voluntary poverty. All are lay Catholics, and almost all are under thirty and will presently leave, after a few years of the work, to go into the world again, usually to get married and raise a family, and their places will be filled by new young volunteers. The movement is thus a kind of university, constantly taking in freshmen and graduating seniors. It is also a large family, in which the voluntary and the involuntary poor, the helpers and the helped, live together in the houses and on the farms with no more distinction in the matter of dress, manners, bed, and board than is to be found in any other family. Miss

Day combines the functions of a headmistress—the cheerful glad-handing, the bringing out of shy individuals, the deft restraining of unruly ones, and even the fund-raising—with those of a fond and watchful mother. She writes a lot and travels a lot, trying to persuade people that it is possible even today to live in peace and brotherhood, and recruiting new members for her staff. Wherever she is and whatever else she does during the day, she always spends from one to two hours in prayer and meditation; her religion is the center of her life, and it is significant that the one touch of luxury in dress she permits herself is a handsome black lace mantilla she sometimes wears to Mass.

By now, Catholic Worker alumni and alumnae are numerous, and their ideas have acted as a leaven on the American Catholic community. There are not many nuns and priests in the United States who have not heard of Dorothy Day. Not long ago, her old friend Mary Heaton Vorse, the labor reporter, was visiting a patient in a small Catholic hospital in Anderson, Indiana, and when the nursing sisters there learned that she knew Miss Day, they crowded excitedly around her, eager to hear more about this woman they all knew and admired by reputation. Although, on principle, Miss Day makes no effort to convert people to her cause, she is an extremely successful evangelist. The effect she produces has been described in this excerpt from a letter written by one of her disciples:

> I was a year out of Harvard, working in Boston, and had been reading the *Catholic Worker* a few months. Dorothy came to Boston and gave a talk at the local C.W. headquarters, a dingy room on lower Washington Street. Before she was through, I had made up my mind. There was nothing spectacular about her oratory—in fact, technically, she was a rather poor speaker. It was a conversational style that stumbled at times but could be enormously direct and forceful. But I think what persuaded me to make a decision that turned my whole life upside down was the fact revealed to me of a humorous, civilized, honest person who was doing a Christian piece of work and having a good time doing it. . . . So, though I had had no such intention when I went to the meeting, I joined up.

The Catholic Workers are religious in a way that is hard for most people even to understand, let alone sympathize with. They practice their faith on Mondays, Tuesdays, Wednesdays, Thursdays, Fridays, and

Saturdays, as well as on Sundays. An eminent theologian has written that for the Anabaptists and Methodists, sects that the Catholic Workers in some ways resemble, religion ceases to be "a matter of outward forms and ordinances" and becomes "an affair of the heart." For the Catholic Workers, too, religion is an affair of the heart, but, far from wanting to free themselves from outward forms and ordinances, they infuse their zeal into their reception of the sacraments and gladly accept the Pope's authority. As one of their admirers recently put it, "Their inner light is refracted through the hard, intricately cut prism of Catholic dogma." This does not mean that they hold Catholics to be any better than anyone else; indeed, on one occasion, Miss Day, in drawing up a list of six of "our representative thinkers and strugglers," named not only the Catholic Saint Vincent de Paul, Saint Francis of Assisi, and Baron von Hügel but three non-Catholics—Gandhi, Tolstoy, and Martin Buber. Catholic Workers believe quite literally in the supernatural. One of their paper's editors, for example, in describing a performance of Gounod's *Faust* he had attended, wrote that he had found it "a terrifying ordeal" because of the way Mephistopheles carried on. "That creature with his machinations took on a lifelike reality," the editor reported, and added that before he retired that night, he took the precaution of sprinkling holy water on his bed. Miss Day knows how the man felt. "I believe in devils as I do in angels," she once wrote in the *Commonweal*.

In some ways, the Catholic Workers do not see eye to eye with their ecclesiastical leaders, a fact that has led to much curious speculation among sideline observers. "How do they stay in the Church?" is the question most often asked about the organization, the runner-up being "What does Spellman think of them?" The latter question, at least, cannot be authoritatively answered, for the Cardinal has maintained a discreet silence on the subject. Like his predecessor, the late Cardinal Hayes, he has endorsed their works of mercy, but he will not be drawn further. Some time ago, at a reception, Miss Day tried. She asked him outright how he felt about the Workers. "You'll find that many of the bishops are on your side," the Cardinal answered, with a diplomatic smile. He could not have been pleased when the *Catholic Worker* attacked him, three years ago, for breaking a gravediggers' strike in a local Catholic cemetery, and added injury to insult by raising funds to meet the rent and grocery bills of the strikers, who were, incidentally, pious Catholics themselves. On most secular issues, from pacifism to psychoanalysis, the

Cardinal and the Workers disagree. Perhaps one reason he doesn't "do something about it," as some people keep expecting him to, is that his disciplinary and supervisory powers over laymen are more limited than many non-Catholics realize. Like the Pope's, they are confined to sitting in judgment on such "matters of faith and morals" as divorce and contraception and ruling on cases of error in connection with such theological dogmas as the Immaculate Conception and the recently proclaimed Assumption of the Virgin. It is true that, as Archbishop of New York, the Cardinal exercises much the same authority over his diocese as the Pope does over the whole Church (any layman has the right to appeal to Rome, but Rome almost always backs up its bishops); it is also true that by stretching a point, or several points, he might get the Workers on a faith-and-morals charge, since they not only advocate radical ideas—not in itself prohibited—but edge into theological territory by presenting these ideas as a logical development of Catholic doctrine. However, he has stayed his hand, whether from conscience or from expediency or because the Church is a house of more mansions than are dreamed of in Paul Blanshard's philosophy.

This is not to say that the Workers' relations with the Chancery—the administrative offices of the diocese, which occupy the old Whitelaw Reid house, across Madison Avenue from St. Patrick's—are always smooth. For a Catholic, a summons to the Chancery is a summons to the headmaster's study. Miss Day has received three such summonses. Once, it was because a priest who had conducted a retreat—that is, a gathering for the purpose of prayer, meditation, and instruction—at one of the organization's farms had fallen into the error of "too vigorous spirituality" through the vehemence with which he denounced liquor, lipsticks, and the movies. Once, it was because some influential laymen had complained about the Workers' anti-capitalist propaganda. In both these instances, Msgr. Edward R. Gaffney, one of the diocesan Vicars-General, simply notified her of the complaints and added his personal admonition. The third time was more serious. In 1948, the *Catholic Worker* advised young men not to register for the draft. Although this was clearly illegal, the editors didn't hear from the F.B.I., but they did hear from Msgr. Gaffney, who summoned Miss Day and "corrected" her—that is, ordered her to cease and desist, which she did.

On a number of occasions, the Workers feel, the Chancery has also exerted indirect pressure. They believe, for example, that its influence was a factor in the removal of the *Catholic Worker* from sale in many Catholic churches in the city when the paper refused to support Franco in 1938. To cite another instance of polite animosity, at one time the Workers' local House of Hospitality was in a building on Mott Street that they rented from a woman active in Catholic charities, and when it was sold, in 1949, they were not offered an opportunity to bid on it. Obliged by the change of ownership to look around for other quarters, the Workers arranged to buy a building from the Paulist Fathers, but at the last minute the deal fell through—because, the Workers are convinced, the Chancery forbade the Fathers to sell. (The New York Workers finally bought their present House of Hospitality, at 223 Chrystie Street, from an Oriental.) There was also the case of the late Father Onesimus Lacouture, a French-Canadian priest who used to hold a famous retreat that was extremist in tendency and greatly influenced the Catholic Workers. His teachings were attacked as Jansenism (a seventeenth-century French heresy similar to Puritanism), and he was accused of exalting grace to far above nature, of overstressing the supernatural, and of "putting the natural to death"—in a word, of being *too* spiritual. Perhaps a weightier, though unexpressed, objection was that by implication he criticized the higher clergy for drinking, smoking, and living luxuriously instead of sharing their food with the hungry and taking the homeless into their episcopal dwellings. At any rate, the hierarchy finally "silenced" Father Lacouture (as it has also silenced a very different sort of priest, Father Coughlin)—in other words, he was forbidden to teach or preach his special doctrines, though he could still perform the ordinary duties of a parish priest.

For all her brushes with authority, however, Miss Day is a Catholic first and a radical second. "The hierarchy permits a priest to say Mass in our chapel," she remarked to a friend not long ago. "They have given us the most precious thing of all—the Blessed Sacrament. If the Chancery ordered me to stop publishing the *Catholic Worker* tomorrow, I would."

The *Catholic Worker* was started, as the name suggests, as a competitor of the Communist *Daily Worker,* and it was no accident that most of its first issue, in 1933, was distributed in Union Square on May Day. In their maiden editorial, which asked, in effect, "Why should the Devil have all the good tunes?," Maurin and Miss Day wrote, "It's time there was a Catholic paper printed for the unemployed. The fundamental aim of most radical sheets is conversion of its readers to radicalism and atheism. Is it not possible to be radical and not atheist?" The Church's social program is contained largely in two papal encyclical letters—the *Rerum novarum,* of Leo XIII (1891), and the *Quadragesimo anno,* of Pius XI (1931). These rebuke the greed of unrestrained capitalism, encourage labor unions, and in general put the interests of the worker above the interests of private property. "Our job is to make the encyclicals click," Maurin once said.

In the thirties, the Catholic Workers were in the thick of events and Miss Day, despite a solid Republican and Episcopalian family background, was in the thickest of them. Whenever she could spare the time, she was out in the streets selling copies of the *Catholic Worker.* "Selling the paper in front of Macy's . . . made one indeed look the fool," she later noted in her autobiography, *The Long Loneliness,* which was published by Harper early this year. (Looking the fool has never bothered Miss Day, one of whose favorite quotations is Saint Paul's pronouncement: "The foolish things of the world hath God chosen, that He may confound the wise.") In a single year—1936—she travelled to Detroit to report on and help along the sitdown strikes out of which came the United Automobile Workers; to Lowell, Massachusetts, where there was a textile strike (the Catholic Workers fed the pickets and supported the strike so enthusiastically that the mayor of Lowell phoned the Chancery in Boston to check up on this crowd of Catholics who were making a noise like Communists; the Chancery reassured him—firmly, if with resignation—that they were Catholics, all right); to Pittsburgh, where the C.I.O. was beginning to organize steel (she and Mary Heaton Vorse, the labor journalist, took a hotel room for a dollar and a half a day and visited every liberal priest in the district, including old Father Adalbert Kazincy, who had been almost alone among the Catholic clergy in backing the 1919 steel strike but now had many priests to keep him company); to Akron, where the rubber workers were striking; to Birmingham, where more steel workers were organizing; and to the Gulf Coast, where there was "trouble" in the shrimp fisheries. That year, the Catholic Workers in New York City spent thousands of dollars feeding and lodging pickets during the seamen's strike that led to the establishing of the National Maritime Union; the fact that Joseph Curran, who became the head of the union, and most of the other leaders were then enjoying active support from the Communists didn't bother them at all. In March, 1937, the Association of Catholic Trade Unionists was formed around a kitchen table in one of the Workers' early headquarters.

• • •

The varied and strenuous activities Miss Day engaged in at that time were not of a kind likely to give comfort to the other members of her family, but then few of her activities ever have been. In the eyes of her father, she was a black sheep almost from the start. She was born in Brooklyn Heights in 1897, the daughter of John I. Day, a peripatetic sportswriter, who later became racing editor of the *Morning Telegraph* and who was instrumental in establishing the Hialeah race track in Florida. Essentially a conservative, Mr. Day contrived to combine respectability with journalism, as have his three sons; one of them is managing editor of the New York *Journal-American,* another is publicity director of the Thoroughbred Racing Association, and the third was, for many years, Riga correspondent for the Chicago *Tribune.* There were also two daughters, one of whom early settled down to married life in Rye. The other found the family pattern unsatisfying. "There was never any kissing in our family, and never a close embrace," Miss Day says in her autobiography. "There was only a firm and austere kiss from my mother every night. . . . We were like most Anglo-Saxons. We could never be free with others, never put our arms around them casually. We were never handholders. We were always withdrawn and alone, unlike Italians, Poles, Jews." Unable to embrace her parents, Miss Day embraced the poor and oppressed. As a young girl in Chicago, where her father was then sports editor of *Inter Ocean,* she began reading radical literature. "Kropotkin especially brought to my mind the plight of the poor, of the workers . . . and made me feel that . . . my life was to be linked to theirs," she writes. "I had received a call, a vocation, a direction to my life. I felt, even at fifteen, that God meant man to be happy." In 1914, shortly before her seventeenth birthday, Miss Day entered the University of Illinois on a scholarship, which she supplemented by caring for children and doing housework. There she joined the Socialist Party—"I was in love with the masses," she says—and made a close friend of a classmate and fellow-rebel, the wealthy and brilliant Rayna Prohme, who later became a Communist, worked with Michael Borodin in China in the middle twenties, died at the age of thirty-three in Moscow, and ended up as the romantic heroine of Vincent Sheean's *Personal History.* In 1916, after two years at the university, Miss Day moved with her family to New York, where her father had taken the job on the *Telegraph.* Soon after they arrived, she went to work as a reporter and columnist on the Socialist *Call.* Her father, who disapproved of career women and was definitely not in love with the masses, tried without success to persuade the editor to fire her. She rented a room on Cherry Street, in the slums of the lower East Side, and never again lived with her family.

On her own at nineteen, Miss Day spent the next ten years in the tumult of Greenwich Village life, which in those days, under the newly ascendant stars of Marx and Freud, was often very tumultuous indeed. The job on the *Call* was followed by one with the Anti-Conscription League; the United States was at war with Germany by then, and she was assigned the enjoyable task of pasting "peace" stickers on the venerable façade of the Union League Club. Presently, she joined the Industrial Workers of the World, because she liked its anarchistic verve and shared its members' distrust of Marx. In the summer of 1917, she became Floyd Dell's assistant on the *Masses,* a lively radical monthly that he and Max Eastman were editing. Her job ended that fall, when the magazine was suppressed and Eastman indicted under the Espionage Act. She was one of about sixty women who in 1917 picketed the White House in protest against the treatment of some suffragettes who had been imprisoned in Washington after staging a demonstration; a batch of the pickets, Miss Day among them, were arrested and sentenced to terms of up to six months in a women's workhouse, where they were manhandled until they staged a hunger strike. Her next job was on the *Liberator,* which Max Eastman's sister Crystal was running as a successor to the *Masses.* Miss Day liked it there well enough but says she found it "more fun to hang around the Provincetown Playhouse, on Macdougal Street, where Eugene O'Neill and others of my friends had plays in rehearsal." The crowd also hung around a Village saloon called the Golden Swan. ("It was a crowd that did a lot of sitting around," according to Miss Day.) In the back room, O'Neill could easily be persuaded to recite "The Hound of Heaven" to the assemblage, which often included the Hudson Dusters, a local gang of mildly sinister repute.

Miss Day spent 1918 as a probationary nurse at Kings County Hospital. ("I hate being Utopian and trying to escape from reality," she wrote to a friend at the time. "Now that we are in the thick of the war and there is so much to be done, I might as well try to do it instead of sitting around playing at writing. And what is my writing now but book reviews, editing, toying with a novel of social significance?") When the war ended, she returned to her Village haunts, throwing herself into the life there with the adventurous ardor that has always been characteristic of her, and without which she almost surely would not have had the courage to start so thankless an enterprise as the Catholic Worker movement. “We made friends with the world,” she says, recalling how she and her companions used to pick up interesting-looking strangers in Washington Square and take them home to dinner. “Dorothy did some foolish things, but she was always protected by the armor of innocence,” one of her acquaintances of that period said the other day. Floyd Dell once described her as “somewhat elfin—that is, not quite human—and very friendly, with a sort of pre-adolescent charm. She was an awkward and charming young enthusiast, tall and slim, with beautiful slanting eyes.” A young poet wrote about her eyes in the *Masses,* and the sitters-around thought she looked like the famous bust of the Egyptian queen Nefretete. Her admirers included Donn Byrne, who later became a novelist, and Mike Gold, then as now a dedicated Communist, to whom she was engaged for several years. They never got married, because Gold, whose ideas on family life were completely bourgeois, thought she was too flighty to make a good mother and housewife.

• • •

In the early twenties, Miss Day divided her time between New York and Chicago, working as a reporter, a proofreader, a librarian, and, during one interlude, a clerk at Montgomery Ward’s. She also underwent one of the most painful experiences of her life when, the victim of a ghastly series of coincidences, she was arrested in Chicago on a charge of prostitution. This occurred one night when she went to stay with a woman friend who, down on her luck, had been exhibiting suicidal tendencies and had taken refuge in a local I.W.W. lodging house ordinarily reserved for visiting male members of the organization. Unfortunately, as Miss Day discovered later, the woman had a police record as a prostitute, and, even more unfortunately, some of United States Attorney General A. Mitchell Palmer’s “Red raiders” stormed the wobblies’ headquarters that night. Finding two women there, the police decided that prostitution would prove to be a tougher rap than revolution, and booked them accordingly. After four days in a cell with a number of real and quite unrevolutionary prostitutes, whom she came to like, if not admire, Miss Day got out on bail, and the case was subsequently dropped. The episode intensified her lifelong sympathy for the underdog.

While holding down her various jobs, Miss Day was writing on the side, and in 1923 A. & C. Boni published her first novel. It was about Village life (the hero and heroine lived in a loft they made habitable by painting everything orange and black), and it was neither a popular nor a critical success. But the Bonis had titled it *The Eleventh Virgin,* and they sold it to Hollywood on the strength of the name. When the movie people got around to reading it, they found the sex—or pay dirt—was all in the title, so they had a completely new story written; then they changed the title. However, the author got twenty-five hundred dollars out of it, which she used to buy a cottage on the shore of Raritan Bay, at Huguenot, Staten Island, where there was a colony that included, as residents or regular visitors, the Kenneth Burkes, the Malcolm Cowleys, Hart Crane, and Mike Gold. Miss Day had just met and fallen in love with a young biology instructor named Forster Batterham, and in 1925 they began living together, in a common-law marriage, in her cottage. The following year, she finished a second novel, about two sisters who were in love with the same man, which was bought by the Bell Syndicate people for newspaper serialization under their title, *What Price Love?*

In March, 1927, Miss Day had a baby, whom she named Teresa. In her autobiography she tells how the birth of her child led her—indeed, compelled her—to become a Catholic. "Forster had made the physical world come alive for me and had awakened in my heart a flood of gratitude," she writes. "The final object of this love and gratitude was God. No human creature could receive or contain so vast a flood of love and joy as I felt after the birth of my child. With this came the need to worship, to adore. I had heard many say they wanted to worship God in their own way and did not need a Church in which to praise Him. . . . But my very experience as a radical, my whole make-up, led me to want to associate myself with others, with the masses, in praising and adoring God. Without even looking into the claims of the Catholic Church, I was willing to admit that for me she was the one true Church." Batterham felt differently. He was deeply irreligious, his temperament being as naturalistic as hers was spiritual. He shared her sympathy for the oppressed, just as she had come to share his passion for observing and studying nature, but his morality, unlike hers, was firmly grounded on this earth; he felt no need to justify or explain the natural world in terms of religion. Since, as a principled atheist, he would have nothing to do with marriage, she had to choose between leaving him and living in mortal sin. "To become a Catholic meant for me to give up a mate with whom I was much in love," she writes. "It was a simple question of whether I chose God or man. I had known enough of love to know that a good healthy family life was as near to Heaven as one could get. . . . It was not because I was tired of sex, satiated, disillusioned, that I turned toward God. Radical friends used to insinuate this. It was because through a whole love, both physical and spiritual, I came to know God." On December 28, 1927, Miss Day was baptized a Catholic in the Church of Our Lady, Help of Christians, in Tottenville, Staten Island. A year later, she was confirmed and after the ceremony she was invited to tea in the rectory parlor, where an earnest nun with whom she had struck up a friendship was one of the guests. Presently, Miss Day told her friend that she must be getting home to her baby. "Oh, I didn't know you were married!" exclaimed the nun. "I'm not," Miss Day said. The nun hurriedly poured herself another cup of tea.

This momentous step of Miss Day's came as a surprise to most of her friends—there was not a Catholic among them—although a few had been conscious of a streak of piety in her. All through her Village days, she had occasionally gone to Mass, and she had chosen the Bible as her reading during the hunger strike in prison that followed the Washington picketing. Cowley remembers that once she suddenly pulled him into a Catholic church in the Village while Vespers was going on, and that at one point during the service he saw tears running down her face. "Many a time, after sitting in taverns all night, or coming at dawn from a ball at Webster Hall, I went to an early-morning Mass at St. Joseph's Church, on Sixth Avenue," Miss Day herself recalls.

Miss Day's conversion made little immediate change in her external life—aside, of course, from her break with Batterham. She worked with the Anti-Imperialist League, and in 1929 she wrote a play dealing with the conflict between Communism and Christianity. An agent sold it to Pathé Films, and, with her daughter, Miss Day spent three months in Hollywood at a hundred and twenty-five dollars a week. In accordance with the local custom, she was given nothing to do; not in accordance with the local custom, she went to no parties, lived cheaply in the Los Angeles slums, and drove around in a second-hand Model T Ford. When her contract was not renewed, she took her baby and a thousand dollars she had saved from her salary and went to Mexico, where she lived for six months, writing a few pieces for the *Commonweal* but mostly getting accustomed to her new life as a mother and a Catholic. In the summer of 1930, she returned, with Teresa, to her cottage in Staten Island, where she earned a little money by interviewing garden owners for the Staten Island *Advance*. She also tried, fruitlessly, to sell short stories to slick-paper magazines. In the fall of 1932, she and Teresa moved into an East Side tenement. There, on the evening of December 10, 1932, Maurin, a stocky, unkempt man, came to call on her with a letter of introduction from a friend of hers.

• • •

Intellectually, Miss Day and Maurin hit it off right from the start. Maurin had a program—"a Utopian Christian communism"—all thought out; Miss Day had the journalistic experience, the practical approach, and the talent for leadership needed to give reality to his vision. It is possible that without that vision, she would never have been stimulated to put her energies behind the Catholic Worker movement; it is certain that without her practical turn of mind, Maurin would have remained an ineffectual eccentric. And it is unlikely that without her journalistic experience, his message would ever have reached many people. One of Maurin's dreams was the setting up of Houses of Hospitality in cities all over the country, in which the needy could be fed, clothed, and lodged without regard to race or creed. Today, the Catholic Workers maintain such a house at 223 Chrystie Street, and keep a benevolent eye on the operation of fourteen similar houses in twelve other cities. Maurin also advocated a back-to-the-land movement, and while if he were alive he would doubtless feel that the organization still has a long way to go in this respect, the Workers do have eight farms in various parts of the country—including one on Staten Island (Peter Maurin Farm) and another near Newburgh, New York (Maryfarm)—where indigent wayfarers are given shelter and city dwellers who are down on their luck are sent for rehabilitation. Neither of these objectives, rural or urban, would ever have materialized had it not been for Miss Day's gifts as an organizer and her ability to get on with people; it is she who, through the years, has recruited the staffs of young Catholic volunteers who run the houses and farms, living in common poverty with the people they help, and it is she who has raised the funds that keep the Workers going.

Under Miss Day's guidance, the Catholic Workers have devised an inexpensive and effective technique of fund-raising: they pray to Saint Joseph, their patron saint. "We appealed to him for help last month," the editors wrote in the second issue of the *Catholic Worker,* "and within two weeks not only our current printing bill was paid but money was there for the February bill, also." Their creditors pray, too. "The printer called us up this morning wanting to know, affably, when we were going to pay our bill," another editorial reads. "We told him he'd better get busy and pray for it hard." Later, the *Worker* reported, "Enough money has come in to pay $300 to our very forbearing printer, and he says he is still praying." Things get behind sometimes—their grocery bill for the Chrystie Street house has run as high as six thousand dollars, and last fall they discovered that they owed two thousand dollars for flour alone—but sooner or later Saint Joseph is always good for the money. Their credit is solid, and their business relations—with their printer (Rogowski, on Pearl Street), their butcher (Kantor Brothers, on Essex Street), and their grocer (Di Falco, at Mott and Hester)—are friendly to the point of sentimentality; the fact that the first two are Jewish firms doesn't seem to make any difference to Saint Joseph. At the very mention of money, Miss Day grows impatient. "That is all in the hands of Saint Joseph," she once wrote in the *Catholic Worker,* apropos of a particularly huge avalanche of debts that was threatening to engulf the organization. "He is our patron and it is up to him. I haven't any doubt about it. I've seen him perform daily miracles around here."

Some of the miracles are chronic. Twice a year, the Workers print an appeal in their paper, and twice a year they get enough donations, all in small sums, to cover their ordinary running expenses. Others are special, as when the Workers wanted to buy the Newburgh farm. "Miraculously, we were given ten thousand dollars by friends, all the money coming in within a month from half a dozen of our readers," Miss Day recalls. Again, when they were wondering whether they could afford to buy the Staten Island farm, Miss Day asked the Lord for a sign by eleven o'clock one morning, and, sure enough, at ten-thirty someone phoned in offering to lend them three thousand dollars. There was also the time in 1950 when, after months of unsuccessful searching for a new headquarters, they sat down and undertook a novena (a kind of prayer marathon), which led them right to 223 Chrystie Street. Sometimes prayer doesn't get results, but then the remedy is clear. "When things go wrong, we know we are not praying enough," Miss Day says. And sometimes Heaven doesn't respond as expected, or, indeed, as wished—a common failing of supernatural agencies, as Macbeth, for one, discovered. Once, needing a thousand dollars in a hurry, Miss Day prayed for it, and got it when her Staten Island cottage, insured for precisely that amount, promptly burned down. Her gratitude was tempered by her affection for the place, and by the fact that it was worth a lot more than a thousand dollars. "Sometimes I wish God weren't quite so literal," she said later.

. . .

Owing in part to the vast changes that have come over the social scene in the last few years, the Catholic Workers are no longer quite as active in public affairs as they once were, and the circulation of their paper has shown a corresponding slump. It is nevertheless still fairly high—fifty-eight thousand, which is about equal to the combined circulations of the *Nation* and the *New Republic*. It is true that the *Catholic Worker* costs only one cent a copy (and twenty-five cents a year, which gives it the perhaps unique distinction of costing more than twice as much to subscribe to as to buy on the newsstands), and it is also true that "bundle orders," which often end up as throwaways, account for many of the copies, and that the business department is dilatory about culling out lapsed subscriptions. But even if only half the copies get into the hands of interested readers, this is quite an achievement for an uncompromisingly high-brow and extremist paper. It has another distinction that is almost unique among crusading periodicals: It just about breaks even.

The *Catholic Worker* is an eight-page tabloid of approximately the same size as the *Daily News*, which it does not otherwise resemble. Typical front-page banner headlines have included "CHRIST THE KING CAN ALONE RECONSTRUCT THE WORLD," "THE PROBLEM OF WAR AND THE OLD TESTAMENT," "THE COMING COLLAPSE OF MODERN INDUSTRIALISM," "THE NATURE OF MAN," and (in an especially gnomic mood) "SEAMEN GO EVERYWHERE." In its coverage of world events the paper's forte is clearly not spot news, except possibly when it gets hold of something like the Holy Father's Christmas Message. Another difference between it and the *News* is that the *Worker*'s staff is unpaid and unprofessional. (Maurin once got to talking with three enthusiastic young men on Columbus Circle, and brought them down to the Chrystie Street house. One became the paper's bookkeeper, another became its circulation manager, and the third married the assistant editor.)

The *Worker*'s contents are schizoid, accurately reflecting the two aspects of the movement—works of mercy and a concern with ultimate philosophical questions. About half its densely printed columns are given over to reports of happenings in the Catholic Worker "family"—a newborn calf at the Newburgh farm, an interesting new face on the bread line, a chat with Jacques Maritain, the French philosopher and theologian—and to columnists of the chatty, rather than the thoughtful, kind. One of the columnists is Ammon Hennacy, a self-styled "one-man revolution." Hennacy is a lean, elderly Ohioan who operates out of Phoenix, Arizona. A Christian anarchist, he rejects all churches, including the Catholic, which doesn't bother the *Worker* in the least. He supports himself and his family by odd jobs and stoop labor in the fields (he has sent two daughters through college), but, in line with the policy of the paper, his real work is bearing witness against war. He stopped paying a federal income tax after the atomic bomb was dropped on Hiroshima, and every year on the anniversary of that event he does penance by embarking upon a six-day fast. His column chronicles in lively detail his efforts to get his fellow-citizens to picket the tax collector's office with the demand that the government put an end to all military expenditures. The result, to date, is a draw, but the authorities know they've been in a fight. There is nothing personal about it, though, for, unlike many crusaders, Hennacy is a man of gentle good will. Some of his best friends are F.B.I. agents, and on his most recent birthday the wife of one of them baked him a cake.

The other half of the *Catholic Worker* is devoted to philosophical discussions of such topics as original sin, the supernatural basis of values, the evolution of capitalism, and the relevance of Freud, Marx, and Kierkegaard to Catholic doctrine. The juxtapositions of these with the homey items are at times dramatic. In one issue, for instance, Miss Day wrote, "Downstairs the baby is crying while Rita gets her breakfast ready: mashed prunes, baby cereal, and milk, all mixed together deliciously," while in an adjoining column Robert Ludlow, one of her fellow-editors, was ruminating along these lines: "And so it is with war, which cannot be said to be *absolutely* opposed to natural morality during certain periods of history, but which of its nature is contrary to the full realization of a natural morality that is based upon the full potentialities of man's nature." Most readers prefer the prunes to the polemics, and Ludlow's cerebrations sometimes bother even Miss Day. "I stand personally behind everything Bob Ludlow writes, though his way of expressing himself is at times peculiar, to say the least," she told a friend not long ago. "I don't think the majority of our readers know what he is talking about when he says, 'The compulsion to revolt can be explained as a manifestation of the libido.'" This kind of frank criticism is frequent among the members of the *Catholic Worker* staff, and extends even to self-criticism. "I dislike writing, due to my lack of talent," wrote one of its columnists a year ago this month. "It kills you when you haven't got it. Right now, I feel cheated by having to meet a deadline with this tripe when I could be listening to the first game of the World Series."

One characteristic common to the two halves of the paper is length.

Whether the contributors are writing about petunias or existentialism, they share a magnificent unconcern about space; it takes them a thousand words just to get warmed up. Another is Miss Day's column, called "On Pilgrimage," which is easily the paper's most popular feature—an odd composite of Pascal's *Pensées* and Eleanor Roosevelt's "My Day." A good hostess on the printed page as well as off, Miss Day in "On Pilgrimage" is constantly introducing the sublime if not to the ridiculous at least to the commonplace. In one installment, after quoting at length from Newman and Saint Teresa of Avila, she continued, "Every time I am making what I consider a thorough confession—that is, telling tendencies that I wish I could overcome, like eating between meals, indulging in the nibbling that women do around a kitchen—and mention it as a venial sin not only in regard to myself but also to my neighbor who is starving all over the world, the confessor makes no attempt to understand but speaks of scruples. . . . These are tendencies to gluttony, and gluttony is one of the seven deadly sins." Only a person who is deeply thoughtful about religion would be likely to see a connection between nibbling in the kitchen and the seven deadly sins, and it is one of Miss Day's outstanding achievements that she has revived the linking of the serious and the trivial that saints and prophets once did so effectively but that long ago went out of fashion. The union of the everyday and the ultimate is the essence of the Catholic Worker movement; even the paper's routine announcements express it, as in this item: "Saturday Work Days and Discussions at Peter Maurin Farm. April 14: Build up low corner of ploughed field and dig cesspool drainage ditch. Discussion: 'No one ever stayed on the land when he could have gone to the city, without a supernatural motive.'"

• • •

Back in the days when the Catholic Workers were playing a conspicuous part in the labor movement, the fight for racial justice, and in the political struggle with the Communists, their paper was full of news and opinion about such matters. Today, when the Workers are less active in these fields, the paper reflects the change. "Many a priest who became famous for his interest in labor," Miss Day says in her autobiography, "felt we had deserted the cause of the union man . . . had departed from our original intention and undertaken work in the philosophical and theological fields that might have been better left to the clergy. . . . Labor leaders felt that in our judgment of war, we judged them also for working in the gigantic armaments race, as indeed we did. Ours is, indeed, an unpopular front." Miss Day might have gone on to point out that, strictly speaking, the Workers did not desert the union man so much as the union man deserted them, partly because he no longer needed their help, partly because in a period of war and disillusionment their radical purity at best bored and at worst shocked him. Their pacifism, for example, was no embarrassment in the thirties, when liberals and Leftists thought in terms of "merchants of death," but in the decade after Pearl Harbor, when "arsenals of democracy" became a more popular phrase, the *Catholic Worker*'s circulation declined slowly but steadily from a hundred thousand in 1939 to its present fifty-eight thousand. The number of Houses of Hospitality has also dwindled, from thirty in 1940 to fifteen today, largely because with the full employment that is the consequence of a chronic state of war, the need for them has become less acute.

Such has been the general trend—a trend with economic overtones. The decline in the popularity of the *Catholic Worker* began, however, with a head-on clash between expediency and principle, in which the Workers, as they always do, clung to principle. The conflict arose over their stand on the Spanish civil war. From the beginning of that war, the entire Catholic hierarchy and the bulk of the lower clergy and the Catholic laity supported Franco, as the champion of religion against infidel Communism and anarchism. The only Catholic publications in New York that refused to support him were the *Worker* and the *Commonweal,* both of which took a neutral position. "There is much right and much wrong on both sides," the *Catholic Worker* editorialized in September, 1936. "Our main concern is that 'the members of Christ tear one another.' This is not a condemnation. It is a cry of anguish, the sob of one who sees his brother in agony." Three months later, the Workers devoted the whole front page of their paper to a translation of an article, written by a Spanish Catholic, which had appeared in *Esprit,* a French radical Catholic magazine, and condemned both sides in the civil war. The Workers' was, indeed, an unpopular front.

Popular or unpopular, the work goes on, and Miss Day goes on with it. "In the last two months, I have visited twenty-seven cities, from Fall River, Mass., to Fargo, North Dakota," she wrote in the *Catholic Worker* last autumn. "I have been bone-tired and mind-tired. I have slept on buses and trains, on boards and beds, in rooms with babies, in dormitories, in solitary splendor. I have eaten in homes where elegance is the rule and at Houses of Hospitality with men from skid row." The only real vacation she has taken since the organization of the Workers was during parts of 1943 and 1944, when she felt that after ten years of uninterrupted work it was spiritually necessary for her to renew acquaintance with herself and with God by meditation. She spent six months in a convent and another six months living quietly in the country with her daughter, who by that time had married and set up housekeeping on a farm in Virginia. A priest told Miss Day that once having put her hand to the plow, she had no right to withdraw it, but she knew better; she felt that she was not the "indispensable leader," or that if she was, it was high time the movement learned to dispense with her. Since her cross-country trip last fall, she has confined her travels to the East and has pretty much let the Chrystie Street house run itself, spending only a night or so a week in the tiny hall bedroom that is reserved for her there. Most of her time has been divided between Peter Maurin Farm and her daughter's present home, a mile down the road; Teresa now has five children of her own, and Miss Day helps with them and with the housework. She is also engaged in writing a book—a biography of Saint Thérèse of Lisieux, a nineteenth-century Carmelite nun. "The sophisticates don't like her," Miss Day says. "They think she is flowery and sentimental. But the common people like her, and so do I."

• • •

"Where there is no love, put in love and you will take out love," wrote Saint John of the Cross. The Catholic Workers quote this and believe it. Usually it works, but when it doesn't, they are not resentful, since they consider love an end and not a means. Some years ago, they rented an apartment in Cleveland to shelter single women; a homeless married couple was temporarily admitted; once in, they wouldn't move out or let anyone else in. The Workers, although they had paid the rent in advance, sighed and looked for another apartment. Perhaps the saddest experience they have had was with their first communal farm, near Easton, Pennsylvania, which, as the years passed, was more and more taken over by down-and-out families, who came to consider the place theirs and to resent the Workers' using it at all. At last, the Workers sold half the farm and gave the rest to the families who had preempted it.

The Workers' abhorrence of coercion extends even to proselytizing. They never ask the religion of the people they help, and the men on the bread line don't have to pray or sing psalms to get fed, nor do their boarders (whose favorite paper is the *Daily News,* not the *Catholic Worker*) have to attend the two brief daily services held in the Chrystie Street house. Any discipline makes Miss Day uneasy. John Cort, a former disciple of the Workers and now a C.I.O. official and labor columnist, once lived with ten other men on the top floor of the old Mott Street house. "Some of them slept late, left their beds in a mess, and shirked their turn to sweep up," he has since recalled. "Finally, I typed out three rules and posted them: 'One, everybody out of bed by 9 A.M. Two, each man is expected to make up his own bed. Three, each man is expected to take turns sweeping up.' One of the fellows there felt these rules were a violation of personalism, a doctrine of inner discipline that Dorothy and Peter were strong for. We took it to Dorothy—the Abbess, as some of us called her—and she agreed with him. The rules came down. I think it possible that she really agreed with me but ruled for this other guy because he was excited about it and she felt his faith in the movement was more brittle than mine. She herself was personal all the way, and she often decided things on a personal basis."

Some of the Workers have at times found freedom oppressive. One of the most energetic toilers on the Easton farm once went on strike because he didn't have a boss. Sitting down under a tree, he announced, "I won't work until someone asks me to and tells me what to do." No one did, and after a time he gave up and grumpily picked up his hoe again. Maurin used to do a lot of heavy work, like breaking rocks for making roads; sometimes he went so far as to leave mauls lying around in conspicuous places, but if no one took the hint, he just swung all the harder. More practical and less principled than Maurin, Miss Day admits that when she gets "really desperate," she actually asks members of her staff to do this or that. If they refuse, however, there is no penalty. "I could stay in my room all day reading or just sitting and no one would say anything," one of her present crop of Workers said not long ago. "After a month, they might act a little cold toward me, of course."

As Cort's story indicates, Miss Day does have a certain authority, but it is an authority that is yielded to her voluntarily, out of love and respect—all too voluntarily, from her point of view, for she is a leader whose chief worry is that her followers have too great a tendency to follow. "Low in mind all day, full of tears," she wrote one evening in 1936 in a journal she has kept since she was a girl. "What with Easton, New York, Boston, Ottawa, Toronto, and Missouri groups all discouraged, all looking for organization instead of self-organization, all weary of the idea of freedom and personal responsibility—I feel bitterly oppressed. I am in the position of a dictator trying to legislate himself out of existence. They all complain that there is no boss. Today I happened to read Dostoevski's 'Grand Inquisitor,' most apropos. Freedom—how men hate it and chafe under it, how unhappy they are with it!"

In the old days, Miss Day used to look at Maurin in moments of discouragement and, with a groan, say, "Why did you have to start all this anyway?" In a gloomy passage in her journal, she remarks, "Sometimes you get discouraged, there's so little change in people. Those who drank go on drinking, those who were ornery go on being ornery." But faith and hope always rise again in her, no matter how great the despair of the moment, and a few pages farther on she is writing, "The goodness of people makes my heart expand in happiness."

NOTES AND COMMENT

E. B. White

JUNE 12, 1954 (ON THE CASE AGAINST SENATOR MCCARTHY)

THE SENATE, BY a simple majority vote, can remove a committee member from the chairmanship of his committee. We think the Senate, when the proper moment comes, should take a vote on Senator McCarthy. We don't know whether he ought to be removed for malpractice, but he certainly ought to be fired for incompetence. His conduct of hearings, as chairman of the Senate Permanent Subcommittee on Investigations, has succeeded only in making the country less secure, and his concept of internal security has kept America in an uproar just when it should have a firm grip on itself. He has tried, with some success, to change the nature and function of Congressional investigation, giving it almost judicial significance and almost executive force. He has become a one-man F.B.I., with his own sources of information, his own stable of informers, his own set of rules governing what a senator is entitled to have in his possession in the way of documents. He is by temperament a sleuth, not a legislator, and he should join a private-eye squad and leave lawmaking to men of thoughtful mien.

. . .

Whether the Army resorted to blackmail, whether McCarthy and Cohn used improper pressure, are questions that interest everybody. But one thing is quite clear: this is no "squabble" (as it is often called) between the Army and McCarthy. This is the showdown on the country's top problem in internal security. It involves the infiltration of Communists into places where nobody wants them to be, and it involves the infiltration of Senator McCarthy into the institutions that he doesn't approve of and would like to rearrange: the Constitution, the White House, the Army, and the Department of Justice; the press and other forms of "extreme Left Wing" dissent; the two-party system (in which you can call the other side anything you want to except "traitor"); the delicate balance between the three main branches of government; due process; and the nice old idea that a citizen isn't guilty of anything just because someone "names" him as guilty.

• • •

The hearings in Washington are structurally bizarre. The committee sits in solemn style, investigating itself, like a monkey looking for fleas. The members sometimes listen thoughtfully to the testimony. At other times, one of them takes the stand, adds to the testimony, then returns to his seat and broods silently on what he has sworn to. Senator Mundt, presumably a conscientious moderator, has a political stake in the hearings. As far as that goes, every senator on the committee does. The Democratic senators, obviously intoxicated by so gaudy a display of Republican embarrassment, have recently been challenged on the score of bias, and Symington has been asked to disqualify himself—as though there had ever been a remote possibility that a committee consisting of Democrats and Republicans could investigate itself dispassionately. Perhaps something useful will emerge from this harlequinade, but if it does, it simply means that this country is, as usual, sort of lucky.

• • •

Although everyone is interested in the specific charges, Army vs. McCarthy, it seems to us that people are even more deeply concerned with finding the answer to the permanent question about the permanent chairman of that permanent subcommittee; namely, must the country continue to be torn to pieces, day by day, week by week, merely because one quick-witted senator has discovered a way to do it and a reason for doing it? That's what America wants to find out, and only the Senate can come up with the answer. If McCarthy were a medium-sized threat to internal security, if he were a bush-league demagogue, if he had done three or four naughty deeds, involving three or four innocent people, perhaps the Senate would be justified in keeping him on in the job. But the Senator's score is imposing and he is not medium-sized—as he well knows. The twenty-years-of-treason junket, the use of the word "guilt" in hearing rooms where nobody is on trial and where no judge sits, the

Zwicker inquisition, the willingness to shatter an army to locate a dentist, the sly substitution of the name "Alger" for the name "Adlai," the labelling of the majority of the press as "extreme Left Wing," the distortion of facts and figures, the challenge of the power of the White House, the use of the grand elision in the phrase "Fifth Amendment Communist," the queer notion that he, and he alone, is entitled to receive raw information that it is illegal for others to have in their possession, the steady attack on national confidence and national faith, as though confidence were evil and suspicion were good—the score is familiar and need not be recited in its long detail. Whatever else can be said for and against the Senator, it has become obvious that he dislikes a great many things about our form of government. To disapprove of these well-loved principles and rules is not a crime, but neither is it a help in performing the duties of a committee chairman in the United States Senate.

THE PSYCHOSEMANTICIST WILL SEE YOU NOW, MR. THURBER

James Thurber

MAY 28, 1955 (ON FIFTIES JARGON)

I BELIEVE THERE ARE no scientific investigators that actually call themselves psychosemanticists, but it is surely time for these highly specialized therapeuticians to set up offices. They must not be carelessly confused with psychosomaticists, who study the effects of mental weather upon the ramparts of the body. The psychosemanticists will specialize in the havoc wrought by verbal artillery upon the fortress of reason. Their job will be to cope with the psychic trauma caused by linguistic meaninglessness, to prevent the language from degenerating into gibberish, and to save the sanity of persons threatened by the onset of polysyllabic monstrosititis.

We have always been a nation of categorizationists, but what was once merely a national characteristic is showing signs of malignancy. I shall not attempt to discover the incipient primary lesion, for I am not a qualified research scholar in this field. Indeed, for having had the impudence to trespass thus far I shall no doubt be denounced by the classificationists as a fractional impactionist (one who hits subjects a glancing blow), an unauthorized incursionist, a unilateral conclusionist, and a presumptuous deductionist. Our national predilection for ponderous phraseology has been traced by one authority as far back as the awkward expression "taxation without representation" (unjust impost). It is interesting to note that the irate American colonists of that period in our history would be categorized today as "anti-taxation-without-representationists."

Not long ago, for the most recent instance in my collection, Senator Lyndon Johnson was described by a Washington newspaperman as a pragmatic functionalist, a term that was used in a laudatory sense. It isn't always easy nowadays to tell the laudatory from the derogatory at first glance, but we should be glad that this Democratic leader is not a dogmatic divisionary or an occlusive impedimentarian. The most alarming incidence of verbal premalignancy occurs, of course, in this very area of politics, but let us skip over such worn and familiar double-jointedisms as creeping Socialists, disgruntled ex-employees, ritualistic liberals, massive retaliationists, agonized reappraisalists, unorthodox thinkers, unwitting handmaidens (male), to name only a few out of hundreds, and take a look at excessive prewar anti-Fascism, a colossal (I use the adjective as a noun, in the manner of television's "spectacular") that was disgorged a few years ago. Here the classificatory degradationists brought a time element into what might be called the post-evaluation of political morality. The operation of this kind of judgment during and after the Civil War would have thrown indelible suspicion upon all the Northern patriots, including Abraham Lincoln, who wanted Robert E. Lee to take command of the Federal Armies in the field. They would be known today as "overenthusiastic pre-Manassas pro-Leeists."

The carcinomenclature of our time is, to be sure, an agglomerative phenomenon of accumulated concretions, to which a dozen different types of elaborative descriptivists have contributed—eminently the old Communist intellectuals, with their "dialectical materialists," "factional deviationists," "unimplemented obscurantists," and so on, and so on. Once the political terminologists of all parties began to cross-infect our moribund vocabulary, the rate of degeneration became appalling. Elephantiasis of cliché set in, synonym atrophied, the pulse of inventiveness slowed alarmingly, and paraphrase died of impaction. Multiple sclerosis was apparent in the dragging rhythms of speech, and the complexion of writing and of conversation began to take on the tight, dry parchment look of death. We have become satisfied with gangrenous repetitions of threadbarisms, like an old man cackling in a chimney corner, and the onset of utter meaninglessness is imminent.

The symptoms of this ominous condition show up most clearly in the tertiary stage of "controversial figure." The most complicated specimen of this type of modern American is the man of unquestionable loyalty, distinguished public service, and outstanding ability and experience who has nonetheless "lost his usefulness." Actually, this victim of verbositosis has not lost his usefulness, his nation has lost it. It doesn't do the national psyche any good to realize that a man may be cut off in the full flower of his usefulness, on the ground that that is not what it is. I trust I have made the urgent need for psychosemanticists apparent, even though I have admittedly become contaminated in the process, and I doubt whether my own psychosemanticist, after treating me, will ever be able to turn to my wife and say cheerfully, "Madam, your husband will write clearly again."

. . .

Before visiting my hypothetical psychosemanticist for a brief imaginary interview, I feel that I should get something reassuring into this survey of depressing ailments of the tongue. We have, then, cured, or at least survived, various incipient mouth maladies in the past. There was a moment when "globaloneyism," growing out of the Timethod of wordoggle, seemed likely to become epidemic, but it fortunately turned out to be no worse than a touch of pig Latin or a slight case of Knock, Knock, Who's There? Congress was not prepared to adopt the telescoping of words, which takes both time and ingenuity, and unless an expression becomes absorbed by Congressionalese, it has little chance of general survival. This brings me to what may easily be the direct cause of my being bundled off to the psychosemanticist's before long: the beating the word "security" is taking in this great, scared land of ours. It is becoming paralyzed. This is bound to occur to any forceful word when it loses its quality of affirmation and is employed exclusively in a connotation of fear, uncertainty, and suspicion. The most frequent use of "security" (I hate to add to its shakiness with quotation marks, which have taken on a tone of mockery in our day) is in "security risk," "weakest link in our chain of security," and "lulled into a false sense of security." Precision of speech and meaning takes a small tossing around in the last of those three phrases. "Lulled" is actually what happens to a nation after it has been argued, tricked, maneuvered, reasoned, coaxed, cajoled, or jockeyed into a false sense of security, but the inflexibility that has descended upon us has ruled out the once noble search for the perfect word and the exact expression. What Eric Partridge calls "a poverty of linguistic resource" is exemplified by the practically exclusive use of two verbs in any public-forum discussion of national security. It is threatened or it is bolstered; I never heard of its being supported, reinforced, fortified, buttressed, or shored up, and only very rarely is it menaced, endangered, or in jeopardy.

The word "insecurity," by the way, seems to have been taken over by the psychiatrists as their personal property. In politics, as in penology, "security" itself has come to mean "insecurity." Take, for example, this sentence: "He was considered a 'maximum security' prisoner because of his police record and was never allowed out of his cell block." Similarly, "security data" means data of the kind calculated to scare the living daylights out of you, if not, indeed, your pants off. I could prove that "maximum," in the case of the prisoner mentioned above, really means "minimum," but I don't want to get us in so deep that we can't get out. The present confused usage of "security" may have originated with the ancient Romans. Anyway, here is what Cassell's Latin Dictionary has to say about *securitas:* "I. *freedom from care.* A. In a good sense, *peace of mind, quiet,* Cic. B. In a bad sense, *carelessness, indifference,* Tac. II. Transf., *freedom from danger, security,* Tac."

• • •

A vital and restless breed of men, given to tapping our toes and drumming with our fingers, infatuated with every new crazy rhythm that rears its ugly beat, we have never truly loved harmony, the graceful structure of shapes and tones, and for this blindness and deafness we pay the awful price of continuous cacophony. It gets into language as well as music; we mug melody for the sake of sound effects, and the louder and more dissonant they are, the better we seem to like them. Our national veins have taken in the singing blood of Italy, Wales, Ireland, and Germany, but the transfusion has had no beneficial effect. Great big blocky words and phrases bumble off our tongues and presses every day. In four weeks of purposeful listening to the radio and reading the newspapers I have come up with a staggering list, full of sound and fury, dignifying nothing: "automation," "roadability," "humature," "motivational cognition" (this baby turned up in a series of travel lectures and was never defined), "fractionalization," "varietism," "redesegregation," "additive," "concertization" (this means giving a concert in a hall, and is not to be confused with cinematization or televisionization). The colloquial deformity "knowledgeable," which should have been clubbed to death years ago, when it first began crawling about like the late Lon Chaney, has gained new life in recent months. It is a dented derby of a word, often found in the scrawny company of such battered straw hats as "do-gooder," "know-how," "update," "uptake" (I recently uptook the iodine uptake test for thyroidism), and others so ugly and strange I can't decipher them in my notes. One of them looks like "de-egghead," which would mean to disintellectualize or mentally emasculate—a crippling operation approved of by an alarming number of squash-heads, in Washington and elsewhere.

During my month of vigil and research, I heard an able physiologist who has a radio program say, quite simply, "We do not use up all the food we take in." He wasn't allowed to get away with that piece of clarity, however. "Ah," cut in his announcer, for the benefit of those no longer able to understand simplicity, "the utilization factor!" I turned from this station to a droning psychologist, just in time to hear him say, "The female is sometimes the sexual aggressor." Here a familiar noun of mental illness and military invasion was clumsily at work beating in the skull of love with a verbal bung-starter. The sweetheart now often wears the fustian of the sick man and the Caesar. In the evening, I tuned in on one of the space-patrol programs that gleefully exude the great big blockyisms. "Your astrogation bank will tell you!" cried the captain of a space ship to another interplanetary pilot, meaning his navigational instruments. In a fairy tale, an astrogation bank would be a "star panel," but the quality of fairy tale is nowhere to be found in these dime novels of the constellations.

One Sunday morning, my head aching with "kiss-close" and "swivel-chair-it," meaning, I guess, "at kissing distance" and "maul it over in your executive brain," respectively, I stumbled upon a small radio station that had been captured by a man of God, ominous and squealful, who was begging his listeners to live on their knees, not as slaves but as supplicants. This particular fundamentalist, or maybe it is fundamentalitarian, had probably never heard of the great protest "I would rather die on my feet than live on my knees." But these yammering eschatologists, and many of their followers, have even less respect for the glory and grace of English than the unsaved politicians. "Let us cease to sugar-coat, let us cease to whitewash, let us cease to bargain-counter the Bible!" the speaker implored us. He finished second in vulgarity, I regret to say, to a reverend I had heard earlier in the year, who shouted, "I didn't cook up this dish, God cooked it up. I'm just dishing it out to ye!" The line between holiness and blasphemy becomes even thinner when some of the lay testimonialists begin ranting. "I own a shoe store in New Jersey," one of them confessed, "but Jesus Christ is my senior partner."

A recent investigation of the worries and concerns of five thousand selected Americans revealed that we are preoccupied almost wholly with the personal and private, and are troubled only mildly by political anxieties, including the danger of war, the state of civil liberties, and the internal Communist threat. This does not come as a surprise to me, since the nature of our national concern about Communism is proved to be personal by such expressions as "anti-anti-Communists" and "anti-anti-anti-Communists." The first actually means men who are against men who are against Communists, and the second, when you unravel it, means men who are against men who are against men who are against Communists. In these wonderful examples of our love of formidable elaborationisms, concept and doctrine are put aside, and personalities take their place. What we have left is pure personalism—a specific reactionary who is against a specific liberal who is against Senator McCarthy, let us say. The multiplicity of prefixes, another sign of linguistic poverty, was touched with a fine and healthful irony in Quincy Howe's invention of the phrase "ex-ex-Communist." (Many will claim that for their own, but Mr. Howe got to it first.) One would think that Americans would be worried, or at least concerned, by a man who may have ceased to be a man who may have ceased to be a Communist, but the Worry Research I have mentioned showed that this isn't so. We are worried about health, family matters, and money, and we have no time for a man who may be lying about lying. Incidentally, a fairly new advertising slogan, "The portable portable," fits neatly into modern jargon: the typewriter that you can carry that you can carry.

While I was exploring the decline of expression in America, I spent a week in a hospital. Medical science has done much for humanity, but not in the area of verbal communication. It should undergo a prefectomy, and have some of its prefixes taken out. I should like to see the "semi" removed from "semi-private," a dispiriting word that originated in hospitals; there must be a less depressing way of describing a room with two or more beds. I am also for taking the "sub" out of "sub-clinical," and starting all over again with the idea in mind of making the word mean something. Incidentally, I discovered at the hospital the difference between "to be hospitalized" and "to become hospitalized." The first means to be placed in a hospital, and the second has two meanings: to get so that you can't stand it in the hospital any longer, and to like it so much there that you don't want to leave.

Lying in bed brooding over these matters, I turned on the radio and heard an American describe another American as "an old-time A.D.A. type of anti-Jeffersonian radical"—a beautiful specimen of bumblery. Sir Winston Churchill, in the exhilarating years of his public life, turned out many phrases as sharp as stilettos—for one example, "squalid gamin." But you can count on your fingers the Americans, since the Thomas Paine of "the summer soldier and the sunshine patriot," who have added bright, clear phrases to our language. If you can bumble an opponent to death why stab him seems to be the general feeling among our politicians, some of whom have got through the ten years since the war ended with only five adjectives of derogation: naïve, hostile, unrealistic, complacent, and irresponsible. All these slither easily, if boggily, into bumblery, and the bumbler is spared the tedious exercising of his mental faculties.

The day I got dressed and was about to leave the hospital, I heard a nurse and an interne discussing a patient who had got something in his eye. "It's a bad city to get something in your eye in," the nurse said. "Yes," the interne agreed, "but there isn't a better place to get something in your eye out in." I rushed past them with my hair in my wild eyes, and left the hospital. It was high time, too.

• • •

When and if I find a reputable psychosemanticist, I want to take up with him something that happened to me one night more than two years ago. It may be the basis of my etymological or philological problems, if that's what they are—words, especially big ones, are beginning to lose their meaning for me. Anyway, I woke up one summer night, from a deep dream of peacelessness, only to realize that I had been startled by nothing whatever into a false sense of insecurity. I had a desperate feeling that I was being closed in on, that there was a menace in the woods behind my house or on the road in front of it, watchful, waiting, biding its time. A few weeks later I bought a .38-calibre Smith & Wesson police revolver, which startled my wife into a genuine sense of insecurity. She hid the gun somewhere, and the cartridges somewhere else, and I still don't know where they are. I have often thought of telling my psychosemanticist about it, and I sometimes have the feeling that I did call on him and that the interview went like this:

"Doesn't your wife's hiding the gun worry you?" he asked.

"No," I said.

"It would me," he confessed.

"It would *what* you?" I demanded.

It seemed to disturb him. "*What* would what me?" he asked cautiously.

I suddenly couldn't think of a thing. I didn't even know what what was, but I had to say something, so I said something: "Ill fares the land, to galloping fears a prey, where gobbledygook accumulates, and words decay."

I had just reached that Goldsmith paraphrase when a sub-researcher brought me the news from Washington that a movement is afoot in the nation's capital to cut down on bumblery, clarify officialese, and discourage certain platitudes (but not enough), in the wistful hope of bringing grace and meaning to the writing of English by government employees. I was glad to discover "finalize" among the banned gargoyles, but I don't see how the lawyers in Washington are going to get along without "predecease." The reformers, by the way, don't seem to know that this monster spawned an equally clumsy offspring, "survivorship." The main reason for this reform is to save filing space and money, but the economic aspect of the project does not depress me too much. It is a hopeful step in the direction of sense and sanity.

Come on, let's go out and get a breath of fresh air.

FROM

A MEETING IN ATLANTA

Bernard Taper

MARCH 17, 1956 (ON AN NAACP ASSEMBLY)

THERE ARE FEW people in this country today, white or black, who have not become seriously concerned about the school-segregation controversy and the turmoil it has aroused. Like just about everyone else, I have been trying to understand, from stories I have read in the papers and from people I have talked with, what is happening and what is at stake. Early last month, on hearing that the National Association for the Advancement of Colored People was about to hold a regional meeting in Atlanta, Georgia, to assess the turbulent situation, I decided to ask permission to attend it, and I was very glad when, presently, my request was granted. I did not, of course, expect to come back from the meeting with the whole story of race relations in the South. Necessarily, what I heard and saw down there would be one-sided. Even so, the N.A.A.C.P. is the organization that had the most to do, directly, with starting all this; its staff pressed cases involving segregation through the inevitable years of litigation, and argued them before the Supreme Court, and won. What I wanted to find out at first hand was how some of its leaders were taking their victory and what they would make of it. This was to be the first Southern regional meeting since the impact of the United States Supreme Court's order of last May requiring local school boards to desegregate had made itself widely felt. A great deal had happened since then.

My travelling companion on the flight to Atlanta, I was pleased to learn, would be Thurgood Marshall, the N.A.A.C.P.'s Special Counsel and the man who pleaded the segregation cases before the Supreme

Court. He is a tall, vigorous man of forty-seven, with a long face, a long, hooked nose above a black mustache, and heavy-lidded but very watchful eyes. He is about as swarthy as a Sikh, and, in fact, rather resembles one when he is in a fierce mood. His mother is a retired schoolteacher; his father, who died eight years ago, was a waiter in Baltimore. In the last fifteen years, Marshall has attained the stature of a semi-legendary folk hero among his people. At the same time, he has earned the deepest respect of sophisticated jurists and students of the law. Since 1938, as the N.A.A.C.P. Special Counsel, he has appeared before the United States Supreme Court to argue sixteen cases. He has won fourteen of them. This would be an extraordinarily high record under any circumstances, but in the light of the fact that in each case Marshall was appealing a lower court's decision, which lawyers consider a much tougher proposition than defending one, and, moreover, was seeking to persuade the highest court in the land to upset established precedent, it may be a unique record. The undisputed dean of constitutional lawyers in our time was the late John W. Davis, once a Democratic Presidential nominee, but the only occasion on which he and Marshall argued on opposite sides before the Supreme Court, Marshall won. That was in connection with the five school-segregation cases on which the court based its momentous ruling. It is as the result of Marshall's victories before the United States Supreme Court that Negroes have won the right to vote in primaries in the South, the right to be free from Jim Crow restrictions when travelling from one state to another, and, now, the right to attend public schools without suffering segregation on the basis of race. Few living individuals have had a greater effect than Marshall on the social fabric of America. Not a scholarly or academic lawyer himself, he has been given credit for assembling a scholarly, painstaking staff and for knowing how to use their research and ideas creatively. No one denies that he is eloquent. He has made his most telling arguments when he has taken off from dry questions of legal precedent to range over the human and social implications of the matter at hand. Out of court, he is informal, colloquial and pungent in his speech, occasionally moody and brusque, sometimes stormy, and often playful, even at serious moments, but without violating his sense of the seriousness of the moment. His courtroom manner is quite different. At such times, his vivid personality does not become muted, but it does become transmuted. In court, he is deferential, respectful, and of a most imposing dignity. His associates say that this alteration of demeanor is not studied but, rather, stems from a profound, almost religious, respect for the law.

• • •

The meeting was to take place on Saturday, February 18th. Marshall and I were to leave New York Friday afternoon. It snowed all that morning. When I set out for LaGuardia Airport to make a four-thirty-five plane, the sky was bleak. Icicles hung from the grilles of parked cars. The snow, already sooty and impure, lingered on the tops of cabs, on the fenders and running boards of trucks, and on the heaps of upturned earth and broken asphalt beside street excavations, around which the clogged traffic flowed sullenly. The pavements were wet, the gutters full of slush. In Queens, as the airport bus rushed along the highway, a freezing rain began to fall, turning to ice under our tires. It was nasty Northern weather. Lots of people were going South that weekend, the clerk who checked my ticket at the airline's counter at LaGuardia told me, and he didn't blame them a bit.

I found Marshall waiting in the plane. Wearing a double-breasted blue suit, he was slouched in his seat, his long legs crossed. I took off my hat and coat and sat down beside him. There was a brief delay while the wings were deiced, and then the plane taxied out onto the field, paused, and roared down the runway. During the takeoff, Marshall sat hunched at the window, gazing with concentration into the heavily overcast sky, as if contributing his will power to the effort to get us off the ground. After the plane was well in the air, he slumped back like a man who had done his part and was now entitled to relax, unfastened his safety belt, lit a cigarette, put on horn-rimmed glasses, and settled down to reading the New York *Post*. He went through it page by page, picking up the continued stories as he came to them. When he had finished, he offered the *Post* to me and took up the *World-Telegram,* remarking, "Now let's see what the other side has to say." He went through that paper in the same way, impartially devoting as much attention to its pages, including the comics, as he had to the *Post*'s. The tumult over segregation in the South loomed up from both newspapers. Stories and editorials talked of racial strife, of violence and threats of violence. Marshall lit another cigarette. "One thing troubles me about this meeting ahead," he said. "We won't be able to smoke. *That's* gonna hurt. The meeting'll be at a Baptist church. The planning committee got together with Reverend Borders a while back, and he said, 'I won't mind if you smoke.' We all looked real happy. And then he said, 'But God will mind—and it's *His* house.' You should've seen our faces fall. We were *sad*." The recollection of his gloom, and the telling of it, made Marshall quite merry for a moment.

Of all the worries that might beset a Negro leader setting out for Georgia, this was one I had not anticipated. I asked Marshall whether he ever had qualms about his safety when he went South. On several occasions in the past, I knew, he had had some close calls. "I'm a Southerner," he told me. "Born and brought up down there. I know my way around. I don't go looking for trouble. I ride in the for-colored-only cabs and in the back end of streetcars—quiet as a mouse. I eat in Negro cafés and don't use white washrooms. I don't challenge the customs personally, because I figure I'm down South representing a client—the N.A.A.C.P.—and not myself. So up until about six months ago I had no qualms when I started out on one of these trips." He paused, rubbing his long nose, and then said, "But I got 'em nowadays. Those boys are playing for keeps. My wife followed me out to the elevator when I left today, begging me to be careful." His laughter over his wife's concern was fond and slightly wistful. Their marriage had taken place only nine weeks before. (It was Marshall's second marriage; his first wife died a year ago.) "There won't be any trouble in Atlanta, though," Marshall added confidently. "I like Atlanta. That's a pretty civilized town."

It was growing dark outside. The stewardess came along the aisle taking orders for drinks—Scotch-and-soda for me, for Marshall coffee. He seemed to feel that the coffee called for an explanation, and said that, as an Episcopalian, he was observing Lent. "It doesn't hurt to take a month off once a year to prove to myself that I don't need liquor," he added. "Having proved it, I can *really* enjoy the stuff the other eleven months." He removed his glasses and put them in his pocket, and then drank his coffee, gulping it rather joylessly, I thought. I asked him if he'd care to give me some sort of summary of the situation in the South as he saw it. He replied that he did not know what the situation was himself. "That's what I'm going down to find out," he said. "That's what the meeting's about." Didn't the N.A.A.C.P. branches send reports to keep him up to date, I asked. "Some do, some don't," he said. "Some are leery about putting everything they know on paper. And when they phone and hear clicking on the line all the time, they get leery about that, too. I can't blame them. It's not safe to be an N.A.A.C.P. leader in some parts of the South today." He lit a cigarette, then turned toward me and said, "Some of them speak out without hesitation, though. I don't know how they do it. They have more courage than I would have in their place." He bent over and picked up a Manila folder from beside his seat. "Here," he said as he opened it. "Here's a letter I got a while ago from one of our people in South Carolina. Would you like to read it?" The letter, typewritten, was from Levi G. Byrd, correspondent and secretary-treasurer of the Cheraw branch of the N.A.A.C.P., Cheraw, South Carolina. It read as follows:

> Mr. Thurgood Marshall
> 20 West 40th Street
> New York 18, N.Y.
>
> Dear Mr. Marshall:
>
> Just a few words to let you know how things is going arond Cheraw, People is not making Much Fuss hear in Chesterfield County But I am obayen just what the Bible says, I am watching First and Prayen with my Eys Open at all times) (at all Times keeps my Power Dry to pretict my House And my Self, God takes cear of all that tryes to take cear of them self's VERY SORRY THAT I LIVE IN A STATE LIKE THIS BUT WE ARE DETERMED TO MAKE IT A DECEN PLACE TO LIVE FOR OUR CHILDREN ALL THAT COMES AFTER US. BY ABAYEN THE LAW OF OUR GREAT AMERICA AS A WHOLE.
>
> The papers. The State has just Published about the Thugs shooting in Rev. Hintons Home Monday Night, People is so Dum at least some of them We will see just what The Gov. of S.C. Will do about this.Nothing of course
>
> Trust that your Office will I know look after this matter in the right way.
>
> AS LONG AS I AND SOME OTHERS THAT HAVE NINE LIVES THE N.A.A.C.P. WILL NEVER DIE IN S.C. RIGHT WILL WIN.
>
> Trusting that you is injoyen your Married life,. I wish you much sucess and a long life.
>
> Very Truly Yours
> Levi G. Byrd, *Corrisp; Secretary-Treas;*

"Mr. Byrd is quite a man," Marshall said, with undisguised admiration, as he glanced over the letter after I handed it back to him. "He knows what's right and nobody can frighten him. He thinks education's real important. He'd like his children to get some." Marshall looked at the letter again and laughed. "'Trusting that you is *in*joyen your married life,'" he repeated with relish. He peered out the window into the darkness. "Where are we now—somewhere over Virginia, North Carolina? Won't be too long before we're over Mr. Byrd's territory." He stubbed out his cigarette and lit another. I could see why he would have wished God to be a little more permissive about what went on in His house.

Marshall talked of how much the N.A.A.C.P. had grown in the past twenty years, to the point where it now has over five hundred thousand members, most of whom pay annual dues of two dollars. "You know, they didn't use to have people like Mr. Byrd in the N.A.A.C.P.," he said. "The organization used to be much more of an élite affair, with everybody trying to be so refined. I remember when I was a kid"—his eyes suddenly gleamed with humor—"we used to say that N.A.A.C.P. stood for the National Association for the Advancement of *Certain* People. There was a redcap at Grand Central Station who brought more than three hundred members into the organization. Somebody proposed that he be put on the executive board. The other board members were horrified. A *redcap*!" Marshall mimicked them, sighting down his nose and pursing his lips fastidiously. "'What college did this person attend? Who are his family?'" His imitation dissolved in laughter.

I asked who the people were that would be taking part in the Atlanta meeting. "Oh, people of all sorts," Marshall replied. "Lots of lawyers, of course, because the law's what this meeting's about, and a few schoolteachers. And then there'll be the state presidents—one works in a post office, one's an undertaker, another's a dentist. And then there's a college president—let's not go to the other extreme and leave *him* out. When I get to this meeting, I'll not only find out from them what the situation is but also find out what *they* want to do about it, because they're the ones that are gonna have to live with any action that's taken. Then I'll try to figure out how to help them do it. That's my part, actually."

• • •

In the lobby of the terminal, J. H. Calhoun, president of the N.A.A.C.P.'s Atlanta branch, was waiting for us. The lobby was a long, crowded room, but it was not hard to find him. Other than Marshall, he was the only

Negro in sight—a large, carefully dressed man, standing with his hat in hand in the middle of the floor, with a small island of space around him. Under the bright lights, his skin gleamed like burnished ebony. He greeted Marshall warmly but respectfully. Then, with grave courtesy, he shook hands with me. Within a few minutes, other newly arrived N.A.A.C.P. representatives had gathered around us—Robert L. Carter, a slender, youngish attorney with a mustache, who is Marshall's chief assistant in the New York office and who argued some aspects of the school-segregation cases before the United States Supreme Court; a slight, jaunty, tea-colored man named James Stewart, an N.A.A.C.P. official from Oklahoma; and two or three others, whose names I did not catch. The delegates started talking about where they would be staying. The matter was complicated. There are only three hotels for Negroes in the city, and they are not considered very satisfactory, even by those in no position to be choosy. At that, I was told, Atlanta is better off in this respect than many Southern cities, several of which have no public accommodations whatever for transient Negroes. Some of the delegates were going to stay at a Negro motel, some would put up at the Negro Y.M.C.A., and some were to be quartered in private houses scattered through Atlanta's colored districts. Marshall and I were to stay in a dormitory at Atlanta University, a university for Negroes, which is the only place in town where, on an occasion such as this, white and Negro visitors can be sheltered under the same roof without public scandal.

Marshall and I got our luggage and then Calhoun ushered us, along with Carter and Stewart, into his car. After we got under way, Stewart congratulated Marshall on his marriage and chaffed him about it. As we drove along, there was a lot of banter and laughter and high-spirited talk among my companions of going out on the town and having themselves a ball tonight. They sounded like Elks Clubbers or American Legionnaires or any other group of conventioneers who have just got together. Calhoun let Marshall and me out at Atlanta University and then the others drove off down the street. I asked Marshall whether he thought they really were going to make a gay night of it. "They might," he said. "But more likely they'll sit around some place and talk back and forth all night about the problems of the N.A.A.C.P."

The University, a privately endowed institution, has a good academic reputation, I understand, and offers quite a varied curriculum. Its red brick buildings looked solid, clean, and comfortable. As we went into the one where we were to stay, we passed a couple of students sitting on the steps—a young man in shirtsleeves and a girl wearing a white cotton dress. Another couple was sauntering up the front walk. In a lounge off the entrance hall, I glimpsed a group of young men sitting about, engaged in a bull session. It all looked, except for the matter of color, very much like any other American college on a balmy Friday night. An attractive co-ed in a loose striped shirt and a dark skirt signed us in and showed us to our rooms. They were spacious and pleasant. I unpacked and showered, then went down the hall to Marshall's room, where we spent the rest of the evening talking and sipping Cokes before windows wide-open to let in the night air. He talked about how, if he and his wife should have children, they would like to move out of their Harlem apartment to some place in the suburbs, because they felt that New York City was not a good place to raise youngsters.

• • •

It was ten-fifteen when we entered the church's assembly room—a quarter of an hour past the scheduled starting time for the meeting. "What's the matter, Thurgood?" a tall, elegant man, paler than most of the people one sees tanning themselves at Miami Beach, asked with mock severity. "Is there a fifteen-minute time differential between here and New York?" Marshall laughed and said, with a wave of his hand, "Hi, Oliver! How are ya?" One of the staff members began passing out copies of the agenda as Marshall took his place at a table in the front of the room, below a small stage on which stood an American flag. On his left was an empty chair, and beyond it sat Roy Wilkins, a slim man with a handsome, sensitive face, successor to the late Walter White as the N.A.A.C.P.'s executive secretary. On Marshall's right was Carter, his chief assistant.

Addressing the meeting in a conversational voice, Marshall said he wasn't going to waste time making a speech—everybody, he observed, had the agenda and had previously received an outline telling what the meeting was about and stressing that it was facts, not rumors, that were wanted, and so now he would suggest that they elect themselves a chairman and then the delegates from the various states could start giving their reports. By acclamation, the delegates chose the Reverend James M. Hinton, of Columbia, South Carolina, for the job. A short, round-faced man with close-cropped white hair, he took the empty chair between Marshall and Wilkins, named a timekeeper, who was to see that none of the states exceeded the fifteen minutes allotted them for their reports, and said they ought to start out by finding what states were represented. One after another, from here and there in the room, people sounded off: "Alabama!" "Maryland!" "Georgia!" "Mississippi!" Mississippi's name brought a murmur from the delegates. Since this group had last convened, less than a year before, two of that state's Negro leaders who had been urging Negroes to register as voters had been shot and killed and a third had been seriously wounded. One of the killings took place in as public a setting as one could well find in the South—in front of a county courthouse on a Saturday afternoon. No one has yet been indicted for any of these crimes.

"Let's call first for a report from the very fine state of Maryland," the Reverend Mr. Hinton said. From the N.A.A.C.P. viewpoint, the news from Maryland was indeed quite encouraging. The Baltimore School Board had voted to end segregation shortly after the Supreme Court, on May 17, 1954, issued its basic constitutional decision that "in the field of public education, the doctrine of 'separate but equal' has no place" and that "separate education facilities are inherently unequal." Baltimore did not wait, as did most other Southern localities, for the Court's implementation order, announced a year later, which stated that desegregation would be a matter for local school authorities to work out but that they would be required to show "good faith," to "make a prompt and reasonable start toward full compliance," and to move "with all deliberate speed." By the time this order was issued, Baltimore had already accomplished the change. Although the state's county boards are moving more slowly, all of them have announced that they will comply with the Supreme Court's decision, and as far as the N.A.A.C.P. is concerned it is mainly a question of making sure they don't take too long about it. In Baltimore, Negro teachers have been assimilated into the revised school system. Several Baltimore schools, in districts that contain no Negro children, now have Negro teachers in charge of all-white classes.

The man presenting the Maryland report was a rather prosperous-looking attorney named Robert B. Watts. Wearing a gray suit with a vest and a red plaid bow tie, he spoke in an easy, matter-of-fact manner. The only incident of any sort in Baltimore, he went on to say, had occurred at Southern High School, in an industrial section of the city, where the students staged a walkout one day in October, 1954. "It was a very warm day, and I think the kids mainly wanted an excuse to get out of school and into the open air," Watts said. "The police commissioner immediately went on TV and warned parents that it was against the law for the youngsters to stay out of school. He said there'd be some arrests made if they didn't go back. They went back right away." Watts announced that he now had a suit pending in Harford County, seeking a court order to require that county's school board to end school segregation. "Edgewood Arsenal and Aberdeen Proving Ground are both in this county, and there are several non-segregated government housing projects," he told the meeting. "We felt that there was certainly no excuse for continuing segregated schools near these places where the races are housed together and the men work and train together." He added that another suit may have to be filed in St. Marys County, and that it is being prepared now. "There the people are more Southern in attitude," he said, rather apologetically.

When Watts had finished, a delegate from one of the Deep South states asked him in a concerned voice whether it was indeed true that Negro students were not doing as well in their achievement tests as their white classmates. From the table, Carter broke in to say, "It's a *fact*. Let's face it."

At the other end of the table, Wilkins, who had spoken little so far, said thoughtfully, "It might be well to clarify our position on this. We don't need to argue the point or be defensive. Some Negroes have flunked out in Baltimore, but some haven't. That's what we care about—the right of each individual to a fair chance." Marshall, who had been quietly making notes during the Maryland report, nodded emphatic agreement. "And *some* Negro students have been making excellent records, including Robert B. Watts, Jr.," Wilkins added. This, everybody realized, was a reference to the Maryland attorney's son. Smiling with fatherly pride, Watts returned to his seat.

The Reverend Mr. Hinton permitted no one to overrun his allotted fifteen minutes, and no one got the floor without his recognition. I had certainly expected more oratorical flourishes, but the slightest hint of anything of this sort was apt to draw from Marshall the warning "Watch out, man, you're using up your own time!" Marshall himself was put firmly in his place when he tried to discuss a point after the Reverend Mr. Hinton had ruled that there would be no further discussion of it. No one in the group seemed to question the chairman's authority, and I, too, in the course of the meeting, came to be powerfully impressed by the strength and firmness of his character, although I would have been hard put to it to say how he communicated these traits, for he never raised his voice and most of the time a mild, kindly smile lingered on his moon-shaped face. This was the Reverend Mr. Hinton mentioned in Levi Byrd's letter from Cheraw. Shotgun blasts had been fired into the minister's house only last January. One night a few years before, he had been kidnapped by an outraged mob and threatened with lynching for leading a protest against segregation in the schools in South Carolina. When asked about that night, he diverts attention from its terrors by smiling gently and recalling that among those Negroes who set out angrily to try to save him were two cars filled with fellow-members of the cloth—a "whole posse of preachers"—and saying that it was a good thing for their immortal souls that they didn't come upon the mob before he was set free. The Reverend Mr. Hinton is one of the people Marshall presumably had in mind when, on the plane down, he had wondered at the courage of the Negro leaders to be found in the South.

• • •

Shortly before one o'clock, the meeting adjourned for lunch, which was served cafeteria-style in a kitchen down the hall and was, as the Reverend Dr. Borders said, "on the house." Each person carried his own loaded tray into a nearby dining room. We had our choice of barbecued ribs or fried chicken. I took the ribs, and they were delicious. One of the last people to come into the dining room was a delegate from West Virginia, a large, very black man who had read his report, full of notable achievements, in a deep, unexcited voice. He stopped in the doorway, tray in hand, looked around at the others, already at table, and meekly inquired, "May colored folks eat here?" Then, smiling broadly, he marched in and sat down.

After lunch, most of the people went outside and stood in the sunshine on the church steps, smoking avidly. I made my way from one group to another, chatting with some and listening to what they had to say. Marshall was scheduled to go to Birmingham, Alabama, on the 29th to plead Miss Autherine Lucy's right to be admitted to the University of Alabama, and he was saying that, frankly, he wasn't looking forward at all to showing himself in that hostile territory. Somebody jokingly urged him to think how much good his becoming a martyr might do the cause, from the long view. "That's too long a view!" Marshall protested. Wilkins laughed and recalled how in the old days when they were sitting around trying to figure out how the organization was going to raise enough money to stay in existence, Walter White used to look speculatively at Marshall and Wilkins and say, "Now, if one of you heroes would just get lynched, I could arrange the finest speaking tour you ever saw."

Presently, I joined a group that was discussing the Montgomery bus boycott. This and the Miss Lucy matter, as might have been expected, were major topics of conversation among the N.A.A.C.P. people that weekend. It was on December 1st that a weary middle-aged Negro seamstress in Montgomery, riding home from work on the bus, refused to get up and give her seat to a white man and was promptly arrested. The bus boycott with which the Negro community responded was in its eleventh week at the time of the meeting. I got the impression from the people I talked to that this passive-resistance movement—with its Gandhian patience, acceptance of physical discomfort, and religious professions of love and tolerance toward the oppressors while refusing to submit to oppression—had taken the N.A.A.C.P. almost as much by surprise as it had the white citizens of Montgomery. The N.A.A.C.P. leaders, many of them lawyers accustomed to working through formal court processes, appeared to me to not know quite what to make of it even while taking pride in the spirit it revealed.

I went down the steps and joined some delegates standing on the sidewalk. They were talking about something the Arkansas delegate had said that morning—that the governors of several Southern states were claiming that most Negroes really didn't want to go to school with whites but preferred to stay among their own kind. One delegate remarked that Senator Eastland, of Mississippi, was fond of saying how happy the "good niggras of Mississippi" would be to have things stay just as they are. A short, serious-looking man, who had been listening to the others in silence, said, "That reminds me of the joke about the good niggra who got put on the radio in Mississippi. The white man drove down to this poor sharecropper's shack and told him he was gonna put him on the radio. 'Put me on the radio, boss? Whaffor?' the sharecropper asks. And the white man says, 'Gonna put you on the radio, Sam, because you're a mighty good niggra for a niggra, and we gonna give you a chance to tell the whole world how fine we treat you-all in Mississippi.' So the two of them drive up to the radio station and they go on in. 'Now, there's the microphone, Sam. Jest talk on into it,' says the white man. 'This the microphone, boss?' 'That's right, Sam.' 'And when I talk, people can hear me?' 'That's right.' 'Outside of Mississippi? All over the world?' 'Sure 'nuff, Sam. Jest go ahead and tell 'em.' So Sam went up to the microphone, took hold of it with both hands, and called, 'Help!'"

• • •

As it happened, the first state scheduled to report when the delegates went back into session after lunch was Mississippi, which was represented by an attorney, wearing slacks, a sports jacket, a bow tie, and horn-rimmed glasses. He had an earnest manner, his stance was square, his gestures simple. He looked as if not too long ago he might have been wearing jeans and doing heavy work. He said that his report on what progress his state was making toward desegregation could be summed up in one word: "None." In fact, he went on, the state officials and legislators, spurred on by the Citizens Councils—a segregationist movement that originated in Mississippi and spread out from there through the South—were devoting most of their energies and their best thinking to making progress in the other direction. "The Mississippi legislature has been meeting since the first Tuesday in January, and they have yet to get around to anything besides ways of strengthening every form of segregation," he said, and, permitting himself the luxury of a modest comment, added, "After they get that taken care of, they'll probably take a couple of weeks to settle the minor affairs of state business." Reading from a sheet of paper, he went over the bills that, he said, the legislature had introduced so far—an act requiring separate waiting rooms for persons travelling on common carriers within the state and forbidding any person to enter a waiting room other than the one marked for his race; an act requiring separate toilet facilities in these waiting rooms; an act conferring upon any person, firm, or corporation engaged in any public business, profession, or trade the right to choose and select the customers, patrons, and clients of such business, and the further right to refuse to sell or render a service to any person, and providing a penalty for any person who refuses to vacate a public place when ordered to do so by the owner or any employee thereof; an act to abolish common-law marriages ("I think the purpose of that bill may be to prevent the children of such unions from suing for their rights," he said. "Aside from that, I don't understand it"); an act making it a felony to hold, or cause to be conducted, athletic contests open to the public wherein Negroes or persons of Mongoloid descent participate with white persons; an act making it unlawful to solicit, advocate, urge, or encourage disobedience to any law of the State of Mississippi or nonconformance to the established traditions, customs, and usages of the State of Mississippi; an act to extend the laws of libel, defamation, and slander so as to prohibit the libelling, slandering, and defaming of states, counties, cities, communities, their inhabitants, their institutions, and their government ("The Jackson newspaper thinks a couple of these bills may be going a little too far"); an act ("Now, this one may deserve careful study") to safeguard for the citizens of the State of Mississippi the rights, privileges, and immunities granted them by the Constitution and laws thereof, to make criminal any violation thereof, and to create a civil-rights section to protect such rights ("I can't understand why they've brought out such a bill," he said. "It seems to me," he went on hopefully, "to offer a strong weapon with which to attack the other segregation laws." "Not a chance," Wilkins assured him. "That's a bill against the N.A.A.C.P. The civil rights that bill protects are the very opposite of what are called civil rights elsewhere"); an act to establish special requirements for out-of-state attorneys ("That's the Thurgood law," somebody in the audience said jocularly); and several other acts. Some of them, the Mississippi delegate said, had already passed both houses and most of the rest were expected to pass shortly. Although the Supreme Court had ruled that segregation was illegal in interstate travel facilities, Mississippi police were continuing to enforce it, he reported. They would arrest a Negro who went through the wrong door in a waiting room and fine him twenty-five dollars. However, if the Negro asked for a trial, an action that would require the court to file a written record of its judgment, the case against him would be dismissed. "So," he said apologetically, "we haven't been able to test in the law courts what they are doing."

"Don't worry about the test," somebody in the audience said. "If they dismiss the case, that's progress in Mississippi, man!" Other delegates laughingly concurred.

There followed reports from Alabama, Florida, Georgia, Louisiana, North Carolina, South Carolina, and Virginia. Like Mississippi, these states were apparently prepared to go to any lengths to defy or circumvent the Supreme Court's ruling that segregation has no rightful place in American public schools. Among other things, the reports brought out that Virginia, South Carolina, and Georgia have made plans to abandon their public-school systems altogether, rather than tolerate Negro and white children in the same classrooms. Georgia has passed a law that would make any school board permitting a non-segregated school to be set up within its jurisdiction guilty of a felony. Prince Edward County, Virginia, evidently guarding against the possibility that a court might order a local school board to desegregate, has refused to approve a yearly school budget and is supplying operating funds on a month-to-month basis. In Georgia, the State Attorney General has filed a suit against the Valdosta School Board, which had implied that it wants to study the situation. The suit seeks, in effect, as one of the N.A.A.C.P. delegates said, "to prevent the school board from even thinking about possibly studying desegregation." Alabama, Louisiana, and North Carolina have passed so-called placement statutes, which give local school boards the power to assign students to schools, ostensibly on the basis of categories other than race—such as health, intelligence, and social adaptability. In the eight recalcitrant states, defiance of the Supreme Court ruling comes not just from the mob but from the highest governing officials. The legislatures of Georgia, Alabama, Mississippi, Virginia, and South Carolina in solemn session have passed interposition, or nullification, resolutions, which declare that the Supreme Court's ruling violates their sovereignty. As Marshall put it, "They don't mean go slow. They mean don't go."

A Kentucky delegate raised a question that interested me: What attitude should be taken toward a school district that had declared that in the interests of gradual and orderly change it planned to abolish segregation in only one school grade at a time? It would start with the first grade next fall; the year after that, as these children were promoted there would be two mixed grades, then three, and so on until 1968, when the whole school system would be on a nonsegregated basis. The reasoning behind this was that such a significant alteration in social attitudes can be effective only if instituted at the earliest possible age, when the child's nature is pliant and unformed. To my ears, the argument had a certain plausibility, but the group rejected the plan. They thought this pace was rather slower than what the Supreme Court meant by "all deliberate speed." And they doubted whether the school board was reasoning in good faith. "In Tennessee, the state colleges have reasoned in just the opposite way," Carter pointed out. "There they said they would start at the graduate level and work down a year at a time. Obviously, they said, only the most mature person can be expected to adjust to so great a social change as this. Both of these arguments seem dreamed up mainly for the purpose of procrastination."

When it came to the eight intransigent states—Mississippi and the rest—there was considerable discussion, but all that it added up to was, I think, aptly summarized by the dapper, bald attorney from Texas who was keeping the minutes. After some time, he stood up and said, "I don't know whether I'm keeping good notes on this. All I can make out of what I've got down here is 'Let's sue!'"

"Those are good notes," Marshall assured him, with a smile.

• • •

At six, the meeting adjourned for two hours, to give a drafting committee, which included Marshall, time to embody the delegates' conclusions in a formal statement. Most of the others drove down to the Negro Y.M.C.A. for dinner. I decided that I would take a walk, to get some exercise and give myself a chance to think things over. In many ways, the meeting had not been at all what I had expected. I had anticipated more speculation, more oratory, more emotional outbursts. Certainly I had been unprepared for the orderliness—indeed, the ordinariness—of the procedure. I wouldn't have been surprised to find deep gloom at the turn events had taken in the last year, and demands for an agonizing reappraisal of the N.A.A.C.P.'s position, or even to hear at least some delegates, frustrated beyond endurance, call for violence or other direct action. But the concreteness, the calm, the serene feeling of assurance that the law would eventually prevail—these I had definitely not expected. As for the humor, I had expected some, but of a different sort. Funny without being escapist, the humor I had heard here reminded me in many ways of Mauldin's G.I.s in the front lines.

Mulling over these things, I walked perhaps a dozen blocks to where the white section of Atlanta begins. There I stopped in at a restaurant opposite the Municipal Auditorium and had a sandwich and a glass of beer. I was unable to get a cup of coffee. "Not much demand for coffee this hot weather," the proprietor said. A thermometer outside the door read seventy-five degrees. In the park in front of the auditorium, the broom hedges were already in bloom, as was the pelargonium in rows along the side. The grass, on which a number of neatly dressed white children were playing, was deep green and lush. As I watched, the fountains were turned on in the park, spouting half a dozen lovely jets from the center of a large marble basin. The sky was pink now, and I started back. It was dark by the time I reached the church.

• • •

"All right, listen to this statement Stewart's going to read," Marshall said when everyone had assembled again. "We're going to debate it, amend it, do anything you want done to it, but we're not getting out of here tonight till we've got something we're agreed on." Much of the document was handwritten, and Stewart stumbled over words as he read it aloud. It was, for the most part, an embodiment of the group's findings as to the progress that had been made and the actions it intended to take where progress had been faltering or nonexistent. When Stewart finished, one of the group said he hoped someone was going to edit out the grammatical errors. "I don't know whether they were in the writing or the reading," Stewart said, and Marshall remarked, "I know at least *one* was in the reading." A number of minor points were debated at some length, and a few changes made, but on the whole the delegates seemed satisfied with the presentation, and shortly after ten they voted their approval.

Now Wilkins, the executive secretary, walked forward and said that since he'd been keeping fairly quiet all day, perhaps he might say a few words in conclusion about the significance of what they were doing here. "I don't want to sound over-heroic, but I have the impression that we who are so close to all this don't comprehend its magnitude," he said. "I don't believe we understand the tremendous effect we are having on the nation. All these little decisions we worked out today are part of a social revolution that is taking place. The whole face of a third of America is changing—and what is achieved here in the South will also help to enhance the status of those who live outside this area and bring all of them closer to that condition we speak of so glibly in the phrase 'first-class citizenship.'" Out of the corner of my eye, I saw a tall young Negro come into the room. He walked down the aisle, spoke a few words to Marshall, who was standing at one side of the room near the platform, and then sat down among the audience. I paid scant attention to him, because I was finding myself engrossed by Wilkins' speech. I suppose his words sound oratorical as I've set them down here, but at that moment they sounded just right. I had got to concentrating on the specific details involved, and had forgotten that these people were engaged in making history. I was, therefore, startled to hear Marshall suddenly interrupt in a rough voice, "Never mind the philosophy, Roy!" Wilkins stopped, and Marshall said, "You don't know the news I've just heard."

Wilkins half turned to him and said, "Yes, I do, Thurgood. I didn't want to say anything about it unless it was definite." He looked back questioningly toward the tall young man, and the young man must have nodded back to him or made some other sign. Then Wilkins said, "Dr. Brewer's just had his head shot off."

For a moment, people sat dumfounded, shocked into silence. But soon they began to blurt out questions: How? Why? Was it definitely Dr. Brewer? The young man stood up and said he didn't have many details—all he knew was what a reporter had told him on the phone. And then someone asked if it had been a racial killing. "He's been getting threats for weeks on the phone," the young man said. "Ever since we started the petition to open the Columbus golf course to Negroes. I have, too, but I didn't pay much attention to them."

Wilkins said he would like to ask a minute's prayer for Dr. Brewer. The delegates stood in silence until Wilkins said "Amen." Then Marshall strode out of the hall. He looked angry. The others followed. And now the calmness and control they had shown all day disappeared. Fears and rumors flew among them as they stood in tense, excited groups on the church steps. Marshall stood off to one side, alone, staring into the darkness. The young man who had brought the news bolted down the steps to his car, to drive to Columbus, a hundred and twenty miles away, where the shooting had taken place; his wife and children were at home all by themselves. Somebody said, "He'd better get there in a hurry. There's liable to be a race riot when the Negroes in Columbus find out what's happened to Dr. Brewer." A large, powerful looking man from Bessemer, Alabama, said a race riot had been threatening in his town for several weeks and might break out at any moment, perhaps even that night. "Everybody is armed there now—white and black both," he said. And a woman standing near me, an N.A.A.C.P. official from Alabama, kept saying she was going to start carrying a gun herself, or get out of Alabama altogether.

Marshall and I were driven by Calhoun, the man who had met us on our arrival, back to our dormitory at Atlanta University. We didn't talk much. A few minutes after we got there, two N.A.A.C.P. attorneys from Virginia arrived—Oliver Hill and Spottswood Robinson. Earlier, they had arranged with Marshall to meet him in his room after the meeting and work out the strategy for two school-segregation lawsuits they had pending, and this still had to be done. They looked drawn and exhausted. Robinson, a former law professor at Howard University, fell asleep in an armchair a few moments after he had sat down, but he roused himself immediately, shook his head, and began fumbling in his briefcase for the legal papers he had brought with him. "All right," Marshall said, "let's start with the Prince Edward County case and go all through that before we take up the other. And I guess we'd better get going on it because we've got a lot to do tonight." I left them and went to bed.

LETTER FROM CHICAGO

Richard H. Rovere

AUGUST 25, 1956 (ON THE DEMOCRATIC CONVENTION)

ADLAI STEVENSON IS, as just about everyone knows, a man much given to self-doubt and hesitation. He has sought the Democratic nomination for almost a year—putting more time and energy into a preconvention campaign than any candidate before him—but there has always been a part of him that didn't want it at all. In 1956, this part of him has clearly been a small one, and if he were to be judged entirely by his public manner and his public words, it might be possible to say that he has suppressed it altogether, or at least reduced it to politically negligible dimensions. Nevertheless, it exists, because it has to; if a man has a sense of the melancholy powerful enough to serve as the basis for a wit as formidable as Stevenson's, he cannot destroy it by an act of will or reason. In any case, this aspect of Stevenson's nature is still sensed and frequently deplored by a number of Democrats, and there are some people, among them Harry Truman and Averell Harriman, who have argued against Stevenson as a candidate because he reckons too much with the chance of defeat and disappointment and finds it difficult, though not quite impossible, to join his party colleagues in their chesty displays of euphoria and confidence. During this past week in Chicago, however, it became clear that Stevenson's ambivalence was a political asset—at least in the circumstances he found himself in when the Democratic Convention opened. It would be going too far to say that his ambivalence won the nomination for him, but it would not be going too far to say that it helped mightily to gain him the nomination on the most enviable terms. If Stevenson's yen for the nomination had been as large and consuming as Governor Harriman's, he would probably have emerged from this gathering not as a candidate who had met and defeated his antagonists on all sides but as a candidate who had won by meeting his antagonists and doing a certain amount of business with them. In the Stevenson camp, there were many advisers who at the start of the week wanted him to engage in an elaborate traffic with Senator Estes Kefauver, Senator Lyndon Johnson, Mr. Truman, and anyone else who might have been worth trafficking with, over the Vice-Presidential nomination, the chairmanship of the Democratic National Committee, planks in the platform, and anything else that might have been negotiable.

The story went the rounds that it was the serious thinkers and the advanced liberals in the Stevenson camp who were the most eager to guarantee a speedy victory by these means, but the stories that go the rounds at political conventions are notoriously unreliable, and anyhow it scarcely matters who counselled compromise and who discouraged it. Stevenson assuredly was given the opportunity to make deals; that, after all, is what conventions are about. The point is that in the days before the convention, and even through the first day it was officially in session, there was a good deal of panic and fright in the Stevenson headquarters, and all during the convention the possibility of total defeat for Stevenson was very gravely calculated by the sort of people who are constantly working over tally sheets and believe that men like Harry Truman and Lyndon Johnson have some rare instinct that prevents them from ever behaving unwisely in political matters—particularly in those political matters that affect their own status. It may be that Stevenson, who has never advanced any serious claims for his own gifts as a strategist, shared the feeling that it was at least conceivable that all his campaigning had been a waste of time. It would certainly have been out of character for him not to have entertained this thought, but in any case he made—as far as it is now possible to tell—not a single one of the deals that were being urged upon him. He determined to let events take their own risky course and to tender Lyndon Johnson, Harry Truman, and other master politicians nothing but the courtesies to which he felt they were entitled. In consequence, he is a candidate free of contractual ties and as free as a loyal Democrat can be of any onus that attaches to the Truman administration. He may again be accused of being Truman's man, but he will have a ready answer. He is free of obligation to Lyndon Johnson or to any of the Southern Democrats. As much as a politician or statesman can ever hope to be, he is today his own man.

It could be argued—and it certainly will be—that it was Stevenson's purity of spirit that triumphed over political baseness. No doubt he will be widely advertised as the man who would rather be right than President. Perhaps he would, and perhaps he is indeed pure of spirit, but the theory that his strength became as the strength of ten because of moral superiority will not bear close investigation. For one thing, there is nothing necessarily base about political trading; alliances are as necessary in the world of party politics as they are among nations. For another thing, Stevenson has made plenty of deals in the past, and he will undoubtedly make plenty in the future. From his point of view, it would have been morally a great deal more defensible and in every respect far more appetizing to promise Senator Johnson control of the Democratic National Committee, which was the main thing Johnson wanted, than to go begging in Georgia, as Stevenson once did, for the approval and support of Herman Talmadge. All that can be said is that at this convention Stevenson gave none of the hostages to fortune that he was being asked to give—and that at one stage or another it might have been prudent to give if he had been determined to eliminate the possibility of defeat. By this course of action, and by having luck from start to finish, he came out stronger and freer than he probably ever thought it was possible for him to be, and he tumbled his opponents in such a way as to cause the political "realists" to rewrite their texts on realism.

The conclusion is almost inescapable that Stevenson was able to gamble in Chicago and to outsit all his opponents because his desire for victory, while great, is not a governing passion. He wants very much to be President of the United States—enough, at least, to lead him to fraternize with Herman Talmadge and with Governor Frank Clement, of Tennessee, and that is quite a lot—but the side of him that resists, the side that dreads the entire prospect of being President and gives him his sombre view of the office, makes it impossible for him to pant for it as Governor Harriman did. Governor Harriman became so desperate in his quest for the nomination that he practically destroyed the rationale of his campaign by coming to terms with people who, on the issues he said he cares most about, stand as far to the right of President Eisenhower as Eisenhower stands to the right of Harriman—the prime example being Governor Gary, of Oklahoma, who placed Harriman's name in nomination. Harriman, of course, gambled more heavily than Stevenson did; in fact, his whole effort was a spectacular race against odds that always seemed long and now seem incalculable. To overcome them, he put in what had every appearance of being a frantic campaign. Stevenson at no point became frantic. It is said that he was deeply troubled by the phrases Harry Truman used in announcing his support of Harriman and his opposition to Stevenson, but he could not be persuaded to make any hasty arrangements with anyone to offset the Truman move. His behavior was clearly that of a man who can tolerate the thought of losing and knows that he can find certain consolations in defeat. It was not necessarily that he would rather be right than President but that he saw an engrossing chance to be both right *and* President, and was willing to take it as a calculated risk. He appears to have been the only man at this convention, apart from Harry Truman, who took a gamble that wasn't dictated by necessity.

Stevenson's luck was better than most people expected it to be. There were a few hours at the start of the convention when it looked as if Harry Truman might have inadvertently delivered his party over to those in it who like him least; no one here, that is, ever thought that Averell Harriman had a prayer, but it did seem to many that Lyndon Johnson's chances would be vastly improved in the event of a deadlock, and that a deadlock was what both Truman and Johnson were promoting. (There are some who insist that Truman does nothing by inadvertence, but they have produced no plausible explanation of why he should want control to pass from the hands of his friends to the hands of people who have never supported him.) One man who thought Lyndon Johnson's chances were excellent was Lyndon Johnson; for somewhere between twelve and eighteen hours on Monday, he waged a perfectly serious and purposeful campaign for the nomination, and he is reliably reported to have thought it more likely than not that he and Senator Russell, of Georgia, could gain control of the Democratic Party and make it a medium for the expression of their views. In that period, a great many people in the Loop hotels and in the International Amphitheatre, where large numbers of obscure Democrats were being given free television time in order to enable them to overcome their obscurity, forgot the wisdom of history, which is that members of the United States Senate almost invariably come to grief when they try to win Presidential nominations for themselves or to manipulate national conventions for any purpose whatever. For many reasons—patronage is one, and control of delegations is another—the big men at conventions are governors and municipal leaders (Carmine De Sapio, of Manhattan, being a striking exception this year), and the governors and urban politicians seldom see things as senators do. And, of course, many people also forgot another general principle, which is that political conventions almost always end the way that logic dictates at the outset. Before the conventions of 1952, it seemed reasonable on the basis of all available evidence to expect the nomination of General Eisenhower by the Republicans and of Governor Stevenson by the Democrats. It was plain from the start that these men were the strongest candidates of their parties, and parties normally nominate the men who appear to have the best chance of winning. At both 1952 conventions, there were periods when the favorites seemed on the point of being rejected, but in the end the suicidal impulses were brought under control and the expected developments developed. This year, all political logic pointed to the renomination of Adlai Stevenson by the Democrats, and the reasoned view of most reasoning observers was that the Party would serve itself best by pairing Estes Kefauver with Stevenson, the theory being that each man has an appeal to precisely those voters who are insensitive to the appeal of the other. As it turned out, Kefauver's nomination was a very chancy thing indeed, and would never have occurred but for a series of altogether unexpected happenings. The fact that he finally made it cannot be used as an argument in favor of the theory that logic generally prevails. Nevertheless, the result was the expected one, and the principle has survived another convention—as it will undoubtedly survive next week's gathering in the Cow Palace in San Francisco.

It is probably a good thing that people tend to cast aside the wisdom of history in the midst of conventions, since to put much stock in it would, for one thing, make the conventions far duller, and, for another, inhibit the attempts to face down the odds that provide all the suspense. This convention has been moderately suspenseful, and hardly ever as thunderously dull as certain conventions of the past. To be sure, the oratory at the International Amphitheatre now and then broke new ground in oppressiveness and witlessness, and the few feeble efforts that were made to hold the attention of the television audience—most notably, the documentary movie on the past glories of the Party—were not marked by brilliance. But while a convention, for most of its participants, is an exercise in histrionics, its drama, when there is any, is not of the sort that can be taken in by the eyes and ears alone. This convention had one scene—the balloting for the Vice-Presidential nomination—that was primarily a theatrical scene, and a very good one, but it seldom happens that things are as compact and vivid as that. The extraordinary interest of this convention has derived from the effect it has had, or seems likely to have, on the biographies of half a dozen leaders of the Democratic Party. Harry Truman, Adlai Stevenson, and Averell Harriman are today very different men from what they were a week ago. It is the strong, though possibly unjust, feeling of most observers that Truman and Harriman are considerably diminished in stature by their defeat, and especially by the way they met defeat. Adlai Stevenson is measurably larger, for he has won a great political victory and sacrificed nothing in the process. Lyndon Johnson's reputation as an uncommonly astute Senate leader remains unimpaired, but the fact has been established—as it was not before—that in the jungle of a national convention he cannot employ the gifts he uses in the Senate. Carmine De Sapio's importance as a figure in national politics is in shreds for the moment, and it has been made clear through his failure that the New York governorship is not quite as formidable politically as it was when it was held by Alfred E. Smith, Franklin D. Roosevelt, and Thomas E. Dewey. Before the convention, it was thought that De Sapio was not too serious about Governor Harriman's Presidential aspirations but was using him as a personification of New York's political power, which is so great that it has almost given the state political sovereignty. New York's political power did the state no good, or at least it did De Sapio no good; he got nothing he wanted from this convention.

• • •

The Truman-Harriman movement here has been one of the most interesting spectacles in recent political history, and there has been an endless amount of conjecture about what led the two men, along with many of their friends, to become involved in so hopeless an adventure. On the surface, at least, the case of Governor Harriman is simpler than that of the ex-President. In the last few years, Harriman has developed an enormous political ambition and a great capacity for political bitterness. The mere fact that he wanted the Presidency is not surprising; most men who get as close to the White House as he got under Franklin Roosevelt and Harry Truman and who meet the constitutional requirements for the office begin to fancy themselves occupying it. It is only his zeal and the passion of his desire for the Presidency that distinguish Mr. Harriman from most men who have held important jobs in the executive branch for any length of time, but this zeal and passion constitute a distinction that is quite extraordinary. It would not surprise anyone who has seen him here this week if they lasted over the next four years and brought him back for a third try in 1960, when he will be sixty-nine. He said the other evening, after his defeat, that he intended to stay in politics and that he looked forward to retaining his present office for "many, many years." His seeking of that office two years ago was itself an index of the intensity of his itch for the Presidency, since it was neither an office that could add much to his stature nor one for which his interests or his impressive talents seemed to qualify him. In order to get it, he pushed out of the way a promising young Democrat, Franklin D. Roosevelt, Jr., whose career would have been greatly advanced by the experience of Albany, and he had been in it only a few months when he began to act like a Presidential candidate. This suited Carmine De Sapio down to the ground, and early this year the State of New York was in business, as it almost always has been, with a candidate of its own.

The team of Harriman and De Sapio now seems never to have had much of a chance, but it might have done a bit better than it did if Harry Truman had not intervened in its behalf. It wasn't until two days before the convention that the ex-President announced his support of Harriman's candidacy, but it had been clear almost since the last election that Truman took a poor view of Adlai Stevenson's 1952 campaign and would find it hard to support him in 1956. Truman may have had some of the technical and professional objections to Stevenson's methods that he wrote about in his memoirs, but his deepest grievance was caused by Stevenson's repudiation of large parts of the Truman record. Frequently in private (though never in public), Stevenson showed both his willingness to concede point after point to critics of the Truman administration and his eagerness to have it thoroughly understood that he had never been part of it. This got back to Mr. Truman, who took it hard, and it was not strange that he should prefer the candidacy of an old associate like Averell Harriman. (He could never, under any circumstances, have turned to the third candidate, Estes Kefauver, who made his reputation by harassing prominent Democrats during the Truman years.) It has happened time after time in American politics that former Presidents and former party leaders have resented and fought against their rightful heirs, and it is possible that even if Harry Truman had not been miffed at Stevenson for disowning large parts of the Fair Deal, he would have opposed him, in tandem with someone like Harriman, for the simple reason that Stevenson is a younger man with a different set of friends and with no need or desire to enlist the talents of such veterans as Judge Samuel Rosenman, the speech writer, and Frank McKinney, the strategist. The only other living ex-President, Herbert Hoover, has often intervened in behalf of the Hooverites in his own party. What was astonishing about the Truman performance was its ineptness and its destructiveness. Truman did positive damage to Harriman by the kind of support he gave him, and thereby contributed to the forging of a coalition behind Stevenson, who had come into the convention with a powerful movement of his own but without benefit of allies. It is most unlikely that Stevenson would have won on the first ballot if Truman had not generated so much hostility by the intemperateness of his anti-Stevenson campaign. Herbert Hoover, though he has consistently opposed the liberals in the Republican Party, has never made a mistake of this magnitude. He has always acted in such a way as to maintain a role for himself not only in his own party but in the government, even when it has been under opposition control.

Adlai Stevenson is a man of almost compulsive charitableness, and he may choose to find a way of restoring some of Truman's political prestige, perhaps by turning up some agreeable chores to keep him from boredom in his advancing years. As of this moment, though, Truman has practically no standing in his own party. The Party will be spoken for by the two men he has fought the hardest, and his friends have been excluded from all roles of importance. If anything comes his way now, it will come as a gift from Adlai Stevenson, and it will come in recognition of his services in the remote past, not in appreciation of anything he has done lately. Moreover, it is fairly certain that Stevenson's efforts to dissociate himself from the Truman record and the Truman approach will no longer be undertaken in private or spoken of sotto voce. In one way or another, he will have to make it clear that he cannot go along with Truman's characterization of the Eisenhower administration as "this bunch of racketeers" and that he does not share Truman's view of Truman as the greatest living expert on everything.

. . .

Stevenson is now in a position to run whatever sort of campaign he wishes. The one serious question about his candidacy is whether he will get from his party the kind of support he needs. Most of the people who have been at the convention feel that it was an apathetic and uninspired gathering. They feel that Stevenson had more votes than enthusiasm behind him. Lack of excitement and inspiration is, of course, the general rule at political conventions, and more often than not any enthusiasm manifested is contrived and bogus. The only real enthusiasm at the convention that nominated General Eisenhower in 1952 was for the man the delegates rejected, Robert A. Taft, who was more beloved by the delegates than Eisenhower, and who was loved with a special fervor and sympathy because it was necessary to deny him the recognition he sought. It has frequently been said this week that while there was no Taft at the 1956 Democratic Convention, Stevenson was its Eisenhower. He was the man the delegates had to choose, because a strong case existed for not giving the prize to any of the other candidates. There is probably something to this, but the comparison with the Republicans in 1952 cannot be made without certain substantial qualifications. Stevenson has acquired four years of seniority since his first appearance, and in view of his lack of shock effect on the delegates it is perhaps surprising that his acceptance speech—which was not felt here to be one of his more felicitous addresses—got as good a response in the convention hall as it did. Moreover, this convention, unlike either convention that took place in 1952, was fully aware that its party's chances for victory are generally thought to be slim. It requires a certain amount of confidence to promote enthusiasm, and the most that any reasonable Democrat believes is that victory is not impossible. The Party faithful can assume that with Adlai Stevenson a free agent the campaign will be an interesting and intellectually stimulating one, but to the people who show up at these affairs, there are a lot of things more important than intellectual stimulation, and the Democrats at the moment don't seem to have many of them. It is conceivable that the spectacle of the Republicans luxuriating in harmony at San Francisco this coming week will gall them into more determination than they have displayed here.

LETTER FROM SAN FRANCISCO

Richard H. Rovere

SEPTEMBER 1, 1956 (ON THE REPUBLICAN CONVENTION)

The Twenty-second Amendment to the Constitution, which was ratified in 1951 and provides that no President shall serve more than two full terms, took practical effect in this handsome city during the past week. Though Mr. Eisenhower enjoyed a great personal triumph here, he suffered, thanks to the new provision in what the classier orators like to call "the basic charter of our liberties," a measurable diminution of power. Nominated for the last possible time, he cannot, from this historic moment on, use the threat of nonsupport or outright reprisal to bring recalcitrants in his party to heel. This is not to say that the moment doesn't belong to him. The Centennial Convention of the Republican Party was nothing less than an ode to his leadership. Indeed, "leadership" is a poor word for the thing that was celebrated from Nob Hill to the Cow Palace by Republican Ciceros, by blaring trumpets and mighty Wurlitzers and Irving Berlin, by bathing beauties and calisthenics teams, and by 2,646 delegates and alternates. At times, the rhetoric was so lavish, the spotlighting was so dazzling, and the mass demonstrations were so massive that the recently imported phrase "personality cult" sprang to many minds—only to be rejected, of course, because the President's true personality, as distinct from that of the near-divinity fabricated by Hollywood and Madison Avenue, does not lend itself to a cult, and because he himself would not tolerate one. (Besides, the Twenty-second Amendment, while open to criticism on many grounds, is fair insurance against this sort of disaster.) Still, there is more to politics than rhetoric and stage management, and the key political fact about the gathering now breaking up is that it has made Richard M. Nixon the symbol, if not the center, of authority in the Republican Party. It was Eisenhower's past that was being honored and Nixon's future that was being assured. In the campaign that is about to open, the President's word will be the command of practically every Republican, but the campaign will be only a short interlude. When it is over, the Vice-President will be the Republican to watch—which would be the case even if the President had never been stricken by a heart attack and ileitis. Of all the men in the Party who can look to 1960 and beyond, Nixon will be the one most courted, most emulated, and most feared.

The President, it is felt here, would do well to take all the comfort he can from the tributes he has received in the past few days and will undoubtedly continue to receive in the next few weeks, for while he may win much praise and many additional honors in the years ahead, his ability to command the Republican organization has reached its peak and can do nothing hereafter but decline. He must be very well aware of this himself. He has learned from harsh experience that there are more orators who will praise him for his "moral and spiritual leadership" than there are politicians who will accept his political counsel. He has had a hard enough time maintaining any sort of party discipline in the years in which every poll and almost every election revealed that the success of the Republican Party was dependent largely on his personal prestige. According to an authorized history of his first administration, he came to recognize this difficulty early in his White House tenancy, and at one time was so nearly overcome by despair that he considered quitting the Republican Party and starting a new party of his own. Nothing is more certain than that he will be given even more cause for despair in the future, since his reappointment as head of the Party on Wednesday put him forever beyond the hope of keeping his associates in line by the most powerful of all his political weapons—the threat of disinheritance. In effect, he is himself disinherited by the Twenty-second Amendment. He has nothing to pass along except the blessing of a President headed for retirement. This may be worth somewhat more than the blessing Harry Truman gave Averell Harriman in Chicago, but that only makes it a little better than nothing. From now on, unless there are forces at work that are unseen by any of the sharp eyes casing the situation here, he will be as dependent on the favors of Republican senators and representatives as they in the past have been dependent on his favors.

• • •

To say, as has been said time and again here, that the really important thing the convention did was to turn control of the Party machinery over to the Vice-President is a crude way of stating a matter of considerable complexity, and there are some people who believe that it puts the cart before the horse. Has Nixon become the head man, they ask, or has he merely served as the agent of a faction whose victory is signalized by his renomination? Will he control the machinery or be controlled by it? A number of Republicans have always looked upon the Vice-President chiefly as a spokesman for a particular tendency within the Party, and they have wished him well or ill according to their view of that tendency. Harold Stassen, for example, before his capitulation on Wednesday morning, insisted that his case was not against Nixon—whom he professed to think a nice enough fellow, and possibly even a friend of Stassenism—but against such things as isolationism and reaction, which he deplores and which he said were riding on Nixon's renomination. Neither Stassen nor the few people who were willing to identify themselves as his supporters argued that they had any serious objection to Nixon's staying on as Vice-President or becoming President. They claimed to be principally concerned about Nixon's friends in the Party, and especially about those friends' influence in the next Congress. In discussing the latter question, they offered a double-barrelled line of reasoning. First, they maintained that Nixon's presence on the ticket would be offensive to enough voters to cost the Republican ticket 6—or, in some estimates, 8—percent of the vote. The President and Nixon, they said, could survive such defections, but large numbers of Congressional candidates could not, and the sure consequence of renominating Nixon would be to deprive the President of a Republican majority. Whenever this analysis was challenged, they were ready with the other barrel. Things would be just as terrible if they were wrong as if they were right, they said, for if a Republican Congress should be elected despite the fact of Nixon's renomination, it would be a Congress controlled by those who had made the greatest effort to keep Nixon in power—Styles Bridges, of New Hampshire; John Bricker, of Ohio; William Jenner, of Indiana, and others of that supposedly sinister breed. At any rate, it was nothing personal, these people went on, but all a matter of high principle, with nation being put above party and party above candidates. And there are good grounds for believing that this is how they really felt about it.

Whether or not they were right in any of their political estimates is something else again. The mere fact that Senator Bridges was deeply gratified by Nixon's renomination does not entitle him to a victor's spoils. Nixon, after all, won by considerably more than a nose. It remains to be seen whether the Republicans can elect a Congress in November. If they fail, it will not be easy to pin the blame on Nixon; they have failed quite a few times when he was not on the ticket. A very strong case could be advanced for the proposition that the Republicans would have damaged their chances more by rejecting Nixon; if, that is, the leading figures in the Stassen demonology are as powerful and determined as Stassen made them out to be, then rebuffing them might have been every bit as destructive as jobbing Nixon.

• • •

Stassen's fight came to nothing except a comic end, but it was one of the two things that had any political interest in a convention that could have done all its business in half a day and that was far from engaging as a spectacle. The other was a small controversy over the civil-rights plank in the platform; this was speedily and effectively stilled when it became clear that the President, far from wishing to insist on language that would sharply distinguish his position from that of the Democrats, was willing to settle for a statement that, like the one adopted in Chicago, would scarcely go beyond acknowledging that the Founding Fathers saddled us with the United States Supreme Court and that we are obliged to honor its decisions—though not necessarily today or tomorrow. The wording that was finally written into the Republican platform came from the White House and was reported to be the last of three formulations suggested by Presidential advisers, each version being slightly less militant than the preceding one. It was plain that the President did not at any time feel himself deeply engaged in the platform controversy and—probably because he figured that he would be able to set the tone of the campaign in speeches prepared under his own direction—could have lived with any of several phrasings. A platform is a lifeless thing, important only until the candidate either identifies himself with it or repudiates it, and there is no reason to suppose that either the President or Adlai Stevenson suffered much anguish over any section of their parties' statements this year; both platforms violate the known beliefs of the candidates at one point or another, but a long and—through usage—honorable tradition exists of overlooking these conflicts.

There is, however, reason to suppose that the President suffered a good deal of anguish over the affair of the Vice-President, and that the real, if perhaps never fully knowable, history of this episode is considerably more interesting than the recorded proceedings of the convention make it appear. Though the Stassen crusade came to an absurd dénouement in the rambling and pointless and generally embarrassing speech of its leader, the facts remain that Mr. Stassen has shown himself to be a fairly astute politician in the past, and that he is in any case not the sort of man to deliberately risk his career in an utterly quixotic cause. Nor is he a man without honor. Even if he were to become involved in a totally misguided adventure, he would not seek to excuse or extricate himself by lying about the encouragement he had received in high places. Stassen never claimed that the President had expressed any hope for the success of his cause, but he did insist that nothing the President said had led him to believe that Mr. Eisenhower would be displeased if Nixon was dropped from the ticket, and neither the President nor anyone else in the White House offered a different interpretation of what had passed between Mr. Eisenhower and his adviser on disarmament. It is also a matter of general knowledge that several people who customarily devote themselves to fulfilling the hopes and wishes of the President to the best of their ability and understanding lent themselves to the Stassen movement at one stage or another, among them General Lucius Clay, Sidney Weinberg, and Paul Hoffman. And if it was necessary to believe Stassen when he said he had found favor in the upper reaches of the administration, it was also necessary to believe his lieutenants here—who are honorable men, too—when they said that their missionary work among the delegates was about as successful as they had expected it to be when they arrived in San Francisco. The fact that they would not reveal to the reporters the names of delegates partial to their cause did not prove that there were no such delegates. In the sort of atmosphere that was developing during the weeks before the convention, it would have taken a bold Republican politician to come out openly against Nixon, and it was only to be expected that those who offered Stassen covert support should have demanded that their names be concealed until the rebellion was a success—at which time, naturally, they would have wished their names listed prominently in every newspaper in the country.

Yesterday afternoon, following Stassen's abandonment of his own movement, there were only Terry Carpenter, of Nebraska, and Joe Smith, a phantasmal creature to everybody but Joe Martin, to give weight to the notion that anyone in the Republican Party thought there might be a case against putting Richard Nixon in line for the most august and powerful office on the face of the earth. Yet there was an obvious malaise surrounding the whole performance of putting him there. The very morning that Governor Christian Herter, of Massachusetts, nominated Nixon, he received with gratitude the assurance of some correspondents that they would have been far happier if Stassen's plan had succeeded and Herter, rather than Nixon, were the candidate. "They had me boxed in," the Governor said. He did not say who "they" were, and his tone of voice suggested that it was an impersonal "they"—the surging forces of history. An instrument of those forces was Leonard Hall, the National Chairman, who, immediately after Stassen's original advocacy of Herter, got Herter to agree to nominate Nixon. But it obviously took more than Hall to convince Herter of the futility of the Stassen movement; the governor of a powerful state owes very little to a National Chairman. Indeed, if the Nixon steamroller had not gathered practically irresistible force by the time Stassen got under way, Stassen would almost certainly never have started; that is to say, Stassen is not the most foresighted of statesmen, or the boldest, and it must have taken a strong conviction of the desperateness of the moment to lead him to jeopardize his own career. Moreover, there has always been an almost visible unease in the President's handling of the Nixon question. Right up to the last minute, he could not be persuaded to assert a preference for Nixon over any other candidate. At the start, this could have been put down to his desire not to give offense to other aspirants, but after a while there were no other aspirants, and when the President persisted in refusing a forthright endorsement, he could hardly have failed to realize that his refusal must give offense to Nixon. Yet he did persist, and as late as yesterday morning, at the extraordinary news conference when he told of Stassen's plan to leap back on the bandwagon by seconding Nixon's nomination, he refused once more—in fact, several times more—to embrace Nixon. He was asked whether, if he found himself serving as a regular delegate from Pennsylvania, he would move the renomination of Nixon, and he hemmed and hawed and said he could give no flat answer, because there were a number of things a delegate would have to think about. At all odds, he could not, standing before the press in the Italian Room of the St. Francis Hotel a few hours before Nixon's scheduled nomination, be led to say that Nixon was his man—or "That's my boy!," as he said on a famous occasion four years ago.

The conclusion drawn by most of the people in the Italian Room was the same as that drawn by most people in Washington during the spring and early summer. It was that the President was of at least two minds about the Vice-President—that he admired Nixon's ability and energy and political cleverness but at the same time had misgivings about Nixon as a possible President of the United States, and was no longer willing, as he had been before the heart attack of last September, to praise him in terms so extravagant that they raised the question of how he could deny him anything. He had once called Nixon "the most valuable member of my team" and "one of the great leaders of men," but that was at a time when his thoughts about the Vice-President probably did not include much speculation about the kind of President he would make. A good many powerful Republicans began thinking that question over last fall, and more than a few of them became jumpy at the prospect of Nixon's renomination. The President seems to have become jumpy, too. It may be that only the spectre of controversy over Nixon raised doubts in his mind about having Nixon on the ticket again; the President is bothered by dissension of any sort and likes, whenever he can, to avert a controversy by removing its cause. At any rate, he seems to have had second thoughts about Nixon, and right up through the weeks before the convention he was careful not to foreclose the possibility of another Vice-Presidential candidate. But as the weeks went by, it became clearer and clearer that Nixon could be stopped only by the President himself. Harold Stassen saw this; his aim was never to secure enough anti-Nixon votes to win for another candidate but, rather, to create an atmosphere in which the President could with propriety ask Nixon to withdraw or could endorse another man in the interests of party unity. Toward the end, Stassen could see, as anyone with normal vision could, that this was hopeless. White House intervention, had it come, would not have averted controversy but would have promoted it.

It was Adlai Stevenson's decision to throw the Democratic nomination for the Vice-Presidency up for grabs that breathed what for a moment looked like new life into the Stassen movement. As things turned out, though, Stevenson's decision probably killed whatever small chances of success Stassen still had. For it would have been a very crass thing indeed if the Republican Convention had at the last minute sought to keep up with the Democratic Joneses by denying the delegates' overwhelming favorite the office they thought he deserved. Stevenson's act in Chicago disturbed the Republicans who were beginning to gather in San

Francisco, and for a day or two they played with several ideas for having an "open" convention. The most promising of these was a scheme to put in nomination a number of other men—Governor McKeldin, of Maryland, and ex-Governor Thornton, of Colorado, were mentioned—and have them withdraw right away. But the other men didn't take kindly to the idea of being used in this way, and almost everyone saw that anything done at so late a stage would be looked upon as bogus—although no one, it is safe to say, was happy about the contrast between Chicago and San Francisco, and the Vice-President was reported to be unhappiest of all. The collapse of the movement to unseat him made his victory on the first ballot a bit too easy to be altogether pleasurable. There is not much doubt that in the last days before his nomination he was wishing Harold Stassen luck—a little luck, anyway.

Stassen had no luck at all—except that he managed not to be drummed out of the regiment on the parade ground here—and speculation about the kind of President that Nixon would make has taken on a new meaning and urgency. The impressions one gathered here during the week were not of the sort to confirm the fears of those who thought that love for the Republic demanded his early elimination. There has always been a certain lack of specificity about these fears; people have been bothered by Nixon without being able to say precisely why, just as the author of the celebrated lines about Dr. Fell was unable to say why he disliked the man. There are doubtless many people who continue to feel that way about Nixon, despite the fact that he has lately been laboring with great zeal to remove any possible reasons for being unloved. He has been very much on his dignity. In his meetings with the state caucuses, he recommended that the 1956 campaign be conducted on the highest possible moral level, and gave the delegates his opinion that Adlai Stevenson and Estes Kefauver were honorable and patriotic Americans who should in no circumstances be accused of having base motives. His acceptance speech was close enough to liberal orthodoxy to qualify him—ideologically, at any rate—for membership on the national board of Americans for Democratic Action. He seemed to stand far to the left of where Henry Wallace stood in 1934. He had barely sat down when his detractors began to explain that it was all subterfuge. His detractors, however, are slightly fewer in number than they were a while back, and there are some people here who think that the new Nixon is an authentic creation. They think that the temper of the times and the magic of the

Presidency are at work upon him. The temper of the times seems to demand that any man in or approaching a high administrative office talk and act like some species of liberal, and the magic of the Presidency, to which he is now so near, seems capable of creating maturity and a sense of responsibility in some of the least promising of men.

LETTER FROM WASHINGTON

Richard H. Rovere

OCTOBER 5, 1957 (ON EISENHOWER AND LITTLE ROCK)

THE PRESIDENT GAVE a full day's notice that he might use federal troops in Little Rock, and that notice, the Washington *Post* said on the following morning—the morning of the day the 101st Airborne Division was flown in—was "what the situation desperately requires." Breathing hard, as most of Washington was, and making heavy demands on its reserve supplies of outraged rhetoric, the *Post* went on to say that "the Faubus-inspired mob which forced the withdrawal of Negro students from the Central High School yesterday is a threat to the supremacy of the United States just as surely as if it had barricaded the White House." Most people here saw matters that way and responded to the President's proclamation on Monday with relief and release; the warning broke the tension, and very little was said in dispraise of Mr. Eisenhower's proclamation, except that it might have come earlier. On Monday, most people still believed that the threat of force would make force itself unnecessary. No doubt the President, who had flown down from Newport that morning for a bit of speechmaking on fiscal problems, returned to Rhode Island confident that he had a way of fixing Governor Faubus and that one more piece of unpleasantness was at an end. Had he thought otherwise—had he thought that his cease-and-desist proclamation would be taken no more seriously than a "No Smoking" sign in a theatre lobby—he would undoubtedly have stayed on.

The militant integrationists could have been pleased with the threat to use troops, but in no quarter is there rejoicing at the soldiers' steely presence in Little Rock. No one who sides with the President is now saying any more than that he did what he had to do, and those who oppose him are almost certainly as aware of the truth of this as anyone else. Senator McClellan and the few other Southern congressmen who happen to be in town are giving out angry statements, but for years the Southern politicians have been affecting a choler on racial matters that few of them really feel, and it is probable that most of them sensed that the President was acting—with Lord knows how much reluctance—only as the situation and his responsibilities required him to act. The Constitution, law and order, elementary justice, the prestige of the country abroad, the political demands of the Cold War, the coordinate theory of government by which he sets so much store—all these demanded the 101st Airborne. Nothing is more certain than that if there had been a less drastic alternative, he would have seized upon it. (There were alternatives as recently as last week, but they seemed drastic for their time, and he didn't want to get into this disagreeable business at all. A few weeks ago, he said, "I can't imagine any set of circumstances that would ever induce me to send federal troops.") He is not an ardent integrationist; unless his whole makeup has changed recently the cause moves him even less than abolitionism for its own sake moved Lincoln. It could not have been with any overpowering sense of self-righteousness that he gave his historic orders to the troops the day before yesterday. He doubtless reckoned, as almost everyone here reckons, that it was a mite better to uphold the courts with bayonets than not to uphold the courts at all. But only a mite, for it is impossible to maintain that either orderly integration or the good name of the country has been very much advanced by his decision. Senator Russell, of Georgia, may have spoken for Southern Bourbonism when he said that the President's action would increase racial tensions throughout the South, but he spoke also for simple common sense. There is a taint on justice whenever it has to be enforced at the point of a gun. To be sure, there is a larger and uglier taint on Governor Faubus and on the mobs whose refusal to disperse forced the President to the step he took so unwillingly, but the mobs can be dispersed by well-armed troops, while the memory that will endure in the community is that it took an army to carry the day.

It may be, of course, that integration in the schools will be more quickly accomplished because of what has happened in Little Rock. Amid the encircling gloom, this now seems the unlikeliest of possibilities. But as much paradox and wayward logic exist in politics as in anything else in life, and there is at least an off-chance that in the litigation that is now bound to occur it will be revealed that the militant resistance movement was organized in the Governor's office and had no real roots anywhere else. It is known that integration in schools and in transportation elsewhere in Arkansas has taken place without undue disturbance, and it is also known that close associates of Governor Faubus were busy rousing the rabble outside Central High School. It is at least conceivable that no more showdowns will be required and that something workable will come out of next week's conference with the Southern governors. Right now, though, the melancholy prospect is that the President's action, no matter what moral and Constitutional justification may be found for it, has made everyone's life, including his own, more difficult.

• • •

In 1952, on the eve of Mr. Eisenhower's first election, Dennis W. Brogan, a leading British authority on American affairs, wrote that the besetting intellectual sin of our politicians and of a fair number of our people was a refusal to come to terms with the fact that "a great many things happen in the world regardless of whether the American people wish them to or not." In an article in *Harper's* called "The Illusion of American Omnipotence," Mr. Brogan, mindful of our discouragement and bitterness over the course of events in Korea, said that the basic fallacy in our thinking was the assumption that "the world must go the American way if the Americans want it strongly enough and give firm orders to their agents to see that it is done." We would suffer less, he went on, and perhaps accomplish more, if we abandoned this view and, in particular, its dangerous corollary, which is "the idea that the whole world, the great globe itself, can be moving in directions annoying or dangerous to the American people only because some elected or non-elected Americans are fools or knaves. When something goes wrong, 'I wuz robbed!' is the spontaneous comment—the American equivalent of that disastrous French cry *'Nous sommes trahis!'*"

Whatever else may be said of the last five years, they have seen the shattering of the illusion of American omnipotence. At least in administration circles, there is today an acute awareness of the limitations of American power (which is, of course, distinct from *force,* of the kind displayed this week), and there are times when it appears that the false pride—if that is what it was—of a few years ago has given way to a conviction that such power as we have is a poor and feeble instrument for dealing with the causes of American distress. Mr. Dulles, for instance, who in 1952 was saying in the Republican platform that sound American policy could have defeated Communism in China, has lately spent much of his time pointing out that there are many parts of the world and many world problems that are beyond the practical reach of American policy. Hungary was last year's leading example; Mr. Dulles's own passion for liberation was well known, and the American will to assist was almost boundless, but the situation, as the White House and the State Department saw it, was one in which there simply wasn't any role for American power except the unacceptable one of going to war with the Soviet Union. The Suez crisis was another example; it grew, according to the administration's analysts, out of conflicts in which we had had no part, and could not possibly have been averted by any American action. (The cry of betrayal was heard all over Washington at the height of the Suez crisis, but it was directed mainly at Anthony Eden and Guy Mollet.) And in recent weeks there have been the cases of Syria and Thailand, where things have been going not at all as we would like them to go. Anyone who now asks at the State Department about the Syrian *coup d'état* and other developments in the Middle East is likely to be read a long Toynbeean lecture on the culture and tradition of the region, on its ancient history of instability, and on the folly of supposing that we Americans can do everything we wish; a Southeast Asia variant of the argument covers the Thailand situation. It is not only beyond the seas that American power has apparently become attenuated; even on our own soil there are areas where it is held to be inoperative. Before the President reluctantly went to the extreme of using federal troops in Little Rock, he repeatedly gave as his reason for failing to intervene in some other way his belief that there was nothing effective he could do. Administration economists protest the unfairness of holding the government responsible for the current inflation; this is a free society, they say, and while the Treasury prints the money and the Federal Reserve Board, which is theoretically independent of the administration, has some control over the discount rates and the amount of money in circulation, the ultimate value of our currency is determined by private citizens—as makers and purveyors and buyers of commodities and services. The President, taking a somewhat different tack in his speech before the directors of the World Bank and the International Monetary Fund earlier this week, said that there is inflation the world over, and that it has to be approached as an essentially global problem. Either way, there is no illusion of omnipotence; the United States government is quick to acknowledge that its ability to control events is far from absolute.

The illusion of omnipotence lies shattered today because the Republican Party has once more grown familiar with authority and responsibility. Out of office for twenty years, and ravening for the kind of issues that would restore them to office, the Republicans created and spread the particular myths that Mr. Brogan deplored in 1952. They were not specifically Republican myths, however, or even specifically American ones. In all countries, out-of-office politicians scour the world for disasters they can charge to the ruling party's account, and if the Democrats should be kept out of the White House as long as the Republicans were, they will create a set of their own myths. Some of them had a go at it in the last campaign, when they talked as if the President were responsible for the presence on earth of Colonel Nasser, and Harry S. Truman has recently argued that a vigorous administration in Washington could have foiled the so-called Captains' Plot in Damascus. Not all Republicans accepted the illusion they sought to create; at the national convention in 1952, Mr. Dulles conceded to reporters that the fall of China to the Communists was an event of somewhat greater complexity than he had made it out to be in the Party platform, but for justification he appealed to the part of the code of political ethics that holds those in power liable for both the credit and the blame for whatever occurs during their tenure. Some Republican politicians, though, did come to accept the illusion, and it was a realization of this that led a number of people here to feel that one excellent reason for giving the Republicans a turn at the helm was to let them learn by experience that the ship of state could not go everywhere its masters and its passengers chose to go.

The Republicans learned with almost breathtaking speed. One of the President's first and most popular acts was the negotiation of a Korean truce whose terms were a denial of omnipotence, and almost every settlement the administration has made or accepted since then, in both domestic and international affairs, has betrayed an acknowledgment of the imperfect and incomplete nature of sovereignty. At Geneva as well as at Panmunjom, in Indo-China and Suez as well as in Korea, in a whole series of appropriations bills as well as in the Civil Rights Act, Mr. Eisenhower and his associates have accepted compromise without apology and have often proclaimed it as victory. A fact that Mr. Brogan, and perhaps the Republican leaders themselves, did not appreciate in 1952 was that the illusion of omnipotence was really alien to the spirit of most Republicans. They could use it as a political gambit, but they could not possibly be governed by it in their political decisions. The core of Republican philosophy is that government is of very limited value in human affairs, that it is generally an impediment to the growth and development of a society, and that political virtue consists largely in the restraint and hobbling of politicians. Republicanism at its most characteristic holds that politics is the art of the possible and that not very much is possible. Robert A. Taft used to say that he actually had no principled objection to government intervention in the economic and social affairs of the country; he simply believed that the federal bureaucracy was too large and unwieldy and remote from the people to be able to do anything the way it ought to be done. Mr. Eisenhower's reasoning may follow a somewhat different line, but he comes out at the same place, and in this sense his credentials as a Republican of the classic breed are unchallengeable.

It is reassuring to know that illusions of omnipotence cannot flourish for very long in American politics, but what alarms some people now is the development of something very much like an illusion of American impotence. Especially in foreign policy, the administration has lately been acting not as if only a few things were possible but, rather, as if nothing were possible. The State Department loudly deplores adverse developments in far parts of the world and then learnedly explains why nothing could have been done to prevent them. The sensible view of history that Mr. Brogan urged on Americans has its political as well as its intellectual advantages (it reduces political hysteria, in addition to being, in all probability, true), but when it is combined in large quantities with the view that the future is almost certainly going to be as refractory as the past, it becomes a kind of soft Machiavellianism, a *Realpolitik* of inaction. We couldn't help what happened in the Middle East last month; *ergo* we can't help what is going to happen there next month, particularly since the policy that covers the area—the Eisenhower Doctrine—requires that we take no action until we are formally requested to by some Middle Eastern power. In the early stages of the Eisenhower administration, disengagement—especially from the Far Eastern conflicts of the period—was a conscious and vigorously pursued policy, whose aim, most people believed, was to permit a more effective engagement in the parts of the world that the President considered more important from the point of view of national interest. We got out of Korea, we stayed out of the war in Indo-China, and we narrowed the range of our commitments to the Chinese Nationalists because we wished to use the strength we had to better effect. But the tempo of disengagement never slackened; we have reduced our commitments not just in a couple of strategic places but very nearly everywhere, and because our commitments have become fewer, we have drastically reduced the power that is our primary resource in foreign policy. Military spending for all services is on the decline; hardly a week goes by without an announcement from the Pentagon of a necessary retrenchment in some program or other. Foreign aid has become almost wholly a matter of military aid to a few Asian and Middle Eastern countries. Aid for economic development consists of little more than a demonstration program here and there. It is not, as some people suppose, a resurgent isolationism that accounts for this. Mr. Eisenhower is not an isolationist of any sort, nor is Mr. Dulles. The President unquestionably believes as earnestly as he ever did in NATO, the United Nations, disarmament, and many other worthy things, and the Secretary of State is as ardent as he ever was about making the world a fit place for the righteous. But they have conducted foreign policy in such a way as to destroy the illusion of omnipotence and to encourage its replacement—in the administration itself, in Congress, and evidently, to a large degree, in the country as a whole—with the illusion that because we can do relatively little with our power, we need relatively little power.

PART FOUR

FAR-FLUNG

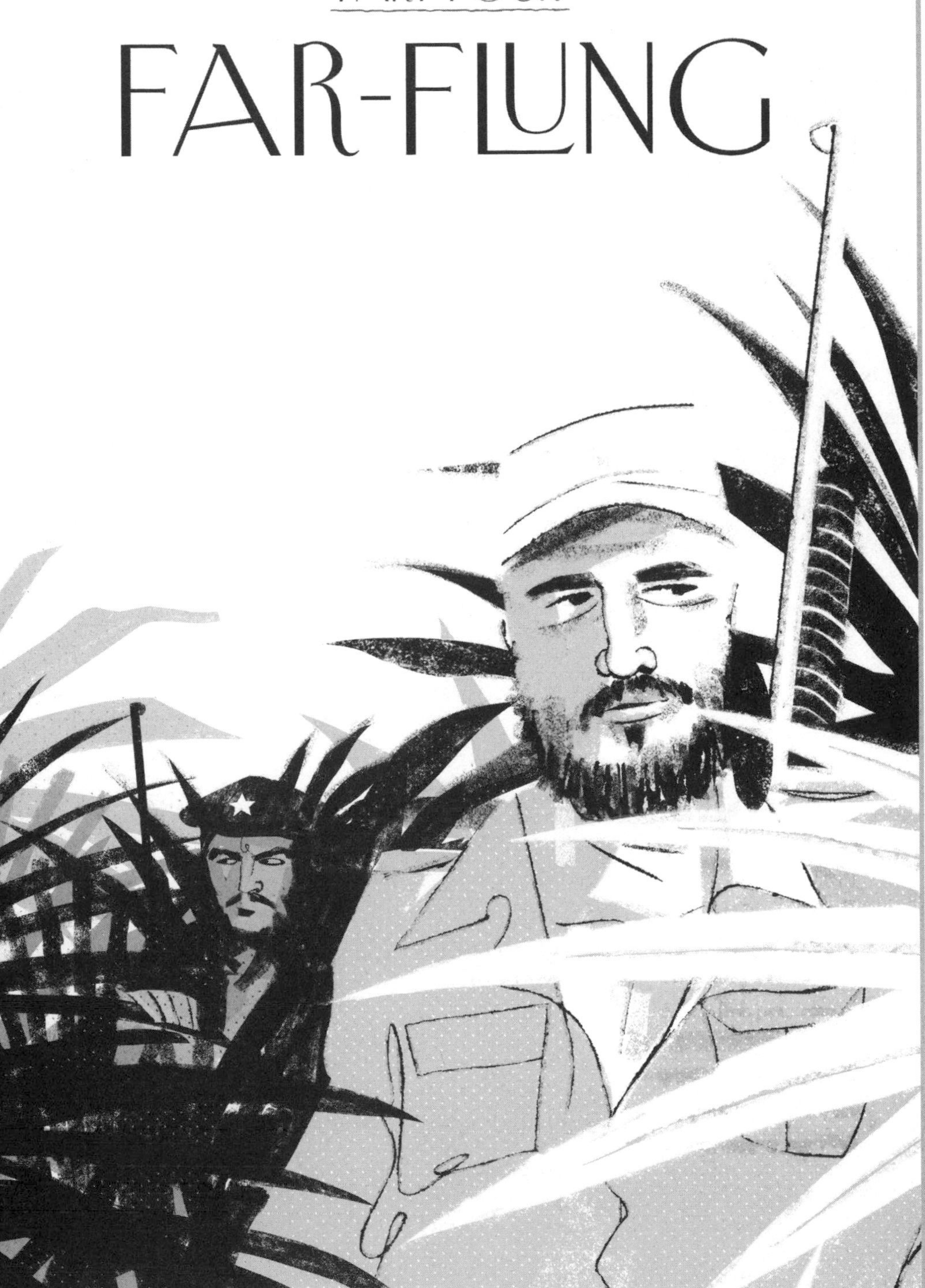

A NOTE BY EVAN OSNOS

IN THE SPRING of 1941, as America braced for war, Harold Ross wrote to E. B. White to lament the "present emergency" and to offer a note of reassurance. "War, after all, is simple. It's black and white," he wrote. "It's peace that is complex." The war was not simple, but the strange new peace that followed was every bit as vexing as Ross had predicted. In a comment in 1945, six months before the bombing of Hiroshima, White wrote, "We feel like a man who left his house to go to a Punch-and-Judy show and, by some error in direction, wandered into *Hamlet*."

The fifties presented *The New Yorker* with a planet that felt larger and more navigable, but also uncertain and inescapable, riven by ideology and energized by an atomic age that carried the prospect of transformative change or unspeakable harm. Members of the staff who had gone to war as greenhorns—St. Clair McKelway, writer and editor, had entered the Army knowing only the three-fingered salute of a Boy Scout—returned with knowledge and curiosity about the world beyond. E. J. Kahn, Jr., had joined the magazine straight from Harvard, but, after he was drafted, he wrote *The Army Life*, which narrated his experience from boot camp to battles in the Pacific. When the Americas and their allies went off to Korea, Kahn followed, in 1951, staying close to the front to describe battles like that of Gloster Hill, in which the surviving members of an outgunned British battalion crawled to safety beneath machine-gun fire in "a ditch about a foot deep."

By age and disposition, Ross was of an earlier era. His instincts were isolationist, but as a newsman he greeted the postwar world as a vast buffet. To W. Averell Harriman, he wrote, "We may sound provincial to you, but we seem like the *International Gazette* to me. We got started on the wide world during the war and can't quit."

For *The New Yorker*, the fifties brought some dividends: advertising had never been more abundant, and a miniature edition of the magazine distributed free to GIs had cultivated hundreds of thousands of new readers. But the decade also brought painful political pressures. E. B. White, Richard Rovere, and others raged in print against Joseph McCarthy's bullying and fearmongering. Critics nicknamed the magazine "The New Worker," and J. Edgar Hoover opened files on the staff. Privately, Ross worried that Janet Flanner, his Paris correspondent, was too congenial to socialism, and, in 1950, she was summoned to New York for some "reorientation." Thomas Kunkel, in *Genius in Disguise,* his biography of Ross, writes that Ross and Flanner met for coffee at the "21" Club and the conversation went poorly. He spoke anxiously about the rise in Europe of "the Commies," as he called them, and urged her to be skeptical of the French, according to her recollection. She offered her resignation, which he rejected, and she eventually returned to Paris and her writing.

There were other accusations. A couple of years later, shortly after William Shawn became the editor, Kay Boyle, a contributor of journalism and fiction, who had signed petitions and donated small sums to Communist-front groups, was called before a "loyalty hearing." Shawn wrote a letter; it attested to her "extraordinary character" but generally offered a muted defense, and he wouldn't pay her legal fees. She had last been published in *The New Yorker* eighteen months prior, and he declined to renew her accreditation as a correspondent in Germany. She blamed that decision for her being blacklisted from American magazines for years to come.

• • •

Beyond the reach of America's political turmoil, the magazine ventured into new territory. Traditions had to adapt. Because of an instinct for secrecy, Shawn was generally reluctant to commit his editorial notes and instructions to letters. But his newly far-flung writers left him no choice but to deliver his notes to Mary McCarthy in Venice by Western Union, in the argot of cable-ese: "EYE ALSO SUGGEST THAT YOU MIGHT CONSIDER RECASTING LAST TWO OR THREE SENTENCES."

The new frontiers created opportunities for new voices, writers with no New York pedigree but the language skills and the local knowledge to get to stories that others could not. Joseph Wechsberg, born in Czechoslovakia, knew only a few hundred words of English when, in 1938, he arrived in America. He had trained as a classical violinist, played in Paris nightclubs, and commanded a machine-gun unit on the Polish front, but he had never written. He soon discovered *The New Yorker* and resolved to write for it someday. Within four years, he had been drafted into the U.S. Army; on his way to Europe in a psychological-warfare division, he dropped by the *New Yorker* offices and offered to send the magazine a piece about his hometown, if he ever reached it. He did, and over the next three decades he published more than a hundred stories, mostly from Europe, where he could capture the often hidden dramas of private life under authoritarianism. To relay the story of East Germany's first popular revolt against Communist rule, in 1953, he recounted one day in the life of Friedrich Schorn, an accountant in a chemical factory, who awoke one morning so cowed by Soviet rule that he was afraid to listen to an illegal radio station. By nightfall, through the improbable chemistry of rebellion, he had emerged as a leader, a fugitive, and a *Barrikadenstürmer*—"a barricade fighter."

In one story or another, the magazine was struggling to make sense of a world in which some of our allies had survived the war only to lose control of their own countries. In 1953, four years after Chiang Kai-shek fled mainland China, defeated by Chairman Mao, Emily Hahn ventured to the island of Taiwan. She found Chiang, the Generalissimo, in reluctant repose—brooding, fussing over ill-fitting dentures, plotting his revenge with aging generals, aching "for the great day of glorious battle they hope will come." Every evening, she watched him pace the hills "in a long gown and a pith helmet," trailed by a fleet of creeping black Cadillacs, poised for the moment when the great man, or his cocker spaniel, had walked enough and the pair would slump into the limousine. Like her subject, Hahn was unsuited to the sedentary life. Brought up in St. Louis, she published her first piece in *The New Yorker* in 1929 and embarked on a foreign adventure that eventually encompassed eight decades and fifty-two books. She wrote of crossing Belgian Congo on foot, of her addiction to opium, of diamonds, and of D. H. Lawrence. She kept her trips to the office in New York to a minimum; on a rare visit to the city, she met the twelve-year-old Roger Angell, who later became an editor and writer, and handed him a monkey—"a small, solemn-faced, greenish-brown" macaque, he recalled. She instructed Angell not to let the monkey bite. "If she does," Hahn said, "bite her right back—bite her on the ear—and she'll never do it again." When Hahn died, in 1997, at the age of ninety-two, the magazine titled its remembrance "Ms. Ulysses."

Six decades later, the Taiwan that Hahn captured—low-slung, rural, remote—has vanished into a blur of high-speed trains and glass-walled skyscrapers. But other portraits that appeared in the *New Yorker* of the fifties astonish us today not because they are unrecognizable but because they are unfathomably unchanged. In 1957, A. J. Liebling visited a novelty of postwar geography, a "thin leg of coastal land now known to the world at large as the Gaza Strip." Nine years after the creation of Israel, the sliver of parched land abutting the Sinai and the Mediterranean was, in Liebling's estimation, already an orphan. To the south, Egyptians offered no citizenship to the Gazans; to the north, a checkpoint on the border with Israel was "a gateway to nowhere for three hundred thousand people." By the end of the century, the population of Gaza had ballooned at least sixfold, to 1.8 million, but its land was no larger, and its predicament endured. Its people remained, much as Liebling had found them, "trapped in a submarine at the bottom of the sea, with an uncertain air supply and no means of egress."

The dispatches of the fifties carry a sense of wonder and apprehension at a world "changed utterly," as Yeats had put it in 1916 in the midst of earlier convulsions. One doesn't find many predictions in the pieces here; rarer still are the predictions that proved to be true. In the spring of 1958, Norman Lewis, a nomadic British writer, set off for the Sierra Maestra in search of Fidel Castro, the young lawyer and intellectual who had gone to the mountains with his band of largely middle-class guerrillas. As a writer, Lewis liked to downplay his own significance; he once said he was as forgettable as "a minor character in an El Greco picture." (His peers disagreed. Auberon Waugh judged him "the greatest travel writer alive, if not the greatest since Marco Polo.") Castro's early experiments in rebellion had been "farcically mismanaged," Lewis wrote. In one battle, the guerrillas were "butchered out of hand by government troops." But, as Lewis stayed on in Cuba, he sensed that the government's confidence was misplaced. When he filed his dispatch, he acknowledged that the regime was determined to hold out. But, he added, "Castro might contrive to hold out even longer."

FROM

NO ONE BUT THE GLOSTERS

E. J. Kahn, Jr.

MAY 26, 1951 (ON A KOREAN WAR BATTLE)

IT IS HARD to tell at this date which battles of the Korean war military historians will ultimately single out for special mention, but it is doubtful whether they can overlook a recent two-and-a-half-day engagement that, whatever name the historians may settle on for it, is known now to those who went through it as the Battle of the Imjin, and that has already been officially characterized as "epic" by the Eighth Army. The battle began, just south of the Imjin River and some twenty-five miles northwest of Seoul, on the night of April 22nd, as the Chinese were launching their spring offensive all across the front, and it continued, without letup, until midafternoon of April 25th. The great majority of the United Nations troops who participated in it were British, of the 29th Brigade, but it was nonetheless a fittingly multinational affair, involving Belgians, South Koreans, and Filipinos, as well as Americans from both the continental United States and Puerto Rico. The 29th Brigade, with a total strength of sixty-six hundred and a front-line fighting strength of four thousand, suffered more than a thousand casualties during that bloody span of time.

Out of something like sixty thousand Chinese who assaulted the seventeen-thousand-yard sector the brigade was holding when the battle started, it is widely, if unofficially, believed that between ten and fifteen thousand were dispatched. And what is perhaps more important—since hordes of dead Chinese were almost as commonplace as hordes of live ones in Korea that particular week—is that the steadfast resistance of the British to this massive assault was very likely the most influential single factor in the dashing of the Communists' probable hope of celebrating May Day in the capital city of the Republic of Korea.

The entire 29th Brigade saw action in the Battle of the Imjin, but the worst assault fell upon one unit, the 1st Battalion of the Gloucestershire Regiment, informally called the Glosters. Of the six hundred and twenty-two Glosters who were in the most advanced of the brigade's three echelons when the fight got under way, just five officers and thirty-four other ranks were available for duty three days afterward, and they only because they had made a near-miraculous withdrawal through enemy fire so intense and enveloping that they subsequently said they felt like human targets in a shooting gallery.

• • •

During the daytime of April 22nd, there were no particular signs of trouble to come. All along the front, to be sure, the United Nations had for several days been awaiting the Chinese offensive, but no one could anticipate precisely when it would be launched, nor did the British seem more or less likely than any other troops in the line to bear the brunt of the attack. On the twenty-first, the British, who had the 1st Republic of Korea Division on their left and the American 3rd Infantry Division on their right, had sent an exploratory patrol across the Imjin. It had travelled ten thousand yards beyond the river and had encountered only a scattering of enemy troops. A British intelligence report took note of a "large undetermined number of enemy north of the river," but concluded that nothing more worrisome than strong enemy probing patrols could be expected on the twenty-third and twenty-fourth. The brigade troops in the line were getting hot meals and, assuming that they would continue to get them, had no combat rations along. That turned out to be unfortunate, for the most any one of them had to eat during the battle was one hard-boiled egg and a slice of bread.

Shortly after midnight of the twenty-second, when Saint George's Day was only half an hour old, Able Company of the Glosters was attacked. By four o'clock, the whole battalion was engaged, and by six the whole brigade. The enemy came in three waves. In the first rush, Able Company lost its commander and two other officers. One walkie-talkie operator, running out of ammunition, used his rifle as a club, swinging it at the Chinese as they came into his foxhole and shouting, "*Banzai,* you bastards! *Banzai!*" A few minutes later, the radioman regained his hereditary reserve and called into his transmitter, with finality, "We're overrun. We've had it. Cheerio." By midmorning, the Glosters had at least a regiment in front of them and, because the South Koreans on their left had been driven back several thousand yards, an indefinite number on the hills behind them. By midday, the Glosters hadn't been budged from the high points they had instructions to hold, but they were completely separated from the rest of the brigade, and the Chinese had penetrated so far back that the battalion's supply echelon was overrun, too, and nine of its men were taken prisoner. Quantities of the things the Glosters needed most desperately—machine guns, ammunition, and medical supplies—were packed into straw-lined bags and dropped to them by six light observation planes. A larger-scale airdrop was set up for the following morning. At dawn on the twenty-fourth, three Flying Boxcars were poised high over the Glosters' positions, waiting for the morning mist to lift so they could descend close enough to drop their cargo accurately. But when the mist rose, the pilots found the Glosters, and not a few Chinese, fighting literally inside a curtain of falling shells that the brigade's gunners and mortarmen were throwing around them. The planes couldn't dip down unless the shelling was halted, and the decision was up to the Glosters. The Glosters waved the hovering Boxcars away.

• • •

There had been three air strikes on Saint George's Day. On the twenty-fourth, there were so many that at noon a young American Air Force lieutenant who was serving as liaison between the brigade and its tactical air support stopped keeping track of individual strikes, as he had been conscientiously doing up to then. Probably some fifty planes gave the brigade a hand that morning. There were plenty of targets available to them. So many Chinese had infiltrated around the Glosters' flanks, both of which were by then exposed, that one air observer spotted some seven hundred of them standing around nonchalantly in a single group, in the open. One dive-bomber seared a Chinese-held hill with napalm. The nine Glosters captured the day before were on it, along with their guards. Several of the guards caught fire, and while they were frantically trying to beat out the flames, seven of the Glosters, who had somehow contrived to avoid being more than uncomfortably warmed, ran down the hill and escaped into the lines held by the Fusiliers and the Rifles. This was a particular relief to one of them, who had spent five years in a Nazi prisoner-of-war enclosure. The Fusiliers and the Rifles were better off than the Glosters, but they were having no picnic, either. There were Chinese behind them, too, and brigade headquarters organized a makeshift reinforcement party to help them out. It was composed of what little could then be mustered for the purpose: eight tanks from the Hussars, some Royal Engineers acting as infantry, a few Royal Army Service Corps lorries—which under normal circumstances wouldn't be sent too near the enemy but whose drivers in this instance volunteered to lumber along behind the tanks right to the front—and forty green replacements who had reported to the brigade that day and had been assigned to the Fusiliers. Some of them never got to report to the Fusiliers. There were so many enemy wandering around the countryside by then that the headquarters was under small-arms fire, and mortars were being lobbed out at the enemy from behind brigade headquarters—which, as a major in charge of the mortars later remarked, was a most ungentlemanly way to wage war.

The Glosters were in pretty bad shape on the morning of the twenty-fourth. The enemy had been at them all night long. Baker Company, which, like the three other rifle companies in the battalion, had a normal strength of a hundred and fifty men, was down to one officer and fifteen other ranks. It was nearly impossible to move out of a foxhole anywhere along the battalion line without drawing machine-gun fire. The Glosters nevertheless reassembled around a hill on which the battalion command post had been established. The line had shrunk from four miles to six hundred yards, but it still hadn't been breached. The Glosters begged several times that day for a helicopter to come and evacuate their more seriously wounded. The enemy, however, was so close on all sides that no helicopter could be sent out with any real hope of accomplishing this mission. That morning, Colonel Carne was asked if he thought a relief column could get through to him. He said no. (Communications with him had been spotty for some hours; artillery fire had knocked out all the telephone wires, and only two gradually fading radios linked the Glosters with the rest of the brigade.) That afternoon, in disregard of the Colonel's opinion, the first of three attempts to rescue the Glosters was made. A battalion of Filipino infantrymen and some supporting tanks got to within fifteen hundred yards of them, and then, in a defile, the lead tank was set afire, and the entire column was blocked and had to withdraw. Neither of the two subsequent relief columns—one composed of Belgian, Filipino, and Puerto Rican infantrymen and elements of the 8th Hussars, and the other of tanks and infantrymen from the American

3rd Division—got even that close. When the third try had failed, the Glosters, by that time seven miles deep in Chinese, were on their own.

• • •

Early on the morning of the twenty-fifth, the brigade was finally instructed to pull back to new defensive positions. It had held up the Chinese long enough to disrupt their timetable all across the front. Those of the Fusiliers and Rifles who could walk managed to withdraw in fairly good order. The non-walking wounded from these units were worse off. Some two hundred of them were loaded onto the backs and sides of eight Centurions, which started off toward the rear through a narrow mountain pass. They were ambushed by the Chinese. The wounded, lying exposed on the tanks, couldn't do anything about it, and the tank crews were almost as impotent. Their vehicles were so slippery with blood and so jammed with sprawled bodies that it was impossible to traverse the gun turrets. On the way out, two tank commanders were wounded. Both remained standing in their hatchways, one fainting there and reassuming command when he came to. An officer riding on the outside of one Centurion, who while aboard ship en route to Korea last fall had entertained at a troop show by putting on a fake mental-telepathy act, was startled when one of the wounded men raised his head and said, "Beg pardon, sir, but there's something I've been wanting to ask you. How'd you do that bloody trick?" The driver of another Centurion, one that had no wounded on it and was, accordingly, buttoned up tight, was surprised to hear a thumping noise overhead. Looking up through his periscope, he saw a Chinese soldier perched above him, pounding on the hatch cover in an effort to open it. Without slowing down, the driver swerved to one side, drove the tank clean through a Korean house, brushing the interloper off, and then resumed his course.

Before daylight each morning during the battle, the Chinese had been sounding the bugle calls with which they customarily herald their armed approach. Before dawn on the twenty-fifth, the three hundred or so Glosters who were still fit to fight counterattacked in just about the only manner left to them: their bugler blew a long reveille. It rang out, clear and astonishing, and it was followed by a series of other calls—short reveille, half-hour dress, quarter-hour dress, cookhouse, and, just for the hell of it, the American variation of reveille. It was an amazing concert. For the few minutes it lasted, both sides stopped firing. Then the Glosters cheered, and the fighting started up again. At five minutes past six, shortly after daybreak, the Glosters were advised by brigade headquarters that they had permission to break out. At six-twenty, the Glosters reported that they were surrounded and couldn't break out. But they still wanted air support, and they got it. By almost split-second coordination between air and artillery, a flight of dive-bombers swooped on the enemy just one and a half minutes after the artillery lifted a barrage it had been laying in. The Glosters by then were down to one small yellow air-ground recognition panel, and it was hard for the diving aircraft to know exactly where to strafe and bomb. But the Glosters threw a couple of smoke grenades out from their perimeter—thirty-five yards is a fair throw with a smoke grenade—and the planes aimed their machine guns where the grenades landed. Then bombs were dropped, at a somewhat, but not terribly much, more circumspect distance. The Chinese were hurt, and momentarily relaxed their pressure.

Colonel Carne summoned his company commanders to a hollow near his headquarters, where fifty or sixty stretcher cases were lying on the ground. He told them that all hope of carrying on as a unit was gone. He said he was going to stay where he was, and he gave them the option of surrendering or fighting their way out in separate groups. The commanders of Able, Baker, and Charlie Companies and their remaining men headed south, toward the United Nations line. It was the commander of Dog Company, Captain Mike Harvey, a twenty-eight-year-old officer from Portsmouth, who led out the group of thirty-nine that got back. He was in charge of Dog Company only by chance; its regular commander, a major, had gone to Japan on April 22nd for a rest. When the major arrived there, he heard that the spring offensive had started and caught the first plane back to Korea. Despite several tries, he was never able to make his way far enough forward to reach his unit. Harvey, a pink-cheeked man with horn-rimmed glasses and an unkempt mustache, is a Reserve officer who was in the Hampshire Regiment during the Second World War; up to April 22nd, he had thought of himself as a Hampshire man on loan to the Gloucestershire Regiment. Now he thinks of himself, without reservation, as a Gloster. He is unusually abstemious for a soldier, forgoing both tobacco and alcohol, principally because he has been interested in judo since the age of twelve and holds one of the highest ratings in the art. After he had assembled his withdrawal party, consisting then of twelve officers and ninety-two other ranks, he let the remnants of the three other companies start off ahead. "I stood on a hill watching them to see if they were really going," he said afterward.

"It was unbelievable that things had come to this pass." He decided not to go south himself but instead to try the unexpected and proceed due north for a mile, straight toward the Chinese rear, and then swing west a couple of miles, in an outflanking movement, before turning south. He warned his group that they would have to travel fast, exhausted though they were, and that there could be no stopping to aid anybody who might be wounded.

Proceeding cautiously, Harvey and his men didn't see a single Chinese for the first three miles. His scheme was working fine. Then, just as they were veering south, they ran into a few Chinese. The Glosters shot them and moved on. When only a few miles from a point where they thought friendly troops would be, they were heartened by the appearance overhead of a Mosquito plane, generally used as liaison between ground forces and fighter aircraft. The Mosquito circled above them and wagged its wings encouragingly, and they waved back. The Mosquito began to guide them homeward through the hills. Harvey was keeping his men on low ground whenever possible, knowing that the Chinese habitually congregate on ridges. Ultimately, they came into one valley, two miles long, that was almost a canyon, with precipitous walls on both sides and a floor about a quarter-mile wide. A stream flowed through it, and they waded along this for a mile or so, until it dwindled away. As they came out on dry ground, thirty or forty machine guns opened up on them, from both flanks. The Glosters made for a ditch about a foot deep and dived into it. By then, the Mosquito had radioed for fighter planes, and they had come buzzing along and were working over the slopes as energetically as they could. But the machine guns didn't let up. The Glosters crawled forward, keeping their heads below the level of the ditch, since raising them as much as an inch above it had already proved fatal to several. The ditch, like the river bed before it, was full of stones, and the soldiers' arms and legs were lacerated. One man's shoes had fallen apart in the river, but he kept going, first in his socks and then, as those disintegrated, barefoot. Every so often, the men came to a four- or five-yard stretch where the ditch petered out, and in the stumbling race for the next ditch more were hit and dropped.

Finally, rounding a bend, they saw some American tanks down the valley, just half a mile away. They crawled ahead eagerly, and got to within five hundred yards of them. The tanks opened up with machine guns and 76-mm. cannon, and the six Glosters in the lead fell. The Mosquito pilot, horrified by this case of mistaken identity—the tank men had no idea any friendly troops were still that far north—flew frantically toward the tanks, diving almost on top of them, but they kept on firing. Harvey's single file of men, on their bellies in the ditch, were receiving fire from the front and both sides, and the men at the rear of the column, most of whom had exhausted their ammunition, were being stabbed by Chinese who had rushed down the valley behind them. Harvey tied his handkerchief and scarf to a stick, put his cap on it, and waved it at the tanks. Simultaneously, the Mosquito made another pass at the tanks and dropped them a note. The tanks, suddenly aware of their error, ceased firing. The remaining Glosters reached the tanks and crouched behind them. Using them as a partial shield against the continuing enemy fire, they withdrew another five hundred yards, to the reverse slope of a small hill. There they climbed on the tanks and rode out, for three more miles under steady enemy fire. The tank men were heartsick over their mistake. One of them took off his shoes and gave them to the Gloster who'd lost his. The lieutenant in command of the tanks kept asking how many of the Glosters his people had wounded. The Glosters, not wanting to make him feel any worse, wouldn't tell him; indeed, they didn't know for sure. The lieutenant was wounded himself getting them out.

As soon as Harvey got to a telephone, he called brigade headquarters. "I thought we had better get back, in case they wanted us again," he explained later. "Then I learned that we were the only survivors and that everyone else was missing. And everyone else is still missing." A week after the battle, the Glosters he had led out invited him to stop by for a beer. He hadn't touched the stuff in over three years, but to please them he drank a glass. "It tasted pretty awful," he said. "Being a judo man, it doesn't suit me."

• • •

The 1st Battalion of the Gloucestershire Regiment began reorganizing the day after the Battle of the Imjin ended. A few days after that, the handful of men from the old battalion and the new replacements lined up in a green Korean field for a simple memorial service. Massed around a table covered with a white cloth and bearing a cross and two candles, they stood with heads bared as their new battalion chaplain walked toward them in a white robe. Captain Harvey, now the battalion's new adjutant, distributed hymnals. The Glosters sang two hymns and, snapping to attention, a stanza of "God Save the King." After a few words from the battalion's new commander, who himself had been shot in the wrist during the Battle of the Imjin, the chaplain recited the names of the known dead, and the names of Colonel Carne and Sergeant Major Hobbs, as symbolic of, respectively, the officers and other ranks listed as missing. Then the chaplain told a story from Ecclesiastes about a city under siege, and how, after all hope was seemingly gone, a good and wise man had saved it. And yet, in spite of that, the chaplain said, the poor wise man was very soon forgotten. "In England, they'll remember for a little while," he went on. "The soldier does have his day. I want to remind you this afternoon that it is not enough to remember now. We've got to show what we think of their sacrifice in the way we conduct ourselves in the days ahead. We are, as it were, a link between our past and the future, and if we are to be faithful to our past, we must hand on to future generations some of the heritage of the past. Having handed it on, we will be in some measure worthy of those who died that we might live."

THE SEVENTEENTH OF JUNE

Joseph Wechsberg

AUGUST 29, 1953 (ON AN UPRISING IN EAST GERMANY)

At half past six on the morning of last June 17th, Friedrich Schorn, a gaunt man of thirty-nine with a bony face and deep-set eyes, left his three-room apartment in Merseburg, a city of forty-five thousand, ten miles west of Leipzig, in the Soviet Zone of Germany, and boarded a streetcar that would take him to his job in the suburb of Leuna. Schorn, a married man and the father of two children, was employed as an accountant at the Leunawerke Walter Ulbricht, which is Soviet Germany's largest chemical concern. The evening before, he had heard rumors that the workers on East Berlin's much publicized housing development on the Stalin-Allee had gone out on strike, and he couldn't help wondering what that might mean. It was well known in the Soviet Zone that the men working on the Stalin-Allee project were *Aktivisten,* hand-picked by the German Communists for their industry and efficiency. Schorn's first thought had been that things must really be bad when even the men on the Stalin-Allee weren't satisfied. But it certainly hadn't occurred to him that evening that for more than seven hours the following day he would be leading a substantial part of the first big known popular uprising against Communist domination, an uprising that Mayor Ernst Reuter of West Berlin has since said ranks in historical significance with the storming of the Bastille.

The Leuna Works, once a segment of the I. G. Farben empire, were taken over in 1945 by the Soviets, as were several important steel and mining operations in the Zone, and made an S.A.G., which officially stands for "Staatliche Aktien Gesellschaft [State Stock Company]" but is more generally and more cynically known as "Sowjet Aktien Gesellschaft," because the Soviet takes a more direct interest in the vital S.A.G. industries than it does in most of the state-owned enterprises. A vast industrial establishment covering five square miles and employing over twenty-eight thousand workers, the Leuna plant produces synthetic gasoline, fertilizers, and many other valuable chemical products, which are widely exported, making it an important earner of hard currency and one of the prizes of the Soviet regime in East Germany. It is the largest plant in the vicinity of Merseburg. The general manager and his principal aides are Russians; the second-echelon men are Germans. The S.E.D. (the Sozialistische Einheitspartei Deutschlands, or Socialist Unity Party, as the Communist Party of East Germany calls itself) is tightly organized inside the plant, and the workers are under constant surveillance by spies, informers, and the *Werkschutz*, a heavily armed industrial militia. The Leuna plant is not the sort of place in which one would expect an outbreak of strikes and open rebellion. Still, it is an S.A.G. operation, so the authorities take a more sophisticated view of things there than in the ordinary state-owned factories. The Russians are more concerned about quantity and quality of output than about loyalty to ideologies. Though the chemists and technicians at the Leuna Works may not be politically reliable, they are highly appreciated—far more so, in fact, than the 100 percent Communist Party men who have no outstanding skills. Specialists at Leuna who earn more than ten thousand Ostmark (six hundred dollars) a year are given contracts and are never harangued about joining the Party or obliged to attend political-indoctrination meetings. As long as they deliver the goods, they are left pretty much alone.

• • •

During the streetcar ride out to the plant that morning, Schorn became aware that something was up. Even more than most people living under the pressures of Soviet Germany, he had developed the technique of listening without turning his head or showing any other indication of interest. Schorn learned to control his facial expressions during four years and two months, from 1946 to 1950, that he spent in the Soviet concentration camp at Buchenwald, an experience that may also account for his emaciated body, on which his clothes hang loosely, and the lines in his thin, ascetic face. So Schorn sat there on the streetcar deadpan while a stranger next to him told everybody within earshot that he'd kept his radio tuned in on RIAS, the American broadcasting station in West

Berlin, all night long. "I heard an appeal by the leader of the West Berlin trade unions," the man was saying. "It was a fine speech. He called on workers everywhere to join the strike of the Stalin-Allee workers. Transportation and railway workers in East Berlin have already joined, he said. The more the better was his idea."

A few people on the streetcar said, "He's right," or nodded approval. Two *Vopos* (members of the *Volkspolizei*, or People's Police) were standing on the rear platform and presumably heard what the man was saying, but they did nothing. That seemed strange to Schorn. In East Germany, listening to RIAS is not forbidden, but repeating what one has heard over it is regarded as a crime against the state. Schorn never listened to RIAS. He was afraid to. His father-in-law is an old-time Communist, who joined the Party back in 1919 and always finds explanations and apologies for the Party's difficulties in East Germany, or simply dismisses them as "children's diseases that every new regime goes through." Schorn's wife, Lieselotte, who has been thoroughly indoctrinated by her father, is a leader in the S.E.D. in Merseburg. Schorn himself, who is the son of a minor official in East Prussia, was a member of the Nazi Party from 1933 to 1935; he then admired Hitler for "doing a lot for the simple workingmen." During the war, Schorn was a flier in the Waffen S.S., the élite troops of the Nazi overlords, and after the fall of Germany he was sent to a British prisoner-of-war camp. He escaped and made his way back to Merseburg, where he found that his wife had excellent connections with the new Communist regime.

It didn't take Schorn long to reach the conclusion that the Communists were not for him. Within a couple of months he became embittered at the way they interfered with his life. Then, during an argument with his father-in-law, he announced that he didn't want to bring up his children "in a Soviet swamp," and a few days later he was arrested by the Soviet secret police and sent to Buchenwald. He doesn't like to talk much about the time he spent there. "But Buchenwald did one good thing for me," he told me not long ago, in West Berlin, to which he escaped after the June 17th uprising was forcibly put down. "It cured me of Nazism forever. Some of the well-known Nazis were prisoners there when I was—men I had once considered gods. I was shocked to see what a cheap, cowardly bunch they were close to."

Schorn and his wife have always been very much attached to each other, despite their political differences, and after he was released from Buchenwald, early in 1950, she helped him get a job in the accounting department of the Leuna Works. He began to study the theory of Communism, though for reasons his wife didn't care much for. "It was clear to me by that time that the Communist system could be beaten only with its own weapons," he told me. "I decided to study dialectics so I could convince the Comrades that they were wrong. I joined the German-Soviet Friendship Society at Leuna and was even elected secretary of its branch at the plant. My wife didn't like that. 'The fact that you can be elected to office in the Society shows a weakness in our system,' she said."

Last May 28th, the German government of the Soviet Zone—the Politburo of the S.E.D.—decreed a 10 percent increase in everybody's production norm. The contents of Schorn's pay envelope the following week shrank almost 15 percent, owing to the loss of a bonus he had been receiving for exceeding his old norm. A few days later, on June 11th, the Communist papers and radio made public an admission by the same Politburo that it had committed "serious mistakes" in failing to provide adequately for the people's standard of living. On June 14th, the S.E.D. paper *Neues Deutschland* printed a severe attack on those in charge of the building industry, accusing them of using "sledge-hammer methods" in their dealings with the workers and warning them against trying to attain the new norms "by threats or force." The Red Army paper, *Tägliche Rundschau,* announced that the East German government "recognized previous errors and failures." One government leader after another publicly confessed that he had been guilty of mistakes. A fundamental revision of economic policies was promised. Farmers were told that the land would be considered theirs and that there would be no more attempts at collectivization. Workers were promised higher wages and better food. Refugees to West Germany were asked to come back, and assured that everything would be forgiven. The *Volkspolizei* became polite.

"It was obvious that something mysterious and possibly very significant was going on," Schorn said to me. "For eight awful years we'd lived in almost constant terror—told what to think, what to eat, what to read. There was no happiness in the Zone, and no hope, only *Galgenhumor* [gallows humor]. Our pastors had been arrested. We'd seen relatives and friends carted away by the Soviet secret police—or been carted away ourselves. Ninety percent of the inhabitants of Soviet Germany had no use for the so-called German Democratic Republic. For years, the government had been promising that living conditions would get better. Instead, they got worse. My wife had a job, and together we earned eight hundred marks a month, which is far better than the average family, but sometimes after the fifteenth of the month we had no money left to buy food. We hadn't seen butter, margarine, or any other fats for months. Potatoes, as you know, mean to a German what spaghetti means to an Italian. Well, potatoes were first rationed and then disappeared entirely. In recent months, there had been less food than ever. Whole villages had been abandoned. The farmers were afraid of collectivization, and ran off to West Germany, leaving their fields to go to seed. The authorities sent Free German Youth boys out to work the fields, but what could those kids do? Our bread became dark and very expensive. Bakers were forbidden to tell their customers what they put into the bread. The price of everything was going up all the time. The distribution system had broken down. Last Christmas, the H.O. [state-owned stores] were selling bathing suits, and when spring came they were selling ski boots. There was a widespread feeling that life simply could not go on like that much longer. But the government was apparently plunged in confusion and didn't seem to know what to do about it. S.E.D. officials went around with a worried look on their faces. The entire Zone was a powder keg, waiting for a spark to touch it off. The strike of the Stalin-Allee workers was the spark."

• • •

Some of the people on the streetcar began to curse Walter Ulbricht, the Moscow-trained Deputy Prime Minister of Soviet Germany, whose name adorns the Leuna Works; as head of the S.E.D., Ulbricht is the most powerful man in the Zone. The two *Vopos* on the rear platform still acted as if they had heard nothing. Upon getting off the streetcar, Schorn made his way to the administration building of the Leuna Works and walked upstairs to the accounting offices, where he at once became convinced that the explosion of the powder keg was imminent. The time was seven-fifteen, the beginning of the day shift. No one was doing any work in the offices; everyone was talking about the Berlin uprising. About 80 percent of the employees at Leuna, whether factory hands or white-collar workers, are not members of the Communist Party. Of the 20 percent who are, three-quarters are "nominal members." People in the Zone make a fine distinction between nominal members—those who have joined only to keep their jobs and whose sole Party activity is to hand over six marks in dues each month—and *Antreiber,* or agitators. Not even all the *Vopos* in the Zone are thoroughgoing Communists;

many of them joined the service primarily because the pay is good and food is always plentiful. The lowest-rank *Vopo* gets four hundred marks a month, which is more than a university professor gets. An *Unterleutnant* in the *Volkspolizei* makes up to twelve hundred marks a month, or more than the manager of a factory, and some of these lieutenants are only nineteen years old.

One of the nominal Party members whispered to Schorn, "Now's the time I'd like to see the regime blown sky-high. We can't go on like this forever—saying one thing and meaning another." Then two confirmed Party men came up, and the nominal member turned to them and said he thought that everything at the plant was under control and that the government should be tough in its attitude toward malcontents. At a nearby desk, a worker said to one who was passing by, "Hans, if I may give you some friendly advice, take your Party emblem off." The other man walked away as if he hadn't heard, but a while later he reappeared minus his Party emblem. Schorn was told by a friend that the members of the plant's S.E.D. district committee had been summoned to an emergency meeting.

Schorn left his office and walked through the plant's workshops. Everywhere the air was charged with tension. He found that some locksmiths in ME 15, the main workshop, were talking of going on strike. ME 15 had been in a rebellious state for the past two weeks, following the arrest by police of the State Security Service of fourteen workmen there who, it was said, were now locked up in prison in Halle, about nine miles away. Several men came up to Schorn and told him they thought the plant should support the Stalin-Allee workers. Schorn cautiously approached a few people in each workshop and asked them what they intended to do. He talked only to those whose Party loyalties he believed to be no more than lukewarm. Without exception, they said they were ready to go out on strike. Schorn walked slowly back to his office, pondering the situation. It was now twenty minutes past nine. Over the *Werkfunk,* the plant's loudspeaker system, came the voice of the S.E.D. district-committee chairman. He asked the men to settle down to work. "You will get more to eat, but you must not stop working," he said. "We must all exceed our norms. Get to work. You need the money." In Schorn's office, people began cursing the S.E.D. man. There were shouts of "Shut up, you *Lump*!" and "Pack your bags, Comrades, and go back to Moscow!" and "We want to be governed by German Germans, not by Russian Germans!" This last was an allusion to Ulbricht and Wilhelm

Pieck, the President of East Germany, both of whom lived for years in Moscow and reportedly became Soviet citizens. The voice of the district-committee chairman was soon drowned out by the shouts and boos.

"Then I happened to look out the window at a large courtyard in front of our building," Schorn recalls. "The big clock there said twenty-eight minutes past nine. Suddenly groups of men came running out of ME 15. They were shouting and waving their arms. I don't remember exactly what happened next, but I found myself running out of the office and down the stairs. Everybody must have had the same thought, for there were people all around me, and when I got to the courtyard, men and women were running toward it from all sides, shouting incoherently. Later that day, I asked some people what had made them run out there, and they all had the same answer—they said they felt they *had* to. They knew that this was the moment they'd been praying for all these years—the great, wonderful moment when they would again do what they wanted to do."

A flight of perhaps a dozen steps led from the courtyard up to an entrance to the headquarters building, where the Russian general manager and the other Russian executives had their offices. The crowd converged on the steps, with Schorn in the vanguard. Some of the men were clutching hammers or other tools that they had neglected to drop when they ran out of the factory, and now they raised them threateningly in the direction of the general manager's office. There were shouts of "The S.E.D. must get out of Leuna!" and "Strike! Let's strike!" and "Down with the higher norms!" Evidently, the men were mostly concerned with better working conditions inside Leuna and had not yet grasped the larger implications of a strike.

At the foot of the steps, Schorn spoke to the men nearest to him. "This isn't a matter of just Leuna," he said. "It's a matter of every German in the Soviet Zone. Everything is at stake. But violence isn't the answer. If we overrun the plant and wreck the machinery, we'll only have to rebuild it later. Let's keep order!" Some of the men nodded in agreement, and two pushed Schorn ahead of them up the steps. Then someone began to sing "Deutschland, Deutschland über Alles," and the crowd joined in. No one has been allowed to sing the "Deutschlandlied" in East Germany since 1945. "Standing there and singing the 'Deutschlandlied' meant the same thing to all of us," Schorn said to me. "It meant that we Germans wanted to be together again—East and West, from the Rhine to the Oder. Men and women put their arms around one another. Women were crying. There were thousands in the courtyard by the time we finished singing the anthem."

The ranking German in the plant—Dr. Eckard—and several of his assistants came out of the headquarters building and stood on a small platform at the top of the steps. These men were skilled engineers, assistant managers, and department heads who, whether motivated by conviction or by opportunism, were on the side of the Russian management; Schorn calls them the *Intelligenz*. Behind the *Intelligenz* stood a couple of members of the *Werkschutz,* holding their guns ready. A microphone, linked to the plant's loudspeaker system, was brought out onto the platform and Dr. Eckard raised his hands and began to speak. He urged the crowd to go back to work and assured them that their demands would be given "immediate consideration." The crowd's answer was a loud and protracted howl. No one moved. Dr. Eckard tried a more conciliatory line, expressing his understanding for "the legitimate demands you people have made," as Schorn recalls his words, but by this time the crowd had become unruly. Again the men were gesticulating with their hammers.

"I was standing not far below Dr. Eckard," Schorn told me. "The crowd had pushed me up there. One of the workers behind me, a fellow I knew, said, 'Take over, Schorn, or something will go wrong.' I stepped up toward Dr. Eckard, who was now talking about the necessity of fulfilling our norms, and said, 'Pardon me, *Herr Doktor,* but I disagree with you.' Then I stopped short. My voice had boomed all over the courtyard. In my excitement, I hadn't realized that I was now standing in front of the microphone. The crowd down below began to yell and applaud. A man just behind me shouted, 'You tell them what we want, Schorn!,' and then Dr. Eckard was somehow pushed away and I found myself standing in his place. I wasn't very representative of the factory workers, of course, but I was well known among them because I'd been in Buchenwald. People in the Zone don't trust one another, but they know that a man who has spent four years in a Soviet concentration camp can be no friend of the system. I was what they call an *eiserner Hasser* [an ironhearted hater] of Communism.

"Well, Dr. Eckard and the *Intelligenz* moved back into the doorway, or perhaps they were pushed back by our men, who by this time were swarming around me. I can still see the surprised look on Dr. Eckard's face. Some of his men appeared to be quite afraid. That encouraged me. I faced the courtyard and said, 'I am taking over the microphone!' An enormous roar went up from the crowd. There must have been twenty thousand people down there. Then I introduced myself and told them that, as they probably knew, there was a strike on in East Berlin and that we workers at Leuna should declare our solidarity with the strikers. There was terrific applause. I said it was no longer a question of going back to work under the old norms, or any norms, and then I brought up the demands that people had told me RIAS was proposing—the immediate resignation of the government, free and secret elections, the unification of Germany, an opportunity for all political parties to operate freely, a higher standard of living for everybody, the immediate release of all political prisoners, the disarming of the *Volkspolizei* and the *Werkschutz,* and the immediate reestablishment of the old norms. That all added up to quite a speech, and after each demand there was much cheering. Sometimes I had to repeat a sentence two or three times before I could make myself heard. While I was talking, somebody hung a big sheet of paper out of a window of the administration building with the words 'WIR FORDERN FREIE WAHLEN [We Demand Free Elections]' and 'SEID EINIG, EINIG, EINIG [Unite, Unite, Unite]' scrawled on it. People down in the courtyard began to shout, 'Let's get out of here! Let's march into town!' I raised my hand, and finally they quieted down a little. I told them that the maintenance crews must stay on the job in the plant. After all, you can't just walk out of a large chemical plant like Leuna and leave it alone for hours. It would blow up and vanish. 'We must be orderly!' I said. 'Let's not do anything illegal. We have a constitutionally guaranteed right to strike, but we must not weaken our cause by crimes against life and property. Our position must remain strong, and it can remain strong only as long as we maintain law and order. Above all, let's not forget that this is a strictly German affair. If we don't offend the Russians, the Russians ought not to interfere.'"

Again the crowd roared enthusiastically. Dr. Eckard and his *Intelligenz* had disappeared. Schorn proposed that three volunteers from each workshop step forward to form a strike committee. The crowd shouted approvingly, and there was considerable shuffling and milling around until this had been accomplished. Then the names of the committee members were announced, and there was another ovation, after which Schorn was elected chairman by general acclamation. He made a short acceptance speech. "Friends," he said. "I'm going to call you friends because we want no more of the *Kollegen* and *Kameraden* we've been hearing around here for the past eight years. Friends, our great Leuna Works will no longer be disgraced by bearing the name of Walter Ulbricht." There was a jubilant outcry, and, with perfect timing, a giant picture of Ulbricht on the façade of the administration building was pulled down. Men and women shouted and embraced in a paroxysm of happiness.

Meanwhile, the members of the *Werkschutz* had surrendered their weapons to some of the ringleaders of the crowd. (In some factories, the *Werkschutz* was disarmed by order of the management. Perhaps the only matter on which the Russians, the government, and the strikers were agreed in East Germany on June 17th was that bloodshed must be avoided.) Schorn issued orders that no one was to carry the weapons surrendered by the *Werkschutz*, and they were shut up in a storeroom. Next, he told the crowd that a group of volunteers was going to Halle immediately to free their fourteen fellow-workers in ME 15 from the prison there. Then the strike committee decided to send a courier to the Buna plant, at Halle, where more than twenty thousand workers were employed producing synthetic rubber. "We're going to ask Buna to join our movement," Schorn said over the loudspeaker. Just then, the main gate leading into the courtyard swung open and a man on a motorcycle drove through. He was from Buna. He was triumphantly taken before the microphone, where he announced that Buna had gone out on a sympathy strike with Berlin. Buna was asking Leuna to join.

"Then the crowd went really wild," Schorn said to me. "I'll never forget that moment. Suddenly everyone realized that all over East Germany at that very moment people were rising and cheering for freedom, just as we were. Obviously, it was not just a coincidence that we and Buna had done the same thing at the same time, though there had been no communication between the two plants. We sensed that ten, fifty, a hundred miles away the same thing was happening in other plants. Here in West Berlin, I've since talked to men from the electrochemical Kombinat in Bitterfeld, the Agfa S.A.G. and the Farbenfabrik in Wolfen, and the Leipzig ball-bearing works. It was the same story everywhere. Yet people say that there can't be a revolutionary mass movement without organized leadership. There was no organized leadership that day."

• • •

It was unanimously decided to march into the city of Merseburg, a couple of miles away, and hold a demonstration on the Uhlandsplatz, a square in the center of the town. Schorn and the other members of the strike committee marched at the head of what was to become a very long parade. "News of the events at Leuna travelled faster than we did," Schorn told me, "and as we approached the city, workers from smaller factories came out of the side streets and fell into line. It turned out that there had been the same spontaneous uprising in every plant in Merseburg, and now the workers in them wanted to join Leuna, the largest plant of all. Housewives with shopping bags, men with briefcases, and carpenters and plumbers still carrying their tools joined us, too. Shopkeepers closed their stores and fell into step. The white-coated salesgirls of the H.O. stores deserted their counters and came with us. As we passed a grade school, we saw boys and girls throwing pictures of Stalin and Pieck out of the windows. Some painters from our plant had brought along buckets of paint and brushes, and when they saw a Communist poster, they would quickly paint it over with our slogans—'NIEDER MIT ULBRICHT [Down with Ulbricht]' or 'LEUNA STREIKT [Leuna on Strike].' They worked so fast that the people behind us in the parade wondered what had become of the Communist posters we'd all grown so accustomed to." Most of the members of the *Volkspolizei* had disappeared, but a few of them tried to stand in the way of the parade. The workers just laughed at them. "Out of the way!" they shouted. "Stand aside or join us!" In two or three instances, the *Vopos* took off their caps and blouses and fell into step with the workers.

When the Leuna column arrived at the Uhlandsplatz, workers from Buna and from the nearby Ammendorferwerke were already there, and so was what seemed to be the entire population of the city. Many people had also come in from the surrounding small towns and villages, and new groups were arriving all the time. Schorn estimates that eventually there were between seventy and eighty thousand men, women, and children there. He discussed the situation with the strike leader from the Buna Works, and they agreed on a course of action. A command post was set up in front of an inn; it consisted of a large truck flanked by two loudspeaker trucks. Schorn got up on an improvised speaker's platform on the big truck and through a microphone linked to the loudspeakers briefly summarized the purpose of the demonstration. "I was surprised by the response," he told me. "There was no doubt that the whole city was backing us up. Ordinarily, the Merseburgers are cool, restrained people, but now they were cheering and singing and applauding like a crowd in Italy or Spain. It was a real *fiesta*."

While members of strike committees representing various factories introduced themselves to the crowd, Schorn and some of the other leaders went around to the local prison. They encountered no resistance there, for the *Vopos* on duty swiftly disappeared and the guards handed over the keys to the cells. "We went into the prison office and checked through the list of prisoners, separating the political prisoners from ordinary criminals," Schorn said. "We liberated all the political prisoners, including the so-called economic criminals—people who had been sentenced to fifteen or twenty years for trumped-up income-tax evasions, so that their businesses could be taken over and nationalized. We did not free the common criminals."

The strike committee sent off two telegrams setting forth the workers' demands—one to the government, in East Berlin, and the other to the Soviet Military Administration, in Karlshorst. "We were very proud of our telegram to Karlshorst, which we thought would convince the Soviet High Command that we were planning no wrong," Schorn said. "In it we asked the High Command to respect the legitimate demands of the workers and to refrain from any measures that might stop our strike. Thus, we said, the Soviet Union would prove its sympathy with the working classes."

A special delegation was sent to the mayor of Merseburg, who, unlike most of the local government officials, had remained in his office. The delegation notified him that the strikers had taken over the city and that he would have to obey their orders. He agreed, and he was told, among other things, to see to it that there was no breakdown in the food-distribution system. While the delegation was issuing its orders, the mayor was called to the phone. When he returned, he said, "That was the Russians. They wanted to know how I am."

"What did you tell them?" one of the strikers asked.

"I told them that I was all right and about to negotiate with you," the mayor replied.

• • •

Shortly before two that afternoon, Schorn was conferring with other strike leaders at the command post when word reached him that some Russian soldiers had driven into the town. They had taken over the prison, and had then arrested a number of strikers and locked them up in it. Schorn reported to the crowd what had happened. A roar of protest went up, and Schorn said, "We will go to the prison with three truckloads of workers and take the prison back from the Russians." Everybody cheered.

By the time Schorn and his men drove up in front of the prison, the Russians, reinforced by several *Vopos,* had barricaded themselves inside it. The Russians turned fire hoses on the strikers through the windows. The strikers retaliated by throwing stones, one of which punctured a hose and put it out of commission. At this point, Schorn demanded to speak to the Russian commandant. After a while, a young lieutenant appeared, and Schorn said, "I warn you that unless you turn the prison back to the workers at once there will be bloodshed." The Russian lieutenant looked out at the street, which was by now chock-full of people. He shrugged and told Schorn to wait. In a few minutes, the door was opened, and the Russian soldiers and the *Vopos* came out. Behind them were the strikers the Russians had arrested. Schorn got up on one of the trucks and admonished the crowd to let the Russian soldiers through. Then he and the workers drove back in triumph to the Uhlandsplatz, where he informed the waiting crowd that their mission had been successful.

"Again there was great jubilation, but it didn't last long," Schorn told me. "A few minutes later, a large number of Russians entered the square. I was standing in front of the microphone, talking to the crowd, when I saw them coming. There were motorized guns, and a long column of trucks filled with infantry soldiers. Most of the people in the crowd were facing the speaker's platform and had no idea they were there. I kept talking—I had to keep talking to give myself time to think. To tell the truth, I was terribly shocked. No one had known for sure what the Russians would do, but some of the optimists had thought that maybe they would help us get rid of the Ulbricht government. Others, like me, had just been hoping and praying that the Russians would not interfere. After all, there had been so much talk about the soft new course the Russians were taking. Surely they would not march against workers! Soviet Russia had always posed as the champion of the working class, and out there in the square the workers were simply demanding their rights."

As word got around that the Russians were there, it grew very quiet in the square. Some people smiled shakily at the newcomers and a few even greeted them, and the Soviet officers smiled back from their jeeps and waved their hands, while the enlisted men sat on their trucks, holding their guns on their knees, and stolidly looked straight ahead. The crowd slowly parted, and the column made its way through the square and came to a halt in front of the speaker's platform. Schorn thereupon asked the people to remain quiet and pointed out again that violence would get them nowhere.

"At first, the strikers did as they were told, but gradually their mood changed," Schorn said to me. "Some began to shout abuse at the Russians and a few spat on their trucks. I knew that things would get out of hand if we stayed there much longer. I stepped back to talk the matter over with the other strike leaders, and they agreed that we had better break it up, so I went to the microphone and told the people that our demonstration had been a success and that the workers would now march back in orderly ranks to their factories. They were to await instructions from their strike committees, which would keep in touch with a central strike committee that was to be set up later that day. No one, I said, should go back to work until the central strike committee gave orders to that effect. The people reacted well. They formed columns and marched off in perfect discipline. The Soviet soldiers, their guns on their knees, still sat on the trucks and stared straight ahead of them."

• • •

Back at the Leuna Works, Schorn found to his relief that things had been quiet there while the demonstration was going on in Merseburg. The maintenance crews had kept things going, and reported that nothing had been damaged. Schorn asked whether RIAS had broadcast any specific strike instructions to the committees in the Zone, and was disappointed to learn that it had not. He felt isolated, and the lack of contact with the outside world made him uncertain what to do next. "You can't move when you don't know what's happening on your flanks," he told me. "There were sporadic bits of news from nearby towns, but no one knew what was going on in Halle, or Magdeburg, or Jena, or Weimar, or Leipzig, or Dresden, or Brandenburg. I knew we had to do something, but the big question was what."

Schorn climbed to the platform at the top of the steps from which he had addressed the crowd earlier in the day. By now, most of the workers had returned from town and were standing or sitting in groups all over the courtyard, waiting for further instructions. The special detachment of strikers that had been sent to Halle returned and reported that the fourteen prisoners from ME 15 had been liberated, and once more cheers went up.

And then the Russians came. It was four-fifteen when the first column appeared outside the main gate. It was made up of truckloads of infantry soldiers armed with machine guns and anti-aircraft guns; there were no tanks. The trucks drove slowly through the gate and stopped. As in Merseburg, the soldiers didn't leave their trucks, or the officers their jeeps. For a while, neither side made a move. Then a few of the workers began to throw stones at the Russians, who continued to sit there quietly. Schorn at once seized the microphone and shouted to the crowd, "Keep calm! Stay where you are! We'll go in and talk to the management." With that, he and three other members of the strike committee went to the office of the Russian general manager. They went in without bothering to knock.

The Russian general manager was sitting behind his desk, surrounded by several of his assistants. He invited Schorn and the other men to sit down, but Schorn said they preferred to stand. Then he announced that the workers at Leuna were going out on a formal strike. The general manager coughed, cleared his throat, and replied that he was no longer in charge. The Soviet Army had taken over the Leuna Works, he said, and the troop commander was now the supreme authority. He sent one of his men to summon the commander. A few minutes later, a Russian colonel entered the room, along with several other officers. Throughout the conference that ensued the Russians—both officers and civilians—were extremely courteous. Schorn admits that the same couldn't be said of him. In the weeks that have passed since then, he has searched his memory for every last detail of what was said at that conference, and he thinks he has reconstructed a fairly complete and accurate version of it.

"*Herr Oberst,*" Schorn began, "do your troops have permission to shoot?"

"No," the colonel replied.

"Why did you bring in your troops?" Schorn asked. "Did we give you any reason to intervene?"

"I have orders to protect Soviet citizens and Soviet property," said the colonel.

"Did we provoke you into coming here?"

"You didn't provoke me."

"We workers of East Germany want to live and work in peace, but we demand decent living and working conditions. This, *Herr Oberst,* is an internal German affair. You shouldn't interfere. This doesn't concern you at all."

At this, the colonel's face got a little red, but he said nothing. Schorn says he realized right then that neither the colonel nor the Russian general manager had received any instructions from higher up as to how to proceed, and were just stalling for time in the hope of getting some. The colonel's evident embarrassment made Schorn decide to keep on the offensive.

"*Herr Oberst,*" Schorn said, "I demand that your troops leave immediately."

"I am unable to comply with your demand," the colonel replied.

Schorn turned to the general manager and said, "*Herr Generaldirektor,* I appeal to you to prevent loss of life. And there will be loss of life if the troops stay here."

"But I am no longer in charge," the general manager protested. "I have handed over the executive power to the colonel."

"*Herr Oberst,*" Schorn said, turning back to the colonel, "if trouble starts, your soldiers will shoot. They will kill many of our workers, but our men will strangle them with their bare hands. There are over twenty thousand workers out there and only four hundred soldiers. I appeal to you to prevent a tragedy."

"I have to await instructions from my headquarters," the colonel said.

"But the crowd will not wait long," Schorn said. "We will give you ten minutes to get your instructions. Within ten minutes, your troops must leave Leuna. Now I'm going outside and tell the workers that you have been so notified."

Schorn and the three men with him turned to go, but the colonel called them back. "I will order the troops to leave," he said.

"Will you guarantee that no reprisals will be taken against the members of our strike committee?" Schorn asked.

"I will," the colonel replied.

Schorn and his three colleagues went back to report to the strikers. "We were exhilarated," he told me. "We all shook hands and told each other we had won a great victory. I think I trusted the colonel at that moment."

. . .

When Schorn and his companions stepped out on the platform overlooking the courtyard, they got a shock. Motorized Russian columns were approaching from two directions. Some of the troops were pouring into the courtyard, while others were encircling the whole plant. Schorn waited a few minutes, expecting a counter command to be given, but the troops did not turn back.

"Then I grew really angry," Schorn told me. "I grabbed the microphone and told the crowd, 'Friends, the Russian troop commander promised me that he would order his troops to leave. You see how he has kept his word. New troops are coming in.' The workers shouted their contempt."

The door behind Schorn opened, and the colonel and his officers came out. Schorn turned to the colonel. "*Herr Oberst,* look!" he said, pointing to the troops. "Do you call this the word of a Russian officer?"

"Don't get excited!" the colonel said tensely.

"I'm not excited," Schorn said. "I've merely stated that you, a colonel of the Red Army, have broken your word. You promised that the troops would leave."

"I have received orders from Karlshorst," said the colonel. "The troops must stay."

"Do you still guarantee the safety of the members of the strike committee?" Schorn asked.

"There will be no reprisals," the colonel said.

Schorn swung around and faced the strikers, who had stood silent, listening to the argument that was taking place in front of the microphone. "You heard what the colonel said," he told them. "All right. It's nearly five o'clock. Go home now. But be back here tomorrow morning at seven. If the members of the strike committee aren't here, you'll know what has happened to them. And then—"

A Russian officer jumped forward and cut the wire to the microphone, and Schorn's voice became all but inaudible in the courtyard. Angrily, he wheeled on the colonel. "Why don't you let me talk to the men?" he asked.

"You've been talking, haven't you?" the colonel said.

"Maybe you didn't notice, *Herr Oberst,* that one of your officers cut this wire," Schorn said. "The workers at Leuna have always been told that the Soviet officers are their friends. They know better now."

Then Schorn turned toward the crowd and held up seven fingers. "Tomorrow at seven!" he shouted. "Everybody right here!"

The men and women moved off in small groups. The colonel and his officers quickly disappeared inside the building. The soldiers were still sitting on their trucks. When Schorn left the courtyard, several workers accompanied him through the main gate and insisted on staying with him until he boarded his streetcar for home. As he rode toward Merseburg, the stimulating influence of the large crowd passed off, and he began to feel tired and depressed. He had no illusions about his future. He suspected that reprisal was both inevitable and imminent; the Russian colonel wouldn't be likely to forget having been humiliated in front of that crowd.

As the streetcar jogged along, a stranger in blue overalls who was sitting next to Schorn leaned over and whispered to him, "My friend, I'm from Leuna. I listened to you today. I've just heard that the Russians have proclaimed martial law in Merseburg. Don't go home tonight. Do you hear me?"

Schorn nodded without turning his head, and the man went on, "If you want to sleep in our place, we've got an extra bed. You'll be safe with us." He whispered an address to Schorn. Then, without saying goodbye, he stood up, and got off at the next stop.

"I didn't know the man, but I trusted him," Schorn told me. "A few months before, my first thought at being addressed by a stranger on a streetcar would have been, Watch out—he may be a spy. But the sincerity of the demonstration earlier in the day had changed all that."

• • •

When the stranger had gone, Schorn got to thinking. All day, he had been so elated by the vision of a new era and by the fervor of the crowd that he had forgotten about his wife and children. Now, in a dazed way, he began to realize the seriousness of what he had done. His wife, a trusted leader in the S.E.D., had turned out to be the wife of a strike leader! And God only knew what they might do to the children! Schorn was well aware that the Russians often make children pay for the offenses of their fathers. Here was a horrible prospect indeed. At first, Schorn thought he would go home, try to explain to his wife what had happened, and then say a regretful goodbye to her and the youngsters. But after his performance that day he might easily jeopardize the safety of his family simply by being with them. If the authorities learned that he had been home and that his wife had not at once done her best to turn him in, they might resort to some very harsh measures. Schorn's mind cleared rapidly, and he could see that there was only one thing for him to do. He got off the car, got on one going in the opposite direction, went to the address the stranger had given him, and spent the night there. In the morning, he went back to the Leuna Works with his host. He knew, of course, that he was taking a chance, but, on the other hand, there was the possibility that he had exaggerated the danger of his position and he felt he could not let the workers down. On the streetcar, he met a neighbor of his, who whispered to him, "Lucky you didn't go home last night. They've been to your house six times."

"Who?" Schorn asked mechanically.

"The *Vopos*," the neighbor replied. "They're looking for you everywhere."

"What about my wife and kids?" Schorn asked.

"They're all right," the neighbor said. "But, of course, your wife is awfully worried about what's happened to you."

Outside the main gate of the plant, Schorn stopped in bewilderment. He thought he'd never seen so much armed strength concentrated in one place. There were Soviet T-34 tanks, anti-aircraft guns, mortars, machine guns, armored reconnaissance cars, and hundreds of infantry soldiers sitting on trucks with their engines running. Schorn learned that troops had been arriving all night long. Two S.E.D. men stood at the gate distributing leaflets asking the workers to return to their jobs and "to help with the arrest of the culprits of yesterday's provocations."

Three workers Schorn knew came running up to him. "You'd better beat it," one of them told him. "Do you know what happened?"

"The Russians and the *Vopos* have arrested every member of the strike committee except you and three others who didn't sleep at home and so couldn't be found. You'd better get away fast. If they find you here, you'll be done for. Try to reach West Berlin. Maybe you can talk to us over RIAS. You can be more help to us alive in Berlin than dead here."

Schorn nodded, and left. He walked to the railroad station. The walls were plastered with posters showing his picture and pictures of the three other missing strike leaders. Underneath was printed an announcement of a reward of five thousand Ostmark for the capture of each of the wanted men, dead or alive. The text that followed accused them of having taken part in "gangster activities against the State and against the population" and of being "handymen of American imperialism." The announcement was signed by a local Russian commander, possibly the colonel Schorn had had dealings with. "It was the first time I had ever seen my own death warrant on a wall," Schorn said to me. "Instead of frightening me, it made me angry, since I had committed no crime. As a matter of fact, if I hadn't kept my head, many people might have been killed and wounded the day before. I was certainly not going to make it easy for them to get me. I turned around, went back a few blocks, and borrowed a bicycle from a man I know. Then I rode to a small town where the guards weren't very alert. There was a train going west, toward Berlin, but I thought I would attract less attention going east, so I bought a ticket to a place near the Polish border where I have a friend."

Schorn reached his friend's place without being recognized, and stayed there two days. A mood of depression hung over the whole community. People walked through the streets with their heads lowered. "If it had only lasted another twenty-four hours," they would say. "Another twenty-four hours and Ulbricht and his crowd would have been wiped out."

After leaving his friend, Schorn made his way slowly to East Berlin; by riding at night on local trains he managed to avoid police patrols. He believes he was not picked up between trains because there is a notable lack of cooperation among the regional branches of the State Security Service, or possibly because the posters calling for his arrest were not properly circulated throughout the Zone. In East Berlin, he found the sector boundaries closed; no one without a *Passierschein,* or special permit, issued by the *Volkspolizei,* could cross over into West Berlin. He stayed for a while with people whom he naturally doesn't want to name. They told him of various spots on the border where escapes had been made to the West. When he investigated a couple of these, he found that others had evidently learned of them before he had, for guards were patrolling them with the utmost vigilance.

Schorn, of course, had no *Passierschein* and was in no position to ask for one, but on the afternoon of June 24th he was strolling by one of the official boundary crossing points, studying the setup, when a sudden thunderstorm broke. The downpour was so great that the *Vopos* on duty retired inside their sentry huts and just glanced out at the *Passierscheine* of the few people who walked by. Schorn saw his opportunity. He waited until two men approached the *Vopos,* holding out their *Passierscheine,* and then moved up close behind them, clutching the simple identity card that every citizen in East Germany is obliged to carry. As he had hoped, the sentries gave his damp identity card only the most cursory glance, and a moment later he'd left them behind. Within half an hour, he was standing in front of a West Berlin official, giving his name and asking for asylum.

. . .

Schorn and several other *Barrikadenstürmer,* or barricade fighters, as the heroes of the seventeenth of June are affectionately called by the West Berliners, now live in a large house overlooking Wannsee. In the beginning, they were known to each other merely by the names of the towns they came from—"Halle," "Jena," "Leipzig," "Dresden," and so on—but now their confidence in one another has grown and they use their own names. Like other political émigrés, they have strong opinions about what should have been done during the crisis, and they don't always agree about what should be done in the future, but they are all remarkable for their complete lack of defeatism. They have refused to be flown out to West Germany, where they would be safer. They want to stay in West Berlin to be close to their friends in the East Zone. "We're going to continue the fight from here," Schorn told me. "Over there in East Germany, the government has started a large-scale campaign of what it calls enlightenment. But the people won't be fooled. I've had news from Leuna. There have been sitdown strikes for weeks. The plant is heavily guarded, but the spirit of our men and women is unbroken. No matter what they are being told now, they won't forget the truth. They were right there listening when that Russian colonel went back on his word. You think they'll ever forget? Never!"

I asked Schorn if he had had any word of his wife and children. He looked away. "I haven't heard from them," he said. "I expect that my wife will ask for a divorce. What else can she do? She must try to protect herself and the children. I miss them terribly, but I've made my decision. I'm still the ironhearted hater. I'll keep fighting. Ulbricht and his crowd are trying to tell the people that the seventeenth of June was the end of the uprising. Don't you believe them. It was just the beginning."

THE OLD BOYS

Emily Hahn

NOVEMBER 7, 1953 (ON CHIANG KAI-SHEK)

THE COHESIVE SPIRIT that characterizes Chiang Kai-shek's court on the crowded island of Formosa—or Taiwan, as it is called in the East—is probably unique among modern governments in exile. This is not to say that the Chinese Nationalists are happy away from the mainland, but simply that, having been driven from one capital to another during the past two decades, they know how to adapt themselves. The main point is that the followers of Chiang who are loyal know from experience that they can expect loyalty in return. Indeed, this reciprocal fidelity actually stands in the way of Free China's war effort, for Taipei, the current capital, is wastefully cluttered with old people who can no longer contribute much of value. American advisers, especially those who are newly arrived and all zealous in the cause, deplore this situation, and so do a few of the old people themselves. "Were you proud of being a general?" I asked a seventy-year-old veteran of the mainland wars who followed the government here. He was showing me his photograph album, and there was a portrait of him in his younger days, splendid in uniform against a background of the Paoting Military Academy. He nodded glumly. "I was," he said. "And now I am proud of *not* being a general. There are too many generals around here."

Little by little, though, the government is beginning to look more youthful, for the old men are slowly being replaced by capable younger officers. The operation is skillfully handled. No bones are broken, no feelings are hurt, and the old-timers are still treated with courtesy and patience. Chiang Kai-shek himself shows no outward sign of weariness with them; he has never been disrespectful to his elders, and undoubtedly today, at sixty-seven, he feels more at ease with his old friends than with the brisk representatives of the new school. The retired generals don't seem redundant to him; they make Taiwan homelike. Even some of the war lords who used to be his enemies are reassuring company on this strange island.

The old-timers didn't all arrive with the Generalissimo when he fled the mainland, in December, 1949. Some of them were here ahead of him, and some came later, with harrowing tales of their escapes. For most of them, retirement did not begin immediately. They were still largely in command when the war started in Korea. Almost all the Nationalists had given up hope by that time, but then America took a new interest in them, advisers were sent in from the States, and the government was streamlined, with younger men taking over important positions. The displaced elders live within easy hailing distance of their leader. In bungalows on the fringes of the city, or up in the series of impressive hills known as Grass Mountain, twelve or thirteen miles from the center of activities, they spend their days talking, reading the newspapers, and planning strategy for the great day of glorious battle they hope will come. At first, life must have seemed strangely full of leisure and tiresomely long to these men, but now they have all developed engrossing side interests. Some of them tend gardens, some of them write memoirs and pamphlets, and some of them have taken new wives. Gambling is frowned on, because the Generalissimo thinks it sets a bad example for the people, so although mah-jongg is still played, it is played furtively. Mostly, the generals indulge in that beguiling pastime of saying, in various ways, "I told you so." Every so often, Chiang holds a conference in his official residence for the benefit of the generals and the war lords and his other old friends, and when they come out of their fastnesses and converge on the place, the roadsides are crowded for a mile around with parked jeeps, Cadillacs, and taxis.

• • •

Chinese, like Americans, seldom refer to their important personages by their formal names, and when speaking English, officials of the Nationalist government have sometimes called the Generalissimo the Gimo, after the fashion of the late W. H. Donald, the Australian who became foreign adviser to the Chiangs back in 1934. More often nowadays, they speak of him affectionately as "the Old Man." Most of the mainland

Chinese on Taiwan are warm supporters of Chiang; otherwise they wouldn't be here. The Old Man is among friends, and they are a picked company. Even so, he has his disagreements with them. Throughout his turbulent life, whenever he has wanted to get away from public affairs for a time or register a protest, he has gone to some mountain hideout. He was born among the hills, in Chekiang Province, and under pressure he reverts to the hills. Fortunately for his spirit, Taiwan is full of hills. There is a secluded spot down toward the middle of the island, at Ta Chi, where a Japanese prince used to seek rest and seclusion in the days when Taiwan belonged to Japan, and Chiang Kai-shek occasionally visits it. It is the only place where he can really find solitude. During the winter months, the Old Man lives in Shihlin, a village on the outskirts of the capital, in a large, Western-style house that was built only seven years ago, for the new governor the Chinese installed in Formosa when the Japanese surrendered. It is hidden from the main road behind a park, guards are stationed at the entrance to the driveway, and there is a little private garden where the Gimo can walk in the evening. During the hottest part of the summer, the Chiang household moves up to Grass Mountain, where the Old Man has a house as secluded as that of any of the generals and war lords sequestered there in mountain crannies. It clings to the side of a precipitous hill, and used to be the guesthouse of a Japanese-owned sugar-refining company, where its executives could relax in Japanese style, sitting on mat floors or in hot baths drawn from the mountain's sulphur springs, and surveying the distant plain. The Generalissimo is in his element there.

Whether in Shihlin or up on Grass Mountain, Chiang follows the same routine he has followed for years, rising at five-thirty to say his prayers, do his exercises, and eat an austere breakfast. At seven-thirty precisely, he leaves for his office, which is in Chieh Shou Hall, in Taipei, with the other government offices. He interviews his American advisers there, holds conversations with his prime minister, Chen Cheng, and officials of the various Yuans, or governmental departments, and studies the news from the outside world, on which his life and his work now depend. He makes a long morning of it, not returning to his house until after one o'clock, but then he stays at home the rest of the day, and, if it becomes necessary, calls in his ministers and other advisers. His intimates say that these calls have become more frequent lately. "He doesn't take advice any more readily than he used to, but he asks for it oftener," one of them told me. The Old Man is still stubborn. When he gets an idea in his head, nothing moves him. But the ideas seem to develop with more deliberation than they used to.

All Chiang's thoughts are, of course, directed to one simple end—a return of his government to the mainland. In May, 1949, when Shanghai fell to the Reds, Chiang is said to have told his friends that if the city wasn't retaken in four months, "I promise you I will commit suicide." This sort of vow is pure convention in China, and no one would have thought of expecting him to keep it, but he probably meant it literally at the time. Now he is suffering deeply from humiliation at the blows of the past four years, but he has been stoic about it, and this is the main reason so many of his followers have stayed with him. "He is really great," one of the young men in the government said to me. "A lesser man probably *would* have committed suicide, years ago. He never gives up hope. That is the great thing." The Generalissimo is too practical to indulge in romantic dreams of a quick reconquest of China. He tells the Americans that if he can land on the mainland, a hundred miles away, establish a beachhead, and hold it against the Reds for three months, or four, or perhaps six, he is confident that the tide will turn; enough people will take the risk of coming over to his side for him to win out.

Everything Chiang does is filled with drama. Although he lives simply and his activities have none of the self-conscious theatricality of some European leaders, the drama seems inevitable. His retinue of household guards and policemen has been growing through the years, not so much because the danger of assassination has increased as because most of the guards who served him on the mainland now have sons and nephews who need jobs. Whenever Chiang moves about, a fleet of black Cadillac limousines moves with him, and the roads he travels on are lined at intervals of a few hundred yards with guards who stand on the alert when he is expected and are practically invisible after he has passed by. Last summer, the sides of the road between Grass Mountain and the city were cleared of underbrush for several paces back into the trees, and its regrowth was discouraged by frequent burning of the grass.

Guards, police, black Cadillacs, and chauffeurs are fairly common sights in the busy streets of Shihlin, but up on the lonely heights of Grass Mountain there is a considerable stir when the Chiangs arrive. The main road to Taipei runs along the top of the hill above Chiang's house, which is off on a side road. The Cadillacs are kept in a long shed near the intersection, where they are constantly attended by uniformed loungers.

There are a few other houses in the vicinity, one of them occupied by the American Ambassador.

In the cool early mornings, when the Chiangs are in residence, servants from the nearest houses drift over to the garage to chat with the Gimo's people. Except for a pillbox commanding the crossroads, it is all very rustic and green, with flowering hedges along the garden walls. Mme. Chiang Kai-shek's cocker spaniel, Blackie, lies napping in the middle of the road. Half-naked babies wander about. A bell rings sharply in the pillbox, once, twice, or three times: the signals are changed periodically. Everyone is galvanized. Domestics disappear behind hedges. Chauffeurs rush to their cars, guards stand at attention, and the Cadillacs whiz down the side road. Again the bell rings. It is seven-thirty sharp. The black cavalcade roars back uphill, swings in to the main road to Taipei, and speeds away. The Old Man is going to his office. Soon the dust has settled, the guards relax, and the servants reappear with their babies. There is another spasm of activity in the early afternoon, when the Gimo returns, and then all is quiet until evening. At six-thirty, the signal bell sounds again. This time, the cars do not go down the hill. Guards pop up all along the way, and a little group of walkers appears, trudging uphill. Blackie, panting proudly, leads the procession. After him, walking quickly, comes Chiang, in a long gown and a pith helmet. Sometimes, and always on Sunday, Madame is with him, slender in her sheath gown, and carrying a parasol, although the sun has already set. Several guards follow them. The Gimo swings up to the highway and on toward a small public park. One of the Cadillacs falls in behind them and follows at a respectful distance. When he has walked long enough, he and his party climb into the car and it drives back down the hill, heralded, as usual, by the bell. Ring! Swish! The Old Man has taken his exercise.

Chiang is beginning to show his age; sixty-seven is quite old for a Chinese. He is not bent or slow or uncertain, but his hair, however close it is cropped, is unmistakably pure white. He is thinner than ever, but his doctor is proud of his condition. A man who never smokes or drinks or overeats might well live forever, the doctor says. There is, however, one significant change. The Generalissimo has taken to smiling quite often. Recently, a visiting journalist commented on it; Chiang Kai-shek's smile, he said, is *cruel*—cold and cruel. "Nonsense," said an American officer who knows Chiang fairly well. "His dentures don't fit, that's all. You'd have a cruel smile, too, if you had to keep those teeth in your mouth."

Chiang's personal pleasures are simple. On Sunday, there are household church services; the Generalissimo, like his wife, is a staunch Methodist. His elder son by a previous marriage, Chiang Ching-kuo, brings his wife and children over for the day. The Old Man is fond of the family and permits himself to relax when nobody from outside is looking. He always retains his severe manner, however, and it impresses most people who come in contact with him. "He has never said we mustn't smoke in his presence," one of his oldest friends, normally a chain smoker, said to me. "The servants even put cigarettes and matches near your hand when you're there, but somehow nobody ever uses them. Just the same, the Old Man is letting up a little. I can see it. He used to drink only hot water. Now, I have observed, he lets his people put a few tea leaves in it."

. . .

Taiwan has not been kind to Mme. Chiang. She suffers from allergies, and shortly after she and her husband took up residence on the island, she developed a severe case of an unpleasant skin disease called disseminated neurodermatitis. One of the new miracle drugs was prescribed for her, and it had a disastrous effect. She went first to Hawaii and then to the United States for treatments, and it was several months before she recovered. During the worst of the attack, her face and body were swollen and her skin turned dark. Now she lives very quietly and follows the latest diet ordained by the specialists—no eggs, no milk, no butter, and so on. Her chief interest outside her home is in the Women's Anti-Aggression League, of which she is chairman. When she goes downtown to its headquarters, the back windows of her car are shrouded with brown curtains, so that she can't be seen. This wish to escape the public eye also accounts for the parasol she carries on her evening walks with the Generalissimo. And when Admiral Arthur W. Radford, the newly appointed Chairman of the Joint Chiefs of Staff, visited Taiwan recently with his wife, Madame's car, with its curtains drawn, drove onto the airport field, where the island's other dignitaries were waiting, at the last minute before the plane landed. Madame appeared as briefly as possible. Mrs. Radford was whisked into the car to share her hostess's obscurity, and driven away in record time. Doubtless, this rather Victoria-like attitude to the public gaze is a hangover from the anxious days when Madame thought she was permanently disfigured. Actually, there is no good reason for her lack of confidence. She was always a pretty woman, but now, even seen at close quarters, she is more than that. At fifty-five, she is, with her thin, graceful figure and her enormous eyes, beautiful.

The Women's Anti-Aggression League is a volunteer organization, but there are few wives of Nationalist officials who would dare not volunteer. Every Chinese lady in Taipei, from the Prime Minister's wife on down, spends one day a week at a sewing machine in the League building, working on clothes for the soldiers and linen for the hospitals. It is a sewing bee that never ends. Women who cannot leave their children at home—and in Taipei, as in New York, baby-sitters are a problem—put them in a nursery next to the sewing-machine room, where a nurse looks after them. In another building, close by, is a nursery school Madame has organized for soldiers' children. The League doesn't publicize its other efforts, such as providing small comforts for wounded guerrillas from outlying islands and training nurses' aides to take care of them. Guerrilla operations are not included in the American-aid program, and they aren't supposed to benefit from American defense funds, so nobody talks about them. But the guerrillas fight a battle now and then, and when the wounded arrive by junk or plane, they are greeted by giggling girls who carry welcoming signs and hand out flowers, cookies, and cigarettes. These ceremonies are never given publicity, and the wounded are quietly hurried off to a hospital.

Like the war lords and generals stranded in Taiwan, Madame used to be much busier than she is now, and, like some of them, she has turned to intellectual pursuits to fill in the time. She has taken up painting. It is not the type of painting that has given solace to Western kings, presidents, premiers, and Führers. Mme. Chiang was educated in America, but she doesn't use water colors or oils; she paints in the Chinese style, with inks. She was late in coming to it. Chinese girls who are brought up at home, instead of being sent abroad—she was sent abroad at the age of ten—take painting lessons as a matter of course, and as they grow older the writing of characters gives them great facility with the brush, but most of them paint a few landscapes in the classic manner and then lose interest, just as elegant English girls in Victorian or Edwardian days used to sketch churches and pretty views but forgot the pastime as soon as they married. It was not like that with Mme. Chiang. Only lately, when illness made her idle, did she think of trying to paint. At first, it is said, her husband was skeptical of the venture. "If you were any good at painting, you would have discovered it before," he is reported to have said. "It's a specialized thing. You'll never be any good at it at your age."

However, Madame persisted. At Taiwan Normal College here, she found a teacher from the mainland, a famous painter named Huang Chun-pi. Under his guidance, she studied the methods of the old Chinese masters and started work. Soon she was surprising Huang, as well as the Generalissimo, with the results. She is really good. Painting has become her chief interest, and she spends hours at it, doing scenes she remembers from the mainland, and a few local landscapes. Chiang has long since admitted that he was mistaken. "I thought you could do it," he is said to have told her, using a time-honored face-saving formula, "but I knew if it sounded too easy, you'd never go ahead with it. I discouraged you on purpose."

. . .

Only a few days after I arrived in Taipei, I began to hear strangely familiar stories. I remember when similar stories centered on the two Chen brothers, who held the imagination of the foreign public in China from the early 1930s until about 1950. They were corrupt, the public agreed—corrupt, cruel, and tremendously powerful. Pro-Communist American journalists had nicknamed them the C-C Clique, and since they stood high in Chiang's council, they came to symbolize the faults people found with his methods. Chiang stands by his friends—it is a Chinese custom—and the Chen brothers were nephews of an old revolutionary companion of his. In spite of American advice, he not only kept them near him but gave them increasingly important posts, which redoubled the gossip about them. The stories I heard might well have concerned them, but one Chen is dead and the other is in America, deeply involved in Moral Re-Armament. The subject of these anecdotes was not a Chen at all but the Generalissimo's son General Chiang Ching-kuo.

"Ching-kuo is a sinister figure," I was told. "He has great influence with the Gimo." Ching-kuo spent much of his life in Russia, people told me, and came back with a Russian wife. There were any number of rumors about him—that he uses Russian methods (what those methods are, no one could say), that he runs the secret police, that he was most corrupt in Shanghai after the war, and that he executed many innocent people at the time of the inflation, which he was supposed to stop. He is in charge of the education of the troops now and, the story goes, isn't doing it democratically. Moreover, they declared, he is Chiang Kai-shek's heir and will no doubt turn the Nationalists over to Russia as soon as he comes into power.

"But how can he be his father's heir?" I asked. "China isn't a kingdom. He's the President's son, that's all. He'd have to be elected. He's no more an heir than James Roosevelt."

As I said, they were the same sort of tales one used to hear about the Chens—full of innuendoes and hints, with nothing very substantial to go on. Chiang Ching-kuo evidently came along in time to fill a conversational vacuum. There was one specific horror story, however. A young American couple employed by the State Department had the misfortune to live across the street from a public radio loudspeaker, which blared all day, much to their distress. To make it worse, the young woman had once recorded a few English lessons for the benefit of the Chinese, and these records were broadcast time after time. "Imagine what it feels like to hear your own voice, stepped up to millions of decibels, all day long," she said in agitated tones. "When we couldn't bear it any longer, we went over to the station and asked them to turn it down, but the man in charge said he couldn't. He said he was playing it loud like that on Chiang Ching-kuo's orders. Well, of course, as soon as we heard that name, we knew it was hopeless."

The Generalissimo's younger son, Chiang Wei-kuo, is a very different character, it seems—a good boy, and one of the pillars of the local Rotary Club. He is fond of a party and a drink, and he likes America. He is there now, on a training mission at Fort Leavenworth.

I decided I would try to meet Chiang Ching-kuo, but I didn't expect I'd be able to manage it. My request was immediately granted, however, perhaps because his advisers had been telling him he was suffering from a bad press and should do something about it. Chiang Ching-kuo occupies a Japanese-style house behind a bamboo fence, as many other generals do. There is a tree in the garden, and attached to it by a long cord when I arrived was a young monkey, who seemed to be spending his time doing setting-up exercises on the edge of the roof. A portrait of Chiang Kai-shek hung on the wall of his son's study—one of the recent ones, in which the Generalissimo is white-haired and smiling. Like his father, the General is not very tall, but he is stocky rather than thin, and his face is not stern or bony. It is a pleasant, open sort of face, and he has a dimple in one cheek.

"Of course I've heard those stories they tell about me," he said readily when I asked him. "Probably I'm better acquainted with them than you are. It's part of my job." He smiled, and then gave me an alert, intelligent look. "You must not think these things are always said behind my back.

Some people criticize to my face. When officials say that my way of doing things is too Russian, I ask them in what way I'm so Russian and they can't reply. After all, I'm the only man here who knows about Russia and has seen the methods of Moscow."

Ching-kuo was sent to Russia as a young boy, in 1925, two years after Sun Yat-sen sent Chiang to Moscow on his famous good-will tour. Chiang wanted his son to study Russian military methods. It was a logical idea; Chiang himself had had four years of training abroad in Japanese military schools. Unfortunately, the Generalissimo's relations with the Soviet took a bad turn, and young Ching-kuo remained a lot longer than anyone had intended—as a hostage. He was there twelve years, and was only returned in 1937, after the Japanese invaded China and relations between Russia and China grew warmer.

"Yes, I know Communism, and the Communists know me," he went on. "When they took over the municipality of Shanghai, they thought of me. They put my picture up in Jessfield Park, as a target for people to throw stones at."

I asked if the game had been popular.

"On the first day, nobody threw anything," he said, grinning. "The second day, they put a few agents in the crowd to encourage the others, and the people followed their lead and began enjoying it. By the third day, everybody was throwing things at my face." He crossed his booted legs, looking thoughtful. "No, rumors don't bother me. People have got to have a scapegoat. There's a Chinese proverb that says good gold doesn't tarnish. My reputation doesn't matter as long as I do my job."

I said the usual things about the importance of publicity: he did not agree. "I'm not fond of publicity," he said. "I don't see the use of it; it looks to me like a sheer waste of time. Still, I know your people think of it in another way. They tell me it's all a part of winning the war. If so, I suppose I ought to take their advice."

"About your American advisers, General," I said. "What do you honestly think of Americans? You've met a lot of them lately."

"Americans are young and vital," he said, "and that's a good thing—that's an excellent thing. I like that liveliness and eagerness for new ideas. We need it in China. There are other things about America that don't seem so attractive. I haven't been there yet myself, but to my mind the American way of life, with its washing machines and big cars and a lot of food, isn't at all the kind of thing we want or need in China. All that luxury, the deep freezes and soft beds—" He broke off and shook his head. “It’s bad for people,” he said flatly. “I don’t admire it. But it doesn’t seem to have spoiled your soldiers. They are capable of genuine discipline. I have seen that for myself, and it surprises me, but it is true.” He paused and looked at me for a minute. “Don’t worry,” he said in a kindly voice. “America’s all right.” Not long after I saw him, he left for a five weeks’ tour of the United States, at the joint invitation of the Defense and State Departments.

• • •

It occurred to me that since there are many historical figures here in Taiwan who are fading into the background, I should take the opportunity to meet and talk to some of them. One of the most restless of the lot is Yolobass Khan, the Governor in Exile of Sinkiang, who would not thank me if I referred to him as an old-timer, although he is sixty-five. He is a great, burly, bearded man, and recently he married a girl of nineteen. This is not his first marriage, by a long shot, but then Yolobass is a Moslem. Chiang appointed him Governor after the Communists overran Sinkiang, and his people here call him Governor, but there have always been more powerful leaders in his province and he is really little more than a chieftain. Sinkiang is a wild country, geographically more a part of Mongolia than of China, and peopled with Mongols, Kazaks, Uigurs, Kirghiz, Manchus, Uzbeks, Tatars, Chinese, and White Russians. Yolobass is a Kazak, and he led thousands of troops on horseback to war against the Reds, both the Chinese and the Russian varieties. He left China by way of the southwestern border in the spring of 1951, and emerged in Kashmir with a band of men, women, and children. He has no desire whatever to remain in Taiwan; he intends to go back home as soon as he can.

“We people of Sinkiang like to fight,” Yolobass declared when I went to see him. He has a big, deep voice, and as he talks, he strokes his long gray whiskers, which are parted in the middle. If his beard were only half as long, I reflected, he would look like a Wild West Charles Evans Hughes. Yolobass talked about his horsemen, and their longing to get back into the fight. “Mongols don’t fear death,” he said in his booming voice, and drew his finger across his throat. I did not doubt him. I could easily think of him on horseback, leading a shrieking troop of his countrymen into battle, but our surroundings interfered with the picture. Yolobass, who should have been giving me an audience in a desert tent, had received me in the sitting room of his Japanese house in a suburb of

Taipei. Its once sparsely furnished interior had been transformed by someone, perhaps his young wife. He talked of valor and death while around him were delicate chairs, plants in pots, and a chubby settee adorned with a lace antimacassar.

Yolobass and his wife graciously gave me a chance to find out what Kazak food is like by asking me to dinner a few nights later. I arrived in some apprehension, for what I had read about Mongols led me to expect that I would have to eat with my fingers. I was so sure of this that I felt rather disappointed when I saw the long table set with knives and forks and spoons. My disappointment did not last long, for it was a most unusual dinner. Yolobass had invited a large number of guests from Sinkiang—enormous, broad-shouldered men all, who didn't look like the Chinese I knew. Another guest, though he is not a Sinkiang man, was General Pai Chung-hsi, of Kwangsi, whose name has figured in Chinese history ever since I can remember. He looked young to be so famous.

Dinner was served. There was a huge plate of cabbage and beef, stewed together. There was a platter of hors d'oeuvres that resembled Russian *zakuska,* and another of flaps of flat bread. We had bowls of soup, and more cabbage and beef, cooked a slightly different way. Then curry, and another kind of soup. At the beginning of dinner I noticed a wine cup at each plate and wondered what it was doing there. Surely we would not drink wine in this Moslem house? Mare's milk? But there are few horses in Taiwan. Actually, we drank lemon pop. We drank lots of lemon pop. The Chinese custom of draining one's glass with every single guest at the party was carefully observed. Each time, I stood up in my place and my drinking companion stood up in his. We bowed, holding out our glasses, we quaffed, and we sat down. Then a servant would spring out of the shadows and fill the glasses with yet more beaded bubbles, and the ceremony continued with the next guest. We went through bottles and bottles.

The meal ended with fried rice. Then we all followed dainty Mrs. Yolobass into the hot, still, mosquito-filled garden. The Khan's house is on a quiet street of Japanese-style houses, each with its little back yard. It struck me as a cozy, bourgeois, fantastically un-Mongol block. What with the temperature, the lightning bugs that flickered in the telephone wires overhead, and the generally cheerful back-yard-on-a-summer-evening atmosphere, I almost fancied myself back in my native St. Louis. Looking around at the strong, swarthy faces of the Sinkiang gentlemen, however, I forgot St. Louis. We sat in a row of chairs forming a sort of horseshoe. I was at the top center. At one end were Mrs. Yolobass and two friends of hers, waving fans of painted, scented wood. At my right was General Pai Chung-hsi. Slices of red watermelon were handed out, and then hot, damp facecloths. After a little desultory chat about the weather, the biggest, fiercest-looking guest began asking me questions. What did the United States think of England's attitude toward Red China? Of the Nationalist future? Of the world situation? His companions chimed in with even more difficult queries, and I stumbled through the catechism as best I could. They nodded politely, if a trifle glumly, at my faltering replies. "What—you don't speak Russian?" one of them asked in simple amazement. "*We* all speak Russian." The light from a lamp inside gleamed on their puzzled faces. Finally, they arrived at the sixty-four-dollar question: Why, since Russia is now patently at her weakest from internal dissension, do we Americans not attack? What are we waiting for? There will never be a better chance, they assured me.

"Well, you see," I began carefully, "fighting is not in the American tradition, as it is in yours. In America, we think, we hope there might be other ways . . ." My voice trailed off, leaving the Sinkiang men in midair, their faces eager, their eyebrows raised.

There was no use talking to generals about such matters, I decided. I turned to Pai Chung-hsi and asked if he had ever been to America. There was a small stir around the garden; the others accepted my diversionary gambit with obvious disgust, but Pai Chung-hsi was willing to go along with me. After all, he is a relatively cosmopolitan fellow, and he had things to talk about. What, he asked me, is the Church of England? Isn't it the same as the Catholic Church? For the rest of the evening, I told General Pai Chung-hsi about Henry VIII. He seemed interested.

• • •

One of the oldest of China's famous wise men, who has been a general, a governor twice over, and, in his time, an enemy of Chiang Kai-shek, is Marshal Yen Hsi-shan. He is now in Taiwan with the rest of the old boys. In addition to his other distinctions, he has also been a war lord, and there aren't many of those still around. The term "war lord" is often employed much too loosely by Westerners. For example, Chiang Kai-shek has been called a war lord, but he isn't one and never has been. A war lord has a private army, which he pays and manages entirely, and uses to maintain his position as dictator of his region. Until Chiang rounded them up, a lot of provincial governors in China, especially in the west, were war lords. They collected the local taxes, dispensed justice according to their lights, and defied any higher authority. When Chiang conquered or otherwise won over a war lord, the private troops were either disbanded or incorporated into the national Army. Some of the war lords were good governors and some were not. Everyone agrees that Yen Hsi-shan was an excellent one. He took over Shansi Province in 1911, and ran it on patriarchal lines. During his tenure, Shansi was one of the most prosperous, peaceful provinces China has ever known. There were not only farms but factories, cottage industries, and mines, and the province was practically self-sufficient. The Governor experimented constantly with social welfare, and while his methods of applying it were unusual, they seemed to work out well.

Marshal Yen is four years older than the Generalissimo. They met in 1928, when Chiang was conducting his great northern drive to unify China under the Nationalists, but they didn't become friends until the Japanese attacked Shansi, in 1937, and no real alliance was formed until the Communists rose up and threatened the entire country. At that time, Shansi occupied a key position between the Communist and the Nationalist spheres of influence, and that made Yen an important ally for either. Unlike Chiang, he sometimes dallied with the Reds and believed their promises; their Socialistic teachings attracted him. That is all over now. He is bitter about the loss of his beloved Shansi, with its mountains and caves. Until he was forced out, he almost never left it, and here in Taiwan he has taken up his abode in an aerie as much like his old home as possible.

The road that wriggles up the mountainside to Marshal Yen's retreat is terrible. The jeep that took me there struggled up bedrock ridges in the middle of the road, and plunged into deep holes on the other side, jangling tinnily. Here and there, it clattered past caves in the cliff where sulphur workers had once dug, and frequently it was brushed by bamboo leaning in from the roadside. Finally, it crawled around a rocky spur and past the rim of a deep gorge, and came out on a flat stretch almost at the top of the mountain. There, just beneath the crest and saved from falling into space by a smooth curve of stone wall, the Marshal's house is perched. The land beneath it swoops westward into a faraway valley and carries on its back a neat hamlet, which is connected to the Marshal's eminence by several hundred stone steps. Between the village and the crest is a farm, which supplies him with vegetables and meat. I looked down on it and saw tiny pigs and people moving among the outbuildings. Beyond, the rocky slope was softened with a green fur of bamboo.

Marshal Yen's home is a Japanese building, made of wood. A typhoon recently took hold of it and gave it several hard shakes, but Yen Hsi-shan was not worried, because he was snug and safe in a sort of storm cellar built for him lower down on the cliff. Whenever the wind gets high, he and his household hurry to this place and wait for it to quiet down. If they are bored, they can while away the time reading a stone tablet, cemented into the wall, that is engraved with a short account, written by Yen, of the Shansi cave dwellings and a discussion of the reasons the Taiwanese never adopted such sensible homes. Yen is fond of writing, and sets down on paper (or, as in this case, on stone) the thoughts that pop into his head.

The day I visited him, there was no typhoon, and I found the Marshal sitting beside a window overlooking the valley. He was reading and fanning himself gently. As I was being led into his presence by his secretary, an intense young woman, I asked her if he had attended Chiang's most recent conference, and she looked depressed. "He couldn't get there," she said. "His motorcar is broken. He doesn't go into Taipei very much, and it's a pity. There isn't even a telephone connection here. Fortunately, he is well looked after and doesn't have to go out for anything. He is a wonderful man for his age. So strong! Like a man of fifty."

We turned and looked admiringly at the Marshal, who nodded agreement and said that he was indeed very strong. He was dressed in a Chinese gown and ceremonial jacket, a costume that usually emphasizes the fragility of the wearer but had no such effect on Yen's sturdy build. He has thick, dark eyebrows and a mobile face, with a high-bridged nose.

"I spend much of my time discussing world affairs with my friends," he told me. "Nearly every day some of them come to see me, and we talk. We talk for hours. At night and in the morning, when they are not with me, I write."

"He writes until one or two in the morning, sometimes," said the secretary. "He doesn't sleep very much."

The Marshal said he had written a number of pamphlets. He called in a manservant and sent him to an inner room to get some of them. The man's face wore a look of devotion, like the secretary's. The Marshal gave me some of the pamphlets, most of which were in English. There was a blue-covered one entitled "How to Prevent Warfare and Establish Foundation of World Unity." A yellow one bore the title "The Impending World Crisis."

"More are being printed," said the Marshal.

There was a brief pause, and I read a few words. "I have read many books, newspaper and magazine articles," Yen Hsi-shan had written. "Summing up what I have learned, there seem to be three main reasons for opposition [to Communism]:

"1. That the Communistic countries are undemocratic, not free.

"2. That the Communist countries are deceitful.

"3. That the Communist countries are cruel and ruthless."

I put the pamphlets aside and said, "That is one thing, at least, that you leaders on Taiwan all have in common; you've always known what the Communists wanted, haven't you?"

"Certainly not," said Yen cheerfully. "They fooled me many times." Then his cheerful look faded. For seventeen years, he said, he has been fighting Communists, and he has lost fifty thousand comrades in the struggle. He said that when the Chinese Reds made their famous Long March, with the Nationalists pursuing them through the mountains toward Shansi, they had thought of settling in his province, where the fields were fertile and they would find life pleasant. But he succeeded in heading them off. That is why they took refuge at last in the neighboring province, Shensi, and lived in the caves of Yenan.

"Marshal Yen, was Soviet Russia slipping secret aid to them all those years they waited in Yenan?" I asked.

Yen shook his head. "They weren't worth helping in those days, so the Russians let them alone," he said. "They couldn't have taken on the Kuomintang troops, and any material given to them would have been wasted."

"But wouldn't Stalin have helped them out of friendship, if nothing else? For the cause?"

The Marshal smiled politely, pitying my ignorance. He explained that friendship played no part in Communist strategy, and that Mao hadn't expected it to. "Then, after the end of the Second World War, everything changed for the Reds," he said. "Mao wielded influence at that time, and Russia began to supply him with arms. What you must not forget—but you *do* forget it—is that the Communists have not stopped cheating you. They never stop cheating." He fanned himself vigorously.

The sun was now lower than the level of the window. I said goodbye, and walked to the door, my arms full of pamphlets. The Marshal and the girl walked with me. “We must go on struggling, no matter how deceptively peaceful things may look from time to time,” he was saying.

When I reached the doorway, I bowed, went down the steps, and started toward the jeep. The granite of the cliff sparkled in the late sunbeams. I turned and waved to the gowned figure in the doorway. “Don’t forget!” he called. “They always cheat!”

FROM

LETTER FROM PARIS

Janet Flanner

JUNE 9, 1956 (ON THE ALGERIAN WAR)

Eleven Frenchmen and one Frenchwoman had their throats slit last Friday by Algerian rebels a few kilometres south of Biskra, in the Sahara, the desert once featured in *The Garden of Allah,* that ancient best-seller that touched on tender relations between natives and whites. Earlier in the week, outside Philippeville, two Moslem families—among them seven women and seven children, one three months old—suspected of loyalty to the French also had their throats cut by rebels, who, furthermore, decapitated their victims' chickens. Most of the Moslem students at the University of Algiers have abandoned their classes, well before their June exams, in response to a rebel slogan declaring, "Examinations make no sense today! Join the Maquis against the French!" Ten days ago, in the gorges near Palestro, seventeen out of twenty-two green French soldiers, in their third week of war, were ambushed and massacred by the rebels they were hunting. After certain Paris newspapers printed not only the names of the boys—eleven came from small towns near Paris—but the horrifying particulars of the mutilations and tortures that killed them, a wartime censorship was set up, forbidding the publication of "morbid details." Premier Guy Mollet is awaiting the results of a three-day Parliamentary debate about the Algerian situation. Grave as that situation is, he is not expected to fall, for though his Rightist political enemies think the war is going badly, no opposition party wants to be nationally responsible, as the Socialists are now, for trying to make it go better—even if any opposition party were sure it knew how. Finance Minister Paul Ramadier has just warned the public that the Algerian campaign will necessitate immediate new temporary taxes, the last adjective being the only part of the statement that sounds optimistic.

This is a cruel, fanatical, démodé Arab holy war, an intimate, hand-to-hand war of native knives and barbaric tortures, in which French helicopters supply the outstanding modern touch, a war of *petits paquets,* with the communiqués mentioning such small parcels of men as to sound ludicrous—except that they are descriptive of the endless, frittering kind of hide-and-seek, hill-and-desert war it really is. One day's communiqué last week featured engagements at Lourmel (rebel band surrounded, fourteen prisoners), Gambetta (three rebels killed), El-Kseur (nineteen rebels killed), and Aurès-Nemencha (skirmish with rebel bands, eleven wounded, two French military killed)—a total of twenty-two dead Algerians and two dead Frenchmen, at a cost of millions of francs, for that day.

The Communists' propaganda here against what they call *la sale guerre* consists of ordering Party members all over France to engage in short protest strikes, which are reported each day in the Communist *Humanité* under headlines demanding a cease-fire, negotiations, and peace in Algeria. There are such items as "Rouen dockers strike, refuse to load war matériel," "Workers in three Marseille factories struck Thursday and paraded to the war monument for the dead," "Tilemakers at Limoux, in the Aude, struck for an hour to protest against the military call-up of three comrades," and "At the Pathé-Marconi works outside Paris, five hundred mechanics struck because four comrades had been called up for Algeria." For weeks now, *Huma* has openly encouraged mass protests against the entraining of conscripts for the war, which is indubitably unpopular with the French working class generally, regardless of political affiliations, and especially with the conscripts' mothers and fiancées, who have been an important propaganda element in such agitated crowds. *Huma* has printed notes like "A thousand citizens at Le Mans protested the departure of the troop convoy" and "Convoy trains were stopped at Nice and Antibes, where the police brutally attacked the crowd." The first ugly riot took place at Grenoble, where troops were being shifted from one train to another. Many militant workmen were injured, and mothers and fiancées threw themselves on the railroad tracks and delayed the train's departure for hours (and upset train schedules on the main line; they are now often being upset in this fashion all over France). On Monday of this week, an outbreak occurred at Saint-

Nazaire, where, according to *Huma,* eight thousand *métallos* and others from the naval shipyards and machine shops, plus local women who lay down on the railroad tracks, staged such a furious protest against the entraining of a batch of conscripts that only two soldiers remained on the train when it finally steamed off toward the war. Patriotic *Figaro,* which cut the number of rioters to three thousand, and some of the other Right Wing papers were forced to mention further painful Monday incidents: a convoy was stopped two hours at Vendôme; the Quimper–Paris express was stopped three hours; the Lyon–Bordeaux express was stopped seventeen times by mutinous soldiers, who pulled the alarm signal. Within the past month, two issues of *Humanité* have been seized by the government and suppressed; after each occasion, *Huma,* parading its martyrdom, burst into print again against "the dirty war." There is no legal method by which a French government can continuously suppress the party organ of 25 percent of the voters, the Republic's biggest solid voting slice, and if a government dared to try it, so many strikes would doubtless break out, from one end of France to the other, that no newspaper could report them all—not even *Humanité.*

The resignation of Pierre Mendès-France from Mollet's Cabinet—where, unfortunately, he had been doing nothing anyhow—brought to light again his "seven significant measures," which he announced in April, and which he still thinks can alone "save the French presence in Algeria." Practically all the French colonials there, and many Frenchmen here, think that if these measures were applied, there would be nearly no Algeria worth saving, as far as French interests go, so why shed blood for such remnants? (An increased war effort is part of the Mendès-France program.) As an economic expert, Mendès proposed the expropriation of all sizable agricultural properties, in order to turn them into small family holdings, and a fundamental reform of agricultural credit that would "extract it from the selfish hands of big owners, who have always profited at the expense of little producers." He wants raised wages, recognition of Moslem labor unions, freedom of opinion for native Arabic newspapers, and the removal of those anti-native French functionaries who from the start have kept everything in their own white hands and out of Arab reach—all this to "promote native confidence and hope in France, without which, sooner or later, we French will be evicted from Algeria and from all of North Africa." Most scandalized French politicians look upon this as a program so bold that only the daring Mendès would risk trying it out, if he should become Premier—an event they are determined not to let happen to France.

Apropos of Mendès' resignation, *Le Monde* dryly remarked that he "is not an accommodating man or at his best except as first fiddle." For the nine years between 1945 and 1954, he played no solo part in Parliament except as a constant, ruthless—and by the outside world unknown—critic of all the French governments. Upon his sudden emergence, two years ago, as France's strong man, he roused the greatest hopes and the greatest devotion—and also the greatest personal hatred on the part of many—of any new French leader of modern times. Now both the former strong men who rose to save France after the war are off the stage—de Gaulle and Mendès-France, two most complex characters, and two incalculable losses for France in her present troubled hour.

LETTER FROM GAZA

A. J. Liebling

MARCH 16, 1957 (ON REFUGEES IN THE STRIP)

THE LARGE TOWN or small city of Gaza sits athwart what the late Earl Wavell, in his book on the Palestine campaigns of the First World War, called "one of the world's oldest and greatest highways, the main route between the earliest known cradles of civilization, the valleys of the Euphrates and of the Nile." From Egypt, he wrote, "its course keeps close to the sea while passing over the inhospitable desert of Sinai; thence it runs up the fertile plains of Philistia and Sharon, leaving the high, rocky fortress of Judaea to the east." The road, in fact, comes straight up from the desert's edge to Gaza through the thin leg of coastal land now known to the world at large as the Gaza Strip. The area was Turkish until 1918, and then part of the British mandate of Palestine until 1948; on the day Israel became free, it was invaded by the Egyptians. Wavell was concerned with Gaza because the British fought three great battles against the Turks there, in March, April, and November, 1917, to force a gateway to Palestine. On the third try, they succeeded. Since early 1949, however, the intercradle road has ended at a checkpoint a couple of miles north of Gaza, which has become a gateway to nowhere for three hundred thousand people. The presence of two-thirds of them was originally caused by a military accident. When the cease-fire came in the 1949 Israeli-Egyptian war, the Egyptian lines extruded from Sinai, which has been officially Egyptian since 1906, into the southwest corner of Palestine. Trapped behind these lines were an estimated quarter-million Arab-speaking refugees from the whole coastal region of Palestine; in their flight, they had followed the historic highway from north to south, and had stopped where they were because they had arrived at a desert. It is unlikely that they would have wished to cross it in any event, since they were Palestinians, not Egyptians, and the breeds are as incompatible as the regions are different. Their exodus, like that of the French civilians in 1940, had been hasty and ill-advised. Many of the last fugitives came from villages a few miles north of what was to become their prison wall. Had peace ensued, or had the Israelis won the Strip before the armistice, the refugees would have been reabsorbed into Israel, returning to their homes within weeks or months. But no treaty followed the armistice, which was never more than an imperfect cease-fire. The state of belligerency between Israel and her opponents continued, and the Gaza refugees, who were belligerent against nobody at all, remained where they are today, as if the French refugees backed up against the Spanish frontier in 1940 had been held ever since within a coastal enclave extending from St.-Jean-de-Luz to Bayonne. During all this time, Egypt has stopped the southern exit from the Strip, never proposing to annex it and never offering the Gazans Egyptian citizenship and freedom to remove to the Nile. Few Gazans might have accepted this option if it had been offered, but none were given a chance to decline. The refugees and the older residents have consequently lived together for eight years like people trapped in a submarine at the bottom of the sea, with an uncertain air supply and no means of egress. When dramatists treat of such situations, they supply lots of dialogue, and they are right; people who can do nothing effectual about their circumstances talk, and that is what the captives of the Gaza Strip have been doing almost incessantly since 1949.

The Strip is not a forbidding prison; most of it is agreeable but unspectacular country, flat except for a low ridge, called Ali Muntar, north and east of Gaza town. From Gaza south, it is green for twenty miles, then begins to go shabby and semi-desertic, and tails off into bleakness at Rafah, the last village. It is roughly twenty-five miles from north to south, and five from west to east, but its arable width is diminished by beaches and sand dunes along the Mediterranean shore. The better soil nourishes orange groves, eucalyptus trees, cactuses, and goats. When the cease-fire caught the refugees here, the tract was already overpopulated. This was because, in addition to the peasants and fishermen it might have normally supported, it contained Gaza, the most considerable place in southern Palestine, with a pre-refugee population of forty thousand, and Gaza's economic life depended on the hinterland, from which the war cut it off. Gaza was, of course, a famous place of old; it belonged to the Philistines and is associated with that Biblical Fanfan la Tulipe, Samson, who is locally alleged to have picked up the pillars of the Philistine temple after he had pulled it down on his head and carried them to the far end of the crest of Ali Muntar, where admiring posterity has erected a marabout as a marker. Gaza was captured at various times by Alexander, Pompey, Napoleon, and Saladin, which shows that it must have been considered worth capturing, and during the Middle Ages it was a textile center that gave its name to French *gaze* and English gauze. Its modern eminence may be gauged by its prison, the largest built by the British in all Palestine. The town is graced by the homes of Moslem landowners whose properties once extended far to the north and east of the present boundaries. With its resident population plus its refugees, it is impossible for the Strip to be self-supporting.

The Israelis, during their four-month occupation of the Strip, which began when they captured it last November 1st and is ending as I write, did nothing to reduce this human edema on their borders beyond shooting a disputed number of civilians when their troops entered and removing twenty-five families compromised by overfriendliness when they left. Their renewed contact with the refugees seemingly offered an opportunity to begin negotiations for the return of some and the compensation of others, but the chance was neglected, and the popular Israeli line on Gaza following the withdrawal may be gleaned from a piece, signed "Diplomatic Correspondent," on the front page of last Tuesday's Jerusalem *Post:* "To continue to administer this island of misery and hate would be a tiresome and costly undertaking for such a small country as this. The best thing for the refugees themselves is, probably, the way chosen by nearly a million Jews—emigration." Diplomatic Correspondent's advice to people trapped in a submarine is to call a taxi.

• • •

My own acquaintance with Gaza dates back only ten days, but I had the good fortune early in my visit to acquire the perspective of a man who had known it a long time. He was General Refet Bele, commander of the Turkish Army corps that defended the city forty years ago against the British. The General sat in the postprandial sun on the terrace of a trim *pension* and regarded with restrained amusement the undamaged villas around him. The *pension* is well removed from the old Arab part of town and stands among the dwellings of the big landowners. A small, thin man with a falcon's head that looked large in proportion to his shrunken neck, he was dapper in a suit of small checks; by his own account, he is seventy-five years old. The General is the Turkish representative on the advisory commission of the United Nations Relief and Works Agency for Palestine Refugees—or UNRWA—and has ambassadorial rank. UNRWA feeds, medicates, and educates the refugee community, which at the last head count totalled 219,423 in the Gaza area. General Bele told me that when Turkey entered his war, he was a major of thirty-three; three years later he was commanding a corps. "As a major, I took a detachment from Palestine to the Suez Canal, at El Kantara," he told me, "but I had not sufficient strength to take the Canal. The British spoke so highly of me, though, that I was promoted." He sighed, as if at a reminiscence he chose not to disclose. "A generous enemy is more helpful than a jealous friend," he added. He spoke in French; he said that he had studied it in Caucasian garrisons from the novels of Pierre Loti and Paul Bourget. He told me that this was his first visit to Gaza since its capture from the Egyptians by the Israelis last year (the Israelis were still there, of course), and then he gave me a clue to the merriment I had seen in his face. "When I defended Gaza," he said, "I left it completely flat. Not one house—not the littlest one—was standing." He moved his right hand in a horizontal arc, palm down. I could see that he was flattered by the deterioration in the quality of war since his day.

I asked him what Palestine had been like under the Ottoman Empire, and he said, "A country of pastoral happiness, where everyone slept on both ears every night. Jew and Arab and Christian lived together in security. They felt they had a father." He felt that the British fomenting of Arab nationalism had opened Pandora's box, and he regretted the passing of the Austro-Hungarian and Ottoman Empires. "They were not sufficiently strong to inspire fear," he said, "but by aiding Germany they balanced the colossus Russia. They have been destroyed, and today one sees the result!" I left him in the sun, the calmest and most reasonable man I have encountered in Gaza. The General, however, is not trapped here. His tour of inspection ended and the battlefields revisited, he will go home bearing presents for his latest child, aged seven.

Even the members of the international staff of UNRWA who are stationed in Gaza suffer from a trapped feeling, though their situation is not as irrevocable as that of their three hundred thousand fellow-inmates. Two planes a week from UNRWA headquarters in Beirut land within the Strip, and a man is always free to ask for a transfer or to resign. Social life was limited before the arrival of the United Nations Emergency

Force—there were eleven "internationals," nine men and two women—at the apex of the staff of three thousand; all the rest were refugees, except for a few Egyptian and Lebanese doctors, nurses, and teachers. In addition, there were within the area half a dozen officer observers of the United Nations, Egypt, and Israel Mixed Armistice Commission, who had had no official duties since the armistice exploded last November, and two American Baptist medical missionaries, who were running a hospital. Some of the UNRWA men had had their families with them before the November fighting, but just before the Israeli attack the families were shipped off by air to Beirut, where they remain. The UNRWA personnel have also felt the lack of a large city for distraction, such as they have in the Arab states that harbor other refugees. But the chief source of the trapped feeling is contagion. It is hard to live long in a prison for three hundred thousand without sometimes feeling claustrophobia.

• • •

Most of the refugees are divided among eight great villages of cabins, built by their labor with UNRWA materials and direction. All the refugees are registered on a ration roster, but of the forty thousand families getting rations, only twenty-four thousand have UNRWA housing, and these occupy thirty-three thousand rooms; it works out to about a room and a third per family, or four persons per room by Arab-peasant standards. The crowding is not as bad as it sounds, but the minority ménages where one man has two or three wives are cramped. The food ration consists basically of just bread—twenty-two pounds of white flour per head per month, which the women bake into flat loaves—plus infinitesimal amounts of lentils or beans, oil or fat, sugar, rice, and occasionally dates. It all comes to fifteen hundred calories a day; children get supplementary meals at school. It isn't brilliant, but, *à la rigueur,* it will indefinitely prevent a human being from dying. The normal refugee, therefore, spends a considerable part of his time on small schemes for bridging the gap between subsistence and getting enough to eat—by working for UNRWA, by working for people who work for UNRWA, by keeping a scraggly hen or goat, or by trading white flour for a greater quantity of the less valuable but equally filling local gray variety. The rest of the time he devotes to political conversation and reflection.

I asked a man who speaks a bit of English to describe his daily routine. "I get up in the morning and I walk around the village and look at nothing," he said. "Then I sit outside a coffee stall, even when I have no money for coffee, and listen to the radio. Also I play trictrac"—a form of ticktacktoe played with stones on sand. The women have hardly more to do, since housekeeping is not complicated. They also bear and scold children. The children are the best off, because they have school to occupy their minds and school meals to bolster their diet. A good half of the population is under the age of sixteen, and at least a quarter of the present refugees must have been born in the Gaza Strip. Officials say that the reason the probable real increase in the refugee population is not reflected in the statistics is that the earlier rosters were inflated by refugees pardonably interested in obtaining extra rations. The gap between the real and the fictitious populations is constantly narrowing, though, as UNRWA checks its figures.

Such picayune details of the refugee's life may tend to belittle him at a range of several thousand miles. A refugee camp is, in fact, a belittling environment; only gas chambers, torture, and starvation can dramatize the human predicament in these latter days, and even they pall easily. But the Palestine Arab peasant—which is what most of the refugees are—is a human type impossible to reduce to a figure of fun. The broadcasts he listens to are all political speeches or news commentary with a political slant: Radios Cairo, Damascus, and Cyprus, the Voice of America, even an Israeli program in Arabic—he is insatiable. The political romanticism of revenge that grew up during his first eight years of such listening suffered considerable shock when the Israelis demonstrated their strength in November, and his hope of a total solution of the refugee problem by force has been shaken. The Egyptians, when they were here, tried to strengthen this romanticism by precluding the hope of any other solution; it was a species of treason, for example, for an individual to admit that he might accept compensation from the Israelis for his land if compensation were offered. Egyptian security agents kept excellent tabs on the interminable public conversations, and there was no temptation to depart from the official doctrine of all or nothing, since there was no possibility of getting past the barrier up the road. In the Egyptian days, no refugee could be found who would say even that he would take his own land back if it meant returning to Israel as an individual and living among Jews. (There is no record, of course, of any such offer's having ever been made.) This legend of the monolithic intransigence of the exiles—not the Gaza lot alone but all the diaspora, in Lebanon, Syria, and Jordan—was in its time useful to Israel, too, because it barred any payments to anybody. The Israeli argument when visitors raise the question of the possibility of piecemeal compensation is that conditions have changed since the Arabs went away—and besides Israel can't spare the money. On the piecemeal resettlement of the refugees in Israel, it is "We need the land for a hundred thousand Jews we expect from Portugal"—or Pimlico or Guatemala; details are unessential. Many Israelis are not only incapable of thinking that this is a paradox but unable to believe that it seems odd to a foreigner. Yet there are Palestinians on the Gaza beach who say, "My land is five miles from here, and they have taken it to give it to men from ten thousand miles away." The difference of opinion is irreconcilable. The degree of intransigence expressed varies, however, with the known political views of your interpreter, who is usually a camp official, and the men among the refugees who have the most substance and education, and who themselves speak English or French, are generally the most reasonable of all. "I would go back and see if I could live happily in the new environment," one such said to me—I had been warned against him as a hothead—"and then see if I couldn't sell out and go where I felt I had more freedom."

The expulsion of the Egyptians last November brought a chance for contact between the present Palestinians and the ex-Palestinians. The chance still exists, as long as the Egyptians don't return. The incursion of the Israeli Army, however, shut off the Strip's most important source of outside revenue, aside from UNRWA's contribution to the economy. This was the money sent home by between five and ten thousand men from the Gaza Strip who work in the oil fields of Saudi Arabia and Kuwait and Qatar. The Egyptian authorities, while they were in command, stopped the Gaza people from coming farther into Egypt than the scabby oasis of El Arish (although they made an exception for Gazans studying at Egyptian universities), but they permitted men to go out of the Strip to work in the oil countries. The Palestinians are often more literate and always more advanced technically than the Arabs of the Hejaz—or, for that matter, than the Egyptians. Their labor is therefore at a premium in primitive Arab lands, and the revenue they sent home was estimated at from twenty-five thousand to a hundred thousand Egyptian pounds monthly. (Gazans, when they talk money, still talk in Egyptian pounds, which are officially worth two dollars and eighty cents. The Israeli pound, officially worth fifty-five cents, found slow acceptance in the Strip, and the day before the withdrawal of the Israeli forces you could get from seven to ten Israeli pounds for one Egyptian pound—a situation that offered a magnificent opportunity for quick profit in what I think is called arbitrage. That same week in Beirut, I was informed, one could buy an Egyptian pound for two dollars. The imagination staggers.)

When the Israelis took over the Strip, all communication with the Arab countries was naturally cut off, since Israel is still technically at war with them. One of the first and most pressing tasks of the United Nations administration at Gaza will be to hold the Strip open to communication and economic exchange at both ends. Maybe we can get those people out of that submarine.

CUBAN INTERLUDE

Norman Lewis

MAY 3, 1958 (ON CUBA AND ITS REBELS)

ALL OVER CUBA, one finds public buildings decorated with murals of a heroic, if lugubrious, nature, depicting the resistance of student revolutionaries to the tyrants of their day. Often, the students are shown facing a firing squad composed of the ferocious volunteers raised by the Spanish colonial authorities or of the no less grim-faced soldiery of one of the early indigenous dictators. None of the macabre episodes portrayed are less than thirty years old, however, and one supposes that at least another thirty years must elapse before the young men who are now carrying on this old student tradition with revolvers and bombs will achieve pictorial commemoration of the same kind. The history of Cuban youth in revolt started a century ago, when students organized a struggle against the senile and brutalized Spanish colonial regime. It was continued sporadically after the liberation from Spain, when the new order so often revealed itself as nothing more than the old order with its recently acquired democratic mask fallen slightly askew. Although in many parts of Latin America the practice of parliamentary democracy is rare, quixotic, and incomplete, Latin-Americans—and Cubans in particular—have never ceased to carry on a nostalgic courtship of the democratic ideal, seen, as it were, as an inaccessible beauty behind an ornamental grille. In periods when something that will just pass muster as democracy is achieved—when elections take place and are not too cynically manipulated, when the press is vocal and the generals are mute—little is heard of student revolutionary action. But when a dictator puts himself in power and stays there too long, the students begin to plot, and soon to throw bombs, and in the end the Army and the police are forced into reprisals of the kind that will one day form the subject matter of yet more depressing murals in provincial town halls. After the period of chaos that attended the overthrow of the detested President Machado in 1933, there followed a fairly quiet quarter of a century, by Cuban standards. Then, late in 1956, the old periodic eruption started again, provoked by what was beginning to look like another immovable dictatorship. Within the ensuing twelve months, there were political assassinations, sabotage, mass demonstrations, and local uprisings, and by the beginning of this year the University of Havana and the other state-supported universities had closed down. Now the jails are full of students, and many idealistic and hotheaded young men—often barely out of their teens—have lost their lives. Nobody seems to have any idea how the thing will end.

When I arrived in Havana not long ago, a fugitive from the chills of London, and more or less a student of Latin-American upheavals, the city was enjoying a brief respite from nightly alarms. The processional crowds of the evening were abroad again, moving in ranks down the Prado under trees full of squawking birds, and then thinning out along the Malecón, past the opulent gray baroque houses, and dodging the whiplash of spray over the low sea wall. Havana was beautiful and noisy, perfumed with cigar smoke and hair oil. People lived clamorously in the streets, under the flame trees in the parks, and in a thousand bars. One remembered T. S. Eliot's "I had not thought death had undone so many." There were gentle-mannered, philosophical pimps at all the street corners—men who, if allowed, would talk of their ancestry first and then describe their wares. This was normality as I remembered it from other visits, but for the past year, I learned, there had been incidents on three nights out of six. There had been bomb throwing and sniping in the streets, and quite frequently the power cables had been cut, blacking out the town and thereby exposing those taken by surprise in the darkened streets to the incidental hazards of gunplay between snipers and police. Even the present lull was an uneasy one, and it was considered foolhardy to visit the cinema or the theatre—inviting places for the planting of bombs—or even to wander far from one's hotel at night. I found fresh bullet holes in the counter of my favorite bar, on the Calle Industria. A few weeks previously, a regular of the establishment had been shot down by a tommy-gunner firing from across the street. One of the barmen had lost a finger in the ragged volley, and, smiling importantly, he held up the stump for inspection. This occurrence had not been bad for business.

In Havana, people like to pop in for a drink at a place where there has been a recent shooting, just as in London they might visit an East End pub once patronized by royalty.

I took a hotel room overlooking the Presidential palace and the garden-filled square in which it stands. The streets around the square had been closed to traffic, and it had become a kind of no man's land, patrolled by police in all sorts of uniforms. There were khaki-colored bulletproof cars at the corners, ready for action, and every so often one would be started up, driven restlessly, with its siren moaning, a few yards up the road, and then brought back. The atmosphere in the neighborhood of the palace was clearly trigger-happy. Visitors to Havana were advised not to loiter as they walked past the front of the palace, or to point cameras in the direction of the machine-gunners crouching behind parapets of sandbags on the palace roof. These exceptional police precautions dated from an afternoon last spring when twenty-one students—who actually brought along their own photographer—had staged an abortive attempt on the regime by driving up to the palace gates in a truck and then dashing through them in the hope of shooting their way up to the President's office, on the second floor. A handful of the attackers almost reached their objective. But the President happened at that moment to be lunching with his wife in his residential quarters, in another part of the building, and there on the landing outside the locked office door the last members of the assault party died. What little chance of success this desperate venture might have had was thrown away, right at the beginning, by a gross lack of coordination. Cuban revolutionary movements are weakened by much internal division. Two separate student organizations had united temporarily to plan the attack, but the larger group, which possessed a bazooka that might have made all the difference, failed to put in an appearance. The hopeless little battle was over in five minutes, but then the government tanks came on the scene, and it was hours before the troops ceased firing their heavy machine guns into the surrounding buildings, in the belief that they harbored snipers. Many motorists, trapped in the line of fire, spent most of the afternoon lying under their cars, and a fair amount of incidental damage—some of a freakish kind—was produced by this protracted bombardment. The abstract sculptures standing in front of the National Museum, which faces the Presidential palace, were badly shot up, and a friend of mine returned to his hotel room facing on the square to find that a couple of the suits hanging in his wardrobe were full of bullet holes. The government paid him a hundred dollars in compensation for these.

• • •

At first, I was inclined to take the view that, apart from a crop of incredible new night clubs (one of them had lawns of spurious grass, and an artificial sky), nothing much had changed in Havana since I first visited the city, almost twenty years ago. In those days, people regarded the topic of democracy with a sort of cynical resignation. In reality, they used to tell you, things weren't a great deal different from the old colonial era, when the ruling Spanish bureaucracy treated the country as a privately owned farm, to exploit in whatever way it thought fit. The main difference was that nowadays it was Cubans who took it out of Cubans—and that was perhaps some slight consolation. Whoever was in power was expected to help himself to the public funds. As long as the administration contented itself with diverting, say, 20 percent of the national revenue into its pockets, its conduct was considered reasonable, if not just, and nobody grumbled much. Nor was it thought particularly scandalous when an outgoing President made it quite evident by his real-estate investments in Miami that he had become a multimillionaire during his term of office. When a government changed, it was a change of personalities, not of principles. The old pernicious, grafting Hispanic system went on. Elections were a sort of white man's version of an African magic ritual that nobody believed in very much any more but that was still carried on, out of ancestral habit. I remembered that at the time of this first visit to Havana an unemployed man's vote cost a peso—one dollar—and I also remember, quite vividly, a remarkable incident that occurred in the Parque Central one day, when the town loafers who congregated there decided to get together and employ a recognized trade-union practice to force the price up to a peso and twenty-five centavos. A politician who had come down to the park with the intention of buying up their votes was stung by this inequitable conduct into threatening them with a tommy gun, and somehow or other it managed to go off. I was just around the corner at the moment, and it was the first time I had ever heard a tommy gun fired on a real-life occasion, although I immediately recognized the sound from my experience of films based on the Chicago scene. Passersby, who had probably gone through this kind of thing before, dropped to the ground and stayed there until the staccato hammering stopped, and then scrambled to their feet and went racing away across the flower beds in the direction of the sound. The siren of a police car howled briefly in the vociferous traffic, and soon policemen, pistols in hand, were herding us away from the sight of whatever had happened. Next day, the newspapers came out with an account of the incident. It seemed that in addition to wounding several down-and-outs, the politician had succeeded—doubtless by the purest mischance—in killing a policeman, and for this he had been lynched by the police in a most gruesome fashion, described in the report with gloating attention to detail. The paper conceded ultimate victory to the loafers. From that time on, it concluded, the price of a vote would be one peso twenty-five. (I understand that it is now double that.) All this was, of course, before the days of Fidel Castro—or, rather, in the days when Fidel Castro was of no more importance than any other scatterbrained young potential revolutionary, and was years away from being the leader of the first genuine maquis, of the Second World War kind, to be organized in the Western Hemisphere.

The Fidel Castro rebellion began with an appallingly disorganized attack, carried out by the leader and a handful of his fellow-conspirators in July, 1953, on the miniature fortress known as the Moncada Barracks, in the city of Santiago de Cuba, capital of Oriente Province, at the east end of the island. At that time, Castro, a lawyer with intellectual interests and without a practice, was twenty-nine years old. He and his little group of followers, armed with a few pistols and rifles, assaulted the barracks in the almost insane belief that once this strong point was in their hands, the town of Santiago—supposedly unfriendly to President Batista—would rise up and join them, and that by some strange talismanic power the revolution would spread itself spontaneously throughout the rest of the island. Amazingly, about half the attackers actually got into the barracks, only to find themselves trapped within a high-walled yard, their escape cut off. For a few moments they stood there, arms raised in surrender, and then the machine guns on the walls opened fire. Castro, who stayed outside the barracks, got away, but was later cornered, and gave himself up. It was the Archbishop of Santiago in person who delivered Castro over to the police, to insure that the young rebel would not also be slaughtered on the spot. This was one of many occasions on which leaders of the Catholic Church in Cuba have shown themselves sympathetic to the anti-Batista revolutionaries. Castro was tried, received a sentence of fifteen years, and was released nineteen months later under a general amnesty decreed by the President. Here is the one and only advantage of being a Cuban revolutionary, as opposed to being a revolutionary in any other country. In Cuban revolutions, the police do not take prisoners if they can help it, and they have been charged—even by judges of the Supreme Court—with the torture of suspects, but anyone who manages to survive the carnage that inevitably follows a failed revolt rarely serves more than a fraction of his prison sentence. As soon as Castro was released, he took refuge in Mexico and there began training a small band of followers in exile—all intellectuals and sons of good middle-class families, like himself—for an invasion of the home country. One of Castro's many tactical errors was to issue propaganda announcements giving the approximate date decided on for this project. Cuba would be freed from the rule of President Batista, he promised, by the end of 1956. By the middle of November, therefore, all garrisons were alerted, Batista's small fleet of armed launches was at sea and on the watch, and his planes continually patrolled the areas where a landing was likely to take place.

Castro's "invasion," when it finally came, was farcically mismanaged—in what would seem to be the tradition of Cuban revolutionary action. There was a good deal of support in Oriente Province for Castro's movement, and on November 30th, the day it had been advertised that he would land, armed revolts took place in Santiago and in the four other principal towns of the province. For several hours, uniformed Castro supporters were in control of the streets, and the police were under siege in their barracks. But Castro and his invaders failed to appear and Army reinforcements began arriving from Havana, so the insurgents lost heart and gradually melted away. Known opponents of the government were subsequently arrested by the hundred, and many were summarily shot. Castro arrived on December 2nd—two days late—after a rough crossing, to find that the last vestige of revolt had been crushed. His total force consisted of eighty-two very seasick men, who were unable to find their landing beach and finally came ashore in a swamp. Batista's air force spotted and strafed the boat as it put in, and the men scrambled away through water and slime, leaving most of their arms, including two anti-tank guns, behind. The survivors, who had only a rough idea of where they were, split up as soon as they reached hard ground. In the distance, they could see the foothills of the Sierra Maestra, but before they could get to the shelter of its tropical forest and its ravines, most of them had been intercepted and butchered out of hand by government troops. Only twelve men, Castro among them, came out of this grisly adventure alive, and it was months before it became generally known that he had indeed escaped and was hinding in the Sierras.

From this unpromising start developed a tough and successfully organized resistance movement. The number of young men now fighting in the Sierras is not known, but it may amount to a thousand, and most of the armed forces of Cuba are kept constantly employed in the effort to contain them, while spectacular coups, such as the recent kidnapping of Juan Fangio, the world motor-racing champion, are frequently carried out by undercover rebel groups in the cities. Castro men like to act in the tradition of the romantic outlaw. Fangio appears to have been charmed with their good manners during his short period of captivity, part of which he spent watching a television broadcast of the race he should have competed in. Three days after the Fangio incident, a party of rebels held up the National Bank of Cuba, in the heart of Havana, but instead of taking any of the cash from the safes, they contented themselves with setting fire to thousands of checks. In the mountains, the men are organized in small bands that keep constantly on the move and avoid sleeping two nights in the same place. The rebels have with them two Catholic priests, a Protestant minister, and several doctors. Castro announced not long ago that for the time being he had no use for further volunteers, unless they could bring their own weapons with them.

The Sierra Maestra is the least known and most neglected area in Cuba; it consists of a seventy-mile range of jungled mountains with peaks rising to over six thousand feet, and is inhabited by a handful of farmers, said to be descendants of outlaws, who live in almost savage simplicity and grow a little coffee for the market. Castro, who is regarded in many parts of Cuba as a sort of Robin Hood, seems to get on well with these backwoodsmen, and he and his band have repaid their good will and protection by organizing schools and medical centers in an area where illiteracy was total and no doctor had ever been seen. The military tactics employed by the rebels are the classic methods of guerrilla warfare, in which head-on engagements with government troops are always avoided, and ammunition and supplies are collected in surprise attacks on Army and police posts. No one has ever discovered that Castro has any war aim other than the elimination of the present dictatorship, in order, he says, to open the way for a new and non-Cuban kind of democracy, which has never been very clearly defined but which is supposed to be in the process of creation by members of Cuban parties in exile in the United States. Castro proposes to achieve his aim by disrupting, if necessary, the economy of the country to such an extent that the United States, to protect its investments, will be compelled to apply pressure for the removal of Batista from power. The remarkable thing is that despite the injury to many private interests that Castro's plan of action involves, his popularity throughout Cuba remains high—even, it seems, with those who suffer actual damage from his acts of sabotage. It is typical of Castro that one of the first plantations he burned belonged to his own family.

• • •

The man against whom Castro's activities are concentrated—President Fulgencio Batista—has either been in office or loomed large behind the scenes in Cuba ever since his extraordinary coup, in 1933. History offers probably no other instance of a sergeant's not only staging a successful mutiny but going on to take over the government of the country. In 1933, Sergeant Batista was a stenographer employed in the Havana garrison. He was noted for his good looks and his persuasive charm. At that time, there was a good deal of unrest among the enlisted men, because of impending pay cuts, and the country was in a state of political turmoil following the downfall of President Machado, who had just bolted in a plane to the United States. Bands of the armed students who had been responsible for Machado's overthrow still roamed the streets, wreaking summary vengeance on supporters of Machado's tyranny. So powerful were these bands that before hatching his plot Batista took care to get on good terms with the students' revolutionary committee, the Directorio Estudiantil, which in those days conducted its own secret courts-martial and once actually executed, by firing squad, a member found guilty of traitorous activities. Having won over the students, Batista put into action a fairly simple plan of his own, which depended for its success on the fact that Cuban officers were then privileged to sleep out of barracks, and practically always did. On this occasion, when the officers of the garrison had gone home for the night Batista simply posted his own picked men on guard duty, with orders not to admit their superiors when they arrived the next day. Then he telephoned every garrison on the island and told the noncommissioned officers on duty that the sergeants were in command.

It seems unlikely that at this juncture Batista thought of himself as the country's eventual leader, and he would probably have been quite ready to treat with a representative of the officers for the redress of the soldiers' grievances. Preliminary discussions were begun, but the officers, believing that the United States would never permit a large-scale mutiny to succeed within what was accepted as its sphere of influence, broke off contact with the mutineers, retired to the Hotel Nacional, and barricaded themselves in. United States warships now appeared off Havana, and Batista, spurred on by militant students who threatened to attack the officers if he did not, and fearing that, in any case, he had gone too far to turn back, gave the order for an assault. His men opened fire on the hotel with old French seventy-fives, sighting their target, it is said, through the barrels of their cannons. Considerable toll was taken among the attackers by accurate rifle fire from the hotel—many of the officers were excellent marksmen—but in the end the defenders' ammunition gave out, they were obliged to surrender, and many of them were massacred in cold blood. No Marines were landed, and Batista, by then a colonel, tightened his grip on the government.

Batista has turned out to be perhaps the most capable and progressive President that Cuba has ever had. His sense of humor is illustrated by his habit, in the old days, when the Communist Party had not been outlawed and was running its own radio station, of giving parties for his friends at which the principal entertainment was listening to the Communist broadcasters' nightly manhandling of the President's private life. Although in recent years Batista has taken openly to a dictatorial form of rule, he is surprisingly free from that brand of dictators' megalomania that makes it impossible for anyone to escape the sight of their portraits in public places and in the press. Batista seems not to care greatly for publicity, and he probably does not even regard himself as an instrument wielded by divine hands to lead the Cuban people forward to their destiny. Nevertheless, the social and labor legislation enacted since his access to power establishes Cuba as one of the most advanced nations in the Americas, and he has repeatedly disappointed business and industry by his failure to abrogate a law that makes it almost impossible to dismiss an employee on any ground—a law that is regarded as one of the greatest deterrents to capital investment on the island. The organized workers—whose wages have now reached their highest point in Cuban history—have repaid Batista by refusing, so far, to respond to Castro's frequent calls for a general strike. On the other hand, Batista has alienated the affections of most middle- and upper-class Cubans by his destruction of civil liberties, his press censorship, his forthright rule by means of the Army, and his toleration of the many repressive excesses indulged in by his police. Although he was once believed to be unattracted by money, charges of immense corruption in his administration are now heard on all sides.

• • •

Censorship in Havana has been so strict lately that a newspaper advertisement for a watch was banned not long ago because the celebrity shown wearing it was a bearded explorer, and every Cuban knows that Castro has a beard (or did have; the story now goes that since the capture of a crate of razors he and his men have been clean-shaven). The news from Oriente Province is heavily censored, and on the rare occasions when the Sierra Maestra is referred to at all, it is usually called, with sly irony, "a certain mountain range." This absence of news has, of course, favored the spread of spectacular rumors. Some weeks ago, well before the most recent flareup in Santiago, where I had spent some time back in 1939, I inquired about what was going on there, and heard such sombre tales of nightly street battles in the city and of a countryside given over to chaos and terror that I decided to go and see for myself. None of the taxi-drivers I talked to would agree to make the trip, and after listening to their stories of wholesale arson and murder in Santiago, I was rather surprised to learn that Cubana Airlines still ran a daily service there. I booked passage on a non-stop flight that left early in the evening, and when I arrived at the Havana airport, the plane, a brand-new four-engine turboprop Viscount, stood waiting on the tarmac, floodlit and under heavy guard. There was half an hour's delay while several parcels brought aboard by the other passengers—there were just four—were untied and found to contain no bombs, and then we took off.

Cuba is one of the gayest of countries to fly over at night. From ten thousand feet, there were always half a dozen brilliantly lit small towns in sight below, scattered over the countryside in a regular pattern, like sparkling modernistic trinkets on the black earth, each with its square-cut central jewel of a plaza. Toward the end of the five-hundred-mile run, with the lights of Santiago ahead and the foothills of the Sierra Maestra off to the right below, I could see a tiny ringworm of fire glowing in the blackness. My fellow-passengers said it was no doubt a burning cane field. (A short time before, Castro had announced that unless Batista resigned, he would burn the cane all over the island as it stood in the fields ready for cutting. "A sugar harvest without Batista, or Batista without a sugar harvest," the slogan went.) A few minutes later, we landed and were hustled into an airport bus, to be driven at a rocking, tire-screeching seventy miles an hour into the center of town. It was now half past nine, and the driver explained to me that when there was to be trouble, the zero hour was inevitably ten o'clock, at which time all the town's lights might be cut off by the insurgents. With half an hour to go, the streets were still ablaze, and small groups of citizens clustered at their doors, like gophers ready to bolt for the shelter of their burrows when the shadow of an eagle fell upon them. Under lamps hung like moons among blossoming trees, other citizens were still performing the decorous ritual of the evening promenade—the women circling the square in one direction and the men in the other. My hotel was on the Parque de Céspedes, in a theatrical setting of ancient colonial buildings. The feeling of being in a theatre was heightened by a row of substantial burghers who sat sipping their Daiquiris along the edge of the hotel veranda. As the cathedral clock struck ten, the promenaders trooped out of the square, as if at the completion of a scene, and on the terrace we waited in our privileged seats to see if more sinister performers would come out on the empty stage. A waiter told me there had been a good deal of shooting the previous night. One of the hotel guests had been caught in the suburbs in the blackout, and had spent half the night under his car while bullets flew in all directions around him. But tonight everything was quiet. At intervals of about half an hour, an Army truck bristling with guns rumbled through the square, but no snipers appeared on the rooftops. One by one, the guests got tired of waiting and took themselves reluctantly off to bed.

It was a relief to find, the next morning, that the gracious old town of Santiago hadn't changed much since I was last there. Neglect and comparative poverty have thus far stemmed the encroachment of the insipid modernism that is fast taking over Havana, and have preserved the near-perfect Céspedes Park and many of the surrounding old houses, with their deep balconies and their enormous, airy rooms, whose ceilings are supported, like Moorish council chambers, by numerous spare and elegant columns. I noted that although the hotel's vast baroque dining room had been defaced by an American-style quick-lunch counter, the huge old Valencian chandeliers, with their bunches of scaly glass flowers, which had survived so many bullets and earthquakes, were still there. The cracks opened in the towers of the Florentine-style cathedral by the 1929 earthquake were only just being filled in.

By day, life went on in Santiago much as usual, although the authorities had thought it wise to remove all the police—even those normally employed on traffic duty—from the streets. A stubbornly festive air hung over the city. Whole barbecued pigs, paraded on wheelbarrows, were rapidly being reduced to sandwiches for consumption on the spot. Many of the shops were decorated with elaborate colored-paper models of airplanes, Colt revolvers, and battleships. The hairdressers were doing a fast trade in de-kinking the hair of the city's fashionable *mulatas,* and there was an all-pervasive background moan of jukeboxes playing barely recognizable American hit tunes. The Cuban obsession with the occult and the pseudo-occult sciences came out more strongly here than in Havana. A department store had a window display of books devoted solely to the significance of numbers. Fortune-telling slot machines abounded. A market stall was heaped with cult objects of Saint Barbara, who has been identified by a Cuban sect known as the Santeros with the African god Chango. And *consultorios espirituales,* with peso-a-trance mediums in attendance, were almost as numerous as barbershops.

Most of the citizens of Santiago appeared to be sympathetic to Castro's cause, not only because he was out to free the whole of Cuba from the dictatorship but because, rightly or wrongly, he symbolized for them the resistance of Oriente Province to what they saw as its exploitation and its neglect by the central authority. I paid a visit to a wealthy local businessman, who openly admitted contributing generously to the war chest of the Castro rebellion. He received me in a cool, palm-shaded patio and presented me with a new aspect of the problem. "It's really all the fault of the English," he said. "I mean your pirates, in the old days. We had to build the city in a low-lying position, where we hoped it wouldn't be seen from the sea. Not that that helped in the long run—your people still managed to sack it half a dozen times. But if the place hadn't turned out so unhealthy, Santiago would have been the capital, not Havana. As things are, we're quite neglected. Oriente is the richest province in Cuba, but all the money goes into the pockets of those gangsters in Havana. Naturally, we're for Castro to a man. What can you expect?"

Castro and his merry men were lurking somewhere in the five hundred square miles of almost unexplored mountain territory that begins just across Santiago Bay. At night, his partisans all over the province were going into the cane fields and planting candles whose bases were wrapped in kerosene-soaked rags. There was a great shortage of food in the mountains, and little water, except for the rank fluid stored in certain tropical plants, so the rebels were renewing their supplies by constant raids on the towns in the vicinity. The most effective troops in use against them on the government side were the *rurales,* a hard-hitting body of men originally formed by one of the early United States occupation forces and steeped in the tradition of shooting first and then asking questions. The *rurales,* I was told, prefer not to take prisoners, and spare no one who is even suspected of being associated with the rebels. Two doctors who were believed to have treated Castro's wounded had just been murdered by the *rurales,* and this had led to an outraged protest to the Batista government from the World Medical Association.

• • •

Despite all the sensational forecasts, it soon became clear that I was unlikely to see any action in Santiago just then, and when, after mooching about its peaceful streets for two days, I received a tip from a rebel sympathizer that an uprising was expected hourly in the town of Manzanillo, about a hundred miles to the west, I hired a taxi—without any difficulty—and drove there. The countryside I drove through was the wonderfully unspoiled Cuba of the last century—or perhaps even the century before. The peasants still built their huts of palm fronds, in the style of the *bohios* of the long-exterminated Siboney Indians, and surrounded them with bowerbird decorations of colored rocks. We passed through tangerine-scented tropical versions of the American frontier towns of the 1850s, with swinging-door saloons, hitching posts, and gun-toting cowboys on white ponies. Two men out of three were going about with fighting cocks tucked under their arms. They fed these birds on scraps of meat and tidbits of hard-boiled eggs soaked in rum, and carried them around mostly for their companionship, it appeared, since cockfights were held only on weekends, in structures built like miniature bull rings, which stood on the outskirts of all the villages. At one crossroads, a distraught-looking female cartomancer had planted herself, to tell fortunes at twenty centavos a clip. Cartomancy is regarded in Cuba as the lowest grade of prediction, and the gloomy cowboys who were this woman's customers flung down their coins and received her austere prognostications without even bothering to dismount. The hills in this area were covered with a light haze from burning fields of sugar cane. Once, we passed a field where a fire had just been put out; the dry grass around its edges was still flaring with the sizzling noise of bacon frying in a pan.

The first *guardia rural* who stopped us, at the small town of Veguitas, was a memorable figure. He was dressed like an American cavalryman of the 1914–18 war, with breeches, leggings, and a Scoutmaster's hat, and he sat under a canopy by the roadside, on an elegant chair upholstered in tooled leather. He held a large automatic pistol in one hand, a tommy gun lay across his knees, and there was a bottle of beer at his side. This proved to be the first of eight such encounters that day, and in one of them—at Bayamo, where everyone predicted freely that a rebel strike was imminent—my luggage was dragged out of the taxi to be searched. This time, it was a pair of consciously tough, swaggering soldiers, members of a whole class of ne'er-do-wells who receive a week or two of training and then, with a gun in their hands and a hundred dollars a month to spend, are let loose upon the countryside. They put on a great show of fury when they found a khaki shirt in my suitcase—apparently it is illegal in Cuba for a civilian to possess such a garment—and one advised the other, in a rattle of slurred Spanish, to "let him have it" if I talked back. At this moment, I remembered only too well that civil rights had been suspended, and that during a tense period a few months previously an N.B.C. man had been flung into jail for eight hours merely because he had had the bad luck to be travelling in the neighborhood at the time. In the end, however, the soldiers let me go, and I reached Manzanillo, which is down on the coast and right under the brow of the Sierras. Here it was perfectly clear, from the sandbag parapets and the manned strong points, that the Army was ready for anything. A uniformed patrol was searching the houses facing the square when I got there, and as soon as I took out my camera, a rifle was levelled at me. I decided that secrecy was not Castro's forte.

The attack came, all right, but it was not at Manzanillo, or at Bayamo, or even at Santiago, as had been variously predicted, but at Veguitas, where the *guardia rural* in the antique cavalryman's outfit had stopped me. A convoy of attackers had descended on the town, and I wondered whether he had tried to intercept them, and what had happened to him. The account I heard was that the Castro men first silenced the opposition and then went around among the stores, loading four trucks with supplies. What is characteristic of this rebellion, although remarkably out of line with tradition, is that the raiders seem actually to pay for all they take, and I felt sure that a proportion of the money they put down in Veguitas had come from my friend the Santiago businessman. It was beginning to look to me as though, in spite of all the early failures, Castro's strategy was more successful than I had supposed, and as though, if the present Cuban dictatorship could perhaps hold out for a long time, Castro might contrive to hold out even longer.

PART FIVE

TAKES

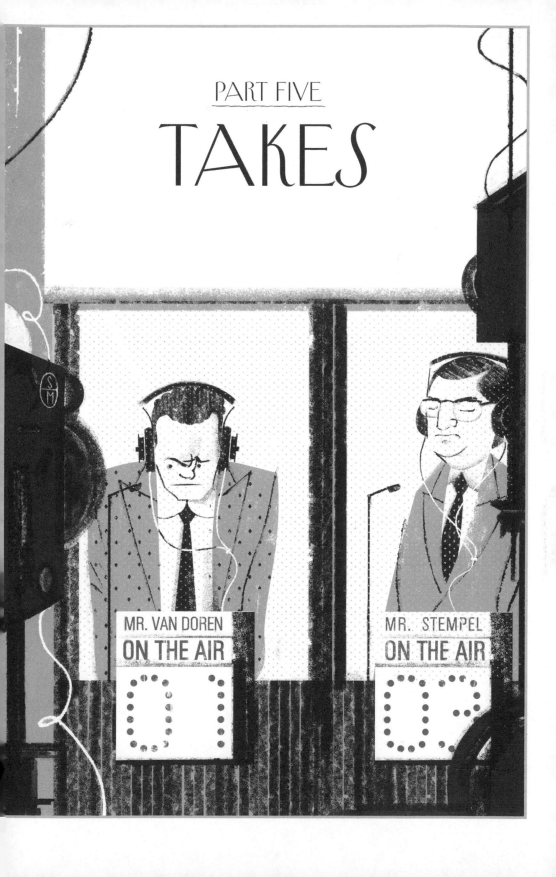

A NOTE BY MALCOLM GLADWELL

"History is written by the victors," Winston Churchill supposedly said, which is a version of the argument that scientists would make a generation later about memory. What we recall, from a given moment or period, is not a videotape of what we actually experienced, pristinely stored in our mental archive. It is a memory overlaid with what we were later told or saw or read, to the point where the initial memory has been revised—often without our realizing it—a thousand times. History is written in the editing room: the victor controls post-production. Keep that in mind when you read what follows. This is not the 1950s. It is *The New Yorker*'s 1950s, and the reason you are reading it is that *The New Yorker* won.

Think about what you know about that decade. Some of you lived through it, but that, the memory experts tell us, has made your recollections all the more subject to post-hoc revision. Many of us were born after it, and for us the problem is much worse. What we do know? Maybe we saw *North by Northwest* and remember that scene where Cary Grant—or was it Jimmy Stewart?—had his secretary bring him his messages while he went for a martini at the Plaza. People drank a lot in the 1950s—or, at least, Madison Avenue advertising executives did, or at least Madison Avenue advertising executives did as imagined by squat, balding, middle-aged British directors who may never have set foot inside a Madison Avenue agency. My elemental 1950s memory was reading Henry Gregor Felsen's 1953 teen masterpiece, *Street Rod,* in rural Canada as a child, which convinced me that, just two decades earlier, the United States was swarming with sixteen-year-olds driving tricked-out roadsters down dusty Midwestern highways at ridiculous speeds. I waited, impatiently, for 1970s Canada to catch up with 1950s America on this particular front. (I'm still waiting.) Felsen, by the way, was the son of Harry and Sabina Felsen of Brooklyn. My vision of the 1950s, in other words, was constructed in southwest Ontario in the 1970s out of the Midwestern fantasies of a Depression-era kid from New York City, whose actual experiences with motorized transport as a seventeen-year-old were probably confined to streetcars and the Q train from Flatbush. We are what we read. It's probably better that way.

So what do these brief vignettes tells us about *The New Yorker*'s 1950s? The twenty-one shorts that follow are drawn largely from The Talk of the Town, which establishes the tenor, although some are excerpts from full-scale stories. By design, they give us a magical, crisply imagined decade that takes place on the island of Manhattan, or on the way to Manhattan—as when Lillian Ross catches up with Ernest Hemingway at the baggage claim at Idlewild. This was the fifties: Kennedy was still a senator and not yet an airport. We get an unforgettable portrait of Toots Shor, whose roost—the restaurant Toots Shor's—was at 51 West Fifty-first Street, eight blocks from the *New Yorker* offices, on Forty-third. Geoffrey Hellman catches up with Frank Lloyd Wright at the Plaza, at Fifty-ninth and Fifth Avenue, where the architect talks a blue streak. There is Mort Sahl at "the apartment of a friend of ours." (Could it be anywhere but the Upper West Side?) And there's Pat Weaver at the NBC building in Rockefeller Center, and Leonard Bernstein at Carnegie Hall on Fifty-seventh.

The New Yorker as a whole has long been a place that rewards the adventurous streak in its writers. Mississippi is good; Bolivia, better. (And if you've got someone who goes from Mississippi to Bolivia and then, after an emotional catharsis of some sort, back again, so much the better.) But The Talk of the Town is the talk of the *town:* it follows the ideology of the city's alternate-side parking rules, which decree that parked cars be moved each day from one side of the street to the other. Travel, in parking terms, is measured in street crossings. That is the rule of the front section of the magazine, and the 1950s, through that prism, is an intimate place. "It was over five years ago that we paid a call on the International Business Machines Selective Sequence Electronic Calculator," one story begins, "in I.B.M. World Headquarters, at Fifty-seventh and Madison." Or: "We marched over to the building housing the firm's electronic laboratory, at 475 Tenth Avenue." Marched! Not even a cab was necessary. As Freud might have put it (had Freud lived on Broadway, not Berggasse), the stories in this section are attuned to the narcissism of small distances.

And that, of course, is their great charm. Our own times are chaotic and confusing enough. Everything is scattered now. The Selective Sequence Electronic Calculator is probably in a server farm in Idaho. Toots Shor would have a place in Vegas. Frank Lloyd Wright would be designing a massive mixed-use development in Dubai. It is more than O.K. to be a little provincial if your province was the New York City of the 1950s, and it's O.K. for us to overwrite our memories with memories as enthralling as this: "Hemingway was wearing a red plaid wool shirt, a figured wool necktie, a tan wool sweater-vest, a brown tweed jacket tight across the back and with sleeves too short for his arms, gray flannel slacks, Argyle socks, and loafers." He was flying in from . . . *Havana*.

Or this: "After our talk with Mrs. Fischer, we made our way to the club." Mrs. Fischer, in case you are wondering, was the mother of Bobby. The "club" is the Manhattan Chess Club on West Sixty-fourth Street. The greatest chess player in the world was fourteen in 1957, and just twenty-one blocks uptown. You could walk over and watch him play. "For four years, I tried everything I knew to discourage him," Mrs. Fischer tells our correspondent, with a sigh. "But it was hopeless." In that era's Talk of the Town, even the mothers of prodigies did not sound like the mothers of prodigies. They sounded so much better. In the pages that follow, everything does.

CHARACTERS

ERNEST HEMINGWAY

Lillian Ross

MAY 13, 1950 (FROM "HOW DO YOU LIKE IT NOW, GENTLEMEN?")

Ernest Hemingway, who may well be the greatest living American novelist and short-story writer, rarely comes to New York. He spends most of his time on a farm, the Finca Vigia, nine miles outside Havana, with his wife, a domestic staff of nine, fifty-two cats, sixteen dogs, a couple of hundred pigeons, and three cows. When he does come to New York, it is only because he has to pass through it on his way somewhere else. Not long ago, on his way to Europe, he stopped in New York for a few days. I had written to him asking if I might see him when he came to town, and he had sent me a typewritten letter saying that would be fine and suggesting that I meet his plane at the airport. "I don't want to see anybody I don't like, nor have publicity, nor be tied up all the time," he went on. "Want to go to the Bronx Zoo, Metropolitan Museum, Museum of Modern Art, ditto of Natural History, and see a fight. Want to see the good Breughel at the Met, the one, no two, fine Goyas and Mr. El Greco's *Toledo*. Don't want to go to Toots Shor's. Am going to try to get into town and out without having to shoot my mouth off. I want to give the joints a miss. Not seeing news people is not a pose. It is only to have time to see your friends." In pencil, he added, "Time is the least thing we have of."

• • •

Time did not seem to be pressing Hemingway the day he flew in from Havana. He was to arrive at Idlewild late in the afternoon, and I went out to meet him. His plane had landed by the time I got there, and I found him standing at a gate waiting for his luggage and for his wife, who had gone to attend to it. He had one arm around a scuffed, dilapidated briefcase pasted up with travel stickers. He had the other around a wiry little man whose forehead was covered with enormous beads of perspiration. Hemingway was wearing a red plaid wool shirt, a figured wool necktie, a tan wool sweater-vest, a brown tweed jacket tight across the back and with sleeves too short for his arms, gray flannel slacks, Argyle socks, and loafers, and he looked bearish, cordial, and constricted. His hair, which was very long in back, was gray, except at the temples, where it was white; his mustache was white, and he had a ragged, half-inch full white beard. There was a bump about the size of a walnut over his left eye. He was wearing steel-rimmed spectacles, with a piece of paper under the nosepiece. He was in no hurry to get into Manhattan. He crooked the arm around the briefcase into a tight hug and said that it contained the unfinished manuscript of his new book, *Across the River and into the Trees.* He crooked the arm around the wiry little man into a tight hug and said he had been his seat companion on the flight. The man's name, as I got it in a mumbled introduction, was Myers, and he was returning from a business trip to Cuba. Myers made a slight attempt to dislodge himself from the embrace, but Hemingway held on to him affectionately.

"He read book all way up on plane," Hemingway said. He spoke with a perceptible Midwestern accent, despite the Indian talk. "He like book, I think," he added, giving Myers a little shake and beaming down at him.

"Whew!" said Myers.

"Book too much for him," Hemingway said. "Book start slow, then increase in pace till it becomes impossible to stand. I bring emotion up to where you can't stand it, then we level off, so we won't have to provide oxygen tents for the readers. Book is like engine. We have to slack her off gradually."

"Whew!" said Myers.

Hemingway released him. "Not trying for no-hit game in book," he said. "Going to win maybe twelve to nothing or maybe twelve to eleven."

Myers looked puzzled.

"She's better book than *Farewell,*" Hemingway said. "I think this is best one, but you are always prejudiced, I guess. Especially if you want to be champion." He shook Myers' hand. "Much thanks for reading book," he said.

"Pleasure," Myers said, and walked off unsteadily.

Hemingway watched him go, and then turned to me. "After you finish a book, you know, you're dead," he said moodily. "But no one knows you're dead. All they see is the irresponsibility that comes in after the terrible responsibility of writing." He said he felt tired but was in good shape physically; he had brought his weight down to two hundred and eight, and his blood pressure was down too. He had considerable rewriting to do on his book, and he was determined to keep at it until he was absolutely satisfied. "They can't yank novelist like they can pitcher," he said. "Novelist has to go the full nine, even if it kills him."

JACKSON POLLOCK

Berton Roueché

AUGUST 5, 1950 ("UNFRAMED SPACE")

WE IMPROVED A shining weekend on eastern Long Island by paying a call on Jackson Pollock—an uncommonly abstract abstractionist and one of seven American painters whose work was tapped for inclusion in the Twenty-fifth International Biennial Exhibition of Figurative Arts, now triumphantly under way in Venice—at his home, a big, gaunt, white clapboard, Ulysses S. Grant–period structure in the fishing hamlet of The Springs. Pollock, a bald, rugged, somewhat puzzled-looking man of thirty-eight, received us in the kitchen, where he was breakfasting on a cigarette and a cup of coffee and drowsily watching his wife, the former Lee Krasner, a slim, auburn-haired young woman who also is an artist, as she bent over a hot stove, making currant jelly. Waving us to a chair in the shade of a huge potted palm, he remarked with satisfaction that he had been up and about for almost half an hour. It was then around 11:30 A.M. "I've got the old Eighth Street habit of sleeping all day and working all night pretty well licked," he said. "So has Lee. We had to, or lose the respect of the neighbors. I can't deny, though, that it's taken a little while. When'd we come out here, Lee?" Mrs. Pollock laughed merrily. "Just a little while ago," she replied. "In the fall of 1945."

"It's marvellous the way Lee's adjusted herself," Pollock said. "She's a native New Yorker, but she's turned into a hell of a good gardener, and she's always up by nine. Ten at the latest. I'm way behind her in orientation. And the funny thing is I grew up in the country. Real country—Wyoming, Arizona, northern and southern California. I was born in Wyoming. My father had a farm near Cody. By the time I was fourteen, I was milking a dozen cows twice a day." "Jackson's work is full of the West," Mrs. Pollock said. "That's what gives it that feeling of spaciousness. It's what makes it so American." Pollock confirmed this with a reflective scowl, and went on to say that at seventeen, an aptitude for painting having suddenly revealed itself to him in a Los Angeles high school, he at once wound up his academic affairs there and headed East. "I spent two years at the Art Students League," he said. "Tom Benton was teaching there then, and he did a lot for me. He gave me the only formal instruction I ever had, he introduced me to Renaissance art, and he got me a job in the League cafeteria. I'm damn grateful to Tom. He drove his kind of realism at me so hard I bounced right into non-objective painting. I'm also grateful to the W.P.A., for keeping me alive during the thirties, and to Peggy Guggenheim. Peggy gave me my first show, in 1943. She gave me two more, and then she took off for Europe, and Lee and I came out here. We wanted to get away from the wear and tear. Besides, I had an underneath confidence that I could begin to live on my painting. I'd had some wonderful notices. Also, somebody had bought one of my pictures. We lived a year on that picture, and a few clams I dug out of the bay with my toes. Since then things have been a little easier." Mrs. Pollock smiled. "Quite a little," she said. "Jackson showed thirty pictures last fall and sold all but five. And his collectors are nibbling at those." Pollock grunted. "Be nice if it lasts," he said.

We asked Pollock for a peep at his work. He shrugged, rose, and led us into a twenty-five-by-fifty-foot living room furnished with massive Italianate tables and chairs and hung with spacious pictures, all of which bore an offhand resemblance to tangles of multicolored ribbon. "Help yourself," he said, halting at a safe distance from an abstraction that occupied most of an end wall. It was a handsome, arresting job—a rust-red background laced with skeins of white, black, and yellow—and we said so. "What's it called?" we asked. "I've forgotten," he said, and glanced inquiringly at his wife, who had followed us in. "*Number Two, 1949*, I think," she said. "Jackson used to give his pictures conventional titles—*Eyes in the Heat* and *The Blue Unconscious* and so on—but now he simply numbers them. Numbers are neutral. They make people look at a picture for what it is—pure painting." "I decided to stop adding to the confusion," Pollock said. "Abstract painting is abstract. It confronts you. There was a reviewer a while back who wrote that my pictures didn't have any beginning or any end. He didn't mean it as a compliment, but it was. It was a fine compliment. Only he didn't know it." "That's exactly what Jackson's work is," Mrs. Pollock said. "Sort of unframed space."

TOOTS SHOR

John Bainbridge

NOVEMBER 11, 1950 (FROM "TOOTS'S WORLD")

TOOTS SHOR, THE burly, impudent, hard-working, high-spirited, sentimental proprietor of the restaurant at 51 West Fifty-first Street that bears his name, is the possessor of a great talent for making friends and enemies. Most of the people who are acquainted with Shor do not simply like him or dislike him; they love him or loathe him. He is capable of making a mild impression on practically nobody. In the eyes of his admirers, Shor is as kind as Saint Francis of Assisi, as generous as Santa Claus, as worldly wise as Bernard Baruch, and as understanding as Dorothy Dix. "I doubt if the world will ever know his true greatness, because so many of his good deeds are sub rosa," Pat O'Brien, the film actor, wrote recently in a letter to a friend. "I call Toots on the phone several times a month. I call him because I'm lonely or to seek advice. As to the lonely reference, Tootsie will always be synonymous with New York, the Manhattan I love and miss, the Gotham close to my ticker. When I say advice, I mean getting his opinion on contracts and stories or a rundown on what goes on in life. It might seem strange that I seek business advice from Toots, but through the years it has paid off. His ideas are always propounded with the mental strength I could never get from other sources. With all his rough exterior, he is gentle and kindly, his friends are legion and loyal, and they will never leave him in the stretch. You can always bet the field when you go to the Shor window, provided you level with him and don't crowd him on the rail. He has more on the ball than Hubbell and more in his heart than just a tick. If he doesn't insult you, he doesn't love you, and if he doesn't love you, you have missed a chunk of life." Shor's detractors are equally vehement. "There's nothing the matter with Toots except that he is an egotistical jughead and as phony as a three-dollar bill," an opinionated man who used to be loved by Shor but who is now, without regret, missing a chunk of life has said. "He's a slob with delusions of grandeur—he wants to be a snob. When his friends are batting three-fifty, Toots can't do enough for them. Then they're real, solid-gold crumb bums. But when they start hitting two hundred, something happens to Toots's eyesight—he can't see the old pals so good any more. He's a guy with the instincts of a bum and the mental outlook of an elephant. He's exactly the kind of guy he'd throw out of his own place." Shor, who has never held himself up as a model of moderation, is neither surprised nor noticeably disturbed by the fact that other people hold immoderate opinions of him. "I have an expression—'Never criticize a guy for something you do yourself,'" he remarked the other day when in a philosophical state of mind. "I'm not like Will Rogers. I've met plenty of guys I didn't like. If I don't like a guy, I wouldn't do nothin' for him. If I like him, there's nothin' I wouldn't do. That's the way it is. Anything I do, I do to excess."

As a host, Shor is, by design, excessively brash. He has acquired the reputation, which he has no trouble living up to, of being a proprietor who ingratiates himself with his customers by being banteringly rude to them. One evening, Louis B. Mayer arrived with a group of friends at Shor's restaurant and, since it was crowded, had to wait fifteen minutes for a table. As his party was being ushered to a table, Mayer passed Shor and said, "I hope we'll find the food has been worth all that waiting." "It'll be better than some of your pictures I've waited in line to see," Shor replied. Charles Chaplin came in for dinner on another busy evening. "You'll have to wait twenty minutes, Charlie," Shor said. "Have a drink and be funny for the people." When Harry Truman was Vice-President, he came to New York to see a prizefight and had dinner beforehand at Shor's, where, during his days as a senator, he had eaten a few times and become friendly with the proprietor. Somewhat awed, Shor began addressing his guest as Mr. Vice-President. Truman smiled and said, "I'm still Harry to my friends." "Jimminy crickets!" Shor said. "Here I was tryin' to give you a buildup." A couple of dapper-looking foreigners, escorting a pair of beautiful domestic blondes, walked into the restaurant one evening and started snapping their fingers for service. Since Shor is rather chauvinistic, holding that American blondes are for Americans, and since he didn't like the way the men were acting, he instructed his headwaiter to take his time seating the party. After they had been kept waiting a short while, one of the men stepped over to the bar, where Shor was having a drink with some friends. "This waiting, this treatment, it is an imposition," the man said. "Yeah?" Shor growled. "Who sent for ya?" Shor takes the position that he is running a restaurant primarily for his friends and that while he doesn't mind letting strangers in, he expects them to appreciate the privilege. "I've been standing here for forty-five minutes while a dozen people who came in after me have been seated," a stranger who hadn't made a reservation complained one night to Shor. "I'm leaving, and I'm never coming back, and furthermore I'm going to tell all my friends." "Go on," Shor said. "Tell him."

A successful manufacturer who is a fairly frequent patron of Shor's has conjectured that the restaurant would double its business (which is already capacity) if the proprietor would change some of his ways. "I like Toots and I like his food," the manufacturer has said, "but sometimes, when you've had a nervous day, you don't feel like going in there and being called a bald-headed bastard and getting swatted on the back and poked in the stomach, even if you know it's a compliment. You just want a quiet meal. Toots is thick. He doesn't understand that. And the way he treats some of the people who come in there, it makes me embarrassed." During lunchtime one day recently, Shor was standing near the bar in his restaurant chatting with a friend from out of town. A man wearing black-rimmed glasses, who had been sitting at the bar, walked over and said, "Excuse me, Mr. Shor. I don't know whether you remember me." He extended his hand. Not taking it, Shor said, "No, I don't remember you." "Well," the man, a doctor from Newark, said, "I was in about three or four weeks ago, and we talked baseball. I used to play, years ago, on the Coast." He stepped back a couple of paces, to afford a better view of himself for identification. Shor looked at him in silence. "I thought you might remember," the Doctor said, taking off his glasses. "I was sitting over there, and we talked for a little while. Not very long." "No, I don't remember," Shor said. "I just thought you might," the Doctor said uneasily. "But I guess you don't." Shor said nothing. The Doctor waited hopefully a moment or two, and then said, "Well, please pardon the interruption. My wife is waiting for me. Excuse me." He walked back to the bar. After he had gone, Shor said, "Those bums. What do they expect me to do—give 'em a lot of soft soap? If I spent two minutes with every one of those guys, I wouldn't have time for nothin' else." Earl Wilson, who visits Shor's twice a day to pick up items for his column, came in and joined Shor and his friend. While they were talking, a ruddy-faced man walked out of the dining room and approached the group. "Hello, Earl," he said to Wilson. "Remember me? I'm from Remington Rand. You did a column about our convention." Wilson acknowledged that he had some recollection of the piece. "Say, Earl, I've been wanting to meet the big boy, here," the Remington Rand man said, indicating Shor with his thumb. "Will you tell him it's all right to say hello to me?" Wilson mumbled something, and his acquaintance continued, "Toots, I've been coming in here for a long time but I never had a chance to meet you. You don't know me, of course, but you probably use some of our machines. I'm with Remington Rand." "The hell with Remington Rand," Shor replied, turning his back. "How do you like that?" he said to his out-of-town friend. "Two creeps in ten minutes." He disappeared into the dining room. The Remington Rand man picked up his hat at the checkroom.

HAROLD ROSS

E. B. White

DECEMBER 15, 1951 ("H. W. ROSS")

Ross died in Boston, unexpectedly, on the night of December 6th, and we are writing this in New York (unexpectedly) on the morning of December 7th. This is known, in these offices that Ross was so fond of, as a jam. Ross always knew when we were in a jam and usually got on the phone to offer advice and comfort and support. When our phone rang just now, and in that split second before the mind focusses, we thought, "Good! Here it comes!" But this old connection is broken beyond fixing. The phone has lost its power to explode at the right moment and in the right way.

Actually, things are not going as badly as they might; the sheet of copy paper in the machine is not as hard to face as we feared. Sometimes a love letter writes itself, and we love Ross so, and bear him such respect, that these quick notes, which purport to record the sorrow that runs through here and dissolves so many people, cannot possibly seem overstated or silly. Ross, even on this terrible day, is a hard man to keep quiet; he obtrudes—his face, his voice, his manner, even his amused interest in the critical proceedings. If he were accorded the questionable privilege of stopping by here for a few minutes, he would gorge himself on the minor technical problems that a magazine faces when it must do something in a hurry and against some sort of odds—in this case, emotional ones of almost overpowering weight. He would be far more interested in the grinding of the machinery than in what was being said about him.

All morning, people have wandered in and out of our cell, some tearfully, some guardedly, some boisterously, most of them long-time friends in various stages of repair. We have amused ourself thinking of Ross's reaction to this flow. "Never bother a writer" was one of his strongest principles. He used to love to drop in, himself, and sit around, but was uneasy the whole time because of the carking feeling that if only he would get up and go away, we might settle down to work and produce something. To him, a writer at work, whether in the office or anywhere in the outside world, was an extraordinarily interesting, valuable, but fragile object; and he half expected it to fall into a thousand pieces at any moment.

The report of Ross's death came over the telephone in a three-word sentence that somehow managed to embody all the faults that Ross devoted his life to correcting. A grief-stricken friend in Boston, charged with the task of spreading the news but too dazed to talk sensibly, said, "It's all over." He meant that Ross was dead, but the listener took it to mean that the operation was over. Here, in three easy words, were the ambiguity, the euphemistic softness, the verbal infirmity that Harold W. Ross spent his life thrusting at. Ross regarded every sentence as the enemy, and believed that if a man watched closely enough, he would discover the vulnerable spot, the essential weakness. He devoted his life to making the weak strong—a rather specialized form of blood transfusion, to be sure, but one that he believed in with such a consuming passion that his spirit infected others and inspired them, and lifted them. Whatever it was, this contagion, this vapor in these marshes, it spread. None escaped it. Nor is it likely to be dissipated in a hurry.

His ambition was to publish one good magazine, not a string of successful ones, and he thought of *The New Yorker* as a sort of movement. He came equipped with not much knowledge and only two books—Webster's Dictionary and Fowler's *Modern English Usage*. These books were his history, his geography, his literature, his art, his music, his everything. Some people found Ross's scholastic deficiencies quite appalling, and were not sure they had met the right man. But he was the right man, and the only question was whether the other fellow was capable of being tuned to Ross's vibrations. Ross had a thing that is at least as good as, and sometimes better than, knowledge: he had a sort of natural drive in the right direction, plus a complete respect for the work and ideas and opinions of others. It took a little while to get on to the fact that Ross, more violently than almost anybody, was proceeding in a good direction, and carrying others along with him, under torrential conditions. He was like a boat being driven at the mercy of some internal squall, a disturbance he himself only half understood, and of which he was at times suspicious.

In a way, he was a lucky man. For a monument he has the magazine to date—one thousand three hundred and ninety-nine issues, born in the toil and pain that can be appreciated only by those who helped in the delivery room. These are his. They stand, unchangeable and open for inspection. We are, of course, not in a position to estimate the monument, even if we were in the mood to. But we are able to state one thing unequivocally: Ross set up a great target and pounded himself to pieces trying to hit it square in the middle. His dream was a simple dream; it was pure and had no frills: he wanted the magazine to be good, to be funny, and to be fair.

We say he was lucky. Some people cordially disliked him. Some were amused but not impressed. And then, last, there are the ones we have been seeing today, the ones who loved him and had him for a friend—people he looked after, and who looked after him. These last are the ones who worked close enough to him, and long enough with him, to cross over the barrier reef of noisy shallows that ringed him, into the lagoon that was Ross himself—a rewarding, and even enchanting, and relatively quiet place, utterly trustworthy as an anchorage. Maybe these people had all the luck. The entrance wasn't always easy to find.

He left a note on our desk one day apropos of something that had pleased him in the magazine. The note simply said, "I am encouraged to go on." That is about the way we feel today, because of his contribution. We are encouraged to go on.

When you took leave of Ross after a calm or stormy meeting, he always ended with the phrase that has become as much a part of the office as the paint on the walls. He would wave his limp hand, gesturing you away. "All right," he would say. "God bless you." Considering Ross's temperament and habits, this was a rather odd expression. He usually took God's name in vain if he took it at all. But when he sent you away with this benediction, which he uttered briskly and affectionately, and in which he and God seemed all scrambled together, it carried a warmth and sincerity that never failed to carry over. The words are so familiar to his helpers and friends here that they provide the only possible way to conclude this hasty notice and to take our leave. We cannot convey his manner. But with much love in our heart, we say, for everybody, "All right, Ross. God bless you!"

SYLVESTER WEAVER

Thomas Whiteside

OCTOBER 16/23, 1954 (FROM "THE COMMUNICATOR")

PEOPLE WHO HAVE the reputation of being philosophers, plentiful though they may be in the poorer-paid professions, are comparatively rare in the radio-and-television industry. In Sylvester L. Weaver, Jr., the president of the National Broadcasting Company, however, the industry has such a man. Weaver, who, for no particular reason, is known to his associates as Pat, is regarded by many people connected with broadcasting not only as the leading showman in the business but also as its most unrelenting thinker and most vocal theorist. "Programwise, the guy is terrific," says a talent agent who has had many dealings with him. "Long-hairwise, he's great, too. With Pat, you can think big even about a cooking show." Weaver has been thinking and theorizing at N.B.C. since 1949, when he joined the organization as a vice-president. He became president last December, taking on a job in which there had recently been a considerable turnover; before Weaver, three men had occupied the office of president in as many years. Weaver's election to the position has been widely interpreted in the trade as not simply another change of leadership but an indication of a change in N.B.C.'s attitude toward the importance of improving its programs. Prior to Weaver, the company's presidents were businessmen first, and their professional talents in the matter of creating radio and television programs were looked upon as relatively incidental to their ability as administrators. Weaver, on the other hand, is a professional program man. "Pat's just what we needed," one N.B.C. producer said not long ago. "He's probably the first top guy we've had here who can dream up a big show, sell a sponsor on the idea, figure out the show's dramatic form, and get the right budget for it and the right script writers, as well as the right talent and the right air time against the right competition. A broad-stroke guy in every respect. Other men, when they have a show on their hands that isn't making dough, will drop it like a hot brick. Pat will take the same kind of show, pour half-a-million bucks into it, and use it like a loss-leader in a chain grocery to gain traffic. Pat knows how to build up a network audience."

. . .

Early one afternoon a while ago, Weaver, splendidly attired as usual and on his way to lunch at "21," was pressing the "Down" button at the bank of elevators on the sixth floor of the R.C.A. Building when a quiet voice behind him said "Pat." Weaver turned, and found himself facing Davidson Taylor, a tall, thin, pleasant-mannered man who is N.B.C.'s vice-president in charge of public affairs.

"Well, Dave!" Weaver said in a tone of pleased surprise. "I'm just segueing out to lunch."

"Good news, Pat," Taylor said. "I just got back from the Detroit client meeting, and came right up to let you know what the big fellows out there are thinking. Detroit wants to buy the football games and the 1954 elections. But you're in a hurry. I'll tell you about it later."

"Good, Dave, good. We'll talk about it," Weaver said. Then, as if he had just remembered something, he quickly added, "Say, Dave! I've been thinking of a big new weekly afternoon show that Detroit is sure to be interested in. I've got the title already. It'll be called *The Wide Wide World,* and it's great, just great. A sure Peabody. I'm writing a memo on it now—" Weaver was interrupted by the arrival of an elevator. He stepped in, and waved jubilantly to Taylor as the door slid closed.

The next morning, a four-page mimeographed memorandum from Weaver dealing with the new program—a program designed to someday take its place alongside such other big-scale Weaver inspirations as *Today, Your Show of Shows, Home,* and the network's current series of color spectaculars—lay on the desks of a number of N.B.C. executives and producers. "We must have the show that gets the most talk in the coming season, that wins the Peabody award, that enables me to keep carrying the fight to the intellectuals who misunderstand our mass-media development, and that can be profitably sold without affecting any of our present business," the memorandum began, soberly enough, and then Weaver began warming up to his subject: "*The Wide Wide World* is what its name is. It takes you OUT. It takes you THERE. It puts you in IT. *The Wide Wide World* uses our five New York remote units . . . plus our other units, plus the remote units of our affiliates, plus our Cadillac unit, plus units aboard helicopters, aboard diving bells, plus vidicon walkie-peepie units on skis, and on surfboards, and on water skis, and watching frogmen, plus candid camera installations here and there but not by chance."

A few days later about fifteen members of the N.B.C. staff gathered in Weaver's office to discuss the proposed program and present their views and suggestions. As the group filed in, Weaver sat comfortably at his desk, at one end of the large room, busily signing mail. Arranged in a casual semicircle in front of the desk were a number of chairs, and off to one side stood Weaver's Bongo Board, a sort of one-man seesaw device on which he exercises regularly to keep in shape. When everyone was settled, Weaver put down his pen, placed his fingertips together, and leaned far back in his swivel chair. "Well, fellows," he said, after a moment, "as you know, we're anxious to establish N.B.C. as it ought to be, and *Wide Wide World* is the sort of show that will do it. The show ought to be on Sunday afternoon. We'll get new money for *Wide Wide World* —there's no use creating a show like this on the usual agency level, where all they're concerned about is the problem of people buying the client's goods. If we did that, the results would be too standard, and, besides, the agencies wouldn't go for the show anyway. You know that, fellows."

Everybody smiled, and Weaver leaned forward and began a detailed dissertation on what he felt were the minimum financial requirements of the program. Then, tilting his chair back again, he surveyed his listeners. "Now, some of you have sent me memos with ideas for *Wide Wide World*," he said. "After reading them, I think that perhaps what didn't come through from *my* memo was what I thought the show was. This isn't to be a point-of-view show but one in which we use television as communications to show the sort of places and events that normal, cultured, well-informed people want to see. Dismal Swamp, the Sadler's Wells Ballet, the Greek Theatre in Los Angeles, playing an ancient Greek play with Greeks—real Greeks, fellows—as performers. Why not? It would be a non-hit, I admit, but it would be real nutsy. We should consider the artistic tastes of the whole populace."

"Pat, a question," Davidson Taylor said. "Is this *The Wide Wide World* or *The Wide Wide U.S.A.*?"

"*Wide Wide World* will be going to London, Moscow, and the Vatican before we're through," Weaver replied. "This program goes *there*."

"Suppose you went to the Greek Theatre in Los Angeles. Would most people *want* to go to the Greek Theatre?" Robert Sarnoff, who is now N.B.C.'s executive vice-president, asked. He was smoking a cigar, and he examined its ash as he awaited an answer.

"This show is not just about what the public wants to do but what you want them to do, Bobby," Weaver said. "You *take* the American people to see the Greek drama, you *take* them to see *King Lear* at Stratford, Ontario. It would be good for them to see Shakespeare, whether they liked it or not." Weaver paused and looked around the room. "I assume you all dig the cultural side of this," he said.

"Would you like some suggestions from our boys in Hollywood?" asked Fred W. Wile, a vice-president of N.B.C. and its West Coast program chief.

"For laughs?" Weaver inquired.

"Well, laughs, too," Wile said. He read a list of suggestions that had been teletyped to him from California.

"Negative," Weaver said when Wile finished. "Negative, negative."

Richard A. R. Pinkham, another vice-president, suggested that the Dance Festival at Jacobs Pillow might make a subject for *The Wide Wide World.*

"An hour and a half of Jacobs Pillow?" Sarnoff asked.

"Maybe there *is* an hour and a half in Jacobs Pillow, Bobby," Weaver said. "Who knows?"

Someone suggested motorboating as a possible subject, and someone else suggested golf.

"Golf is a possibility, but motorboating is better," Weaver said. "Golf is a game, but motorboating is a way of life. With a motorboat, you *go* places."

"Isn't going down the Hudson something you see in the newsreels?" Ted Mills, another producer, asked.

"We don't care about the newsreels," Weaver replied. "The important thing is the opening on the world."

"How about a murder trial at a county seat in Georgia?" Mills asked.

"On Sunday afternoon?" Weaver raised his eyebrows. "Anyway, in urbane life I see no reason why such subjects should come up."

"What do you mean by urbane, exactly?" Mills asked, in a puzzled tone.

"Why, you know, Ted," Weaver said in an exaggerated drawl. "New York–type stuff."

Everybody laughed, and then Weaver went on earnestly, "I think I know what I want but I'm not sure that you all do. I want a show that will give people a chance to go out of their homes to almost every part of our wide world that is America and participate in all of our activities—

a show that people will say has enabled us to become more mature, more cultured, and more urbane, and that will be the conversation piece wherever people meet. That is why I say no to hunger and no to Chicago, but boating, yes—and if everybody was a member of the élite he'd have seen the show. Nobody would watch *Wide Wide World* all the time unless he was paralyzed, but he would see it occasionally and it would do him good. Fellows, don't you see I'm trying to get something *civilized*?"

EMILY POST

Geoffrey T. Hellman

MAY 14, 1955 ("MRS. POST'S PARTY")

THE NINTH EDITION and eighty-second printing of Emily Post's *Etiquette: The Blue Book of Social Usage,* which was originally issued in 1922 under the title *Etiquette: In Society, in Business, in Politics and at Home,* is just out. We celebrated its advent by attending a reception and buffet luncheon "to meet Emily Post," given by its publishers, Funk & Wagnalls, in the Louis XVI Room of the St. Regis. Mrs. Post, who is eighty-one, received her forty-odd guests sitting on a settee next to her grandson, William Goadby Post, who is in his thirties and was wearing a Countess Mara tie crawling with monkeys. A Funk & Wagnalls publicity lady presented the guests to her; each time the guest was a woman, Mrs. Post rose. We buttonholed her son, Edwin M. Post, Harvard '16, who was wearing a plain gray silk tie, and asked him for a few words about his mother and her book.

"There have been five major revisions in thirty-three years, and this is the most extensive one," Mr. Post said. "We started from scratch this time. We made entirely new plates; expense was no object. Mother's syndicated column, which appears in a hundred and sixty papers seven days a week, brings in about three thousand letters weekly, and some of them have suggested new material that has been incorporated into the latest edition. The Emily Post Institute, which has an office in her apartment, answers routine letters and relays the non-routine ones—about five percent of the total—to her to answer. She spends over six months a year in her house in Edgartown, where she keeps a secretary the year round. The first really warm day in spring, she flies up there with her cook, waitress, and parlormaid. Her house is in the middle of town. You can see the sea only from its widow's walk. Crazy, isn't it? You might just as well be in New York. I have a place at Westhampton Beach, where I can see the sea from my downstairs windows."

"I gather Mrs. Post doesn't want the age of the chaperon again," a lady guest said. "I suspect she's a rather forward-looking individual."

"I think the thing she regrets most is the loss of the art of conversation," Mr. Post said. "Discussing a book doesn't exist today. No one's read a book."

Mr. William Roulet, Funk & Wagnalls' vice-president, who was standing near him, frowned. "The advance sale is three times that of any previous revision," he said. "We've never permitted any cheap commercialism in connection with the book. No reprints. No book clubs."

We went into an adjoining dining room, which contained a number of small tables, and sat down between Miss Anne H. Lincoln, assistant to the editor of the *Woman's Home Companion,* and Miss Christie Thompson, assistant to the editor of the *Companion*'s teen-age department.

"Mrs. Post is wearing a straw hat with red grosgrain trim and a black crêpe dress with red-and-white silk pleating," Miss Lincoln advised us.

"I told her it was a sort of what-the-hell costume, and she told me *she* occasionally says 'What the hell,' too," Miss Thompson said. "I use her book all the time to answer questions from teen-agers about how to address invitations, how to run a tea, what does the groom pay for, and so on."

"She allows unmarried girls to go to bachelors' apartments," said Miss Lincoln.

"Provided they leave at a reasonable hour," said Miss Thompson.

We downed chicken consommé, chicken Tetrazzini, and ice-cream cake, and noted with regret the absence of water glasses.

"Mother loves desserts, especially ones with chocolate and whipped cream," said Mr. Post, who had taken a seat at our table. "She doesn't like the rest of the meal at all. Very few people read her book all the way through. They buy it to look up the particular thing they want to know; for instance, how to address the headmaster of a boys' school. Nobody can keep all such details in his head."

“What a luncheon party she had in Edgartown for her cookbook a few years ago!” a lady opposite us said. “Thirty-two women’s-page writers flown up in a DC-3 by Funk & Wagnalls!”

“Everything cooked out of her cookbook,” Mr. Post said.

We got a glass of water from the bar and made our adieux.

FRANK LLOYD WRIGHT

Geoffrey T. Hellman

JUNE 16, 1956 (“WRIGHT REVISITED”)

FRANK LLOYD WRIGHT had his eighty-seventh birthday last Friday, and we called on him a few days earlier, at Suite 223 of the Plaza, which he is using as his New York headquarters while the new Guggenheim Museum is being built. We found him in a large room, facing east. He was seated at a large table, going over plans marked “Archeseum for the Solomon R. Guggenheim Foundation” with Mr. Medley G. B. Whelpley, a trustee of the Foundation and a former Guggenheim Brothers partner. Mr. Wright’s daughter, Iovanna, was taking phone calls for him and making herself generally useful.

“We’ve had ‘colosseum’ and ‘Rameseum,’ so I thought, Why not ‘archeseum’?” said Mr. Wright, who was wearing a brown suit, a tie tied like a shoelace, no glasses, and a commanding expression. “Why should ‘colosseum’ ever be spelled ‘coliseum’—with an ‘i’? It should always be with an ‘o,’ after ‘colossus.’ The word looks like a medicine. The Rameseum is where Rameses reposes. No one knows what words mean. You know, the architects come around to see me, the youngsters, and I say, ‘Boys, you know what this word means—“architect”?’ Silence. I nod to their bellwether and say, ‘Surely your leader knows.’ Silence. Well, it means ‘the master of the know-how.’ A free translation, but a good one. A museum is where you seek the work inspired by the Muses. ‘Arch’ means ‘the high.’ An archeseum is where you go to see the highest. It seemed a natural word, so I proposed it to Mr. Harry Guggenheim, chairman of the board of trustees of the Foundation. He has since advised me that it has not been accepted by the trustees."

"I looked it up in the dictionary, but it isn't there," said Mr. Whelpley.

"Toilets on every floor," said Mr. Wright. "Seven floors and a below-ground auditorium. A capacious elevator. Gravity employed so as to give you quiet, easy access to whatever show is on. Light so tempered and arranged as to suit the taste of the curator. We have dramatized the pictures. Control of lights makes them more naturally lighted in a less lighted place. We're not going to have those big buncombe frames around the pictures. The building will be the frame. The entrance has an air-conditioned grating that sucks down and will take the dust off your shoes and trousers. I've always wanted to take the dust off people. It will pull the ladies' skirts down, not blow them up."

"No place for Marilyn Monroe," said Mr. Whelpley.

"It's what the old gentleman wanted," Mr. Wright said, and we realized that he meant the late S. R. Guggenheim. "I first showed him the plans twelve years ago. He believed that a depression was in the offing, and that building costs would go down, so we waited. The depression never came."

"Mr. Guggenheim knew that if the depression didn't come, his stocks would go up," said Mr. Whelpley.

"He left a bequest of eight or nine million for the Museum," Mr. Wright said. "Now it's more, isn't it, Mr. Whelpley?"

"Much more," said Mr. Whelpley.

A phone rang in another room, and Miss Wright, who answered it, told her father it was for him. He took the call and returned after a brief conversation. "Man wanted a job on the Museum as a lighting expert," he said. "An expert is a man who has stopped thinking. Why? He *knows*. I had the exquisite pleasure of firing seven experts when I built the Imperial Hotel, in Tokyo, or it never would have been built."

Mr. Wright went back to the large table. "This is the literature of the building," he said, turning the great sheets of the plan, floor by floor. "Writers and artists try to reflect man, but architecture alone presents man as he is. That's why we architects look down on writers and artists. Twelve years of concentrated devotion and emotion over the Museum! A whirlpool of antagonism, defamation, and admiration! Seven hundred and sixty-nine buildings I've been given to do, and they say he isn't practical! How could I be here at eighty-seven with this work in my hand if I'd been impractical? The contract has been let to the Euclid Contracting Corporation, and the building will be up in eighteen months. I hope I'll be there to see it open. I spend a week a month here. I'm going to Wisconsin for my birthday. There will be quite a party this year—pageantry and fireworks. I go to bed at nine. I still drink Old Bushmills. One glass Saturday night and one Sunday night. They're trying to get me down to one a week. I'd become a drinker if I had to live in New York. It's badly oversized. I consider it *fin de siècle.* For a place that is doomed, as this is, it's well to get out of it what you can. Bob Moses keeps putting in more parking places. The more parking places you have, the sooner the place is going to end. This is the old Diamond Jim Brady suite. It's the best part of New York."

Mr. Wright turned to a window, looked out at the plaza, and said, "I asked Bob Moses if he wouldn't get the fountain going. I see there are workmen down there now. Perhaps they are doing something about it."

A waiter brought in coffee and cookies, Mr. Wright's daughter poured, and we all took seats around a small table.

"I'm a guest preacher at the Universalist Church of the Divine Paternity, on Central Park West, this Sunday," Mr. Wright said. "I'm building a million-dollar synagogue in Philadelphia, and I'm doing three private houses around here—in White Plains, Rye, and New Canaan. I love American humor. I've tried to get movie producers to do Mark Twain's *The Man That Corrupted Hadleyburg,* but they won't."

"Mother and I read aloud to Daddy," Miss Wright said.

"I always fly to Wisconsin and back," Mr. Wright said. "American trains are no good. They rattle. European trains don't rattle. They have a gadget that keeps them from rattling. Why don't we? Our motorcars are like ferryboats coming down the street. They stick out at all corners. If a fish did this, it would be floating on the surface, dead. That's why I drive a Mercedes. I've designed an automobile and an airplane and a taxicab. The taxi is designed like an old hansom. It can turn on a dime. It's going to be manufactured. It's like the Museum—you have to wait and wait and wait."

"Mr. Guggenheim's stocks did go up," said Mr. Whelpley.

"The University of Wales is giving me a degree of Doctor of Laws this summer," Mr. Wright said, nibbling a cookie. "They offered it *in absentia,* contrary to precedent, if I wanted, but I'm going to pack up Mrs. Wright and our old kit bag in July and go over and get it. We've worked together for thirty years, and I don't think either of us would know what to do without the other. I already have thirty-two honorary degrees, but this is the one that touches me the most. It would have delighted my mother, who was Welsh. It would have delighted my Welsh grandfather and all my Welsh uncles."

We finished our coffee, wished him a happy birthday, and left.

BOBBY FISCHER

Bernard Taper

SEPTEMBER 7, 1957 ("PRODIGY")

THE LATEST PRODIGY of the chess world is a fourteen-year-old Brooklyn boy named Robert Fischer, who a few weeks ago, at a tournament held in Cleveland, upset some two hundred of his elders and putative betters, including a number of the country's top-ranking players, to win the United States Open Chess Championship. There have been chess prodigies in this country who flashed to prominence when considerably younger than Fischer, but none has ever captured a major title at such an early age. Honors are beginning to pile up for Robert. The United States Chess Federation has elevated him to the rank of master (some of the wits among his teen-age friends now address him as Master Master Fischer); he has been invited to be one of the ten distinguished players, from all over the world, who will participate in the highly regarded invitation tournament at Hastings, in England, this Christmas; and shortly after that he is scheduled, if the Chess Federation's present plans work out, to visit the Soviet Union and show off his prowess before the world's most discriminating mass audience, the Russians having been notorious chess addicts for centuries.

Young Fischer took to the game of chess from the time the moves were first explained to him. This was when he was six, and his teacher was his elder sister, Joan. Before that, his only hint of precocity had been his authoritative war with jigsaw puzzles. He entered his first tournament at the age of nine, and has twice won the United States Junior Chess Championship. His most striking achievement before the United

States Open Championship was winning the brilliancy prize last year in the Lessing J. Rosenwald Tournament here, for a game so inspired that it was hailed on the cover of *Chess Review* as "the game of the century." When he started playing in tournaments, he burst into tears each time he lost a game, but now he merely bites his fingernails and glowers. The United States Open Champion is at present in his second year at Erasmus High School. Though school tests have shown him to have generally superior intelligence, he does no better than average in his studies, displaying little interest in most of the subjects taught and being restless in class. His teachers are amazed when they hear of his chess victories—not so much at his revealing mental powers that they hadn't suspected as at his being able to sit still for the five hours a tournament game may last. "In my class, Bobby couldn't sit still for five *minutes,*" one of them says. A chessboard, with pieces set up on it, is always beside his bed. From the moment he wakes up, he works at chess problems—even during meals and while watching television.

Most of this intelligence we gleaned from Robert's mother, Mrs. Regina Fischer, when we talked with her one evening recently. We also gathered that Mrs. Fischer, though proud of her son's triumphs, is by no means convinced that his devotion to chess is a good thing. "For four years, I tried everything I knew to discourage him," she said, with a sigh, "but it was hopeless." She told us that almost any evening during the summer vacation her son was to be found at the Manhattan Chess Club, on West Sixty-fourth Street—a venerable institution, with an imposing number of champions and chess masters in its membership. "That's Bobby's favorite hangout," Mrs. Fischer said. "Sometimes I have to go over there at midnight to haul him out of the place." Robert's mother and father have been divorced for some years.

After our talk with Mrs. Fischer, we made our way to the club. In the hushed, gray-walled main chamber, several games were in progress, but none of the men brooding over their boards came within three or four decades of resembling a teen-ager. A white-haired man in his sixties approached us with soft, slow steps and introduced himself, in a whisper, as Hans Kmoch, the club's secretary. When we asked about young Fischer, he whispered, "Bobby's out, getting a soda or something. He'll be back." In the club's tournament room—a small, square alcove just off the main room—an important challenge match was being played between Samuel Reshevsky, an international grand master, who is considered perhaps the finest player in the Western world, and was once himself a dazzling child prodigy, and Donald Byrne, a leading American player. We stepped into the alcove to join six or eight spectators of the game. Here the silence was solemn. The game had been in progress over two hours, and the players had made sixteen moves. It was Reshevsky's move now. A tiny man in his late forties, with a huge bald head, he sat with his hands tightly clasped in his lap, frowning at the board. Unclasping his hands, he half lifted one of them. The spectators leaned forward. The scorekeeper tensed, and picked up his pencil to write down the move. A minute passed, and then Reshevsky let his hand fall into his lap. The spectators settled back. The scorekeeper laid down his pencil. Suddenly, we heard a most unexpected sound from the other room—a burst of exuberant laughter. Stepping through the open doorway, we saw Kmoch making shushing gestures at a group of people gathered about a table in the far corner of the room. "Just can't keep those boys quiet," he muttered as we came up to him. "You want to see Bobby play? He's over there in the middle of that gang. They just came back." He led us to the group, introduced us, and then left us.

We sat down to watch what was going on. Young Fischer, whom we discovered to be a lanky lad with a mischievous, rather faunlike face, was playing against a stout, elegant man in his middle twenties—an Argentine named Dr. Dan J. Beninson, who, we were told, is scientific secretary of the United Nations' Scientific Committee on the Effects of Atomic Radiation. They were playing chess such as we had never seen before—making their moves with split-second rapidity, while exchanging banter with each other and the kibitzers, most of whom were of college age. Within a few minutes, they had finished one game and were launched on another, and Fischer was asserting, with a triumphant grin, as he pushed his queen, "You're dead now." "That's what you think, Bobby, my boy," Dr. Beninson answered, instantly bringing his bishop across the board—an unexpected stroke, apparently, since it caused young Fischer to clap a hand to his head and brought a burst of laughter from the kibitzers. Everybody seemed to be having a high time. Once, when Dr. Beninson lingered over a move for perhaps three seconds, Fischer threw up his hands in feigned disgust and groaned, "It's no fun to play chess if you take all year over a move."

We asked what they called this kind of hopped-up chess. "Blitz," replied Fischer, and added, making several moves in the course of his brief reply, "That's what we all play for fun. Much more fun than tough, slow chess." Every few minutes, the elderly Kmoch padded over to the group and whispered, ineffectually, "Sh-h-h, boys!" We watched the lad and Dr. Beninson breeze through a dozen of these lightning, carefree games, involving perhaps as many as a thousand moves, in the half hour or so we stayed there. On the way out, we looked into the tournament room. All was exactly as before—silent, solemn, tense. Checking the score sheet, we saw that Reshevsky still hadn't made his move.

MORT SAHL

Whitney Balliett

NOVEMBER 30, 1957 ("FREE ASSOCIATION")

MORT SAHL, THE lightning, inexhaustible thirty-year-old monologuist and nonconformist's nonconformist from California, is back in town and doing a full-house business at the Village Vanguard, near Sheridan Square. There, armed only with the bulldog edition of the *News* or the *Mirror* and dressed in a red sweater, a white open-necked shirt, and gray slacks, he improvises non-stop several times a night, for as much as an hour at a crack, on such sacred and profane themes as foreign policy, hi-fi, spies, sports cars, and integration; raps knuckles on the Right, Center, and Left along the way; and speaks at top speed a language that is a unique cross between a philology paper and the argot of modern jazz. We tracked Sahl down one afternoon last week at the apartment of a friend of ours, and found him a thin, compact, jumpy, hawk-faced man with deep-set eyes and dark hair, a hair-trigger laugh, and a broad smile that creases his face into enormous, identical parentheses. He was wearing a yellow open-necked shirt, a tan jacket, and dark-brown slacks, and for three non-stop hours he talked, pausing only to catch his breath. "I couldn't get a thing going when I came here for the first time, in 1952," he said. "I lived in a hotel on West Forty-seventh Street on eighteen dollars a week, which covered room, laundry, and loaves of day-old bread from the A. & P. I'd been starving on the University of California campus, in Berkeley, for a couple of years, auditing courses, and graduating by osmosis. I'd got a B.S. from the University of Southern California, in Los Angeles, in 1950 in public administration, with a minor in civil engineering, and I was really doing graduate work there on street-traffic engineering. But I scuffled up to the U. of C. all the time because my family was putting this dollars-and-cents thing on my back and the base period of bohemianism was just starting around there, and nobody judged you. I was trying to be a writer. I wrote four one-act plays that were produced in L.A. I wrote a novel and a lot of short stories. I even wrote an oratorio for Stan Kenton—a big, heavy, serious, epic thing for half a dozen actors and the full band. I bound it up nicely in a book and showed it to Stan, and he was stunned. I wrote eighteen sets of lyrics for some songs one of his arrangers was doing. I used words like 'misanthrope,' and *he* was stunned. But I had a very jealous attitude toward my writing. I sat on it. Then I discovered I had to *talk*. I'd go into the strip joints in L.A. and ask them to let me perform for free during intermissions. I did intermissions at the Palladium when Kenton was there, before four thousand people. Despite all the folklore about the faith of friends in the struggling young artist, my friends constantly discouraged me. 'What do you think you're doing?' and 'How are you going to make it doing that?' I became very bitter.

"Suddenly I got my first job, as a vacation replacement at a very bohemian place out in North Beach called the hungry i, all in lower case—the hungry intellectual, yes, and under the bohemianism and the nonconformism the anxious asp—at seventy-five a week. That was Christmas, 1953, and I laid a very big egg. They were interested in the folk singer on the bill—one of those guys with their shirt open to the waist—and I guess they didn't think I had any right to be so caustic when I didn't show any self-confidence, even though I had a latent Christlike vision of myself. Knocking the pharisees and publicans. I was so nervous I began bringing a newspaper onstage with all my cues stapled to the inside pages. I was free-associating, indicting all the bright young people. Then, one night, somebody laughed. I think he was an economist connected with the National Labor Relations Board. Then somebody else laughed—the conformist—and the thing started building. I stayed eight months, because the owner never had the courage to fire me. I was already losing discipline as a performer. I'd get going within the cadence of the audience's laughter, and sometimes I'd build for a solid thirty minutes and still never reach the core of what I wanted to say. I don't kid myself. I'm not a comedian. I don't build jokes around myself. There's too much to say about everything else, and nobody is saying it. I began getting discovered when I went to Chicago. I've been discovered—and dropped—six or seven times, all over the place. Eddie Cantor ('Don't wear that red sweater. Wrong associations'), Groucho Marx ('I love your act, but it'll never go'), Ed Sullivan, Perry Como. I was on Jack Paar's television show, and he spent two hours backstage before it demoralizing me by telling me not to be esoteric. He said the audiences were made up of Rotarians. I was on nine and a half minutes, being esoteric, and had to stop six times for applause.

"I need the therapy of doing a lot of different things, especially since discovering that I'm suffering from what Paul Desmond, the alto saxophonist, calls 'erosion of identity.' No personal life—that sort of jazz. When I finish my show, I buy all the newspapers and magazines and read till six in the morning. Natural curiosity. I'm going to do a novel. There's less quicksand in the written word. I've never had a big reverence for poetry, though. Kenneth Rexroth standing up before a jazz group in San Francisco and saying, 'Do the dead know what time it is?' Man! I'm working on an L.P. idea with the trombonist Bill Russo—a little satire on jazz. Things are building. Adlai Stevenson told me one night in Chicago, 'You're more successful with free association than I am with painstaking editing.' Bill Blair, his old buddy and law partner; James Jones; Dr. Carl Binger, the Harvard psychiatrist; Leonard Bernstein—they've all been into the Vanguard. Audiences are in an oxcart until someone chooses to propel it."

LEONARD BERNSTEIN

Robert Rice

JANUARY 11, 1958 (FROM "THE PERVASIVE MUSICIAN")

As publicly as circumstances have allowed over the last twenty-nine years—and for the last fourteen of them that has been very publicly indeed—Leonard Bernstein, a formidably gifted and communicative thirty-nine-year-old Bostonian, has been, in his phrase, "making love" to music. The affair has been incessant, ardent, triumphant, and, one might say, comprehensive. In the course of it, Bernstein has embraced the Muse (name of Euterpe) as a concert pianist, as a conductor, as a composer of both concert pieces and Broadway shows, and as a musical pedagogue on television. Last October, Bernstein was in Tel Aviv, leading the Israel Philharmonic. He had flown there the day after the opening of *West Side Story,* his latest musical show and one of Broadway's biggest current hits. He had spent the day before the opening writing the introduction to a book of his, concerned mainly with Euterpe, that Simon & Schuster hopes to publish this year. (This is not the first year that Simon & Schuster has hoped to publish it; its title was originally to have been "Conversations at 30.") Also in October, Columbia issued two records of Bernstein's; one was *West Side Story* and the other consisted of two piano concertos, a Bach and a Beethoven, in which he had conducted a special recording orchestra, with Glenn Gould as the soloist. When Bernstein returned from Israel, early in November, he took on a few new chores: learning the score of the Shostakovich Second Piano Concerto, which he played with the Philharmonic as pianist-conductor just a few days ago; preparing himself to conduct seven weeks of Philharmonic concerts, four in January and three in April; and writing five or six television scripts—four of them for the Philharmonic's Young People's Concerts, which he will lead Saturday afternoons this winter, and one or two of them for the television program *Omnibus,* which frequently features him as a freewheeling lecturer on various aspects of music. It was a little over a year ago that Bernstein was hired to share with Dimitri Mitropoulos the musical directorship of the Philharmonic-Symphony Society of New York, and it was late in November that Mitropoulos announced his resignation, to take effect after the present season, and Bernstein was appointed to take over next fall as sole musical director of the Philharmonic—probably the most important musical job in the country. This is the first time ever that that exalted post has been given to a man born in the United States. It is also the first time ever that it has been given to the composer of a song called "Wrong Note Rag."

Outwardly, Bernstein has much of the actor about him. The bones of his face are arranged so theatrically that in shifting light he gives the impression, without moving a muscle, of being an entire cast of characters; it is hard to find two photographs of him that are clearly of the same man. His skin is dark, and his hair is thick and black, with a distinguished flecking of silver beginning to appear in it. His posture is erect and his figure is trim. (Few conductors ever get fat; leading an orchestra is stiff work.) His speech, too, could be an actor's; his voice is baritone, with a suspicion of vibrato in it, and his diction is precise and of that curiously cosmopolitan sort that combines the broad "a" with the hard "r" and is therefore indigenous to no place or background except show business. Most people meeting him for the first time are surprised that he is quite short—he stands five feet eight and a half—since in a tailcoat on a podium, or as the subject of a television cameraman's artistic angle shots, he looks statuesque. He is fond of clothes and is always carefully turned out; as a matter of fact, he can become as exuberant over adding to his wardrobe as over any other activity he engages in, and he has been known to invite friends to fittings he regards as especially momentous. ("Lenny's dress rehearsals," one guest has called them.) In the early days of his fame, his dress tended to be fiery, but in recent years it has become conspicuously cool. A few months ago, when he appeared on *Omnibus* to expound Bach, the jacket of his suit was so uncompromisingly three-button that it left almost no shirt front visible. Socially, Bernstein generally manages to be downstage center; he is cheerful, informal, gregarious, and a star player of parlor games and jazz piano. "Lenny is not a person it takes you six months to get to know," an old friend has said; practically no one—not even the musicians who work for him, or, for that matter, his doctor's office nurse—calls him anything but Lenny.

Onstage, Bernstein is even less sombre than he is off. His directions to an orchestra during rehearsals tend to be facetious, and are often phrased in pure Tin Pan Alleyese: "I want the next four bars *sehr* square," or "No! No! Not rallentando, just relaxo." One day recently, after listening to a soprano run through a larynx-breaking aria from the Mozart Requiem, he inquired, "First timesies?" And when the singer confessed that it was, he exclaimed joyously, "Marvellusio! Couragiosa!" One of his *Omnibus* lectures last winter—which attracted an audience estimated at eleven million people—was on the subject of contemporary music. In the course of it, he said tonality was like a baseball field, with the tonic note as home plate, and he illustrated dissonance with such parlor tricks as playing the melody of the "Habanera" from *Carmen* in one key and the accompaniment in another, and then playing the melody of "The Star-Spangled Banner" with his right hand and the melody of "America" with his left—at which the vice-presidents in the sponsor's booth became rigid with consternation over the deluge of protests that were bound to come from patriotic societies. (None ever came.) Finally, Bernstein remarked, "And so we have the two warring camps of tonalists and atonalists, with Stravinsky and Schoenberg as the heap big chiefs." On a previous *Omnibus* show, "The World of Jazz," he pointed out that a blues song was a succession of twelve-bar stanzas, each stanza being a musical setting for a rhymed couplet in iambic pentameter with the first line repeated. Then, to illustrate what he meant, he rendered the following stanza from what he called the "Macbeth Blues":

> "I will not be afraid of death and bane;
> I said I will not be afraid of death and bane.
> 'Til Birnam forest come to Dunsinane."

It is while leading a symphony orchestra in full cry, however, that Bernstein reaches his peak as an actor—and, of course, in the estimation of most critics, as a musician as well. To say the least, he conducts *con moto*. Attending a Bernstein concert is an optical as well as an aural experience. His technique of communicating with an orchestra involves the hands, the arms, the shoulders, the pelvis, and the knees, to say nothing of the forehead, the eyes, and the teeth, and until last week's Philharmonic concerts he had rarely, if ever, been known to use a baton on the podium—apparently considering a stick supererogatory. He is rather aggrieved by the fact that a discussion of his bodily movements is a feature of almost any review of a concert of his. "'Acrobatic' and 'choreographic' are two of the most tiresome adjectives in the language," he remarked plaintively not long ago. He claims that he is quite unaware of what he does when he conducts—that he simply reacts to the music. Lately, though, he seems to have been keeping guard over his reactions, to some extent anyway, for his performances are almost decorous compared with those of his younger days, when Thomson, describing a series of hairbreadth escapes that Bernstein had enacted on the podium, called him "our musical Dick Tracy." One important reform, in the opinion of some spectators, is the result of his marriage, six years ago, to the actress Felicia Montealegre; she cuts his hair, and she cuts it often. Though reviewers continue to carp, and one small and queasy section of the public still insists that the way to listen to a Bernstein concert is with the eyes tightly closed, there is no denying that Bernstein has always been good box-office as a conductor. Indeed, his external graces are powerful enough to be a continuing source of allure to certain bobby-soxers—a minority group, to be sure, but one that is equipped, like the majority, with dog-eared autograph books, shrill voices, and unrequited passion.

LORRAINE HANSBERRY

Lillian Ross

MAY 9, 1959 ("PLAYWRIGHT")

WE HAD A talk recently with Lorraine Hansberry, the twenty-eight-year-old author of the hit play *A Raisin in the Sun*. Miss Hansberry is a relaxed, soft-voiced young lady with an intelligent and pretty face, a particularly vertical hairdo, and large brown eyes, so dark and so deep that you get lost in them. At her request, we met her in a midtown restaurant, so that she could get away from her telephone. "The telephone has become a little strange thing with a life of its own," she told us, calmly enough. "It's just incredible! I had the number changed, and gave it to, roughly, twelve people. Then I get a call from a stranger saying 'This is So-and-So, of the B.B.C.'! It's the flush of success. Thomas Wolfe wrote a detailed description of it in *You Can't Go Home Again*. I must say he told the truth. I enjoy it, actually, so much. I'm thrilled, and all of us associated with the play are thrilled. Meanwhile, it does keep you awfully *busy*. What sort of happens is you just hear from *everybody*!"

Miss Hansberry gave a soft, pleased laugh. "I'm going to have some scrambled eggs, medium, because, as far as I know, I haven't had my breakfast yet," she went on. "I live in the Village, and the way it's been, people sort of drop in on me and my husband. My husband is Robert Nemiroff, and he, too, is a writer. Yesterday, I got back to writing, and I wrote all day long. For the first time in weeks. It was wonderful. We have a ramshackle Village walkup apartment, *quite* ramshackle, with living room, bedroom, kitchen, bath, and a little back workroom, and I just stayed in that little old room all day and wrote. I may even get time now to do some of my housework. I don't want to have anyone else to do my housework. I've always done it myself. I believe you *should* do it yourself. I feel very strongly about that."

The medium scrambled eggs arrived, and Miss Hansberry sampled them vaguely and went on to tell us something of what life has been like since her play opened, a few weeks ago. "I now get twenty to thirty pieces of mail a day," she said. "Invitations to teas, invitations to lunches, invitations to dinners, invitations to write books, to adapt mystery stories for the movies, to adapt novels for Broadway musicals. I feel I have to answer them, because I owe the people who wrote them the courtesy of explaining that this is not my type of thing. Then, there are so many organizations that want you to come to their meetings. You don't feel silly or bothered, because, my God, they're all doing such important work, and you're just delighted to go. But you're awfully busy, because there are an awful lot of organizations. The other morning, I came downstairs to walk my dog—he's sort of a collie, and he'll be six in September—and there, downstairs, were the two most charming people, a middle-aged couple who wanted me to have dinner with the New Rochelle Urban League before it went to see the play. I just couldn't say no. Meanwhile, I'd been getting telegrams from Roosevelt University, in Chicago, which is a very wonderful institution back home, asking me to come and speak. I kept sending telegrams back saying I couldn't come, and then they got me on the phone, and they had me. Once I'm on the phone, I just can't say no. I sometimes find myself doing things for three or four organizations in one day. The other morning, I started the day by taping a television program. Then I went to the National Association of Negro Business and Professional Women's Clubs Founders' Day Tea, at the Waldorf, where they were giving out Sojourner Truth Awards—awards named for Sojourner Truth, who was a very colorful orator who went up and down New England and the South speaking against slavery. Then I went home and went to the Square with my dog. When I got back home, I fed the dog and put on a cocktail dress, and my husband and I had dinner in a new Village steak house. Then we went to a reception for a young Negro actor named Harold Scott, who had just made a record album of readings from the works of James Weldon Johnson. A very beautiful album. Then we went home and had banana cream pie and milk and watched television—a program with me on it, as a matter of fact. It was terrifying to see. I had no idea I used my face so much when I talked, and I decided that that was the end of my going on television. The next day was quiet.

I had only one visitor—a young Negro writer who wanted to drop off a manuscript for me to read. We had a drink and a quick conversation, and he was off. I actually got to cook dinner—a pretty good one, with fried pork chops, broccoli *au gratin*, salad, and banana cream pie. I'm mad for banana cream pie. Fortunately, there's a place in the neighborhood that makes marvellous ones."

Miss Hansberry told us that she had written her play between her twenty-sixth and twenty-seventh birthdays, and that it had taken her eight months. "I'd been writing an awful lot of plays—about three, I guess—and this happened to be one of them," she told us. "We all know now that people like the play, including the critics. Most of what was written about the play was reasonable and fine, but I don't agree that this play, as some people have assumed, has turned out the way it has because just about everybody associated with it was a Negro. I'm pleased to say that we went to great pains to get the best director and the best actors for this particular play. And I like to think I wrote the play out of a specific intellectual point of view. I'm aware of the existence of Anouilh, Beckett, Dürrenmatt, and Brecht, but I believe, with O'Casey, that real drama has to do with audience involvement and achieving the emotional transformation of people on the stage. I believe that ideas *can* be transmitted emotionally."

"Agreed," we said, and asked Miss Hansberry for some autobiography.

"I was born May 19, 1930, in Chicago," she told us. "I have two brothers and one sister. I'm the baby of the family. My sister Mamie is thirty-five and has a three-year-old daughter, Nantille, who is divine and a character. She was named for my mother, whose name is Nannie, and her other grandmother, Tillie. My older brother, Carl, Jr., is forty, and my other brother, Perry, Sr., is thirty-eight and has an eighteen-year-old daughter, who is starting college and is very beautiful. Carl, Perry, and Mamie run my father's real-estate business, Hansberry Enterprises, in Chicago. My father, who is dead now, was born in Gloster, Mississippi, which you can't find on the map, it's so small. My mother comes from Columbia, Tennessee, which *is* on the map, but just about. My father left the South as a young man, and then he went back there and got himself an education. He was a wonderful and very special kind of man. He died in 1945, at the age of fifty-one—of a cerebral hemorrhage, supposedly, but American racism helped kill him. He died in Mexico, where he was making preparations to move all of us out of the United States. My brother Carl had just come back from Europe, where he fought with Patton's army. My father wanted to leave this country because, although he had tried to do everything in his power to make it otherwise, he felt he still didn't have his freedom. He was a very successful and very wealthy businessman. He had been a U.S. marshal. He had founded one of the first Negro banks in Chicago. He had fought a very famous civil-rights case on restricted covenants, which he fought all the way up to the Supreme Court, and which he won after the expenditure of a great deal of money and emotional strength. The case is studied today in the law schools. Anyway, Daddy felt that this country was hopeless in its treatment of Negroes. So he became a refugee from America. He bought a house in Polanco, a suburb of Mexico City, and we were planning to move there when he died. I was fourteen at the time. I'm afraid I have to agree with Daddy's assessment of this country. But I don't agree with the leaving part. I don't feel defensive. Daddy really belonged to a different age, a different period. He didn't feel free. One of the reasons I feel so free is that I feel I belong to a world majority, and a very assertive one. I'm not really writing about my own family in the play. We were more typical of the bourgeois Negro exemplified by the Murchison family that is referred to in the play. I'm too close to my own family to be able to write about them.

"I mostly went to Jim Crow schools, on the South Side of Chicago, which meant half-day schools, and to this day I can't count. My parents were some peculiar kind of democrats. They could afford to send us to private schools, but they didn't believe in it. I went to three grade schools—Felsenthal, Betsy Ross, and A. O. Sexton, the last of them in a white neighborhood, where Daddy bought a house when I was eight. My mother is a remarkable woman, with great courage. She sat in that house for eight months with us—while Daddy spent most of his time in Washington fighting his case—in what was, to put it mildly, a very hostile neighborhood. I was on the porch one day with my sister, swinging my legs, when a mob gathered. We went inside, and while we were in our living room, a brick came crashing through the window with such force it embedded itself in the opposite wall. I was the one the brick almost hit. I went to Englewood High School and then to the University of Wisconsin for two years. Then I just got tired of going to school and quit and came to New York, in the summer of 1950. The theatre came into my life like *k-pow!*" Miss Hansberry knocked a fist into the palm of her other hand. "In Chicago, on my early dates, I was taken to see shows like *The Tempest*, *Othello*, and *Dark of the Moon*, which absolutely flipped me, with all that witch-doctor stuff, which I still adore. In college, I saw plays by Strindberg and Ibsen for the first time, and they were important to me. I was intrigued by the theatre. Mine was the same old story—sort of hanging around little acting groups, and developing the feeling that the threatre embraces everything I like all at one time. I've always assumed I had something to tell people. Now I think of myself as a playwright."

COMPUTERS

I.B.M.'S NEW BRAIN

John Brooks

MARCH 4, 1950 ("NEVER STUMPED")

WE'VE PAID A call on the International Business Machines Selective Sequence Electronic Calculator, which is housed in a room on the ground floor of the I.B.M. Building, at Fifty-seventh Street and Madison, and for the past couple of years has been tackling problems brought to it by scientists and industrialists from all over the world. I.B.M. offers the services of its big brain free to scientists whose questions are hard enough and important enough for the calculator to bother with; businessmen who wish to use it have to pay the operating cost, which comes to three hundred dollars an hour. In both cases, of course, the questions must be capable of expression in the austere mathematical terms the calculator is designed to handle. People who just want to look at the calculator, as we did, are always welcome.

We were introduced to the brain by Robert R. Seeber, Jr., who helped invent it and is, or thinks he is, its boss. Seeber told us that it is the fastest and most complex general computer now in use, cost $750,000 to build, and when in full cogitation requires two operators. The principal cerebral parts of the machine are tubes and wires behind glass panels, covering three walls of the room. Two hoppers, looking rather like oversize mailboxes, stand near the middle of the room. One is the "in" hopper, into which questions are inserted on punched cards or tapes; the other is the "out" hopper, from which, if all goes well, the answer emerges. High on one wall of the room is a large sign reading "THINK," but this admonition isn't addressed to the calculator.

So far, Seeber told us, the calculator has solved five weighty problems in pure science, the most recent of them having to do with the uranium atom. Some time ago, Niels Bohr, the Danish physicist, advanced the theory that the behavior of the nucleus of an atom of uranium was in many respects similar to that of a drop of liquid, such as water. It was thought, however, that this notion might have to be discarded, because a drop of liquid—we're talking about a mathematical drop now, not a real one—appeared to split evenly, whereas the uranium nucleus splits unevenly. Two Princeton physicists whipped the problem into shape for the calculator, and the calculator was able to demonstrate that, by George, a mathematical drop of liquid splits *une*venly. This opens the way to further presumably fruitful speculation. The calculator took a hundred and three hours to solve the problem. A hypothetical man with an ordinary desk calculator and an iron constitution would have been at the job about a century and a half, Seeber told us. The calculator has tackled any number of commercial problems. When we arrived, it was just warming up for one that involved a means of getting more oil out of oil fields.

Seeber took us on a quick tour of the brain. "This is the number-reading section," he said, tapping one of the glass panels. "You feed two things into the calculator, factors and instructions, both in numerical form. The factors are 'read' and put into the memory section, where they're later dealt with by the various computing sections, according to what the instructions say." As we moved along, relays began to rattle in a carefree manner and patterns of light danced across the panels. "The oil problem," Seeber said. At the memory section, he flipped on a switch, and a pattern of lights appeared behind one of the panels. "That's a number it has to remember," Seeber said. "Happens to be plus 12,788,400." Peering behind the panel, we noticed several loose wires. We pointed them out to Seeber, and he nodded and said, "Yes, it's a funny thing about those wires—nobody knows what they're doing there."

We asked Seeber to tell us some of the calculator's limitations. He said that it can't reason and hence can't have any new ideas, and that though its memory is more reliable than human memory, it is less persistent. It exercises a certain amount of discretion, but only if a human being first establishes what choices are open to it. "You have to tell it every simple little fact," Seeber said, in what seemed to us a slightly petulant tone. "You even have to tell it whether to add or subtract." We inquired about a story we'd heard, to the effect that an electronic calculator had once been asked, as a lark, to prove that one equals zero; according to the story, it had made several gallant attempts to do the job and had then suffered a breakdown, from which it was months recovering. "Our machine has never been stumped," Seeber said. "But then it has never been baited. We've been too busy to try mathematical posers on it. It *is* subject to normal wear and tear and to breakdowns from constant overwork. The first things to go are the tubes, then the relays and resistors. If the calculator makes a minor mistake because of a defective part, it goes on automatically trying to do the same part of the computation over and over again. In case of a really serious mistake, it shuts itself off. During the severe strain of solving that nucleus-of-uranium problem, it blew a part every four hours or so. We'd fix the part and then give the whole brain a rest—sometimes ten minutes, sometimes a couple of hours."

THE NIM MACHINE

Rex Lardner

AUGUST 2, 1952 ("IT")

THE PEOPLE OVER at the W. L. Maxson Corporation, which is primarily in the business of developing and manufacturing secret electric, electronic, and electromechanical equipment for the government but also puts out, for commercial users, such things as Unimax switches, Langevin transformers, and Maxson precision phasemeters, were kind enough a few days back to invite us to come over and have a go at their Nim machine. "A California guided-missiles man built a ticktacktoe machine," the Maxson gentleman who proffered the invitation said, "so we built a Nim machine. Our machine is a very strong player, so watch out." In spite of our poor record against machines of *any* sort, we marched over to the building housing the firm's electronic laboratory, at

475 Tenth Avenue, the next day, rode up to the fourteenth floor, and, wondering all the while what Nim might be, stated our business, signed in, had a huge badge pinned on our lapel, and were conducted by three solemn, bespectacled young men into a cubicle with light-green walls. There we were confronted with a walnut box, thirty inches high and eighteen inches deep, whose front was studded with light bulbs and push buttons. The box was sitting inscrutably on a table. In the upper right-hand corner of the front panel was printed the word "Nim." Below this inscription were two legends that could be illuminated. One was "You Win," the other "You Lose." Below them was a button marked "New Game." The greater part of the panel was taken up by four rows of seven bulbs each. There was a button at the end of each row, and below *them* were, at one side, a button labelled "Machine Play" and, at the other, a bulb labelled "You Play," which was also lighted. In the upper left-hand corner of the contrivance was a bulb with the word "Tilt" over it. The three young men were labelled Eugene Grant, Herbert Koppel, and Howard Baller. Grant started off by explaining to us that Nim is an old game for two people, usually played with several rows of counters; the number of rows and the number of counters is immaterial. Each player takes a turn at removing one or more counters from a single row. The player who removes the last counter of the whole bunch wins. "Other forms of Nim are played with a single row of, say, matchsticks," Baller told us. "Then you're limited to taking one, two, or three matches at a time, and the idea is to make your opponent pick up the last one." "The origins of the game are shrouded in the mists of antiquity," Koppel said, "but it seems to come from the Orient. The Anglo-Saxon word for 'to take' or 'to filch' is *'niman.'* In *The Beggar's Opera,* one of the characters says, 'I expect the Gentleman about this snuff-box that Filch nimm'd two nights ago in the park.' Charles L. Bouton, the mathematician, called it a game with a complete mathematical theory. On our machine, we use lights instead of counters."

Grant told us the machine was all set to play and briefed us on procedure: Every time we pressed the button to the right of a row of lights, one of the bulbs in that row would go dark; if we pressed buttons in two rows without allowing the machine a turn, the "Tilt" button would light up and we would lose on a foul. With some trepidation, we pressed the button governing the second row twice. Two lights went off. At Koppel's nod, we pressed the "Machine Play" button, and with haughty efficiency the machine put out several more lights in the same row. "It's now impossible for you to win," Baller announced witheringly. Nevertheless, we doggedly kept pressing buttons, and soon there were only two lights left—one in the first row and one in the third. "It's your turn," Koppel said. "Press a button." We did. The light in the first row went out. We pressed the "Machine Play" button, the last light went out, and "You Lose" triumphantly flashed on.

"The way the machine's arranged now," said Koppel, "a player can win by pure luck five percent of the time." "It ought to be explained," said Baller, "that, mathematically, each play you make produces either a safe or an unsafe condition—that is, relative to your position in regard to the rest of the bulbs. If the condition is safe, and you keep it that way for the rest of the game, you can't lose. If it's unsafe just once, you can't win, no matter what, because the machine never makes a mistake." "The machine is so keen on winning that sometimes it cheats a little bit," said Koppel. "It makes the 'You Play' bulb light up without taking its turn. Or it puts out lights in two rows at once without flashing the 'Tilt' bulb. It also plays a nerve-racking game of attrition when it's up against an expert, putting out only one bulb at a time. Wears you down." "The way to maintain the safe condition," said Grant, "is to see to it that each power of two appears an even number of times in the aggregate of all rows. That is, you are safe when the sums of all individual binary digits are even numbers. The formula is—" We urged him to let it go. "When William Maxson, the son of the founder of the firm, played it," Baller said, "Koppel, who made the machine from plans by Grant and me, gave him special instructions, and he beat the pants off it. At the end of about the fourth game, the machine started clicking and clacking something terrible." "Oh, it has a temper," Koppel said.

The machine weighs fifty pounds, cost two thousand dollars to build, and is loaded with small electronic tubes, germanium crystals, and wires. It was completed, after three months' work, in time to go on display at the recent National Conference of Airborne Electronics Engineers, in Dayton. "Most of our stuff is so hush-hush we can't exhibit it," Grant told us. "So we built this to show people interested in engineering what we could produce in the way of a simple digital computer. Turned out to be the biggest draw in Dayton. It—we call it It—played about fifteen hundred games and only lost a hundred and fifty. That was against some of the best engineering minds in the country. You want a return match?" We said no, thanks, walked out, and handed in our badge.

DATA PROCESSING SYSTEMS

John Brooks

AUGUST 6, 1955 ("MENTAL")

IT WAS OVER five years ago that we paid a call on the International Business Machines Selective Sequence Electronic Calculator in I.B.M. World Headquarters, at Fifty-seventh and Madison, so when I.B.M. announced a couple of weeks ago that it now has a whole integrated team of big and small electronic brains up there, standing ready to tackle the big and small problems of businessmen and scientists, we decided to repeat our visit. We have now done so, and have found that things had really moved along up on Fifty-seventh Street during our absence. In the first place, the term "electronic calculator" has given way to a more exact one—"electronic data-processing machine." Secondly, the data processors are now being rented to business organizations at profitable rates, just like other I.B.M. machines, instead of being offered for use either free or at cost, the way our old, superseded acquaintance the S.S.E.C. was. Thirdly, the new devices lack one of the most endearing components of the S.S.E.C.; namely, some loose ends of wire, inexplicable even to I.B.M. men, sticking out of its memory section. The integrated team, which we found on the ground floor of the I.B.M. Building after passing an amiable receptionist and an implacable "THINK" sign, consists chiefly of a lot of shoulder-high closed cabinets purring smoothly in a couple of blandly pleasing rooms with aluminum ceilings and red walls. There is scarcely a wire in sight, let alone one not connected to anything.

In the larger of these rooms, where a dozen men were clustered expectantly around the "out" end of a machine, we had the good fortune to fall in with Dr. Cuthbert C. Hurd, I.B.M.'s director of electronic data-processing, and thus coach of the integrated team. Dr. Hurd, a youngish-looking, sparse-haired man, told us that the star players are the 701, which rents for three hundred dollars an hour, and the 702, which rents for four hundred and forty-five dollars. The 701 has been available for rental for a couple of years, but the 702 is brand-new. "They resemble twins having different mental characteristics," Dr. Hurd told us. "They both use megacycle circuitry, of course, and they both use the same kind of printers, punches, card readers, and magnetic tapes. On the other hand, they look different, except for their memories, which look exactly alike."

Dr. Hurd showed us the 702's memory, a big, handsome gray box, and then, leading us into the other room, showed us the 701's memory. Sure enough, they looked exactly alike. "Now, as to their mental characteristics," Dr. Hurd went on, like a doting father, "the 701 has much more arithmetical facility, and can, for example, add many columns of figures simultaneously. The 702, on the other hand, adds the same way you and I do, but it can accept information from the outside world much more readily than the 701, and it can understand the language that an accountant uses. In a word, the 701 has a scientific turn of mind—it's particularly good on theoretical problems—and the 702 has a practical business orientation. Those men you see around the console of the 702 are businessmen waiting for it to finish solving their problem, but to preserve business security I'd better not tell you who they are or what their problem is. In fact, I don't *know* what their problem is." Dr. Hurd explained that I.B.M. encourages users of its data-processing machines to operate them for themselves, after first taking a three-week course the company offers in how they work. When I.B.M. has to do the operating for clients, it charges extra. We asked Dr. Hurd if he could give us a general notion of some business problems submitted to the 702 that he *did* know about, and he said he could. "For example, one of the airlines wants to optimize the assignment of its maintenance help," he said. "The 702 is being asked to simulate the random arrival of planes at airports. Can do! Then, there's a large chemical concern looking for names for new products. It is feeding the 702 a set of rules—names must be chemically logical, must not have too many consonants, and so on. The 702 will absorb the information and rattle off a list of all possible names, from which the company executives can make their selections."

Dr. Hurd rattled off some statistics to prove how much more advanced the 701 and 702 are than the S.S.E.C. was, but, thank God, we have forgotten them. As we were preparing to leave, we noticed that the men around the 702 console were examining with satisfied expressions some punch cards coming out of it. Dr. Hurd plucked at our sleeve and said modestly, "I ought to mention that the 701 and 702 have their limitations.

There is no evidence yet that they or any machine can be taught to do program analysis, otherwise known as programming, otherwise known as creative thinking."

ELECTION RESULTS VIA UNIVAC

Philip Hamburger

NOVEMBER 17, 1956 ("BRAIN")

Our man Stanley, wearing a mechanical, nonpartisan smile, came into the office the day after election and left the following message:

"Spent Election Night in company of Univac, giant Remington-Rand electronic brain, at Remington-Rand Building, on lower Fourth Avenue. Univac that people saw on C.B.S. television not actual Univac—just blinking, flashing facsimile of control board of brain itself. Real brain sweating like Einstein downtown, giving results that were subsequently phoned to C.B.S. correspondents at studio uptown, then read over air. Went downtown after supper, entered control room for big brain through closely guarded door. Room a madhouse. Close to a hundred human brains, attached to bodies, occupied room, some bending over teletype machines, others poring over stacks of papers at desks, others standing before restaurant-refrigerator-type machines with glass fronts and whirring discs inside. Control boards everywhere—red, green, amber. Terrifying. Was mercifully taken in hand by Dr. Max Woodbury, of New York University's College of Engineering Mathematics Department. Dr. Woodbury a tall, tense brain, with minute reddish-brown mustache—one of several scientists in charge of Univac operation. 'Univac has a great mind,' he said. His voice was filled with awe. 'All these people are servicing Univac, helping her to reach her conclusions,' he said. 'We began stuffing statistics into Univac in 1952 and 1954. Originally, we went back to Bryan and free silver for statistics, but they didn't seem to have any appreciable pertinence, so we confined ourselves ultimately to data from 1928 onward. Mostly Presidential-election figures—data from states and districts, paying special attention to unique counties, such as Wayne County, Michigan; Polk County, Iowa; San Francisco County; and the five boroughs of New York. Univac knows a unique county when she sees one,' he said cryptically.

"'Brain working now?' I asked.

"'Working?' he said. 'Like a dream.'

"'How does she work?' I asked.

"'Briefly,' said Dr. Woodbury, 'raw material comes in from the teletypes, is processed by people at that circular desk, is broken down into precincts—possibility of human error here, you know—and is transferred to Univac digital recording magnetic tape. The tapes are placed in one of the ten servos, and then translated to Univac herself. Univac compares current data with accumulated data and comes out with the answers.' Courier bearing white slip of paper interrupted Dr. Woodbury. Dr. Woodbury scanned paper. 'Univac predicts, on basis of one million votes counted, three hundred and ninety-eight electoral votes for Ike, sixty-eight for Stevenson, with the balance in doubt. Perfectly splendid! Right on the beam! Univac is willing to go a hundred to one for Eisenhower! And now I'll show you Univac herself—the works—through glass, of course.'

"Went to end of room and looked through window at what seemed like dozen or more airplane engines, millions of coils and lights. 'The brain!' said Dr. Woodbury. 'We have to cool her off with air.' Quiet-looking man stepped up. 'Meet Dr. John Mauchly,' said Dr. Woodbury. 'Dr. Mauchly, here, is a co-inventor of Univac.'

"'Univac costs one million dollars to purchase outright,' said Dr. Mauchly. 'Twenty-five thousand dollars a month to rent.' Told Dr. Mauchly I'd think it over. 'Univac is going smoothly,' said Dr. Mauchly.

"'One thing worries me,' said Dr. Woodbury. 'Univac says Tennessee is going Democratic, I say Tennessee is going Republican.' Courier arrived with United Press dispatch that Tennessee was going Republican. 'The machine is slightly wrong,' said Dr. Woodbury, tugging at his mustache.

"Evening wore on, machines whirred, lights flashed. On basis of 2,600,000 votes counted, Univac predicted 383 electoral votes for Eisenhower, 90 for Stevenson, 58 doubtful. On basis of 3,773,000 votes counted,

Univac predicted 405 electoral votes for Eisenhower, 81 for Stevenson, 45 in doubt. Drs. Mauchly and Woodbury beamed. Courier arrived and whispered something into Dr. Woodbury's ear. 'The machine has goofed,' said Dr. Woodbury. 'Mechanical failure, but just possibly an input goof.'

"'She has become persnickety about accepting some data,' said Dr. Mauchly. 'Often, she regurgitates unacceptable data into her post-mortem file.'

"'That's how we catch the goofs,' said Dr. Woodbury. He was now tugging fiercely at his mustache.

"'The brain is smart,' said Dr. Mauchly, his voice like cold steel, 'but the brain is also stupid. Stuff her with something wrong and she'll go right ahead with it.'

"'Sometimes a surprising trend disturbs her, and then she has to make a decision,' said Dr. Woodbury. 'Often, she says, "I will not accept this decision," and that's where the post-mortem file comes in.'

"'Really, *we* make the value judgments,' said Dr. Mauchly.

"'No,' said Dr. Woodbury, 'we do the creation.'

"'I can give her the rules,' said Dr. Mauchly.

"'I feel we are following the decision rules,' said Dr. Woodbury. Group of anxious technicians huddled over a control board. Red lights were flashing wildly. 'Error lights,' said Dr. Woodbury.

"'Easy to blame the machinery,' said Dr. Mauchly. 'Could be human failure.'

"'The trouble is in the Senate,' said Dr. Woodbury. 'She's goofed on the Senate.'

"Drs. Woodbury and Mauchly joined technicians at control board. I went home and listened to returns on radio. Eisenhower by landslide."

THE PERCEPTRON SIMULATOR

Harding Mason

DECEMBER 6, 1958 ("RIVAL")

HAVING TOLD YOU about the giant digital computer known as I.B.M. 704 and how it has been taught to play a fairly creditable game of chess, we'd like to tell you about an even more remarkable machine, the perceptron, which, as its name implies, is capable of what amounts to original thought. The first perceptron has yet to be built, but it has been successfully simulated on a 704, and it's only a question of time (and money) before it comes into existence. This about-to-be marvel is a lot more subtle than the 704; indeed, it strikes us as the first serious rival to the human brain ever devised, and our own brain is thoroughly dazzled by the things it's said to do. The begetters of the prodigy are Dr. Frank Rosenblatt, of the Cornell Aeronautical Laboratory, and Dr. Marshall C. Yovits, of the Office of Naval Research, in Washington. Dr. Rosenblatt was passing through town recently, on his way to a consultation with Dr. Yovits, and we conned him, over a cup of coffee, into a brief exegesis of their brilliant offspring. "Our success in developing the perceptron means that for the first time a nonbiological object will achieve an organization of its external environment in a meaningful way," Dr. Rosenblatt said. "That's a safe definition of what the perceptron can do. My colleague disapproves of all the loose talk one hears nowadays about mechanical brains. He prefers to call our machine a self-organizing system, but, between you and me, that's precisely what any brain is."

Digital computers, Dr. Rosenblatt said, are equipped to solve certain problems more quickly and accurately than human beings can, but the problems must be prepared and, in effect, spoon-fed to them by specialists; being basically adding machines, the computers lack creativity. The distinctive characteristic of the perceptron is that it interacts with its environment, forming concepts that have not been made ready for it by a human agent. Biologists claim that only biological systems see, feel, and think, but the perceptron behaves *as if* it saw, felt, and thought. Both computers and perceptrons have so-called memories; in the latter, however, the memory isn't a mere storehouse of deliberately selected and accumulated facts but a free, indeterminate area of association units, connecting, as nearly as possible at random, a sensory input, or eye, with a very large number of response units.

If a triangle is held up to the perceptron's eye, the association units connected with the eye pick up the image of the triangle and convey it along a random succession of lines to the response units, where the image is registered. The next time the triangle is held up to the eye, its image will travel along the path already travelled by the earlier image. Significantly, once a particular response has been established, all the connections leading to that response are strengthened, and if a triangle of a different size and shape is held up to the perceptron, its image will be passed along the track that the first triangle took. If a square is presented, however, a new set of random lines is called into play and a new response results. The more images the perceptron is permitted to scan, the more adroit its generalizations in respect to those images become. Dr. Rosenblatt picked up a silver cream pitcher beside his coffee cup. "I recognize this as a pitcher, though I've never seen it before," he said. "That process of thought may seem simple to you, but in fact it's immensely complicated. The perceptron is able to draw subtle conclusions of that sort. It can tell the difference between a dog and a cat, though so far, according to our calculations, it wouldn't be able to tell whether the dog was to the left or right of the cat. We still have to teach it depth perception and refinements of judgment."

Of what practical use, we asked, would the perceptron be? "At the moment, none whatever," Dr. Rosenblatt said cheerfully. "Someday we may find it useful to send one out into space to take in impressions for us. In these matters, you know, use follows invention. Something called an Interdisciplinary Conference on Self-Organizing Systems has been scheduled for May. It'll bring together biologists, psychologists, physicists, and social scientists from all over, and we'll see what happens when they all get to thinking and talking about perceptrons." What, we asked, *wasn't* the perceptron capable of? Dr. Rosenblatt threw up his hands. "Love," he said. "Hope. Despair. Human nature, in short. If we don't understand the human sex drive, why should we expect a machine to?"

CURIOUS DEVELOPMENTS

THE HOME FREEZER

Brendan Gill

MAY 30, 1953 ("FROZEN")

WE MENTIONED A while ago the case of a housewife who bought a large home freezer and, while attending a night-school course in Freezer Management, learned that the best way to clean spinach before cooking and freezing it is to give it a whirl in a washing machine. Now we've been to see the conductor of the course and have gathered further information on the multiple uses to which home appliances can be put. The course in Freezer Management is offered as part of the night-school curriculum of the Long Island Agricultural and Technical Institute, in Farmingdale, a branch of the State University of New York, and is taught by an ingenious fellow named George G. Cook, who is forty and the holder of a B.S. and M.S. in agriculture and education from Cornell. As we entered the classroom, he was winding up a demonstration of the proper way to prepare a Baked Alaska. "As far as I know, this is the first course in Freezer Management ever offered," he told us, tucking the Baked Alaska away in one of nine gleaming white freezers scattered about the room. "I've been interested in food preservation through freezing ever since 1946, and I like to pass along to my classes some of the little tricks I've picked up over the years. For example, I recommend the washing machine not only for spinach but for beet greens, turnip greens, kale, and Swiss chard. The swirling action of the machine gets the dirt off the undersides of the leaves faster and more thoroughly than hand washing. I also recommend that the housewife spin-dry the vegetables before removing them from the washer. Less mess. As for peas, I suggest that they be shucked by boiling them in the pods for a minute and then passing them through a clothes wringer."

Cook's next self-imposed chore was to bone a turkey, and as he boned he predicted to us that the freezer would shortly become as indispensable to the kitchen as the refrigerator and stove. Over five million home freezers are already in operation throughout the country, he said, and the eating habits of *Homo americanus* are, as a result, being radically altered. "Back in the old, pre-freezer days," he explained, "the usual thing was to buy a ham, have baked ham one night, sliced cold ham the next, ham hash or ham loaf on the third night, and maybe a ham-bone soup on the fourth. Ham, ham, ham! Nowadays, you can have ham one night and freeze the remainder till you're good and ready for it." The key to successful freezer management, he went on, giving the turkey a terrible wrench, is to buy a big enough freezer. "Allow five to six cubic feet per family member," he said. "Since the cost of stocking it once a year is prohibitive, unless you raise your own vegetables, stock it as often as you can with as much as you can. But stock! Stock! Bake eight pies in one oven heating and freeze seven. Or eight loaves of bread. Freezing bread actually makes it taste fresher, and I advise the women in my classes to buy day-old bread, pies, cakes, and sweet rolls at bakeries for a few cents off, then freeze them. A dollar saved is a dollar earned. People with freezers stop throwing away leftovers. Do you know what happens to waffles that don't get eaten? They get put into moistureproof bags and frozen—*frozen,* do you hear?"

We may have looked slightly ill, for Mr. Cook hurriedly left leftovers to speak instead of his classes, which average thirty-two members and meet for two hours one evening a week for twelve weeks. There's a registration fee of four dollars and a laboratory fee of two dollars for the materials used; otherwise, the course is free. He provides all the food that his pupils prepare, except meat, and the students get their two dollars' worth of food back the last night of the course. The price of meat being what it is, he fears that if he were to give it away, a certain number of artful dodgers might take his course merely in order to pick up a nice cut of beef. His counsel in class ranges all the way from blanching food to the use of dry ice in case of power failure. A negative advantage of home freezers, he said, as he got the turkey ready for *its* moistureproof bag, is that they keep housewives out of grocery stores, where they're subject to impulse buying. A positive advantage is that housewives not only are spared the horror of becoming hopeless impulse buyers but don't get trichinosis. "Matter of fact," Cook said, "my wife always leaves blankets and winter clothes in our freezer for forty-eight hours before storing them for the summer. That's guaranteed to kill moths in all stages. Think what an advantage that is! Furthermore, the freezer is an ideal place in which to put valuable papers. The thick walls of the freezer make it practically fireproof. Or hide your cash and securities in a frozen-food container at the bottom of the freezer, and how is a thief to find them? He's not going to empty the whole darned thing looking for them—not with frosty haddock fillets and ice-cold succotash sticking to his fingers. Safe as a bank."

JAZZ CLASS AT COLUMBIA

Whitney Balliett

DECEMBER 25, 1954 ("MAGNETIC FORCE")

WE'VE BEEN UP to Columbia to attend a class in "Adventures in Jazz," a course sponsored by the Institute of Arts and Sciences and conducted by a jazz mandarin named Sidney Gross. He meets his pupils in a room in the School of Journalism Building, to which we repaired a few minutes before classtime, which we knew to be 7:30 P.M. The room had blackboards on three walls and was furnished with a baby-grand piano, a record-player, and Mr. Gross, a handsome fellow with dark hair and piercing light-green eyes. We pressed him for a thumbnail autobiography, and he replied that he was born in London thirty-nine years ago; became a student of jazz at twelve, on hearing a Jimmy Dorsey recording of "Praying the Blues"; studied the violin for two years, then switched to the ukulele, and then to the guitar; and in 1939 joined the R.A.F. as a musician. "During the Battle of Britain, we used to send the pilots up full of jazz and hot rhythms," he said. "After the war, I started a series of weekly jazz concerts at the Adelphi Theatre, in London. We took in more money there than the London Philharmonic did. I came to this country five years ago. Been fooling around in radio and records ever since."

Mr. Gross told us that his course, the first of its kind ever offered by Columbia, has an enrollment of sixty-five students of all ages and occupations, including a real-estate man, a dentist, and a female anesthetist. The course lasts only ten weeks and provides no credits toward a degree, but Mr. Gross feels sure that every college in the country will eventually have to come to terms with jazz, and take it as seriously as history or French. A feature of his course is guests, who perform before the class. "Tonight the star performer will be the drummer Louie Bellson," Mr. Gross said. "I've rented a whole drum kit for him. Excuse me while I go fetch it." He scooted out of the room to fetch the drum kit, and by the time he had returned, the room was jammed with students. After greeting them, he read aloud from a paper on jazz that had been contributed by a member of the class named Walda Klay. We noted in the reading such statements as "Jazz is a sixth sense," "Jazz has inescapable magnetic force," and "Jazz is worth living, loving, and listening to." At the end of the reading, the class burst into applause, and Mr. Gross asked Walda Klay to stand. A girl with a blond horsetail got up, bowed to Mr. Gross, and hurriedly resumed her seat.

Mr. Gross announced that the topic of the evening would be bebop. "In the evolution of life, people often reach out too far too suddenly," he said. "That is what happened to jazz in 1941, when bebop was being conceived. Among our guests tonight is Nat Hentoff, the New York editor of *Down Beat*. Nat, will you come up and say a few words?" Mr. Hentoff, a tall, shy-appearing man, walked to the front of the room and shook hands with Mr. Gross. "Tell the class which way jazz is heading, Nat," Mr. Gross said.

"Jazz is heading in several different directions at once," Mr. Hentoff said, not at all disapprovingly. "One of these directions is, I believe, a search for more form."

A student raised his hand and inquired, "Mr. Hentoff, do you think the West Coast modern movement will become as important as the Chicago school was?"

"The so-called West Coast movement doesn't exist," Mr. Hentoff said. "It's no different from jazz anywhere else."

"What about Turk Murphy and his San Francisco jazz?" Mr. Gross asked.

"All that people like Turk Murphy are doing out there is copying the records of people like Jelly Roll Morton, right down to the surface scratches," Mr. Hentoff replied. "What happens to revivalists is that they tend to get homesick for places they've never been."

Another guest, Thelonius Monk, was introduced as a pianist, a composer, and an early booster of bebop. At Mr. Gross's urging, Mr. Monk sat down at the piano and struck a few chords. "Those are old-style chords," he said. "Now here's a new-style chord—a G seventh." He banged the keys smartly. "That's what the chords we're using nowadays sound like," he said. "I'll play a chorus of 'Just You, Just Me,' and see how you like it." When he finished the piece, the class applauded wildly. In rapid succession, Mr. Gross introduced some more new-style guests: Oscar Pettiford, who came forward bearing a bass fiddle; Jimmy Hamilton, who bore a clarinet; and the great Louie Bellson, who stepped into the classroom just as his name was spoken and, taking off his overcoat, seated himself like a banker back of the rented drums. Mr. Gross said that Bellson, Monk, Pettiford, and Hamilton would play "Just You, Just Me," and that still another guest, the poet Langston Hughes, would then read from his works certain passages having to do with jazz in general and the birth of bebop in particular. "Give us a C," Hamilton called out to Monk. Monk gave his companions a C, and they were off. The music slammed back and forth, louder and louder, inside the long classroom, and Professor Gross sat at his desk and beamed.

VACCINATING AGAINST POLIO

John McNulty

APRIL 23, 1955 ("WIPE AND JAB")

PLANS FOR THE polio vaccination of some two hundred and eighty thousand New York City children have been brewing since last October, at which time the Health Department forehandedly established a Polio Task Force, under the command of Dr. Morris Greenberg, chief of its Bureau of Preventable Diseases. It was in October that the National Foundation for Infantile Paralysis announced it would provide Salk vaccine for mass inoculations *if* the Francis report was favorable. "If the report had been unfavorable—and I assure you we had no advance information—we'd have been saddled with some seventy-two thousand dollars' worth of supplies," Dr. Greenberg told us the other morning at his office on Worth Street—a busy place, made all the busier by a couple of hundred phone calls each day from citizens wanting to know about some phase of the vaccine situation. "But we had to act as if we knew the report would show maximum effectiveness. We had to be fully prepared for the best, and we are."

The Polio Task Force, composed of representatives from the National Foundation for Infantile Paralysis, the local office of the Foundation, the Public Health Nursing Bureau, and the Bureau of Handicapped Children, was helped in making its happily justified preparations by last year's experimental injections. More than forty thousand city children got shots then, half of them receiving authentic Salk vaccine and the other half placebo. (The Health Department's estimate of the public's intelligence was vastly increased when it found not a single instance of parents' trying to pull strings to make sure their children got the real stuff.) All the placebo kids are, of course, eligible for genuine Salk this time. Among the things Dr. Greenberg and his associates learned from last year's experience were how many children one doctor can conveniently inject in a single hour (thirty-three and a third) and how few children can be expected to faint at the sight or prick of a needle (considerably under the normal rate for the nation's armed forces). On the basis of these and other pertinent findings, the Task Force plunged ahead, and had soon stockpiled 4,500 syringes, 16,255 hypodermic needles, 156 gallons of alcohol, 800,000 cotton balls, 30,000 gauze pads, 1,300 enamel trays, 1,400 pairs of small forceps, 30 quart cans of detergent, 1,525 rubber-stamp-and-stamp-pad sets, 1,100 white enamel mugs (to hold alcohol for sterilizing), and 170,000 envelopes (in which to keep sterilized needles and syringes). All this matériel was stored in the basement at Worth Street, pending word from Ann Arbor.

Concurrently, letters went out to all school principals, alerting them to the probable state of affairs. A form letter was written for distribution to appropriate parents. Doctors were recruited, and windshield placards prepared to keep them from getting parking tickets while administering vaccine at schools. Through Parent-Teacher Associations, volunteers were lined up to transport vaccine to schools from municipal district health centers—there are twenty-one of these, scattered throughout the city—and to take used needles and syringes back to the centers for resterilization.

Within a day after the great communiqué from Michigan, the Task Force began to roll. Dr. Greenberg, who was in Albany, personally carried back from there a two-foot-high stack of green papers, as well as various corollary documents, indicating, in code, which of last year's inoculated children had received what. At once, the Health Department began decoding the lists and notifying those parents whose children *were* vaccinated. Unnotified parents of children who participated in the 1954 tests can assume that their children got placebo. "This year's operation is enormously simplified," Dr. Greenberg said. "Last year, to control the test properly, we had to be certain that each child got his second and third shots out of the same bottle as his first, and that made for complicated bookkeeping. This year, it'll just be wipe and jab, wipe and jab, as fast as we can go."

In fairness to the armed forces, we ought perhaps to observe that more children might have keeled over last year if the authorities hadn't distracted them from thoughts of pain by offering them a selection of lollipops of assorted colors. It has been concluded that the necessity of making a choice absorbed the kids so deeply that they tended to forget about the needle.

MARKETING MILTOWN

Thomas Whiteside

MAY 3, 1958 (FROM "GETTING THERE FIRST WITH TRANQUILLITY")

EQUANIL AND MODERIL, Pacatal and Dartal, Suavitil and Harmonyl, Compazine and Sparine, Atarax and Ultran, Trilafon and Deprol—these are representative of the trade names designating the multitude of new tranquillizing agents, and on behalf of them, and tranquillity, their manufacturers have been waging unrelenting warfare against each other, not only with fusillades of pills but also, on many sectors, with kaleidoscopic bursts of promotional literature and volleys of publicity. While this war has been raging as fiercely as any of the struggles between the manufacturers of soap, the general public is not nearly as conscious of it, for the makers of prescription drugs—or ethical drugs, as they are called in the profession—are prevented by venerable medical custom from advertising their products directly to the laity. They may, however, plant stories in the lay press—as long as these do not constitute paid advertising—and, even more important, they are free to advertise their drugs to doctors with all the zest, ingenuity, and cash at their command.

In keeping with the grand themes involved, much of the printed matter extolling drugs is marked by lavish layout and elegant typography. It is also marked by a use of visual symbolism so determined that it has perhaps been equalled only by the jackets of long-playing phonograph records. The symbolism used in pushing tranquillizers, for instance, ranges from a spiky-looking black-and-white drawing of a hand nervously stubbing out a cigarette in an ashtray full of twisted butts—denoting pre-tranquillized humanity—to large photographs tinted in what one company calls "precisely the right psychological shade of blue" and showing cool, refreshing vistas of snowclad mountains and pine-fringed lakes to represent post-tranquillizer serenity. One favorite visual device is a highly stylized, multicolored human brain, its nerves—thin, red, and aquiver with tension—extending downward into an expanse of white space. Another is humanity itself in as jittery a state as the ad men can dream up; male and female models are shown being bawled out by the boss, climbing into the dentist's chair, waiting to be put on the operating table, and even, in one case, groping through a mauve labyrinth on which is superimposed, in gray halftone, a dizzying montage of office clocks, medicine bottles, Martini glasses, and rumpled bedclothes.

Equanil is one brand of meprobamate, and another brand—the original one, in fact—is put out by Wallace Laboratories, a fairly small and until three years ago altogether obscure pharmaceutical company that is a division of Carter Products, Inc., of New Brunswick, New Jersey, the makers of, among other things, Carter's Little Liver Pills. The Wallace brand is called Miltown, and it is one of the paradoxes of the tranquillizer industry that, while Equanil outsells Miltown by at least two to one, Miltown is by far the better-known drug. During the three years that Miltown has been on the market, its name has been bandied about not only as a handy label for tranquillizing drugs in general but as a synonym for tranquillity itself; indeed, it seems at times that Miltown has as many semantic uses as pharmacological ones. "Be my little Miltown," one of last year's more enterprising valentines read, employing the word in a blissful sense, but it has also been used to convey the idea of far from blissful conditions, as in the title of S. J. Perelman's latest book—*The Road to Miltown*.

Henry H. Hoyt, the president of Carter Products, Inc., a short, somewhat wizened middle-aged man, had, through shrewd merchandising and endless repetition of the old slogan "Wake Up Your Liver Bile!," brought the company to a state of glowing financial health. Now he was in the process of expanding operations beyond the limits of patent medicine. Hoyt decided to strike for Miltown while the iron was hot. He asked Ted Bates & Co., which had been touting Little Liver Pills for a number of years, to take on Miltown, too, not only placing ads in the pages of the medical journals but also furnishing stories and background material to the lay press. In the fall of 1955 swarms of articles about tranquillizing drugs, which gave considerable space to Miltown—and little to Equanil—began to appear in newspapers and national magazines.

As the winter progressed, dramatic shortages of the drug developed in many parts of the country. Toward the end of January, the Charlotte, North Carolina, *Observer* published an article, subheaded "CAROLINIANS LINE UP FOR NEW DRUG," in which a local wholesale druggist was quoted as remarking that Miltown pills were in such short supply "that we are having to ration them out on a wartime basis." Shortly thereafter, the

Louisville *Courier-Journal* quoted a physician as saying that the local drugstores had run so short of Miltown that some of his patients had orders waiting at two or three stores. The paper also reported, in an interview with another doctor, this example of the effectiveness of Miltown:

> A Louisville truck driver was the excitable type and would get "mad" when another driver cut in front of him. He would cuss out the other driver and perhaps run into his car. But since he has been taking the new drug, he remains calm and hasn't had an accident.

Truck drivers were not the only people of volatile disposition to give Miltown a whirl. Toward the end of 1955, the drug had begun to be fashionable in show business, a highly nervous field of endeavor; then, around February, the craze hit the motion-picture colony in Los Angeles. Everybody—producers, directors, actors, writers—seemed to be talking about tranquillizers at studios, restaurants, and social gatherings, and when they talked about tranquillizers, they generally talked about Miltown. Some actors took to swallowing Miltown by the fistful, and since the supply was still running far behind the demand, many people were willing to pay black-market prices for their pills. Some drugstores sold the drug without a prescription—and, of course, at a stiff markup. The arrival of fresh supplies in Hollywood drugstores became an important local event. "YES, WE HAVE MILTOWN!" a sign in huge letters running the length of a plate-glass window triumphantly proclaimed on the front of a big drugstore at Sunset and Gower, and another establishment took out an ad in *Daily Variety* promising free and fast delivery of Miltown upon receipt of a call from the reader's physician. Miltown tablets were sometimes served to the guests at Hollywood and New York theatrical parties, and Frances Kaye, a publicity woman, described for the press a party in Palm Springs, at which tranquillizers "were passed around like peanuts," adding, "Some of the people drank what they called a Miltown cocktail—a tranquillizing pill mixed with a Bloody Mary." Kendis Rochlen, who reports on motion pictures for the Los Angeles *Mirror-News,* pretty well summed up the atmosphere in Hollywood at the time when she wrote, "I went from Ginger Rogers' party to José Ferrer's party to a dinner party, and everywhere they were talking about it [Miltown]. My husband is on it now. He used to be very nervous, really just miserable. Now he doesn't get mad as quick or stay mad as long. He has no energy, of course."

From its victory in Hollywood, Miltown had no trouble moving on to triumph after triumph in television. One of the product's earliest gratuitous public endorsements came from Milton Berle, a theretofore far from subdued personality, whom the February 27, 1956, issue of *Time* quoted as saying, "It's worked wonders for me. In fact, I'm thinking of changing my name to Miltown Berle." It was not long before the air was clogged with gags about "happy pills" and "I-don't-care pills," and in these the name Miltown invariably figured. The monitored script of an N.B.C. television program featuring Bob Hope affords a sufficient example of the Miltown jokes splashing from the home screen that spring:

> HOPE: Whether you like them or not, Khrushy and Bulgy are two of the smartest Russians alive. [Laughter.] The fact that they're alive still proves it. Now they want to come to the United States and sell us peace. Is this a switch? They must be spiking their vodka with Miltown. [Laughter.]
>
> Have you heard about Miltown? The doctors call Miltown the "I-don't-care" pill. The government hands them out with your income-tax blanks. [Laughter.]

While some of these comments scarcely tended to add to the dignity of a prescription drug, Hoyt, who over the years had spent millions on brief plugs for Little Liver Pills, could not help being impressed by the babble of publicity that Miltown was getting free. "I was frankly amazed at all the exposure we were getting," he said not long ago. "We had never anticipated such a development. Those television actors—hell, we hadn't even sent them free Miltown, or anything."

Altogether, the Wallace people thought that the publicity was wonderful. It did not occur to them until a little later on, when the full impact of the Miltown promotion had made itself felt, that it might be almost too wonderful. The unfortunate truth, it developed, was that many physicians were becoming increasingly hesitant about putting the word Miltown on prescriptions, because it was so familiar and easy to recognize—a clear breach of the hallowed medical tradition of not telling patients what they are getting. As a result, quite a few doctors who had been prescribing Miltown switched to the comfortably cryptic Equanil.

It was a hard thing for the Wallace people, after all their educational efforts, to find themselves thus hoist with their own petard, and Hoyt, in particular, was chagrined at the new twist of events. "I think it was primarily the unusual name of the product that caused us trouble," he said a while ago. "All those jokes on television—Miltown Berle! It was my own fault. I suppose I just shouldn't have got that idea of using the code name as a product name; I should have picked something more technical-sounding, I guess. It seemed like a good idea at the time, but it wasn't. Hell, when we went into research on shaving creams we code-named one of our experimental pressurized shaves Yonkers. Do you think we called it Yonkers? No, we called it Rise, and it's the best-seller in its field! Of course, I had no idea how the name Miltown was going to catch on. Frankly, I had no idea at the outset of the potential size of the meprobamate market. Well, the more I see in this business the more I know I just don't know. Let me tell you, when you're dealing with the general public, you're dealing with the great unknown. You're dealing with the public's subconscious, and when you're dealing with that, you just never know where you are. Never. Boy, if you ever *really* hit on the source of human motivations, you'd have something—you'd hit the jackpot."

ROCK 'N' ROLL'S YOUNG ENTHUSIASTS

Dwight Macdonald

NOVEMBER 29, 1958 (FROM "A CASTE, A CULTURE, A MARKET")

ROCK 'N' ROLL—the very term is orthographically unsettling. Here teenism reaches its climax, or its nadir—at any rate, its least inhibited expression. Here one may observe in their purest forms the teenagers' defiance of adult control, their dominance of certain markets, their tendency to set themselves up as a caste, and the tribal rituals and special dialect they have evolved. "The Big Beat is here to stay. The music market, for the first time in history, is completely dominated by the young set." So wrote Mr. Charles Laufer, editor of *'Teen.* In a later issue, a couple of tribesmen responded from Danbury, Connecticut: "We *absolutely, positively* agree that rock 'n' roll *has* to be here to stay. It's *our* music! The older generation has a tendency to go for classical music and standards. They have their place but so does rock 'n' roll, so why do they knock the beat? Rock 'n' roll is our way of showing how we feel. Fast music is a way of keeping up with the pace of the world. The world will be ours in a few years—so why fight it?" This tocsin rings ominously in adult ears, which find rock 'n' roll even less interesting musically than the insipid ballads that Crosby and Sinatra crooned to earlier generations of adolescents. It seems to consist of nothing but a simple beat and lots of noise; submerged in the pounding surf of rhythm, the tune is as hard to find as it is in Schoenberg.

Almost the only adult—except the adults making money from it—who regards rock 'n' roll as something more than a pain in the neck is the British anthropologist Geoffrey Gorer, who published some speculations on the subject in the magazine *Encounter* about a year ago. While he agreed that rock 'n' roll is musically dull ("remarkable only for its resolute rejection of the rhythmic complications and subtleties of jazz and ragtime"), he saw in the craze a great deal more than mere foolishness or perversity. Taking off from Nietzsche's contrast between Apollonian and Dionysian types (in the former "the values are order and proportion," in the latter "sensation and self-abandonment"), he suggested that rock 'n' roll is a Dionysian revolt against a predominantly Apollonian society, an instinctive effort to redress a balance that has swung too far from spontaneity, ecstasy, and "the full use . . . of the striped muscles."

One of the many reasons adults dislike rock 'n' roll is that it has largely driven other kinds of popular music off the airwaves. The disc jockeys play only the most popular records (the Top Twenty is the usual formula), and because their largest and most enthusiastic audience is teenage, rock 'n' roll seems to pound out twenty-four hours a day. There are now some three thousand disc jockeys—it is hard to believe that before 1935, when Martin Block invented the art form, there wasn't a single one—and they are a powerful force in the music market. Mr. Miller, of Columbia Records, thinks they have abused their power. Not long ago, he spoke bluntly to a convention of disc jockeys: "You went and abdicated your programming to the eight-to-fourteen-year-olds, to the preshave crowd that makes up twelve percent of the country's population and zero percent of its buying power, once you eliminate pony-tail ribbons, Popsicles, and peanut brittle. Youth must be served—but how about some music for the rest of us?"

Perhaps the chief adult objection to rock 'n' roll is to the sexy nature of the lyrics—*Variety* calls them "leerics"—and of the bumps and grinds executed by certain singers. The sexual overtones are odd, considering that the rock-'n'-roll audience is now believed to lie mostly between the ages of eight and fifteen—much younger than the crowd that listened to the crooners twenty years ago. Perhaps this is another instance of the striking tendency of the young in America to mature—or, anyway, to act independently of adult control—at an increasingly early age. The damage, however, may be less than alarmed parents fear. For all its Dionysian verve, rock-'n'-roll dancing is curiously sexless. "Despite the pelvic contortions of a few singers, and the double meanings in the words of some lyrics," Mr. Gorer writes, "I should consider rock 'n' roll the least sexual type of social dancing which Europe has seen in the last couple of centuries; instead of a stylisation of courtship and wooing, there is practically no physical contact nor opportunity for conversation; the dance can only be performed if the pair are in good rapport before they step on to the dance floor." The accuracy of this analysis may be verified by a look at a current television hit show—Dick Clark's *American Bandstand,* in which young Mr. Clark, a former disc jockey, presides over the revels of a roomful of teenagers, who rock 'n' roll to songs like "Skinny Minnie" ("She ain't skinny, she's tall, that's all"). The show has eight million look 'n' listeners, half of them adults (another example of the blurring of age lines), and provokes forty-five thousand letters a week, or the equivalent of four people sitting down to write Mr. Clark every minute of the day and night—God knows what about.

"The feeling that it's their own," mentioned by Mr. Miller, is largely an illusion. The Children's Crusade undoubtedly threw up some inspired teenage leaders, but the very notion of a crusade came from the grown-ups. Similarly, a fifteen-year-old may write or sing a rock-'n'-roll number, but, whether he knows it or not, his elders have been there before him. The term was coined by an adult disc jockey, Alan Freed—still a high priest of rock 'n' roll—who in 1949 began plugging, on Station WJW, in Cleveland, what were then called "race records"; that is, "rhythm" and "blues" numbers that appealed especially to Negroes. Freed thought whites might also go for this kind of music if it had a broader name, so he called his program "The Moondog Rock 'n' Roll Party." (The original

Moondog, a Times Square personage, eventually enjoined him from using that name, but no one has contested his right to "Rock 'n' Roll.") In 1952, Freed gave the first of several Moondog Balls, in the Cleveland Arena—or, rather, he intended to do so. The Arena has a capacity of ten thousand, and thirty thousand showed up, the result being a mild riot, no ball, and lots of publicity. In 1954, Freed made his first rock-'n'-roll broadcast over WINS, in New York, and the following year he gave two dances at the St. Nicholas Arena, into which seven thousand teenagers, or double the hall's capacity, jammed each time. In 1956, Columbia released the first rock-'n'-roll movie, *Rock Around the Clock,* starring Freed. In 1957, Freed put on a Christmas show at the New York Paramount, and it drew the biggest crowds in that theatre's history. There are now said, by not disinterested observers, to be four thousand Alan Freed Clubs here and abroad, and Freed is said, by the same observers, to receive ten thousand fan letters a week.

The great symbol of rock 'n' roll, of course, is not Alan Freed but Elvis Presley, the Southern back-country boy who began his big-time career only two years ago and who, before he was drafted, last March, received fifty thousand dollars for three brief TV appearances. As Freed stands for the blues-rhythm-Negro element of rock 'n' roll, so Presley stands for the country-music element—hillbilly songs, folk tunes, and cowboy ballads, most of them composed in Tin Pan Alley and all of them heavily corned with sentiment. Of the current rock 'n' rollers, Presley is by far the most vulgar, to use the word in its good sense (earthy) as well as its bad (coarse). Imitators on the order of Jerry Lee Lewis, recently extruded from England when it became known that his bride and travelling companion was thirteen, are just vulgar-bad. But Presley has a Greek profile, an impressive physique, lots of animal magnetism, and a not disagreeable singing voice; in fact, it is rumored that he had some talent before Hollywood and television got hold of him. Because of his uninhibited pelvic movements and the vulgar-good-bad way he sings his "leerics," most parents take an even dimmer view of Presley than of other rock 'n' rollers. For somewhat the same reasons, he has the most enthusiastic teenage following in the business. Wherever he sings, "I LIKE ELVIS" buttons sprout like mushrooms after rain.

Rock 'n' roll plays one more important part in the teenage syndrome. It is the teenagers' link to the nihilism of our time—to the Beat Generation and hipsterism. Except for a few precocious sports (in both senses of the word), even the rank-and-file hipsters are well out of their teens, while some of their leaders are positively venerable; Jack Kerouac is pushing forty, and Kenneth Rexroth will never see fifty again. Hipsters dig cool, or progressive, jazz, which is as intellectual as rock 'n' roll is primitive. Their culture heroes run from Buddha to the late Charlie Parker, a Negro saxophoning genius who had a lot to do with inventing progressive jazz, but definitely do not include Elvis, although there is a romantic feeling for the late James Dean, whom the teenagers have a super-romantic feeling for. Nor can it be said that rock 'n' roll is the kindergarten of hipsterism, since, in contrast to the Flaming Youth of the twenties, most teenagers quickly turn into Nice Young Married Couples. Hipsterism is a postgraduate course—the novelist Norman Mailer thinks "the hipsters may be the beginning of a new world revolution, like the Early Christians"—and most Americans never get beyond high school. Nevertheless, there is a connection. Rock-'n'-rolling teenagers are likely to express themselves—or, rather, to not express themselves—in the "hip" vocabulary, which is as eloquent as a stammer, as meaningful as a grunt. And they share the hipsters' contempt for respectability; they, too, feel alienated from adult culture (including spelling and grammar), and they, too, value Dionysian sensation as The Greatest and ever strive to Get With It. In the struggle with Apollo, the teenager is the temporary ally of the hipster, even if later on, in his twenties, he becomes the most Apollonian of credit managers.

THE PUSH-BUTTON PHONE

Harriet Ben Ezra

JULY 18, 1959 ("VARIABLES")

THE TELEPHONE PEOPLE are thinking—just thinking, mind you—of someday replacing dial telephones with push-button telephones, and have recently installed, on a trial basis, several hundred push-button telephones in Connecticut and Illinois. Dedicated as we are to bringing our readers the news behind the news, we no sooner got wind of this world-shaking development than we arranged to pay a call on Dr. John E. Karlin, head of the Human Factors Engineering Group of the Bell Telephone Laboratories, in Murray Hill, New Jersey. A native of South Africa, who started off in music at the University of Cape Town and wound up with a Ph.D. in psychology from the University of Chicago, Dr. Karlin was the first research psychologist ever to join Bell, an event that took place back in 1945. To give you some idea of the success he has since enjoyed in New Jersey, we will mention that it was Karlin who, in a series of brilliant experiments involving the latest type of dial telephone (the one that has the exchange letters and digits outside the dial wheel), discovered that people tended to dial more efficiently when they had a target to aim their fingers at, and therefore decreed that *a single white dot be placed under every hole on the wheel*! He has also played in the first-violin section of the Colonial Little Symphony, of Madison, New Jersey.

Dr. Karlin prefaced our discussion of push-button telephones with a glance at the big push-button picture. "Ours is a push-button era, but what do most people actually know about push buttons?" he asked. "They look simple enough, but the truth is that they bristle with scores of fascinating technological and psychological problems. It doesn't follow, for example, that an easy push button is the best push button. What if a push button controlling a mechanism of the greatest importance required so little effort that one became careless in its operation? It's especially necessary to have just the right kind of push buttons where human beings are under stress, as in, say, the Armed Forces. In my opinion, the relationship between men and push buttons epitomizes the fundamental relationship between men and machines. We at Bell have been carrying out a study of push buttons on an unprecedented scale, and we feel that our researches fill a crucial gap not only in the company's knowledge but in the knowledge of mankind as a whole."

Dr. Karlin indicated that Bell had first made sure that push-button telephones were technologically superior to dial telephones, then set out to discover whether they were psychologically superior as well. "We don't bring out new models every year, as the car people do," he said. "When we make a change, we have to be absolutely confident that it's a good change. Now, push-button telephones can get a number a lot faster than dial telephones. The average person can tap out a number with push buttons in about five seconds, which is a saving of four seconds over the dial system, and that not only increases efficiency at the central office but also, we were interested to learn, increases the user's efficiency. The faster you can get a number the easier it is to get it right, because memory falls off very rapidly with time, and just waiting for the dial wheel to return to position causes many people to forget a digit or two of an unfamiliar number. This matter of memory is only one aspect of the problem; all told, we've studied thirty-eight human-factor variables, in three categories."

The first of the three categories, Dr. Karlin told us, was configuration, or the pattern in which the push buttons were to be disposed. Should they be arranged like digits on a Comptometer, or like digits on an automobile speedometer, or like digits on a clockface? "We polled people at random, inviting design suggestions, then made up samples of the most popular choices—triangles, half-moons, and the like," he said. "Oddly enough, a lot of crosses turned up, but in practice they worked out very badly. We tested the various arrangements according to speed, accuracy, and how the users felt about them. The three samples that scored highest were an arrangement of push buttons similar to the present dial wheel; an arrangement of two horizontal rows of five buttons each; and an arrangement of three rows of three buttons each, with a single button below. Under laboratory conditions, all three seemed equally promising. We decided to use the three-rows-and-a-button-below arrangement in our field tests, because it's considered best from an engineering point of view."

The second category of human-factor variables involved what Dr. Karlin called "force displacement." "The things you have to know about the dynamics of push buttons!" he exclaimed. "How far should the button project from the surface of the phone? How far should it move? How much force should you have to exert to set it in motion? What about final force, which is the force you continue to exert once the button has been set in motion? What about snap, which is the click that can be mechanically put into a button to tell the pusher that he has pushed far enough for the action to take place? Snap happens in the middle of the button's downward journey. Should it be smooth or jerky? Finally, what kind of bottoming action do you want? Would you like a thud at the end, or would you prefer to sink gently into an imaginary ooze?"

Having settled these vexatious questions to their satisfaction, Dr. Karlin and his cohorts had to deal with the third category of variables, which he described as something of a catchall, dominated by the shape of the button top. "How big should a button top be?" he asked, again launching interrogatories to which we could supply no answers. "Should it be rectangular, square, or circular? Should it be flat or concave? Should it have a glossy or matte finish? And what color should it be? Suffice it to say that the buttons we're using in our field tests are about half an inch square and an eighth of an inch apart, are rectangular and flat, have a matte finish, and are white with black letters. Whether push-button phones will be in general use next year, or five years from now, or never is no concern of this department's. Our job was to state the human-factor requirements for the best possible push button, and we're pretty sure that nobody on earth knows more about them than we do."

THE ARRIVAL OF VIDEOTAPE

Louis P. Forster

AUGUST 8, 1959 ("TAPED")

THE UNEXPECTED DEBATE with which Premier Khrushchev and Vice-President Nixon opened the American National Exhibition in Moscow served to call attention to an extraordinary process that not only is revolutionizing commercial television but is having a marked effect on worlds as far apart as horse racing and medical education; to wit, Videotape recording. The Moscow debate got under way with Mr. Nixon explaining to Mr. Khrushchev that their words and images, the latter in color, were being set down on tape and would be played back immediately; Mr. Khrushchev appeared delighted, like a ham actor who can never see too much of himself. The subsequent discussion between the two having caused a sensation, the tape was rushed to this country by plane that very evening, and on the following evening innumerable duplicates, with an English translation of Khrushchev's remarks dubbed in over his voice, were being telecast from coast to coast.

Prompted by this transatlantic episode, we've been pestering the Ampex Corporation, whose prodigious baby Videotape recording is, to tell us something of its history and how it works. To begin with, the first experimental device for recording sound magnetically, on wire, was constructed by the Danish scientist Valdemar Poulsen, back in the nineties, but magnetic recording didn't catch on in a big way until the Second World War, when the Germans developed methods of recording on tape instead of on wire. The tape, a plastic coated with minute particles of iron oxide in a resinous base, is drawn over a recording head, where a magnetic field fluctuates in response to variations in the incoming electrical voltage, and the iron particles are instantaneously magnetized in a pattern conforming to those variations. The technical superiority of magnetic tape over other forms of recording, Ampex says, in a characteristically Latinic business prose, "is attributable to its capacity to record any variable which can be expressed as an electrical signal, over an extremely wide frequency range, and with minimum distortion of the recorded signal on reproduction. Magnetic tape is an unvarying and permanent record. Accuracy . . . does not deteriorate through repeated use; unwanted recordings may simply be erased by demagnetizing and the tape reused almost indefinitely. Magnetic tape is easily spliced and edited."

Ampex got into tape recording after the war. Urged on by Bing Crosby, who was tired of doing his radio shows "live" and was enchanted by the possibility of recording them in advance, at his convenience and yet with a happy minimum of distortion, the company produced, in 1948, "the first professional quality, high-fidelity tape recorder to be made in America" and promptly sold twenty to Crosby's employer, the American Broadcasting Company. With the rise of TV, it became obvious that TV shows should also enjoy the advantages of being recorded in advance; filming them, however, proved technically unsuccessful, for even the best kinescopes have always managed to look rather like forty-year-old Westerns. Ampex set to work developing a tape recorder capable of handling pictures as well as sound. Its engineers must have been a little dashed to discover that while a good sound tape recorder handles from fifteen to twenty thousand electrical impulses a second, a good picture tape recorder would have to handle *four million*. To fit this appalling number of impulses onto a conventional tape would mean using up a reel of tape as big as an automobile tire every ninety seconds. Ampex solved the problem by constructing a machine with four recording heads, all travelling at the rate of a hundred and six miles an hour and recording on separate channels of a two-inch-wide tape. An entire frame of a TV picture can be duplicated on a half inch of this tape, and an hour-long

TV show can be recorded on a single reel with a twelve-and-a-half-inch diameter. Ampex brought out its first Videotape recorder in 1956, priced at forty-five thousand dollars, and within five days had orders for four and a half million dollars' worth. The price is still forty-five thousand for a black-and-white job; a Videotape recorder like the one on display in Moscow, capable of recording and playing back in color, will cost you an extra twenty-nine thousand.

We mentioned that Videotape is a boon not only to commercial TV but to other worlds as well. The Ford Foundation, for example, is experimenting with Videotape in public-school education; astronomers are using Videotape to measure the cosmic field; closed-circuit televising of Videotaped surgical operations is becoming commonplace in medical schools and at medical conventions; and, last and most certainly least, race tracks all over the country are installing Videotape to record races, instead of filming them. The time saved at Yonkers Raceway by using Videotape, which can be instantly played back if a protest is made, instead of film, which must be laboriously processed, has made it possible for the track to schedule nine races a day instead of eight, for an increased gross of some thirty thousand dollars a day; thus the Yonkers recorder paid for itself halfway through the second day.

By way of postscript, we can't help wondering whether Khrushchev, hamming it up at the Exhibition, would have been amused, or only made more querulous, to learn that the founder of the Ampex Corporation is himself a Russian—Alexander M. Poniatoff, a flier in the Russian Navy during the First World War, who left Russia at the time of the Revolution and became an American citizen in 1932, and whose initials, combined with the "ex" in "excellence," gave the company its name.

THE QUIZ-SHOW SCANDALS

John Updike

OCTOBER 24, 1959 ("NOTES AND COMMENT")

FOR A LONG time now, we have suspected that there was something fundamentally wrong with the American political system, but we weren't sure what it was until the returns from the recent election in Great Britain had been analyzed. "Sir Oswald Mosley, Britain's Fascist leader of prewar years, was trounced in North Kensington so badly that he forfeited his deposit," said a short paragraph toward the end of a dispatch from London that appeared in the New York *Times* a day or two after that election. And the next day the *Times* noted that a number of Communist candidates had been similarly humiliated. In other words, these candidates had lost not only the election but their deposits. Ladies and gentlemen, friends and fellow-Americans, we give you the Deposit Plan. It would make every single one of our politicians think twice before deciding to take a chance. Whether a man wholeheartedly desired to be a candidate or was drafted by a reckless crowd of admirers, he would have to put up or shut up. And he would know that if he put up, he might he obliged to forfeit his deposit. Details, of course, would have to be worked out, but in general we favor a high deposit for all candidates for all public offices—equal, let us say, to the percentage of annual income that a thirty-thousand-dollar-a-year worker has to contribute toward the support of the federal government. A candidate shouldn't be penalized for excessive unpopularity, though. Under the Deposit Plan, a man who lost by a whisker would forfeit his deposit right along with the man who was badly trounced. What should be done in the case of the winners is, as they say in political circles, a question that requires further study.

. . .

The mysterious and awful thing about the television quiz scandals is not that the jaded souls who ran the show were hoaxers but that dozens, and perhaps hundreds, of contestants, almost all of whom must have applied in the simplicity of good faith, were successfully enrolled in the hoax. Now, as we remember the flavor and ethos of that innocent era, we realize that the contestants, aside from their freakish passion for Hittite history or skeet-shooting statistics, were meant to be us—you and me and the bright boy next door. This was America answering. This was the mental wealth behind the faces you saw in a walk around the block. The appeal of the programs, with the rising challenge of Soviet brain power as a backdrop, was ultimately patriotic; the contestants were selected to be a cross-section of our nation just as deliberately as the G.I.s in a war movie are. There we bravely sat in our living rooms, sweating it out with this or that Shakespeare-reading poultry farmer or chemistry-minded chorus girl, and there they were on the other side of the blurred little screen, patting (not wiping) their brows with handkerchiefs, biting their tongues as instructed, stammering out rehearsed answers, gasping with relief at the expected cry of congratulation. And we sat there, a nation of suckers, for years. It's marvellous how long it went on, considering the number of normal Americans who had to be corrupted to keep the cameras whirring. In all this multitude, not one snag, not one audible bleat, not one righteous refusal that made the news. The lid didn't blow off until, years afterward, a winner, disgruntled because he had not won more, was moved to confess and purge his guilt.

We are fascinated by the unimaginably tactful and delicate process whereby the housewife next door was transmogrified into a paid cheat. We picture her coming into the studio, a little weary still from yesterday's long plane trip, a bit flustered by the noise and immensity of the metropolis—Dorothy Dotto, thirty-eight, happily married for nineteen years, the mother of three, a member of the Methodist Church, the Grange, and the Ladies' Auxiliary. She lives, and has lived all her life, in the town of Elm Corners, somewhere in the Corn Belt; as a child, she won seven consecutive pins for perfect Sunday-school attendance, and she graduated with good grades from a public school where the remarkable truthfulness of George Washington and the durable axioms of Benjamin Franklin were often invoked. Her father, Jesse, who is retired but still alive (bless him), for forty years kept above his desk at the feed mill a sign declaring, "Honesty Is the Best Policy."

Our heroine meets the show's producer, dapper, dimpled Leonard Blough (pronounced "Bluff"), who takes her into a little room walled with aluminum and frosted glass:

Blough (*smiling and lifting from her arms a bundle, containing her lunch, that she has been clutching awkwardly*): Well, Mrs. Dotto, you did very well on the qualifying tests. Very well indeed.

Mrs. D. (*blushing*): Thank you. My dad always told me I had a good head for books; he wanted me to go on to normal school and be a teacher, but then I met Ralph, and—well, one thing led to another . . . (*Blushes more deeply*)

Blough: Ah, yes. Young love, young love. Well, Dorothy— You don't mind if I call you Dorothy?

Mrs. D.: Sakes, no!

Blough: We look forward to having you on our show. We know you're going to be a wonderful contestant.

Mrs. D.: Well, I hope so. It's a wonderful honor for me. When I think of all those folks back in Elm Corners watching, I'm afraid I'll get so nervous I won't be able to make a word come out of my mouth. We all watch, you know, every day, fair weather or foul.

Blough (*dimpling profusely*): That's the kind of tribute we value most. Dotty, I know you won't be nervous; we're a very close and friendly family on this show. By the way, the capital of Paraguay is Asunción.

Mrs. D.: Eh?

Blough (*consulting a paper on his desk*): A-s-u-n-c-i-o-n. Asunción. Better practice the Spanish accent in your hotel room tonight.

Mrs. D. (*flustering*): But— But— You think I might be asked that?

Blough (*his eyes narrowing thoughtfully*): Let's put it this way, Dot. The odds on your being asked the capital of Paraguay are as good as the odds on your being asked anything else. Do you follow me?

Mrs. D.: I— I— I'm not sure.

Blough (*looking her right in the eyes—a devastating effect*): I think you do. And—oh, yes—an animal that carries its young in a pouch is a marsupial. M-a-r-s—

Mrs. D.: Yes, I know that. But why are you telling me?

Blough (*leaning back in his chair and staring at the ceiling, which is one great fluorescent panel*): Let me try to express myself. I like you, honey. I think you have what it takes.

Mrs. D.: But you mean that all this is a fake—that all those people answering questions are told the answers ahead of time?

Blough: Come, come, let's not be nai-*eev*, dear. That's show biz.

Mrs. D.: But I thought— The whole idea— I mean what made it interesting—

Blough (*cunningly*): It *is* interesting, isn't it? I mean it's a good show. Now, it wouldn't be a good show if the clucks out there *knew,* but they don't *know,* so they're *happy*. Aren't they?

Mrs. D.: Well, but my daddy always had this sign over his desk—

Blough: And we don't want them to be *un*happy, do we? We don't want them, say, to have their own Mrs. D. show up as a dope tomorrow, do we? Listen, Sister, we can lace questions into you you won't even know what they *mean*. Now, listen to reason. Be a doll.

Mrs. D.: Well, I've come all this way—

Blough (*jubilant*): That's the girl! You're on! And when the time comes to take your dive, you'll take it, won't you? Huh?

Mrs. D. (*growing fairly cunning herself*): Not this side of three grand I won't.

Blough (*standing up, arms akimbo*): Baby! It's a deal! (*They embrace, and, as the Curtain Falls, the West Declines noticeably.*)

PART SIX

THE CRITICS

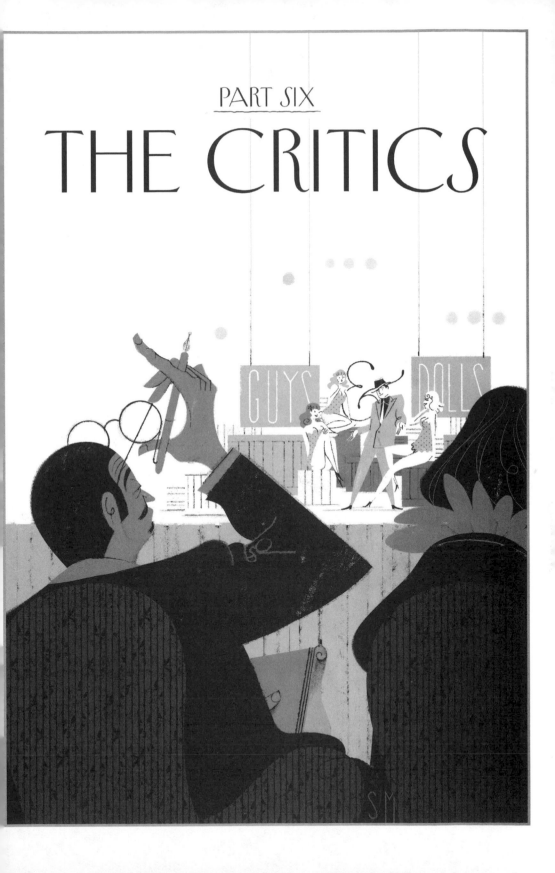

A NOTE BY ADAM GOPNIK

THE *NEW YORKER* began in the 1920s as a magazine of reporting and humor, and then, in the thirties, evolved into a magazine of reporting, humor, and serious, if mostly short, fiction. Only over time did it become what most of its readers think of it as now, a magazine of reporting, humor, longish short fiction, and serious—at times, strenuous—criticism. The 1950s, the decade we have under inspection here, was the time when that big change, already in motion the decade before, got fixed in place—the moment when a weekly dose of ambitious criticism became integral to the magazine's identity. But it is also nice to recall that in the fifties the magazine's original vein of cabaret criticism still flourished.

For a long time, criticism sneaked into the pages mostly if it could pass as humor. It often did, sometimes unforgettably so. Robert Benchley on the theatre, Dorothy Parker on books—these very good things were essentially there to entertain, certainly not to argue a professorial point, and much less to make a scholarly argument available to a bigger audience. They were fun in the first instance, and wise in the second. Wolcott Gibbs, who remained *The New Yorker*'s theatre critic throughout most of the fifties, at a time when this was generally considered the top critic's job, is here as a remaining master of that kind of criticism, and exhibits its special virtues. Critics like Gibbs are sometimes patronized as mere joke-makers, although in truth making the right jokes about the right works is even harder than making the right judgments about them, since the right jokes have to contain the judgments and be funny, too. What is easy to miss is the ease of the erudition underlining the entertainment: Gibbs's rapturous review of the opening night of *My Fair Lady* is credible because Gibbs knows Shaw inside out, and so can register what's tinny or un-Shavian in the show while taking true joy in something as purely Broadway as "The Rain in Spain."

Edmund Wilson on books and Lewis Mumford on architecture, along with the slightly-later-arriving Dwight Macdonald, were something different, actual big-league highbrows. They were men of letters (and of seminar rooms) in a way that their predecessors were not. This crucial passage in the magazine's life had already begun, best marked by the moment, in 1944, when Wilson replaced Clifton Fadiman as the magazine's most visible book critic. (Fadiman, it should be said, was by no means the mere book taster of later dismissals; Wilfrid Sheed remembered him as the most highbrow of the Book-of-the-Month Club judges. But he did become a Book-of-the-Month Club judge.) Wilson's mission, more or less openly stated, was to bring to the magazine serious discussion of the monuments of modernism—of the kind that he had already done so much to advance, in books like *Axel's Castle*. To read some of his admirers, one might imagine him to be a bilious and beetle-browed writer. In truth, Wilson was at his best when he was on fire and when he was having fun. Though not a particularly poetic writer—the basic Wilson sentence is foursquare to the point of sometimes being flat-footed—he remained a terrific judge of true and false poetry in others. In his specific judgments, he now seems to have batted around .300, which is the best anybody ever does (he got Tolkien and Kafka wrong; Dawn Powell and the Marquis de Sade exactly right), but his values seem nearly perfectly tuned. Though very much a man of the old school, he was an instinctive feminist, full of praise for and discernment regarding Powell and Edna Millay and Anita Loos.

Wilson was a distinguished literary historian—the kind of critic for whom historical criticism is always the most interesting kind of criticism. The publication in English of Pasternak's samizdat novel *Doctor Zhivago* was a big occasion: he rose to it, and pulled the magazine up with him. He had lots of historical work to do, explaining the evolution of the Russian state and its transformation by Leninism; and he had lots of literary work to do, too, explaining Pasternak's remnant Christian symbolism and Russian sources. Though many readers now might agree with Wilson's friend and correspondent Nabokov that *Doctor Zhivago* isn't as good as Wilson wanted it to be—he had a weakness for Big Books that expressed Significant Crises—the occasion was, in a way, even bigger than the book. His review was a milestone in the life of *The New Yorker,* the moment when the magazine became the place you went to find out how to start thinking about the big book everyone was talking about. If, in the forties, such criticism came in the side, it was soon walking right through the front door.

• • •

A question that must have kept William Shawn up nights, as editors are kept awake by such worries, was what to make of the popular culture that had taken such a surprising turn in the fifties. The magazine had always been up to its armpits in pop culture, being the source, addled or not, of a great many movies, from *Mister 880* to *The Secret Life of Walter Mitty,* not to mention Broadway hits like *Life with Father, My Sister Eileen, Wonderful Town,* and so on. What was new in the fifties was that pop culture now was becoming youth culture, a different thing. In a curious way, you can see an attempt to grapple with that youth culture in the playwright and diarist S. N. Behrman's review of J. D. Salinger's *The Catcher in the Rye*—one *New Yorker* regular reviewing the work of a younger regular, who was already one of the magazine's stars, and struggling to grasp a style and a sound as new to him as Brando's acting and Elvis's voice would soon become to everybody else. What comes through is both Salinger's originality of tone (the passages from *Catcher* that Behrman quotes seem to be coming from some completely new, contemporary planet) and Behrman's good will in coming to grips with it.

If there is a common preoccupation in the magazine's criticism during this decade, it is a distinctly American one, the great "middlebrow" question. Addressing that question is exactly what those big-browed critics were doing there in the back of the book. The fifties were a time when middlebrow culture, or "midcult," as Dwight Macdonald had dubbed it, was a living, even a dominant, form. What did "middlebrow" mean? These pages suggest that it referred to two things. One thing it meant was the fossilized reverence for relics of the literary and philosophical past, seen as monuments to admire rather than as living things to relish. This is the middlebrow of the once bestselling anthologist Mortimer Adler, and it is one that Dwight Macdonald mocks in a famous review collected here. Macdonald makes fun of the respect given to works of prestige, where most of the respect derived from the prestige and the prestige from the respect, in a hall-of-mirrors genuflection where no real art objects could be seen or touched or explored, or get much love or real attention for the charm or mischief or magic they contained. But then there is a second sense of what middlebrow could be, equally alive in the pages—a belief that art and ways of living once restricted to the rich should be available to the aspiring middle classes. It was this other form of middlebrow—the one that made Leonard Bernstein's conducting the Philharmonic front-page news—that *The New Yorker* itself was a part of. So, in the constant back-and-forth on middlebrow culture, we actually have a kind of civil war among its sects, with Macdonald our Josephus, the Jew turned Roman.

As with other things much mocked in their decade—train travel and piano bars belong here, too—this kind of midcult looks a lot better now that it's largely gone than it did when it was the one thing going. This midcult (which is as visible in the cartoons making puzzled fun of modern art, and in the magazine's ad pages of the era, where French perfumes and English riding boots are on sale for all) had its silly side, as aspirational cultures always do. But it helped to make a coherent whole that we look back on only in envy. Bad middlebrow makes people feel bad about what they don't know; the good kind makes people feel happy about what they *can* know. The first kind of middlebrow may be, as Macdonald believed, only a form of salesmanship, but the second is a base for citizenship. A country where people are expected to admire hard texts and remote authors, to read books they don't know and find that they like them more than they thought they might, is a country in pretty good shape culturally. One kind of middlebrow culture in the fifties produced dead volumes sitting on the shelf; another produced *My Fair Lady* and a readership desperate to know what to think about Russian dissident literature. The first, status-anxious kind of middlebrow helped to create the conditions for the second, aspirational-minded kind—anxiety about status helped feed an appetite for art.

The right tone was everything, as it always is. Like most cultural moments, the good and the bad in the fifties are all mixed up, with Mortimer Adler's Aristotle and Lerner and Loewe's Shaw singing from essentially the same hymnbook, though one sings solemnly and the other sings sweetly. Back in the fifties, many kinds of critics struck tuning forks of different notes. John Lardner pioneered television criticism for the magazine, and found a tone of sardonic disbelief nicely mingled with surprised appreciation. Lardner was Ring's son, and, as with the father, the son's newspaper background helped him toward a wise-guy style not too infatuated with itself, rather like that of Murray Kempton later on. (Lardner later devoted himself to an understandably unfinished history of drinking in America.)

Whitney Balliett, just beginning his five-decade career as a nonpareil jazz writer, simply assumed that jazz was art. He set himself the task of fine description, for which one needed the gifts of a poet and the patience of a private eye on a stakeout. Sitting in the back of bars and nightclubs, Balliett returned with the essential id of several generations of jazz musicians. Robert M. Coates, meanwhile, wrote art criticism with an astonishing clarity of eye. His forte was not the historical dimension—the grasp (which his successor Harold Rosenberg notably possessed) of how the avant-garde picture stands in relationship to what came before it and what now comes after it—but his grasp of what's before you when you actually look at a Pollock remains thrilling.

Finally, Kenneth Tynan, the Angry Young Man arriving from London to take over the theatre job after Gibbs's death, in 1958, turned out to be a cavalier dandy, showing himself, against expectations, to be a passionate lover of that quintessential middlebrow form, the musical comedy. One of the things that made the young men so angry in London, it seems, was that all the British musical shows were so creaky, compared with the American ones. In his review here of the Sondheim-Styne masterpiece *Gypsy,* Tynan shows that he was aware that he would need to think and write about these things in a self-conscious way that his predecessor hadn't, but the thoughts he had weren't so far removed from where Gibbs, the cabaret critic, ended up in writing on *My Fair Lady.* Tynan's judgment on *Gypsy* is simple and right and solves the midcult equations perfectly: "a machine has been assembled that is ideally fitted to perform this task and no other," he says, and "since the task is worth while, the result is art." It was then, and remains now, the only sure sanity on the subject.

BOOKS

S. N. BEHRMAN

THE VISION OF THE INNOCENT

AUGUST 11, 1951 (ON *THE CATCHER IN THE RYE* BY J. D. SALINGER)

HOLDEN CAULFIELD, THE sixteen-year-old protagonist of J. D. Salinger's first novel, *The Catcher in the Rye,* which has been published by Little, Brown and chosen by the Book-of-the-Month Club, refers to himself as an illiterate, but he *is* a reader. One of the tests to which he puts the books he reads is whether he feels like calling the author up. He is excited about a book by Isak Dinesen and feels like calling her up. He would like to call up Ring Lardner, but an older brother has told him Lardner is dead. He thinks *Of Human Bondage* is pretty good, but he has no impulse to put in a call to Maugham. He would like to call up Thomas Hardy, because he has a nice feeling about Eustacia Vye. (Nobody, evidently, has told him the sad news about Hardy.) Mr. Salinger himself passes his unorthodox literary test with flying colors; this reader would certainly like to call *him* up.

Mr. Salinger's brilliant, funny, meaningful novel is written in the first person. Holden Caulfield is made to tell his own story, in his own strange idiom. Holden is not a normal boy. He is hypersensitive and hyperimaginative (perhaps these are synonymous). He is double-minded. He is inexorably self-critical; at various times, he refers to himself as yellow, as a terrible liar, a madman, a moron. He is driven crazy by "phoniness," a heading under which he loosely lumps not only insincerity but snobbery, injustice, callousness to the tears in things, and a lot more. He is a prodigious worrier. ("When I really worry about something, I don't just fool around. I even have to go to the bathroom when I worry about something. Only, I don't go. I'm too worried to go.") He is moved to pity unconscionably often. He has few defenses. For example, he is driven frantic by a scrawled obscenity some vandal has chalked on the wall of his ten-year-old sister Phoebe's school. Grown men sometimes find the emblazoned obscenities of life too much for them, and leave this world indecorously, so the fact that a sixteen-year-old boy is overwhelmed should not be surprising. When another boy steals his gloves, Holden can't just go up to the boy's room, accuse him of stealing his gloves, and hit him in the jaw. He is scared by what he imagines the culprit's face will look like while his jaw is being demolished. ("I can't stand looking at the other guy's face, is my trouble. It wouldn't be so bad if you could both be blindfolded or something.") He is also worried by the lack of an acute sense of ownership; he didn't really care about losing the gloves in the first place.

The book covers Holden's last day at Pencey, a fashionable prep school, from which he has flunked out, and the following two days, which he spends in hiding in New York City. Stradlater, Holden's roommate, is handsome, gross, and a successful amorist. On Holden's last night at school, a Saturday night, he is in a frenzy of jealousy because Stradlater has dated up Jane Gallagher, with whom Holden is in love. The hero and heroine of this novel, Holden's dead brother Allie and Jane Gallagher, never appear in it, but as they are always in Holden's consciousness, together with his sister Phoebe—these three constitute his emotional frame of reference—the reader knows them better, finally, than the characters Holden encounters, who are, except for Phoebe, marginal. It is characteristic of Holden that although he is crazy about Jane, always thinking of her, always wanting to call her up, he never does call her up. He is always about to but doesn't, because he's never "in the mood." ("You really have to be in the mood for that stuff.") Perhaps he means that circumstances and his feelings are always too chaotic at the particular moment—that he wants to appear before Jane when everything is in order and he is in control of himself. Or perhaps he wishes to keep his memory of Jane inviolate and consecrated, like his memory of Allie; perhaps he is afraid of finding her innocence tarnished—not in a sexual sense, because eventually he is sure that Stradlater didn't "get to first base with her," but simply of finding her no longer what she was, possibly finding that she has become, in short, a phony. He keeps calling up a girl named Sally Hayes, whose manifest phoniness gives him "a royal pain," but he writes that off as the overhead of sex. He can never risk it with Jane.

While Stradlater is shaving before going to meet Jane, he asks Holden to write a classroom composition for him. "Anything descriptive," Stradlater says. "A room. Or a house. . . . Just as long as it's as descriptive as hell. . . . Just don't do it *too* good, is all. . . . I mean don't stick all the commas and stuff in the right place." The implication that all there is to writing a composition is a sense of direction about commas also gives Holden "a royal pain." "I mean," he explains, "if you're good at writing compositions and somebody starts talking about commas. Stradlater was always doing that. He wanted you to think that the only reason *he* was lousy at writing compositions was because he stuck all the commas in the wrong place. . . . God, how I hate that stuff!"

While Stradlater is out with Jane, Holden, knowing his roommate's technique on the back seats of cars, takes terrific punishment from his imagination. Nevertheless, he sits down to write a composition for the absent Don Juan:

> The thing was, I couldn't think of a room or a house or anything to describe the way Stradlater said he had to have. I'm not too crazy about describing rooms and houses anyway. So what I did, I wrote about my brother Allie's baseball mitt. It was a very descriptive subject. It really was. My brother Allie had this left-handed fielder's mitt. He was left-handed. The thing that was descriptive about it, though, was that he had poems written all over the fingers and the pocket and everywhere. In green ink. He wrote them on it so that he'd have something to read when he was in the field and nobody was up at bat. He's dead now. He got leukemia and died when we were up in Maine, on July 18, 1946. You'd have liked him. He was two years younger than I was, but he was about fifty times as intelligent. He was terrifically intelligent. His teachers were always writing letters to my mother, telling her what a pleasure it was having a boy like Allie in their class. . . . They really meant it. But it wasn't just that he was the most intelligent member in the family. He was also the nicest, in lots of ways. He never got mad at anybody. . . .

When Allie died, Holden took it hard:

> I was only thirteen, and they were going to have me psychoanalyzed and all, because I broke all the windows in the garage. I don't blame them. I really don't. I slept in the garage the night he died, and I broke all the goddam windows with my fist, just for the hell of it. . . . It was a very stupid thing to do, I'll admit, but I hardly didn't even know I was doing it, and you didn't know Allie. My hand still hurts me once in a while, when it rains and all, and I can't make a real fist any more—not a tight one, I mean—but outside of that I don't care much. I mean I'm not going to be a goddam surgeon or a violinist or anything *any*way.

Holden copies Allie's poems from his baseball mitt. He tells you casually, "I happened to have it with me, in my suitcase." Very much later, we discover that the only person to whom Holden has ever shown this mitt is Jane. ("She was interested in that kind of stuff.") Allie is always there. Sitting in his hotel room in New York, Holden feels he is sunk, and he starts talking to Allie. He remembers that he and another boy were going on a bicycle jaunt with their BB guns, and Allie asked to come along, and Holden wouldn't let him:

> So once in a while, now, when I get very depressed, I keep saying to him, "Okay. Go home and get your bike and meet me in front of Bobby's house. Hurry up." It wasn't that I didn't use to take him with me when I went somewhere. I did. But that one day, I didn't. He didn't get sore about it—he never got sore about anything—but I keep thinking about it anyway, when I get very depressed.

Holden is always regretting that you didn't know Allie. "You'd have liked him," he keeps saying: the human impulse to make a silent voice audible to others, a lost essence palpable.

By the time Stradlater returns from his date with Jane, Holden is sure that he has slept with her, and Stradlater helps him to think so, without being actually caddish. Stradlater asks for the composition; he is furious when he reads it, because it is about a baseball glove rather than a room or a house. Holden tears the composition up. He has a fight with Stradlater and gets a bloody nose. Shortly after that, he decides he can't stay another minute in Pencey and will go to New York, though his parents don't expect him until Wednesday.

Holden goes to say goodbye to Mr. Spencer, his nice old history teacher. It worries the boy that while his teacher is saying edifying valedictory things to him, he becomes acutely concerned about the winter quarters of the ducks in the Central Park lagoon. ("I was wondering if it [the lagoon] would be frozen over when I got home, and if it was, where did the ducks go. I was wondering where the ducks went when the lagoon got all icy and frozen over. I wondered if some guy came in a truck and took them away to a zoo or something. Or if they just flew away.") This worry about the ducks stays with Holden all through his adventures in New York. On his second night, he has an irresistible impulse to go to Central Park and see what the ducks are doing. In his avidity to find them, he pokes in the grass around the lagoon, to see if they are sleeping there, and nearly falls in the water. No ducks. Beginning to shiver, he is sure he is going to die of pneumonia, and he decides to sneak into his parents' apartment to see Phoebe once more before he dies.

This Phoebe is one of the most exquisitely created and engaging children in any novel. She is herself a prolific novelist, who is not deterred from starting a new book merely because she hasn't finished the last one. They are all about an attractive girl detective named Hazle Weatherfield. Hazle's father is "a tall attractive gentleman about 20 years of age." When Holden tiptoes into Phoebe's room, she is asleep. As befits an author, Phoebe has numberless notebooks. Before Holden wakes Phoebe, he has a look at her notebooks and her schoolbooks. Phoebe's middle name is Josephine, but Holden finds "Phoebe Weatherfield Caulfield 4B–1" written on the flyleaf of her *Arithmetic Is Fun!* Phoebe keeps changing her middle name, according to caprice. In a little list of variations, Holden finds "Phoebe Weatherfield Caulfield, Esq." "Kids' notebooks kill me," Holden says. He devours Phoebe's.

Holden wakes Phoebe. The moment she opens her eyes, she wants to know whether Holden has received her letter announcing that she is going to appear in a school play, *A Christmas Pageant for Americans*. "It stinks but I'm Benedict Arnold," she tells him excitedly. "I have practically the biggest part." Then, after her theatrical excitement simmers down, she remembers that Holden wasn't expected home until Wednesday, and she learns that he has been kicked out of school. She hits him with her fist. "Daddy'll *kill* you!" she cries. Holden lights a cigarette and tries to explain, but can't get much further than saying that the school was full of phonies and they depressed him. "You don't like *anything* that's happening," she says. This accusation, in which Holden recognizes that there is a fundamental truth, also depresses him. He tries desperately to justify himself. He enumerates things and people he does like—his brother Allie, for instance. Phoebe replies sagely that it is easy to like people who are in Heaven. Holden, miserable, cannot marshal all his likes. There was, he remembers, a frail boy who was so bullied by some thug schoolmates that he jumped out of a window to escape them. A teacher, Mr. Antolini, picked the boy up and put his own coat around him—"He didn't even give a damn if his coat got all bloody"—and for this teacher Holden has always had a special feeling. Near Phoebe, Holden begins to feel better. They turn on the radio and dance. Holden's parents come back from a late party, and Holden hides in a closet. Phoebe, to allay her mother's suspicions, says she has been smoking. Then, when Holden is about to leave, she gives him her Christmas money. She is terribly distressed by her brother's plight, but she cannot resist flaunting a private triumph:

> While I was walking towards the door, old Phoebe said, "Holden!" and I turned around.
>
> She was sitting way up in bed. She looked so pretty. "I'm taking belching lessons from this girl, Phyllis Margulies," she said. "Listen."
>
> I listened and I heard *something* but it wasn't much. "Good," I said.

Everybody, says Holden, accuses him of acting twelve years old. It's partly true, he admits, but not all true, because "sometimes I act a lot older than I am—I really do—but people never notice it." These perpetual insistences of Holden's—"I really am," "I really do," "It really does"—after he has explicitly said something, reveal his age, even when he is thinking much older, as when he says, "People always think something's *all* true." Although Holden thinks lots of things are funny, he hasn't much sense of humor; he has the deadpan literalness and the all-or-nothing combativeness of the passionate adolescent. Salinger's use of reiteration and redundancy in Holden's self-communion conveys this. After a passage describing his schoolmate Robert Ackley as pimply, dirty, disgusting, and nasty, and as having a terrible personality, he tells you, "I wasn't too crazy about him, to tell you the truth." He had been to the movies, which he hates, with this boy and another, and they both "laughed like hyenas at stuff that wasn't even funny," and then he tells you, after this harrowing experience, "I didn't even enjoy sitting next to them in the movies." The "even" is odd and characteristic. After a full confession about how he feels when Jane and Stradlater are out in the car, he tells you, "I don't even like to talk about it, if you want to know the truth." He is so aware of the danger of slipping into phoniness himself that he has to repeat over and over "I really mean it," "It really does." When he is not communing with himself but is in actual situations, these reiterations disappear; the dialogue and the descriptions are economical and lean.

The literalness and innocence of Holden's point of view in the face of the tremendously complicated and often depraved facts of life make for the humor of this novel: serious haggles with belligerent taxi-drivers; abortive conversational attempts with a laconic prostitute in a hurry; an "intellectual" discussion with a pompous and phony intellectual only a few years older than himself; an expedition with Sally Hayes, which is one of the funniest expeditions, surely, in the history of juvenilia. Holden's contacts with the outside world are generally extremely funny. It is his self-communings that are tragic and touching—a dark whirlpool churning fiercely below the unflagging hilarity of his surface activities. Holden's difficulties affect his nervous system but never his vision. It is the vision of an innocent. To the lifeline of this vision he clings invincibly, as he does to a phonograph record he buys for Phoebe (till it breaks) and a red hunting cap that is dear to him and that he finally gives to Phoebe, and to Allie's baseball glove. He has a hunger for stability. He loves the Museum of Natural History because the figures in the glass cases don't change; no matter how often you go, the Eskimo is still there catching fish, the deer drinking out of the water hole, the squaw weaving the same blanket. You change the circumstances of your visit—you have an overcoat on one time when you didn't before, or you may have "passed by one of those puddles in the street with gasoline rainbows in them," but the squaw and the deer and the Eskimo are stable. (It was the reason Keats liked the suspended attitudes of the figures on the Grecian urn.) Holden knows things won't remain the same; they are dissolving, and he cannot reconcile himself to it. He hasn't the knowledge to trace the process of dissolution or the mental clarity to define it; all he knows is that he is gasping in the avalanche of disintegration around him. And yet there is an exhilaration, an immense relief in the final scene of this novel, at the Central Park carrousel with Phoebe. ("I felt so damn happy all of a sudden, the way old Phoebe kept going around and around.") Holden will be all right. One day, he will probably find himself in the mood to call up Jane. He will even become more tolerant of phonies—it is part of the mechanics of living—as he has already had to endure the agony of saying "Glad to've met you" to people he isn't glad to have met. He may even, someday, write a novel. I would like to read it. I loved *this* one. I mean it—I really did.

V. S. PRITCHETT

GREEN ON DOTING

MAY 17, 1952 (ON HENRY GREEN)

SINCE HE WROTE *Living,* in 1928, we have had in Mr. Henry Green a novelist who has gone off on his own. He has been the most curious imagination in the English novel during the last twenty years, for though Miss Compton-Burnett's dramatic confection of Greek tragedy and Jane Austen is stranger, it has never altered, whereas Mr. Henry Green's aquariums always contain different fish. He changes the water, the greenery, the exquisite or the plain inhabitants, from book to book. His people are often bizarre, but that is because they are normal; they live in the backs of their minds. He belongs to the mad tradition in English literature—Sterne, Carroll, Firbank, and Mrs. Woolf are predecessors. The strain seems to spring from the injury done to certain English minds by the main, conventional emphases of English life. During high periods, this has produced lyrical poetry; in prose, it has led to fantasy and wit. This morbid mind often underlies the fierce, light-headed polish of artificial comedy, and here Mr. Henry Green has, not surprisingly, arrived in his last two books. In *Nothing* and, now, *Doting* (Viking) one seems to hear a quietly raging Congreve, or some other Restoration dramatist, exposing his freaks, terrors, and brutalities as he carries his comedy to formal perfection. Like *Nothing, Doting* is a classical comedy of manners; it has the hard streak of upper-class life. In stringently cutting these books down to arabesques of dialogue, he has taken the English novel back to one of its sources—the theatre. And there every word has to point, every situation has to tell.

The matter and machinery of classical comedy is always deceptively trivial; what counts is the texture. In *Doting* this lies in Mr. Green's phenomenal ear for the follies of talk. The scene is hardly described—two smartish London flats, an expensive restaurant, a bar, a couple of night clubs. The characters are types—a middle-aged couple, the raffish, cliché-uttering friend of the family, all in the higher taxation group: a son home from school, and two young girls. Plot: the casual-seeming but unsleeping intrigue of the wife, keeping both men off the girls and dishing everyone, with the naïve hypocrisy, the tender but relentless cunning, of the undefeatable English lady. The shocked ghost of Henry James will appear to the reader as he treads a world so superficially familiar but so shot to pieces. Society has vanished. The "young person" on the brink of life is still eager to begin, but there is nowhere to begin. She is innocent still, despite her heavy talk of "bed"; the game of innocence has not changed now all the cards are on the table.

Then, in default of values or personal security, we have "arrangements." Mr. and Mrs. Middleton have their sacred arrangement about "going out" on their own. (Mrs. Middleton "never counts teas.") There is always something someone doesn't count. Annabel and Claire have their arrangement to meet so many times a week and tell lies about their love affairs. (Who knows when a poor girl will be asked out next? Only the middle-aged can afford it.) Addinsell, the old friend of the family—a considerable character—has a peculiar arrangement about death: the memory of his wife, who died in childbirth, is a sacred injustice. ("Not her fault, good God! If anything, might have been mine, or equally the fault of each of us, in actual practice.") He relies on the defense of this singularity:

> "You've never been left with a child on your hands."
>
> "Well, no, I suppose not."
>
> "So there you are."
>
> "But you mustn't hold it against your wonderful Penelope."
>
> "Don't know what you mean. No one's fault when they die in bed, is it? Can't see how that could be."

> "Then why not marry a second time?" Ann asked, in a bewildered voice. "Another mother for your child?"
>
> "Might die again" the man replied with obvious distaste.

Naturally, he makes an ass of himself with a girl smart enough to say her parents are dead. We laugh, but the Middletons and Addinsell are worried hunters in the wilderness of middle age, bewildered by time and by their lost significance, condemned to be tragic as well as absurd. Their conversation is beautifully inadequate to their condition.

The Middleton couple have their love. Their double bed is the centerpiece of the book. But love itself is a habit constructed by eighteen years—Mr. Middleton calls it nineteen when he is in a temper—and to a young girl like Annabel it seems like an institution the middle-aged have made in order to escape from their private terrors. By a fluke, the brainless little piece is right; in all his novels Henry Green's characters are eaten alive by time and are terrified of it. And time does not merely eat; it snaps like a shark. They see death, like a bad joke, everywhere—the scream of the cancer ward, the crunch of the road accident, old Arthur Morris in *Nothing* having his leg cut off bit by bit. Pain gives a maniacal edge to the wild laughter that lies between the absurd lines.

The consolation is doting. Doting may simply be the schoolboy angrily doting on his food; everyone, he snarls, is trying to starve him. Or doting may start with Arthur Middleton asking Annabel to open her mouth:

> Her wet teeth were long and sharp, of an almost transparent whiteness. The tongue was pointed also and lay curled to a red tip against her lower jaw, to which the gums were a sterile pink. Way back behind, cavernous, in a deeper red, her uvula seemed to shrink from him. But it was the dampness, the cleanliness, the fresh-as-wet-paint must have made the man shut his lips tight, as, in his turn, he leaned over hers and it was then, or so he, even, told his wife after, that he got, direct from her throat, a great whiff of flowers.

"Sex!" cries Arthur Middleton, in a line of proper Restoration annoyance and brutality. "How they wave it about at you."

Again, doting may start because, nowadays, with no hostesses, no dances, and no money, how else is a girl to meet people? Addinsell dotes girls into bed with his tragic face, after talking about wonderful dead Penelope. Mrs. Middleton dotes on people she intends to dish, because she is doing it "all for dear Peter," her son. The comedy begins when doting leads to cross-doting, when the partners of the comedy of manners change and rechange. Here Mr. Green is superbly clever, quick, and surprising. In the jealous quarrels of Mr. and Mrs. Middleton, for example, he has Molière's trick of the repeated or echoing line.

"But Arthur, your *hand*!" accuses Mrs. Middleton, as yet again she remembers the scene in her bedroom when she caught Arthur kneeling beside Annabel, who had taken her skirt off to wash out the stain of the coffee Arthur had spilled on her. We join in Mrs. Middleton's incantation. "Your hand, Arthur!" we cry, too. Where *was* Arthur's hand? *Qu'est-elle allée faire dans cette galère?* Arthur may deny. Arthur may explain. But no; once again "Your hand, Arthur—I saw it." Arthur is as hypnotized by this invention of his wife's as we are. How brilliant of Mr. Green, after this, to show Mrs. Middleton rushing off in the full glory of jealousy to go one better and tell old Addinsell, "I found them naked in my bed."

As an oblique study of *mœurs* and a discreet exposure of character, *Doting* is as ingenious as *Nothing* was. It is true there is no scene as rich in folly as the ludicrous birthday party in *Nothing,* nor is Mrs. Middleton, who is a doting, respectable wife with her claws out, quite as deep in folly as that aging octopus of the twenties, Mrs. Weatherby. Taxation keeps down the tone. But *Doting* is both tenderer and more spirited, and each character comes to precise, foolish bloom. The boy Peter, public-school-stunned, is excellent; a minor character, he has three dimensions and pretty well kicks a hole in the book with his clumsy boots. Mrs. Middleton stops one of her wifely scenes dead to remark that Peter has caught his first salmon, and goes to bed with her husband at once. After eighteen years, marriage in the English upper classes is agreeably unlike *The Kreutzer Sonata.*

Mr. Henry Green is not a satirist like Waugh. He is not a conventional moralist off the peg like Maugham. He is not outside, he is inside the human zoo, preoccupied with it, and occasionally giving a sad, startled look at the bars he had momentarily forgotten. He is not—despite appearances in *Nothing* and *Doting*—a true artificial writer, for he is fundamentally sympathetic, and his real interest is in the blurred, the lethargic, inarticulate part of human beings, the wound that becomes their quotidian poetry. The groping soldier returned from the prisoner-of-war camp in *Back,* with his maimed memory; the mean servants of *Loving,* who nevertheless drool the poetry of self-interest like a collection of stumbling and deceiving doves; the woman dimming toward death in *Party Going*—these are people whose fantasies and inner fever he has invaded by way of the comedy of their muddled minds. He is a kind of psychologist-poet who begins to make people out of blots. In these books he has a compassion and sensibility that are cut down in *Nothing* and *Doting,* perhaps because the upper classes have a surface harder to penetrate, perhaps because, in contemporary Society, they have become too automatically the funny class that servants used to be. Certainly the people and their interests are trivial, when they are compared with the people in *Back,* but so are Congreve's. The comedy of manners depends on the supply of idiotic, normal blanks.

ANTHONY WEST

BLACK MAN'S BURDEN

MAY 31, 1952 (ON *INVISIBLE MAN* BY RALPH ELLISON)

RALPH ELLISON'S FIRST novel, *Invisible Man* (Random House), is an exceptionally good book and in parts an extremely funny one. That is not to say that it is without defects, but since they are almost entirely confined to the intolerably arty prologue and epilogue, and to certain expressionist passages conveniently printed in italics, they can easily be skipped, and they should be, for they are trifling in comparison with its virtues. What gives it its strength is that it is about being colored in a white society and yet manages not to be a grievance book; it has not got the whine of a hard-luck story about it, and it has not got the blurting, incoherent quality of a statement made in anger. What gives it its character is a robust courage; it walks squarely up to color the way seventeenth-century writing walks up to mortality and death, to look it in the face as a part of the human situation that has to be lived with. Mr. Ellison's hero is a Negro of the South who starts out with the naïve illusion that what stands between him and the whites is a matter of education. He is given a scholarship to a Southern college that has been endowed by Northern philanthropists, and he goes to it in great delight, thinking that what he will learn there will pare away all his disabilities and disadvantages. He finds that the college cannot do that for him and does not even try to do it; it is concerned only with helping him make realistic adjustments to things as they are. He gets into a mess of trouble and is expelled. Before expelling him, the dean tells him just what the facts of colored life are:

> "You have some vague notions about dignity. . . . You have some white folk backing you and you don't want to face them because nothing is worse for a black man than to be humiliated by white folk. I know all about that too. . . . But you'll get over it; it's foolish and expensive and a lot of dead weight. You let the white folk worry about pride and dignity—you learn where you are and get yourself power, influence, contacts with powerful and influential people—then stay in the dark and use it!"

He is too young and too nobly stubborn to believe that this is the best that can be done with his life, and the rest of the book deals with his attempts to force the world to accept him on a pride-and-dignity basis, and with his final realization that he has to stay in the dark as an invisible man. This could easily be a glum and painful performance, but Mr. Ellison has the real satirical gift for handling ideas at the level of low comedy, and when he is most serious he is most funny. The technique is that of which *Candide* is the supreme example, but there is nothing archaic about the writing, which has an entirely contemporary vitality and a quite unexpected depth.

The first chapter is a little slow, but the second and third, which describe the trouble that leads to the hero's expulsion, convince one that Mr. Ellison is a writer with much more than promise. The hero is asked by the dean to drive one of the white Northern patrons of the college on a brief afternoon airing. By an unlucky chance, he takes the man past the house of the most notorious Negro no-good in the neighborhood, a man who is the embodiment of what Negro progressives call, and with hatred, field niggerism. The Northerner insists on stopping and talking to the monster, and a scene ensues that is an extraordinary piece of comic invention. Even when it is read over in a cold, analytical frame of mind and its purely entertaining aspects are set aside, it stands out as a startlingly good piece of writing. The monster's account of his misdeeds is in itself a tour de force—at once a brilliant parody of a kind of Southern genre writing about Negroes and an acute description of a psychopath's feeling about his actions, which includes, in a couple of sentences, a deadly cartoon of the relations between a genuine psychopathic criminal and members of the more optimistic schools of psychiatry. But excellent as that is, it is nothing to what Mr. Ellison makes the passage do on a more serious level. The student's reaction to the monster's story takes one deep into the feeling of one sort of Negro about another, but his reaction to the Northerner's reception of it takes one even further—into the heart of the very complex feeling between races. The Northerner's philanthropic interest in Negro education is a cover for a form of prurience, a voyeur's fascination. His real interest is in the Negro as an inferior kind of man, closer to the animal, more capable of letting drive on the lines of instinctive impulse and less restrained by civilized morality and patterns of conduct. Giving money to the college offers him a high-toned way of getting as close to these dark possibilities as he dares. It is easy to accuse Mr. Ellison of letting racial paranoia get out of hand in this particular character, and of producing an overdrawn caricature in consequence. But the attitude he is describing is a fairly common one, and is often given direct expression—even by writers of great delicacy and sensibility—despite its offensiveness. A poem called "The African," in the Literary Supplement of the London *Times* a while ago, put it very flatly:

> . . . I fell to brooding
> On bronze-dark features facing me, the glazed
> Soft shine of jet-black eyes; on what a London
> His Congo-born, his secret vision gazed
> So gently, mournfully; beyond his waking
> Quiet behavior what still potent background
> Vast and primeval worked, what violence
> Ancestral under silences profound.

The poem, presumably toying with some symbolism about a gracious innocence, went on to compare the man to swans on a pond, but even so it is hard to think that it would be pleasant to be on the receiving end of this sort of thing. Mr. Ellison tries to show just what it is like to take it from behind bronze-dark features, and does so remarkably well.

A good deal of the book is concerned with penetrating to the unease and self-consciousness that underlie a great many earnest white progressive approaches to The Question. After the student is kicked out of college, he goes North to try to make his way in New York, and his adventures are told in a highly imaginative, picaresque story, but, though the storytelling is excellent, in the end the impressive thing is the analysis of attitudes that rises out of each situation; there are always such sharpness of observation, such awareness of shades of feeling, at work. The hero is caught up in what is clearly an agitprop apparatus of the Communist Party (Mr. Ellison does not, though, give it that name) that is exploiting the color situation in Harlem. He is a natural speaker and he is made use of in campaigns as a front for the white committee. There is not only perceptive writing about the feeling between Negro and white in this part of the book but there is also perhaps the best description of rank-and-file Communist Party activity that has yet appeared in an American novel. The endless committee discussions of tactics, and the post-mortems after the hero's speeches, in which the nature and extent of his departures from "correct" lines are thrashed out, have an absolute authenticity. So has the picture of the way in which the interplay of personalities inside the movement, and the constant intriguing to use the Party disciplinary machinery to advance one clique and set back another, takes place. At last, the hero discerns the rank stink of falsity in the Party line about color, partly through catching on to the way in which a white Comrade who has married a colored girl makes play with the fact to strengthen his hand in policy discussions of district tactics, partly through a realization that the white Comrades have used him as a lure, as a Negro gull to gull other Negroes. He sees that his district leader, Brother Jack, is just as much Marse Jack as a field boss in a white-supremacy state. The description of his disillusion with the Party, a true agon, which is also his final understanding that there is no external machine that can produce any ready-made solution either to the color problem or to his own perplexities, is as moving and vivid a piece of writing on this difficult subject as one could wish to read.

The book ends with a second tour de force, as successful as the brilliant comedy scene in the Southern college town that is, in effect, the book's starting point. The Party has lost control of its agitation campaign as a result of what at first seems to the hero to be a typical tactical blunder, and the mass support that it has won drifts over to a straight anti-Communist and anti-white agitator called Ras, whose wild speeches bring on a wave of rioting and looting. The drift into disorder and the spread of violence are astonishingly well described in realistic terms, and through it all Mr. Ellison never loses touch with his gift for comic invention. As the riot builds up, the hero realizes that not only have the Communists an unfriendly interest in him but that he is due for unpleasantness from Ras's strong-arm men, who have him marked down as their enemy and a tool of the whites. He disguises himself in bourgeois finery, but the colored glasses and white hat he dons to put him across the class frontier also turn him into the double of a numbers racketeer called Rinehart, who is heavily involved in quite enough trouble for two men. The hero's evasions as all Harlem comes apart have a real nightmare humor. And in the middle of it all, as the riot squads and the mounted police move in and shooting begins, he suddenly sees what is happening. The Party has not made a tactical blunder at all; it has deliberately surrendered its mass following to Ras in order to provoke violence, so that colored martyrs, shot down by the police, can be exploited in the next phase of agitation in the district. The hero emerges in his own identity to warn the innocents he has helped to fool what is being done to them. But Mr. Ellison has a tight grip on his satiric comedy, and he is not going to let his buffoon hero escape into tragedy; martyrdom is not to be *his* fate. A gang of white looters chase him up a dark street, and he falls through an open manhole into a coal cellar. The whites, enraged by this surprising vanishing trick, slam the manhole cover down and leave him lying there helpless while the riot burns itself out above.

Few writers can have made a more commanding first appearance. Up to a point, *Invisible Man* resembles Céline's *Death on the Installment Plan*. Its humor recalls the jokes that hang on Céline's fraudulent scientist, with his ascents in worn-out and patched balloons, his absurd magazine, and his system of electromagnetic plant culture, but Ellison's jokes are on the whole funnier, and his satire is much more convincing because there is clearly visible behind it—as there is not in Céline—a positive alternative to the evils he is attacking, the knowledge of a better way without which all satire becomes merely an empty scolding. It is a pity that Mr. Ellison's direct statement of the better way takes the form it does in the prologue and the epilogue, since they are the two worst pieces of writing. But the ideas toward which they fumble are as dignified as they are impressive, and it is perhaps unnecessary to have this direct statement, as they are so plainly implied in the rest of the book. It is not merely the Negro who has to realize that the only escape from the rattrap of worry about what one is or is not is to abandon the constant tease of self-consciousness. The Invisible Man of Mr. Ellison's title is the unattached man of Aldous Huxley's Perennial Philosophy, the man with courage to be utterly indifferent to himself and to his place in the world, the man who is alone free to be fully a man.

DWIGHT MACDONALD

THE BOOK-OF-THE-MILLENNIUM CLUB

NOVEMBER 29, 1952 (ON MORTIMER ADLER'S GREAT BOOKS SET)

FOR $249.50, WHICH is (for all practical purposes) $250, one can now buy a hundred pounds of Great Books: four hundred and forty-three works by seventy-six authors, ranging chronologically and in several other ways from Homer to Dr. Mortimer J. Adler, the whole forming a mass amounting to thirty-two thousand pages, mostly double-column, containing twenty-five million words squeezed into fifty-four volumes. The publisher of this behemoth, which cost almost two million dollars to produce, is the Encyclopædia Britannica, which is jointly owned by Senator William Benton of Connecticut and the University of Chicago. The books were selected by a board headed by Dr. Robert Hutchins, formerly chancellor of the University of Chicago and now an associate director of the Ford Foundation, and Dr. Adler, who used to teach the philosophy of law at the University of Chicago and who now runs the Institute for Philosophical Research, an enterprise largely financed by the Ford Foundation. The novelty of the set and to a large extent its raison d'être is the Syntopicon, a two-volume index to the Great Ideas in the Great Books. The Syntopicon ("collection of topics") was constructed by a task force commanded by Dr. Adler, who also contributes 1,150 pages of extremely dry essays on the Great Ideas, of which, according to his census, there are exactly a hundred and two. It also contains 163,000 page references to the Great Books, distributed under 2,987 topical subdivisions of the Great Ideas, plus an Inventory of Terms (which includes 1,690 ideas found to be respectable but not Great), plus a Bibliography of Additional Readings (2,603 books that didn't make the grade), plus an eighty-page essay by Dr. Adler on "The Principles and Methods of Syntopical Construction," and it cost the Encyclopædia just under a million dollars. If these facts and figures have an oppressive, leaden ring, so does this enterprise.

"This set of books," says Dr. Hutchins in *The Great Conversation,* a sort of after-dinner speech that has somehow become Volume I of Great Books, "is the result of an attempt to reappraise and reembody the tradition of the West for our generation." For some, this might take a bit of doing, but Dr. Hutchins makes it sound as easy as falling off a log (with Mark Hopkins on the other end): "The discussions of the Board revealed few differences of opinion about the overwhelming majority of the books in the list. The set is almost self-selected, in the sense that one book leads to another, amplifying, modifying, or contradicting it." But if the criterion of selection really was whether a book amplifies, modifies, or contradicts another book, one wonders how any books at all were eliminated. Actually, the Board seems to have shifted about between three criteria that must have conflicted as often as they coincided: which books were most influential in the past, which are now, which ought to be now. Cicero and Seneca were more important in the past than Plato and Aeschylus but are less important today; in excluding the former and including the latter, the Board honored the second criterion over the first. On the other hand, devoting two volumes apiece to Aristotle and Aquinas could be justified only by their historical, not their contemporary, interest. The third criterion was involved here, too; these philosophers are important to the Adler-Hutchins school of thought, and the Board doubtless felt that if they are not important in modern thought, they damned well should be. My objection is not to this method of selection—jockeying back and forth between conflicting criteria is the essence of the anthologist's craft—but to the bland unawareness of it shown by the impresarios, Dr. Hutchins and Dr. Adler, who write as if the Truth were an easy thing to come by. This doctrinaire smugness blinds them to the real problems of their enterprise by giving them mechanical, ready-made solutions that often don't fill the bill.

• • •

The wisdom of the method varies with the obviousness of the choice, being greatest where there is practically no choice; that is, with the half of the authors—by no means "the overwhelming majority"—on which agreement may be presumed to be universal: Homer, the Greek dramatists, Plato, Aristotle, Thucydides, Virgil, Plutarch, Augustine, Dante, Chaucer, Machiavelli, Rabelais, Montaigne, Shakespeare, Cervantes, Bacon, Descartes, Spinoza, Milton, Pascal, Rousseau, Adam Smith, Gibbon, Hegel, Kant, Goethe, and Darwin. A large second category seems sound and fairly obvious, though offering plenty of room for discussion: Herodotus, Lucretius, Epictetus, Marcus Aurelius, Tacitus, Aquinas, Hobbes, Locke, Berkeley, Hume, Swift, Montesquieu, Boswell, Mill, Marx, Tolstoy, Dostoevski, and Freud. The rest of the list depended entirely upon the Board, and in this case the choice seems to be mostly foolish. Only two selections are both daring and sound: *Moby Dick* and William James' *Psychology*. The former is, of course, well known but could easily have been passed over; the latter is an extraordinarily rich and imaginative work that has been overshadowed by the Freudian vogue. The Freud volume, with no less than eighteen books and papers in it, gives an excellent conspectus of Freud's work; the Marx volume, on the other hand, contains only the Communist Manifesto and Volume I of *Capital* (misleadingly titled, so that it suggests it is the whole work), which is barely the ABC of Marx's political thought. This unevenness of editing is prevalent. There is a provincial overemphasis on English literature at the expense of French; we get Boswell, *Gulliver, Tristram Shandy,* and *Tom Jones* but no Molière, Corneille, or Racine, and no Stendhal, Balzac, or Flaubert. This is what might be called an accidental eccentricity, the kind of error any board of fallible mortals might make. But most of the eccentricities are systematic rather than accidental, springing from dogma rather than oversight.

A fifth of the volumes are all but impenetrable to the lay reader, or at least to this lay reader—the four devoted to Aristotle and Aquinas and the six of scientific treatises, ranging from Hippocrates to Faraday. "There is a sense in which every great book is always over the head of the reader," airily writes Dr. Hutchins. "He can never fully comprehend it. That is why the books in this set are infinitely rereadable." I found these ten volumes infinitely unreadable. There is a difference between not fully comprehending Homer and Shakespeare (in that one is always discovering something new on rereading them) and not even getting to first base with either a writer's terminology or what he is driving at. Aristotle and Aquinas should have been included, I would say, but four volumes is excessive. Furthermore, no expository apparatus is provided, no introduction relating their *Weltanschauung* to our own, no notes on their very special use of terms and their concepts. Lacking such help, how can one be expected to take an interest in such problems, vivid enough to Aquinas, as "Whether an Inferior Angel Speaks to a Superior Angel?," "Whether We Should Distinguish Irascible and Concupiscible Parts in the Superior Appetite?," "Whether Heavenly Bodies Can Act on Demons?," and "Whether by Virtue of Its Subtlety a Glorified Body Will No Longer Need to Be in a Place Equal to Itself?" In fact, even *with* help, one's interest might remain moderate. In the case of a philosopher like Plato, essentially a literary man and so speaking a universal human language, the difficulty is far less acute, but Aquinas and Aristotle were engineers and technicians of philosophy, essentially system builders whose concepts and terminology are no longer familiar. The difficulty is much more urgent in the six volumes of scientific work, so urgent that almost no expository apparatus would suffice. A scientific work differs from a literary, historical, or philosophical work (the three categories, aside from science, into which the Great Books fall) partly because it is written in a language comprehensible only to the specialist (equations, diagrams, and so on) and partly because its importance is not in itself but in its place in the development of science, since it has often been revised, edited, and even superseded by the work of later scientists. Milton, on the other hand, does not supersede Homer; Gibbon represents no advance over Thucydides. All this is pretty obvious, but in this one instance, the editors of the Great Books exhibit a remarkable capacity for overlooking the obvious. Their dogma states that all major cultural achievements are of timeless, absolute value, and that this value is accessible to the lay reader without expository aids if he will but apply himself diligently. Because science is clearly part of our culture, they have therefore included these six useless volumes without asking themselves what benefit the reader will get from a hundred and sixty double-column pages of Hippocrates ("We must avoid wetting all sorts of ulcers except with wine, unless the ulcer be situated in a joint." "In women, blood collected in the breasts indicates madness." "You should put persons on a course of hellebore who are troubled with a defluction from the head." "Acute disease come [*sic*] to a crisis in fourteen days") or how he can profit from or even understand Fourier's *Analytical Theory of Heat* and Huygens' *Treatise on Light* without a special knowledge of earlier and later work in these fields.

Another drawback is the fetish for Great Writers and complete texts, which results in a lot of the same thing by a few hands instead of a more representative collection. Minor works by major writers are consistently preferred to major works by minor writers. Thus nearly all Shakespeare is here, including even *The Two Gentlemen of Verona,* but not Marlowe's *Dr. Faustus* or Webster's *Duchess of Malfi* or Jonson's *Volpone.* Nearly all Milton's poetry is here, but no Donne, no Herrick, no Marvell, or, for that matter, any other English poetry except Chaucer and Shakespeare. We get Gibbon in two huge volumes but no Vico, Michelet, or Burckhardt; six hundred pages of Kant but no Nietzsche or Kierkegaard; two volumes of Aquinas but no Calvin or Luther; three hundred pages of Montesquieu's *Spirit of Laws* but no Voltaire or Diderot. Even if in every case the one right author had been elected to the Great Writers' Club, which is not the situation, this principle of selection would give a distorted view of our culture, since it omits so much of the context in which each great writer existed.

. . .

So much for the selection, which, for all its scholastic whimsicality, is the most successful aspect of the enterprise.[1] Having caught your goose, you

1. It is certainly much sounder than the selection offered by its long-established and still active competitor, Dr. Eliot's celebrated Five-Foot Shelf, the Harvard Classics. Half the authors on Dr. Adler's shelf (which also measures, by chance or ineluctable destiny, five feet) appear on Dr. Eliot's, but only eight are represented by the same works; the rest appear in extracts or in shorter works, for if Dr. Adler overdoes the complete text, Dr. Eliot goes to the opposite extreme. Among the Great Books authors whose work doesn't appear in the Classics at all (if one ignores a few snippets) are Aristotle, Thucydides, Aquinas, Rabelais, Spinoza, Gibbon, Hegel, Marx, Tolstoy, Dostoevski, and Freud. On the other hand, since Dr. Eliot went in for variety above all, he did include, though often in unsatisfactory snippets, many writers omitted by Dr. Adler. No less than ten of his fifty volumes are anthologies, and while this is overdoing it, surely the Great Books would have been enriched by a few, such as one of English poetry and one of political writing since the French Revolution. Some of Dr. Eliot's choices are as eccentric as some of Dr. Adler's (though Eliot produced nothing as fantastic as the six volumes of scientific treatises): Robert Burns gets a whole volume, Manzoni's *I Promessi Sposi* another, and Dana's *Two Years Before the Mast* a third. But in some ways the Classics are a better buy. For one thing, they cost only half as much. And for another, there is an amateurish, crotchety, comfortable atmosphere about them that is more inviting than the ponderous professionalism of the Great Books. Moreover, while Dr. Eliot is overfond of the brief sample, the chief practical use of such collections may well be as a grab bag of miscellaneous specimens, some of which may catch the reader's fancy and lead him to further explorations on his own. When I was a boy, I enjoyed browsing in the family set of the Classics, but browsing in the Great Books would be like browsing in Macy's book department.

must cook it. But the editors are indifferent cooks. They have failed to overcome the two greatest barriers to a modern reader's understanding and enjoyment of the Great Books—that their authors were largely foreigners in both place and time.

Only a third of them wrote in English; almost all of them were citizens of strange countries fifty to three thousand years away. Except for a few scientific works, apparently no translations were commissioned for this undertaking. The existing translations of prose writers are probably adequate, and some are classic. But just two of the verse translations seem good to me: Rogers' Aristophanes and Priest's *Faust.* (I speak of reading pleasure, not of their fidelity. But I assume, first, that a work of art is intended to give pleasure, and that if it does not, the fault lies either with the writer, a thought too unsettling to be entertained in the case of the Great Books, or with the translator; and, second, that if any writer, Great or not, wrote verse he must have had in mind the effect of verse, in which the unit of form is the rhythmical line rather than the sentence or the paragraph, and that a prose rendering which runs the lines together produces something that is to poetry as marmalade is to oranges.) Rhoades' Virgil and Cookson's Aeschylus are in verse, but they are dull and mediocre, the former smoothly so and the latter clumsily so. Charles Eliot Norton's prose Dante is unbelievably graceless ("In my imagination appeared the vestige of the pitilessness of her who . . ." "While I was going on, my eyes were encountered by one, and I said straightway thus . . ."). Jebb's Sophocles and E. P. Coleridge's Euripedes are in that fantastic nineteenth-century translator's prose ("Yon man . . ." "Ay me! And once again, Ay me!" "Why weepest thou?" "Thus stands the matter, be well assured." "In fear of what woe foreshown?"). Homer is in Samuel Butler's translation, the best prose version extant, except for T. E. Lawrence's *Odyssey,* and far better than the Wardour Street English of Butcher-Lang-Leaf-Myers, but it is still prose, and Homer was a poet. In prose, he reads like a long-winded novel. It is not as if there were no excellent modern verse renderings of the Greeks: Richmond Lattimore's *Iliad,* published last year by Dr. Hutchins' own University of Chicago, and the eleven plays by various hands in Dudley Fitts' *Greek Plays in Modern Translation,* put out by Dial in 1947. At modest expenditure, the editors could have used these translations and commissioned others that would have for the first time made all the Greeks, Virgil, and Dante readable in English. However, since to the editors the classics are not works of art but simply quarries to be worked for Ideas, they chose instead to spend a million dollars in compiling that two-volume index, or Syntopicon.

On principle, they have ignored the other barrier, time. "The Advisory Board," Hutchins writes, "recommended that no scholarly apparatus be included in the set. No 'introductions' giving the editors' views of the authors should appear. The books should speak for themselves, and the reader should decide for himself. Great books contain their own aids to reading; that is one reason why they are great. Since we hold that these works are intelligible to the ordinary man, we see no reason to interpose ourselves or anybody else between the author and the reader." (The Doctor doesn't explain why scholarly introductions represent an editorial interposition between author and reader while a two-volume Syntopicon does not.) It is true that our age tends to read about the classics instead of reading them, to give such emphasis to the historical background that the actual text is slighted, and the Adler-Hutchins school is quite right in combatting this tendency. But surely, without distracting the reader from the text, a "scholarly apparatus" could have given the essential information about the historical and cultural context in which each work appeared and have translated terms and concepts whose meaning has changed with time. For example, while some of the theories advanced in James' *Psychology* are still fruitful, others are not—a fact that the modest and admirably pragmatic James would have been the first to accept—and the general reader would profit from such an expert discussion of the point as is provided in Margaret Knight's introduction to a recent Pelican anthology of James' writings on psychology. By presenting the complete text with no comment or exposition, the Board of Editors implies it is a "classic," timeless and forever authoritative, which of course is just what they want to suggest. This is not my concept of a classic. Nor do I agree with Dr. Hutchins when he implies that indoctrination ("giving the editors' views") is the only function of an introduction. There is a difference between informing the reader and telling him what to think that seems to escape Dr. Hutchins, possibly because in his case there isn't any difference.

• • •

We now come to the question: Why a set at all? Even if the selection and the presentation were ideal, should the publishers have spent two million dollars to bring out the Great Books, and should the consumer spend $249.50 to own them? Some of the more enthusiastic Great Bookmanites seem to think The Books have been preserved for us only through the vigilance of their leaders. Last spring, Clifton Fadiman, in the expansive atmosphere of a Waldorf banquet for the founding subscribers, saluted those present as "you who are taking upon yourselves . . . the burden of preserving, as did the monks of early Christendom, through another darkening . . . age the visions, the laughter, the ideas, the deep cries of anguish, the great eurekas of revelation that make up our patent to the title of civilized man" (applause). But with or without the present enterprise, the eurekas and the deep cries of anguish would continue to resound. The publishers themselves state that all but twenty-one of the four hundred and forty-three works are "generally available in bookstores and libraries." Most of the Great Books can be had in inexpensive reprints, and almost all the rest can be bought for less than the five dollars a volume they cost in this set. This presents a dilemma: Those who are truly interested in books probably already have most of these, while those who don't may be presumed not to be ardent readers, and not in a mood to spend two hundred and fifty dollars. Even when need and desire coincide, as in the case of young bookworms (if such there still are), it is more fun—and cheaper—to buy the books separately. Not only that, but sets, especially of different authors, are monotonous and depressing; books, like people, look better out of uniform. It bothers me to see *Tristram Shandy* dressed like the *Summa Theologica*. Milton should be tall and dignified, with wide margins; Montaigne smaller, graceful, intimate; Adam Smith clear and prosaic; and so on. Mr. Rudolph Ruzicka has done his best, by varying the type faces and the title pages, to give variety and distinction to the set. In this respect, and in the binding, he has made a vast advance over the Harvard Classics (no great feat). But he has put nearly everything into double columns, which I find textbookish and uninviting. (Even the Classics are not double-column.) This was doubtless necessary for the lengthier books, but such slim volumes as Homer, Dante, Hegel, Bacon, and Rabelais get the same treatment. Rabelais looks particularly grotesque in this textbook format. There is, however, one work in the set to which double columns are admirably suited: Dr. Adler's Syntopicon.

. . .

With this formidable production I shall now grapple. I have already pointed out that insofar as the set has a raison d'être, the Syntopicon is it. It is, however, a poor substitute for an introductory apparatus. According to Dr. Adler, "this gargantuan enterprise" represents "about 400,000 man-hours of reading . . . over seventy years of continuous reading, day and night, seven days a week, week in and week out from birth on." Since he did not start reading at birth and is not seventy, he had to call in some help; the Syntopicon is "the product of more than one hundred scholars working for seven years," which is to say that a hundred scholars worked on it at one time or another during the seven years of preparation. (The staff fluctuated between twenty and fifty people.)

The first step was to select not some Great Ideas but The Great Ideas. A list of seven hundred was whittled down to a hundred and two, extending from Angel to World and including Art, Beauty, Being, Democracy, Good and Evil, Justice, Logic, Man, Medicine, Prudence, Same and Other, Theology, and Wisdom.[2] These were broken down into 2,987 "topics," the top sergeants in this ideological army, the link between the company commanders (the hundred and two Great Ideas) and the privates (the 163,000 page references to the Great Books). Thus the references under "Art" are arranged under twelve topics, such as "3. Art as imitation," "7a. Art as a source of pleasure or delight," "8. Art and emotion: expression, purgation, sublimation." With Dr. Adler as field marshal, coach, and supreme arbiter, the "scholars" (bright young graduate students who needed to pick up a little dough on the side and latched on to this latter-day W.P.A.) dissected the Great Ideas in the Great Books and, like mail clerks, distributed the fragments among the topical pigeonholes, the upshot being that, in theory, every passage on "Art as a source of pleasure or delight" in the Great Books from Homer to Freud ended up in "Art 7a." Finally, Dr. Adler has prefaced the references under each Great Idea with a syntopical essay that summarizes the Great Conversation of the Great Writers about it and that reads like the Minutes of the Preceding Meeting as recorded by a remarkably matter-of-fact secretary.

2. Inevitably, the choice was more than a little arbitrary: to the naked eye, such rejected ideas as Fact, Faith, Sex, Thought, Value, and Woman seem as "great" as some of those included. However, the Doctor has appended to his Syntopicon those sixteen hundred small ideas, running from A Priori to Zoology via such way stations as Gluttony (see Sin), Elasticity, Distinctness, Circumcision (see God), and Daydreaming (see Desire). This Inventory relates each of these small ideas to the Great Ideas (or Great Idea) under which references pertinent to the small ideas can be found, and all one needs to find one's way around in the Syntopicon is some sort of idea, Great or small (plus, naturally, plenty of time and determination).

The Syntopicon, writes Dr. Adler, is "a unified reference library in the realm of thought and opinion," and he compares it to a dictionary or an encyclopedia. Words and facts, however, can be so ordered because they are definite, concrete, distinguishable entities, and because each one means more or less the same thing to everyone. Looking them up in the dictionary or encyclopedia is not a major problem. But an idea is a misty, vague object that takes on protean shapes, never the same for any two people. There is a strong family resemblance between the dictionaries of Dr. Johnson, Mr. Webster, and Messrs. Funk & Wagnalls, but every man makes his own Syntopicon, God forbid, and this one is Dr. Adler's, not mine or yours. To him, of course, ideas seem to be as objective and distinct as marbles, which can be arranged in definite, logical patterns. He has the classifying mind, which is invaluable for writing a natural history or collecting stamps. Assuming that an index of ideas should be attempted at all, it should have been brief and simple, without pretensions to either completeness or logical structure—a mere convenience for the reader who wants to compare, say, Plato, Pascal, Dr. Johnson, and Freud on love. Instead, we have a fantastically elaborate index whose fatal defect is just what Dr. Adler thinks is its chief virtue: its systematic all-inclusiveness. (He apologizes because it is not inclusive enough: "It is certainly not claimed for the references under the 3,000 topics that they constitute a *full* collection of the relevant passages in the great books. But the effort to check errors of omission was diligent enough to permit the claim that the references under each topic constitute an adequate representation of what the great books say on that subject.") This approach is wrong theoretically because the only one of the authors who wrote with Dr. Adler's 2,987 topics in mind was Dr. Adler. And it is wrong practically because the reader's mental compartmentation doesn't correspond to Dr. Adler's, either. Furthermore, one needs the patience of Job and the leisure of Sardanapalus to plough through the plethora of references. Those under Science, which take up twelve and a half pages, begin with four lines of references to Plato, which took me an hour to look up and read. Sometimes, as when one finds sixty-two references to one author (Aquinas) under one subdivision of one topic under one idea (God), one has the feeling of being caught in a Rube Goldberg contraption. Again, under Justice ("2. The precepts of justice: doing good, harming no one, rendering to each his own, treating equals equally"), one is referred to "Chaucer, 225a–232a, esp. 231b–232a," which turns out to be the entire "Reeve's Tale," a bit of low comedy that one of the mail clerks threw into this pigeonhole apparently because Chaucer stuck on a five-line moral at the end ("esp. 231b–232a"). The one method of classification that would have been useful was not employed; there is no attempt to distinguish between major and minor references. An important discussion of Justice in Plato has no more weight than an aside by Uncle Toby in *Tristram Shandy,* although it is common practice to make such a distinction by using different type faces or by putting the major references first.

"What the Corpus Juris does for the legal profession," Dr. Adler has said, "the Syntopicon will do for everyone." That is, as lawyers follow a single point of law through a series of cases, the reader can follow one topic through the Great Books. The Doctor is simply carrying on his mistaken analogy with the dictionary. The structure of law, although intricate, is a rigid framework within which concepts are so classified and defined that they mean exactly the same thing to everybody. Yet Dr. Adler actually suggests that the best way for the beginning reader, wholly unfamiliar with the Great Books, to get acquainted with them is to follow chosen topics through a series of works whose context he knows nothing about.

It is natural for Dr. Adler to compare his Syntopicon with the Corpus Juris, since he has been a teacher of the philosophy of law and a writer about it, and his mind is essentially a legalistic one. He aspires to be the great codifier and systematizer of Western culture, to write its Code Napoléon. The Syntopicon is merely the first step toward this goal. At his Institute for Philosophical Research, another group of scholars is working with him, using the Syntopicon, to produce "a dialectical summation of Western thought, a synthesis for the twentieth century." The most celebrated attempt at such a summation was, of course, the *Summa Theologica* of Thomas Aquinas, Dr. Adler's guide and inspirer. Aquinas had certain advantages over his disciple; the culture he summarized was homogeneous, systematically articulated, and clearly outlined, because of the universal acceptance of the Roman Catholic faith as expressed in the Bible and by the Church Fathers. Dr. Adler cannot bring these qualities to and make them a part of twentieth-century thought, but he proceeds as if he could, and he has run up his own homemade substitutes for the sacred writings. Thus the true reason for his set of Great Books becomes apparent. Its aim is hieratic rather than practical—not to make the books accessible to the public (which they mostly already were) but to fix the canon of the Sacred Texts by printing them in a special edition. Simply issuing a list would have been enough if practicality were the only consideration, but a list can easily be revised, and it lacks the dramatic, totemistic force of a five-foot, hundred-pound array of books. The Syntopicon is partly a concordance to the Sacred Texts, partly the sort of commentary and interpretation of them the Church Fathers made for the Bible.

In its massiveness, its technological elaboration, its fetish of The Great, and its attempt to treat systematically and with scientific precision materials for which the method is inappropriate, Dr. Adler's set of books is a typical expression of the religion of culture that appeals to the American academic mentality. And the claims its creators make are a typical expression of the American advertising psyche. The way to put over a two-million-dollar cultural project is, it seems, to make it appear as pompous as possible. At the Great Bookmanite banquet last spring, Dr. Hutchins said, "This is more than a set of books. It is a liberal education. . . . The fate of our country, and hence of the world, depends on the degree to which the American people achieve liberal education. [It is] a process . . . of placing in the hands of the American people the means of continuing and revitalizing Western civilization, for the sake of the West and for the sake of all mankind." This is Madison Avenue cant—Lucky Strike Green Has Gone to War, The Great Books Have Enlisted for the Duration. It is also poppycock. The problem is not placing these already available books in people's hands (at five dollars a volume) but getting people to read them, and the hundred pounds of densely printed, poorly edited reading matter assembled by Drs. Adler and Hutchins is scarcely likely to do that.

EDMUND WILSON

FROM

DOCTOR LIFE AND HIS GUARDIAN ANGEL

NOVEMBER 15, 1958 (ON *DOCTOR ZHIVAGO* BY BORIS PASTERNAK)

IN DEALING WITH *Doctor Zhivago*, the novel by Boris Pasternak, the reviewer—not to end on a dampening note—proposes to reverse the usual procedure and discuss the translation first. This translation was made in England by Max Hayward and Manya Harari (though the poems which compose the last chapter are translated by Bernard Guilbert Guerney); the copyright page of the American edition (Pantheon) shows that it was revised over here; and a lack of coordination between these several hands may be part of the explanation of the unsatisfactoriness of this English version. But, comparing it with the Russian text—which has been announced for December publication by the University of Michigan Press—one has the impression that a project which, if properly carried out, might well have taken many months has been put through in too much of a hurry and without the translators' having beforchand sufficicntly studicd thc book.

All this is not said, however, to discourage you from reading the novel, which is one of the very great books of our time. Tolstoy and Turgenev first made their impression in translations that were sometimes far less competent than that of Harari and Hayward. The good thing that can be said for this version is that it reads well, it does not sound translated. And it is the triumph, in any case, of the literary genius of the Russians, master storytellers, master moralists, that they have been able to leave their language and a good deal of their style behind, to submit to be stripped of so much, and yet hold the world spellbound.

. . .

Doctor Zhivago has no doubt been much read—like other books that promise to throw some light on the lives of our opposite numbers in the

Soviet Union—out of simple curiosity. But it is not really a book about Russia in the sense that the newspaper accounts of it might lead the reader to expect; it is a book about human life, and its main theme is death and resurrection.

Dr. Zhivago is the hero of the story, and though Zhivago is a real Russian name—there was a nineteenth-century painter called Zhivago—it is obvious that Pasternak wants to suggest *zhivoy,* "alive, living" (to one form of which it almost corresponds), as well as *zhizn',* "life," and *zhit',* "to live." These words are constantly used by Zhivago in his arguments against the deadness of political abstractions and the tyranny of government control. One is reminded, in reading *Zhivago,* of Yeats's constant insistence on the importance in literature of "the crooked way of life" as distinguished from "inorganic, logical straightness." One may not at first notice this dominant theme, though it is first announced on page 9 (of the translation) and repeated on page 67. One is likely to be so much surprised at finding a book from the Soviet Union which pays no deference to the official ideology, which has been written completely outside it on assumptions that have nothing in common with Marxism, that one does not at first quite know where one is. Then one realizes that where one is with Pasternak is exactly where one is oneself, at home in the great literary tradition of bold thinking and original art.

Pasternak is as much an example of the intellectual man of the world as Pushkin or Turgenev or Tolstoy, yet he is saturated with Russian life and language in a way that makes most Soviet writing look like diagrams drawn up in offices. His father was a painter, his mother a musician; he studied philosophy in Germany, and he evidently, like Zhivago, before the first war, lived a good deal in Eastern Europe. At the time of the Revolution, he was twenty-seven—that is, his mind was already formed. That this mind should have continued to function for forty years in the Soviet Union, judging the events in Russia and continuing to think in terms of the whole sweep of human history, is likely to seem as astonishing as that the mammoths preserved in Siberian ice should still have their flesh intact. We find that we are reading a contemporary and peer of Faulkner, Malraux, and Auden, and we are so eager to see how such a mind will deal with the Bolshevik seizure of power, the dictatorship of the proletariat, the Civil Wars, the Soviet state after Lenin's death, the purges, and the war against Germany that we may not notice at first that his interest in these matters is, in a sense, incidental. For though he touches on all these events and though his comment on them is breathtakingly explicit, and as enlightening as it is unexpected, there is developed throughout the novel, consistently and step by step, a point of view that is universal, that does not cater to Soviet officialdom or even to Russian patriotism and from which war and revolution are seen as striking local occurrences that have made Russia loom larger to the rest of the world as well as to the Russians themselves but that must be taken in a wider perspective as the transient phenomena they are. It will be well, then, before coming to the story itself, to try to give some account of Pasternak's general view as it is gradually built up for the reader in conversations between Zhivago and the other characters.

It ought to be explained at the outset that Pasternak—though a Jew or part Jewish—has evidently been brought up in the Greek Orthodox Church; that the ritual and the doctrine of the Church represent for him the fundamental moral realities. Yet his religious position is peculiar. It is as if his Jewish authority had somehow made it possible for him to reinvent Christianity—which, to this non-religious reviewer, is made here to seem a good deal more impressive than in the works of the literary converts: a force of regeneration that has given Pasternak the faith to survive and the moral courage to write this book. Since it is usually Zhivago or his uncle, whose line of thought the nephew is supposed to be following, who develops this point of view, I shall not, I think, be misrepresenting it if I summarize it by putting together the utterances of several characters at different ages and in various circumstances.

It is possible, then, we are told at the beginning, "to be an atheist, not to know whether God exists or why there should be one," and yet to believe that Jesus has brought to man the supreme revelation. By displacing the moral emphasis from the society, from the nation, from the people in the sense of the *populus Romanus* to the individual soul, to "the idea of the free personality and the idea of life as a sacrifice," he for the first time rescued man from the rest of nature and inaugurated a society that was truly human. It has been the great mistake of the Jews—it is a Jewish character who makes this point—not to recognize this revelation, which has been their own chief gift to humanity. The doctrine of the salvation of the individual disregards, supersedes nationalities, yet the Jews, with all their social idealism, have remained professional nationalists and have paid for this with unnecessary suffering.

But Jesus also brought immortality. One must be "faithful to immortality, which is another word for life, a somewhat intensified word." The resurrection of all humanity in another world is unthinkable and ridiculous. We should be animals still craving our animal life, and our removal from the continuum of the universe would leave it and God without meaning. But life, which pervades the universe, does incessantly renew itself in its innumerable different forms. Our birth is a resurrection, and we shall rise again in our children as well as in our work. (The translators make Zhivago say to his love when they part for the last time, "Farewell . . . until we meet in the next world," but this is not in the text and would be contrary to Zhivago's cosmology. What Pasternak makes him say is that he will never see her again "in life"; he merely bids her "farewell in this world," which does not imply meeting in Heaven.)

The approach to human problems of the official Soviet philosophy has been based on a crude misconception. It has always talked about "remaking life," but "people who can talk in this way—even though they may have seen a good deal of the world—have never known life at all, have never felt its spirit, its soul. For them, human existence is a lump of raw material which has not been ennobled by their touch, which has never been worked over by them. But life is not a material, it is not a substantial thing. It is something that eternally renews itself, a principle that is always taking different shapes; it is always remaking and re-creating itself; it is away out of reach of our stupid theories." The Communists are always thinking in terms of "building new worlds, transition periods. . . . That is all they have been taught, and it is all they understand. And do you know why they make all this fuss about these eternal preparations? From sheer lack of any definite competence, from the absence of real ability. Man is born to live and not to prepare to live. And life itself, the phenomenon of life, the gift of life is such an absorbing and serious matter! So why try to substitute for it this childish harlequinade of immature fantasies," such escapades as that of the schoolboys in Chekhov's story, who decide to run away to America but who never get farther than the nearest Russian town. (The translators have omitted this amusing reference.)

As for Marxism: when a provincial lawyer who professes the official creed while continuing to carry on his bourgeois business tells Zhivago that Marxism is "a positive science, the study of reality, the theory of historical conditions," "Marxism a science?" the Doctor replies. "To argue that with someone one hardly knows is of course rather imprudent—but never mind about that. Marxism is too little in control of itself to be considered a science. The sciences are better equilibrated. Marxism and objectivity? I don't know of any movement more completely shut in upon itself and remoter from the facts than Marxism. Everybody is preoccupied with proving himself in practice, and the people who are in power are compelled by the fable of their infallibility to exert their utmost efforts to keep their eyes averted from the truth. Politics mean nothing to me. I cannot care for people who are indifferent to truth." The whole attempt on the part of Marxism to see everything in terms of classes, to force people into social camps and to align them against one another—Reds against Whites, peasants and workers, on the one hand, against nobility and bourgeoisie, on the other—is contrary to the real character of human nature. It disregards the fundamental Christian truth: that the vital unit is the individual. The very self-discipline, to some degree heroic, which has transformed the railroad worker's young son into an uncompromising commissar imposes a false mold which in the long run would prove fatal. The thing that redeems him as a human being is that he cannot quite submit to this mold. When Zhivago confronts him, the Doctor discovers that this young man is not quite what his formidable reputation has led Zhivago to expect to meet. "It is a good thing," Zhivago says, "when a man fails to live up to your expectation, when he is different from your previously conceived idea. To run true to type is the extinction of a man, his condemnation to death. If he cannot be assigned to a category, if he is not a model of something, a half of what is needed is there. He is still free from himself, he has acquired an atom of immortality."

• • •

But now let us proceed to the story itself to see how this immortality is realized.

The first chapters—except for the poetic impressionism—sound rather like Dos Passos's *Manhattan Transfer*. You are quickly switched from one to another of several groups of characters: a little boy attends his mother's funeral and spends the night with his uncle in a monastery; a little Jewish boy, travelling with his lawyer father, sees a man throw himself out of the train; a little girl comes to Moscow with her French mother, a widow in reduced circumstances, who takes over a dressmaking business; a railroad workers' strike on the eve of the 1905 revolution; a big Christmas-tree celebration in a well-to-do Moscow home. All these characters are interconnected, but one does not at first get the hang of them. In childhood and adolescence, we do not yet know whom we see, where we stand in relation to one another; we are simply a lot of young people together. But the pattern of the narrative soon changes with the coming of the First World War. Young Yury Andreyevich studies medicine and becomes Dr. Zhivago; he marries the daughter of a chemistry professor whose grandfather was an industrialist and landowner. Larisa, the daughter of the impoverished Frenchwoman, marries the studious son of a railroad worker who has been exiled for his political activities. The narrative now concentrates on Zhivago and Larisa; they emerge as the hero and heroine. Though married to others, they are separated from their families and thrown together at intervals by the vicissitudes of the war and the Revolution, and their intermittent, inescapable, and mutually inspiring love affair provides the vitalizing central charge that makes them resistant to pressures and clairvoyant in the midst of confusion. When the great social crisis comes, the background of their cultivated bourgeois world melts away, with many of its figures; other figures fall into place in the drama of the Civil Wars and the establishment of the new society; but Yury Andreyevich and Larisa Fyodorovna are both at once too much individualists, too much naturally immune to the materialistic doctrine, and too much products of the old education—and Larisa is not even a Russian—to accept the Communist creed and that method of dealing with human problems which it suggests to uneducated men recently risen to power.

It should be noted in this connection that one of the most startling features of the book is Pasternak's abstention—in spite of the sympathy with which he presents them—from any idealization, of either Tolstoy's or Lenin's kind, of the peasantry, "the toiling masses." Not that the bourgeoisie is flattered. Nobody is flattered, nor is anyone condemned on the basis of office or class. There are no caricatures and no glorifications. The author never departs from his Christian ideal of taking every individual seriously as a soul which must be respected. Komarovsky, the shady lawyer, who stands for the worst of the old bourgeoisie, who is more or less responsible for the suicide of Zhivago's reckless father (the man who throws himself off the train), who sets up Larisa's mother in business and then seduces the daughter, is shown struggling against a real love for Larisa. And Pasha, the railroad worker's son, whom Larisa afterward marries, is first made sympathetic by reason of his diligence and ambition; then arrogant and unpleasant when, having taken the name of Strelnikov (which suggests shooting people), he appears as the formidable commissar the very mention of whose name creates terror, and baits Zhivago in a menacing way as a potential counter-revolutionary;

then made a pathetic figure when the Party authorities are after him and he takes refuge in the same house as Zhivago.

There is a wonderful scene here: "They had been talking a long time, for hours, as only Russians in Russia talk, as talked particularly the frightened and anxious, the frantic and raving people that all Russians were at that time. . . . He was unable to stop talking, he held on as tightly as he could—in order not to be alone—to his conversation with the Doctor. Was he afraid of the gnawing of conscience or of his load of depressing memories, or was he burdened by the self-dissatisfaction in which a man becomes unbearable and hateful to himself and ready to die of shame. . . . This was the malady of the age, the revolutionary madness of the period. What really went on in their minds was quite different from their words and their outward appearance. The conscience of no one was clean. Everyone had good grounds for feeling that he was as guilty as possible, a secret criminal, an unmasked impostor. As soon as any pretext presented itself, there would burst forth and run to extravagant lengths a debauch of self-torturing imagination. People would run on into fantasies, they would falsely denounce themselves, not merely from the working of fear but as the result of a morbid destructive impulse, deliberately, in a state of metaphysical trance and that passion for self-condemnation which cannot be stemmed when one has once given way to it."

The commissar, now under suspicion, has hoped to clear himself of the charges against him, but he knows from his own methods with others that he will not be given a chance to defend himself. The interesting point is made that he has elicited so many confessions of counter revolutionary guilt that he is tempted by the guilt of his inhuman acts to make a "self-unmasking" confession not of these but of political offenses which he has not committed. He shoots himself in the morning, but not before, in the talk of the previous night, he has poured out—it is the first time in the novel that we have had a full statement of this—the whole apologia for his generation. This passage is too long to quote, but in its insight into the sources of the Communist faith of the early days of the Revolution, it is as important as the negative passages of Pasternak's political commentary which are currently being printed in the press, out of context and in a way that is quite misleading. Zhivago, Pasha-Strelnikov begins by telling him, cannot understand his point of view: he has grown up in a different world from the one that Pasha came out of; and Pasha describes this world of overcrowding and dirt and privation, and describes the animus it gave the young people, who had always been aware of the indifference to them of the rich in the smart streets, to turn the social world upside down. Marxism has shown them "the root of the evil and where to find the remedy for it." This resentment had been seething all over Europe through the whole of the nineteenth century, and the great revolutionary movement—with "its pitiless instruments devised in the name of pity"—had found its full expression in Lenin, with the result that "the immense figure of Russia, impossible to disregard," had "suddenly risen before the eyes of the world, blazing up like a candle of redemption for all the slackness and the misfortunes of humanity."

Pasha has been wrecked as a human being by his attempt to play a Marxist role. Zhivago and Larisa, who do not attempt roles, will outlive him, but they, too, are to be destroyed. Life in Moscow becomes so difficult in the days after the Revolution that Yury Andreyevich decides to get as far away as possible, to take his family to the Ural Mountains, where his father-in-law had had an estate and where he hopes to find some peace of mind. But the East, he finds, is even more disrupted and dangerous. He is kidnapped and pressed into service by a band of wandering partisans who are fighting the White leader Kolchak in Siberia. He has come upon Larisa again in the nearby town of Yuratin, in which, before Pasha's enlistment, she had been living with him and teaching school. She had married her young proletarian out of a kind of feeling of duty that she ought, on account of her own disadvantages, to identify her interests with his, yet her natural "affinity," her deep understanding, is all with Yury Andreyevich. Pasha had already become aware that Larisa could not really love him—"he was jealous of her very thoughts, of the mug from which she drank, of the pillow on which she lay"—and he goes away to the war to prove himself to himself, to impress her, to compete with what she represents (and this in spite of the fact that his original revolutionary impulse has been spurred by his desire to protect her, a finer nature than his, from the indignity of her early helplessness). Missing in action and supposed to be dead, he has escaped from his German captors and re-created himself as "Strelnikov"—also, as Larisa knows, partly to build up something so strong that she cannot refuse to admire it. But he has never—for all his impressive exterior—succeeded in getting his inner morale to the point where he dares to come back to her. And in the meantime, Yury Andreyevich, escaped from the partisan band, *has* returned to Larisa. His wife, as the result of his disappearance, has made her way back to Moscow and so to Paris. He had already been having a love affair with Larisa, and he now begins living with her in Yuratin. But they both now come under suspicion, she as "Strelnikov's" wife, he on account of his original thinking. While working in a local hospital, he lectures on evolution, and his views about the adaptation of organisms to environment are not sufficiently mechanical for the provincial Marxists. Though he is valued as a diagnostician, he finds that when he talks about intuition, they begin to shy away from him: they are afraid of a trap, a heresy. He and Larisa do not have "the right attitude." A counter-revolutionary group with a hidden store of arms is discovered at this point in Yuratin, and they know that they may be pounced upon at any moment. They get away to the place in the country—the estate of his wife's father—in which Yury Andreyevich has lived with his family.

This episode of their life in the country—the last, desperate phase of their love—is unlike anything else in fiction: full of the tension of anguish and terror yet also of nobility and exaltation. It is winter; the house is freezing. Zhivago has to keep the stove going; Larisa has to clean up the rooms. Larisa's little daughter is with them. Her mother tries to give her lessons, and sometimes, when she is out with her sled, the lovers' hands happen to touch, and they drop their time-consuming housework for interludes of passionate tenderness. (The translators have castrated this passage by omitting "the minutes ran into hours" and by changing its whole rhythm.) They know that it is only a question of time before the police will find them. Yet Zhivago, when Larisa has gone to bed, returns to his early poetry, and in the course of these nocturnal sessions, his creative activity renews itself. "After two or three stanzas that came pouring and several metaphors by which he was himself surprised, the work took possession of him, and he began to feel the presence of what is called inspiration. The correlation of the forces that govern artistic genius had as it were been turned upside down. It is no longer the man and the state of his soul, for which he is seeking expression, that are in the ascendancy now, but the language with which he seeks to express it. This language, which is the place of origin and the repository of beauty and meaning, itself begins to think and to speak for the man and is completely transformed into music, not in terms of outward audible sonorities but in terms of the impetuosity and the power of its inward current. Now, like the great rolling mass of the torrent of a river, by its own movement turning as if on a lathe the stones that lie on its bed and revolving the wheels of mills, the onrushing speech itself, by force of its own laws, molds in its course, in passing, the music and the rhythm of the poem, and a thousand other forms and configurations which are even more important than these but which have not yet been recognized or taken into consideration, which have not yet even been given names. At such moments, Yury Andreyevich felt that the main work was not done by him but somehow somewhere above him, that it had found him and taken control of him—the poetry and thought of the world in its present phase and that which is coming, that which is following in orderly progression, the next step which has become inevitable in poetry's historical development. And he felt himself only the occasion, the *point d'appui,* for it to get itself into movement." He looks at the girl and Larisa asleep side by side in their bed. "The cleanness of the linen, the cleanness of the rooms [the achievement of the *women's* work], the purity of their features, fusing with the purity of the night, the snow and the stars" make him "exult and weep with a feeling of the triumphant purity of existence." Then at three o'clock he is torn from his concentration by a plaintive and dismal sound. He sees far off, over the wild waste of snow, four shadows that make little marks on it. Starved wolves have smelled the horse in the stable.

This chapter, at the end of which Zhivago is to lose Larisa, is the emotional climax of this extraordinary book, in which everyone is degraded or ruined or crushed but in which the positive values—Christianity and love and art—are presented with such overwhelming power that the barbarities against which they must assert themselves seem lacking in long-range importance. But Komarovsky, the indestructible rascal who has been both Larisa's and her mother's lover, and whom Larisa has once tried to shoot, eventually turns up in Yuratin, and Zhivago—to save Larisa's life—allows him to take her to the Far East. To induce her to go, he has promised her to follow, but when she has left, he makes his furtive and difficult way—mostly on foot—back to Moscow, where it is possible for him only to a limited extent to pick up his former life. His old friends have managed to adapt themselves. One of them has been arrested, imprisoned, and exiled for his unorthodox opinions, and he sickens Yury Andreyevich by telling him how much good has been done him by a brainwashing at the hands of the examining magistrate. Zhivago has lost first his family, then Larisa; though he continues to practice medicine, he has no chance for a real career, and though he publishes, in a semi-private way, a few papers on historical and scientific subjects, and though these papers make a certain impression, his work cannot be freely accepted. He marries the daughter of his former servant.

• • •

It is impossible, however, to summarize, in an article such as this, what happens in *Doctor Zhivago,* and any attempt at a thorough analysis would be likely to reach almost the proportions of the studies devoted to Joyce. The story itself is so long and complex—it covers so much ground—that a mere recapitulation would be impossible within the scope of a review, and one finds, threaded in and out of the story, a phase-by-phase chronicle of Soviet policy, and a discussion of the development of Russian literature which touches on almost all its great figures from Pushkin to the school of modern poetry which is represented by Pasternak himself. There is also involved in the story a historical-political fable—see Larisa's relations with Zhivago, Komarovsky, and Pasha—of the kind that since the time of Turgenev has been traditional in Russian fiction, as well as (what for Pasternak is far more important) a kind of religious parable. The reader will not at first notice this last, though it constitutes the core of the novel. The incidents succeed one another with so much invention and vivacity, with such range of characterization and description, each submerges us so completely in the atmosphere of its moment of Russian life, we are carried along so absorbedly by the vodka parties, the unexpected encounters, the journeyings (the chaotic interminable train trip of Zhivago and his family to the Urals that occupies a whole long chapter), the campaigns (the adventures of the partisans in the forest is a whole story in itself), the conversations (the nocturnal talks, both comic and desolating, between Zhivago, bored, irritated, and sleepy, and the fervent young partisan leader, who shoots his men for distilling vodka but has discovered the virtues of cocaine as an ideological stimulus and is depleting the Doctor's medical store and keeping him awake at night with his hopped-up pep talks), and the intensely personal love affairs, at once so exciting and so dolorous, that are always being broken up by public events—we have so much the illusion of following life that we only come gradually to realize the poetic significance of these happenings. For if Gogol's *Dead Souls* is, as he called it, a "poem," *Doctor Zhivago* is also a poem. Though we may think, when we begin it, that we are entering again the familiar world of social fiction—the "group" novel of intertwined strands, such as Sartre's Existentialist series, "Les Chemins de la Liberté," which has now been bogged down for so long, simply, it would seem, for the reason that Sartre has changed his political line, or Leonov's *Road to the Ocean,* in which a real Russian talent falsifies and nullifies itself by submitting to a Soviet formula—we presently become aware that *Doctor Zhivago* is more like an epic than even *War and Peace,* that the landscapes, the personalities, the tragic outbursts, the comic anecdotes (usually as much horrible as comic) are poetic in their relief and their meaning. This book, in which everything seems real, is not at all "realistic." It exhibits, in fact—as a whole as well as in individual episodes—in spite of its immediacy of detail, of all the costumes and accents and jargon and paraphernalia and living conditions of twentieth-century Russia, something of the technique and the spirit of the *skazka,* the Russian folk tale. The narrative is full of coincidences, each of which is in itself quite plausible but the repeated occurrence of which might shake our "suspension of disbelief" if we were not so much under the spell of what is really a legend, a fable. We are no more surprised or put out by the fact that the characters of *Doctor Zhivago* are always meeting one another again in different guises and changed states of mind than we are in a fairy tale when the wretched old crone whom the youngest of three brothers has been the first to treat with courtesy turns out to be a powerful spirit who can determine success or failure.

The most *skazka*-like element in the story is Zhivago's half brother Evgraf, who is really a supernatural figure. Evgraf is introduced so unobtrusively that we do not at first pay attention to him, and we have to go back later to look him up. Zhivago's unreliable father has left his wife for a princess with the hybrid name of Stolbunova-Enrici, by whom he has had a son. The half-celestial personality of the son is evidently adumbrated when we are told that the mother is *"mechtatel' nitsa i sumasbrodka,"* "a dreamer and rather mad (or erratic)." Yury Andreyevich's mother is characterized with similar brevity as *"myagkaya . . . mechtatel' nitsa,"* "gentle, a dreamer." (The translator has muffed this significant repetition by combining the two epithets of the first of these descriptions into the single blank word "eccentric.") The Princess and her illegitimate son live far away, on the outskirts of Omsk, in Siberia. The Princess never goes out, and nobody knows what they live on. Yury Andreyevich has seen a photograph of their house, with five plate-glass windows and stucco medallions, and has felt that it was staring at him in a hostile way across all the thousands of versts and that sooner or later its glance will be fatal. Partly out of fear of this, partly out of contempt for litigation, he refuses to contest the claims to his father's estate of this princess and another of his father's mistresses, and he is rewarded for his renunciation by the strange intervention in his favor at critical times in his life of his mysterious half brother from the East. At the time of the victory of the workers in the fighting of the October days and the transfer of power to the Soviets, the Doctor walks out at night in the midst of a heavy snowstorm and buys a paper which carries the news. In order to get light to read it, he goes into the entrance hall of an unknown building. An eighteen-year-old boy comes downstairs in a Siberian fur coat and fur cap. He has narrow Kirghizan eyes but something aristocratic in his face—"the shy ray, the hidden delicacy, which is sometimes found in persons of mixed and complicated stock and which seems to have been brought from afar." Zhivago does not know that it is his half brother Evgraf, but the apparition afterward haunts him. This is the moment of his most wholehearted enthusiasm for the success of the Revolution. He feels that there is something characteristic of Russia in the drastic directness, the rude courage, of the sweeping away of the old order—"something of the uncompromising clarity of Pushkin, of the unevasive fidelity to facts of Tolstoy." One imagines at this point that Evgraf is meant to represent something sound, at once popular and noble, in Russia, and as the story goes on one suspects that he may even be intended to embody the old conception of "Holy Russia." One becomes more and more aware that Pasternak's book is studded with the symbolism of the Orthodox Church. The five barless windows of the house in Siberia are the five wounds of Jesus. (The number five elsewhere appears, and always with sinister significance: the five-o'clock train from which the older Zhivago throws himself, the five conspirators in the forest who try to murder the partisan leader.) Evgraf is a guardian angel, but he is also, with his dark face, the angel of death. And yet death is always followed by resurrection. Three times, like the fairy in the folk tale, he comes to Yury Andreyevich's rescue. First when, before Zhivago has taken his family away, he collapses in Moscow with typhus; again, when he is marooned with his family in the Urals, before he has been kidnapped by the partisans; and finally when, returned to Moscow, unwanted and unassimilable, he is on the point of petering out. On this last occasion, Evgraf induces him to leave for a time his devoted lower-class wife and provides him with lodgings in which to write. We never know what Evgraf is or how he accomplishes his miracles; he is always an important person whose authority is felt at once, never questioned; he can always produce food, secure for his half brother conditions of leisure. Yet we do not know what office he holds, why he is always so sure of himself, how he has managed to escape the purges. On his third intervention, he brings death in the flesh. The Doctor, now hidden from his family, does not survive his last creative liberation, but Evgraf preserves his manuscripts, the poems in which Yury lives again. Since "Yury" is a Russian equivalent for "George," the Russian reader will have guessed by this time that Zhivago is St. George, the martyr, who is supposed to have paid with his life for his audacity in arguing Christianity with Diocletian. He has written in the Urals, with the wolves on the horizon, a queer poem with an unexpected ending, about the battle of St. George with the Dragon, which we shall read in the final chapter. (One suspects that the legends of St. Larisa and St. Eugraphos, after whom the heroine and Evgraf are named, would reveal further connections between the characters and the hagiography of the Orthodox Church. A mythological Larisa is supposed to have been the wife of Poseidon, and Pasternak's Larisa is associated with the sea by Zhivago—for reasons which, however, I have not grasped.) Evgraf, a general now, appears for the last time toward the end of the second great war to rescue the daughter of Larisa and Yury, born after her flight with Komarovsky and abandoned with a peasant family, who has been partially reduced to the level of a peasant and yet knows that she is something else. Evgraf will see that she is educated (the importance of education is emphasized all through the book).

By this time, we are quite aware that the theme of death and resurrection, slipped into the first pages, is central to the whole book, repeated in all sorts of variations and with ever stronger positive force. Again and again the characters are entombed and rise from the tomb. Evgraf is the angel at the grave. The father, enmeshed in the financial ruin entailed by his emotional instability, has leaped out of the train; Yury Andreyevich, the son, with sclerosis of the heart, is suffocating on a crowded tram, tries to get a window up, then forces his way out and drops dead on the curb. And in the interval between these two deaths, the incidents that join them together are now seen to compose a sequence of images, sometimes physical, sometimes spiritual, of the cycle of extinction and survival. The vodka and pancakes of Shrovetide—which in Russia is dedicated both to the dead and to the renewal of life by marriage—are a ritual symbol of the theme. The second of these references is a herald of Evgraf's second intervention. The Jewish boy in the station who is thinking about "what it means to be a Jew" and paying no attention to the man who has just then committed suicide—he later adapts himself to the Moscow regime, though not with the same enthusiasm as the non-Jewish friend who has been brainwashed—is meant to illustrate the author's conception of the too self-centered role of the Jews. The book begins with the burial of Yury's mother and the night in the monastery, in which no special ray of light is yet seen; and we have afterward the escape from the train of the prisoners condemned to forced labor; the shooting, on the edge of a precipice, of the vodka distillers and other offenders, of whom one, a backward boy, survives; the burial of the old woman by her murderer in the pit in which she has been hoarding potatoes, and the escape, through taking refuge in an underground cave, in the raid that follows the murder, of a boy who is suspected already of having committed it; and the trapping in the cellar of the murderer of the husband of the peasant woman with whom the daughter of Zhivago and Larisa has been living. Pasternak keeps too close to real life to perpetrate a monotonous allegory. In this last-mentioned instance of burial, there is no resurrection for the brute. He is held prisoner by the woman whose husband has been killed, and she allows him to strangle her little boy, whom he has taken down with him as a hostage. The abandoned daughter of Zhivago and Larisa flags a passing train—the husband of the woman was a signalman—and the trainmen bring out the murderer, tie him to the tracks, and run over him. The woman, as a result of all this, goes mad. Here it is the girl who escapes from the household which has for her been a tomb.

The last chapter is composed of Zhivago's poems, which have been published after his death. The reader, when he faces this chapter, may be somewhat puzzled and dubious as to why what is ostensibly a story should be prolonged by what looks like an appendix; but by the time we have finished these poems, we see that they are needed to complete the book, that the theme only now gets its full, triumphant statement. These poems fall into two series, which alternate and echo one another and merge. One sequence recapitulates certain incidents of Zhivago's life and grows darker with the parting from Larisa and the darkness of the oppression of Stalin: "For this in early spring my friends and I gather together, and our evenings are farewells, our feasts are testaments, in order that our hidden stream of suffering may warm the cold of existence." The other of these sequences commemorates the holy days of the Church and the main events of the life of Jesus. The gloomy poem quoted above is followed by "Evil Days," the entrance of Christ into Jerusalem and giving him up for judgment to the dregs of society by "the dark forces of the Temple," and his memory at this moment, of his bounty at Cana and his bringing Lazarus back from the tomb; then two poems on Mary Magdalene, with whom we have already had some intimation that Larisa is to be identified (after all, she could never get away from Komarovsky, whom she has married in the Far East). The last magnificent poem of this sombre yet affirmative series gives us Jesus in the Garden of Gethsemane. "I shall descend into the grave," it ends, "and on the third day I shall rise again and as rafts float along the river, so the centuries, like the barges of a caravan, shall, for my judgment, float down out of darkness."

• • •

I assume that by this time everybody knows that *Doctor Zhivago* has not been published in Russia, that the manuscript was brought out of the Soviet Union by the Italian Leftist publisher Feltrinelli, that Pasternak was awarded the Nobel Prize, and that the anti-creative bureaucrats who are allowed in the Soviet Union to interfere in matters of literature—sounding much like those Mississippi newspapers which raised a howl against Faulkner in the same situation—have compelled him to refuse this reward. I do not, however, in paying my respects to the official mediocrities of Moscow, want to adopt the self-righteous attitude toward Russia which has become official in the United States. On hearing of this literary crisis, Secretary Dulles said that "it illustrates what I said last night. The system of international Communism insists on conformity not only in deed but in thought. Anything a little out of line they try to stamp out." *Doctor Zhivago* is not merely a little out of line with the assumptions of the Soviet Union; it presents a radical criticism of all our supposedly democratic but more and more centralized societies. The criticism of Pasternak's novel is directed at conditions and tendencies which are in evidence all over the world and which have lately become pronounced in the United States. Here is a quotation from Pasternak which might equally apply to us: "It was then," says Larisa of the First World War, "that untruth came to the land of Russia. The first disaster, the root of future evil, was the loss of faith in one's own opinion. They imagined that the time had passed for them to pay attention to the promptings of moral feeling, that one now had to sing with the general voice and to live by the general notions that were being thrust upon one."

Doctor Zhivago will, I believe, come to stand as one of the great events in man's literary and moral history. Nobody could have written it in a totalitarian state and turned it loose on the world who did not have the courage of genius. May his guardian angel be with him! His book is a great act of faith in art and in the human spirit. As for his enemies in his fatherland, I predict that their children, over their vodka and tea, will be talking about the relations between Larisa Fyodorovna and Pasha and Yury Andreyevich as their parents, and I don't doubt they themselves, have talked about Tatiana and Lensky and Evgeny Onegin, and Natasha and Prince André and Pierre.

THE CURRENT CINEMA

JOHN MCCARTEN

GOOD TOUGH STUFF

JULY 31, 1954 (ON *ON THE WATERFRONT*)

On the Waterfront is based solidly and most satisfactorily on the New York *Sun* articles about labor conditions along the New York docks, which won for Malcolm Johnson, their author, a Pulitzer Prize. As dramatized by Budd Schulberg, Mr. Johnson's findings add up to the sort of galvanic movie we used to get when the Warner Brothers were riding herd on Al Capone and his associates. The locale of Mr. Schulberg's story is Hoboken, for which in the lovely past I used to have the same malty affection Romberg had for Heidelberg. The stratum of Hoboken society that Mr. Schulberg depicts—and bear in mind that the script is, if anything, a rather gentle depiction of real happenings—consists of people among whom even Senator McCarthy's Indian might be considered effete; mayhem and murder are as lightly regarded in this crowd as traffic violations are in more civilized circles. To deal with this violent, brawling, and terrifying littoral—the Cro-Magnon depths of our social structure—Mr. Schulberg has assembled a lot of full-bodied characters, and given them motivations far more plausible than we have come to expect in movies like this. Contributing to the credibility of *On the Waterfront,* which had the good fortune to be directed by Elia Kazan, is the fact that it was actually made in Hoboken; in none of the scenes is there a trace of the fictitious background that can be so unsettling in films with documentary origins.

The tale that Mr. Schulberg has woven together to sustain Mr. Johnson's brutal discoveries centers on a classic situation—the redemption of a sinner through love. This particular sinner is a longshoreman, no brighter than the next, who has dreamed long dreams of being a champion boxer and winds up wielding a baling hook on the sufferance of hopelessly corrupt labor bosses. I won't try to describe the intricacies of the pattern Mr. Schulberg has invented to show how our hero emerges from the awful wallow that circumstance has plunged him into, but I will say that in the person of Marlon Brando he is a thoroughly convincing individual. Indeed, I'd give cozy odds that no actor this year is going to match Mr. Brando's performance here. At that, he's only a short length ahead of some of his colleagues in this enterprise. As a priest who comes to the realization that the hold of a ship is just as good a place for religion as any temple, Karl Malden is superb, and as the lady who does most to redeem Mr. Brando, Eva Marie Saint is altogether captivating. Mr. Schulberg, who, I've been informed, used to own a piece of a fighter, has garnished *On the Waterfront* with a good deal of pugilistic argot, and he—or maybe Mr. Kazan—has had the courage to include in the cast such battlers as Tony Galento, Tami Mauriello, and Abe Simon. All of them, it seems to me, do better here than they ever did in the ring. To spell out in detail all the other worthies involved in *On the Waterfront* —and among them Lee J. Cobb is conspicuously competent—would be an impossibility in this space, but I must say a word for the score Leonard Bernstein composed to accompany this movie. It is at once pertinent and unobtrusive, and it always serves to step up the dramatic points the film is making.

NO SANCTUARY

NOVEMBER 28, 1959 (ON *THE 400 BLOWS*)

THE FRENCH FILM called *The 400 Blows* was produced, directed, and written (in collaboration with Marcel Moussy) by a young man named François Truffaut, who is almost as capable as Vittorio De Sica at depicting a small boy's confusion when trying to face up to an adult world that is no more enlightened than a jungle. (I'm thinking of *Bicycle Thief*.) The boy whose short and sad career M. Truffaut outlines here is a prepossessing twelve-year-old, portrayed by Jean-Pierre Léaud, a lad who has had no previous experience as an actor but is altogether the perfect type to represent a bewildered small fry, alternately mischievous and pathetic, intransigent and affectionate. This small fry is a product of the most sordid circumstances. (*"Faire les quatre cents coups"* is the French equivalent of "hell-raising.") His handsome mother (Claire Maurier), who bore him out of wedlock, is now married to a foolish man (Albert Rémy) who ignores her infidelities while devoting himself to the petty activities of an automobile club. Living in close quarters with this pair, our boy obviously never gets a chance to establish any stable values, and eventually, having stirred up the wrath of his schoolmaster with his pranks, he becomes an outlaw on the loose in Paris. M. Truffaut apparently has a very low opinion of the teaching methods of Parisian public schools, and I think you will, too, after witnessing some of the educational exercises he puts on view. But worse is to come. As a fugitive in Paris, living uncertainly by his wits, young Jean-Pierre has only one friend (Patrick Auffay) upon whom he can depend. Adept at petty thievery, he sustains himself for a while by pinching clocks and the like (his chum, whose mother is a drunk and whose father is a horseplayer, knows all about the art of pawning things), but when he finally tries a big job—the theft of a typewriter from his stepfather's office—he is arrested. M. Truffaut's attitude toward lower-echelon French educators is nothing short of admiration compared to what he thinks of the French police. Jean-Pierre is literally thrown into a chicken-wire pen, after being fingerprinted as if he were the prize criminal catch of the age. His companions are thieves and prostitutes, and when, at length, his parents are called in to make some sort of decision about his fate, neither of them can do anything more charitable than surrender him to the court, to be sent to a juvenile-delinquent home for observation.

Having here and there revealed that his young hero, when given a chance, has a broad ability to enjoy the simple things of life—he is at his happiest when attending a movie with his mother and her husband—M. Truffaut now leads us to a grim conclusion. One of our boy's ambitions is to tell a story in the manner of Balzac; another, and more driving one, is to have a look at the sea. In the juvenile home, he is questioned extensively about a nonexistent sex life, regimented, and brutalized, and finally he takes off in search of peace and freedom—freedom to think about Balzac, if nothing more. Running with the strength of the demented, he finally comes upon the sea, and there M. Truffaut stops his camera, revealing to us, in one corrosive still-shot, a boy with no place to go. In fact, it could be said that the whole film is corrosive, for it leaves an etching on the mind that deepens with time.

The performances in *The 400 Blows* are all superior, but, in a cast of superb actors, the amateur Jean-Pierre stands out with authority.

THE THEATRE

WOLCOTT GIBBS

BOUQUETS, BRICKBATS, AND OBITUARIES

DECEMBER 2, 1950 (ON *GUYS AND DOLLS*)

I DON'T THINK I ever had more fun at a musical comedy than I had the other night, when an association of strangely gifted men put on a Broadway epic known as *Guys and Dolls*. There have been loftier moral and aesthetic experiences, like *Show Boat* and *South Pacific;* there have been more enduring musical accomplishments, like *Porgy and Bess;* there have been occasions when the humor was clearly on a more ambitious level, like *Of Thee I Sing;* there have been more sensational individual performances, like practically anything involving Miss Ethel Merman. There has, however, been nothing I can remember that sustained a higher general level of sheer entertainment than the operation at the Forty-sixth Street Theatre. In form and content, the closest thing to it was *Pal Joey,* but even that fine essay in jocular corruption had its moments when I wished the cast would move on to something else. There were none such—for me, at least—in *Guys and Dolls.* The credits on the program note that the piece was produced by Cy Feuer and Ernest H. Martin; that the book was adapted, by Jo Swerling and Abe Burrows, from a story by the late Damon Runyon; that the music and lyrics were the work of Frank Loesser; that the settings were designed by Jo Mielziner and the costumes by Alvin Colt; that the dances were staged by Michael Kidd; and that George S. Kaufman was responsible for the direction. There isn't a man on this list who hasn't my deepest admiration and gratitude.

I haven't any idea how closely the story Mr. Swerling and Mr. Burrows have chosen follows the original, since it is one of the holes in my culture that I have read very little Runyon, whose idiom I always suspected—wrongfully, I'm sure—of being more or less synthetic, like Milt Gross's approximation of the vernacular of the Bronx, and whose plots, or at least the few with which I am familiar, leaned heavily on the old O. Henry switch at the end. Both these faults, if they are faults, are visible in the play version. The speech employed by the characters is a heightened parody, and not a very accurate one, of that used by the Broadway types, including a good many horseplayers, of my acquaintance, and the switch is certainly present, especially when the toughest gambler of them all turns up as a member of a mission band. I don't think these things make any difference, and it may even be that what were flaws in fiction are virtues on the stage, where broad strokes and slapstick techniques are practically obligatory.

Mr. Swerling and Mr. Burrows, to get down to a rough outline of the facts, are primarily interested in two romances—one between Nathan Detroit, the impresario of the oldest floating crap game in New York, and a blonde, to whom he has been engaged for fourteen years, who heads the floor show in a joint called the Hot Box; the other between the gambler mentioned above, whose name is Sky Masterson, and the young lady in charge of the mission. Detroit, who needs a thousand dollars to rent a suitable site for his crap game, makes a bet for that amount with Masterson, who gambles on his ability to persuade the girl from the mission to accompany him to Havana. He succeeds, but, yielding to a soft impulse brought on by love, gallantly denies that he did, thus enabling the boys to get on with their game. Somehow or other (the details would just mix you up), everything works out satisfactorily, at least from the feminine point of view, and the final curtain falls on a rash of weddings. It is as simple as that.

I can list only a few of the brilliant and hilarious things that ornament this framework. Vivian Blaine, as the night-club singer, has two numbers, one explaining how emotional frustration can give a girl a bad cold in her head, and the other an indignant ditty known as "Take Back Your Mink" ("to from whence it came"), that are as funny and as impressively delivered as anything you'll hear this season. Isabel Bigley, as the evangelist, has a face, a voice, and a figure that are all astonishing, to put it mildly, and her material, especially two sentimental songs called "If I Were a Bell" and "I'll Know," and a frivolous duet with Miss Blaine labelled "Marry the Man Today," is well worthy of all these talents. There is a memorable scene in which fifteen or twenty gamblers are tricked somehow into the mission and presently find themselves carolling something called "Follow the Fold," and another, involving some excellent dancing, in which they are all happily congregated in a sewer, shooting dice. The guys and dolls, in addition to those already named, bear such names as Nicely-Nicely Johnson, Benny Southstreet, Harry the Horse, and Angie the Ox. They are all hoarse in their speech, disreputable in their ways, and seriously misguided in the matter of shirts and ties. The actors who impersonate Detroit and Masterson are Sam Levene and Robert Alda, respectively, and they are superb at capturing that indefinable blend of terrible sentimentality and brassy sophistication that characterizes the Times Square man of distinction. The others include Stubby Kaye, Johnny Silver, Tom Pedi, and B. S. Pully, and I found each of them awe-inspiring, too. Among the virtuous members of the company are Paul Reed, as a hard-boiled detective; Netta Packer, as the commanding officer of the mission band; and Pat Rooney, Sr., who, as one of her lieutenants, sings a song, called "More I Cannot Wish You," that is one of the pleasantest things in the show.

SOMETHING TO REMEMBER US BY

APRIL 2, 1955 (ON *CAT ON A HOT TIN ROOF*)

On the whole, this has been a barren year in the theatre (it has, in fact, been so barren that there has been scarcely a play I couldn't imagine having written myself, suitably stimulated), and it is therefore a pleasure to announce that Tennessee Williams, well known to you, I'm sure, for *The Glass Menagerie* and *A Streetcar Named*

Desire, has written an almost wholly admirable play called *Cat on a Hot Tin Roof,* recently unveiled at the Morosco.

The story Mr. Williams has to tell is hard to summarize very intelligibly, because it deals with emotions rather outside our common, or at least acknowledged, experience. The play begins with a scene between a young woman and her husband, who has withdrawn from any real participation in life. In college, he reached a kind of limited excellence as a football player, and had a never quite explicitly homosexual relationship with another student, which makes it impossible for him to accept a world that seems to fall so far and disgustingly (this word is Mr. Williams') short of his adolescent dream. Anyway, he has taken to drink and has injured himself in a childish and drunken effort to recapture the athletic splendors of the past. His wife loves him, but her physical advances are repugnant to him and he is much too remote to appreciate the desperate humor of her conversation. There is no conceivable method of communication between them, and although it appears to me that Mr. Williams' specific dilemma is a little bizarre, his underlying thought is just as simple as this: the profound and tragic mystery that every man is to every other man in the world, and even to himself.

The plot is not much more than a serviceable mechanism for conveying the author's ideas. A rich old man, the hero's father, has come back, on his sixty-fifth birthday, to the family plantation. While an erroneous laboratory report has led him to suppose that he still has a good many years to live, the fact is that he is dying of cancer, and when he finds that out, he is obliged to make a final settlement of his affairs. This involves choosing as his heir either a boy whom he recognizes as an alcoholic and probably a homosexual or a son who is a competent bore with five existing children and another imminent. In a way, Mr. Williams has stacked his cards a little too obviously, since his corrupted idealist is as picturesque and charming a figure as any the theatre has recently produced and his bore isn't much more than a standard low-comedy caricature. There is never any question about the old man's real emotional commitment, and I should say that in this particular, too much legitimate dramatic suspense may have been sacrificed for a kind of self-conscious literary integrity. Mr. Williams, that is, has in general scornfully declined to write anything that could possibly be defined as a "commercial" play, and has, indeed, turned out something that occasionally seems like a parody of one. There are villains, but they are far too ludicrous to concern anybody much. If you really care about who gets the ten million dollars and the twenty-eight thousand acres of the most fertile land this side of the Nile, the Morosco is not the theatre you're looking for. The play there has to do with what an extremely sensitive writer has been able to make of a fragment of human experience. Any resemblance it may have to *The Desperate Hours* or any other shapely exercise of the year is the result of a compromise that I'm sure the author deplores exactly as much as I do.

Overlooking its mistakes, which seem to me many and important, *Cat on a Hot Tin Roof* is unquestionably a distinguished play. The scene in the first act between the hero and his wife is an impressive tour de force (it amounts essentially to a half-hour monologue, in which a semi-literate woman gives the whole history of the disaster that has overtaken them both to a man who stopped hearing living people talk quite a while ago), and a subsequent encounter, between the hero and his father, is on a level that few playwrights can approach. Much of Mr. Williams' thought is permanently inscrutable to me, but I think he intends to suggest that the partial knowledge men have of one another is infinitely preferable to the truth, which no one can face without seeing all the illusions by means of which he's managed to sustain himself destroyed. In any case, it is a piece of writing to be respected, and it seems a long time since I've been able to say that of anything.

Critics are notoriously half-witted in their appraisals of performances, and I would like to report only that Barbara Bel Geddes understands the technique of her trade better than any other young actress I can name (this includes Audrey Hepburn); that Ben Gazzara, in a part that demands an odd quality of low vitality, plays the husband with what struck me as a decent regard for the author's intention rather than any consideration of his own growing reputation; and that Burl Ives, as the father, is believable even when he is talking about the time he was seduced by a five-year-old Arab girl, which must have been quite a trick, on the whole. Among the others are Mildred Dunnock, Madeleine Sherwood, Pat Hingle, and Fred Stewart. They play more than acceptably the parts that Mr. Williams neglected to write, and Elia Kazan's direction indicates only occasionally that he was aware he had a Master on his hands. Jo Mielziner and Lucinda Ballard did the scenery and costumes, in that order. They are very gifted people.

BEEP THE MEEM

OCTOBER 1, 1955 (ON MARCEL MARCEAU)

THE TOPIC FOR discussion this week is the art of pantomime and, specifically, a Gallic practitioner of it called Marcel Marceau, who is now on exhibition at the Phoenix. This essay will be brief and, I'm afraid, unilluminating, partly because "mime," which most of the first-night audience chose to rhyme with "steam," is a special, hothouse art form that calls for a technical vocabulary a little outside my range, and partly because I suspect that the apathy I feel toward it is the product of a cultural inadequacy of my own and I am reluctant to expose it at any length. Several years ago, a Profile writer in these pages described his subject, Mr. Walter Winchell, as a "thrilling bore." With the addition of the word "intermittently," I think this odd phrase says approximately what is on my mind about M. Marceau. There were times in the course of the two-hour program when I was aware that he was doing something precise, difficult, and rather beautiful, in a manner rigidly stylized by tradition, and at those moments I was emotionally satisfied, in the direction of either comedy or pathos.

For the greater part of the evening, however, I found M. Marceau rather a trial. I had no doubt that he was performing in strict accordance with a set of ancient and remarkably exacting rules, but my appreciation of his work was academic at best. My attitude was presumably like that of a man at his first bullfight, who understands that a great and complicated ritual is involved but actually sees nothing except a man going enormously out of his way to kill a bull. This Philistine response was probably caused to some extent by the fact that a good deal of Marceau's material has to do with Continental customs and backgrounds bafflingly outside my experience, but the monotonous exercise of a single and to me not particularly fascinating skill had a lot to do with it, too.

Several of my colleagues, who apparently had hell's own time at the Phoenix, found occasion to compare the performer very favorably with Chaplin, and a similarity certainly exists, in the sense that the same technique is employed and the same essential personality created—a touchingly inadequate figure in conflict with a contemptuously hostile society. The primary difference, I should say, is in degree of talent, Chaplin being a man of delicate and subtle perception and extraordinary comic invention, and Marceau a far broader, more conventionally inspired, and considerably less appealing clown. The secondary one, of course, has to do with the method of presentation. The current exhibit is pantomime in its purest form. Marceau, that is, works alone, wearing a chalk mask and a variety of baggy costumes, and he employs no props except a wooden box or two. Chaplin, on the other hand, was assisted not only by elaborate scenery and a surrounding cast but also by a full-scale plot. It is obvious that the former is an infinitely more demanding form, and its self-imposed limitations probably put it in a higher category of art, at least in the eyes of proper aesthetes. It is my own opinion that no basis for serious comparison exists, but since it has been made, I can only say that I have an idea I will be remembering that little business with the forks and the rolls in *The Gold Rush* long after I have forgotten who Marceau was or what he did. I even suspect that I'll still remember old Joe Jackson, too, but then, of course, *he* had that bicycle.

There were fifteen items on M. Marceau's bill the night I was there. The eight that composed the first section were described in the program as "style pantomimes," and among their titles were "Walking Against the Wind," "The Public Garden," "At the Clothiers," "The Dice-Players," and "Youth, Maturity, Old Age, and Death." The second section was devoted to the activities of a character called Bip, who appears, variously, as a butterfly hunter, an amateur artist, a lion tamer, a tightrope walker, a railway passenger, a skater, a guest at a dance hall, and, simultaneously, David and Goliath. Most of these offerings are sufficiently defined by their headings, and I will describe them only to the extent of remarking that M. Marceau did indeed look amazingly like a man struggling uphill in a high wind or trying on a tight pair of gloves or annoying a lion, as the case might be. They were exact, polished, and particularly impressive to me in the feeling they gave of almost perfect timing and muscular control. Standing out above these feats of simple physical mimicry were "Youth, Maturity, Old Age, and Death," which actually and miraculously compressed the essence of a lifetime into something like two minutes, and "David and Goliath," which was one of the funniest and most ingenious double impersonations I have ever seen. I haven't anything else to say about M. Marceau, except that every now and then, for a disconcerting instant, he reminded me very strongly of Miss Judith Anderson as Medea. I have no reason to suppose that this was intentional.

SHAW WITH MUSIC

MARCH 24, 1956 (ON *MY FAIR LADY*)

JUST ABOUT THE most brilliantly successful scene I remember seeing in a musical comedy turns up somewhere about halfway through *My Fair Lady,* the adaptation of Shaw's *Pygmalion* at the Mark Hellinger. Eliza Doolittle, the Cockney flower girl whom Professor Henry Higgins is grooming to talk like a lady, suddenly manages to say "The rain in Spain falls mainly on the plains" with all its treacherous vowels intact, and so enchanted are her listeners that they go into a triumphant little tango by way of celebration. It is a moment that has practically everything—charm, style, wit, gaiety—and I will cherish it as long as I live. The rest of the play never quite achieves this magic level, but it is still all wonderfully entertaining, and extraordinarily welcome in a season that previously offered no musicals except two glum exploits called *The Vamp* and *Pipe Dream.*

My Fair Lady is meritorious in every department, but probably its greatest accomplishment lies in its remarkable humanization of Mr. Shaw, who has been transformed from an amiable but fundamentally sardonic observer of human behavior into a beaming old sentimentalist, as warm and lovable as Santa Claus. The changes and elisions that Alan Jay Lerner has made in the text are surprisingly few, considering the peculiar demands of musical comedy, but there is certainly a new sympathy for love. In *Pygmalion,* the approach, while by no means hostile, was still pretty chilly and vegetarian, giving the impression that the author was quite willing to tolerate sex but rather preferred to discuss the caste system. Mr. Lerner has remedied that. The science of phonetics and the general absurdity of hereditary aristocracy get into *My Fair Lady* all right, but the real emphasis is enthusiastically on romance. It seems to me that here and there something has been lost—Eliza's raffish papa, for instance, is a healthier and much less complicated scoundrel than he was in the original—but on the whole it is a highly intelligent and tremendously engaging piece of work. An only slightly smaller miracle has been accomplished with the songs, whose lyrics, by Mr. Lerner, if not precisely Shavian, are always cheerfully in key with the rest of the proceedings, and whose melodies, composed by Mr. Frederick Loewe, are as bright and stylish as everything else about the production. In addition to its pleasant sound, *My Fair Lady* is entrancing to look at. Oliver Smith's sets, ranging from the crazy squalor of Covent Garden to the icy grandeur of an embassy ballroom, are handsome, posterlike inventions, and Cecil Beaton's costumes—by far the best we've seen this year—show impressive wit and imagination. People really looked like something in 1912, I thought, surveying my neighbors in the opening-night audience, who seemed to have gone out of their way to dress in a singularly melancholy and uninspiring fashion.

As Eliza, Julie Andrews fulfills all the promise she showed last year in *The Boy Friend.* The part, of course, could hardly be more gratifying to an actress, since the transition from the screeching Cockney slattern of the early scenes to the composed and majestic elocutionist of the later ones is almost guaranteed sorcery, but Miss Andrews goes far beyond the obvious effects. She turns very satisfactorily from a howling savage into a suitable companion for duchesses, but there remains a fine suggestion of incorruptible vulgarity smoldering somewhere inside. Even when her poise and accent are most implacable, she still seems just on the verge of a yell. It is a hilarious and at the same time singularly touching performance. Rex Harrison, who plays Higgins, is rumored to have resisted even the slightest tampering with the original text, and there are times when he appears to be condescending somewhat to Mr. Lerner's version of the role. Nevertheless, it is generally an attractive effort, and he talks his songs at least as effectively as a lot of actors would sing them. Stanley Holloway, as Doolittle, is marvellously funny in his rendering of two numbers called "With a Little Bit of Luck" and "Get Me to the Church on Time," and there are other valuable contributions by Robert Coote, as a stuffy bulwark of the Empire; Cathleen Nesbitt, as a handsome Mayfair matron; and Viola Roache, Philippa Bevans, and John Michael King, in more or less subordinate assignments. Moss Hart has directed the cast of thirty-one with his customary skill, and Hanya Holm has staged at least two dances that struck me as being as lovely as dreams.

KENNETH TYNAN

POINTS WEST

MARCH 21, 1959 (ON *A RAISIN IN THE SUN*)

THE SUPREME VIRTUE of *A Raisin in the Sun,* Lorraine Hansberry's new play at the Ethel Barrymore, is its proud, joyous proximity to its source, which is life as the dramatist has lived it. I will not pretend to be impervious to the facts; this is the first Broadway production of a work by a colored authoress, and it is also the first Broadway production to have been staged by a colored director. (His name is Lloyd Richards, and he has done a sensible, sensitive, and impeccable job.) I do not see why these facts should be ignored, for a play is not an entity in itself, it is a part of history, and I have no doubt that my knowledge of the historical context predisposed me to like *A Raisin in the Sun* long before the house lights dimmed. Within ten minutes, however, liking had matured into absorption. The relaxed, freewheeling interplay of a magnificent team of Negro actors drew me unresisting into a world of their making, their suffering, their thinking, and their rejoicing. Walter Lee Younger's family lives in a roach-ridden Chicago tenement. The father, at thirty-five, is still a chauffeur, deluded by dreams of financial success that nag at the nerves and tighten the lips of his anxious wife, who ekes out their income by working in white kitchens. If she wants a day off, her mother-in-law advises her to plead flu, because it's respectable. ("Otherwise they'll think you've been cut up or something.") Five people—the others being Walter Lee's progressive young sister and his only child, an amiable small boy—share three rooms. They want to escape, and their chance comes when Walter Lee's mother receives the insurance money to which her recent widowhood has entitled her. She rejects her son's plan, which is to invest the cash in a liquor store; instead, she buys a house for the family in a district where no Negro has ever lived. Almost at once, white opinion asserts itself, in the shape of a deferential little man from the local Improvement Association, who puts the segregationist case so gently that it almost sounds like a plea for modified togetherness. At the end of a beautifully written scene, he offers to buy back the house, in order—as he explains—to spare the Youngers any possible embarrassment. His proposal is turned down. But before long Walter Lee has lost what remains of the money to a deceitful chum. He announces forthwith that he will go down on his knees to any white man who will buy the house for more than its face value. From this degradation he is finally saved; shame brings him to his feet. The Youngers move out, and move on; a rung has been scaled, a point has been made, a step into the future has been soberly taken.

Miss Hansberry's piece is not without sentimentality, particularly in its reverent treatment of Walter Lee's mother; brilliantly though Claudia McNeil plays the part, monumentally trudging, upbraiding, disapproving, and consoling, I wish the dramatist had refrained from idealizing such a stolid old conservative. (She forces her daughter, an agnostic, to repeat after her, "In my mother's house there is still God.") But elsewhere I have no quibbles. Sidney Poitier blends skittishness, apathy, and riotous despair into his portrait of the mercurial Walter Lee, and Ruby Dee, as his wife, is not afraid to let friction and frankness get the better of conventional affection. Diana Sands is a buoyantly assured kid sister, and Ivan Dixon is a Nigerian intellectual who replies, when she asks him whether Negroes in power would not be just as vicious and corrupt as whites, "I *live* the answer." The cast is flawless, and the teamwork on the first night was as effortless and exuberant as if the play had been running for a hundred performances. I was not present at the opening, twenty-four years ago, of Mr. Odets' *Awake and Sing,* but it must have been a similar occasion, generating the same kind of sympathy and communicating the same kind of warmth. After several curtain calls, the audience began to shout for the author, whereupon Mr. Poitier leaped down into the auditorium and dragged Miss Hansberry onto the stage. It was a glorious gesture, but it did no more than the play had already done for all of us. In spirit, we were up there ahead of her.

CORNUCOPIA

MAY 30, 1959 (ON *GYPSY*)

Quite apart from considerations of subject matter, perfection of style can be profoundly moving in its own right. If anyone doubts that, he had better rush to the Broadway Theatre and buy a ticket for *Gypsy,* the first half of which brings together in effortless coalition all the arts of the American musical stage at their highest point of development. So smooth is the blending of skills, so precise the interlocking of song, speech, and dance, that the sheer contemplation of technique becomes a thrilling emotional experience. It is like being present at the triumphant solution of some harsh architectural problem; stone after massive stone is nudged and juggled into place, with a balance so nice that the finished structure seems as light as an exhalation, though in fact it is earthquakeproof. I have heard of mathematicians who broke down and wept at the sight of certain immaculately poised equations, and I have actually seen a motoring fanatic overcome with feeling when confronted by a vintage Rolls-Royce engine. *Gypsy,* Act I, confers the same intense pleasure, translated into terms of theatre. Nothing about it is superfluous; there is no display of energy for energy's sake. No effort is spared, yet none is wasted. Book, lyrics, music, décor, choreography, and cast seem not—as so often occurs—to have been conscripted into uneasy and unconvinced alliance but to have come together by irresistible mutual attraction, as if each could not live without the rest. With no strain or dissonance, a machine has been assembled that is ideally fitted to perform this task and no other. Since the task is worth while, the result is art.

As everyone must surely be aware, the show is based on the memoirs of Gypsy Rose Lee, the renowned kimonophobe (to use a word of George Jean Nathan's) whose intellectual aspirations were gently pinked by Rodgers and Hart in a song called "Zip." Miss Lee's account of her early life in vaudeville and her subsequent transition to burlesque stripping was dominated by the eccentric, outspoken, and wildly propulsive figure of Rose, her mother. The latter, a nightmare incarnation of Noël Coward's Mrs. Worthington, put her two daughters on the stage as soon as they could walk, and kept them there, as a coy and piping child act, until both were well into their teens. They had no formal—and very little informal—education. Their parents were divorced when Gypsy, the elder of the sisters, was four years old, and although their mother afterward ran through two other husbands, the liaison in each case was brief, and it cannot be said that the girls ever felt truly fathered. Rose's pride and cynosure was her younger daughter, Baby June, who has recently published, under her present stage name of June Havoc, an autobiography in which her mother appears as a total monster, forever pressing the children's noses to the grindstone of her own frustrated ambitions. The show at the Broadway takes Miss Lee's view, which is rather more temperate; the element of vicarious fulfillment is unmistakably there, but we are encouraged to admire Rose's shrewdness as much as to dislike her possessiveness. The miraculous first half deals with her obsessive attempts to make Baby June a star, and ends when the child elopes, at the age of fourteen, with one of the boys in the act. As the curtain comes down, Rose has erased June from her mind and transferred her fantasies of fame to the gauche, neglected elder sibling. I don't know that I shall ever forget the way Sandra Church, as Gypsy, quails and shakes when she encounters her mother's heady, appraising stare and guesses what is in store for her. It is like watching a rabbit petrified by the headlights of a silently onrushing car.

Although Miss Church happens to be acting better than anyone else of her age on Broadway, a lot of people are equally responsible for the wonder of that first act. Jule Styne, the most persistently underrated of popular composers, has contributed to it nine songs, all of which are both exciting in themselves and relevant to the action—from the opening chorus, "May We Entertain You?," a splendid pastiche of ragtime vapidity, to "Everything's Coming Up Roses," in which Rose, whistling in the dark, tries to persuade herself that life without June is going to be just peachy. In addition, we have "Small World," an elastically swaying tune used by Rose to seduce Herbie, the agent who becomes her lover; "Little Lamb," sung by Gypsy to one of her mother's menagerie of pets; "You'll Never Get Away from Me," Rose's jovial assertion of her man's dependence; "If Momma Was Married," in which the daughters complain about their enslavement; and "All I Need Is a Girl," a song-and-dance number in the Astaire manner, performed by a young man who wants to leave Momma's troupe and go out on his own. He demonstrates his routine to Gypsy, and invites her to dance with him. This being a musical, she does, but, this being no ordinary musical, she does not know the steps, and the partners end up in a state of mild, enjoyable confusion.

The credit for this stroke, and for the whole physical gesture of the evening, belongs to Jerome Robbins, who, as director and choreographer, has poured into *Gypsy* the same abundance of invention with which he galvanized *West Side Story*. From the latter show he has borrowed a lyricist, Stephen Sondheim, and a librettist, Arthur Laurents, both of whom have brought to their new jobs an exemplary mixture of gaiety, warmth, and critical intelligence. A passing genuflection will suffice as tribute to Jo Mielziner, who must by now be aware that he is a superlative scenic designer, but I feel I should dwell longer on the cast. On Jacqueline Mayro, for instance, who plays Baby June, the cavorting tot, with a mask of dutiful glee and an absolute mastery of applause-milking devices, such as the pretense of breathlessness after a not particularly exhausting routine. On Lane Bradbury, too, who plays June grown up and ready to bolt. (The aging process is handled superbly, like a movie dissolve; the children dance in a flickering spotlight and are replaced, one at a time, by their adolescent selves.) And, above all, we must linger on Ethel Merman, the most relaxed brass section on earth, singing her heart out and missing none of her own inimitable tricks, among them her habit of sliding down to important words from a grace note above, which supplies the flick that precedes the vocal whipcrack. But Miss Merman not only sings; she acts. I would not say that she acts very subtly; Rose, after all, with her dreams of glory, her kleptomania, her savage parsimony, and her passion for exotic animals and Chinese breakfasts, is scarcely a subtle character. Someone in the show describes her as "a pioneer woman without a frontier," and that is what Miss Merman magnificently plays.

The second half, which is briefer, is also less effective. There are several reasons for this. One has to do with plot; having seen the grooming of Baby June, we now watch the grooming of Gypsy, and this makes for redundancy. Another is that Act II contains only three new songs; the rest are reprises. A third is the lack, felt ever more urgently as the hours tick by, of a good, solid male singer; Jack Klugman, the show's nearest approach to a hero, is an amiable actor, but his voice is no more than an amplified snore. Fourth, Sandra Church is too chaste in demeanor to reproduce the guileful, unhurried carnality with which the real Gypsy undressed. Fifth, we have the finale. Rejected by both her daughters, Miss Merman plods onto the empty stage and bursts into a song about how she could have been better than either of them, given the chance. No sooner has she embarked on what promises to be a burlesque routine of staggering panache than the authors cut in to remind her of their purpose, which is to demonstrate the beastliness of managing mothers. Accordingly, she breaks off in mid-phrase, and sets about lacerating herself in prose. This, I felt, was a case of integrity carried too far. Once Miss Merman has started to sing, nothing short of an air-raid warning should be allowed to interrupt her. To mute her at this point is an act of presumption, and the evening suffers from it. The latter half has in its favor a flamboyant trio of strippers, one of whom peels with her left hand while playing a trumpet with her right. But I don't see how anyone could deny that the show tapers off from perfection in the first act to mere brilliance in the second.

TELEVISION

PHILIP HAMBURGER

PEEPING FUNT

JANUARY 7, 1950 (ON *CANDID CAMERA*)

A GENTLEMAN NAMED ALLEN Funt, who presents a television program entitled *Candid Camera,* has succeeded, I think, in reducing the art, the purpose, and the ethics of the "documentary" idea to the level of the obscene. Mr. Funt, who airs his program Monday evenings over C.B.S. and who is sponsored by Philip Morris, employs a simple, deadly formula. Equipped with a hidden movie camera and microphone and a crew of assistant snoopers, he roams the city in various poses, pretending to be, say, a banker, a bootblack, or a mattress salesman. He records on film the words and actions of unsuspecting people, and, when he has finished with them, tells them what he has done to them, asks permission to televise the pictures, and explains that they will be paid off in cash and, I guess, in some dubious fame. For the purposes of his program, he then throws together a half hour of selected shots. Not long ago, for example, a lady entered the mattress department of R. H. Macy & Co. with nothing more in mind than the purchase of a mattress. Approaching what she thought was a salesman, she asked him to show her some mattresses. She naturally thought that the fellow was just another salesman employed by R. H. Macy & Co., but—you're right—he was Allen Funt, the Candid Camera Man, and he had been hanging around the mattress department, evidently with the jovial connivance of R. H. Macy & Co., ready to pounce on just such an innocent party. Without the customer's knowledge, he switched on his equipment, and from that moment forward almost everything possible was done to make her look foolish. The salesman (Funt) wondered who was to use the mattress. An old lady, said the customer. How does she sleep, asked the salesman. "Well," said the customer, "she generally sleeps on her back with her toes up." "With her toes up!" exclaimed the incredulous salesman (Funt). "We have no mattresses for sale here for people who sleep on their backs with their toes up." The customer was flabbergasted, but, being a lady and wanting to buy a mattress, she was patient with the salesman. He next wanted to know whether the old lady snored. "Sometimes," said the customer. "Try the mattress for comfort," said the salesman (Funt). "Bounce up and down on it." The customer bounced up and down on the mattress, right there in the mattress department of R. H. Macy & Co. What a gimmick! She thought she was just testing a mattress, see, but actually she was bouncing up and down, potentially, in the view of thousands of Peeping Toms watching her on television. Finally, Funt confessed to her that her every word and her every action had been recorded, and her embarrassment at this disclosure was likewise recorded.

For the same program, which was broadcast last week, Funt posed as a businessman and called up a messenger service and asked to have a boy sent around to his "office" to pick up a package he wanted delivered. When the messenger arrived, Funt handed him an unwrapped dead fish and ordered him to take it to a certain address. The messenger wondered, politely, whether he might wrap the fish. Nix, said the man (Funt), deliver it *as is*. "Holy cow!" said the messenger. "Down Fifth Avenue you want me to deliver this fish, walking down Fifth Avenue with fish—holy cow!" He was terribly, terribly embarrassed, and he wondered if he might call his office and find out whether he had to fulfill this dreadful mission. He called his office, and somebody at the other end of the line apparently told him to go ahead and deliver it. I shall not soon forget the essential nobility of this messenger. Mr. Funt had faced him with a painful situation. Obviously, his inclination was to tell the man (Funt) to go to hell, throw the fish in his face, and depart. But the messenger had a job, and, I gathered, needed the job, and at unknown risk to his self-respect he said, "O.K., I'll take the fish." Preparing to leave, humiliated, fish in hand, he remarked, quietly and expressively, "It would be different, you know, if I had caught this fish myself, somewhere out in the country."

Mr. Funt and C.B.S. and Philip Morris feel, I suppose, that Mr. Funt is giving the television audience portraits of "life in the raw," pictures of ordinary human beings trapped by strange circumstances and reacting like "people." In reality, he is demonstrating something that spies have known about since spies began to operate; namely, that most people are fundamentally decent and trusting and, sad to tell, can readily be deceived. Mr. Funt bases his program, purely and simply, upon deceit. Persuading his subjects that he is something he is not, he succeeds in making them look foolish, or in forcing them to struggle, against unfair odds, for some vestige of human dignity. For my money, *Candid Camera* is sadistic, poisonous, anti-human, and sneaky. The men who control television have tremendous opportunities for recording our times; they can go into people's homes and offices and factories, they can go through the great cities or take their cameras to remote parts of the country, as Robert Flaherty did in *Louisiana Story,* and show us how people live and behave. The catch is that the true documentarian must respect his fellow-man and feel that what he has to say is worth hearing. For years, radio has been showing its basic contempt for the dignity of man, and now television, with *Candid Camera* as a conspicuous example, is following suit.

JOHN LARDNER

BANANAS IN GENERAL

APRIL 19, 1958 (ON TV COMEDIANS)

I WROTE A CONSIDERABLE number of words here recently to the effect that Sid Caesar, in his Sunday-evening program *Sid Caesar Invites You,* is the only performer on television at present who does true, undiluted comedy on a regular basis. That's a broad and hazy proposition, and also, perhaps, by implication a gloomier one than I meant it to be. In the first place, it raises questions of definition, and of boundary lines. Jack Benny, for instance, provides regularly a program that goes beyond the limitations of mere situation comedy; it has certain of the outward marks of true comedy. Bob Hope, regardless of the quality of his work, adheres bravely and steadily to the comic tone; he's an undiluted comedian. Besides these two, there are many people in the field—some of them, to my mind, less synthetic than Mr. Benny and more original than Mr. Hope—who are funny by fits and starts. The fact that they can't, or don't, sustain the quality over a full, exacting season of television doesn't by any means cancel their usefulness or their importance. The material of television these days is generally so grim, so stiff with discretion, and so doughy with portent that it needs comedy to make it fit for human consumption. I didn't intend, when I first discussed Mr. Caesar's show, to suggest that comedy on the air had to be done his way—with a kind of desperate consecutiveness, by weekly performers—or not at all. There must be other, easier ways of bringing the supply of comic talent to bear. What's required, I think, is a formula that will allow as many good comedians as possible to do their stuff when and as best they can. The formula should also (this is a vital point) allow them to be wholly, unremittingly comic in character, with no forced excursions into sentimentality or public-spiritedness or that strange, degrading line of behavior that might be described as announcerism.

To get back for a moment to the question of definition: The reason Mr. Caesar is able to produce pure, unmixed, spontaneous comedy week after week is, I believe, that his work is essentially creative; that is, his humor comes primarily from his own special view of life, rather than from plots, props, jokes, and other contrivances of writers. Creative comedians are scarce. There have probably been no more than a dozen or so in this century. (In addition to W. C. Fields, Bobby Clark, Ed Wynn, Jimmy Durante, Groucho Marx, and Harpo Marx, whom I've mentioned before, the list might well include Beatrice Lillie, Victor Moore, Frank Tinney, Fannie Brice, Bert Williams, Bert Lahr, and a singing satirist of fifty years ago named Charlie Case. And, to be sure, Charlie Chaplin.) Most of them formed their styles and working habits in mediums more static and leisurely than television. Among comedians who have specialized, more or less, in television, perhaps only Jackie Gleason and Milton Berle, besides Mr. Caesar, have been even touched by the spirit of true, creative comedy; and Mr. Gleason and Mr. Berle, although they scrambled gamely against the odds of so-called exposure, were obliged in the long run to fall back on situation comedy or joke-book material or both, and then to retire—temporarily, I hope—from the wars to lick their wounds. I spoke a little earlier of Jack Benny as a performer who has managed to present a comic program at regular intervals. His stamina and his success have, of course, been prodigious, in television as well as in the calmer field of radio. Since his program is only superficially situation comedy—it qualifies, in part, because of the star's skill and influence, as the straight, personal comedy of the comic virtuoso—Mr. Benny's case calls for a word or two of explanation from me in defense of my first proposition. The fact is, I consider Mr. Benny to be not a true, creative clown but a shrewd politician and an immensely resourceful mechanic. On the face of it, his comedy is satiric, and thus genuine, because he dwells on human frailties: vanity, greed, arrogance, selfishness. But it seems to me that he forfeits any claim to the creation of sound social satire by spelling out the weaknesses of his characters, including himself, as though they were labels; and by taking care to show, quickly and consistently, that it isn't true, that it's all in fun. His program is an expert job of commercial demagogy. It represents, I feel, Mr. Benny's idea of just how far character study can be carried in front of a mass audience; and the stopping point is as carefully timed and calculated as every other phase of the Benny technique. At that point, Mr. Benny and his cast say "We're kidding." And they are. The show (*The Jack Benny Show,* Channel 2, 7:30–8 P.M., alternate Sundays) is, in short, a charade, a game of make-believe social criticism. It avoids the strains and risks of complete, uncompromising comedy, and therefore, as I see it, fails to challenge the bold loneliness of Mr. Caesar.

I have, nonetheless, a strong respect for Mr. Benny's good humor, mechanical or not. He is loyal to the mood of comedy. I also admire the doggedly fun-loving spirit of Mr. Hope (*The Bob Hope Show,* Channel 4), who is, if not the last, certainly the most tireless and confident of the stand-up comedians, or gagmen. There are, as I've said, comedians in circulation who strike me as being potentially funnier than either of these steadfast technicians. But the others—largely, I guess, through no fault of their own—are not doing themselves justice. Their activities are sporadic, or shamefully mixed. It's depressing, for example, to see a wit and comedian of the calibre of Steve Allen (*The Steve Allen Show,* Channel 4, 8–9 P.M., Sundays) performing the chores of an Ed Sullivan or a John Daly—introducing guests, promoting causes, running commercial errands, leading troops in the rating wars, behaving at times as blandly and institutionally as any other master of ceremonies. To take an austere view of the matter, it doesn't become an honest comedian to present *Photoplay*'s awards of the year to movie actors . . . or to plug even such respectable authors as J. Edgar Hoover, whose books expose, as Mr. Allen was saying the other night, "that ugly philosophy" . . . or to wish the world a happy St. Patrick's Day . . . or to use the industry's key word, "wonderful," fifty times in an evening. "You speak wonderful English," we find Mr. Allen saying. And "What do you like to do? Collect stamps? Wonderful!" And "You come from Denver? Wonderful!" And, by way of sweeping the board, "I'd like to thank all our wonderful guests!" It's possible, though not medically certain, that a comedian can injure himself organically by too much master-of-ceremonies work. As for some of the other present-day sidelines of comedians, they are patently dangerous. It's hard to see how George Gobel, for instance, who shares his program with a singer, can survive the experience with his native talent uninfected, in an age when singers are gaily and ruthlessly poisoning the wellsprings of humor.

And yet comedy—true, expert, original comedy—does continue to exist in television, in small lodes and veins that must be earnestly dug for. You'll find it on the Allen show, among others, if you're patient. Mr. Allen, when his mind is free of his hostly duties, is not only a smooth and versatile comedian himself but a patron and a collector of comedy. I've seen at least three excellent comic skits on his program in recent weeks, in which he ably and unselfishly played straight man. In one of these, Keenan Wynn analyzed different types of waiters. In another, Peter Ustinov analyzed national types of customs officials. In the third, Mr. Allen's panel of house comedians—whose work is sometimes a little blatant and hard on the nerves—were very funny, with Mr. Allen's help, as members of a research board called the Allen Bureau of Standards. Jack Paar (*The Jack Paar Show*, Channel 4, 11:15 P.M.–1 A.M., Mondays through Fridays) has also given valuable service as a collector and exhibitor of fragments of true comedy. Mr. Paar's own performance has in the last few months, I'm sorry to say, taken on an unaccountably sullen, tired, and arrogant tone that has done his program no good at all; a man of his ability and intelligence should not be using the audience-needling routine, which consists of remarks like "Are you dead out there?" and "Maybe I should try that again." But he does occasionally unearth a sound, fresh comedian whom the public might not otherwise see or know about; one such was a brash and nonsensical fellow named Charlie Weaver, whom Mr. Paar has been putting through his paces. And Mr.

Hope, in one of his shows in early February, made his audience a handsome and unexpected present of two sketches—a rock-'n'-roll parody, and a burlesque of *Lassie*—involving Wally Cox, an exceptionally deft and polished clown.

Since there are comedians available, it would seem that the problem is, first, to segregate them and, second, to find a way to put them to steady, sensible, organized use. Those who are now bogged down in serial stories or variety shows or ceremonial duties should be separated from their sticky surroundings at least for short, stated periods; as noted, a comedian, to be completely effective, must be completely comic, and completely uncommitted to anyone's mood or style but his own. History indicates that few true comedians—Mr. Caesar being the current exception—can beat the odds of exposure for any length of time with a weekly, or even a monthly, program. If that's the case, other means of distribution can be found. I devoutly hope that some network—or some high-minded combination of networks—will see its way soon to scheduling a full thirty-nine-week season of comedy, with a different comedian dominating each show. Small efforts have been made in this direction before, but none, as far as I know, that was thoroughly and ambitiously planned. The program might be staged biweekly, at a given time on a given night, to alternate with another kind of theatrical show, perhaps a play. In that event, only twenty major comedians would be needed for the comedy program. The quota, I'm reasonably sure, could be filled without trouble.

The comedians—that is, the dominating comedians—would be the best comedians. If Mr. Caesar were still fully engaged with his own show, as I trust he would be, I'd exempt him from the extra work. There would be a show apiece for, among others, Mr. Durante, Mr. Clark, the Marx Brothers, Miss Lillie, Mr. Moore, Mr. Lahr, Mr. Wynn (I'm speaking of Ed Wynn, but I'd be glad to see him supported by Keenan Wynn), Mr. Cox, Mr. Gleason, Mr. Berle (if he stuck to his historic, early-television form), and Mr. Allen. Because of Mr. Allen's special gift for the management and promotion of comedians, I'd expect him to bring along and manipulate his own private herd. I'd expect the same of Mr. Hope, if he were given a show, and Mr. Paar. Since Mr. Cox has proved that situation comedy, which he once practiced, does not necessarily destroy the reflexes and muscles needed for real comedy, I'd be willing to extend amnesty to Phil Silvers, and perhaps to Danny Thomas. I'd like to see Mr. Benny have an hour in which to demonstrate his slick but consummate art. I think the freedom of the hall might be awarded, for a full hour or less apiece, to three men of marked, if dissimilar, gifts, all television comedians emeritus—Ernie Kovacs, Henry Morgan, and Red Buttons.

The formula of limited exposure, of the once-a-year show, has been developed with particular skill by still another comedian, Victor Borge. I regard the comedy of Mr. Borge as being on the artificial and tricky side. I think it relies heavily on a bogus effect—on the kidding or negation of a serious accomplishment of his own, on the exploitation of his musicianship. The late Fred Stone exploited athleticism in the same way, and passed as a comedian. But, because Mr. Borge has paved the way for one-shot showmanship on television, I'll concede him a place on the new program, provided he remembers one of the program's rules: Don't mix in with the salespeople. In his last show, he did commercials. I've heard it said that the commercials were amusing, because Mr. Borge did them only semi-seriously. I defy any man, including Bob and Ray, to make a commercial funny if he is 1 percent serious—if, for that matter, he as much as mentions the product's name.

THOUGHTS ON RADIO-TELEVESE

JUNE 6, 1959 (ON ON-THE-AIR LANGUAGE)

INTERVIEWING GOVERNOR ROCKEFELLER recently on Station WMCA, Barry Gray, the discless jockey, felt the need to ask his guest a certain question. He also felt a clear obligation to put the inquiry in radio-televese, the semi-official language of men who promote conversation on the air. Though it is more or less required, this language is a flexible one, leaving a good deal to the user's imagination. "Governor," Mr. Gray said, after pausing to review the possibilities of the patois, "how do you see your future in a Pennsylvania Avenue sense?" I thought it was a splendid gambit. Another broadcaster might have said "How do you see yourself in the electoral-college picture?" or "How do you project yourself Chief Executive–wise?" The Gray formula had the special flavor, the colorful two-rings-from-the-bull's-eye quality, that I have associated with the work of this interviewer ever since I began to follow it, several years ago. For the record, Governor Rockefeller replied, "I *could* be happier where I am." He might have meant Albany, he might have meant the WMCA studio. As you see, radio-televese is not only a limber language, it is contagious.

The salient characteristic of remarks made in radio-televese is that they never coincide exactly with primary meanings or accepted forms. For instance, Mr. Gray, a leader in the postwar development of the lingo, has a way of taking a trenchant thought or a strong locution and placing it somewhere to the right or left of where it would seem to belong. "Is this your first trip to the mainland? How do you feel about statehood?," I have heard him ask a guest from the Philippines on one of his shows (the program runs, at present, from 11:05 P.M. to 1 A.M.). On the topic of Puerto Ricans in New York, he has said, "How can we make these people welcome and not upset the décor of the city?" On a show a few years ago, he described an incident that had taken place in a night club "that might be called a bawd." A drunk at a ringside table, Mr. Gray said, "interrupted the floor show to deliver a soliloquy." "When did the chink begin to pierce the armor?" he once asked, in connection with a decline in the prestige of former Mayor O'Dwyer. "The fault, then," he said on another occasion, "is not with Caesar or with his stars but with certain congressmen." Speaking of the real-life source of a character in a Broadway play, he has observed, "He was the clay pigeon on whom the character was modelled." When Mr. Gray called Brussels "the Paris of Belgium," I was reminded of an editorial I had read in a Long Island newspaper long ago in which Great Neck was called "the Constantinople of the North Shore." There is an eloquence and an easy confidence in Mr. Gray's talk that stimulates even his guests to heights of radio-televese. Artie Shaw, a musician, in describing the art of another performer to Mr. Gray, said, "He has a certain thing known as 'presence'—when he's onstage, you can see him." Another guest declared that the success of a mutual friend was "owing to a combination of luck and a combination of skill." "You can say that again," Mr. Gray agreed, and I believe that the guest did so, a little later. The same eloquence and the same off-centerism can be found today in the speech of a wide variety of radio and television regulars. "Parallels are odious," Marty Glickman, a sports announcer, has stated. "The matter has reached a semi-head," a senator—I couldn't be sure which one—said at a recent televised Congressional hearing. "I hear you were shot down over the Netherlands while flying," a video reporter said to Senator Howard Cannon, a war veteran, on a Channel 2 program last winter. "Where in the next year are we going to find the writers to fill the cry and the need?" David Susskind demanded not long ago of a forum of TV directors. "Do you have an emotional umbilical cord with Hollywood?" Mr. Susskind asked a director on the same show.

Mr. Susskind's second question raises the point that metaphor is indispensable in radio-televese. "Wherein water always finds its own level, they should start hitting soon," a baseball announcer said about the Yankees the other day. In an earlier year, Red Barber, analyzing a situation in which a dangerous batter had been purposely walked, with the effect of bringing an even more dangerous batter to the plate, remarked that it was a case of "carrying coals to Newcastle, to make use of an old expression." I suspect that Mr. Barber meant that it was a case of the frying pan and the fire, and I also suspect that if he had thought of the right metaphor afterward, he would have corrected himself publicly. He is a conscientious man, and therefore by no means a typical user of radio-televese. The true exponent never retraces his steps but moves from bold figure to bold figure without apology. There have been few bolder sequences (or "seg-ways," as they are sometimes called on the air) than the one that Mr. Gray achieved in 1957, during a discussion of the perils faced by Jack Paar in launching a new program. I think I have quoted this passage here once before; it still fills me with admiration. "It's like starting off with a noose around your neck," Mr. Gray said. "You've got twenty-six weeks to make good, or they'll shoot you. That sword of Damocles can be a rough proposition." As most of you know by now, Mr. Paar eventually made good before the sword could explode and throttle him.

Perhaps the most startling aspect of radio-televese is its power to move freely in time, space, and syntax, transposing past and future, beginnings and endings, subjects and objects. This phase of the language has sometimes been called backward English, and sometimes, with a bow to the game of billiards, reverse English. Dorothy Kilgallen, a television panelist, was wallowing in the freedom of the language on the night she said, "It strikes me as funny, don't you?" So was Dizzy Dean when he said, "Don't fail to miss tomorrow's doubleheader." Tommy Loughran, a boxing announcer, was exploring the area of the displaced ego when he told his audience, "It won't take him [the referee] long before I think he should stop it." Ted Husing was on the threshold of outright mysticism when he reported, about a boxer who was cuffing his adversary smartly around, "There's a lot more authority in Joe's punches than perhaps he would like his opponent to suspect!" It is in the time dimension, however, that radio-televese scores its most remarkable effects. Dizzy Dean's "The Yankees, as I told you later . . ." gives the idea. The insecurity of man is demonstrated regularly on the air by phrases like "Texas, the former birthplace of President Eisenhower" and "Mickey Mantle, a former native of Spavinaw, Oklahoma." I'm indebted to Dan Parker, sportswriter and philologist, for a particularly strong example of time adjustment from the sayings of Vic Marsillo, a boxing manager who occasionally speaks on radio and television: "Now, Jack, whaddya say we reminisce a little about tomorrow's fight?" These quotations show what can be done in the way of outguessing man's greatest enemy, but I think that all of them are excelled by a line of Mr. Gray's, spoken four or five years ago: "What will our future forefathers say?"

It is occasionally argued in defense of broadcasters (though they need and ask for no defense) that they speak unorthodoxly because they must speak under pressure, hastily, spontaneously—that their eccentricities are unintentional. Nothing could be farther from the truth. Their language is proud and deliberate. The spirit that has created it is the spirit of ambition. Posterity would have liked it. In times to come, our forebears will be grateful.

ART & ARCHITECTURE

ROBERT M. COATES

EXTREMISTS

DECEMBER 9, 1950 (ON JACKSON POLLOCK ET AL.)

THE CRITIC CONFRONTED with such a phenomenon as Jackson Pollock, whose new paintings are now on view at the Betty Parsons Gallery, is obliged to cling more tightly than usual to his basic beliefs if he is to review the man's work with reasonable intelligence. He must remind himself that artists are rarely humorous, at least where their painting is concerned, and, despite what the cynical may say, they are still less likely to devote themselves to a lifetime of foisting off practical jokes on the public, especially when they make very little money in the process. He should recall that even the most extravagant technical innovations generally have some artistic justifications, and remember, too, that no matter how fantastic and unconventional they may seem, there are always, underneath the surface, some linkages with the past. So although Mr. Pollock—along with others of the new "wild" school of moderns, like Hans Hofmann, Richard Pousette-Dart, and Louis Schanker—has been accused of pretty much everything, from a disgracefully sloppy painting technique to out-and-out chicanery, we can afford to disregard or discount most of the charges. His unorthodox manner of applying pigment (he is reported to work with the canvas flat on the floor, and just dribble the paint on straight from the can or tube) and his fondness for such unusual materials as aluminum paint, asphalt roofing cement, and Duco enamel, though both were probably at the start gestures of rebellion against conventional procedures, have a certain wry relation to the brisker industrial practices, in which the brush is also abandoned in favor of directer methods and new materials are constantly being experimented with. Odd and mazy as it is, his painting style is far from sloppy, for the overlying webs on webs of varicolored lines that make up most of his pictures are put on with obvious sureness, while the complaint that it's all a vast hoax falls to the ground, it seems to me, because of the size and, to date, the unprofitableness of his enterprise.

The question still remains: What is Pollock getting at? Here, I think, as is true of others of the general school he belongs to, the concept of design makes understanding the work a bit difficult. To most of us, form means outline, and, conversely, when we see an outline on canvas, we try to make it contain a form. This is, it happens, a situation that the Cubists and such early Non-Objectivists as van Doesburg and Mondrian were up against, but because their designs were either angular or precisely curved, they instantly suggested the outlines and forms of simple geometry, and acquired for the spectator—by association, as it were—a feeling of inevitability and austere logic. In Pollock's work, though, the drawing is irregular and sinuously curved, while the composition, instead of being orderly and exact, is exuberant and explosive. Both suggest the organic, and since the lines of natural forms are varied and unpredictable, we search longer for the recognizable outline (which, of course, isn't there) and are all the more baffled when we cannot find it.

It is partly because of this difference, I believe, that Pollock's paintings, while they are actually no more arbitrary in their design than, say, Mondrian's, seem so much more difficult to "get into" immediately, but it is true, too, that the younger man has hardly yet acquired the wisdom and maturity of the other. It's still possible, though, to get past the apparent obscurities of Pollock's work, and the new show, which contains some thirty canvases, all but one of them dated this year, gives an excellent chance to observe both the strengths and the weaknesses of his work. Among the faults, I think—and this one is a failing of the whole school—is a tendency to let the incidental rule at the expense of the overall concept, with the result that the basic values of a composition are lost in a clutter of more or less meaningless embellishment. (All the pictures in the show are simply numbered, by the way, which makes reference to them here a bit dull.) This fault is particularly evident in the two large canvases numbered 30 and 31, while in some of the smaller ones, notably No. 15, a really exquisite rhythmic quality in the design is almost totally obscured by the same sort of overelaboration.

There is, as well, a slight repetitiousness in Pollock's color patterns. His favorite compositional device is the overlying webs and striations that I have mentioned, and though this gives an air of depth and spaciousness to his canvases that is quite distinctive, it seems to me that too often the progression is up from a background of blue-greens and reds, through a network of whites, to a bolder pattern in black, and I am grateful when occasionally, as in the lacy and delicate No. 1 and the snowy-looking No. 27, he varies the sequence. By no means all of the work is repetitious, however, as one can see if one turns from the boldly black No. 32 to No. 27, or to the friezelike, somewhat smaller No. 7, and in general the work shows a healthy imaginativeness of attack. Pollock's main strength, though, lies in an exuberance and vitality that, though hard to define, lend a sparkle and an excitement to his painting. I felt this particularly in such pieces as the green-and-black No. 19 and the lively, small No. 18. But it's a quality that is apparent all through the show, and I hope that he doesn't end up by letting it run away with him.

STYLES AND PERSONALITIES

JANUARY 17, 1959 (ON AN ABSTRACT EXPRESSIONISM SHOW)

DIVISIONISM IS A crime in the Communist countries, but I've always felt that in a school of art it's a healthy manifestation—as the survey now on at the Sidney Janis, of a group of our top Abstract Expressionist painters, indicates. The development of any school of art, I've noticed, follows a fairly fixed pattern. First comes the breakaway, the time when about the only thing the artists feel is an acute dissatisfaction with the established painting purposes and procedures. But this is only the negative phase, and as the positive search for new methods begins it is followed by the theoretical, or let's-all-get-together-and-work-out-a-better-system, period. Then artistic personalities are lost in a welter of generalization—really lost, for to abandon a traditional style is like abandoning a well-travelled highway in a desert, fog-bound. It takes courage. But since no one knows for sure which way to head now, there is at first a tendency to huddle, and it's not till the fog lifts, or—to wrestle this metaphor back to its bearing on art again—till the mistier part of the theorizing clears and the new direction becomes plainer, that the artists' separate personalities can begin to emerge.

This, I think, is the danger point in any school's development, for this is the time for wider exploration, and the school's tenets and aims must be broad and well-founded enough to allow for it. The artists can no longer even go single file; they must be able to branch out on side excursions of their own, and if they can't do that and still retain a certain coherence within their group, then the school itself will surely die—as Orphism died, and Dynamism, Suprematism, and a number of the other once promising abstract movements that sprang up in the early part of this century. This is the "divisionist" phase. It's a testing phase, which may be one reason the Communists don't like it, since its effect in the end is to prove how strong or weak the school's philosophic basis is, by trying out its adaptability to broad individual interpretation. It seems to me that Abstract Expressionism is in that phase now, and the fact that it stands up as well as it does under the test is an indication of its vitality as a method.

The exhibit at the Sidney Janis is a case in point. Eight artists are represented, each with a single canvas, and two of them, Josef Albers and Arshile Gorky, are not strictly Abstract Expressionist. Gorky, though, was a forerunner, and as his painting (untitled) demonstrates, with its floating, indeterminate figures and flowing pattern, he was unquestionably an influence on the school in its formative days. And while Albers' firm addiction to the geometric approach might appear to rule him out as an influence, one has only to compare his *Homage to the Square* with the blurred geometry of Mark Rothko's *Red, White and Brown*—both built on rectangular patterns and both striving for vibrant tonal effects—to see a definite affinity between the older man and the younger one. The five other paintings show further variations in the Abstract Expressionist approach. There has always been a good deal of diversification in the group, the distinction at its broadest being between the more or less calligraphic style of Franz Kline, say, and the flamboyantly colorful manner affected by Willem de Kooning. Both these men are in the show, Kline with a slashingly powerful black-and-white oil, *Delaware Gap,* and de Kooning with a gentler study based on landscape motifs, *Suburb in Havana,* which to me has a suggestion of van Gogh. Philip Guston's *The Return,* a kind of waterfall of greenish lacery, doesn't show him at his best, and the same must be said of Robert Motherwell's lumpish *The Wedding.* But to make up for that there's a handsome, intricate large *Frieze,* by Jackson Pollock.

• • •

Hans Hofmann, at seventy-eight, is the undisputed dean (and in a sense even the founder) of Abstract Expressionism, and his paintings, now at the Kootz, have an authority that is fully commensurate with his position. The exhibition is a two-part affair. The first section, closing this Saturday, is given over to his paintings of the past year, about twenty in number, while the second, running through the rest of January, will be devoted to a display of his earlier works, dated from 1940 to 1947. As for his current production, I must say that it seems to be his finest performance so far. Hofmann has always been primarily a colorist; indeed, the interplay of tonalities, one upon the other, has always been the factor that "made" his paintings, far more than any formal structure. His color now is fully as varied as ever. But he has succeeded in sharpening his compositional values, so the paintings seem stronger and denser in design. Exuberance is still one of the key words for Hofmann's manner, however, and there are times when, inevitably, it spills over into sheer flamboyance, as in the rather hectic *Towering Clouds,* or into mere clutteredness, as in the awkwardly planned *Blue Spell.* I feel, too, that the artist depends to excess upon tiered slabs of crusty color, laid on with the palette knife, for textural effect; used to excess, they seem to weight the over-all compositional fabric down, and I thought the otherwise admirable *Golden Blaze* suffered because of this. One can have little but praise, though, for such paintings as *Equinox* (with its climbing, varicolored patterns), the beautifully blue *Oceanic,* and the handsomely organized *The Phantom.*

LEWIS MUMFORD

THE MUD WASPS OF MANHATTAN

MARCH 25, 1950 (ON TALL BUILDINGS GONE WRONG)

During the past year there has been an eruption of tall office buildings in midtown Manhattan. Once more, office buildings, at least those under thirty stories high, are profitable investments, or, at all events, a lot of people seem to think so. To an old New Yorker such an outbreak is quite commonplace, and it is a shock to realize that except for Rockefeller Center and the postwar Universal Pictures Building, at Park Avenue and Fifty-seventh, these are almost the first tall office buildings to go up in New York in twenty years. Twenty years is a long time, and architecture everywhere has advanced rapidly in that span. Naturally, this spate of construction makes one wonder how much New York has learned in that time—whether the people of the city now understand the forces that are making Manhattan unlivable, whether investors and builders have contemplated the limited achievements of Rockefeller Center and considered how far they are prepared to go beyond it. The answer is that nobody seems to have learned anything. The new skyscrapers are being built by people who reason like the mud wasp; their chain reflexes will not let them do anything their ancestors have not done a thousand times before. Fortunately for the mud wasp, his humble dwelling is still habitable; unfortunately for New Yorkers, the skyscrapers they persist in building will ultimately ruin the city almost as effectively as any H-bomb.

Let us examine in detail three of the new crop of buildings—the one at the northeast corner of Park Avenue and Fifty-ninth Street, which I shall call Buff, after the color of its brick facing; the white whale of a building, No. 488, that raises its hump over the west side of Madison Avenue between Fifty-first and Fifty-second Street; and the Crowell-Collier Building, at Fifth Avenue and Fifty-first Street. Like the Universal Pictures and the McGraw-Hill Buildings, Buff and 488 differ from the skyscrapers of the boom period in that they stress horizontal and not vertical lines; none of these buildings was conceived, to recall Louis Sullivan's famous description of the skyscraper, as a "proud and soaring thing." The continuous window without any visible columns or walls to interrupt its flow was first used, if memory does not betray me, by Eric Mendelsohn in his design for the Schocken department store in Chemnitz, Germany, a generation ago. That façade carried a step further Hans Poelzig's robust treatment of a Breslau office building in 1912. When the interior of an office or a factory is so shallow that sunlight can penetrate its full depth, there is good reason for using this system of fenestration. In the case of Buff and 488, strip windows are used apparently just because they are fashionable; after all, these buildings are so deep that sunlight cannot completely penetrate, and they have to rely upon artificial lighting at all hours of the day. The one good reason for using this type of window in such structures has been ignored. Kahn & Jacobs, in their design for the Universal Pictures Building, excellently expounded that reason. Using the narrow columns in the frames of their strip window for vertical support, these architects did away with bulky columns in or near the outer wall. This permits a most flexible use of floor space, since partitions may be placed almost at will. Neither Buff nor 488 takes advantage of this innovation in construction. The supporting columns from which the floors are cantilevered out are only a couple of feet from the windows, and the floor space is even less adaptable than it would be if the designers had kept to the old-fashioned practice of placing big supporting columns in the outer walls. Unless the strip window is a building's major source of light and air, there is nothing in particular to be said in favor of using it instead of more conventional fenestration; in this city of torrid summer temperatures, the balance is a little on the side of the latter. The one thing that can be said for the strip windows of Buff and 488 is that they seem to have tempted the architects to turn their corners with a curve rather than a right angle. But why this aesthetic effect should appeal to hardheaded businessmen I do not know, since it causes them to lose a small yet appreciable amount of floor space at the most valuable part of a building, where the light and ventilation come from two sides. The strip window also can have a tricky optical effect, one that was first noticeable some years ago in the McGraw-Hill Building and that is quite plain in 488: While 488's topmost setback, which houses the elevator and air-conditioning machinery, is rather well done, the strip window beneath creates the illusion that the setback is leaning over. Happily, the building offers some photogenic passages in compensation. On the Fifty-first Street side, the smooth black-and-white walls break into a series of setbacks; visually, these curving waves of black and white dash against the smooth, unbroken rear walls of Best's. In bright sunlight, the effect is exhilarating, but like so many good subjects for photography, it is almost innocent of architectural intention. If there were no zoning restrictions to establish setbacks, the façade would have been unbroken.

Externally, as a piece of metropolitan stage decoration, 488 is "clean," unlike most of the city's skyscrapers between 1908 and 1931, or from the Singer Building to the Irving Trust Company. But that mere absence of insipid or irrelevant detail, which in the mid-twenties would have been a triumph, is by now a minimal requirement of large-scale urban architecture. The architect has thoughtfully used for contrast with his continuous glass windows smooth horizontal hands of cream-white brick rather like the brick used in the neighboring Best's, and he has most delicately underlined the horizontal accent by inserting two bands of headers—bricks laid with their ends showing—for the bond. He has, I think, carried the principle of unity too far by employing for the lowest band of masonry, above the big show windows of the ground floor, a granite of almost the same tone and textural reticence as the brick. Here a treatment much richer in color or texture might have been used to separate the great mass of 488 from its base. Verdict: a good architect pitted against a problem of site incapable of a sound organic solution.

• • •

The Crowell-Collier Building is another matter. It is indecisive in aesthetic intention, confused and contradictory in detail, lacking in visual relation to its Rockefeller Center neighbors, and embellished (over its side entrance) with some extremely depressing ornamental sculpture. I have looked at this building repeatedly without discovering what the designers were doing, or even what they thought they were doing. The base of the building is dedicated to the National City Bank: great oblong upright windows, opening on a very spacious interior—an interior that is classicism without Corinthian columns, dignity "humanized" by some insipidly colossal and colossally insipid wall paintings, of the kind indigenous to insurance calendars and banks. The architects are not to blame for these last embellishments, but they are nevertheless in keeping with the side-entrance sculpture.

Viewed a few blocks away, from the south, the profile of the building is rather handsome, but its planes and setbacks seem all awry when approached from the east. The facing is a fine-grained limestone, almost smooth enough to be called marble. At certain points, the blocks are shaped and laid to emphasize the horizontal, but the uprights between some of the window panels are carved to emphasize the vertical. This aesthetic indecision characterizes the whole structure. The best feature of the Crowell-Collier Building is probably the lobby—smooth, unostentatious, wholly consistent. In sum, this building is an example of eclecticism without conviction. In attempting to reconcile the traditional and the modern, it has managed to combine the saddest features of each.

• • •

But my most serious objections to these buildings are not aesthetic objections, and the blame does not lie with their architects. These buildings fail as sound architecture, philosophically speaking, because their builders committed themselves to an obsolete program of land development based upon getting hold of a few lots, originally plotted for single-family residences, and covering them completely with buildings designed to afford the maximum possible amount of rentable space. That is the formula that produced New York's present chaos, and though it still seems to suit the investors it has become a headache for everyone else. As long as land values are what they are in the midtown section, there is no way of making a fresh start; in fact, no one investor can afford to do anything but what he is now doing. Unfortunately, every new building that follows this obsolete pattern imposes new burdens upon the city as a whole: traffic delays, increased cost of delivering goods, higher taxes to pay for all the fresh engineering palliatives that must be introduced to repair the immediate effects of congestion without ever bringing about a cure—in short, economic waste and human frustration. Inevitably, some drastic step must be taken to nullify the damage that is being done. Our zoning and heights-of-buildings regulations are almost farcical because of their failure to deal with the acute problems of overbuilding, but their existence has long lulled people into thinking that something has in fact been done. There are no effective laws to restrain builders and investors from overcrowding the land; the City Planning Commission, though it has the legal power to control heights, can in practice do this properly only where land values are low, and it hardly makes more than a pretense of doing it anywhere. The city's whole tax structure is based on congested densities and high land values, so the city, no less than the investor, is caught in a vicious circle of our own making. Furthermore, there has been no private or public effort to assemble parcels of land the size of Rockefeller Center on which an efficient group of office buildings, more conducive to successful business as well as to successful architecture, could be erected. Only the mud-wasp mind has been working. The result is neither architecture nor civic order.

If we wish to keep traffic from complete coagulation in Manhattan, we shall have to impose strict limitations on the height and plot coverage of all future office buildings. They may, perhaps, have to be less than ten stories, at least along the midtown streets. The place for new office groups is on the outskirts of our overcrowded business districts, in the derelict areas east of Third Avenue, west of Eighth Avenue, and south of Washington Square. The City Planning Commission has always had some able men, but as a body it has lacked the courage and the imagination to buck the tide that is rapidly undercutting the foundations of the city. The Commission should ask the state legislature for the power to condemn land for business purposes, and it should then replan the proper sections of town expressly for office buildings of the proper height and size. This would do more to overcome the strangulation of its activities than a dozen Robert Moseses pushing through a dozen more super-colossal arterial highways.

In the midtown area, between eleven in the morning and six in the evening, it is often quicker to walk anywhere than to take a taxi or bus. If the custom of overloading the land with twenty- and thirty-story skyscrapers persists, even walking will be reduced to the best speed one can now achieve on Broadway during the theatre rush—a mile an hour. Though there has been little construction of buildings for twenty years, the multiplication of motorcars has been enough to bring on a creeping paralysis, and now that this congestion is being aggravated by a series of new office buildings in mid-Manhattan, the grim end is in sight. As the city nears strangulation, because of the congestion of its streets, the overcrowding of its transit lines, and the lack of off-street parking space, our builders are cheerfully tightening the hangman's noose by creating buildings that not only augment the traffic on the streets they abut but do not provide any off-street parking space for the vehicles of their occupants and visitors.

Some weeks ago, in these columns, I pointed out a minor example of intelligent long-term planning and canny business acumen—the Parke-Bernet Galleries Building, owned by the City Investing Company. Our midtown business district desperately needs an even bolder and more imaginative approach. Instead, someone will soon be tearing down the Ritz to supplant it with a temporarily more profitable office building—replacing a fine hotel in the right place with a plethora of offices in the wrong place. That process will go on until the citizens of New York decide that they must begin planning for their own survival.

THE ROARING TRAFFIC'S BOOM

APRIL 2, 1955 (ON A CONGESTED METROPOLIS)

WHAT HAPPENS IN New York to the art of building is bound up with what happens to the city as a place to work and live in. If it ceases to be a milieu in which people can exist in reasonable contentment instead of as prisoners perpetually plotting to escape a concentration camp, it will be unprofitable to discuss its architectural achievements—buildings that occasionally cause people to hold their breath for a stabbing moment or that restore them to equilibrium by offering them a prospect of space and form joyfully mastered. For a whole generation, New York has become steadily more frustrating and tedious to move around in, more expensive to do business in, more unsatisfactory to raise children in, and more difficult to escape from for a holiday in the country. The subway rides grow longer and the commuting trains carry their passengers from more distant suburbs, until as much time is spent in transporting the human carcass as is gained by diminishing the work week. Because urban surface transportation often comes almost to a standstill, the cost of delivering anything to anyone is rising steeply and the futility of owning a car for any purpose but fleeing the city over the weekend is becoming clearer and clearer. Meanwhile, the distant dormitory areas of New York describe ever wider arcs. By 1975, the Regional Plan Association's experts calculate, more people will be living in the suburbs within fifty miles of New York than will live in the city itself. When that happens, it will be impossible to build enough highways to accommodate the weekend exodus, just as it is already impossible to provide enough internal traffic arteries to handle Manhattan's present congestion. And obviously, even if people could escape, they would then have no place within easy distance to go, since there would be no choice for recreation but metropolitan jam or suburban jelly.

Fifty years ago, the upper-income groups here, as in most other big towns, began to move out of the city along the railroad lines, to provide their families with peace and quiet, open spaces and gardens, and tree-lined roads that brought them quickly into the country for a walk or a picnic. *Life with Father* took on a rural tinge, though Father rarely got home in time to do more than say good night to the children. Since then, the desire to escape the city has filtered down into every other economic group, and as a result of the suburb's popularity in satisfying this desire, that haven of refuge is itself filling up. Despite village zoning laws, skyscraper apartments overtop the trees in regions that were rural only yesterday, and the load of metropolitan traffic on the parks and highways around New York, abetted by the subdivider busily turning farms into building lots, has enormously cut down the open spaces that gave the suburb, despite its inconveniences, an edge over the city.

Were the eruption of vehicles and buildings in and around New York a natural phenomenon, like Vesuvius, there would be little use discussing it; lava inexorably carves its own channels through the landscape. But the things that spoil life in New York and its environs were all made by men, and can be changed by men as soon as they are willing to change their minds. Most of our contributions to planned chaos are caused by private greed and public miscalculation rather than irrational willfulness. During the nineteenth century, when more cities were built than ever before, the business of assembling them was entirely in the hands of those who were thinking only of their immediate needs or their immediate profit. "Officers and all do seek their own gain, but for the wealth of the Commons not one taketh pain," a late-medieval poet commented at the very beginning of this urban breakdown. By now, hundreds of millions of dollars are poured every year into clearly obsolete and ineffectual efforts to overcome the ensuing congestion—street widenings, double-deck bridges, cloverleaf intersections, subways, garages—and the sole result of these improvements is to accelerate the disorder they are supposed to alleviate. Manhattan will soon be in the same predicament as imperial Rome; it will have to banish private wheeled traffic from the midtown area in daytime, as Julius Caesar did in Rome, to permit a modicum of public transportation and pedestrian movement. This will mean, as in Rome, the delivery of goods by night. That may temporarily relieve the congestion, but it will permanently increase insomnia, as Juvenal sardonically noted after Caesar issued his traffic ordinance.

I have put the whole urban picture within this ample frame to counteract the current habit of looking at one small corner of the problem—congestion at the Jersey end of the George Washington Bridge at 8:45 A.M. or at the intersection of Seventh Avenue and Thirty-fifth Street at 3 P.M.—and attempting to solve that. Perhaps the wisest words on the complexity of the traffic problem were uttered long ago by Benton MacKaye, who fathered the Appalachian Trail. To relieve the congestion of traffic in Times Square, he remarked, it might be necessary to reroute the flow of wheat through the Atlantic ports. But our one-eyed specialists continue to concoct grandiose plans for highway development, as if motor transportation existed in a social vacuum, and as if New York were a mere passageway or terminal for vehicles, with no good reasons of its own for existence. To these experts, a successful solution of the traffic problem consists of building more roads, bridges, and tunnels so that more motorcars may travel more quickly to more remote destinations in more chaotic communities, from which more roads will be built so that more motorists may escape from these newly soiled and clotted environments. If these planners realized that it is as much the concern of good planning to prevent traffic from going into areas that should remain secluded and stable as it is to bring new traffic into areas that should be developed, they would never have offered their recent proposal for undermining what is left of rural Long Island. About that particular outrage, I shall have more to say in a later article.

The fact is that motor transportation is the sacred cow of the American religion of technology, and in the service of this curious religion no sacrifice in daily living, no extravagance of public expenditure, appears too great. Motor transportation is not merely an object of public worship; it has succeeded the railroad as the most powerful tool for either distributing or congesting the population—and it currently does both. Like any other tool, it must be used for some human purpose beyond the employment of the tool itself, and that further purpose represents the difference between carving and mere whittling. Our transportation experts are only expert whittlers, and the proof of it is that their end product is not a new urban form but a scattered mass of human shavings. Instead of curing congestion, they widen chaos.

• • •

The best way to understand what has to be done to make both the city itself and the surrounding region livable and workable is to begin our exploration of the problem at the center of the town and work outward to the country. The same principles of modern planning apply to both areas, and are just as difficult to put into action. The problem affects the working of every organ of the city, and neither gentle poultices nor brutal surgery (like the latest roadway encroachments on Central Park) will restore the city to health. The gridiron plan of New York, with its standard block, two hundred feet wide by six hundred feet long, and its numerous intersections, is a product of the age of the public stagecoach, the private carriage, and the common cart. The massive network of streets and avenues that, back in 1811, the City Planning Commissioners projected up as far as 155th Street was more than adequate for its original job. In fact, it was actually wasteful of land in residential areas, for it gave these quarters the same vehicular space it gave the busiest commercial districts, and thus sacrificed land that should have been dedicated to squares and parks and schools. But as long as only horses and carriages used the streets and only a fraction of the population could afford a private turnout, the streets of New York—at least above Washington Square—met the demands of transportation. This is not to say that there were not occasional traffic snarls and bottlenecks. For the safety of the pedestrian, the municipality in 1867 built a four-pronged footbridge over Broadway at Fulton Street, and if laziness had not prevailed over prudence, it might have built a series of footways over every busy intersection, like those that now span the East River Drive.

What caused traffic to become a serious problem was first the development of the multi-story building after the 1880s and then the rapid spread of the motorcar after 1915. There were forty persons per motor vehicle in the United States in 1915, a little over ten in 1920, and about five in 1925, and though at first New York didn't go in for automobile ownership as wholeheartedly as other parts of the country, its density of population produced the same problems here just as quickly. During the Second World War, owners were permitted to use the public streets gratis all week long for parking, and since then the number of cars quartered along our curbs has grown year by year. Our streets and avenues were designed to serve a density of population no greater than could be accommodated in buildings four stories high. But in a large part of Manhattan we have overlaid the land with so many high buildings that we have in effect piled from three to ten early Manhattans on top of each other. If the average height of these buildings was only twelve stories, the roadway and sidewalks flanking them should, according to the original ratio, be two hundred feet wide, which is the entire width of the standard New York block. In other words, to alleviate the pressure of traffic, we should be tearing down all the existing buildings in certain areas instead of putting up still taller ones.

As the city grew, the elevateds and subways took some of the load of traffic off the streets and temporarily stalled off strangulation of Manhattan's north and south traffic, but these facilities effected practically no improvement in its crosstown traffic. Because our subway lines have opened up new sections of the Bronx, Brooklyn, and Queens and are pouring the rising population of these districts into Manhattan, these lines now ease the difficulties of uptown-and-downtown circulation here only during the non-rush hours. The present area of our streets and avenues cannot be increased without adding to our already monstrous deficiencies in public parks and playgrounds in residential areas where the population densities have mounted to between two hundred and four hundred and fifty people an acre. After all, the most feasible means of expansion, the river and belt-line drives, have already been resorted to. The only way, therefore, of providing space for all the present-day transportation, short of resorting to even more elevated highways, and thus creating a hell of noise and shadowed buildings far worse than the one our "L"s produced, is to build multiple-level tunnels under every congested street and avenue—which, as Euclid used to say, is absurd, since even a fraction of this construction would land the municipality in irremediable bankruptcy. We could, however, make better use of the land in Manhattan by replanning our residential neighborhoods into great superblocks, with fewer streets and fewer intersections, and all but purely local traffic confined to wider arteries that run past but not through these neighborhoods. We have the beginnings of this kind of development in Stuyvesant Town and many of our public housing developments, but nowhere has it been done systematically enough to provide wider arteries for even crosstown traffic. No piecemeal improvements, however valuable in themselves, can take the place of a scheme that will consider the city and its problems as a whole, not as something to be patched up here and there while the rest of it goes to ruin.

• • •

Instead of the city's preventing the internal traffic flood at the place where it originates, traffic engineers wait till traffic has reached the flood crest and then build ditches and canals to carry it away. These ditches merely add to the congestion, since traffic, unlike rivers, flows in two directions, and the wider the new exit route, the more traffic flows into it. All the current plans for dealing with congestion are based on the assumption that it is a matter of highway engineering, not of comprehensive city and regional planning, and that the private motorcar has priority over every other means of transportation, no matter how expensive it is in comparison with public transportation, or how devastating its by-products. In most cities, current plans for "traffic relief" include adding central parking areas, often tunnelling under public squares and parks, as in San Francisco's Union Square Park, or of building handsome garages, like the one Philadelphia's special commission has lately opened on Rittenhouse Square, but all these devices merely invite more traffic. Our Park Commissioner, Mr. Robert Moses, has happily resisted this kind of encroachment on our own parks, but he is convinced that more garages should be built in the core of congested areas or just outside them. And only the other day Mr. T. T. Wiley, our Traffic Commissioner, put forth a proposal to provide room for forty thousand cars in public parking lots and garages, mostly at the edge of the city—as if this invitation to fill the highways coming into New York would magically take a load off the streets within the city. Proposals for off-street parking space in new office buildings continue to pop up, too, and the practice of providing at least enough parking space for the higher executives is fast becoming standard practice. One of the latest suggestions, by a firm of local architects, offers a slight variant on Mr. Moses' scheme—a series of huge garages, up to six hundred feet long and seven floors tall, astride the city's river drives. This scheme, too, would halt many incoming cars at the edges of Manhattan, but it suggests no means for enabling the dismounted motorist to reach his urban destination by swift public transport. Even if it did, it would still have the common failing of traffic schemes—it would encourage more vehicles on overburdened arteries. People, it seems, find it hard to believe that the cure for congestion is not more facilities for congestion.

While only a quack would pretend to have a pat solution for this complicated problem, there is no reason that we should not explore alternatives to the course we have been so blindly following. As Mr. Robert Mitchell, one of our few intelligent traffic experts, lately remarked, when a municipal counsellor in Philadelphia expressed shock at the modesty of the budget he proposed for further research, "What we need is not more traffic counts but more thought—and thinking is cheap." A little thought may disclose that with traffic, as with many other matters, there is no swift and simple answer—"the longest way round is the shortest way home." Before we can promise to restore the normal facilities of transportation to our blocked avenues and our almost paralyzed metropolis we may have to take even more drastic measures than rerouting the continental flow of wheat. Most of these measures, happily, will increase the habitability of the city and relieve the almost neurotic compulsion to get out of it. But one cannot promise that this public gain will produce a private profit.

THE LESSON OF THE MASTER

SEPTEMBER 13, 1958 (ON THE SEAGRAM BUILDING)

THERE IS A quick but accurate way of describing the new skyscraper office building at 375 Park Avenue. It is everything that most of the office buildings that have been going up in the midtown area in the last few years are not. That the new work gains by this contrast is, happily, the least that can be said in its favor. Almost any piece of sober craftsmanship, however humble its pretensions, would gain by such contrasting, and Seagram's new building, far from being humble, is perhaps the most quietly ostentatious one in the city. But to appreciate the virtues of this building, sheathed in bronze and topaz-tinted glass, one should make a summary canvass of its contemporaries—one can hardly call them its rivals. Among them are greedy buildings, hogging every cubic foot of space the law allows; flashy buildings, with murals in the lobby whose winking leer at art has something less than honorable intentions; gaudy buildings, whose unpleasant colors resemble Detroit's recent favorite hues and in a few years will look similarly old-fashioned; buildings slickly covered with sheets of pressed metal, which are cheaper than stone or brick and which, despite all the decorative embossments, look just that—magnificently cheap; and corner-cutting buildings, often with ceilings so low that their claims to being adequately air-conditioned must be considered brazen effrontery, as their inmates have doubtless been discovering.

Out of this stalled, rush-hour clutter of new structures, brightly sordid, meretriciously up-to-date, the Seagram building has emerged like a Rolls-Royce accompanied by a motorcycle escort that gives it space and speed. To an even greater degree than its elegant neighbor, Lever House, 375 has *ambiance*. From three sides, it is wholly visible to the eye and approachable by foot; instead of using up space, it creates space. This act of detachment from the surrounding buildings was the most daring of all the innovations its chief architectural designer, Mies van der Rohe, made; by a heavy sacrifice of profitable floor area he achieved for this single structure an effect that usually is created only when a group of buildings are placed together on a plat even larger than a city block, as in Rockefeller Center. Some of that openness will disappear when the vacant block to the north is occupied, but some of it will remain, as in the case of its modest traditional neighbor, St. Bartholomew's Church, a block below on Park Avenue.

In accounting for the qualities that distinguish this edifice, one is safe in assuming that they derive, directly or indirectly, from the Master himself. To acknowledge this is not to diminish the contribution made by his associate, Philip Johnson, an avowed if by now an independent disciple, nor does it minimize the necessary donation of practical architectural experience made by those veterans in office-building design, Kahn & Jacobs. The spirit that pervades the building as a whole, the spirit that makes it a whole, is that of Mies van der Rohe; it has the aesthetic impact that only a unified work of art carried through without paltry compromises can have. In their willingness to accept van der Rohe's judgment, rather than that of their realty experts, the Seagram executives deserve, in the cause of art, a special salute.

The Seagram building—which, landscaping and all, occupies an entire blockfront on Park Avenue and half the land between that street and Lexington Avenue—presents itself, first of all, as a single shaft of bronze and glass, thirty-eight stories high (set well back from both Park Avenue and the side streets), roughly a hundred and fifty feet wide and less than ninety feet deep, with five-story wings at either side, and, in the rear, a narrower ten-story wing, which is not visible from the Park Avenue front. Now, when other contemporary architects are still, thirty years later, imitating Mendelsohn's innovation of unbroken horizontal bands of wall and window or van der Rohe's all-glass façade boxed by steel, van der Rohe himself has gone back to Louis Sullivan's concept of the skyscraper as a "proud and soaring thing" and has designed one with unqualified emphasis on the vertical. The prototype of this building was van der Rohe's own project, nearly forty years old, for a glass skyscraper, but, apart from that, this tower is such a divergence from the mode of his Farnsworth house, his Illinois Institute of Technology, and his Lake Shore apartment houses that it must give all the little micelike Mieses who have been coming forth from the architectural schools a touch of panic, for this is not the particular academic cliché they have so sedulously identified with modern architecture. To make the departure even more unmodish, van der Rohe has also rejected the now standard thin, slab-shaped building, with its long sides acting as a wall that blocks off the vision of the beholder, and with its shallow layout offering a suggestion of openness that becomes insincere once sealed windows, air-conditioning, and day-long indoor lighting have been installed. In the development of van der Rohe, the Seagram building is almost as much of a departure for him as the chapel at Ronchamp was for Le Corbusier, but, unlike Ronchamp, the new building reveals no sloppy abandonment of discipline.

The upward movement of the unbroken central prism is accentuated by the use of narrow, vertical bronze fins, or mullions, not only to separate all the windows, which run from floor to ceiling, but to multiply the vertical lines that rise above the glass-walled ground floor right to the roof; even the bronze plates of the great columns that frame the Park Avenue entrance are incised with vertical lines. This sheathing is in direct contrast to the underlying structure, whose powerful frame, when bare, gave more visual weight to the horizontal beams than to the vertical columns. The windows are set in bays almost thirty feet wide between heavy columns, six windows to a bay, and the faces of the building, instead of being an expression of the structure, are frankly and boldly a mask, designed to give pleasure to the eye and to complement, rather than to reveal, the coarser structural form behind it. This is, after all, a logical treatment of the curtain wall, for the very nature of a curtain is to be detached from the structure, not to support it; if anyone should doubt this detachment, the barely visible segmentation of those vertical fins, to allow for the expansion and contraction of the metal they are made of, should settle the matter.

The original renderings of the building showed the floors, which the large windows make completely visible from without, lighter in tone than the metal panels between the banks of windows, and this suggested a contrast between the vertical and the horizontal elements of the structure, but that contrast is, fortunately, almost nonexistent in the finished product. Even the fluorescent-lighting fixtures in the ceilings, which might break the upward movement, are only dimly apparent; the glass, thanks to the happy choice of color—presenting a much pleasanter interior view than the usual blue-green glass would—carries through the sombre bronze note that unifies the whole façade. I shall come back to the color in a moment. But first let me note that no small part of the aesthetic impact of this façade derives from its undeviating austerity both in idea and in execution. There are only two departures from bronze and glass: the use of dull-green stone plaques in the vertical column of blank panels (in lieu of windows) that run all the way up the northeast and southeast corners of the tower—panels that conceal an elaborate complex of windbracing—and the use of unbroken dark bronze sheathing as the facing for the windowless top stories, where the mechanical equipment is housed. The central structure is a shaft and nothing but a shaft, straightforward in concept, solemn in color, sober in execution, a building whose absolute simplicity and consistency has only one rival I can call to mind—John Root's Monadnock Building (1889–91), in Chicago, the last of the great masonry skyscrapers, and one that is equally free from a meretricious use of color or ornament. Until 375 was finished, I had doubts about the use of dark bronze for sheathing; if any considerable area of the city were to blossom forth in this material, the total effect would be a bit depressing. But if one accepts the fact that this is not just another business building but a singular monument, that its aloof, aristocratic qualities are not likely to be often repeated in a city where—to resort to that classic confession of the realty financier—"money does not look ahead more than five years," this choice of dark bronze, meant to deepen in tone but not change, even under our heavy sootfall, is justified. Here is the effect that Raymond Hood aimed at, but did not quite achieve, in his design for the American Radiator Building, built of black brick, which faces Bryant Park. Van der Rohe's tower was designed to flout the fashions and to weather indifferently all changes, including changes in the weather. That choice, like the form itself, was one of the many lessons of the Master. The relief is almost as welcome as a serious and thoughtful face in a news photograph. (Whether the architect's intention will eventually be betrayed by the particular bronze alloy used for the facing is another matter, still, alas, in doubt.)

• • •

As one crosses the open plaza that intervenes between Park Avenue and the building, in a few steps one is lifted out of the street so completely that one has almost the illusion of having climbed a long flight of stairs. One faces a vast, continuous wall of plate glass, two stories high, behind the columns that mark the entrance. This glass curtain encloses the ground floor but reveals the travertine-covered inner walls and the elevator shafts, all of which emphasize the transparency of the outer wall. The columns—six of them, square, covered in bronze, and striated by vertical lines a few inches apart—define the entrance with a becoming massiveness and dignity, which also increase the diaphanous air of the outer wall. A canopy above the entrance juts forward, with rectangular severity, to indicate the function of the opening and to bathe the space below, at night, with its inset lights. The pavement of the plaza, of granite divided into large, unemphatic squares, continues right into the building—no attempt here at a change of texture, at color, at irrelevant decoration; outside and inside are simply the same. The noble scale of the entrance is not just an outside pretense but an inside reality; again the clients showed themselves ready to sacrifice rentable space to achieve an aesthetic effect that does more to set this building apart than the most lavish murals or the most exuberant horticultural display. The serene effect of pure space itself, now vanished from the great railroad stations of New York, and even from the New York Public Library, has once again been recaptured; the design itself wars against the "noisy crowding up of things," which in the days of Rome's decadence sent men into the monastery to find visible peace and order. Even the black bands of the cove lighting in the lobby ceiling, which is of multi-toned gray mosaic, serve to point up, by their sharp contrast, the firm, undeviating integrity—and masculinity—of this design. Such purity and dignity are completely lacking in most contemporary metropolitan architecture, with its endeavor to humanize what is inhuman and to refine what remains so patently vulgar. One must almost go back to Palladio's San Giorgio Maggiore, in Venice, for anything like the same quality of mind and expression. Only at a single point is the purity of this design betrayed, and then by the very rigor of its execution. Since the side streets slope toward Lexington Avenue, the entrances from them are by way of a flight of steps covered with a glass canopy, of transparent glass and perilously elegant, and leading to revolving doors. But a transparent glass roof in New York is a drawing-board dream; even a daily hosing down of the canopy would not guarantee a transparent surface a few hours later—and what looks dirtier than even slightly soiled glass? The lobby terminates in a glass wall, behind which a restaurant is destined to open. Of that spacious approach and that setting one can utter only this sentiment: May the food and the service be worthy of it!

• • •

Since this building was designed, first of all, to meet the needs of the corporation, producer of many whiskeys, that built it, one is tempted to appraise the quality of the corporation's own quarters, done directly under the eyes of the architects, and I turn aside from that beguiling path with reluctance, all the more because there is a certain warmth and fantasy in the decoration, of a sort that is usually absent from van der Rohe's almost surgically aseptic designs. However pure this building is, it is not a pure Mies building, and I am not sure that it is the worse for this. Purity, the perfection of a single aesthetic idea to the neglect of all the other human requirements that enter into a many-dimensioned work of architecture, has gradually developed into a grave weakness in van der Rohe's work—so grave, in fact, that it very nearly undermines his claim to being still a practitioner of architecture. (This vice is usually even more conspicuous in the work of his disciples, who come forth with waxen imitations of the Master's sterile white flowers.) Van der Rohe's famous motto, "Less is more," comes to mean, in the end, "Nothing is even better," so that he reaches in his later buildings the final terminus, where architecture dissolves into constructive sculpture and sculpture itself deliberately disappears into a geometric void. (At this point, it remains for Hans Andersen's little boy to remark that the Emperor wears no clothes.) The virtue of the flawless treatment of the structure of 375 lies precisely in the discipline it imposes upon those who must minister to other than formal aesthetic needs. I think none the worse of the decorators because they have covered one wall of the main Seagram reception office with glass cases in which a variety of liquor bottles form a repeating pattern (this is both an honest symbol and a handsome one), nor, on another floor, would I look down my nose at the abstract mural that turns out to be a chart of production flow in a Seagram plant, though I can well imagine that both these embellishments might cause van der Rohe exquisite pain. But it is the Miesian background that makes these and similar modifications so grateful to the eye—the textured woven-bronze-wire and stainless-steel sheathing of the elevator interiors, the wood panelling of the conference rooms, the excellent lettering and numbering (at once small and bold), and even some of the abstract paintings. After a fast, the simplest meal has the effect of a feast. I have not yet had the opportunity to see how far his chaste example has influenced the people who designed other offices of the building.

It is at ground level, in the public spaces, that van der Rohe's sense of architectural order remains unqualified and supreme, and here again his lesson is a salutary one. The fact that 375 is set back from Park Avenue some ninety feet not merely makes it visible but makes it approachable, and the open plaza in front, plus the arbored green rectangles at the sides, gives the same satisfaction that the building itself does. This plaza is open without being formidable; the absence of any kind of ornament, except the tall bronze flagpole, seventy-five feet high, slightly to the right of the main entrance, and the fountains and rectangular, step-rimmed pools of water on either side, only emphasizes the quality of the space itself. In spite of the towering shaft, the plaza, thanks partly to the treatment of the ground floor, maintains the human scale, and its emptiness is a part of its serenity, while the impending tower itself disappears from the observer's field of vision. It needs no ornamental fixtures other than those it has in order to increase this human quality; all it needs—and it already has these, both by day and by night—is people capable of enjoying the primal aesthetic pleasures: ordered space, air, the spray of the fountains on one's face, and sunlight or the regal mixture of black and gold that greets one from the lighted building at night. Small plazas like this, if repeated often enough about the city, would accomplish more for recreation than thousands of distant wild acres hardly worth the effort of a crawling Sunday journey.

This post-Whistler nocturne, by public consensus, is perhaps the highest aesthetic achievement of the building, more than justifying its daytime reserve by its unexpected nighttime splendor. The nocturnal brilliance is enhanced by the amber window glass, which takes the curse of coldness off the fluorescent lights, and it gives one a hint of what such integral illumination, divorced from advertising, might do to enliven the townscape at night.

Unfortunately, the least error in such a simple design hurts like a splinter under one's fingernail, and there are two or three lapses that call for correction. One is a purely aesthetic error: the use of weeping beeches for ornamental greenery at either side of the building—beeches whose writhing forms (already, such is the New York climate, apparently in the agonies of death) seem closer to the spirit of Salvador Dalí than to that of Mies van der Rohe. This is fashionable claptrap, which defiles the whole spirit of the design. Another error is a practical one. In creating this plaza, the architects beckoned the passerby to loaf and invite his soul, but they absurdly failed to provide any benches, which they no doubt thought might mar its spatial purity. Though the pools and the ivy-covered rectangular beds are edged by long marble walls, parallel to the side streets, the designers seemingly never imagined that they were thus providing a natural seat for those who would enjoy the play of water and air and green branches; as a result, one can find a seat only by stepping hazardously along the narrow stone rim of the pool. Grievous as this oversight is, it could be overcome merely by lowering the water in the pools until the next level in the step-rimmed basin emerges. This brings me to the final error, a strangely gross defect in a design as refined and costly as this one: the materials and execution of the pool and its fountains. The pools, composed of large, square granite slabs, are shallow, and it is obvious that some of the blocks have been defectively laid, for there are smudges of cement filling the cracks; even worse, the pipes that feed the jets are just so much raw plumbing. The fact that the workmanship, here so exposed, is not as impeccable as in the rest of the building, and that the pipes themselves are not concealed, seems almost beyond explanation. Where close contemplation demands perfect craftsmanship, such a failure becomes an aesthetic enormity.

• • •

In appraising this design, I have confined myself to its manifest aesthetic qualities. I have not considered the practical and functional demands that must be integrated in any complete work of architecture, nor have I asked at what cost or sacrifice these aesthetic qualities were achieved. Like so much architecture of today, 375 falls into the category of the Pyramid—a building that exhausts every resource of art and engineering to create an imposing visible effect out of all proportion to its human significance. This error is not the architects'; it characterizes our whole civilization, which now sacrifices on the altar of the bureaucratic functions and engineering services what it once gave, in awe and exaltation, only to divinities. What Mies van der Rohe has demonstrated in this building is how to do, with superb aesthetic aplomb and with all but unerring taste, what his colleagues do coarsely and clumsily, in a spirit of tepid compromise with forces to which they have surrendered all too complaisantly in advance. For once, an outstanding human personality got the better of a system that places a premium upon self-effacing conformity and impersonality. And the result is a building that will not be cheapened by imitation—as Lever House was so quickly, if unsubtly, caricatured by the building directly north of it on Fifty-fourth Street. Nevertheless, the thirty-eight-story Seagram tower, for all its prodigal disinclination to occupy every square inch of its site, has a few urban drawbacks. Its municipally sanctioned congestion of occupancy, its lack of visual outlook for all but the occupants of outside offices, its wasteful disproportion of elevator shafts to usable floor space, and its inevitable over-mechanization make it not a desirable model for the city of the future. Yet its positive qualities demonstrate what such a city might be, once whole blocks and quarters, themselves limited in height, were characterized by occasional towers that have the same cavalier attitude toward quick returns and high profits from the investment. Taken with all its inherent limitations, this seems to me the best skyscraper New York has seen since Hood's Daily News Building; in classic execution it towers above the doubled height of the Empire State Building, while its nearest later rival, Lever House, more package than Pyramid, looks curiously transitory and ephemeral when one turns from one to the other. Sombre, unsmiling, yet not grim, 375 is a muted masterpiece—but a masterpiece.

MUSIC

WHITNEY BALLIETT

JAZZ RECORDS

JUNE 15, 1957 (ON SONNY ROLLINS AND THELONIOUS MONK)

Possibly the most incisive and influential jazz instrumentalist since Charlie Parker is a twenty-seven-year-old tenor saxophonist named Sonny Rollins, whose bossy, demanding style has made him the unofficial leader of a new and burgeoning school of modern jazz known as hard bop. Most of the members of the movement, which includes Horace Silver, Sonny Stitt, and Art Blakey, came to the front during the height of bebop, and as a result they largely formed their styles on Parker, Dizzy Gillespie, Lester Young, and Bud Powell. At the same time, they absorbed much of the nervous hotness of this music, which—though often regarded as an unduly complex type of jazz, what with its extended melodic lines, broadened chord structures, and jerky, rhythmic base—in many ways was a direct return to the pushing, uncomplicated vigor of Louis Armstrong's Hot Five. Rollins, who continues to use standard bop frameworks and instrumentation, has, however, developed a solo style that makes bop sound as placid as Handel's *Water Music*. At first, there is something almost repellent about his playing, for his bleak, ugly tone—reminiscent, at times, of the sad sounds wrestled by beginners out of the saxophone—is rarely qualified by the gracefulness of a vibrato or by the use of dynamics. He seems, in fact, to blat out his notes as if they were epithets, and his solos often resemble endless harangues. After a time, though, it becomes clear that most of this staccato braying is a camouflage for a tumultuous and brilliant musical imagination and a rhythmic sense that probably equals Parker's.

Rollins is in his fearful prime in a new recording, *Saxophone Colossus* (Prestige LP-7079), made in company with Tommy Flanagan, piano; Doug Watkins, bass; and Max Roach, drums. Of the five numbers on the record—three are by Rollins—the best are "Moritat," from *The Threepenny Opera,* which he turns into a surprising combination of the brusque and the tender, and Rollins' "Blue Seven," a long, rolling medium-tempo blues that features, in addition to his brooding variations, a remarkable solo by Roach, in which he ticks off on every part of his equipment a compelling, metronomic series of beats, the difficult tempo notwithstanding. Flanagan is a delicate, pearly-sounding pianist and Watkins is a firm new bassist. Both are impeccable throughout, and even manage to be more than foils for Rollins' red-necked vigor.

• • •

Thelonious Monk, the extraordinary and iconoclastic pianist and composer who was one of the founders of bop in the early forties, has made a recording, *Brilliant Corners: Thelonious Monk* (Riverside RLP-12-226), that is as provocative as any he has produced in recent years. In three of the five numbers he is joined by Ernie Henry (alto saxophone), Rollins, Oscar Pettiford (bass), and Roach, and in one by Clark Terry (trumpet), Rollins, Paul Chambers (bass), and Roach. The fifth, "I Surrender, Dear," is an unaccompanied piano solo. The rest of the tunes, in all of which Monk had a hand, are, like his earlier ones, queer, moody, humorous compositions (dissonant, bumping ensembles, a variety of subtle rhythms, and an over-all needling piquancy), and they have a tortuous, concentrated power that produces a curious effect: the soloists, no matter how vigorous, seem secondary to their materials. As a result, although Rollins plays with much of his customary vibrancy, there is a subdued air about his work that fortunately balances the frenetic saxophone of Henry, who at his calmest (in an ingratiating blues called "Ba-lue Bolivar Ba-lues-are") plays in a wild, chanting fashion that is undeniably effective. Monk is superb in "I Surrender, Dear," in which, free of a rhythm section, he produces a straggling army of flatted chords and off-notes that continually poke at and prick the melody. Chambers and Pettiford are satisfactory, but Roach occasionally becomes so energetic behind the soloists that he appears to be uncontrollably soloing rather than providing sympathetic support.

WINTHROP SARGEANT

MAN WITH A MANNER

MARCH 22, 1958 (ON GLENN GOULD AT CARNEGIE HALL)

Owing to the enormous and conflicting traffic of events that confronts a New York concertgoer, I had not, up to one of the Philharmonic's performances in Carnegie Hall last week, had an opportunity to witness the playing of the now rather celebrated young Canadian pianist Glenn Gould. I had heard a number of his recordings, and while all of them had seemed to me to be the work of an artist of extraordinary gifts, they had scarcely prepared me for the visual spectacle Mr. Gould presents as he displays these gifts before an audience. The spectacle is, to say the least, somewhat eccentric compared with the formal platform manner of the average concert performer. To begin with, Mr. Gould is a lanky, slightly dishevelled, and intensely earnest-looking young man, who sits on a remarkably low stool at a piano that has been raised several inches on jacks, bringing the keyboard almost to the level of his chin. When he is at rest, he leans back, allowing his long arms to dangle listlessly to the floor. When he is not at rest, he gives the impression of a man subduing a piano by jujitsu. He staves it off with upraised feet, pummels it, feints with elaborate motions that seem designed to distract its attention, recoils from it as if it were a hot stove, beats time with one hand while playing with the other, and croons the music, inaudibly but very visibly, throughout the performance. When he rises to take his bows, he does so with a sort of awkward casualness, saluting the orchestra and shrugging with a "Shucks, fellas, 'taint nothin'" air, which seems to imply that the whole business has been an episode in a hoedown.

It would be easy to dismiss all this as deliberate exhibitionism, but after watching it with some amusement the other night, and listening to what emerged from the piano, I concluded that Mr. Gould's manner is a perfectly sincere expression of his *Gesamtpersönlichkeit*. He is obviously an original, whom one must accept on his own terms, and I would be quite happy to see him stand on his head if he felt such a posture necessary to the projection of his musical ideas. For the fact is that none of his physical flamboyance enters into what one hears. On the contrary, his performance of Bach's D Minor Concerto for Piano and Orchestra was a masterpiece of coherence, control, and fine musical taste. Mr. Gould is the possessor of a tremendous pianistic technique, and though it may be highly unconventional, it enables him to bring off all the feats of speed, power, delicacy, contrast, and nuance that one expects from virtuosos of the first rank. He also has a penetrating intelligence, evident in the clean, unambiguous quality of his phrasing; an engaging masculine robustness; and the kind of authority that indicates a profound knowledge of the art of music. These attributes, in a twenty-five-year-old, are impressive indeed, and I look forward with great interest to Mr. Gould's future appearances.

When Mr. Gould had finished the Bach concerto, he embarked with equal fervor and dedication on Schoenberg's Piano Concerto, and almost, but not quite, convinced me that its arid mathematical formulas contain something identifiable as musical meaning. Certainly, if I remained unconvinced, it was through no fault of Mr. Gould's, for he played the concerto with what, had it been music of a more rewarding sort, I should describe as real eloquence. Dimitri Mitropoulos, who was in charge of the orchestra, performed his role in this work with his customary energy and enthusiasm. I thought, however, that his performance as the accompanist of the Bach concerto was slapdash and coarse—an impression perhaps intensified by the fact that he used a huge, ponderous aggregation of instrumentalists, instead of reducing the ensemble to the small dimensions appropriate to this kind of music.

The rest of Mr. Mitropoulos' program was also unusual and generally interesting. It began with a Prologue and Fugue by the Brazilian composer Camargo Guarnieri, which seemed to me merely fashionable in more or less the style of Aaron Copland, and ended with Samuel Barber's *Medea's Meditation and Dance of Vengeance,* a familiar and worthwhile work, which I have previously discussed. The most absorbing item of the evening was the somewhat belated New York première of Gustav Mahler's unfinished Tenth Symphony. This composition has been the subject of considerable controversy, several later musicians—among them Ernst Křenek—having had a hand in editing the original score, which was in a very fragmentary form when Mahler died. There has also been a lot of discussion about the symphony's autobiographical implications, based on a number of exclamations and other marginal notes that Mahler appended to the manuscript. Mahler, it appears, knew when he wrote it that he was dying; the notes seem to indicate the tortured frame of mind with which he approached death, and for those who like to examine the mental processes of an extremely complex musical genius, the work is unquestionably a document of great psychological significance. Personally, however, I preferred to listen to the symphony simply as music. Considered from this point of view, it is indeed a fragmentary affair, consisting of one solid and fairly finished movement—the opening Andante—and another movement, very tentative and not entirely satisfying, which is obviously unfinished. To what extent the opening Andante has been tampered with by its editors I am not in a position to say, but, as it stands, it is as noble an episode as ever came from Mahler's pen, and, like all Mahler's music, it has a strong individuality that sets it apart from the music of any other composer. The agony with which Mahler viewed the subject of death is undoubtedly expressed in it, but Mahler did a good deal of gloomy thinking about death throughout his life, and I see very little in this composition that has not been touched on or prefigured in his earlier symphonies. At any rate, the Andante is a magnificent, tragic preamble by an artist who ranks, in my mind, as the last of the really great symphonists, and Mr. Mitropoulos and the Philharmonic performed a valuable service in giving it a hearing.

WHITNEY BALLIETT

JAZZ RECORDS

JUNE 27, 1959 (ON COLEMAN HAWKINS)

IMPROVISATION, THE VERY seat of jazz, is a remorseless, bullying art that demands of the performer no less than this: that, night in and night out, he spontaneously invent original music based upon certain given themes and confined within certain limitations, by putting in perfect balance—with the speed of light—emotion and intelligence, form and content, and tone and attack, all of which, to succeed, must both charge and entertain the spirit of the listener. Improvisation comes in various shapes and colors. There is the melodic embellishment of Louis Armstrong and Vic Dickenson; the similar but far more complex thematic improvisation of Lester Young; the improvisation upon chords, as practiced by Coleman Hawkins and Charlie Parker; and the rhythmic-thematic-chordal convolutions now being put forward by Thelonious Monk and Sonny Rollins. There are, too, the collective improvisations, such as the New Orleans ensemble, a superbly intricate homemade device that, sadly, is all but defunct, and its contrapuntal descendants, which are thriving in the hands of John Lewis and Charlie Mingus. Great improvisation is a miraculous explosion that occurs once in a blue moon; bad improvisation, which is really not improvisation at all but a rerun or imitation of old ideas, happens all the time. There is no more precarious and dominating art. Indeed, there is evidence that the gifted jazz musicians who have either died or dried up in their twenties, thirties, or forties are primarily victims not of drugs and alcohol but of the insatiable furnace of improvisation. Thus, such consummate veteran improvisers as Armstrong, Dickenson, Hawkins, Buck Clayton, and Monk deserve considerable awe. In addition to being imaginative master craftsmen, they are remarkable endurance runners. Perhaps the hardiest of these unique beings is Hawkins, who, now fifty-four, continues to play with all the freshness, vitality, and authority that he demonstrated during the Harding administration as a member of Mamie Smith's Jazz Hounds.

Hawkins, in fact, is a super jazz musician, for he has been an originator of the boldest sort, a masterly improviser, a shepherd of new movements, and a restless, steadily developing performer. A short, dapper, contained man, whose rare smiles have the effect of a lamp suddenly going on within, he was the first to prove that jazz could be played on the saxophone, which until then had been largely a purveyor of treacle. He did this with such conviction and breadth of imagination that by the mid-thirties he had founded one of the two great schools of saxophone playing. (The other, which was to have fewer members, because of the inimitable style of its leader, Lester Young, arrived later.) Its pupils, many of the more recent ones now diluted by other products, include such performers as Herschel Evans, Chu Berry, Ben Webster, Don Byas, Harry Carney, Johnny Hodges, Lucky Thompson, Charlie Parker, and Sonny Rollins. In 1939, Hawkins set down, as an afterthought at a recording session, a version of "Body and Soul" that almost achieves the impossible—perfect art. A few years later, he repeated this success with superlative refashionings of "Sweet Lorraine" and "The Man I Love."

Unlike many other celebrated jazz musicians, who are apt to regard anything new with defensive animosity, Hawkins has always kept an ear to the ground for flutters of originality, and as a result he led, in 1944, the first official bebop recording session, which involved men like Dizzy Gillespie, Max Roach, and the late Clyde Hart. Soon afterward, he used the largely unknown Monk in some equally important recordings. Then his playing inexplicably began to falter and he went into semi-eclipse, from which he rocketed up, without warning, in the early fifties, landing on his feet with a brand-new style (his third), which, in its occasional all-embracing febrility, suggests the exuberance of a man several decades younger.

Hawkins' early style was rough and aggressive. His tone tended to be harsh and woody, and he used a great many notes, which bumped up and down the scale in the unremitting, staccato manner of a pneumatic drill. Unlike a similar contemporary trumpet player, Jabbo Smith, whose musical pyrotechnics grew more and more gaudy, Hawkins eventually simmered down, and by the mid-thirties he had entered his second and most famous phase. His heavy vibrato suggested the wingbeats of a big bird, while his tone, which grew to alarming proportions, suggested enormous rooms hung with dark velvet and lit by huge fires. He was now the despair of his imitators, who often sounded like old bellows. His technique had become infallible. He never fluffed a note, his tone never shrank or overflowed—as did Chu Berry's, say—and he gave the impression that he had enough equipment to state in half a dozen different and equally finished ways what was in his head. This proved to be remarkable, particularly in his handling of slow ballads, a lyrical approach largely originated by him and equalled by only a handful of musicians on any instrument.

Hawkins would often begin such a number by playing one chorus of the melody, as if he were testing its resilience. He would stuff its fabric with tone to see how much it would take, eliminate certain notes, sustain others, slur several, and add new ones. Then, satisfied, he would shut his eyes, as if blinded by the vision of what he was about to play, and launch into pure improvisation with a concentration that pinned one down by its very intensity. (Hawkins' total lack of tentativeness—the exhilarating, blindman tentativeness of Pee Wee Russell or Roy Eldridge—invariably suggested that he had written out and memorized his solos long before playing them.) He would construct—out of phrases crowded with single notes, glissandos, abrupt stops, and his corrugated vibrato—long, hilly figures that sometimes lasted until his breath gave out. Immediately refilling his lungs, often with an audible wind-tunnel ferocity, he would be off again—bending notes, dropping in little runs like steep, crooked staircases, adding decorative, almost calligraphic flourishes, emphasizing an occasional phrase by perversely allowing it to vanish into puffs of breath. He often closed these solos with roomy codas, into which he would squeeze a stream of fresh and frequently fancy ideas that gave the impression of being worthy material that had simply been crowded out of his earlier ruminations. If another soloist was to follow him, he might terminate his own statement with an abrupt ascending figure that catapulted his successor neatly into space. When Hawkins had finished, his solo, which had been anchored directly and emphatically to the beat (as opposed to the method of Lester Young, who was always pulling the beat inside out, as if he were hunting lost change in it), had been worked into a tight yet elaborate super-version of the original melody, as though he had fitted a rococo Victorian mansion over a modern ranch house. At fast tempos, Hawkins merely forced the same amount of music into a smaller space. There seemed to be no pause at all between phrases or choruses, and this produced a thunderhead intensity that appeared to thicken the beat and whose vehemence was occasionally indicated by sustained sandpaper growls. Yet for all this teeming, agile enthusiasm, Hawkins' playing during this period often left the listener vaguely dissatisfied. Perhaps it was because his style had an unceasing—and, for that time, unusual—intellectual quality, with the forbidding glint of perfection and a viselike unwillingness to let any emotion seep out, lest it spoil the finish on his work. At any rate, one kept waiting for the passion pumping away beneath the surface to burst through, but it never did—until five years ago.

Like a man fresh out of prison, Hawkins can now be volcanic. His present style is marked primarily by a slight tightening of tone, which occasionally resembles the sound he achieved at the outset of his career; the use of certain rather harsh and inflexible notes and phrases that, not surprisingly, suggest aspects of Charlie Parker and Sonny Rollins; and an open display of emotion that, when it does not go awry, can rock foundations. But this exuberance has been costly. In his pursuit of pure flame, Hawkins sometimes misses notes or plays them badly, and he falls back, perhaps out of temporary middle-aged fatigue, on stock phrases of his own, such as a series of abrupt, descending triplets, which sound like a hard-rubber ball bounding down a hall. When everything is in mesh, however, the results are peerless.

This happens more than once in two recent Hawkins recordings—*The High and Mighty Hawk* (Felsted FA J 7005) and *Coleman Hawkins Soul* (Prestige 7149). Despite a few flat spots, the first recording, in which Hawkins is joined by Buck Clayton, Hank Jones, Ray Brown, and the drummer Mickey Sheen, is one of his superior efforts. There are a blues, three originals, and two standards. The blues, taken at a pleasant medium tempo, is a tour de force in the best sense of that expression. After the opening ensemble, Hawkins slides, with another-day, another-dollar casualness, into a soliloquy that lasts for no less than seventeen unbroken choruses, each of them totally different and each giving the feeling that it could fit only where it happens to fall. All of the best qualities of his present work are in evidence—the gradual, unremittingly logical development of a three- or four-note figure (the first five choruses), the near-parodying reflections of the work of the modern tenor saxophonist John Coltrane (tenth chorus), the tremendous bustle (eleventh and twelfth choruses), and the emotion (fifteenth and sixteenth choruses). It is remarkable improvisation. Hawkins matches this perfection in "You've Changed," a slow ballad, which, however, does not receive the glossy, ten-gun treatment he might have offered it a decade ago. Instead, for only a chorus and a half, he pokes at the melody in a soft, cautious, exploratory way, savoring its pleasant design, making minor improvements here and there, and infusing it with a warmth and a lyricism that are wholly affecting. Clayton and Brown, in particular, play with considerable beauty. Indeed, Brown's long solo in the blues number has an ingenious mixture of darting runs, exaggerated pauses, and half-time retarding phrases that very nearly top Hawkins' solo.

The second record is aptly named. Hawkins is accompanied by Kenny Burrell on guitar, Ray Bryant on piano, Wendell Marshall on bass, and Osie Johnson on drums. There are seven numbers, most of them blues. The longest is a very slow one, which is so blue—it is filled with swollen tremolos, gospel rhythms, stirrings of rock-and-roll, and screaming blue notes—that it becomes at once the epitome of all slow blues and a caricature of all slow blues. Hawkins takes a short, plaintive solo near the opening and returns later for an extraordinary chorus, in which, after some quiet, moody, chantlike phrases, he abruptly emits an astonishing wail that sounds like an exhalation from the bottom of Hell. No more unsettling moment has occurred on a jazz record. The shortest number on the record is totally dissimilar—a classic revitalization of the sixteenth-century "Green Sleeves." Hawkins simply plays embellishments on the melody, but with such pathos and blueslike feeling that one constantly fears he will break down before it is finished. Instead, instantaneously plumbing his three and a half decades of playing, Hawkins turns it into a kind of Gettysburg Address on improvisation. It's an indelible statement.

PART SEVEN

POETRY

A NOTE BY PAUL MULDOON

WHEN THE FEBRUARY 16, 1957, issue of *The New Yorker* ran a Profile of Marianne Moore, with the title "Humility, Concentration, and Gusto," it was clear, if only from the deployment of that serial comma, that Harold Ross was still in his heaven and all was still fairly right with the world. "The serial comma is important because it is almost exclusively *The New Yorker*'s, and is a mildly controversial thing," Ross once wrote. "But we're right, and all the rest are wrong."

Although William Shawn had now taken over from Ross as editor, with Howard Moss as poetry editor throughout the decade, the poems from the 1950s suggest only subtly that the lines between right and wrong might be blurring. Some of the era's predilections and aspirations could be read in the magazine's advertisements. Jules Kuti was ensconced at the piano in Café Nino, at 10 East Fifty-second Street. At Hutton's Murray Hill, meanwhile, Charles Albert was at the piano "nitely." Readers were invited to try the new, extra-rich, 97 percent caffeine-free Sanka Coffee, "delicious in either instant or regular form," and to eat Birds Eye fish bites, "also salubrious as a main course." It was an era in which the Asti Restaurant, at 13 East Twelfth Street, could unself-consciously advertise "gay singing from 7:30 P.M." in a program ranging from "Pagliacci to Tin Pan Alley." Other cultural currents remained subterranean.

Moss's taste as poetry editor was quite wide-ranging, extending eventually even to publishing his own work. W. H. Auden and Chester Kallman may have been questioning his catholicity in their famous squib:

TO THE POETRY EDITOR OF THE NEW YORKER

Is Robert Lowell
Better than Noel
Coward,
Howard?

The cod couplets in which this is written are the mainstay of much of the verse of the era, be it Hayden Carruth's Pagliaccian "Sparrows" or Ogden Nash's Tin Pan Alley–esque "Just How Low Can a Highbrow Go When a Highbrow Lowers His Brow?" with its splendid wordplay:

> For the most part, my feelings about him I silently conceal,
> But when he comments that *The Power of Positive Thinking*
> burns with a hard, gemlike flame, I can only cry that he is
> robbing Pater to paw Peale.

The couplet continues to be a mainstay of Marianne Moore's "The Arctic Ox," the rhyme at the end of each stanza clinching the deal on the animal's admirable constancy and self-containment. Another great formalist, Richard Wilbur, is already adept in combining tact with surprise tactics in "Boy at the Window," while Karl Shapiro shows himself to be a poet of startling unconventionality working within a conventional form. In "Voices from the Other World," James Merrill lets loose "a horde / Of voices gathered above the Ouija board" to upset any rhyme scheme that attempts to establish itself.

It's clear from this selection of poems that in the fifties free verse was very much in the ascendant. William Carlos Williams offers for our delectation a wonderfully elegant poetic "entrechat." Theodore Roethke has given up his sub-Yeatsian mode for the bright and breezy tone of "Frau Bauman, Frau Schmidt, and Frau Schwartze." Sylvia Plath, a poet much influenced by Roethke, is in terrific form in "Mussel Hunter at Rock Harbor," as she describes crabs:

> Each wore one
> claw swollen to a shield large
> as itself—no fiddler's arm
> grown Gargantuan by trade,
>
> but grown grimly, and grimly
> borne, for a use beyond my
> guessing of it.

We may detect trace elements of Elizabeth Bishop in Plath's poem, yet she is very much her own woman. Bishop herself is represented by "Questions of Travel," a poem beginning to question what is meant by "home."

Other things were coming into question, too. In "Living in Sin," Adrienne Rich registers the tremors of the seismic shift in sexual mores. And, at the end of the decade, Anne Sexton brilliantly summons the mood of disquiet over "that thing in the sky" that has forced itself into the 1950s consciousness. In 1957, indeed, the thing in the sky had become more than merely metaphorical when the Russians tested an intercontinental ballistic missile. Now, Sexton sensed, a looming threat to survival was "going around / like a persistent rumor / that will get us yet."

BOY AT THE WINDOW

Seeing the snowman standing all alone
In dusk and cold is more than he can bear.
The small boy weeps to hear the wind prepare
A night of gnashings and enormous moan.
His tearful sight can hardly reach to where
The pale-faced figure with bitumen eyes
Returns him such a godforsaken stare
As outcast Adam gave to Paradise.

The man of snow is, nonetheless, content,
Having no wish to go inside and die.
Still, he is moved to see the youngster cry.
Though frozen water is his element,
He melts enough to drop from one soft eye
A trickle of the purest rain, a tear
For the child at the bright pane surrounded by
Such warmth, such light, such love, and so much fear.

—*Richard Wilbur*
January 5, 1952

FRAU BAUMAN, FRAU SCHMIDT, AND FRAU SCHWARTZE

(SCENE: A GREENHOUSE IN MY CHILDHOOD)

Gone the three ancient ladies
Who creaked on the greenhouse ladders,
Reaching up white strings
To wind, to wind
The sweet-pea tendrils, the smilax,
Nasturtiums, the climbing
Roses, to straighten
Carnations, red
Chrysanthemums; the stiff
Stems, jointed like corn,

They tied and tucked—
These nurses of nobody else.
Quicker than birds, they dipped
Up and sifted the dirt;
They sprinkled and shook;
They stood astride pipes,
Their skirts billowing out wide into tents,
Their hands twinkling with wet;
Like witches they flew along rows,
Keeping creation at ease;
With a tendril for needle
They sewed up the air with a stem;
They teased out the seed that the cold kept asleep—
All the coils, loops, and whorls.
They trellised the sun; they plotted for more than
themselves.

I remember how they picked me up, a spindly kid,
Pinching and poking my thin ribs
Till I lay in their laps, laughing,
Weak as a whiffet;
Now, when I'm alone and cold in my bed,
They still hover over me,
These ancient leathery crones,
With their bandannas stiffened with sweat,
And their thorn-bitten wrists,
And their snuff-laden breath blowing lightly over me in my
first sleep.

—*Theodore Roethke*
March 29, 1952

LOVE FOR A HAND

Two hands lie still, the hairy and the white,
And soon down ladders of reflected light
The sleepers climb in silence. Gradually
They separate on paths of long ago,
Each winding on his arm the unpleasant clew
That leads, live as a nerve, to memory.

But often, when too steep her dream descends,
Perhaps to the grotto where her father bends
To pick her up, the husband wakes as though
He had forgotten something in the house.
Motionless he eyes the room that glows
With the little animals of light that prowl

This way and that. Soft are the beasts of light
But softer still her hand that drifts so white
Upon the whiteness. How like a water plant
It floats upon the black canal of sleep,
Suspended upward from the distant deep
In pure achievement of its lovely want.

Quietly then he plucks it and it folds
And is again a hand, small as a child's.
He would revive it, but it barely stirs,
And so he carries it off a little way
And breaks it open gently. Now he can see
The sweetness of the fruit, his hand eats hers.

—Karl Shapiro
October 4, 1952

THE ARTIST

Mr. T
      bareheaded
                  in a soiled undershirt
his hair standing out
      on all sides
                  stood on his toes
heels together
      arms gracefully
                  for the moment
curled above his head!
      Then he whirled about
                  bounded
into the air
      and with an entrechat
                  perfectly achieved
completed the figure.
      My mother
                  taken by surprise
where she sat
      in her invalid's chair
                  was left speechless.
"Bravo!" she cried at last
      and clapped her hands.
                  The man's wife
came from the kitchen:
      "What goes on here?" she said.
                  But the show was over.

—*William Carlos Williams*
November 28, 1953

LIVING IN SIN

She had thought the studio would keep itself—
No dust upon the furniture of love.
Half heresy, to wish the taps less vocal,
The panes relieved of grime. A plate of pears,
A piano with a Persian shawl, a cat
Stalking the picturesque, amusing mouse
Had been her vision when he pleaded "Come."
Not that, at five, each separate stair would writhe
Under the milkman's tramp; that morning light
So coldly would delineate the scraps
Of last night's cheese and blank, sepulchral bottles;
That on the kitchen shelf among the saucers
A pair of beetle eyes would fix her own—
Envoy from some black village in the moldings. . . .
Meanwhile her night's companion, with a yawn,
Sounded a dozen notes upon the keyboard,
Declared it out of tune, inspected, whistling,
A twelve hours' beard, went out for cigarettes,
While she, contending with a woman's demons,
Pulled back the sheets and made the bed and found
A fallen towel to dust the tabletop,
And wondered how it was a man could wake
From night to day and take the day for granted.
By evening she was back in love again,
Though not so wholly but throughout the night
She woke sometimes to feel the daylight coming
Like a relentless milkman up the stairs.

—Adrienne Cecile Rich
January 23, 1954

QUESTIONS OF TRAVEL

There are too many waterfalls here; the crowded streams
hurry too rapidly down to the sea,
and the pressure of so many clouds on the mountaintops
makes them spill over the sides in soft slow-motion,
turning to waterfalls under our very eyes.
—For if those streaks, those mile-long, shiny, tearstains,
aren't waterfalls yet,
in a quick age or so, as ages go here,
they probably will be.
But if the streams and clouds keep travelling, travelling,
the mountains look like the hulls of capsized ships,
slime-hung and barnacled.

Think of the long trip home.
Should we have stayed at home and thought of here?
Where should we be today?
Is it right to be watching strangers in a play
in this strangest of theatres?
What childishness is it that while there's a breath of life
in our bodies, we are determined to rush
to see the sun the other way around?
The tiniest green hummingbird in the world?
To stare at some inexplicable old stonework,
inexplicable and impenetrable,
at any view,
instantly seen and always, always delightful?
Oh, must we dream our dreams
and have them, too?
And have we room
for one more folded sunset, still quite warm?

But surely it would have been a pity
not to have seen the trees along this road,
really exaggerated in their beauty,
not to have seen them gesturing
like noble pantomimists, robed in pink.
—Not to have had to stop for gas and heard

the sad, two-noted, wooden tune
of disparate wooden clogs
carelessly clacking over
a grease-stained filling-station floor.
(In another country the clogs would all be tested.
Each pair there would have identical pitch.)
—A pity not to have heard
the other, less primitive music of the fat brown bird
who sings above the broken gasoline pump
in a bamboo church of Jesuit baroque:
three towers, five silver crosses.
—Yes, a pity not to have pondered,
blurr'dly and inconclusively,
on what connection can exist for centuries
between the crudest wooden footwear
and, careful and finicky,
the whittled fantasies of wooden cages.
—Never to have studied history in
the weak calligraphy of songbirds' cages.
—And never to have had to listen to rain
so much like politicians' speeches:
two hours of unrelenting oratory
and then a sudden golden silence
in which the traveller takes a notebook, writes:

*"Is it lack of imagination that makes us come
to imagined places, not just stay at home?
Or could Pascal have been not entirely right
about just sitting quietly in one's room?*

*Continent, city, country, society:
the choice is never wide and never free.
And here, or there . . . No. Should we have stayed at home,
wherever that may be?"*

*—Elizabeth Bishop
January 21, 1956*

SPARROWS

Spring comes and autumn goes
But we still have the town of sparrows.

Under the eaves and in the ivy
These folk keep continually busy.

If someone speaks, someone demurs;
They are indomitable bickerers.

One can easily imagine them
Asquabble in the copses when brave William

Led his band by; or even, once,
In the dust near Hannibal's elephants.

Maybe in the primeval firs
They went at it: What's his, what's hers?

Apparently they do not welcome
Finality in sparrowdom.

Now, in the ivy, they are all upset;
This argument isn't settled yet.

—Hayden Carruth
December 8, 1956

FIRST THINGS FIRST

Woken, I lay in the arms of my own warmth and listened
To a storm enjoying its storminess in the winter dark
Till my ear, as it can when half asleep or half sober,
Set to work to unscramble that interjectory uproar,
Construing its airy vowels and watery consonants
Into a love speech indicative of a proper name.

Scarcely the tongue I should have chosen, yet, as well
As harshness and clumsiness would allow, it spoke in your praise
Kenning you a godchild of the Moon and the West Wind,
With power to tame both real and imaginary monsters,
Likening your poise of being to an upland county,
Here green on purpose, there pure blue for luck.

Loud though it was, alone as it certainly found me,
It reconstructed a day of peculiar silence
When a sneeze could be heard a mile off, and had me walking
On a headland of lava beside you, the occasion as ageless
As the stare of any rose, your presence exactly
So once, so valuable, so very new.

This, moreover, at an hour when only too often
A smirking devil annoys me in beautiful English,
Predicting a world where every sacred location
Is a sand-buried site all cultured Texans "do,"
Misinformed and thoroughly fleeced by their guides,
And gentle hearts are extinct like Hegelian bishops.

Grateful, I slept till a morning that would not say
How much it believed of what I said the storm had said
But quietly drew my attention to what had been done—
So many cubic metres the more in my cistern
Against a leonine summer—putting first things first:
Thousands have lived without love, not one without water.

—W. H. Auden
March 9, 1957

VOICES FROM THE OTHER WORLD

Presently, at our touch, the teacup stirred,
Then circled lazily about
From A to Z. The first voice heard
(If they are voices, these mute spellers-out)
Was that of an engineer

Originally from Cologne.
Dead in his 22nd year
Of cholera in Cairo, he had "known
No happiness." He once met Goethe, though.
Goethe had told him: *Persevere.*

Our blind hound whined. With that, a horde
Of voices gathered above the Ouija board,
Some childish and, you might say, blurred
By sleep; one little boy
Named Will, reluctant, possibly in a ruff

Like a large-lidded page out of El Greco, pulled
Back the arras for that next voice,
Cold and portentous: "All is lost.
Flee this house. Otto von Thurn und Taxis.
Obey. You have no choice."

Frightened, we stopped; but tossed
Till sunrise striped the rumpled sheets with gold.
Each night since then, the moon waxes,
Small insects flit round a cold torch
We light, that sends them pattering to the porch . . .

But no real Sign. New voices come,
Dictate addresses, begging us to write;
Some warn of lives misspent, and all of doom,
In ways that so exhilarate
We are sleeping sound of late.

Last night, the teacup shattered in a rage.
Indeed, we have grown nonchalant
Toward the other world. In the gloom here,
Our elbows on the cleared
Table, we talk and smoke, pleased to be stirred

Rather by buzzings in the jasmine, by the drone
Of our own voices and poor blind Rover's wheeze,
Than by those clamoring overhead,
Obsessed or piteous, for a commitment
We still have wit to postpone

Because, once looked at, lit
By the cold reflections of the dead
Risen extinct but irresistible,
Our lives have never seemed more full, more real,
Nor the full moon more quick to chill.

—James Merrill
June 29, 1957

MUSSEL HUNTER AT ROCK HARBOR

I came before the water-
colorists came to get the
good of the Cape light that scours
sand grit to sided crystal
and buffs and sleeks the blunt hulls
of the three fishing smacks beached
on the bank of the river's

backtracking tail. I'd come for
free fish bait: the blue mussels
clumped like bulbs at the grass-root
margin of the tidal pools.
Dawn tide stood dead low. I smelt
mud stench, shell guts, gulls' leavings;
heard a queer crusty scrabble

cease, and I neared the silenced
edge of a cratered pool bed.
The mussels hung dull blue and
conspicuous, yet it seemed
a sly world's hinges had swung
shut against me. All held still.
Though I counted scant seconds,

enough ages lapsed to win
confidence of safe-conduct
in the wary otherworld
eying me. Grass put forth claws;
small mud knobs, nudged from under,
displaced their domes as tiny
knights might doff their casques. The crabs

inched from their pygmy burrows
and from the trench-dug mud, all
camouflaged in mottled mail
of browns and greens. Each wore one
claw swollen to a shield large
as itself—no fiddler's arm
grown Gargantuan by trade,

but grown grimly, and grimly
borne, for a use beyond my
guessing of it. Sibilant
hordes, mass-motived, they sidled
out in a converging stream
toward the pool mouth, perhaps to
meet the thin and sluggish thread

of sea retracing its tide-
way up the river basin.
Or to avoid me. They moved
obliquely with a dry-wet
sound, with a glittery wisp
and trickle. Could they feel mud
pleasurable under claws

as I could between bare toes?
That question ended it—I
stood shut out, for once, for all,
puzzling the passage of their
absolutely alien
order as I might puzzle
at the clear tail of Halley's

comet, coolly giving my
orbit the go-by, made known
by a family name it
knew nothing of. So the crabs
went about their business, which
wasn't fiddling, and I filled
a big handkerchief with blue

mussels. From what the crabs saw,
if they could see, I was one
two-legged mussel picker.
High on the airy thatching
of the dense grasses, I found
the husk of a fiddler crab,
intact, strangely strayed above

his world of mud—green color
and innards bleached and blown off
somewhere by much sun and wind;
there was no telling if he'd
died recluse or suicide
or headstrong Columbus crab.
The crab face, etched and set there,

grimaced as skulls grimace—it
had an Oriental look,
a samurai death mask done
on a tiger tooth, less for
art's sake than God's. Far from sea—
where red-freckled crab backs, claws,
and whole crabs, dead, their soggy

bellies pallid and upturned,
perform their shambling waltzes
on the waves' dissolving turn
and return, losing themselves
bit by bit to their friendly
element—this relic saved
face, to face the bald-faced sun.

—Sylvia Plath
August 9, 1958

JUST HOW LOW CAN A HIGHBROW GO WHEN A HIGHBROW LOWERS HIS BROW?

Take the intellectual prig;
For his pretensions I do not care a whit or a fig.
I am content that he should know what name Achilles
 assumed among the women, and do his crosswords
 in Esperanto,
And ostentatiously comprehend the inner meaning of
 Pound's obscurest canto.
It does not disturb me that he can distinguish between
 "flaunt" and "flout," and "costive" and "costate,"
What does disturb me is his black-sheep brother, the
 intellectual prig apostate.
Such a one is so erudite that he frequently thinks in Aramaic,
But he expresses himself in slang long passé in Passaic.
His signature is purple ink in an illegible curlicue,
And he compares baseball to ballet, and laments the passing
 of burlesque, which he refers to as burlicue.
He has a folksy approach to the glory that was Greece,
And professes to find more social and sociological
 significance in *Li'l Abner* than in *War and Peace.*
For the most part, my feelings about him I silently conceal,
But when he comments that *The Power of Positive Thinking*
 burns with a hard, gemlike flame, I can only cry that
 he is robbing Pater to paw Peale.

—Ogden Nash
August 30, 1958

THE ARCTIC OX

(Derived from "Golden Fleece of the Arctic," an article in the Atlantic Monthly, *by John J. Teal, Jr., who rears musk oxen on his farm in Vermont)*

To wear the arctic fox
you have to kill it. Wear
    qiviut—the underwool of the arctic ox—
pulled off it like a sweater;
your coat is warm, your conscience better.

I would like a suit of
qiviut, so light I did not
    know I had it on, and in the
course of time another,
since I had not had to murder

the "goat" that grew the fleece
that grew the first. The musk ox
    has no musk and it is not an ox—
illiterate epithet.
Bury your nose in one when wet.

It smells of water, nothing else,
and browses goatlike on
    hind legs. Its great distinction
is not egocentric scent
but that it is intelligent.

Chinchillas, otters, water rats,
and beavers keep us warm.
    But think! A "musk ox" grows six pounds
of *qiviut;* the cashmere ram,
three ounces—that is all—of *pashm.*

Lying in an exposed spot,
basking in the blizzard,
        these ponderosos could dominate
the rare-hairs market in Kashan, and yet
you could not have a choicer pet.

They join you as you work,
love jumping in and out of holes,
        play in water with the children,
learn fast, know their names,
will open gates and invent games.

While not incapable
of courtship, they may find its
        servitude and flutter too much
like Procrustes' bed,
so some decide to stay unwed.

Camels are snobbish
and sheep unintelligent,
        water buffaloes neurasthenic,
even murderous,
reindeer seem overserious.

Whereas these scarce *qivies,*
with golden fleece and winning ways,
        outstripping every fur bearer—
there in Vermont quiet—
could demand Bold Ruler's diet:

Mountain Valley water,
dandelions, carrots, oats;
        encouraged as well, by bed
made fresh three times a day,
to roll and revel in the hay.

Insatiable for willow
leaves alone, our goatlike
        qivi-curvi-capricornus
sheds down ideal for a nest.
Songbirds find *qiviut* best.

Suppose you had a bag
of it; you could spin a pound
        into a twenty-four- or five-
mile thread—one, forty-ply,
that will not shrink in any dye.

If you fear that you are
reading an advertisement
        you are. If we can't be cordial
to these creatures' fleece,
I think that we deserve to freeze.

—Marianne Moore
September 13, 1958

THE GOODNIGHT

He stood still by her bed
Watching his daughter breathe,
The dark and silver head,
The fingers curled beneath,
And thought: Though she may have
Intelligence and charm
And luck, they will not save
Her life from every harm.

The lives of children are
Dangerous to their parents
With fire, water, air,
And other accidents;
And some, for a child's sake,
Anticipating doom,

Empty the world to make
The world safe as a room.

Who could endure the pain
That was Laocoön's?
Twisting, he saw again
In the same coil his sons.
Plumed in his father's skill,
Young Icarus flew higher
Toward the sun, until
He fell in rings of fire.

A man who cannot stand
Children's perilous play,
With lifted voice and hand
Drives the children away.
Out of sight, out of reach,
The tumbling children pass;
He sits on an empty beach,
Holding an empty glass.

Who said that tenderness
Will turn the heart to stone?
May I endure her weakness
As I endure my own.
Better to say goodnight
To breathing flesh and blood
Each night as though the night
Were always only good.

—Louis Simpson
January 24, 1959

LYING AWAKE

This moth caught in the room tonight
Squirmed up, sniper-style, between
The rusted edges of the screen;
Then, long as the room stayed light,

Lay here, content, in some cornerhole.
Now that we've settled into bed,
Though, he can't sleep. Overhead,
He throws himself at the blank wall.

Each night, hordes of these flutterers haunt
And climb my study windowpane;
Fired by reflection, their insane
Eyes gleam; they know what they want.

How do the petulant things survive?
Out in the fields they have a place
And proper work, furthering the race;
Why this blind, fanatical drive

Indoors? Why rush at every spark,
Cigar, head lamp, or railroad warning,
Break a wing off and starve by morning?
And what could a moth fear in the dark

Compared with what you meet inside?
Still, he rams the fluorescent face
Of the clock, thinks that's another place
Of light and families, where he'll hide.

We ought to trap him in a jar,
Or come like the white-coats with a net
And turn him out toward living. Yet
We don't; we take things as they are.

—W. D. Snodgrass
June 13, 1959

THE ROAD BACK

The car is heavy with children
tugged back from summer,
swept out of their laughing beach,
swept out while a persistent rumor
tells them nothing ends.
Today, we fret and pull
on wheels, ignore our regular loss
of time, count cows and others,
while the sun moves over
like an old albatross
we must not count or kill.

There is no word for time.
Today, we will not think
to number another summer
or watch its white bird into the ground.
Today, all cars,
all fathers, all mothers, all
children and lovers will
have to forget
about that thing in the sky
going around
like a persistent rumor
that will get us yet.

—Anne Sexton
August 29, 1959

PART EIGHT

FICTION

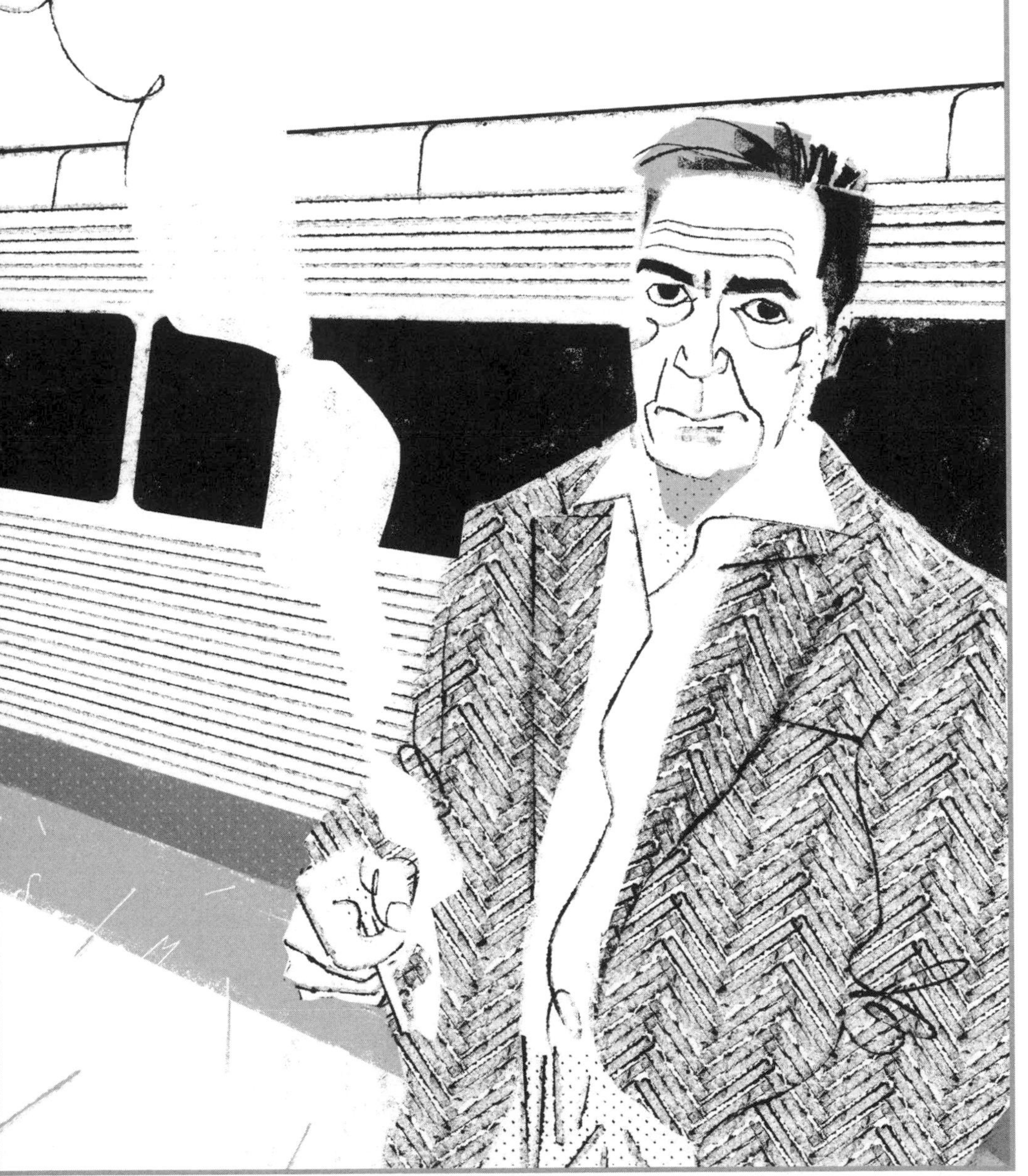

A NOTE BY JONATHAN FRANZEN

THE FIFTIES WERE a key decade in the evolution of American magazine fiction. Earlier in the century, there had been a large stable of magazines to which writers like Katherine Anne Porter and F. Scott Fitzgerald could make a fine living by selling short stories. Later in the century, *The New Yorker* was preeminent; placing a story in its pages was the grail of budding writers, the ultimate validation. By the end of the century, the magazine essentially had the commercial market for short fiction to itself.

It was also in the fifties that "the *New Yorker* story" emerged, quite suddenly, as a distinct literary genus. What made a story *New Yorker* was its carefully wrought, many-comma'd prose; its long passages of physical description, the precision and the sobriety of which created a kind of negative emotional space, a suggestion of feeling without the naming of it; its well-educated white characters, who could be found experiencing the melancholies of affluence, the doldrums of suburban marriage, or the thrill or the desolation of adultery; and, above all, its signature style of ending, which was either elegantly oblique or frustratingly coy, depending on your taste. Outside the offices of *The New Yorker,* its fiction editors were rumored to routinely delete the final paragraph of any story accepted for publication.

The heyday of "the *New Yorker* story" coincided so neatly with the tenure of William Shawn, who succeeded Harold Ross as editor in 1952 and presided until 1987, that it might instead be called "the Shawn story." The one story from the Ross era in this volume, Roald Dahl's "Taste," is written in an older and more conventional register. Its setting—the dinner party of a parvenu stockbroker—is still recognizable and relevant today, but its high-concept premise and its O. Henry ending hark back to the decades when magazine fiction supplied the sort of popular entertainment now considered television's province. The fifties put an end to that, and "the *New Yorker* story," with its emphasis on sentence craft and its rejection of neatly tied-up endings, can be understood, in part, as a retreat from the pressure of commercial TV, a retrenchment in provinces beyond the reach of visual media.

In the fifties, and for a long time afterward, *The New Yorker* didn't identify its fiction as fiction. The author's name appeared only at the end, in small capital letters, the same way the magazine's journalists and critics were credited. What began, perhaps, as an affectation of Harold Ross's became an emblem of the magazine's definition of itself: the writing literally came first, the author's ego-bearing name last. Although fiction in those days was usually given pride of place at the front of the magazine (rather than being secreted near the back, as is the case today), the number of short stories varied from issue to issue, which left it to the reader to determine whether the text in front of her was fiction or nonfiction. The respect the magazine thereby accorded fiction writers—the implication that what mattered about a piece was its sentence-by-sentence excellence, not its genre, not the weight of its subject matter—was part of what made *The New Yorker* the place every young American story writer dreamed of being published.

"The *New Yorker* story" was a stereotype, of course, and inevitably an unfair one—Shawn ran dozens of shtetl stories by I. B. Singer and Irish country stories by Frank O'Connor, and he devoted most of one issue to the experimental novel *Snow White,* by Donald Barthelme, who at the time was not well known. But it was "the *New Yorker* story," as it developed in the fifties, that became the model for aspiring writers, because it seemed to be the key to getting into the magazine, and by the seventies the model was so dominant that it generated mockery and backlash. Too many stories about mopey suburbanites. Too many well-off white people. A surfeit of descriptions, a paucity of action. Too much privileging of prose for the sake of prose, too little openness to rougher energies. And those endings? A style repeated too often devolves into a tic. After Shawn retired and the magazine's fiction section became more of a free-for-all, more multivalent and multiethnic, "the *New Yorker* story" began to look like a form in well-deserved retirement—a relic of an era when subscribers had still had the patience and the time, in New Canaan, in Armonk, on a beach in the Hamptons, to read slow-moving stories in which nothing much happened at the end.

It's therefore instructive to reread John Cheever's "The Country Husband," published in 1954. It's to Cheever, even more than to *The Man in the Gray Flannel Suit,* that we owe a core-cultural suite of images of the fifties: the fathers working in Manhattan, the commuter trains, the autumn leaves on suburban lawns, the overwhelmed young mothers, the willfully forgotten war, the drinking. Along with John Updike and Ann Beattie, Cheever was the paradigmatic "*New Yorker* story" writer. "The Country Husband" is set in an affluent Hudson Line suburb, concerns an obscurely troubled marriage, contains many paragraphs of precise description, and ends obliquely. Even if you've never read it, you might think you've read it all before. But you haven't, because Cheever was a true writer, which is to say, a writer who had skin in the game. Even as he was laying down the very template for "the *New Yorker* story," in 1954, he was chafing against the confines of the stereotype, exploiting the fact of these confines by letting his main character chafe against them, and thereby implicitly justifying the template.

The story's main character, Francis Weed, superficially recalls James Thurber's Walter Mitty, from an earlier *New Yorker* decade: the domesticated middle-class man yearning for adventure. But Thurber's story, though it's written with charm and warmed by empathy, is basically an extended prose version of a thirties *New Yorker* cartoon; the humor is gentle and draws on stock cultural assumptions. This older humor was still present in the cartoons running alongside "The Country Husband" in 1954—in one of them, a housewife has dented her husband's car—but the fiction writer, Cheever, was registering an altogether different level of suburban desperation. Where Walter Mitty waited meekly for his wife and imagined heroics, Francis Weed survives an emergency plane landing and contemplates rape. What lurks beneath his unsatisfying life as a father and husband isn't fantasy. It's true chaos, and Weed's creator seems to know it intimately. Cheever's careful, ironic descriptions of Weed's neighbors and domestic life read like litanies of torment. The most appealing figure in the story is a neighbor's dog, Jupiter, who recognizes no boundaries and leaves destruction in his wake. "The Country Husband" is a reminder of why "the *New Yorker* story" became so dominant. In a country recovering from one war and entering others, living under a nuclear shadow, awaiting large-scale social upheavals, no scream could do justice to the American middle-class predicament. Only understatement could.

While Cheever and Updike were creating the main template for "the *New Yorker* story," regional variants were flourishing. We have here Eudora Welty's tour de force "No Place for You, My Love," which consists so entirely of description that not even its two (nameless) main characters seem to know what they're doing in it. "Below New Orleans there was a raging of insects from both sides of the concrete highway, not quite together, like the playing of separated marching bands": the setting is a long way from Cheeverland, but the quality of the writing isn't. Welty was *The New Yorker*'s favored fictional voice from the South, Mavis Gallant her cooler-eyed counterpart from expat Paris, Harold Brodkey the sui generis reporter from the two frontiers of St. Louis and over-the-top narcissism. Vladimir Nabokov makes a welcome appearance, with the hilarious opening chapter of his novel *Pnin,* to confirm his status as the grand master of linguistic dexterity and childhood memory. Nadine Gordimer is here, too, writing about South African injustice with an irony so brutal that it hurts.

Finally, at the end of the decade, Philip Roth storms into the magazine with his early story "Defender of the Faith." Loosely written, lacking in vivid description, linear in plot, unambiguous in ending, "Defender" is the least "*New Yorker* story" in this volume. It's a story in a hurry to get somewhere, because its author himself was in a hurry. Roth had discovered such a large and untapped store of fictional fuel—had found in himself such a capacity for honesty about the American Jewish experience, the self-hatred, the tribal loyalties—that his stories came out of him in a rocketlike jet. Even as he was arriving at *The New Yorker,* his trajectory was taking him away from it and into the wider spaces of the novel. "Defender" is an exceptional blast, illuminating not only the direction that American fiction would take in the sixties but, by implication, the many modes of fifties writing—Mailer, Gaddis, Kerouac, Flannery O'Connor—that weren't represented in the magazine. It's a testament to the vitality of fiction in the fifties that so much could be left out and still leave so much brilliance.

TASTE

Roald Dahl

THERE WERE SIX of us to dinner that night at Mike Schofield's house in London: Mike and his wife and daughter, my wife and I, and a man called Richard Pratt.

Richard Pratt was a famous gourmet. He was president of a small society known as the Epicures, and each month he circulated privately to its members a pamphlet on food and wines. He organized dinners where sumptuous dishes and rare wines were served. He refused to smoke for fear of harming his palate, and when discussing a wine, he had a curious, rather droll habit of referring to it as though it were a living being. "A prudent wine," he would say, "rather diffident and evasive, but quite prudent." Or, "a good-humored wine, benevolent and cheerful—slightly obscene, perhaps, but nonetheless good-humored."

I had been to dinner at Mike's twice before when Richard Pratt was there, and on each occasion Mike and his wife had gone out of their way to produce a special meal for the famous gourmet. And this one, clearly, was to be no exception. The moment we entered the dining room, I could see that the table was laid for a feast. The tall candles, the yellow roses, the quantity of shining silver, the three wineglasses to each person, and, above all, the faint scent of roasting meat from the kitchen brought the first warm oozings of saliva to my mouth.

As we sat down, I remembered that on both Richard Pratt's previous visits Mike had played a little betting game with him over the claret, challenging him to name its breed and its vintage. Pratt had replied that that should not be too difficult, provided it was one of the great years. Mike had then bet him a case of the wine in question that he could not do it. Pratt had accepted, and had won both times. Tonight I felt sure that the little game would be played over again, for Mike was quite willing to lose the bet in order to prove that his wine was good enough to be recognized, and Pratt, for his part, seemed to take a grave, restrained pleasure in displaying his knowledge.

The meal began with a plate of whitebait, fried very crisp in butter, and to go with it there was a Moselle. Mike got up and poured the wine himself, and when he sat down again, I could see that he was watching Richard Pratt. He had set the bottle down in front of me so that I could read the label. It said, "Geierslay Ohligsberg, 1945." He leaned over and whispered to me that Geierslay was a tiny village in the Moselle, almost unknown outside Germany. He said that this wine we were drinking was something unusual, that the output of the vineyard was so small that it was almost impossible for a stranger to get any of it. He had visited Geierslay personally the previous summer in order to obtain the few dozen bottles that they had finally allowed him to have.

"I doubt anyone else in the country has any of it at the moment," he said. I saw him glance again at Richard Pratt. "Great thing about Moselle," he continued, raising his voice, "it's the perfect wine to serve before a claret. A lot of people serve a Rhine wine instead, but that's because they don't know any better. A Rhine wine will kill a delicate claret, you know that? It's barbaric to serve a Rhine before a claret. But a Moselle—ah!—a Moselle is exactly right."

Mike Schofield was an amiable, middle-aged man. But he was a stockbroker. To be precise, he was a jobber in the stock market, and, like a number of his kind, he seemed to be somewhat embarrassed, almost ashamed, to find that he had made so much money with so slight a talent. In his heart he knew that he was not really much more than a bookmaker—an unctuous, infinitely respectable, secretly unscrupulous bookmaker—and he knew that his friends knew it, too. So he was seeking now to become a man of culture, to cultivate a literary and aesthetic taste, to collect paintings, music, books, and all the rest of it. His little sermon about Rhine wine and Moselle was a part of this thing, this culture that he sought.

"A charming little wine, don't you think?" he said. He was still watching Richard Pratt. I could see him give a rapid, furtive glance down the table each time he dropped his head to take a mouthful of whitebait. I could almost *feel* him waiting for the moment when Pratt would take his first sip, and look up from his glass with a smile of pleasure, of astonishment, perhaps even of wonder, and then there would be a discussion and Mike would tell him about the village of Geierslay.

But Richard Pratt did not taste his wine. He was completely engrossed in conversation with Mike's eighteen-year-old daughter, Louise. He was half turned toward her, smiling at her, telling her, so far as I could gather, some story about a chef in a Paris restaurant. As he spoke, he leaned closer and closer to her, seeming in his eagerness almost to impinge upon her, and the poor girl leaned as far as she could away from him, nodding politely, rather desperately, and looking not at his face but at the topmost button of his dinner jacket.

We finished our fish, and the maid came around removing the plates. When she came to Pratt, she saw that he had not yet touched his food, so she hesitated, and Pratt noticed her. He waved her away, broke off his conversation, and quickly began to eat, popping the little crisp brown fish quickly into his mouth with rapid jabbing movements of his fork. Then, when he had finished, he reached for his glass, and in two short swallows he tipped the wine down his throat, and turned immediately to resume his conversation with Louise Schofield.

Mike saw it all. I was conscious of him sitting there, very still, containing himself, looking at his guest. His round, jovial face seemed to loosen slightly and to sag, but he contained himself and was still and said nothing.

• • •

Soon the maid came forward with the second course. This was a large roast of beef. She placed it on the table in front of Mike, who stood up and carved it, cutting the slices very thin, laying them gently on the plates for the maid to take around. When he had served everyone, including himself, he put down the carving knife and leaned forward with both hands on the edge of the table.

"Now," he said, speaking to all of us but looking at Richard Pratt. "Now for the claret. I must go and fetch the claret, if you'll excuse me."

"You go and fetch it, Mike?" I said. "Where is it?"

"In my study, with the cork out—breathing."

"Why the study?"

"Acquiring room temperature, of course. It's been there twenty-four hours."

"But why the study?"

"It's the best place in the house. Richard helped me choose it last time he was here."

At the sound of his name, Pratt looked around.

"That's right, isn't it?" Mike said.

"Yes," Pratt answered, nodding gravely. "That's right."

"On top of the green filing cabinet in my study," Mike said. "That's the place we chose. A good draft-free spot in a room with an even temperature. Excuse me, now, will you, while I fetch it."

The thought of another wine to play with had restored his humor, and he hurried out the door, to return a minute later, more slowly, walking softly, holding in both hands a wine basket in which a dark bottle lay. The label was out of sight, facing downward. "Now!" he cried as he came toward the table. "What about this one, Richard? You'll never name this one!"

Richard Pratt turned slowly and looked up at Mike; then his eyes travelled down to the bottle, nestling in its small wicker basket, and he raised his eyebrows, a slight, supercilious arching movement of the brows, and with it a pushing outward of the wet lower lip, suddenly imperious and ugly.

"You'll never get it," Mike said. "Not in a hundred years."

"A claret?" Richard Pratt asked, condescending.

"Of course."

"I assume, then, that it's from one of the smaller vineyards?"

"Maybe it is, Richard. And then again, maybe it isn't."

"But it's a good year? One of the great years?"

"Yes, I guarantee that."

"Then it shouldn't be too difficult," Richard Pratt said, drawling his words, looking exceedingly bored. Except that, to me, there was something strange about his drawling and his boredom: between the eyes a shadow of something evil, and in his bearing an intentness that gave me a faint sense of uneasiness as I watched him.

"This one is really rather difficult," Mike said. "I won't force you to bet on this one."

"Indeed. And why not?" Again the slow arching of the brows, the cool, intent look.

"Because it's difficult."

"That's not very complimentary to me, you know."

"My dear man," Mike said, "I'll bet you with pleasure, if that's what you wish."

"It shouldn't be too hard to name it."

"You mean you want to bet?"

"I'm perfectly willing to bet," Richard Pratt said.

"All right, then, we'll have the usual. A case of the wine itself."

"You don't think I'll be able to name it, do you?"

"As a matter of fact, and with all due respect, I don't," Mike said. He was making some effort to remain polite, but Pratt was not bothering overmuch to conceal his contempt for the whole proceeding. And yet, curiously, his next question seemed to betray a certain interest.

"You like to increase the bet?"

"No, Richard. A case is plenty."

"Would you like to bet fifty cases?"

"That would be silly."

Mike stood very still behind his chair at the head of the table, and he was still carefully holding the bottle in its ridiculous wicker basket. There was a trace of whiteness around his nostrils now, and his mouth was shut very tight.

Pratt was lolling back in his chair, looking up at him, the eyebrows raised, the eyes half closed, a little smile touching the corners of his lips. And again I saw, or thought I saw, something distinctly disturbing about the man's face, that shadow of intentness between the eyes, and in the eyes themselves, right in their centers, where it was black, a small, slow spark of shrewdness, hiding. "So you don't want to increase the bet?"

"As far as I'm concerned, old man, I don't give a damn," Mike said. "I'll bet you anything you like."

• • •

The three women and I sat quietly, watching the two men. Mike's wife was becoming annoyed; her mouth had gone sour and I felt that at any moment she was going to interrupt. Our roast beef lay before us on our plates, slowly steaming.

"So you'll bet me anything I like?"

"That's what I told you. I'll bet you anything you damn well please, if you want to make an issue out of it."

"Even ten thousand pounds?"

"Certainly I will, if that's the way you want it." Mike was more confident now. He knew quite well that he could call any sum Pratt cared to mention.

"So you say I can name the bet?" Pratt asked again.

"That's what I said."

There was a pause while Pratt looked slowly around the table, first at me, then at the three women, each in turn. He appeared to be reminding us that we were witness to the offer.

"Mike!" Mrs. Schofield said. "Mike, why don't we stop this nonsense and eat our food. It's getting cold."

"But it isn't nonsense," Pratt told her evenly. "We're making a little bet."

I noticed the maid standing in the background holding a dish of vegetables, wondering whether to come forward with them or not.

"All right, then," Pratt said. "I'll tell you what I want you to bet."

"Come on, then," Mike said, rather reckless. "I don't give a damn what it is—you're on."

Pratt nodded, and again the little smile moved the corners of his lips, and then, quite slowly, looking at Mike all the time, he said, "I want you to bet me the hand of your daughter in marriage."

Louise Schofield gave a jump. "Hey!" she cried. "No! That's not funny! Look here, Daddy, that's not funny at all."

"No, dear," her mother said. "They're only joking."

"I'm not joking," Richard Pratt said.

"It's ridiculous," Mike said. He was off balance again now.

"You said you'd bet anything I liked."

"I meant money."

"You didn't *say* money."

"That's what I meant."

"Then it's a pity you didn't say it. But anyway, if you wish to go back on your offer, that's quite all right with me."

"It's not a question of going back on my offer, old man. It's a no-bet anyway, because you can't match the stake. You yourself don't happen to have a daughter to put up against mine in case you lose. And if you had, I wouldn't want to marry her."

"I'm glad of that, dear," his wife said.

"I'll put up anything you like," Pratt announced. "My house, for example. How about my house?"

"Which one?" Mike asked, joking now.

"The country one."

"Why not the other one as well?"

"All right, then, if you wish it. Both my houses."

At that point, I saw Mike pause. He took a step forward and placed the bottle in its basket gently down on the table. He moved the saltcellar to one side, then the pepper, and then he picked up his knife, studied the blade thoughtfully for a moment, and put it down again. His daughter, too, had seen him pause.

"Now, Daddy!" she cried. "Don't be *absurd*! It's too silly for words. I refuse to be betted on like this."

"Quite right, dear," her mother said. "Stop it at once, Mike, and sit down and eat your food."

Mike ignored her. He looked over at his daughter and he smiled, a slow, fatherly, protective smile. But in his eyes, suddenly, there glimmered a little triumph. "You know," he said, smiling as he spoke, "you know, Louise, we ought to think about this a bit."

"Now, stop it, Daddy! I refuse even to listen to you! Why, I've never heard anything so ridiculous in my life!"

"No, seriously, my dear. Just wait a moment and hear what I have to say."

"But I don't want to hear it."

"Louise! Please! It's like this. Richard, here, has offered us a serious bet. *He* is the one who wants to make it, not me. And if he loses, he will have to hand over a considerable amount of property. Now, wait a minute, my dear, don't interrupt. The point is this. *He cannot possibly win*."

"He seems to think he can."

"Now, listen to me, because I know what I'm talking about. The expert, when tasting a claret—so long as it is not one of the famous, great wines like Lafite or Latour—can only get a certain way towards naming the vineyard. He can, of course, tell you the Bordeaux district from which the wine comes, whether it is from St. Emilion, Pomerol, Graves, or Médoc. But then each district has several communes, little counties, and each county has many, many small vineyards. It is impossible for a man to differentiate between them all by taste and smell alone. I don't mind telling you that this one I've got here is a wine from a small vineyard that is surrounded by many other small vineyards, and he'll never get it. It's impossible."

"You can't be sure of that," his daughter said.

"I'm telling you I can. Though I say it myself, I understand quite a bit about this wine business, you know. And anyway, heavens alive, girl, I'm your father and you don't think I'd let you in for—for—for something you didn't want, do you? I'm trying to make you some money."

"Mike!" his wife said sharply. "Stop it now, Mike, please!"

Again he ignored her. "If you will take this bet," he said to his daughter, "in ten minutes you will be the owner of two large houses."

"But I don't want two large houses, Daddy."

"Then sell them. Sell them back to him on the spot. I'll arrange all that for you. And then, just think of it, my dear, you'll be rich! You'll be independent for the rest of your life!"

"Oh, Daddy, I don't like it. I think it's silly."

"So do I," the mother said. She jerked her head briskly up and down as she spoke, like a hen. "You ought to be ashamed of yourself, Michael, ever suggesting such a thing! Your own daughter, too!"

Mike didn't even look at her. "Take it!" he said eagerly, staring hard at the girl. "Take it, quick! I'll guarantee you won't lose."

"But I don't like it, Daddy."

"Come on, girl. Take it!"

Mike was pushing her hard. He was leaning toward her, fixing her with two hard, bright eyes, and it was not easy for the daughter to resist him.

"But what if I lose?"

"I keep telling you, you can't lose. I'll guarantee it."

"Oh, Daddy, must I?"

"I'm making you a fortune. So come on now. What do you say, Louise? All right?"

For the last time, she hesitated. Then she gave a helpless little shrug of the shoulders and said, "Oh, all right, then. Just so long as you swear there's no danger of losing."

"Good!" Mike cried. "That's fine! Then it's a bet!"

"Yes," Richard Pratt said, looking at the girl. "It's a bet."

• • •

Immediately, Mike picked up the wine, tipped the first thimbleful into his own glass, then skipped excitedly around the table filling up all the others. Now everyone was watching Richard Pratt, watching his face as he reached slowly for his glass with his right hand and lifted it to his nose. The man was about fifty years old and he did not have a pleasant face. Somehow, it was all mouth—mouth and lips—the full, wet lips of the professional gourmet, the lower lip hanging downward in the center, a pendulous, permanently open taster's lip, shaped open to receive the rim of a glass or a morsel of food. Like a keyhole, I thought, watching it; his mouth is like a large, wet keyhole.

Slowly he lifted the glass to his nose. The point of the nose entered the glass and moved over the surface of the wine, delicately sniffing. He swirled the wine gently around in the glass to release the bouquet. His concentration was intense. He had closed his eyes, and now the whole top half of his body, the head and neck and chest, seemed to become a kind of huge, sensitive smelling-machine, receiving, filtering, analyzing the message from the sniffing nose.

Mike, I noticed, was lounging in his chair, apparently unconcerned, but he was watching every move. Mrs. Schofield, the wife, sat prim and upright at the other end of the table, looking straight ahead, her face tight with disapproval. The daughter, Louise, had shifted her chair away a little, and sidewise, facing the gourmet, and she, like her father, was watching closely.

For at least a minute, the smelling process continued; then, without opening his eyes or moving his head, Pratt lowered the glass to his mouth and tipped in almost half the contents. He paused, his mouth full of wine, getting the first taste; then he permitted some of it to trickle down his throat, and I saw his Adam's apple move as it passed by. But most of it he retained in his mouth. And now, without swallowing again, he drew in through his lips a thin breath of air, which mingled with the fumes of the wine in the mouth and passed on down into his lungs. He held the breath, blew it out through his nose, and finally began to roll the wine around under the tongue, and chewed it, actually chewed it with his teeth, as though it were bread.

It was a solemn, impressive performance, and I must say he did it well.

"Um," he said, putting down the glass, running a pink tongue over his lips. "Um—yes. A very interesting little wine—gentle and gracious, almost feminine in the aftertaste."

There was an excess of saliva in his mouth, and as he spoke he spat an occasional bright speck of it onto the table.

"Now we can start to eliminate," he said. "You will pardon me for doing this carefully, but there is much at stake. Normally I would perhaps take a bit of a chance, leaping forward quickly and landing right in the middle of the vineyard of my choice. But this time— I must move cautiously this time, must I not?" He looked up at Mike and he smiled, a thick-lipped, wet-lipped smile. Mike did not smile back.

"First, then, which district in Bordeaux does this wine come from? That is not difficult to guess. It is far too light in the body to be from either St. Emilion or Graves. It is obviously a Médoc. There's no doubt about *that.*

"Now—from which commune in Médoc does it come? That also, by elimination, should not be too difficult to decide. Margaux? No. It cannot be Margaux. It has not the violent bouquet of a Margaux. Pauillac? It cannot be Pauillac, either. It is too tender, too gentle and wistful for a Pauillac. The wine of Pauillac has a character that is almost imperious in its taste. And also, to me, a Pauillac contains just a little pith, a curious, dusty, pithy flavor that the grape acquires from the soil of the district. No, no. This—this is a very gentle wine, demure and bashful in the first taste, emerging shyly but quite graciously in the second. A little arch, perhaps, in the second taste, and a little naughty also, teasing the tongue with a trace, just a trace, of tannin. Then, in the aftertaste, delightful—consoling and feminine, with a certain blithely generous quality that one associates only with the wines of the commune of St. Julien. Unmistakably this is a St. Julien."

He leaned back in his chair, held his hands up level with his chest, and placed the fingertips carefully together. He was becoming ridiculously pompous, but I thought that some of it was deliberate, simply to mock his host. I found myself waiting rather tensely for him to go on. The girl Louise was lighting a cigarette. Pratt heard the match strike and he turned on her, flaring suddenly with real anger. "Please!" he said. "Please don't do that! It's a disgusting habit, to smoke at table!"

She looked up at him, still holding the burning match in one hand, the big, slow eyes settling on his face, resting there a moment, moving away again, slow and contemptuous, and, bending her head, she blew out the match, but continued to hold the unlighted cigarette in her fingers.

"I'm sorry, my dear," Pratt said, "but I simply cannot have smoking at table."

She didn't look at him again.

"Now, let me see—where were we?" he said. "Ah, yes. This wine is from Bordeaux, from the commune of St. Julien, in the district of Médoc. So far, so good. But now we come to the more difficult part—the name of the vineyard itself. For in St. Julien there are many vineyards, and as our host so rightly remarked earlier on, there is often not much difference between the wine of one and the wine of another. But we shall see."

He paused again, closing his eyes. "I am trying to establish the 'growth,'" he said. "If I can do that, it will be half the battle. Now, let me see. This wine is obviously not from a first-growth vineyard—nor even a second. It is not a great wine. The quality, the—the— what do you call it? —the radiance, the power, is lacking. But a third growth—that it could be. And yet I doubt it. We know it is a good year—our host has said so—and this is probably flattering it a little bit. I must be careful. I must be very careful here."

He picked up his glass and took another small sip.

"Yes," he said, sucking his lips, "I was right. It is a fourth growth. Now I am sure of it. A fourth growth from a very good year—from a great year, in fact. And that's what made it taste for a moment like a third- or even a second-growth wine. Good! That's better! Now we are closing in! What are the fourth-growth vineyards in the commune of St. Julien?"

Again he paused, took up his glass, and held the rim against that sagging, pendulous lower lip of his. Then I saw the tongue shoot out, pink and narrow, the tip of it dipping into the wine, withdrawing swiftly again—a repulsive sight. When he lowered the glass, his eyes remained closed, the face concentrated, only the lips moving, sliding over each other like two pieces of wet, spongy rubber.

"There it is again!" he cried. "Tannin in the middle taste, and the quick astringent squeeze upon the tongue. Yes, yes, of course! Now I have it! This wine comes from one of those small vineyards around Beychevelle. I remember now. The Beychevelle district, and the river and the little harbor that has silted up so the wine ships can no longer use it. Beychevelle . . . Could it actually be a Beychevelle itself? No, I don't think so. Not quite. But it is somewhere very close. Château Talbot? Could it be Talbot? Yes, it could. Wait one moment."

He sipped the wine again, and out of the side of my eye I noticed Mike Schofield and how he was leaning farther and farther forward over the table, his mouth slightly open, his small eyes fixed upon Richard Pratt.

"No. I was wrong. It is not a Talbot. A Talbot comes forward to you just a little quicker than this one; the fruit is nearer to the surface. If it is a '34, which I believe it is, then it couldn't be a Talbot. Well, well. Let me think. It is not a Beychevelle and it is not a Talbot, and yet—yet it is so close to both of them, so close, that the vineyard must be almost in between. Now, which could that be?"

He hesitated, and we waited, watching his face. Everyone, even Mike's wife, was watching him now. I heard the maid put down the dish of vegetables on the sideboard behind me, gently, so as not to disturb the silence.

"Ah!" he cried. "I have it! Yes, I think I have it!"

For the last time, he sipped the wine. Then, still holding the glass up near his mouth, he turned to Mike and he smiled, a slow, silky smile, and he said, "You know what this is? This is the little Château Branaire-Ducru."

Mike sat tight, not moving.

"And the year, 1934."

We all looked at Mike, waiting for him to turn the bottle around in its basket and show the label.

"Is that your final answer?" Mike said.

"Yes, I think so."

"Well, is it or isn't it?"

"Yes, it is."

"What was the name again?"

"Château Branaire-Ducru. Pretty little vineyard. Lovely old château. Know it quite well. Can't think why I didn't recognize it at once."

"Come on, Daddy," the girl said. "Turn it round and let's have a peek. I want my two houses."

"Just a minute," Mike said. "Wait just a minute." He was sitting very quiet, bewildered-looking, and his face was becoming puffy and pale, as though all the force was draining slowly out of him.

"Michael!" his wife called sharply from the other end of the table. "What's the matter?"

"Keep out of this, Margaret, will you please."

Richard Pratt was looking at Mike, smiling with his mouth, his eyes small and bright. Mike was not looking at anyone.

"Daddy!" the daughter cried, agonized. "But, Daddy, you don't mean to say he's guessed it right!"

"Now, stop worrying, my dear," Mike said. "There's nothing to worry about."

I think it was more to get away from his family than anything else that Mike then turned to Richard Pratt and said, "I'll tell you what, Richard. I think you and I better slip off into the next room and have a little chat?"

"I don't want a little chat," Pratt said. "All I want is to see the label on that bottle." He knew he was a winner now; he had the bearing, the quiet arrogance, of a winner, and I could see that he was prepared to become thoroughly nasty if there was any trouble. "What are you waiting for?" he said to Mike. "Go on and turn it round."

• • •

Then this happened: The maid, the tiny, erect figure of the maid, in her white-and-black uniform, was standing beside Richard Pratt, holding something out in her hand. "I believe these are yours, sir," she said.

Pratt glanced around, saw the pair of thin horn-rimmed spectacles that she held out to him, and for a moment he hesitated. "Are they? Perhaps they are. I don't know."

"Yes sir, they're yours." The maid was an elderly woman—nearer seventy than sixty—a faithful family retainer of many years standing. She put the spectacles down on the table beside him.

Without thanking her, Pratt took them up and slipped them into his top pocket, behind the white handkerchief.

But the maid didn't go away. She remained standing beside, and slightly behind, Richard Pratt, and there was something so unusual in her manner and in the way she stood there, small, motionless, and erect, that I, for one, found myself watching her with a sudden apprehension. Her old, gray face had a frosty, determined look, the lips were compressed, the little chin was out, and the hands were clasped together tight before her. The curious cap on her head and the flash of white down the front of her uniform made her seem like some tiny, ruffled, white-breasted bird.

"You left them in Mr. Schofield's study," she said. Her voice was unnaturally, deliberately polite. "On top of the green filing cabinet in his study, sir, when you happened to go in there by yourself before dinner."

It took a few moments for the full meaning of her words to penetrate, and in the silence that followed I became aware of Mike and how he was slowly drawing himself up in his chair, and the color coming to his face, and the eyes opening wide, and the curl of the mouth, and the dangerous little patch of whiteness beginning to spread around the area of the nostrils.

"Now, Michael!" his wife said. "Keep calm now, Michael, dear! Keep calm!"

December 8, 1951

NO PLACE FOR YOU, MY LOVE

Eudora Welty

THEY WERE STRANGERS to each other, both fairly well strangers to the place, now seated side by side at luncheon—a party combined in a free-and-easy way when the friends he and she were with recognized each other across Galatoire's. The time was a Sunday in summer—those hours of afternoon that seem Time Out in New Orleans.

The moment he saw her little blunt, fair face, he thought that here was a woman who was having an affair. It was one of those odd meetings when such an impact is felt that it has to be translated at once into some sort of speculation.

With a married man, most likely, he supposed, slipping quickly into a groove—he was long married—and feeling more conventional, then, in his curiosity as she sat there, leaning her cheek on her hand, looking no further before her than the flowers on the table, and wearing that hat.

He did not like her hat, any more than he liked tropical flowers. It was the wrong hat for her, thought this Eastern businessman who had no interest whatever in women's clothes and no eye for them; he thought the unaccustomed thing crossly.

It must stick out all over me, she thought, so people think they can love me or hate me just by looking at me. How did it leave us—the old, safe, slow way people used to know of learning how one another feels, and the privilege that went with it of shying away if it seemed best? People in love like me, I suppose, give away the short cuts to everybody's secrets.

Something, though, he decided, had been settled about her predicament—for the time being, anyway; the parties to it were all still alive, no doubt. Nevertheless, her predicament was the only one he felt so sure of here, like the only recognizable shadow in that restaurant, where mirrors and fans were busy agitating the light, as the very local talk drawled across and agitated the peace. The shadow lay between her fingers, between her little square hand and her cheek, like something always best carried about the person. Then suddenly, as she took her hand down, the secret fact was still there—it lighted her. It was a bold and full light, shot up under the brim of that hat, as close to them all as the flowers in the center of the table.

Did he dream of making her disloyal to that hopelessness that he saw very well she'd been cultivating down here? He knew very well that he did not. What they amounted to was two Northerners keeping each other company. She glanced up at the big gold clock on the wall and smiled. He didn't smile back. She had that naïve face that he associated, for no good reason, with the Middle West—because it said "Show me," perhaps. It was a serious, now-watch-out-everybody face, which orphaned her entirely in the company of these Southerners. He guessed her age, as he could not guess theirs: thirty-two. He himself was further along.

Of all human moods, deliberate imperviousness may be the one most quickly communicated—it may be the most successful, most fatal signal of all. And two people can indulge in imperviousness as well as in anything else. "You're not very hungry either," he said.

The blades of fan shadows came down over their two heads, as he saw inadvertently in the mirror, with himself smiling at her now like a villain. His remark sounded dominant and rude enough for everybody present to listen back a moment; it even sounded like an answer to a question she might have just asked him. The other women glanced at him. The Southern look—Southern mask—of life-is-a-dream irony, which could turn to pure challenge at the drop of a hat, he could wish well away. He liked naïveté better.

"I find the heat down here depressing," she said, with the heart of Ohio in her voice.

"Well—I'm in somewhat of a temper about it, too," he said.

They looked with grateful dignity at each other.

"I have a car here, just down the street," he said to her as the luncheon party was rising to leave, all the others wanting to get back to their houses and sleep. "If it's all right with— Have you ever driven down south of here?"

Out on Bourbon Street, in the bath of July, she asked at his shoulder, "South of New Orleans? I didn't know there was any south to *here.* Does it just go on and on?" She laughed, and adjusted the exasperating hat to her head in a different way. It was more than frivolous, it was conspicuous, with some sort of glitter or flitter tied in a band around the straw and hanging down.

"That's what I'm going to show you."

"Oh—you've been there?"

"No!"

His voice rang out over the uneven, narrow sidewalk and dropped back from the walls. The flaked-off, colored houses were spotted like the hides of beasts, and breathed their heat down onto them as they walked to the car parked there.

"It's just that it couldn't be any worse—we'll see."

"All right, then," she said. "We will."

So, their actions reduced to amiability, they settled into the car—a faded-red Ford convertible with a rather threadbare canvas top, which had been standing in the sun for all those lunch hours.

"It's rented," he explained. "I asked to have the top put down, and was told I'd lost my mind."

"It's out of this world. *Degrad*ing heat," she said and added, "Doesn't matter."

The stranger in New Orleans always sets out to leave it as though following the clue in a maze. They were threading through the narrow and one-way streets, past the pale-violet bloom of tired squares, the brown steeples and statues, the balcony with the live and probably famous black monkey dipping along the railing as over a ballroom floor, past the grillwork and the latticework to all the iron swans painted flesh color on the front steps of bungalows outlying.

Driving, he spread his new map and put his finger down on it. At the intersection marked Arabi, where their road led out of the tangle and he took it, a small Negro seated beneath a black umbrella astride a box chalked "Shou Shine" lifted his pink-and-black hand and waved them languidly goodbye. She didn't miss it, and waved back.

• • •

Below New Orleans there was a raging of insects from both sides of the concrete highway, not quite together, like the playing of separated marching bands. The river and the levee were still on her side, waste and jungle and some occasional settlements on his—poor houses. Families bigger than housefuls thronged the yards. His nodding, driving head would veer from side to side, looking and almost lowering. As time passed and the distance from New Orleans grew, girls ever darker and younger were disposing themselves over the porches and the porch steps, with jet-black hair pulled high, and ragged palm-leaf fans rising and falling like rafts of butterflies. The children running forth were nearly always naked ones.

She watched the road. Crayfish constantly crossed in front of the wheels, looking grim and bonneted, in a great hurry.

"How the Old Woman Got Home," she murmured to herself.

He pointed, as it flew by, at a saucepan full of cut zinnias which stood waiting on the open lid of a mailbox at the roadside, with a little note tied onto the handle.

They rode mostly in silence. The sun bore down. They met fishermen and other men bent on some local pursuits, some in sulphur-colored pants, walking and riding; met wagons, trucks, boats in trucks, autos, boats on top of autos—all coming to meet them, as though something of high moment were doing back where the car came from, and he and she were determined to miss it. There was nearly always a man lying with his shoes off in the bed of any truck otherwise empty—with the raw, red look of a man sleeping in the daytime, being jolted about as he slept. Then there was a sort of dead man's land, where nobody came. He loosened his collar and tie. By rushing through the heat at high speed, they brought themselves the effect of fans turned onto their cheeks. Clearing alternated with jungle and canebrake like something tried, tried again. Little shell roads led off on both sides; now and then a road of planks led into the yellow-green.

"Like a dance floor in there." She pointed.

He informed her, "In there's your oil, I think."

There were thousands, millions of mosquitoes and gnats—a universe of them, and on the increase.

A family of eight or nine people on foot strung along the road in the same direction the car was going, beating themselves with the wild palmettos. Heels, shoulders, knees, breasts, backs of the heads, elbows, hands, were touched in turn—like some game, each playing it with himself.

He struck himself on the forehead, and increased their speed. (His wife would not be at her most charitable if he came bringing malaria home to the family.)

More and more crayfish and other shell creatures littered their path, scuttling or dragging. These little samples, little jokes of creation, persisted and sometimes perished, the more of them the deeper down the road went. Terrapins and turtles came up steadily over the horizons of the ditches.

Back there in the margins were worse—crawling hides you could not penetrate with bullets or quite believe, grins that had come down from the primeval mud.

"Wake up." Her Northern nudge was very timely on his arm. They had veered toward the side of the road. Still driving fast, he spread his map.

Like a misplaced sunrise, the light of the river flowed up; they were mounting the levee on a little shell road.

"Shall we cross here?" he asked politely.

. . .

He might have been keeping track over years and miles of how long they could keep that tiny ferry waiting. Now skidding down the levee's flank, they were the last-minute car, the last possible car that could squeeze on. Under the sparse shade of one willow tree, the small, amateurish-looking boat slapped the water as, expertly, he wedged on board.

"Tell him we put him on hub cap!" shouted one of the numerous olive-skinned, dark-eyed young boys standing dressed up in bright shirts at the railing, hugging each other with delight that that last straw was on board. Another boy drew his affectionate initials in the dust of the door on her side.

She opened the door and stepped out, and, after only a moment's standing at bay, started up a little iron stairway. She appeared above the car, on the tiny bridge beneath the captain's window and the whistle.

From there, while the boat still delayed in what seemed a trance—as if it were too full to attempt the start—she could see the panlike deck below, separated by its rusty rim from the tilting, polished water.

The passengers walking and jostling about there appeared oddly amateurish, too—amateur travellers. They were having such a good time. They all knew each other. Beer was being passed around in cans, bets were being loudly settled and new bets made, about local and special subjects on which they all doted. One red-haired man in a burst of wildness even tried to give away his truckload of shrimp to a man on the other side of the boat—nearly all the trucks were full of shrimp—causing taunts and then protests of "They good! They good!" from the giver. The young boys leaned on each other thinking of what next, rolling their eyes absently.

A radio pricked the air behind her. Looking like a great tomcat just above her head, the captain was digesting the news of a fine stolen automobile.

At last a tremendous explosion burst—the whistle. Everything shuddered in outline from the sound, everybody said something—everybody else.

They started with no perceptible motion, but her hat blew off. It went spiralling to the deck below, where he, thank heaven, sprang out of the car and picked it up. Everybody looked frankly up at her now, holding her hands to her head.

The little willow tree receded as its shade was taken away. The heat was like something falling on her head. She held the hot rail before her. It was like riding a stove. Her shoulders dropping, her hair flying, her skirt buffeted by the sudden strong wind, she stood there, thinking they all must see that with her entire self all she did was wait. Her set hands, with the bag that hung from her wrist and rocked back and forth—all three seemed objects bleaching there, belonging to no one; she could not feel a thing in the skin of her face; perhaps she was crying, and not knowing it. She could look down and see him just below her, his black shadow, her hat, and his black hair. His hair in the wind looked unreasonably long and rippling. Little did he know that from here it had a red undergleam like an animal's. When she looked up and outward, a vortex of light drove through and over the brown waves like a star in the water.

He did after all bring the retrieved hat up the stairs to her. She took it back wordlessly and held it to her skirt. What they were saying below was more polite than their searchlight faces.

"Where you think he come from, that man?"

"I bet he come from Lafitte."

"Lafitte? What you bet, eh?"—all crouched in the shade of trucks, squatting and laughing.

Now his shadow fell partly across her; the boat had jolted into some other strand of current. Her shaded arm and shaded hand felt pulled out from the blaze of light and water, and she hoped humbly for more shade for her head. It had seemed so natural to climb up and stand in the sun.

The boys had a surprise—an alligator on board. One of them pulled it by a chain around the deck, between the cars and trucks, like a toy—a hide that could walk. He thought, Well, they had to catch one sometime. It's Sunday afternoon. So they have him on board now, riding him across the Mississippi River. . . . The playfulness of it beset everybody on the ferry. The hoarseness of the boat whistle, commenting briefly, seemed part of the general appreciation.

"Who want to rassle him? Who want to, eh?" two boys cried, looking up. A boy with shrimp-colored arms capered from side to side, pretending to have been bitten.

What was there so hilarious about jaws that could bite? And what danger was there once in this repulsiveness—so that the last worldly evidence of some old heroic horror of the dragon had to be paraded in capture before the eyes of country clowns?

He noticed that she looked at the alligator without flinching at all. Her distance was set—the number of feet and inches between herself and it mattered to her.

Perhaps her measuring coolness was to him what his bodily shade was to her, while they stood pat up there riding the river, which felt like the sea and looked like the earth under them—full of the red-brown earth, charged with it. Ahead of the boat it was like an exposed vein of ore. The river seemed to swell in the vast middle with the curve of the earth. The sun rolled under them. As if in memory of the size of things, uprooted trees were drawn across their path, sawing at the air and tumbling one over the other.

When they reached the other side, she felt that they had been racing around an arena in their chariot, among lions. The whistle took and shook the stairs as they went down. The young boys, looking taller, had taken out colored combs and were combing their wet hair back in solemn pompadour above their radiant foreheads. They had been bathing in the river themselves not long before.

The cars and trucks, then the foot passengers and the alligator, waddling like a child to school, all disembarked and wound up the weed-sprung levee.

Both respectable and merciful, their hides, she thought, forcing herself to dwell on the alligator as she looked back. Deliver us all from the naked in heart. (As she had been told.)

When they regained their paved road, he heard her give a little sigh and saw her turn her straw-colored head to look back once more. Now that she rode with her hat in her lap, her earrings were conspicuous too. A little metal ball set with small pale stones danced beside each square, faintly downy cheek.

Had she felt a wish for someone else to be riding with them? He thought it was more likely that she would wish for her husband if she had one (his wife's voice) than for the lover in whom he believed. Whatever people liked to think, situations (if not scenes) were usually three-way—there was somebody else always. The one who didn't—couldn't—understand the two made the formidable third.

He glanced down at the map, flapping on the seat between them, up at his wristwatch, out at the road. Out there was the incredible brightness of four o'clock. On this side of the river, the road ran beneath the brow of the levee and followed it. Here was a heat that ran deeper and brighter and more intense than all the rest—its nerve. The road grew one with the heat as it was one with the unseen river. Dead snakes stretched across the concrete like markers—inlaid mosaic bands, dry as feathers, which their tires licked at intervals that began to seem clocklike.

No, the heat faced them—it was ahead. They could see it waving at them, shaken in the air above the white of the road, always at a certain distance ahead, shimmering finely as a cloth, with running edges of green and gold, fire and azure.

"It's never anything like this in Syracuse," he said.

"Or in Toledo, either," she replied with dry lips.

They were driving through greater waste down here, through fewer and even more insignificant towns. There was water under everything. Even where a screen of jungle had been left to stand, splashes could be heard from under the trees. In the vast open, sometimes boats moved inch by inch through what appeared endless meadows of rubbery flowers.

Her eyes overcome with brightness and size, she felt a panic rise, as sudden as nausea. Just how far below questions and answers, concealment and revelation, they were running now—that was still a new question, with a power of its own, waiting. How dear—how costly—could this ride be?

"It looks to me like your road can't go much further," she remarked cheerfully. "Just over there, it's all water."

"Time out," he said, and with that he turned the car into a sudden road of white shells that rushed at them narrowly out of the left.

They bolted over a cattle guard, where some rayed and crested purple flowers burst out of the vines in the ditch, and rolled onto a long, narrow, green, mowed clearing: a churchyard. A paved track ran between two short rows of raised tombs, all neatly whitewashed and now brilliant as faces against the vast flushed sky.

The track was the width of the car with a few inches to spare. He passed between the tombs slowly but in the manner of a feat. Names took their places on the walls slowly at a level with the eye, names as near as the eyes of a person stopping in conversation, and as far away in origin, and in all their music and dead longing, as Spain. At intervals were set packed bouquets of zinnias, oleanders, and some kind of purple flowers, all quite fresh, in fruit jars, like nice welcomes on bureaus.

They moved on into an open area beyond, of violent-green grass, spread before the green-and-white frame church with worked flower beds around it, flowerless poinsettias growing up to the window sills. Beyond was a house, and left on the doorstep of the house a fresh-caught catfish the size of a baby—a fish wearing whiskers and bleeding. On a clothesline in the yard, a priest's black gown on a hanger hung airing, swaying at man's height, in a vague, trainlike, ladylike sweep along an evening breath that might otherwise have seemed imaginary from the unseen, felt river.

With the motor cut off, with the raging of the insects about them, they sat looking out at the green and white and black and red and pink as they leaned against the sides of the car.

"What is your wife like?" she asked. His right hand came up and spread—iron, wooden, manicured. She lifted her eyes to his face. He looked at her like that hand.

Then he lit a cigarette, and the portrait, and the right-hand testimonial it made, were blown away. She smiled, herself as unaffected as by some stage performance; and he was annoyed in the cemetery. They did not risk going on to her husband—if she had one.

Under the supporting posts of the priest's house, where a boat was, solid ground ended and palmettos and water hyacinths could not wait to begin; suddenly the rays of the sun, from behind the car, reached that lowness and struck the flowers. The priest came out onto the porch in his underwear, stared at the car a moment as if he wondered what time it was, then collected his robe off the line and his fish off the doorstep and returned inside. Vespers was next.

• • •

After backing out between the tombs he drove on still south, in the sunset. They caught up with an old man walking in a sprightly way in their direction, all by himself, wearing a clean bright shirt printed with a pair of palm trees fanning green over his chest. It might better be a big colored woman's shirt, but she didn't have it. He flagged the car with gestures like hoops.

"You're coming to the end of the road," the old man told them. He pointed ahead, tipped his hat to the lady, and pointed again. "End of the road." They didn't understand that he meant, "Take me."

They drove on. "If we do go any further, it'll have to be by water—is that it?" he asked her, hesitating at this odd point.

"You know better than I do," she replied politely.

The road had for some time ceased to be paved; it was made of shells. It was leading into a small, sparse settlement like the others a few miles back, but with even more of the camp about it. On the lip of the clearing, directly before a green willow blaze with the sunset gone behind it, the row of houses and shacks faced out on broad, colored, moving water that stretched to reach the horizon and looked somehow like an arm of the sea. The houses on their shaggy posts, patchily built, some with plank runways instead of steps, were flimsy and alike, and not much bigger than the boats tied up at the landing.

"Venice," she heard him announce, and he dropped the crackling map in her lap.

They rolled down the brief remainder. The end of the road—she could not remember ever seeing a road simply end—was a spoon shape, with a tree stump in the bowl to turn around by.

Around it, he stopped the car, and they stepped out, feeling put down in the midst of a sudden vast pause or subduement that was like a yawn. They made their way on foot toward the water, where at an idle-looking landing men in twos and threes stood with their backs to them.

The nearness of darkness, the still uncut trees, bright water partly under a sheet of flowers, shacks, silence, dark shapes of boats tied up, then the first sounds of people just on the other side of thin walls—all this reached them. Mounds of shells like day-old snow, pink-tinted, lay around a central shack with a beer sign on it. An old man up on the porch there sat holding an open newspaper, with a fat white goose sitting opposite him on the floor. Below, in the now shadowless and sunless open, another old man, with a colored pencil bright under his hat brim, could still see to mend a sail.

When she looked clear around, thinking they had a fire burning somewhere now, out of the heat had risen the full moon. Just beyond the trees, enormous, tangerine-colored, it was going solidly up. Other lights just striking into view, looking farther distant, showed moss shapes hanging, or slipped and broke matchlike on the water that so encroached on the rim of ground they were standing on.

There was a touch at her arm—his, accidental.

"We're at the jumping-off place," he said.

She laughed, having thought his hand was a bat, while her eyes rushed downward toward a great pale drift of water hyacinths—still partly open, flushed and yet moonlit, level with her feet—through which paths of water for the boats had been hacked. She drew her hands up to her face under the brim of her hat; her own cheeks felt like the hyacinths to her, all her skin still full of too much light and sky, exposed. The harsh vesper bell was ringing.

"I believe there must be something wrong with me, that I came on this excursion to begin with," she said, as if he had already said this and she were merely in hopeful, willing, maddening agreement with him.

He took hold of her arm, and said, "Oh, come on—I see we can get something to drink here, at least."

But there was a beating, muffled sound from over the darkening water. One more boat was coming in, making its way through the tenacious, tough, dark flower traps, by the shaken light of what first appeared to be torches. He and she waited for the boat, as if on each other's patience. As if borne in on a mist of twilight or a breath, a horde of mosquitoes and gnats were singing and striking at them first. The boat bumped, men laughed. Somebody was offering somebody else some shrimp.

Then he might have cocked his dark city head down at her; she did not look up at him, only turned when he did. Now the shell mounds, like the shacks and trees, were solid purple. Lights had appeared in the not-quite-true window squares. A narrow neon sign, the lone sign, had come out in bright blush on the beer shack's roof: "Baba's Place." A light was on on the porch.

The barnlike interior was brightly lit and unpainted, looking not quite finished, with a partition dividing it.

One of the four cardplayers at a table in the middle of the floor was the newspaper reader; the paper was in his pants pocket. Midway along the partition was a bar, in the form of a pass-through to the other room, with a varnished, second-hand fretwork overhang. He and she crossed the floor and sat, alone there, on wooden stools. An eruption of humorous signs, newspaper cutouts and cartoons, razor-blade cards, and personal messages of significance to the owner or his friends decorated the overhang, framing where Baba should have been but wasn't.

Through there came a smell of garlic and cloves and red pepper, a blast of hot cloud escaped from a cauldron they could see now on a stove at the back of the other room. A massive back, presumably female, with a twist of gray hair on top, stood with a ladle akimbo. A young man joined her and stole something from the pot with his fingers and ate it. At Baba's they were boiling shrimp.

When he got ready to wait on them, Baba strolled out to the counter, young, black-headed, and in very good humor.

"Coldest beer you've got. And food— What will you have?"

"Nothing for me, thank you," she said. "I'm not sure I could eat, after all."

"Well, I could," he said, shoving his jaw out. Baba smiled. "I want a good solid ham sandwich."

"I could have asked him for some water," she said, after he had gone.

While they sat waiting, it seemed very quiet. The bubbling of the shrimp, the distant laughing of Baba, and the slap of cards, like the beating of moths on the screens, seemed to come in fits and starts. The steady breathing they heard came from a big rough dog asleep in the corner. But it was bright. Electric lights were strung riotously over the room from a kind of spider web of old wires in the rafters. One of the written messages tacked before them read, "Joe! At the boyy!!" It looked very yellow, older than Baba's Place. Outside, the world was pure dark.

Two little boys, almost alike, almost the same size, and just cleaned up, dived into the room with a double bang of the screen door, and circled around the card game. They ran their hands into the men's pockets.

"Nickel for some pop!"

"Nickel for some pop!"

"Go 'way and let me play, you!"

They circled around and shrieked at the dog, ran under the lid of the counter and raced through the kitchen and back, and hung over the stools at the bar. One child had a live lizard on his shirt, clinging like a breast pin—like lapis lazuli.

Bringing in a strong odor of geranium talcum, some men had come in now—all in bright shirts. They drew near the counter, or stood and watched the game.

When Baba came out bringing the beer and sandwich, "Could I have some water?" she greeted him.

Baba laughed at everybody. She decided the woman back there must be Baba's mother.

Beside her, he was drinking his beer and eating his sandwich—ham, cheese, tomato, pickle, and mustard. Before he finished, one of the men who had come in beckoned from across the room. It was the old man in the palm-tree shirt.

She lifted her head to watch him leave her, and was looked at, from all over the room. As a minute passed, no cards were laid down. In a far-off way, like accepting the light from Arcturus, she accepted it that she was more beautiful or perhaps more fragile than the women they saw every day of their lives. It was just this thought coming into a woman's face, and at this hour, that seemed familiar to them.

Baba was smiling. He had set an opened, frosted brown bottle before her on the counter, and a thick sandwich, and stood looking at her. Baba made her eat some supper, for what she was.

"What the old fellow wanted," said he when he came back at last, "was to have a friend of his apologize. Seems church is just out. Seems the friend made a remark coming in just now. His pals told him there was a lady present."

"I see you bought him a beer," she said.

"Well, the old man looked like he wanted *something*."

All at once the juke box interrupted from back in the corner, with the same old song as anywhere. The half-dozen slot machines along the wall were suddenly all run to like Maypoles, and thrown into action—taken over by further battalions of little boys.

There were three little boys to each slot machine. The local custom appeared to be that one pulled the lever for the friend he was holding up to put the nickel in, while the third covered the pictures with the flat of his hand as they fell into place, so as to surprise them all if anything happened.

The dog lay sleeping on in front of the raging juke box, his ribs working fast as a concertina's. At the side of the room a man with a cap on his white thatch was trying his best to open a side screen door, but it was stuck fast. It was he who had come in with the remark considered ribald;

now he was trying to get out the other way. Moths as thick as ingots were trying to get in. The cardplayers broke into shouts of derision, then joy, then tired derision among themselves; they might have been here all afternoon—they were the only ones not cleaned up and shaved. The original pair of little boys ran in once more, with the hyphenated bang. They got nickels this time, then were brushed away from the table like mosquitoes, and they rushed under the counter and on to the cauldron behind, clinging to Baba's mother there. The evening was at the threshold. She and he were quite unnoticed now. He was eating another sandwich, and she, having finished part of hers, was fanning her face with her hat. Baba had lifted the flap of the counter and come out into the room. Behind his head there was a sign lettered in orange crayon: "Shrimp Dance Sun. PM." That was tonight, still to be.

And suddenly she made a move to slide down from her stool, maybe wishing to walk out into that nowhere down the front steps to be cool a moment. But he had hold of her hand. He got down from his stool, and, patiently, reversing her hand in his own—just as she had had the look of being about to give up, faint—began moving her, leading her. They were dancing.

"I get to thinking this is what we get—what you and I deserve," she whispered, looking past his shoulder into the room. "And all the time, it's real. It's a real place—away off down here . . ."

He patted her between the shoulder blades. *He* at one time had got to thinking it was symbolic or something, but it would outdo her to say so.

They danced gratefully, formally, to some song carried on in what must be the local patois, while no one paid any attention as long as they were together, and the children poured the family nickels steadily into the slot machines, walloping the handles down with regular crashes and troubling nobody with winning.

She said rapidly, as they began moving together too well, "One of those clippings was an account of a shooting right here. I guess they're proud of it. And that awful knife Baba was carrying . . . I wonder what he called me," she whispered in his ear.

"Who?"

"The one who apologized to you."

If they had ever been going to overstep themselves, it would be now as he held her closer and turned her, when she became aware that he could not help but see the bruise at her temple. It would be not six inches from his eyes. She felt it come out like an evil star. (Let it pay him back, then, for the hand he had stuck in her face when she'd tried once to be sympathetic, when she'd asked about his wife.) They danced on still as the record changed, after standing wordless and motionless, linked together in the middle of the room, for the moment between.

Then, they were like a matched team—like professional, Spanish dancers wearing masks—while the slow piece was playing.

Surely even those immune from the world, for the time being, need the touch of one another, or all is lost. Their arms encircling each other, their bodies circling the odorous, just-nailed-down floor, they were, at last, imperviousness in motion. They had found it, and had almost missed it: they had had to dance. They were what their separate hearts desired that day, for themselves and each other.

They were so good together that once she looked up and half smiled. "For whose benefit did we have to show off?"

Like people in love, they had a superstition about themselves almost as soon as they came out on the floor, and dared not think the words "happy" or "unhappy," which might strike them, one or the other, like lightning.

In the thickening heat they danced on while Baba himself sang with the mosquito-voiced singer in the chorus of *"Moi pas l'aimez ça,"* enumerating the *ça*'s with a hot shrimp between his fingers. He was counting over the platters the old woman now set out on the counter, each heaped with shrimp in their shells boiled to iridescence, like mounds of honeysuckle flowers.

The goose wandered in from the back room under the lid of the counter and hitched itself around the floor among the table legs and people's legs, never seeing that it was neatly avoided by two dancers—who nevertheless vaguely thought of this goose as learned, having earlier heard an old man read to it. The children called it Mimi, and lured it away. The old thatched man was again drunkenly trying to get out by the stuck side door; now he gave it a kick, but was prevailed on to remain. The sleeping dog shuddered and snored.

It was left up to the dancers to provide nickels for the juke box; Baba kept a drawerful for every use. They had grown fond of all the selections by now. This was the music you heard out of the distance at night—out of the roadside taverns you fled past, around the late corners in cities half asleep, drifting up from the carnival over the hill, with one odd little strain always managing to repeat itself. This seemed a homey place.

Bathed in sweat, and feeling the false coolness that brings, they stood finally on the porch in the lapping night air for a moment before leaving. The first arrivals of the girls were coming up the steps under the porch light—all flowered fronts, their black pompadours giving out breathlike feelers from sheer abundance. Where they'd resprinkled it since church, the talcum shone like mica on their downy arms. Smelling solidly of geranium, they filed across the porch with short steps and fingers joined, just in time to turn their smiles loose inside the room. He held the door open for them.

"Ready to go?" he asked her.

• • •

Going back, the ride was wordless, quiet except for the motor and the insects driving themselves against the car. The windshield was soon blinded. The headlights pulled in two other spinning storms, cones of flying things that, it seemed, might ignite at the last minute.

He stopped the car and got out to clean the windshield thoroughly with his brisk, angry motions of boredom. Dust lay thick and cratered on the roadside scrub.

Under the now ash-white moon, the world travelled through very faint stars—very many slow stars, very high, very low.

It was a strange land, amphibious—and whether water-covered or grown with jungle or robbed entirely of water and trees, as now, it had the same loneliness. He regarded the great sweep—like steppes, like moors, like deserts (all of which were imaginary to him); but more than it was like any likeness, it was South. The vast, thin, wide-thrown, pale, unfocussed star-sky, with its veils of lightning adrift, hung over this land as it hung over the open sea. Standing out in the night alone, he was struck as powerfully with recognition of the extremity of this place as if all other bearings had vanished—as if snow had suddenly started to fall.

He climbed back inside and drove. When he moved to slap furiously at his shirtsleeves, she shivered in the hot, licking night wind that their speed was making. Once the car lights picked out two people—a Negro couple, sitting on two facing chairs in the yard outside their lonely cabin—half undressed, each battling for self against the hot night, with long white rags in endless, scarflike motions.

In peopleless open places there were lakes of dust, smudge fires burning at their hearts. Cows stood in untended rings around them, motionless in the heat, in the night—their horns standing up sharp against that glow.

At length, he stopped the car again, and this time he put his arm under her shoulder and kissed her—not knowing ever whether gently or harshly. It was the loss of that distinction that told him this was now. Then their faces touched unkissing, unmoving, dark, for a length of time. The heat came inside the car and wrapped it still, and the mosquitoes had begun to coat their arms and even their eyelids.

Later, crossing a large open distance, he saw at the same time two fires. He had the feeling that they had been riding for a long time across a face—great, wide, and upturned. In its eyes and open mouth were those fires they had had glimpses of, where the cattle had drawn together: a face, a head, far down here in the South—south of South, below it. A whole giant body sprawled downward then, on and on, always, constant as a constellation or an angel. Flaming and perhaps falling, he thought.

She appeared to be sound asleep, lying back flat as a child, with her hat in her lap. He drove on with her profile beside his, behind his, for he bent forward to drive faster. The earrings she wore twinkled with their rushing motion in an almost regular beat. They might have spoken like tongues. He looked straight before him and drove on, at a speed that, for the rented, overheated, not at all new Ford car, was demoniac.

It seemed often now that a barnlike shape flashed by, roof and all outlined in lonely neon—a movie house at a crossroads. The long white flat road itself, since they had followed it to the end and turned around to come back, seemed able, this far up, to pull them home.

• • •

A thing is incredible, if ever, only after it is told—returned to the world it came out of. For their different reasons, he thought, neither of them would tell this (unless something was dragged out of them): that, strangers, they had ridden down into a strange land together and were getting safely back—by a slight margin, perhaps, but margin enough. Over the levee wall now, like an aurora borealis, the sky of New Orleans, across the river, was flickering gently. This time they crossed by bridge, high above everything, merging into a long light-stream of cars turned cityward.

For a time afterward he was lost in the streets, turning almost at random with the noisy traffic until he found his bearings. When he stopped the car at the next sign and leaned forward frowning to make it out, she sat up straight on her side. It was Arabi. He turned the car right around.

“We’re all right,” he muttered, allowing himself a cigarette now.

Something that must have been with them all along suddenly, then, was not. In a moment, tall as panic, it rose, cried like a human, and dropped back.

“I never got my water,” she said.

She gave him the name of her hotel, he drove her there, and he said goodnight on the sidewalk. They shook hands.

“Forgive . . .” For, just in time, he saw she expected it of him.

And that was just what she did, forgive him. Indeed, had she waked from a deep sleep in time, she would have told him her story. She disappeared through the revolving door, with a gesture of smoothing her hair, and he thought a figure in the lobby strolled to meet her. He got back in the car and sat there.

He was not leaving for Syracuse until early in the morning. At length, he recalled the reason; his wife had recommended that he stay where he was this extra day so that she could entertain some old, unmarried college friends without him underfoot.

As he started up the car, he recognized in the smell of exhausted, body-warm air in the streets, in which the flow of drink was an inextricable part, the signal that the New Orleans evening was just beginning. In Dickie Grogan’s, as he passed, the well-known Josefina at her organ was charging up and down with “Clair de Lune.” As he drove the little Ford safely to its garage, he remembered for the first time in years when he was young and brash, a student in New York, and the shriek and horror and unholy smother of the subway had its original meaning for him as the lilt and expectation of love.

September 20, 1952

THE OTHER PARIS

Mavis Gallant

By the time they decided what Carol would wear for her wedding (white with white flowers), it was the end of the afternoon. Mme. Germaine removed the sketchbooks, the scraps of net and satin, the stacks of *Vogue;* she had, already, a professional look of anxiety, as if it could not possibly come out well. One foresaw seams ripped open, extra fittings, even Carol's tears.

Odile, Carol's friend, seemed disappointed. "White isn't *original,*" she said. "If it were me, I would certainly not be married in all that rubbish of lace, like a First Communion." She picked threads from her skirt fastidiously, as if to remove herself completely from Carol and her unoriginal plans.

I wonder if anyone has ever asked Odile to marry him, Carol thought, placidly looking out the window. As her wedding approached, she had more and more the engaged girl's air of dissociation: nothing mattered until the wedding, and she could not see clearly beyond it. She was sorry for all the single girls of the world, particularly those who were, like Odile, past thirty. Odile looked sallow and pathetic, huddled into a sweater and coat, turning over samples of lace with a disapproving air. She seemed all of a piece with the day's weather and the chilly air of the dressmaker's flat. Outside, the street was still damp from a rain earlier in the day. There were no trees in sight, no flowers, no comforting glimpse of park. No one in this part of Paris would have known it was spring.

"Even *blue,*" said Odile. But there was evidently no conversation to be had with Carol, who had begun to hum, so she said to the dressmaker, "Just imagine! Miss Frazier came to Paris to work last autumn, and fell in love with the head of her department."

"Non!" Mme. Germaine recoiled, as if no other client had ever brought off such an extraordinary thing.

"Fell in love with Mr. Mitchell," said Odile, nodding. "At first sight, *le coup de foudre*."

"At first sight?" said the dressmaker. She looked fondly at Carol.

"Something no one would have expected," said Odile. "Although Mr. Mitchell is charming. *Charming*."

"I think we ought to go," said Carol.

Odile looked regretful, as if she had more to say. Carol made an appointment for the following day, and the two left the flat together, Odile's sturdy heels making a clatter as they went down the staircase.

"Why were you so funny just then?" Odile said. "I didn't say anything that wasn't true, and you know how women like that love to hear about weddings and love and everything. And it's such a wonderful story about you and Mr. Mitchell. I tell it to everyone."

This, Carol thought, could not be true, for Odile was rarely interested in anyone but herself, and had never shown the least curiosity about Carol's plans, other than offering to find a dressmaker.

"It was terribly romantic," Odile said, "whether you admit it or not. You and Mr. Mitchell. Our Mr. Mitchell."

It penetrated at last that Odile was making fun of her.

• • •

People had assured Carol so often that her engagement was romantic, and she had become so accustomed to the word, that Odile's slight irony was perplexing. If anyone had asked Carol at what precise moment she fell in love, or where Howard Mitchell proposed to her, she would have imagined, quite sincerely, a scene that involved all at once the Seine, moonlight, barrows of violets, acacias in flower, and a confused, misty background of the Eiffel Tower and little crooked streets. This was what everyone expected, and she had nearly come to believe it herself.

Actually, he had proposed at lunch, over a tuna-fish salad. He and Carol had known each other less than three weeks, and their conversation until then had been limited to their office—an American government agency—and the people in it. Carol was twenty-two; no one had proposed to her before, except an unsuitable medical student with no money and eight years' training still to go. She was under the illusion that in a short time she would be so old no one would ask her again. She accepted at once, and Howard celebrated by ordering an extra bottle of wine. Both would have liked champagne, as a more emphatic symbol of the unusual, but each was too diffident to suggest it.

The fact that Carol was not in love with Howard Mitchell did not dismay her in the least. From a series of helpful college lectures on marriage she had learned that a common interest, such as a liking for Irish setters, was the true basis for happiness, and that the illusion of love was a blight imposed by the film industry, and almost entirely responsible for the high rate of divorce. Similar economic backgrounds, financial security, belonging to the same church—these were the pillars of the married union. By an astonishing coincidence, the fathers of Carol and Howard were both attorneys and both had been defeated in their one attempt to get elected a judge. Carol and Howard were both vaguely Protestant, although a serious discussion of religious beliefs would have gravely embarrassed them. And Howard, best of all, was sober, old enough to know his own mind, and absolutely reliable. He was an economist who had had sense enough to attach himself to a corporation that continued to pay his salary during his loan to the government. There was no reason for the engagement or the marriage to fail.

Carol, with great efficiency, nearly at once set about the business of falling in love. Love required only the right conditions, like a geranium. It would wither exposed to bad weather or in dismal surroundings; indeed, Carol rated the chances of love in a cottage or a furnished room at zero. Given a good climate, enough money, and a pair of good-natured, *intelligent* (her college lectures had stressed this) people, one had only to sit back and watch it grow. All winter, then, she looked for these right conditions in Paris. When, at first, nothing happened, she blamed it on the weather. She was often convinced she would fall deeply in love with Howard if only it would stop raining. Undaunted, she waited for better times.

Howard had no notion of any of this. His sudden proposal to Carol had been quite out of character—he was uncommonly cautious—and he alternated between a state of numbness and a state of self-congratulation. Before his engagement he had sometimes been lonely, a malaise he put down to overwork, and he was discontented with his bachelor households, for he did not enjoy collecting old pottery or making little casserole dishes. Unless he stumbled on a competent housemaid, nothing ever got done. This in itself would not have spurred him into marriage had he not been seriously unsettled by the visit of one of his sisters, who advised him to marry some nice girl before it was too late. “Soon,” she told him, “you'll just be a person who fills in at dinner.”

Howard saw the picture at once, and was deeply moved by it. Retreating by inches, he said he knew of no one who would do.

Nonsense, his sister said. There were plenty of nice girls everywhere. She then warned him not to marry a French girl, who might cause trouble once he got her home to Chicago, or a Catholic, because of the children, and to avoid anyone fast, nervous, divorced, or over twenty-four. Howard knew a number of girls in Paris, most of whom worked in his office or similar agencies. They struck him as cheerful and eager, but aggressive—not at all what he fancied around the house. Just as he was becoming seriously baffled by this gap in his life, Carol Frazier arrived.

He was touched by her shy good manners, her earnest college French. His friends liked her, and, more important, so did the wives of his friends. He had been seriously in love on earlier occasions, and did not consider it a reliable emotion. He and Carol got on well, which seemed to him a satisfactory beginning. His friends, however, told him that she was obviously in love with him and that it was pretty to see. This he expected, not because he was vain but because one took it for granted that love, like a harmless familiar, always attended young women in friendships of this nature. Certainly he was fond of Carol and concerned for her comfort. Had she complained of a toothache, he would have seen to it that she got to a dentist. Carol was moved to another department, but they met every day for lunch and dinner, and talked without discord of any kind. They talked about the job Howard was returning to in Chicago; about their wedding, which was to take place in the spring; and about the movies they saw together. They often went to parties, and then they talked about everyone who had been there, even though they would see most of them next day, at work.

It was a busy life, yet Carol could not help feeling that something had been missed. The weather continued unimproved. She shared an apartment in Passy with two American girls, a temporary ménage that might have existed anywhere. When she rode the Métro, people pushed and were just as rude as in New York. Restaurant food was dull, and the cafés were full of Coca-Cola signs. No wonder she was not in love, she would think. Where was the Paris she had read about? Where were the elegant and expensive-looking women? Where, above all, were the men, those men with their gay good looks and snatches of merry song, the delight of English lady novelists? Travelling through Paris to and from work, she saw only shabby girls bundled into raincoats, hurrying along in the rain, or men who needed a haircut. In the famous parks, under the drizzly trees, children whined peevishly and were slapped. She sometimes thought that perhaps if she and Howard had French friends . . . She suggested it to him.

"You have a French friend," said Howard. "How about Odile?"

But that was not what Carol had meant. Odile Pontmoret was Howard's secretary, a thin, dark woman who was (people said) the niece of a count who had gone broke. She seldom smiled and, because her English was at once precise and inaccurate, often sounded sarcastic. All winter she wore the same dark skirt and purple pullover to work. It never occurred to anyone to include her in parties made up of office people, and it was not certain that she would have come anyway. Odile and Carol were friendly in an impersonal way. Sometimes, if Howard was busy, they lunched together. Carol was always careful not to complain about Paris, having been warned that the foreign policy of her country hinged on chance remarks. But her restraint met with no answering delicacy in Odile, whose chief memory of her single trip to New York, before the war, was that her father had been charged twenty-four dollars for a taxi fare that, they later reasoned, must have been two dollars and forty cents. Repeating this, Odile would look indignantly at Carol, as if Carol had been driving the taxi. "And there was no service in the hotel, no service at all," Odile would say. "You could drop your nightgown on the floor and they would sweep around it. And still expect a tip."

These, her sole observations of America, she repeated until Carol's good nature was strained to the limit. Odile never spoke of her life outside the office, which Carol longed to hear about, and she touched on the present only to complain in terms of the past. "Before the war, we travelled, we went everywhere," she would say. "Now, with our poor little franc, everything is finished. I work to help my family. My brother publicizes wines—*Spanish* wines. We work and work so that our parents won't feel the change and so that Martine, our sister, can study music."

Saying this, she would look bewildered and angry, and Carol would have the feeling that Odile was somehow blaming her. They usually ate in a restaurant of Odile's choice—Carol was tactful about this, for Odile earned less than she did—where the food was lumpy and inadequate and the fluorescent lighting made everyone look ill. Carol would glance around at the neighboring tables, at which sat glum and noisy Parisian office workers and shop clerks, and observe that everyone's coat was too long or too short, that the furs were tacky.

There must be more to it than this, she would think. Was it possible that these badly groomed girls liked living in Paris? Surely the sentimental songs about the city had no meaning for them. Were many of them in love, or—still less likely—could any man be in love with any of them?

Every evening, leaving the building in which she and Howard worked, she would pause on the stair landing between the first and second floors to look through the window at the dark winter twilight, thinking that an evening, a special kind of evening, was forming all over the city, and that she had no part in it. At the same hour, people streamed out of an old house across the street that was now a museum, and Carol would watch them hurrying off under their umbrellas. She wondered where they were going and where they lived and what they were having for dinner. Her interest in them was not specific; she had no urge to run into the street and introduce herself. It was simply that she believed they knew a secret, and if she spoke to the right person, or opened the right door, or turned down an unexpected street, the city would reveal itself and she would fall in love. After this pause at the landing, she would forget all her disappointments (the Parma violets she had bought that were fraudulently cut and bound, so that they died in a minute) and run the rest of the way down the stairs, meaning to tell Howard and see if he shared her brief optimism.

On one of these evenings, soon after the start of the cold weather, she noticed a young man sitting on one of the chairs put out in an inhospitable row in the lobby of the building, for job seekers. He looked pale and ill, and the sleeves of his coat were short, as if he were still growing. He stared at her with the expression of a clever child, at once bold and withdrawn. She had the impression that he had seen her stop at the window on the landing and that he was, for some reason, amused. He did not look at all as if he belonged there. She mentioned him to Howard.

"That must have been Felix," Howard said. "Odile's friend." He put so much weight on the word "friend" that Carol felt there was more, a great deal more, and that, although he liked gossip as well as anyone else, he did not find Odile's affairs interesting enough to discuss. "He used to wait for her outside every night. Now I guess he comes in out of the rain."

"But she's never mentioned him," Carol protested. "And he must be younger than she is, and so pale and funny-looking! Where does he come from?"

Howard didn't know. Felix was Austrian, he thought, or Czech. There was something odd about him, for although he obviously hadn't enough to eat, he always had plenty of American cigarettes. That was a bad sign. "Why are you so interested?" he said. But Carol was not interested at all.

• • •

After that, Carol saw Felix every evening. He was always polite and sometimes murmured a perfunctory greeting as she passed his chair. He continued to look tired and ill, and Carol wondered if it was true that he hadn't enough to eat. She mentioned him to Odile, who was surprisingly willing to discuss her friend. He was twenty-one, she said, and without relatives. They had all been killed at the end of the war, in the final bombings. He was in Paris illegally, without a proper passport or working papers. The police were taking a long time to straighten it out, and meanwhile, not permitted to work, Felix "did other things." Odile did not say what the other things were, and Carol was rather shocked.

That night, before going to sleep, she thought about Felix, and about how he was only twenty-one. She and Felix, then, were closer in age than he was to Odile or she herself was to Howard. When I was in school, he was in school, she thought. When the war stopped, we were fourteen and fifteen. . . . But here she lost track, for where Carol had had a holiday, Felix's parents had been killed. Their closeness in age gave her unexpected comfort, as if someone in this disappointing city had some tie with her. In the morning she was ashamed of her disloyal thoughts—her closest tie in Paris was, after all, with Howard—and decided to ignore Felix when she saw him again. That night, when she passed his chair, he said "Good evening," and she was suddenly acutely conscious of every bit of her clothing: the press of the belt at her waist, the pinch of her earrings, the weight of her dress, even her gloves, which felt as scratchy as sacking. It was a disturbing feeling; she was not sure that she liked it.

"I don't see why Felix should just sit in that hall all the time," she complained to Howard. "Can't he wait for Odile somewhere else?"

Howard was too busy to worry about Felix. It occurred to him that Carol was being tiresome, and that this whining over who sat in the hall was only one instance of her new manner. She had taken to complaining about their friends, and saying she wanted to meet new people and see more of Paris. Sometimes she looked at him helplessly and eagerly, as if there were something he ought to be saying or doing. He was genuinely perplexed; it seemed to him they got along well and were reasonably happy together. But Carol was changing. She hunted up odd, cheap restaurants. She made him walk in the rain. She said that they ought to see the sun come up from the steps of the Sacré-Cœur, and actually succeeded in dragging him there, nearly dead of cold. And, as he might have foreseen, the expedition came to nothing, for it was a rainy dawn and a suspicious gendarme sent them both home.

At Christmas, Carol begged him to take her to the carol singing in the Place Vendôme. Here, she imagined, with the gentle fall of snow and the small, rosy choirboys singing between lighted Christmas trees, she would find something—a warm memory that would, later, bring her closer to Howard, a glimpse of the Paris other people liked. But, of course, there was no snow. Howard and Carol stood under her umbrella as a fine, misty rain fell on the choristers, who sang over and over the opening bars of "Il est né, le Divin Enfant," testing voice levels for a broadcast. Newspaper photographers drifted on the rim of the crowd, and the flares that lit the scene for a newsreel camera blew acrid smoke in their faces. Howard began to cough. Around the square, the tenants of the Place emerged on their small balconies. Some of them had champagne glasses in their hands, as if they had interrupted an agreeable party to step outside for a moment. Carol looked up at the lighted open doorways, through which she could see a painted ceiling, a lighted chandelier. But nothing happened. None of the people seemed beautiful or extraordinary. No one said, "Who *is* that charming girl down there? Let's ask her up!"

Howard blew his nose and said that his feet were cold; they drifted over the square to a couturier's window, where the Infant Jesus wore a rhinestone pin, and a worshipping plaster angel extended a famous brand of perfume. "It just looks like New York or something," Carol said, plaintive with disappointment. As she stopped to close her umbrella, the wind carried to her feet a piece of mistletoe and, glancing up, she saw that cheap tinsel icicles and bunches of mistletoe had been tied on the street lamps of the square. It looked pretty, and rather poor, and she thought of the giant tree in Rockefeller Center. She suddenly felt sorry for Paris, just as she had felt sorry for Felix because he looked hungry and was only twenty-one. Her throat went warm, like the prelude to a rush of tears. Stooping, she picked up the sprig of mistletoe and put it in her pocket.

"Is this all?" Howard said. "Was this what you wanted to see?" He was cold and uncomfortable, but because it was Christmas, he said nothing impatient, and tried to remember, instead, that she was only twenty-two.

"I suppose so."

They found a taxi and went on to finish the evening with some friends from their office. Howard made an amusing story of their adventure in the Place Vendôme. She realized for the first time that something could be perfectly accurate but untruthful—they had not found any part of that evening funny—and that this might cover more areas of experience than the occasional amusing story. She looked at Howard thoughtfully, as if she had learned something of value.

• • •

The day after Christmas, Howard came down with a bad cold, the result of standing in the rain. He did not shake it off for the rest of the winter, and Carol, feeling guiltily that it was her fault, suggested no more excursions. Temporarily, she put the question of falling in love to one side. Paris was not the place, she thought; perhaps it had been, fifty years ago, or whenever it was that people wrote all the songs. It did not occur to her to break her engagement.

She wore out the winter working, nursing Howard's cold, toying with office gossip, and, now and again, lunching with Odile, who was just as unsatisfactory as ever. It was nearly spring when Odile, stopping by Carol's desk, said that Martine was making a concert début the following Sunday. It was a private gathering, a subscription concert. Odile sounded vague. She dropped two tickets on Carol's desk and said, walking away, "If you want to come."

"If I *want* to!"

Carol flew away to tell Howard at once. "It's a sort of private musical thing," she said. "There should be important musicians there, since it's a début, and all Odile's family. The old count—everyone." She half expected Odile's impoverished uncle to turn up in eighteenth-century costume, his hands clasped on the head of a cane.

Howard said it was all right with him, provided they needn't stand out in the rain.

"Of course not! It's a *concert*." She looked at the tickets; they were handwritten slips bearing mimeographed numbers. "It's probably in someone's house," she said. "In one of those lovely old drawing rooms.

Or in a little painted theatre. There are supposed to be little theatres all over Paris that belong to families and that foreigners never see."

She was beside herself with excitement. What if Paris had taken all winter to come to life? Some foreigners lived there forever and never broke in at all. She spent nearly all of one week's salary on a white feather hat, and practiced a few graceful phrases in French. *"Oui, elle est charmante,"* she said to her mirror. *"La petite Martine est tout à fait ravissante. Je connais très bien Odile. Une coupe de champagne? Mais oui, merci bien. Ah, voici mon fiancé! M. Mitchell, le Baron de . . ."* and so forth.

She felt close to Odile, as if they had been great friends for a long time. When, two days before the concert, Odile remarked, yawning, that Martine was crying night and day because she hadn't a suitable dress, Carol said, "Would you let me lend her a dress?"

Odile suddenly stopped yawning and turned back the cuffs of her pullover as if it were a task that required all her attention. "That would be very kind of you," she said, at last.

"I mean," said Carol, feeling gauche, "would it be all right? I have a lovely pale-green tulle that I brought from New York. I've only worn it twice."

"It sounds very nice," said Odile.

Carol shook the dress out of its tissue paper and brought it to work the next day. Odile thanked her without fervor, but Carol knew by now that that was simply her manner.

"We're going to a private musical début," she wrote to her mother and father. "The youngest niece of the Count de Quelquechose. . . . I've lent her my green tulle." She said no more than that, so that it would sound properly casual. So far, her letters had not contained much of interest.

• • •

The address Odile had given Carol turned out to be an ordinary, shabby theatre in the Second Arrondissement. It was on an obscure street, and the taxi-driver had to stop and consult his street guide so often that they were half an hour late. Music came out to meet them in the empty lobby, where a poster said only "J. S. Bach." An usher tiptoed them into place with ill grace and asked Carol please to have some thought for the people behind her and remove her hat. Carol did so while Howard groped for change for the usher's tip. She peered around: the theatre was less than half filled, and the music coming from the small orchestra on the stage had a thin, echoing quality, as if it were travelling around an empty vault. Odile was nowhere in sight. After a moment, Carol saw Felix sitting alone a few rows away. He smiled—much too familiarly, Carol thought. He looked paler than usual, and almost deliberately untidy. He might at least have taken pains for the concert. She felt a spasm of annoyance, and at the same time her heart began to beat so quickly that she felt its movement must surely be visible.

What ever is the matter with me, she thought. If one could believe all the arch stories on the subject, this was traditional for brides-to-be. Perhaps, at this unpromising moment, she had begun to fall in love. She turned in her seat and stared at Howard; he looked much as always. She settled back and began furnishing in her mind the apartment they would have in Chicago. Sometimes the theatre lights went on, startling her out of some problem involving draperies and Venetian blinds; once Howard went out to smoke. Carol had just finished papering a bedroom green and white when Martine walked onstage, with her violin. At the same moment, a piece of plaster bearing the painted plump foot of a nymph detached itself from the ceiling and crashed into the aisle, just missing Howard's head. Everyone stood up to look, and Martine and the conductor stared at Howard and Carol furiously, as if it were their fault. The commotion was horrifying. Carol slid down in her seat, her hands over her eyes. She retained, in all her distress, an impression of Martine, who wore an ill-fitting blue dress with a little jacket. She had not worn Carol's pretty tulle; probably she had never intended to.

Carol wondered, miserably, why they had come. For the first time, she noticed that all the people around them were odd and shabby. The smell of stale winter coats filled the unaired theatre; her head began to ache, and Martine's violin shrilled on her ear like a penny whistle. At last the music stopped and the lights went on. The concert was over. There was some applause, but people were busy pulling on coats and screaming at one another from aisle to aisle. Martine shook hands with the conductor and, after looking vaguely around the hall, wandered away.

"Is this all?" said Howard. He stood up and stretched. Carol did not reply. She had just seen Felix and Odile together. Odile was speaking rapidly and looked unhappy. She wore the same skirt and pullover Carol had seen all winter, and she was carrying her coat.

"Odile!" Carol called. But Odile waved and threaded her way through the row of seats to the other side of the theatre, where she joined some elderly people and a young man. They went off together backstage.

Her family, Carol thought, sickening under the snub. And she didn't introduce me, or even come over and speak. She was positive now that Odile had invited her only to help fill the hall, or because she had a pair of tickets she didn't know what to do with.

"Let's go," Howard said. Their seats were near the front. By the time they reached the lobby, it was nearly empty. Under the indifferent eyes of the usher, Howard guided Carol into her coat. "They sure didn't put on much of a show for Martine," he said.

"No, they didn't."

"No flowers," he said. "It didn't even have her name on the program. No one would have known."

It had grown dark, and rain poured from the edge of the roof in an unbroken sheet. "You stay here," said Howard. "I'll get a taxi."

"No," said Carol. "Stay with me. This won't last." She could not bring herself to tell him how hurt and humiliated she was, what a ruin the afternoon had been. Howard led her behind the shelter of a billboard.

"That dress," he went on. "I thought you'd lent her something."

"I had. She didn't wear it. I don't know why."

"Ask Odile."

"I don't care. I'd rather let it drop."

He agreed. He felt that Carol had almost knowingly exposed herself to an indignity over the dress, and pride of that nature he understood. To distract her, he spoke of the job waiting for him in Chicago, of his friends, of his brother's sailboat.

Against a background of rain and Carol's disappointment, he sounded, without meaning to, faintly homesick. Carol picked up his mood. She looked at the white feather hat the usher had made her remove and said suddenly, "I wish I were home. I wish I were in my own country, with my own friends."

"You will be," he said, "in a couple of months." He hoped she would not begin to cry.

"I'm tired of the way everything is here—old and rotten and falling down."

"You mean that chunk of ceiling?"

She turned from him, exasperated at his persistently missing the point, and saw Felix not far away. He was leaning against the ticket booth, looking resignedly at the rain. When he noticed Carol looking at him, he said, ignoring Howard, "Odile's backstage with her family." He made a face and went on, "No admission for us foreigners."

Odile's family did not accept Felix; Carol had barely absorbed this thought, which gave her an unexpected and indignant shock, when she realized what he had meant by "us foreigners." It was rude of Odile to let her family hurt her friend; at the same time, it was even less kind of them to include Carol in a single category of foreigners. Surely Odile could see the difference between Carol and this pale young man who "did other things." She felt that she and Felix had been linked together in a disagreeable way, and that she was floating away from everything familiar and safe. Without replying, she bent her head and turned away, politely but unmistakably.

"Funny kid," Howard remarked as Felix walked slowly out into the rain, his hands in his pockets.

"He's horrible," said Carol, so violently that he stared at her. "He's not funny. He's a parasite. He lives on Odile. He doesn't work or anything, he just hangs around and stares at people. Odile says he has no passport. Well, why doesn't he *get* one? Any man can work if he wants to. Why are there people like that? All the boys I ever knew at home were well brought up and manly. I never knew anyone like Felix."

She stopped, breathless, and Howard said, "Well, let Odile worry."

"Odile!" Carol cried. "Odile must be crazy. What is she thinking of? Her family ought to put a stop to it. The whole thing is terrible. It's bad for the office. It ought to be stopped. Why, he'll never marry her! Why should he? He's only a boy, an orphan. He needs friends, and connections, and somebody his own age. Why should he marry Odile? What does he want with an old maid from an old, broken-down family? He needs a good meal, and—and help." She stopped, bewildered. She had been about to say "and love."

Howard, now beyond surprise, felt only a growing wave of annoyance. He did not like hysterical women. His sisters never behaved like that.

"I want to go *home,*" said Carol, nearly wailing.

He ran off to find a taxi, glad to get away. By "home" he thought she meant the apartment she shared with the two American girls in Passy.

For Carol, the concert was the end, the final *clou*. She stopped caring about Paris, or Odile, or her feelings for Howard. When Odile returned her green dress, nicely pressed and folded in a cardboard box, she said only, "Just leave it on my desk." Everyone seemed to think it normal that now her only preoccupation should be the cut of her wedding dress. People began giving parties for her. The wash of attention soothed her fears. She was good-tempered, and did not ask Howard to take her to tiresome places. Once again he felt he had made the right decision, and put her temporary waywardness down to nerves. After a while, Carol began lunching with Odile again, but she did not mention the concert.

As for Felix, Carol now avoided him entirely. Sometimes she waited until Odile had left the office before leaving herself. Again, she braced herself and walked briskly past him, ignoring his "Good evening." She no longer stopped on the staircase to watch the twilight; her mood was different. She believed that something fortunate had happened to her spirit, and that she had become invulnerable. Soon she was able to walk by Felix without a tremor, and after a while she stopped noticing him at all.

• • •

"Have you noticed winter is over?" Odile said. She and Carol had left the dressmaker's street and turned off on a broad, oblique avenue. "It hasn't rained for hours. This was the longest winter I remember, although I think one says this every year."

"It was long for me, too," Carol said. It was true that it was over. The spindly trees of the avenue were covered with green, like a wrapping of tissue. A few people sat out in front of shops, sunning themselves. It was, suddenly, like coming out of a tunnel.

Odile turned to Carol and smiled, a rare expression for her. "I'm sorry I was rude at Mme. Germaine's just now," she said. "I don't know what the matter is nowadays—I am dreadful to everyone. But I shouldn't have been to you."

"Never mind," said Carol. She flushed a little, for Howard had taught her to be embarrassed over anything as direct as an apology. "I'd forgotten it. In fact, I didn't even notice."

"Now you are being nice," said Odile unhappily. "Really, there is something wrong with me. I worry all the time, over money, over Martine, over Felix. I think it isn't healthy." Carol murmured something comforting but indistinct. Glancing at her, Odile said, "Where are you off to now?"

"Nowhere. Home, I suppose. There's always something to do these days."

"Why don't you come along with me?" Odile stopped on the street and took her arm. "I'm going to see Felix. He lives near here. Oh, he would be so surprised!"

"Felix?" Automatically Carol glanced at her watch. Surely she had

something to do, some appointment? But Odile was hurrying her along. Carol thought, Now, this is all wrong. But they had reached the Boulevard de Grenelle, where the Métro ran overhead, encased in a tube of red brick. Light fell in patterns underneath; the boulevard was lined with ugly shops and dark, buff-painted cafés. It was a far cry from the prim street a block or so away where the dressmaker's flat was. "Is it far?" said Carol nervously. She did not like the look of the neighborhood. Odile shook her head. They crossed the boulevard and a few crooked, narrow streets filled with curbside barrows and marketing crowds. It was a section of Paris Carol had not seen; although it was on the Left Bank, it was not pretty, not picturesque. There were no little restaurants, no students' hotels. It was simply down-and-out and dirty, and everyone looked ill-tempered. Arabs lounging in doorways looked at the two girls and called out, laughing.

"Look straight ahead," said Odile. "If you look at them, they come up and take your arm. It's worse when I come alone."

How dreadful of Felix to let Odile walk alone through streets like this, Carol thought.

"Here," said Odile. She stopped in front of a building on which the painted word "Hôtel" was almost effaced. They climbed a musty-smelling staircase, Carol taking care not to let her skirt brush the walls. She wondered nervously what Howard would say when he heard she had visited Felix in his hotel room. On a stair landing, Odile knocked at one of the doors. Felix let them in. It took a few moments, for he had been asleep. He did not look at all surprised but with a slight bow invited them in, as if he frequently entertained in his room.

The room was so cluttered, the bed so untidy, that Carol stood bewildered, wondering where one could sit. Odile at once flung herself down on the bed, dropping her handbag on the floor, which was cement and gritty with dirt.

"I'm tired," she said. "We've been choosing Carol's wedding dress. White, and *very* pretty."

Felix's shirt was unbuttoned, his face without any color. He glanced sidelong at Carol, smiling. On a table stood an alcohol stove, some gaudy plastic bowls, and a paper container of sugar. In the tiny washbasin, over which hung a cold-water faucet, were a plate and a spoon, and, here and there on the perimeter, Felix's shaving things and a battered toothbrush.

"Do sit on that chair," he said to Carol, but he made no move to take away the shirt and sweater and raincoat that were bundled on it. Everything else he owned appeared to be on the floor. The room faced a court and was quite dark. "I'll heat up this coffee," Felix said, as if casting about for something to do as a host. "Miss Frazier, sit down." He put a match to the stove and a blue flame leaped along the wall. He stared into a saucepan of coffee, sniffed it, and added a quantity of cold water. "A new PX has just been opened," he said to Odile. He put the saucepan over the flame, apparently satisfied. "I went around to see what was up," he said. "Nothing much. It is really sad. Everything is organized on such a big scale now that there is no room for little people like me. I waited outside and finally picked up some cigarettes—only two cartons—from a soldier."

He talked on, and Carol, who was not accustomed to his conversation, could not tell if he was joking or serious. She had finally decided to sit down on top of the raincoat. She frowned at her hands, wondering why Odile didn't teach him to make coffee properly and why he talked like a criminal. For Carol, the idea that one might not be permitted to work was preposterous. She harbored a rigid belief that anyone could work who sincerely wanted to. Picking apples, she thought vaguely, or down in a mine, where people were always needed.

Odile looked at Carol, as if she knew what she was thinking. "Poor Felix doesn't belong in this world," she said. "He should have been killed at the end of the war. Instead of that, every year he gets older. In a month, he will be twenty-two."

But Odile was over thirty. Carol found the gap between their ages distasteful, and thought it indelicate of Odile to stress it. Felix, who had been ineffectively rinsing the plastic bowls in cold water, now poured the coffee out. He pushed one of the bowls toward Odile; then he suddenly took her hand and, turning it over, kissed the palm. "*Why* should I have been killed?" he said.

Carol, breathless with embarrassment, looked at the brick wall of the court. She twisted her fingers together until they hurt. How can they act like this in front of me, she thought, and in such a dirty room? The thought that they might be in love entered her head for the first time, and it made her ill. Felix, smiling, gave her a bowl of coffee, and she took it without meeting his eyes. He sat down on the bed beside Odile and said happily, "I'm glad you came. You both look beautiful."

Carol glanced at Odile, thinking, Not beautiful, not by any stretch of good manners. "French girls are all attractive," she said politely.

"Most of them are frights," said Felix. No one disputed it, and no one but Carol appeared distressed by the abrupt termination of the conversation. She cast about for something to say, but Odile put her bowl on the floor, said again that she was tired, lay back, and seemed all at once to fall asleep.

Felix looked at her. "She really can shut out the world whenever she wants to," he said, suggesting to Carol's startled ears that he was quite accustomed to see her fall asleep. Of course, she might have guessed, but why should Felix make it so obvious? She felt ashamed of the way she had worried about Felix, and the way she had run after Odile, wanting to know her family. This was all it had come to, this dirty room. Howard was right, she thought. It doesn't pay.

At the same time, she was perplexed at the intimacy in which she and Felix now found themselves. She would have been more at ease alone in a room with him than with Odile beside him asleep on his bed.

"I must go," she said nervously.

"Oh, yes," said Felix, not stopping her.

"But I can't find my way back alone." She felt as if she might cry.

"There are taxis," he said vaguely. "But I can take you to the Métro, if you like." He buttoned his shirt and looked around for a jacket, making no move to waken Odile.

"Should we leave her here?" said Carol. "Shouldn't I say goodbye?"

He looked surprised. "I wouldn't think of disturbing her," he said. "If she's asleep, then she must be tired." And to this Carol could think of nothing to say.

He followed her down the staircase and into the street, dark now, with stripes of neon to mark the cafés. They said little, and because she was afraid of the dark and the Arabs, Carol walked close beside him. On the Boulevard de Grenelle, Felix stopped at the entrance to the Métro.

"Here," he said. "Up those steps. It takes you right over to Passy."

She looked at him, feeling this parting was not enough. She had criticized him to Howard and taught herself to ignore him, but here, in a neighborhood where she could not so much as find her way, she felt more than ever imprisoned in the walls of her shyness, unable to say "Thank you," or "Thanks for the coffee," or anything perfunctory and reasonable. She had an inexplicable and uneasy feeling that something had ended for her, and that she would never see Felix, or even Odile, again.

Felix caught her look, or seemed to. He looked around, distressed, at the Bar des Sportifs, and the *sportifs* inside it, and said, "If you would lend me a little money, I could buy you a drink before you go."

His unabashed cadging restored her at once. "I haven't time for a drink," she said, all briskness now, as if he had with a little click dropped into the right slot. "But if you'll promise to take Odile to dinner, I'll lend you two thousand francs."

"Fine," said Felix. He watched her take the money from her purse, accepted it without embarrassment, and put it in the pocket of his jacket.

"Take her for a nice dinner somewhere," Carol repeated.

"Of course."

"Oh!" He exasperated her. "Why don't you act like other people?" she cried. "You can't live like this all the time. You could go to America. Mr. Mitchell would help you. I know he would. He'd vouch for you, for a visa, if I asked him to."

"And Odile? Would Mr. Mitchell vouch for Odile too?"

She glanced at him, startled. When Felix was twenty-five, Odile would be nearly forty. Surely he had thought of this? "She could go, too," she said, and added, "I suppose."

"And what would we do in America?" He rocked back and forth on his heels, smiling.

"You could work," she said sharply. She could not help adding, like a scold, "For once in your life."

"As cook and butler," said Felix thoughtfully, and began to laugh. "No, don't be angry," he said, putting out his hand. "One has to wait so long for American papers. I know, I used to do it. To sit there all day and wait, or stand in the queue—how could Odile do it? She has her job to attend to. She has to help her family."

"In America," said Carol, "she would make more money, she could help them even more." But she could not see clearly the picture of Felix and Odile combining their salaries in a neat little apartment and faithfully remitting a portion to France. She could not imagine what on earth Felix would do for a living. Perhaps he and Odile would get married; something told her they would not. "I'm sorry," she said. "It's really your own business. I shouldn't have said anything at all." She moved away, but Felix took her hand and held it.

"You mean so well," he said. "Odile is right, you know. I ought to have been killed, or at least disappeared. No one knows what to do with me or where I fit. As for Odile, her whole family is overdue. But we're not—how does it go in American papers, under the photographs?—'Happy Europeans find new life away from old cares.' We're not that, either."

"I suppose not. I don't know." She realized all at once how absurd they must look, standing under the Métro tracks, holding hands. Passersby looked at them, sympathetic.

"You shouldn't go this way, looking so hurt and serious," he said. "You're so nice. You mean so well. Odile loves you."

Her heart leaped as if he, Felix, had said he loved her. But no, she corrected herself. Not Felix but some other man, some wonderful person who did not exist.

Odile loved her. Her hand in his, she remembered how he had kissed Odile's palm, and she felt on her own palm the pressure of a kiss; but not from Felix. Perhaps, she thought, what she felt was the weight of his love for Odile, from which she was excluded, and to which Felix now politely and kindly wished to draw her, as if his and Odile's ability to love was their only hospitality, their only way of paying debts. For a moment, standing under the noisy trains on the dark, dusty boulevard, she felt that she had at last opened the right door, turned down the right street, glimpsed the vision toward which she had struggled on winter evenings when, standing on the staircase, she had wanted to be enchanted with Paris and to be in love with Howard.

But that such a vision could come from Felix and Odile was impossible. For a moment she had been close to tears, like the Christmas evening when she found the mistletoe. But she remembered in time what Felix was—a hopeless parasite. And Odile was silly and immoral and old enough to know better. And they were not married and never would be, and they spent heaven only knew how many hours in that terrible room in a slummy quarter of Paris.

No, she thought. What she and Howard had was better. No one could point to them, or criticize them, or humiliate them by offering to help.

She withdrew her hand and said with cold shyness, "Thank you for the coffee, Felix."

"Oh, that." He watched her go up the steps to the Métro, and then he walked away.

• • •

Upstairs, she passed a flower seller and stopped to buy a bunch of violets, even though they would be dead before she reached home. She wanted something pretty in her hand to take away the memory of the room and the Arabs and the dreary cafés and the messy affairs of Felix and Odile. She paid for the violets and noticed as she did so that the little scene—accepting the flowers, paying for them—had the gentle, nostalgic air of something past. Soon, she sensed, the comforting vision of Paris as she had once imagined it would overlap the reality. To have met and married Howard there would sound romantic and interesting, more and more so as time passed. She would forget the rain and her unshared confusion and loneliness, and remember instead the Paris of films, the street lamps with their tinsel icicles, the funny concert hall where the ceiling collapsed, and there would be, at last, a coherent picture, accurate but untrue. The memory of Felix and Odile and all their distasteful strangeness would slip away; for "love" she would think, once more, "Paris," and, after a while, happily married, mercifully removed in time, she would remember it and describe it and finally believe it as it had never been at all.

April 11, 1953

SIX FEET OF THE COUNTRY

Nadine Gordimer

MY WIFE AND I are not real farmers—not even Lerice, really. We bought our place, ten miles out of Johannesburg on one of the main roads, to change something in ourselves, I suppose; you seem to rattle about so much within a marriage like ours. You long to hear nothing but a deep satisfying silence when you sound a marriage. The farm hasn't managed that for us, of course, but it has done other things, unexpected, illogical. Lerice, who I thought would retire there in Chekhovian sadness for a month or two, and then leave the place to the servants while she tried yet again to get a part she wanted and become the actress she would like to be, has sunk into the business of running the farm with all the serious intensity with which she once imbued the shadows in a playwright's mind. I should have given it up long ago if it had not been for her. Her hands, once small and plain and well-kept—she was not the sort of actress who wears red paint and diamond rings—are hard as a dog's pads.

I, of course, am there only in the evenings and on weekends. I am a partner in a luxury-travel agency, which is flourishing—needs to be, as I tell Lerice, in order to carry the farm. Still, though I know we can't afford it, and though the sweetish smell of the fowls Lerice breeds sickens me, so that I avoid going past their runs, the farm is beautiful in a way I had almost forgotten—especially on a Sunday morning when I get up and go out into the paddock and see not the palm trees and fishpond and imitation-stone bird bath of the suburbs but white ducks on the dam, the lucerne field brilliant as window dresser's grass, and the little, stocky, mean-eyed bull, lustful but bored, having his face tenderly licked by one of his ladies. Lerice comes out with her hair uncombed, in her hand a stick dripping with cattle dip. She will stand and look dreamily for a moment, the way she would pretend to look sometimes in those plays. "They'll mate tomorrow," she will say. "This is their second day. Look how she loves him, my little Napoleon." So that when people come out to see us on Sunday afternoon, I am likely to hear myself saying as I pour out the drinks, "When I drive back home from the city every day, past those rows of suburban houses, I wonder how the devil we ever did stand it. . . . Would you care to look around?" And there I am, taking some pretty girl and her young husband stumbling down to our riverbank, the girl catching her stockings on the mealie-stooks and stepping over cow-turds humming with jewel-green flies while she says, ". . . the *tensions* of the damned city. And you're near enough to get into town to a show, too! I think it's wonderful. Why, you've got it both ways!"

And for a moment I accept the triumph as if I *had* managed it—the impossibility that I've been trying for all my life—just as if the truth was that you could get it "both ways," instead of finding yourself with not even one way or the other but a third, one you had not provided for at all.

But even in our saner moments, when I find Lerice's earthy enthusiasms just as irritating as I once found her histrionical ones, and she finds what she calls my "jealousy" of her capacity for enthusiasm as big a proof of my inadequacy for her as a mate as ever it was, we do believe that we have at least honestly escaped those tensions peculiar to the city about which our visitors speak. When Johannesburg people speak of "tension," they don't mean hurrying people in crowded streets, the struggle for money, or the general competitive character of city life. They mean the guns under the white men's pillows and the burglar bars on the white men's windows. They mean those strange moments on city pavements when a black man won't stand aside for a white man.

• • •

Out in the country, even ten miles out, life is better than that. In the country, there is a lingering remnant of the pretransitional stage; our relationship with the blacks is almost feudal. Wrong, I suppose, obsolete, but more comfortable all round. We have no burglar bars, no gun. Lerice's farm boys have their wives and their piccanins living with them on the land. They brew their sour beer without the fear of police raids. In fact, we've always rather prided ourselves that the poor devils have nothing much to fear, being with us; Lerice even keeps an eye on their children, with all the competence of a woman who has never had a child of her own, and she certainly doctors them all—children and adults—like babies whenever they happen to be sick.

It was because of this that we were not particularly startled one night last winter when the boy Albert came knocking at our window long after we had gone to bed. I wasn't in our bed but sleeping in the little dressing-room-*cum*-linen-room next door, because Lerice had annoyed me and I didn't want to find myself softening toward her simply because of the sweet smell of the talcum powder on her flesh after her bath. She came and woke me up. "Albert says one of the boys is very sick," she said. "I think you'd better go down and see. He wouldn't get us up at this hour for nothing."

"What time is it?"

"What does it matter?" Lerice is maddeningly logical.

I got up awkwardly as she watched me—How is it I always feel a fool when I have deserted her bed? After all, I know from the way she never looks at me when she talks to me at breakfast the next day that she is hurt and humiliated at my not wanting her—and I went out, clumsy with sleep.

"Which of the boys is it?" I asked Albert as we followed the dance of my torch.

"He's too sick. Very sick, *Baas,*" he said.

"But who? Franz?" I remembered Franz had had a bad cough for the past week.

Albert did not answer; he had given me the path, and was walking along beside me in the tall dead grass. When the light of the torch caught his face, I saw that he looked acutely embarrassed. "What's this all about?" I said.

He lowered his head under the glance of the light. "It's not me, *Baas.* I don't know. Petrus he send me."

Irritated, I hurried him along to the huts. And there, on Petrus's iron bedstead, with its brick stilts, was a young man, dead. On his forehead there was still a light, cold sweat; his body was warm. The boys stood around as they do in the kitchen when it is discovered that someone has broken a dish—uncooperative, silent. Somebody's wife hung about in the shadows, her hands wrung together under her apron.

I had not seen a dead man since the war. This was very different. I felt like the others—extraneous, useless. "What was the matter?" I asked.

The woman patted at her chest and shook her head to indicate the painful impossibility of breathing.

He must have died of pneumonia.

I turned to Petrus. "Who was this boy? What was he doing here?" The light of a candle on the floor showed that Petrus was weeping. He followed me out the door.

When we were outside, in the dark, I waited for him to speak. But he didn't. "Now, come on, Petrus, you must tell me who this boy was. Was he a friend of yours?"

"He's my brother, *Baas*. He come from Rhodesia to look for work."

• • •

The story startled Lerice and me a little. The young boy had walked down from Rhodesia to look for work in Johannesburg, had caught a chill from sleeping out along the way, and had lain ill in his brother Petrus's hut since his arrival three days before. Our boys had been frightened to ask us for help for him because we had never been intended ever to know of his presence. Rhodesian natives are barred from entering the Union unless they have a permit; the young man was an illegal immigrant. No doubt our boys had managed the whole thing successfully several times before; a number of relatives must have walked the seven or eight hundred miles from poverty to the paradise of zoot suits, police raids, and black slum townships that is their *Egoli,* City of Gold—the Bantu name for Johannesburg. It was merely a matter of getting such a man to lie low on our farm until a job could be found with someone who would be glad to take the risk of prosecution for employing an illegal immigrant in exchange for the services of someone as yet untainted by the city.

Well, this was one who would never get up again.

"You would think they would have felt they could tell *us,*" said Lerice next morning. "Once the man was ill. You would have thought at least—" When she is getting intense over something, she has a way of standing in the middle of a room as people do when they are shortly to leave on a journey, looking searchingly about her at the most familiar objects as if she had never seen them before. I had noticed that in Petrus's presence in the kitchen, earlier, she had had the air of being almost offended with him, almost hurt.

In any case, I really haven't the time or inclination any more to go into everything in our life that I know Lerice, from those alarmed and pressing eyes of hers, would like us to go into. She is the kind of woman who doesn't mind if she looks plain, or odd; I don't suppose she would even care if she knew how strange she looks when her whole face is out of proportion with urgent uncertainty. I said, "Now I'm the one who'll have to do all the dirty work, I suppose."

She was still staring at me, trying me out with those eyes—wasting her time, if she only knew.

"I'll have to notify the health authorities," I said calmly. "They can't just cart him off and bury him. After all, we don't really know what he died of."

She simply stood there, as if she had given up—simply ceased to see me at all.

I don't know when I've been so irritated. "It might have been something contagious," I said. "God knows?" There was no answer.

I am not enamored of holding conversations with myself. I went out to shout to one of the boys to open the garage and get the car ready for my morning drive to town.

• • •

As I had expected, it turned out to be quite a business. I had to notify the police as well as the health authorities, and answer a lot of tedious questions: How was it I was ignorant of the boy's presence? If I did not supervise my native quarters, how did I know that that sort of thing didn't go on all the time? Et cetera, et cetera. And when I flared up and told them that so long as my natives did their work, I didn't think it my right or concern to poke my nose into their private lives, I got from the coarse, dull-witted police sergeant one of those looks that come not from any thinking process going on in the brain but from that faculty common to all who are possessed by the master-race theory—a look of insanely inane certainty. He grinned at me with a mixture of scorn and delight at my stupidity.

Then I had to explain to Petrus why the health authorities had to take away the body for a post-mortem—and, in fact, what a post-mortem was. When I telephoned the health department some days later to find out the result, I was told that the cause of death was, as we had thought, pneumonia, and that the body had been suitably disposed of. I went out to where Petrus was mixing a mash for the fowls and told him that it was all right, there would be no trouble; his brother had died from that pain in his chest. Petrus put down the paraffin tin and said, "When can we go to fetch him, *Baas*?"

"To fetch him?"

"Will the *Baas* please ask them when we must come?"

I went back inside and called Lerice, all over the house. She came down the stairs from the spare bedrooms, and I said, "*Now* what am I going to do? When I told Petrus, he just asked calmly when they could go and fetch the body. They think they're going to bury him themselves."

"Well, go back and tell him," said Lerice. "You must tell him. Why didn't you tell him then?"

When I found Petrus again, he looked up politely. "Look, Petrus," I said. "You can't go to fetch your brother. They've done it already—they've *buried* him, you understand?"

"Where?" he said slowly, dully, as if he thought that perhaps he was getting this wrong.

"You see, he was a stranger. They knew he wasn't from here, and they didn't know he had some of his people here, so they thought they must bury him." It was difficult to make a pauper's grave sound like a privilege.

"Please, *Baas,* the *Baas* must ask them?" But he did not mean that he wanted to know the burial place. He simply ignored the incomprehensible machinery I told him had set to work on his dead brother; he wanted the brother back.

"But, Petrus," I said, "how can I? Your brother is buried already. I can't ask them now."

"Oh, *Baas*!" he said. He stood with his bran-smeared hands uncurled at his sides, one corner of his mouth twitching.

"Good God, Petrus, they won't listen to me! They can't, anyway. I'm sorry, but I can't do it. You understand?"

He just kept on looking at me, out of his knowledge that white men have everything, can do anything; if they don't, it is because they won't.

And then, at dinner, Lerice started. "You could at least phone," she said.

"Christ, what d'you think I am? Am I supposed to bring the dead back to life?"

But I could not exaggerate my way out of this ridiculous responsibility that had been thrust on me. "Phone them up," she went on. "And at least you'll be able to tell him you've done it and they've explained that it's impossible."

She disappeared somewhere into the kitchen quarters after coffee. A little later she came back to tell me, "The old father's coming down from Rhodesia to be at the funeral. He's got a permit and he's already on his way."

Unfortunately, it was not impossible to get the body back. The authorities said that it was somewhat irregular, but that since the hygiene conditions had been fulfilled, they could not refuse permission for exhumation. I found out that, with the undertaker's charges, it would cost twenty pounds. Ah, I thought, that settles it. On five pounds a month, Petrus won't have twenty pounds—and just as well, since it couldn't do the dead any good. Certainly I should not offer it to him myself. Twenty pounds—or anything else within reason, for that matter—I would have spent without grudging it on doctors or medicines that might have helped the boy when he was alive. Once he was dead, I had no intention of encouraging Petrus to throw away, on a gesture, more than he spent to clothe his whole family in a year.

When I told him, in the kitchen that night, he said, "Twenty pounds?"

I said, "Yes, that's right, twenty pounds."

For a moment, I had the feeling, from the look on his face, that he was calculating. But when he spoke again I thought I must have imagined it. "We must pay twenty pounds!" he said in the faraway voice in which a person speaks of something so unattainable that it does not bear thinking about.

"All right, Petrus," I said in dismissal, and went back to the living room.

The next morning before I went to town, Petrus asked to see me. "Please, *Baas*," he said, awkwardly handing me a bundle of notes. They're so seldom on the giving rather than the receiving side, poor devils, that they don't really know how to hand money to a white man. There it was, the twenty pounds, in ones and halves, some creased and folded until they were soft as dirty rags, others smooth and fairly new—Franz's money, I suppose, and Albert's, and Dora the cook's, and Jacob the gardener's, and God knows who else's besides, from all the farms and small holdings round about. I took it in irritation more than in astonishment, really—irritation at the waste, the uselessness of this sacrifice by people so poor. Just like the poor everywhere, I thought, who stint themselves the decencies of life in order to insure themselves the decencies of death. So incomprehensible to people like Lerice and me, who regard life as something to be spent extravagantly and, if we think about death at all, regard it as the final bankruptcy.

• • •

The servants don't work on Saturday afternoon anyway, so it was a good day for the funeral. Petrus and his father had borrowed our donkey cart to fetch the coffin from the city, where, Petrus told Lerice on their return, everything was "nice"—the coffin waiting for them, already sealed up to save them from what must have been a rather unpleasant sight after two weeks' interment. (It had taken all that time for the authorities and the undertaker to make the final arrangements for moving the body.) All morning, the coffin lay in Petrus's hut, awaiting the trip to the little old burial ground, just outside the eastern boundary of our farm, that was a relic of the days when this was a real farming district rather than a fashionable rural estate. It was pure chance that I happened to be down there near the fence when the procession came past; once again Lerice had forgotten her promise to me and had made the house uninhabitable on a Saturday afternoon. I had come home and been infuriated to find her in a pair of filthy old slacks and with her hair uncombed since the night before, having all the varnish scraped off the living-room floor, if you please. So I had taken my No. 8 iron and gone off to practice my approach shots. In my annoyance, I had forgotten about the funeral, and was reminded only when I saw the procession coming up the path along the outside of the fence toward me; from where I was standing, you can see the graves quite clearly, and that day the sun glinted on bits of broken pottery, a lopsided homemade cross, and jam jars brown with rain water and dead flowers.

I felt a little awkward, and did not know whether to go on hitting my golf ball or stop at least until the whole gathering was decently past. The donkey cart creaks and screeches with every revolution of the wheels and it came along in a slow, halting fashion somehow peculiarly suited to the two donkeys who drew it, their little potbellies rubbed and rough, their heads sunk between the shafts, and their ears flattened back with an air submissive and downcast; peculiarly suited, too, to the group of men and women who came along slowly behind. The patient ass. Watching, I thought, You can see now why the creature became a Biblical symbol. Then the procession drew level with me and stopped, so I had to put down my club. The coffin was taken down off the cart—it was a shiny, yellow-varnished wood, like cheap furniture—and the donkeys twitched their ears against the flies. Petrus, Franz, Albert, and the old father from Rhodesia hoisted it on their shoulders and the procession moved on, on foot. It was really a very awkward moment. I stood there rather foolishly at the fence, quite still, and slowly they filed past, not looking up, the four men bent beneath the shiny wooden box, and the straggling troop of mourners. All of them were servants or neighbors' servants whom I knew as casual, easygoing gossipers about our lands or kitchen. I heard the old man's breathing.

I had just bent to pick up my club again when there was a sort of jar in the flowing solemnity of their processional mood; I felt it at once, like a wave of heat along the air, or one of those sudden currents of cold catching at your legs in a placid stream. The old man's voice was muttering something; the people had stopped, confused, and they bumped into one another, some pressing to go on, others hissing them to be still. I could see that they were embarrassed, but they could not ignore the voice; it was much the way that the mumblings of a prophet, though not clear at first, arrest the mind. The corner of the coffin the old man carried was sagging at an angle; he seemed to be trying to get out from under the weight of it. Now Petrus expostulated with him.

The little boy who had been left to watch the donkeys dropped the reins and ran to see. I don't know why—unless it was for the same reason people crowd round someone who has fainted in a cinema—but I parted the wires of the fence and went through, after him.

Petrus lifted his eyes to me—to anybody—with distress and horror. The old man from Rhodesia had let go of the coffin entirely, and the three others, unable to support it on their own, had laid it on the ground, in the pathway. Already there was a film of dust lightly wavering up its shiny sides. I did not understand what the old man was saying; I hesitated to interfere. But now the whole seething group turned on my silence. The old man himself came over to me, with his hands outspread and shaking, and spoke directly to me, saying something that I could tell from the tone, without understanding the words, was shocking and extraordinary.

"What is it, Petrus? What's wrong?" I appealed.

Petrus threw up his hands, bowed his head in a series of hysterical shakes, then thrust his face up at me suddenly. "He says, 'My son was not so heavy.'"

Silence. I could hear the old man breathing; he kept his mouth a little open, as old people do.

"My son was young and thin," he said at last, in English.

Again silence. Then babble broke out. The old man thundered against everybody; his teeth were yellowed and few, and he had one of those fine, grizzled, sweeping mustaches that one doesn't often see nowadays, which must have been grown in emulation of early Empire builders. It seemed to frame all his utterances with a special validity, perhaps merely because it was the symbol of the traditional wisdom of age—an idea so fearfully rooted that it carries still something awesome beyond reason. He shocked them; they thought he was mad, but they had to listen to him. With his own hands he began to prize the lid off the coffin and three of the men came forward to help him. Then he sat down on the ground; very old, very weak, and unable to speak, he merely lifted a trembling hand toward what was there. He abdicated, he handed it over to them; he was no good any more.

They crowded round to look (and so did I), and now they forgot the nature of this surprise and the occasion of grief to which it belonged, and for a few minutes were carried up in the delightful astonishment of the surprise itself. They gasped and flared noisily with excitement. I even noticed the little boy who had held the donkeys jumping up and down, almost weeping with rage because the backs of the grownups crowded him out of his view.

In the coffin was someone no one had ever seen before: a heavily built, rather light-skinned native with a neatly stitched scar on his forehead—perhaps from a blow in a brawl that had also dealt him some other, slower-working injury, which had killed him.

• • •

I wrangled with the authorities for a week over that body. I had the feeling that they were shocked, in a laconic fashion, by their own mistake, but that in the confusion of their anonymous dead they were helpless to put it right. They said to me, "We are trying to find out," and "We are still making inquiries." It was as if at any moment they might conduct me into their mortuary and say, "There! Lift up the sheets; look for him—your poultry boy's brother. There are so many black faces—surely one will do?"

And every evening when I got home, Petrus was waiting in the kitchen. "Well, they're trying. They're still looking. The *Baas* is seeing to it for you, Petrus," I would tell him. "God, half the time I should be in the office I'm driving around the back end of the town chasing after this affair," I added aside, to Lerice, one night.

She and Petrus both kept their eyes turned on me as I spoke, and, oddly, for those moments they looked exactly alike, though it sounds impossible: my wife, with her high, white forehead and her attenuated Englishwoman's body, and the poultry boy, with his horny bare feet below khaki trousers tied at the knee with string and the peculiar rankness of his nervous sweat coming from his skin.

"What makes you so indignant, so determined about this now?" said Lerice suddenly.

I stared at her. "It's a matter of principle. Why should they get away with a swindle? It's time these officials had a jolt from someone who'll bother to take the trouble."

She said, "Oh." And as Petrus slowly opened the kitchen door to leave, sensing that the talk had gone beyond him, she turned away, too.

I continued to pass on assurances to Petrus every evening, but although what I said was the same and the voice in which I said it was the same, every evening it sounded weaker. At last, it became clear that we would never get Petrus's brother back, because nobody really knew where he was. Somewhere in a graveyard as uniform as a housing scheme, somewhere under a number that didn't belong to him, or in the medical school, perhaps, laboriously reduced to layers of muscle and strings of nerve? Goodness knows. He had no identity in this world anyway.

It was only then, and in a voice of shame, that Petrus asked me to try and get the money back.

"From the way he asks, you'd think he was robbing his dead brother," I said to Lerice later. But as I've said, Lerice had got so intense about this business that she couldn't even appreciate a little ironic smile.

I tried to get the money; Lerice tried. We both telephoned and wrote and argued, but nothing came of it. It appeared that the main expense had been the undertaker, and after all he had done his job. So the whole thing was a complete waste, even more of a waste for the poor devils than I had thought it would be.

The old man from Rhodesia was about Lerice's father's size, so she gave him one of her father's old suits, and he went back home rather better off, for the winter, than he had come.

May 23, 1953

PNIN

Vladimir Nabokov

THE ELDERLY PASSENGER sitting on the north-window side of that inexorably moving railway coach, next to an empty seat and facing two empty ones, was none other than Professor Timofey Pnin. Ideally bald, suntanned, and clean-shaven, he began rather impressively with that great brown dome of his, tortoise-shell glasses (masking an infantile absence of eyebrows), apish upper lip, thick neck, and strongman torso in a tightish tweed coat, but ended, somewhat disappointingly, in a pair of spindly legs (now flannelled and crossed) and frail-looking, almost feminine feet.

His sloppy socks were of scarlet wool with lilac lozenges; his conservative black oxfords had cost him about as much as all the rest of his clothing (flamboyant goon tie included). Prior to the 1940s, during the staid European era of his life, he had always worn long underwear, its terminals tucked into the tops of neat silk socks, which were clocked, soberly colored, and held up on his cotton-clad calves by garters. In those days, to reveal a glimpse of that white underwear by pulling up a trouser leg too high would have seemed to Pnin as indecent as showing himself to ladies minus collar and tie, for even when decayed Mme. Roux, the concierge of the squalid apartment house in the Sixteenth Arrondissement of Paris where Pnin had lived for a score of years after escaping from Leninized Russia, happened to come up for the rent while he was without his *faux col,* prim Pnin would cover his front stud with a chaste hand. All this underwent a change in the heady atmosphere of the New World. Nowadays, at fifty-five, he was crazy about sunbathing, wore sports shirts and slacks, and when crossing his legs would carefully, deliberately, brazenly display a tremendous stretch of bare shin. Thus he might have appeared to a fellow-passenger, but except for a soldier asleep at one end and two women absorbed in a baby at the other, Pnin had the coach to himself.

Now a secret must be imparted. Professor Pnin was on the wrong train. He was unaware of it, and so was the conductor, already threading his way through the train to Pnin's coach. As a matter of fact, Pnin at the moment felt very well satisfied with himself. When inviting him to deliver a Friday-evening lecture at Cremona—some two hundred versts west of Waindell, Pnin's academic perch—the vice-president of the Cremona Women's Club, a Miss Judith Clyde, had advised our friend that the most convenient train left Waindell at 1:52 P.M., reaching Cremona at 4:17. But Pnin—who, like so many Russians, was inordinately fond of everything in the line of timetables, maps, catalogues, and collected them, helped himself freely to them with the bracing pleasure of getting something for nothing, took especial pride in puzzling out schedules for himself—had discovered, after some study, an inconspicuous reference mark against a still more convenient train, "Lv. Waindell 2:19 P.M., Ar. Cremona 4:32 P.M."; the mark indicated that Fridays, and Fridays only, the two-nineteen stopped at Cremona on its way to a distant and much larger city, graced likewise with a mellow Italian name. Unfortunately for Pnin, his timetable was five years old and in part obsolete.

He taught Russian at Waindell College, a somewhat provincial institution characterized by an artificial lake in the middle of a landscaped campus, by ivied galleries connecting the various halls, by murals displaying recognizable members of the faculty in the act of passing on the torch of knowledge from Aristotle, Shakespeare, and Pasteur to a lot of monstrously built farm boys and farm girls, and by a huge, active, buoyantly thriving German Department, which its head, Dr. Hagen, smugly called (pronouncing every syllable very distinctly) "a university within a university."

The enrollment in the Russian Language course consisted of three students only: Josephine Malkin, whose grandparents had been born in Minsk; Charles McBeth, a graduate student, whose prodigious memory had already disposed of ten languages and was prepared to entomb ten more; and languid Eileen Lane, whom somebody had told that by the time one had mastered the Russian alphabet one could practically read "*Anna Karamazov*" in the original. As a teacher, Pnin was far from being able to compete with those stupendous Russian ladies scattered all over academic America who, without having had any formal training at all, manage somehow, by dint of intuition, loquacity, and a kind of maternal bounce, to infuse a magic knowledge of their difficult and beautiful tongue into a group of innocent-eyed students in an atmosphere of Old Mother Volga songs, red caviar, and tea; nor did Pnin, as a teacher, even presume to approach the lofty halls of modern scientific linguistics—that temple wherein earnest young people are taught not the language itself but the method of teaching others to teach that method. No doubt Pnin's approach to his work was amateurish and lighthearted, depending as it did on a book of exercises in grammar brought out by the head of the Slavic Department in a far greater college than Waindell—a venerable fraud whose Russian was a joke but who would generously lend his dignified name to the products of anonymous drudgery. Pnin, despite his many shortcomings, had about him a disarming old-fashioned charm, which Dr. Hagen, his staunch protector, insisted before morose trustees was a delicate, imported article worth paying for in domestic cash. Whereas the degree in sociology and political economy that Pnin had obtained with some pomp at the University of Prague around 1920 had become by mid-century a doctorate in desuetude, he was not altogether miscast as a teacher of Russian. He was beloved not for any essential ability but for those unforgettable digressions of his, when he would remove his glasses to beam at the past while massaging the lenses of the present. Nostalgic excursions in broken English. Autobiographical tidbits. How Pnin came to the *Soedinyonnïe Shtatï* (the United States). "Examination on ship before landing. Very well! 'Nothing to declare?' 'Nothing.' Very well! Then political questions. He asks: 'Are you Anarchist?' I answer [time out on the part of the narrator for a spell of cozy mute mirth]: 'First, what do we understand under "Anarchism"? Anarchism practical, metaphysical, theoretical, mystical, abstract, individual, social? When I was young,' I say, 'all this had for me signification.' So we had a very interesting discussion, in consequence of which I passed two whole months on Ellis Island [abdomen beginning to heave; heaving; narrator convulsed]."

But there were still better sessions in the way of humor. With an air of coy secrecy, benevolent Pnin, preparing the children for the marvellous treat that he had once had himself, and already revealing, in an uncontrollable smile, an incomplete but formidable set of tawny teeth, would open a dilapidated Russian book at the elegant leatherette marker he had carefully placed there; he would open the book, whereupon as often as not a look of the utmost dismay would alter his plastic features; openmouthed, feverishly, he would flip right and left through the volume, and minutes might pass before he found the right page—or satisfied himself that he had marked it correctly after all. Usually, the passage of his choice came from some old and naïve comedy of merchant-class habitus rigged up by Ostrovski almost a century ago, or from an equally ancient but even more dated piece of trivial Leskovian jollity dependent on verbal contortions. He delivered these stale goods with the rotund gusto of the classical Alexandrinka Theatre in Petersburg, rather than with the crisp simplicity of the Moscow Artists, but since to appreciate whatever fun those passages still retained one had to have not only a sound knowledge of the vernacular but also a good deal of literary insight, and since his poor little class had neither, the performer would be alone in enjoying the associative subtleties of his text. The heaving we have already noted in another connection would become here a veritable earthquake. Directing his memory, with all the lights on and all the masks of the mind a-miming, toward the days of his fervid and receptive youth (in a brilliant cosmos that seemed all the fresher for having been abolished by one blow of history), Pnin would get drunk on his private wines as he produced sample after sample of what his listeners politely surmised was Russian humor. Presently, the fun would become too much for him; pear-shaped tears would trickle down his tanned cheeks. Not only his shocking teeth but an astonishing amount of pink upper-gum tissue would suddenly pop out, as if a jack-in-the-box had been sprung, and his hand would fly to his mouth while his big shoulders shook and rolled. And although the speech he smothered behind his dancing hand was now doubly unintelligible to the class, his complete surrender to his own merriment would prove irresistible. By the time he was helpless with it, he would have his students in stitches, with abrupt barks of clockwork hilarity coming from Charles, and a dazzling flow of unsuspected lovely laughter transfiguring Josephine, who was not pretty, while Eileen, who was, dissolved in a jelly of unbecoming giggles.

All of which does not alter the fact that Pnin was on the wrong train.

• • •

How should we diagnose Pnin's sad case? He, it should be particularly stressed, was anything but the type of that good-natured German platitude of last century, *der zerstreute Professor* (the absent-minded professor). On the contrary, he was perhaps too wary, too persistently on the lookout for diabolical pitfalls, too painfully on the alert lest his erratic surroundings (unpredictable America) inveigle him into some bit of preposterous oversight. It was the world that was absent-minded and it was Pnin whose business it was to set it straight. His life was a constant war with insensate objects that fell apart, or attacked him, or refused to function, or viciously got themselves lost as soon as they entered the sphere of his existence. He was inept with his hands to a rare degree, but because he could manufacture in a twinkle a one-note mouth organ out of a pea pod, make a flat pebble skip ten times on the surface of a pond, shadowgraph with his knuckles a rabbit (complete with blinking eye), and perform a number of other tame tricks that for some reason or other Russians have up their sleeves, he believed himself endowed with considerable manual and mechanical skill. On gadgets he doted with a kind of dazed, superstitious delight. Electric devices enchanted him. Plastics swept him off his feet. He had a deep admiration for the zipper. But after a storm in the middle of the night had paralyzed the local power station, the devoutly plugged-in clock would make nonsense of his morning. The frame of his spectacles would snap in mid-bridge, leaving him with two identical pieces, which he would vaguely attempt to unite, in the hope, perhaps, of some organic marvel of restoration coming to the rescue. The zipper a gentleman depends on most would come loose in his puzzled hand at some nightmare moment of haste and despair.

And he still did not know that he was on the wrong train.

A special danger area in Pnin's case was the English language. Except for such not very helpful odds and ends as "The rest is silence," "Never more," "weekend," *"Who's Who,"* and a few ordinary words and phrases like "eat," "street," "fountain pen," "gangster," "the Charleston," and "marginal utility," he had had no English at all at the time he left France for the States. Stubbornly he sat down to the task of learning the language of Fenimore Cooper, Edgar Allan Poe, Edison, and thirty-one Presidents. In 1945, at the end of one year of study, he was proficient enough to use glibly terms like "wishful thinking" and "okey-dokey." By 1946, he was able to interrupt his narrations with the phrase "To make a long story short." By the time Truman entered his second term, Pnin could handle quite a number of elegant clichés, but otherwise progress seemed to have stopped despite all his efforts, and in 1953 his English was still full of flaws. That autumn, he supplemented the usual courses of his academic year by delivering a weekly lecture in a so-called symposium ("Wingless Europe: A Survey of Contemporary Continental Culture") directed by Dr. Hagen. All our friend's lectures, including sundry ones he gave out of town, were edited by one of the younger members of the

German Department. The procedure was somewhat complicated. Professor Pnin laboriously translated his own Russian verbal flow, teeming with idiomatic proverbs, into patchy English. This was revised by young Miller. Then Dr. Hagen's secretary, a Miss Eisenlohr, typed it out. Then Pnin deleted the passages he could not understand. Then he read it to his weekly audience. He was utterly helpless without the prepared text, nor could he use the ancient system of dissimulating his infirmity by moving his eyes up and down—snapping up an eyeful of words, reeling them off to his audience, and drawing out the end of one sentence while diving for the next. Pnin's worried eye would be bound to lose its bearings. Therefore he read his lectures, his gaze glued to his text, in a slow, monotonous baritone that seemed to climb one of those interminable flights of stairs used by people who dread elevators.

• • •

The conductor, a gray-headed, fatherly person with steel spectacles placed rather low on his simple, functional nose and a bit of soiled adhesive tape on his thumb, had now only three coaches to deal with before reaching the last one, where Pnin rode.

Pnin in the meantime had yielded to the satisfaction of a special Pninian craving. He was in a Pninian quandary. Among other articles indispensable for a Pninian overnight stay in a strange town, such as shoe trees, apples, and dictionaries, his Gladstone bag contained a relatively new black suit he planned to wear that night for the lecture ("Are the Russian People Communist?") before the Cremona ladies. It also contained next Monday's symposium lecture ("Don Quixote and Faust"), which he intended to study the next day, on his way back to Waindell, and a paper by a graduate student, Betty Bliss ("Dostoevski and Gestalt Psychology"), that he had to read for Dr. Hagen. The quandary was as follows: If he kept the Cremona manuscript—a sheaf of typewriter-size pages, carefully folded down the center so as to fit into a pocket of his coat—on his person, in the security of his body warmth, the chances were, theoretically, that he would forget to transfer it from the coat he was wearing to the one he would wear. On the other hand, if he placed the lecture in the pocket of the suit in the bag *now*, he would, he knew, be tortured by the possibility of his luggage being stolen. On the third hand (these mental states sprout additional forelimbs all the time), he carried in the inside pocket of his present coat a precious wallet with two ten-dollar bills, the newspaper clipping of a letter he had, with my help, written to the *Times* in 1945 anent the Yalta conference, and his certificate of naturalization, and it was physically possible to pull out the wallet, if needed, in such a way as to fatally dislodge the folded lecture. During the twenty minutes he had been on the train, our friend had already opened his bag twice to play with his various papers. When the conductor reached the car, diligent Pnin was perusing with difficulty Betty's latest effort, which began, "When we consider the mental climate wherein we all live, we cannot but notice—"

The conductor entered, did not awake the soldier, promised the women he would let them know when they were about to arrive, and presently was shaking his head over Pnin's ticket. The Cremona stop had been abolished two years before.

"Important lecture!" cried Pnin. "What to do? It is a cata-stroph!"

Gravely, comfortably, the gray-headed conductor sank into the opposite seat and consulted in silence a tattered book full of dog-eared insertions. Finally he said that in a few minutes—namely, at three-eight—Pnin would have to get off at Whitchurch; this would enable him to catch the four-o'clock bus that would deposit him, around six, at Cremona.

"I was thinking I gained twelve minutes, and now I have lost nearly two whole hours," said Pnin bitterly. Upon which, clearing his throat and ignoring the consolation offered by the kind gray-head ("You'll make it"), he collected his stone-heavy bag and repaired to the vestibule of the car, to wait there for the confused greenery skimming by to be cancelled and replaced by the definite station he had in mind.

• • •

Whitchurch materialized as scheduled. A hot, torpid expanse of cement and sun lay beyond the geometrical solids of various clean-cut shadows. The local weather was unbelievably summery for October. Alert, Pnin entered a waiting room of sorts, with a needless stove in the middle, and looked around. In a solitary recess one could make out the upper part of a perspiring young man who was filling out forms on the broad wooden counter before him.

"Information, please," said Pnin. "Where stops four-o'clock bus to Cremona?"

"Right across the street," briskly answered the employee, without looking up.

"And where possible to leave baggage?"

"That bag? I'll take care of it."

And with the national informality that always nonplussed Pnin, the young man shoved the bag into a corner of his nook.

"Quittance?" queried Pnin, Englishing the Russian for "receipt"—"*kvitantzia.*"

"What's that?"

"Number?" tried Pnin.

"You don't need a number," said the fellow, and resumed his writing.

Pnin left the station, satisfied himself about the bus stop, and entered a coffee shop. He consumed a ham sandwich, ordered another, and consumed that, too. At exactly five minutes to four, having paid for the food but not for an excellent toothpick, which he carefully selected from a neat little cup in the shape of a pine cone near the cash register, Pnin walked back to the station for his bag.

A different man was now in charge. The first had been called home, the new man explained, to drive his wife in all haste to the maternity hospital. He would be back in a few minutes.

"But I must obtain my valise!" cried Pnin.

The substitute was sorry but could not do a thing.

"It is there!" cried Pnin, leaning over and pointing.

This was unfortunate. He was still in the act of pointing when he realized that he was claiming the wrong bag. His index wavered. That hesitation was fatal.

"My bus to Cremona!" cried Pnin.

"There is another at eight," said the man.

What was our poor friend to do? Horrible situation! He glanced streetward. The bus had just come. The engagement meant an extra fifty dollars. His hand flew to his right flank. It was there, *slava Bogu* (thank God)! Very well! He would not wear his black suit, *vot i vsyo* (that's all). He would retrieve it on his way back. He had lost, dumped, shed many more valuable things in his day. Energetically, almost lightheartedly, Pnin boarded the bus.

He had endured this new stage of his journey for only a few city blocks when an awful suspicion crossed his mind. Ever since he had been separated from his bag, the tip of his left forefinger had been alternating with the proximal edge of his right elbow in checking a precious presence in his inside coat pocket. All of a sudden, he brutally yanked out the folded sheets. They were Betty's paper.

Emitting what he thought were international exclamations of anxiety and entreaty, Pnin lurched out of his seat. Reeling, he reached the exit.

With one hand, the driver grimly milked out a handful of coins from his little machine, refunded him the price of the ticket, and stopped the bus.

Poor Pnin landed in the middle of a strange town. He was less strong than his powerfully puffed-out chest might imply, and the wave of hopeless fatigue that suddenly submerged his top-heavy body, detaching him, as it were, from reality, was a sensation not utterly unknown to him. He found himself in a damp green park, of the formal and funereal type, with the stress laid on sombre rhododendrons, glossy laurels, sprayed shade trees, and closely clipped lawns, and hardly had he turned in to an alley of chestnut and oak, which the bus driver had curtly told him led back to the railway station, than that eerie feeling, that tingle of unreality, overpowered him completely. Was it something he had eaten? That pickle with the ham? Was it a mysterious disease that none of his doctors had yet detected? My friend wondered, and I wonder, too.

• • •

I do not know if it has ever been noted before that one of the main characteristics of life is discreteness. Unless a film of flesh envelops us, we die. Man exists only insofar as he is separated from his surroundings. The cranium is a space traveller's helmet. Stay inside or you perish. Death is divestment, death is communion. It may be wonderful to mix with the landscape, but to do so is the end of the tender ego. The sensation poor Pnin experienced was something very like that divestment, that communion. He felt porous and pregnable. His chest hurt. He was sweating. He was terrified. A stone bench among the laurels saved him from collapsing on the sidewalk. Was his seizure a heart attack? I doubt it. For the nonce, I am his physician, and let me repeat, I doubt it. My patient was one of those singular and unfortunate people who regard their heart ("a hollow, muscular organ," according to the gruesome definition in Webster's New Collegiate Dictionary, which Pnin's orphaned bag contained) with a queasy dread, a nervous repulsion, a sick hate, as if it were some strong, slimy, untouchable monster that one had to put up with, alas. Occasionally, when puzzled by his tumbling and tottering pulse, doctors had examined him more thoroughly, and the cardiograph had outlined fabulous mountain ranges and indicated a dozen fatal diseases that excluded one another. He was afraid of touching his own wrist. He never attempted to sleep on his left side, even in those dismal hours of the night when the insomniac longs for a third side after trying the two he has.

And now, in the park of Whitchurch, Pnin felt what he had felt already on August 10, 1942, and May 18, 1937, and May 18, 1929, and July 4, 1920—that the repulsive automaton he lodged had developed a consciousness of its own, and not only was grossly alive but was causing him pain and panic. He pressed his poor bald head against the stone back of the bench and recalled all the past occasions of similar discomfort and despair. Could it be pneumonia this time? He had been chilled to the bone a couple of days before in one of those hearty American drafts that a host treats his guests to after the second round of drinks on a windy night. And then suddenly Pnin (was he dying?) found himself sliding back into his childhood. This sensation had the sharpness of retrospective detail that is said to be the dramatic privilege of drowning individuals, especially in the former Russian Navy—a phenomenon of suffocation that a veteran psychoanalyst, whose name escapes me, has explained as being the subconsciously evoked shock of one's baptism, which causes an explosion of intervening recollections between the first immersion and the last. It all happened in a flash, but there is no way of rendering it in less than so many consecutive words.

• • •

Pnin came from a respectable, fairly well-to-do St. Petersburg family. His father, Dr. Pavel Pnin, an eye specialist of some repute, had once had the honor of treating Leo Tolstoy for a case of conjunctivitis. Timofey's mother, a frail, nervous little person with a waspy waist and bobbed hair, was the daughter of the once famous revolutionary Umov (rhymes with "zoom off") and of a German lady from Riga. Through his half swoon, Pnin saw her approaching eyes. It was a Sunday in midwinter. He was eleven. He had been preparing lessons for his Monday classes at the First *Gymnasium* when a strange chill pervaded his body. His mother took his temperature, looked at her child with a kind of stupefaction, and immediately called her husband's best friend, the pediatrician Sokolov. He was a small, beetle-browed man, with a short beard and a crew cut. Easing the skirts of his frock coat, he sat down on the edge of Timofey's bed. A race was run between the Doctor's fat golden watch and Timofey's pulse (an easy winner). Then Timofey's torso was bared, and to it the Doctor pressed the icy nudity of his ear and the sandpapery side of his head. Like the flat sole of some monopode, the ear ambulated all over Timofey's back and chest, gluing itself to this or that patch of skin and then stomping on to the next. No sooner had the Doctor left than Timofey's mother and a robust servant girl with safety pins between her teeth encased the distressed little patient in a strait-jacket-like compress. It consisted of a layer of soaked linen, a thicker layer of absorbent cotton, and another of tight flannel, with a sticky, diabolical oilcloth—the hue of urine and fever—coming between the clammy pang of the linen next to his skin and the excruciating squeak of the cotton around which the outer layer of flannel was wound. A poor cocooned pupa, Timosha (Tim) lay under a mass of additional blankets; they were of no avail against the branching chill that crept up his ribs from both sides of his frozen spine. He could not close his eyes because his eyelids stung so. Vision was but oval pain with oblique stabs of light; familiar shapes became the breeding places of evil delusions. Near his bed was a four-section screen of varnished wood, with pyrographic designs representing a lily pond, a bridle path felted with fallen leaves, an old man hunched up on a bench, and a squirrel holding a reddish object in its front paws. Timosha, a methodical child, had often wondered what that object could be (a nut? a pine cone?), and now that he had nothing else to do, he set himself to solve this dreary riddle, but the fever that hummed in his head drowned every effort in pain and panic. Still more oppressive was his tussle with the wallpaper. He had always been able to see that in the vertical plane a combination made up of three different clusters of purple flowers and seven different oak leaves was repeated a number of times with soothing exactitude; but now he was bothered by the undismissible fact that he could not find what system of inclusion and circumscription governed the horizontal recurrence of the pattern; that such a recurrence existed was proved by his being able to pick out here and there, all along the wall from bed to wardrobe and from stove to door, the reappearance of this or that element of the series, but when he tried travelling right or left from any chosen set of three inflorescences and seven leaves, he forthwith lost himself in a meaningless tangle of rhododendron and oak. It stood to reason that if the evil designer—the destroyer of minds, the friend of fever—had concealed the key of the pattern with such monstrous care, that key must be as precious as life itself and, when found, would regain for Tim his everyday health, his everyday world, and this lucid—alas, too lucid—thought forced him to persevere in the struggle.

A sense of being late for some appointment as odiously exact as school, dinner, or bedtime added the discomfort of awkward haste to the difficulties of a quest that was grading into delirium. The foliage and the flowers, with none of the intricacies of their warp disturbed, appeared to detach themselves in one undulating body from their pale-blue background, which, in its turn, lost its papery flatness and dilated in depth till the spectator's heart almost burst in response to that expansion. He could still make out through the autonomous garlands certain parts of the nursery more tenacious of life than the rest, such as the lacquered screen, the gleam of a tumbler, the brass knobs of his bedstead, but these interfered even less with the oak leaves and rich blossoms than would the reflection of an inside object in a windowpane with the outside scenery perceived through the same glass. And although the witness and victim of these phantasms was tucked up in bed, he was, in accordance with the twofold nature of his surroundings, simultaneously seated on a bench in a green-and-purple park. During one melting moment, he had the sensation of holding at last the key he had sought, but, coming from very far, a rustling wind, its soft volume increasing as it ruffled the rhododendrons, confused whatever rational pattern Timofey Pnin's surroundings had once had. He was alive and that was sufficient. The back of the bench against which he still sprawled felt as real as his clothes, or his wallet, or the date of the Great Moscow Fire—1812.

A gray squirrel sitting on comfortable haunches on the ground before him was sampling a peach stone. The wind paused, and presently stirred the foliage again.

The seizure had left him a little frightened and shaky, but he argued that had it been a real heart attack, he would have surely felt a good deal more unsettled and concerned, and this roundabout piece of reasoning completely dispelled his fear. It was now four-twenty. He blew his nose and trudged back to the station.

The initial employee was back. "Here's your bag," he said cheerfully. "Sorry you missed the Cremona bus."

"At least"—and what dignified irony our unfortunate friend tried to inject into that "at least"—"I hope everything is good with your wife?"

"She'll be all right. Have to wait till tomorrow, I guess."

"And now," said Pnin, "where is located the public telephone?"

The man pointed with his pencil as far out and sidewise as he could without leaving his lair. Pnin, bag in hand, started to go, but he was called back. The pencil was now directed streetward.

"Say, see those two guys loading that truck? They're going to Cremona right now. Just tell them Bob Horn sent you. They'll take you."

• • •

Some people—and I am one of them—hate happy endings. We feel cheated. Harm is the norm. Doom should not jam. The avalanche stopping in its tracks a few feet above the cowering village behaves not only unnaturally but unethically. Had I been reading about this mild old man, instead of writing about him, I would have preferred him to discover, upon his arrival at Cremona, that his lecture was not this Friday but the next. Actually, however, he not only arrived safely but was in time for dinner—a fruit cocktail to begin with, mint jelly with the anonymous meat course, chocolate syrup with the vanilla ice cream. And soon afterward, surfeited with sweets, wearing his black suit, and juggling three papers, all of which he had stuffed into his coat so as to have the one he wanted among the rest (thus thwarting mischance by mathematical necessity), he sat on a chair near the lectern while, at the lectern, Judith Clyde, an ageless blonde in aqua rayon, with large, flat cheeks stained a beautiful candy pink and two bright eyes basking in blue lunacy behind a rimless pince-nez, presented the speaker.

"Tonight," she said, "the speaker of the evening— This, by the way, is our third Friday night; last time, as you all remember, we all enjoyed hearing what Professor Moore had to say about agriculture in China. Tonight we have here, I am proud to say, the Russian-born, and citizen of this country, Professor—now comes a difficult one, I am afraid—Professor Pun-neen. I hope I have it right. He hardly needs any introduction, of course, and we are all happy to have him. We have a long evening before us, a long and rewarding evening, and I am sure you would all like to have time to ask him questions afterward. Incidentally, I am told his father was Dostoevski's family doctor, and he has travelled quite a bit on both sides of the Iron Curtain. Therefore I will not take up your precious time any longer and will only add a few words about our next Friday lecture in this program. I am sure you will all be delighted to know that there is a grand surprise in store for all of us. Our next lecturer is the distinguished poet and prose writer Miss Linda Lacefield. We all know she has written poetry, prose, and some short stories. Miss Lacefield was born in New York. Her ancestors on both sides fought on both sides in the Revolutionary War. She wrote her first poem before graduation. Many of her poems—three of them, at least—have been published in *Response,* a collection of a hundred love lyrics by American women. In 1922, she published her first collection, *Remembered Music.* In 1924, she received the cash prize offered by—"

But Pnin was not listening. A faint ripple stemming from his recent seizure was holding his fascinated attention. It lasted only a few heartbeats, with an additional systole here and there—last, harmless echoes—and was resolved in demure reality as his distinguished hostess invited him to the lectern. But while it lasted, how limpid the vision was! In the middle of the front row of seats he saw one of his Baltic aunts, wearing the pearls and the lace and the blond wig she had worn at all the performances given by the great ham actor Khodotov, whom she had adored from afar before drifting into insanity. Next to her, shyly smiling, sleek dark head inclined, gentle brown gaze shining up at Pnin from under velvet eyebrows, sat a dead sweetheart of his, fanning herself with her program. Murdered, forgotten, unrevenged, incorrupt, immortal, many old friends were scattered throughout the dim hall among more recent people, such as Miss Clyde, who had modestly regained a front seat. Vanya Bedniashkin, shot by the Reds in 1919, in Odessa, because his father had been a liberal, was gaily signalling to his former schoolmate from the back of the hall. And in an inconspicuous situation Dr. Pavel Pnin and his anxious wife, both a little blurred but on the whole wonderfully recovered from their obscure dissolution, looked at their son with the same life-consuming passion and pride that they had looked at him with that night in 1912 when, at a school festival commemorating Napoleon's defeat, he had recited (a bespectacled lad all alone on the stage) a poem by Pushkin.

The brief vision was gone. Old Miss Herring, retired professor of history, author of *Russia Awakes* (1922), was bending across one or two intermediate members of the audience to compliment Miss Clyde on her speech, while from behind that lady another twinkling old party was thrusting into her field of vision a pair of withered, soundlessly clapping hands.

November 28, 1953

THE STATE OF GRACE

Harold Brodkey

THERE IS A certain shade of red brick—a dark, almost melodious red, sombre and riddled with blue—that is my childhood in St. Louis. Not the real childhood, but the false one that extends from the dawning of consciousness until the day that one leaves home for college and manhood. That one shade of red brick and green foliage is St. Louis in the summer (the winter is just a gray sky and a crowded school bus and the wet footprints on the brown linoleum floor at school), and that brick and a pale sky is spring. It's also heartbreak and loneliness and the queer, self-pitying wonder that children whose families are having catastrophes feel.

I can remember that brick best on the back of our apartment house; it was on all the apartment houses on that block, and also on the apartment house where Edward lived. Edward was a small boy I took care of on the evenings when his parents went out. As I came up the street from school, past the boulevard and its ugliness (the vista of shoe-repair shops, dime stores, hairdressers', pet shops, the Tivoli Theatre, and the closed Piggly Wiggly, about to be converted into a Kroger's), past the place where I could see the Masonic Temple, built in the shape of some Egyptian relic, and the two huge concrete pedestals flanking the boulevard (what they supported I can't remember, but on both of them, in brown paint, was a large heart and the information that someone named Erica loved someone named Peter), past the post office, built in W.P.A. days of yellow brick and chrome, I hurried toward the moment when at last, on the other side, past the driveway of the garage of the Castlereagh Apartments, I would be at the place where the trees began, the apartment houses of dark-red brick, and the empty stillness.

In the middle of that stillness and red brick was my neighborhood, the terribly familiar place where I was more comfortably an exile than anywhere else. There were two locust trees that were beautiful to me—I think because they were small and I could encompass them (not only with my mind and heart but with my hands as well). Then came an apartment house of red brick (but not quite the true shade) where a boy I knew lived, and two amazingly handsome brothers, who were also strong and kind, but much older than I and totally uninterested in me. Then came an alley of black macadam and another vista, which I found shameful but drearily comfortable, of garages and ashpits and telephone poles and the backs of apartment houses—including ours—on one side, the backs of houses on the other. I knew many people in the apartments but none in the houses, and this was the ultimate proof, of course, to me of how miserably degraded I was and how far sunken beneath the surface of the sea. I was on the bottom, looking up through the waters, through the shifting bands of light—through, oh, innumerably more complexities than I could stand—at a sailboat driven by the wind, some boy who had a family and a home like other people.

I was thirteen, and six feet tall, and I weighed a hundred and twenty-five pounds. Though I fretted wildly about my looks (my ears stuck out and my hair was like wire), I also knew I was attractive; girls had smiled at me, but none whom I might love and certainly none of the seven or eight goddesses in the junior high school I attended. Starting in about second grade, I always had the highest grades—higher than anybody who had ever attended the schools I went to—and I terrified my classmates. What terrified them was that so far as they could see, it never took any effort; it was like legerdemain. I was never teased, I was never tormented: I was merely isolated. But I was known as "the walking encyclopedia," and the only way I could deal with this was to withdraw. Looking back, I'm almost certain I could have had friends if I'd made the right overtures, and that it was not my situation but my forbidding pride that kept them off; I'm not sure. I had very few clothes, and all that I had had been passed to me from an elder cousin. I never was able to wear what the other boys wore.

Our apartment was on the third floor. I usually walked up the back stairs, which were mounted outside the building in a steel framework. I preferred the back stairs—it was a form of rubbing at a hurt to make sure it was still there—because they were steep and ugly and had garbage cans on the landings and wash hanging out, while the front door opened off a court where rosebushes grew, and the front stairs were made of some faintly yellow local marble that was cool and pleasant to the touch and to the eye. When I came to our back door, I would open the screen and call out to see if my mother was home. If she was not home, it usually meant that she was visiting my father, who had been dying in the hospital for four years and would linger two more before he would come to terms with death. As far as I know, that was the only sign of character he ever showed in his entire life, and I suppose it was considerable, but I hoped, and even sometimes prayed, that he would die—not only because I wouldn't have to visit the hospital again, where the white-walled rooms were filled with odors and sick old men (and a tangible fear that made me feel a falling away inside, like the plunge into the unconscious when the anesthetic is given), but because my mother might marry again and make us all rich and happy once more. She was still lovely then, still alight with the curious incandescence of physical beauty. There was a man who had loved her for twenty years and who loved her yet and wanted to marry her. I wished so hard my father would die, but he just wouldn't. If my mother was home, I braced myself for unpleasantness, because she didn't like me to sit and read; she hated me to read. She wanted to drive me outdoors, where I would become an athlete and be like other boys and be popular. It filled her with rage when I ignored her advice and opened a book; once, she rushed up to me, her face suffused with anger, took the book (I think it was *Pride and Prejudice*), and hurled it out the third-story window. At the time, I sat and tried to sneer, thinking she was half mad, with her exaggerated rage, and so foolish not to realize that I could be none of the things she thought I ought to be. But now I think—perhaps wistfully—that she was merely desperate, driven to extremes in her anxiety to save me. She felt—she knew, in fact—that there was going to come a moment when, like an acrobat, I was going to have to climb on her shoulders and on the shoulders of all the things she had done for me, and leap out into a life she couldn't imagine (and which I am leading now), and if she wanted to send me out wrapped in platitudes, in an athletic body, with a respect for money, it was because she thought that was the warmest covering.

But when I was thirteen, I only wondered how anyone so lovely could be so impossible. She somehow managed it so that I hated her far more than I loved her, even though in the moments before sleep I would think of her face, letting my memory begin with the curving gentleness of her eyelid and circle through all the subtle interplay of shadows and hollows and bones, and the half-remembered warmth of her chest, and it would seem to me that this vision of her, always standing in half light (as probably I had seen her once when I was younger, and sick, perhaps, though I don't really remember), was only as beautiful to me as the pattern in an immeasurably ancient and faded Persian rug. In the vision, as in the rug, I could trace the lines in and out and experience some unnamed pleasure, but it had almost no meaning, numbed as I was by the problems of my sonhood.

Being Jewish also disturbed me, because it meant I could never be one of the golden people—the blond athletes, with their easy charm. If my family had been well off, I might have felt otherwise, but I doubt it.

My mother had a cousin whom I called Aunt Rachel, and we used to go and see her three or four times a year. I hated it. She lived in what was called the Ghetto, which was a section of old houses in downtown St. Louis with tiny front porches and two doors, one to the upstairs and one to the downstairs. Most people lived in them only until they could move to something better; no one had ever liked living there. And because of that, the neighborhood had the quality of being blurred; the grass was never neat, the window frames were never painted, no one cared about or loved the place. It was where the immigrants lived when they arrived by train from New York and before they could move uptown to the apartments near Delmar Boulevard, and eventually to the suburbs—to Clayton, Laclede, and Ladue. Aunt Rachel lived downstairs. Her living room was very small and had dark-yellow wallpaper, which she never changed. She never cleaned it, either, because once I made a mark on it, to see if she would, and she didn't. The furniture was alive and frightening. It was like that part of the nightmare where it gets so bad that you decide to wake up. I always had to sit on it. It bulged in great curves of horsehair and mohair, and it was dark purple and maroon and dark green, and the room had no light in it anywhere. Somewhere on the other side of the old, threadbare satin draperies that had been bought out of an old house was fresh air and sunshine, but you'd never know it. It was as much like a peasant's hut as Aunt Rachel could manage, buying furniture in cut-rate furniture stores. And always there were the smells—the smell of onion soup and garlic and beets. It was the only place where I was ever rude to my mother in public. It was always full of people whom I hardly ever knew, but who knew me, and I had to perform. My mother would say, "Tell the people what your last report card was," or "Recite them the poem that Miss Huntington liked so well." That was when the feeling of unreality was strongest. Looking back now, I think that what frightened me was their fierce urgency; I was to be rich and famous and make all their tribulations worth while. But I didn't want that responsibility. Anyway, if I were going to be what they wanted me to be, and if I had to be what I was, then it was too much to expect me to take them as they were. I had to go beyond them and despise them, but first I had to be with them—and it wasn't fair.

It was as if my eyelids had been propped open, and I had to see these things I didn't want to see. I felt as if I had taken part in something shameful, and therefore I wasn't a nice person. It was like my first sexual experiences: What if anyone knew? What if everyone found out? . . . How in hell could I ever be gallant and carefree, like the blond athletes?

I had read too many books by Englishmen and New Englanders to want to know anything but graceful things and erudite things and the look of white frame houses on green lawns. I could always console myself by thinking my brains would make me famous (brains were good for something, weren't they?), but then my children would have good childhoods—not me. I was irrevocably deprived, and it was the irrevocableness that hurt, that finally drove me away from any sensible adjustment with life to the position that dreams had to come true or there was no point in living at all. If dreams came true, then I would have my childhood in one form or another, someday.

• • •

If my mother was home when I came in from school, she might say that Mrs. Leinberg had called and wanted me to baby-sit, and I would be plunged into yet another of the dilemmas of those years. I had to baby-sit to earn money to buy my lunch at school, and there were times, considering the dilemma I faced at the Leinbergs', when I preferred not eating, or eating very little, to baby-sitting. But there wasn't any choice; Mother would have accepted for me, and made Mrs. Leinberg promise not to stay out too late and deprive me of my sleep. She would have a sandwich ready for me to eat, so that I could rush over in time to let Mr. and Mrs. Leinberg go out to dinner. Anyway, I would eat my sandwich reading a book, to get my own back, and then I would set out. As I walked down the back stairs on my way to the Leinbergs', usually swinging on the railings by my arms to build up my muscles, I would think forlornly of what it was to be me, and wish things were otherwise, and I did not understand myself or my loneliness or the cruel deprivation the vista down the alley meant.

There was a short cut across the back yards to the apartment house where the Leinbergs lived, but I always walked by my two locust trees and spent a few moments loving them; so far as I knew, I loved nothing else.

Then I turned right and crossed the street and walked past an apartment house that had been built at right angles to the street, facing a strange declivity that had once been an excavation for still another apartment house, which had never been built, because of the depression. On the other side of the declivity was a block of three apartment houses, and the third was the Leinbergs'. Every apartment in it had at least eight rooms, and the back staircase was enclosed, and the building had its own garages. All this made it special and expensive, and a landmark in the neighborhood.

Mr. Leinberg was a cosmetics manufacturer and very successful. I thought he was a smart man, but I don't remember him at all well (I never looked at men closely in those days but always averted my head in shyness and embarrassment; they might guess how fiercely I wanted to belong to them) and I could have been wrong. Certainly the atmosphere then, during the war years—it was 1943—was that everyone was getting rich; everyone who could work, that is. At any rate, he was getting rich, and it was only a matter of time before the Leinbergs moved from that apartment house to Laclede or Ladue and had a forty-thousand-dollar house with grounds.

Mrs. Leinberg was very pretty; she was dark, like my mother, but not as beautiful. For one thing, she was too small; she was barely five feet tall, and I towered over her. For another, she was not at all regal. But her lipstick was never on her teeth, and her dresses were usually new, and her eyes were kind. (My mother's eyes were incomprehensible; they were dark stages where dimly seen mob scenes were staged and all one ever sensed was tumult and drama, and no matter how long one waited, the lights never went up and the scene never was explained.) Mrs. Leinberg would invite me to help myself in the icebox, and then she would write down the telephone number of the place where she was going to be. "Keep Edward in the back of the apartment, where he won't disturb the baby," she would tell me. "If the baby does wake up, pick her up right away. That's very important. I didn't pick Edward up, and I'll always regret it." She said that every time, even though Edward was lurking in the back hallway, waiting for his parents to leave so he could run out and jump on me and our world could come alive again. He would listen, his small face—he was seven—quite blank with hurt and the effort to pierce the hurt with understanding.

Mrs. Leinberg would say, "Call me if she wakes up." And then, placatingly, to her husband, "I'll just come home to put her back to sleep, and then I'll go right back to the party—" Then, to me, "But she almost always sleeps, so don't worry about it."

"Come on, Greta. He knows what to do," Mr. Leinberg would say impatiently.

I always imagined contempt in his voice—contempt for us both. I would be standing by the icebox looking down on the two little married people. Mr. Leinberg had a very red mouth. "Come on, Greta," it would say. "We'll be back by eleven," it would say to me.

"Edward goes to bed at nine," Mrs. Leinberg would say, her voice high and birdlike, but tremulous with confusion and vagueness. Then she would be swept out the front door, so much prettily dressed matchwood, in her husband's wake. When the door closed, Edward would come hurtling down the hall and tackle my knees if I was staring after his parents, or, if I was facing him, leap onto my chest and into my arms.

"What shall we play tonight?"

He would ask that and I would have to think. He trembled with excitement, because I could always make the games wonderful to him—like his daydreams, in fact. Because he was a child, he trusted me almost totally, and I could do anything with him. I had that power with children until I was in college and began at last to be like other people.

In Edward's bedroom was a large closet; it had a rack for clothes, a washstand, a built-in table, and fifteen or twenty shelves. The table and shelves were crowded with toys and games and sports equipment. I owned a Monopoly board I had inherited from my older sister, an old baseball glove (which was so cheap I never dared use it in front of my classmates, who had real gloves signed by real players), and a collection of postcards. The first time I saw that closet, I practically exploded with pleasure; I took down each of the games and toys and played with them, one after another, with Edward. Edward loved the fact that we never played a game to its conclusion but would leap from game to game after only a few moves, until the leaping became the real game and the atmosphere of laughter the real sport.

It was comfortable for me in the back room, alone in the apartment with Edward, because at last I was chief; and not only that, I was not being seen. There was no one there thinking of me or what I should be or how I should behave; and I have always been terrified of what people thought of me, as if what they thought was a hulking creature that would confront me if I should turn a corner.

There were no corners. Edward and I would take his toy pistols and stalk each other around the bed. Other times, we were on the bed, the front gun turret of a battleship sailing to battle the Japanese fleet in the Indian Ocean. Edward would close his eyes and roll with pleasure when I went "Boom! Boom! BOOOOM!"

"It's sinking! It's sinking, isn't it?"

"No, stupid. We only hit its funnel. We have to shoot again. Boom, Boom—"

Edward's fingers would press his eyelids in a spasm of ecstasy; his delirious, taut, little boy's body would fall backward on the soft pillows and bounce, and his back would curve; the excited breathy laughter would pour out like so many leaves spilling into spring, so many lilacs thrusting into bloom.

Under the bed, in a foxhole (Edward had a Cub Scout hat and I had his plastic soldier helmet), we turned back the yellow hordes from Guadalcanal. Edward dearly loved to be wounded. "I'm hit!" he'd shriek. "I'm hit!" He'd press his hand against his stomach and writhe on the wooden floor. "They shot me in the guts—"

I didn't approve of his getting wounded so soon, because then the scene was over; both his and my sense of verisimilitude didn't allow someone to be wounded and then get up. I remember how pleased he was when I invented the idea that after he got wounded, he could be someone else; so, when we crawled under the bed, we would decide to be eight or twelve or twenty Marines, ten each to get wounded, killed, or maimed as we saw fit, provided enough survived so that when we crawled out from under the bed we could charge the Japanese position under the dining-room table and leave it strewn with corpses.

Edward was particularly good at the detective game, which was a lot more involved and difficult. In that, we would walk into the kitchen, and I would tell him that we had received a call about a murder. Except when we played Tarzan, we never found it necessary to be characters. However, we always had names. In the detective game, we were usually Sam and Fred. We'd get a call telling us who was murdered, and then we'd go back to the bedroom and examine the corpse and question the suspects. I'd fire questions at an empty chair. Sometimes Edward would get tired of being my sidekick and he'd slip into the chair and be the quaking suspect. Other times, he would prowl around the room on his hands and knees with a magnifying glass while I stormed and shouted at the perpetually shifty suspect: "Where were you, Mrs. Eggnogghead [giggles from Edward], at ten o'clock, when Mr. Eggnogghead [laughter, helpless with pleasure, from Edward] was slain with the cake knife?"

"Hey, Fred! *I found bloodstains.*" Edward's voice would quiver with a creditable imitation of the excitement of radio detectives.

"Bloodstains! Where, Sam? Where? This may be the clue that breaks the case."

Edward could sustain the *commedia dell'arte* for hours if I wanted him to. He was a precocious and delicate little boy, quivering with the malaise of being unloved. When we played, his child's heart would come into its own, and the troubled world where his vague hungers went unfed and mothers and fathers were dim and far away—too far away ever to reach in and touch the sore place and make it heal—would disappear, along with the world where I was not sufficiently muscled or sufficiently gallant to earn my own regard. (What ever had induced my mother to marry that silly man, who'd been unable to hang on to his money? I could remember when we'd had a larger house and I'd had toys; why had she let it get away?) It angered me that Edward's mother had so little love for him and so much for her daughter, and that Edward's father should not appreciate the boy's intelligence—he thought Edward was a queer duck, and effeminate. I could have taught Edward the manly postures. But his father didn't think highly of me: I was only a baby-sitter, and effeminate, too. Why, then, should Edward be more highly regarded by his father than I myself was? I wouldn't love him or explain to him.

That, of course, was my terrible dilemma. His apartment house, though larger than mine, was made of the same dark-red brick, and I wouldn't love him. He wasn't as smart as I'd been at his age, or as fierce. At his age, I'd already seen the evil in people's eyes, and I'd begun the construction of my defenses even then. But Edward's family was more prosperous, and the cold winds of insecurity (*Where will the money come from?*) hadn't shredded the dreamy chrysalis of his childhood. He was still immersed in the dim, wet wonder of the folded wings that might open if someone loved him; he still hoped, probably, in a butterfly's unthinking way, for spring and warmth. How the wings ache, folded so, waiting; that is, they ache until they atrophy.

So I was thirteen and Edward was seven and he wanted me to love him, but he was not old enough or strong enough to help me. He could not make his parents share their wealth and comfort with me, or force them to give me a place in their home. He was like most of the people I knew—eager and needful of my love; for I was quite remarkable and made incredible games, which were better than movies or than the heart could hope for. I was a dream come true. I was smart and virtuous (no one knew that I occasionally stole from the dime store) and fairly attractive, maybe even very attractive. I was often funny and always interesting. I had read everything and knew everything and got unbelievable grades. Of course I was someone whose love was desired. Mother, my teachers, my sister, girls at school, other boys—they all wanted me to love them.

But I wanted them to love me first.

None of them did. I was fierce and solitary and acrid, marching off the little mile from school, past the post office, all yellow brick and chrome, and my two locust trees (water, water everywhere and not a drop to drink), and there was no one who loved me first. I could see a hundred cravennesses in the people I knew, a thousand flaws, a million weaknesses. If I had to love first, I would love only perfection. Of course, I could help heal the people I knew if I loved them. No, I said to myself, why should I give them everything when they give me nothing?

How many hurts and shynesses and times of walking up the back stairs had made me that way? I don't know. All I know is that Edward needed my love and I wouldn't give it to him. I was only thirteen. Many sins can be forgiven a boy of thirteen, but I'm not thinking of the sin; I'm thinking of all the years that might have been—if I'd only known then what I know now. The waste, the God-awful waste.

Really, that's all there is to this story. The boy I was, the child Edward was. That and the terrible desire to suddenly turn and run shouting back through the corridors of time, screaming at the boy I was, searching him out, and pounding on his chest: Love him, you damn fool, love him.

November 6, 1954

THE COUNTRY HUSBAND

John Cheever

To begin at the beginning, the airplane from Minneapolis in which Francis Weed was travelling East ran into heavy weather. The sky had been a hazy blue, with the clouds below the plane lying so close together that nothing could be seen of the earth. Then mist began to form outside the windows, and they flew into a white cloud of such density that it reflected the exhaust fires. The color of the cloud darkened to gray, and the plane began to rock. Francis had been in heavy weather before, but he had never been shaken up so much. The man in the seat beside him pulled a flask out of his pocket and took a drink. Francis smiled at his neighbor, but the man looked away; he wasn't sharing his painkiller with anyone. The plane had begun to drop and flounder wildly. A child was crying. The air in the cabin was overheated and stale, and Francis' left foot went to sleep. He read a little from a paper book that he had bought at the airport, but the violence of the storm divided his attention. It was black outside the ports. The exhaust fires blazed and shed sparks in the dark, and, inside, the shaded lights, the stuffiness, and the window curtains gave the cabin an atmosphere of intense and misplaced domesticity. Then the lights flickered and went out. "You know what I've always wanted to do?" the man beside Francis said suddenly. "I've always wanted to buy a farm in New Hampshire and raise beef cattle." The stewardess announced that they were going to make an emergency landing. All but the child saw in their minds the spreading wings of the Angel of Death. The pilot could be heard singing faintly, "I've got sixpence, jolly, jolly sixpence. I've got sixpence to last me all my life . . ." There was no other sound.

The loud groaning of the hydraulic valves swallowed up the pilot's song, and there was a shrieking high in the air, like automobile brakes, and the plane hit flat on its belly in a cornfield and shook them so violently that an old man up forward howled, "Me kidneys! Me kidneys!" The stewardess flung open the door, and someone opened an emergency door at the back, letting in the sweet noise of their continuing mortality—the idle splash and smell of a heavy rain. Anxious for their lives, they filed out of the doors and scattered over the cornfield in all directions, praying that the thread would hold. It did. Nothing happened. When it was clear that the plane would not burn or explode, the crew and the stewardess gathered the passengers together and led them to the shelter of a barn. They were not far from Philadelphia, and in a little while a string of taxis took them into the city. "It's just like the Marne," someone said, but there was surprisingly little relaxation of that suspiciousness with which many Americans regard their fellow-travellers.

In Philadelphia, Francis Weed got a train to New York. At the end of that journey, he crossed the city and caught, just as it was about to pull out, the commuting train that he took five nights a week to his home in Shady Hill.

He sat with Trace Bearden. "You know, I was in that plane that just crashed outside Philadelphia," he said. "We came down in a field . . ." He had travelled faster than the newspapers or the rain, and the weather in New York was sunny and mild. It was a day in late September, as fragrant and shapely as an apple. Trace listened to the story, but how could he get excited? Francis had no powers that would let him re-create a brush with death—particularly in the atmosphere of a commuting train, journeying through a sunny countryside where already, in the slum gardens, there were signs of harvest. Trace picked up his newspaper, and Francis was left alone with his thoughts. He said good night to Trace on the platform at Shady Hill and drove in his second-hand Volkswagen up to the Blenhollow neighborhood, where he lived.

• • •

The Weeds' Dutch Colonial house was larger than it appeared to be from the driveway. The living room was spacious and divided like Gaul into three parts. Around an ell to the left as one entered from the vestibule was the long table, laid for six, with candles and a bowl of fruit in the center. The sounds and smells that came from the open kitchen door were appetizing, for Julia Weed was a good cook. The largest part of the living room centered around a fireplace. On the right were some bookshelves and a piano. The room was polished and tranquil, and from the windows that opened to the west there was some late-summer sunlight, brilliant and as clear as water. Nothing here was neglected; nothing had not been burnished. It was not the kind of household where, after prying open a stuck cigarette box, you would find an old shirt button and a tarnished nickel. The hearth was swept, the roses on the piano were reflected in the polish of the broad top, and there was an album of Schubert waltzes on the rack. Louisa Weed, a pretty girl of nine, was looking out the western windows. Her younger brother Henry was standing beside her. Her still younger brother, Toby, was studying the figures of some tonsured monks drinking beer on the polished brass of the wood box. Francis, taking off his hat and putting down his paper, was not consciously pleased with the scene; he was not that reflective. It was his element, his creation, and he returned to it with that sense of lightness and strength with which any creature returns to its home. "Hi, everybody," he said. "The plane from Minneapolis . . ."

Nine times out of ten, Francis would be greeted with affection, but tonight the children are absorbed in their own antagonisms. Francis has not finished his sentence about the plane crash before Henry plants a kick in Louisa's behind. Louisa swings around, saying "*Damn* you!" Francis makes the mistake of scolding Louisa for bad language before he punishes Henry. Now Louisa turns on her father and accuses him of favoritism. Henry is always right; she is persecuted and lonely; her lot is hopeless. Francis turns to his son, but the boy has justification for the kick—she hit him first; she hit him on the ear, which is dangerous. Louisa agrees with this passionately. She hit him on the ear, and she *meant* to hit him on the ear, because he messed up her china collection. Henry says that this is a lie. Little Toby turns away from the wood box to throw in some evidence for Louisa. Henry claps his hand over little Toby's mouth. Francis separates the two boys but accidentally pushes Toby into the wood box. Toby begins to cry. Louisa is already crying. Just then, Julia Weed comes into that part of the room where the table is laid. She is a pretty, intelligent woman, and the white in her hair is premature. She does not seem to notice the fracas. "Hello, darling," she says serenely to Francis. "Wash your hands, everyone. Dinner is ready." She strikes a match and lights the six candles in this vale of tears.

This simple announcement, like the war cries of the Scottish chieftains, only refreshes the ferocity of the combatants. Louisa gives Henry a blow on the shoulder. Henry, although he seldom cries, has pitched nine innings and is tired. He bursts into tears. Little Toby discovers a splinter in his hand and begins to howl. Francis says loudly that he has been in a plane crash and that he is tired. Julia appears again, from the kitchen, and, still ignoring the chaos, asks Francis to go upstairs and tell Helen that everything is ready. Francis is happy to go; it is like getting back to headquarters company. He is planning to tell his oldest daughter about the airplane crash, but Helen is lying on her bed reading a *True Romance* magazine, and the first thing Francis does is to take the magazine from her hand and remind Helen that he has forbidden her to buy it. She did not buy it, Helen replies. It was given to her by her best friend, Bessie Black. Everybody reads *True Romance.* Bessie Black's father reads *True Romance.* There isn't a girl in Helen's class who doesn't read *True Romance.* Francis expresses his detestation of the magazine and then tells her that dinner is ready—although from the sounds downstairs it doesn't seem so. Helen follows him down the stairs. Julia has seated herself in the candlelight and spread a napkin over her lap. Neither Louisa nor Henry has come to the table. Little Toby is still howling, lying face down on the floor. Francis speaks to him gently: "Daddy was in a plane crash this afternoon, Toby. Don't you want to hear about it?" Toby goes on crying. "If you don't come to the table now, Toby," Francis says, "I'll have to send you to bed without any supper." The little boy rises, gives him a cutting look, flies up the stairs to his bedroom, and slams the door. "Oh dear," Julia says, and starts to go after him. Francis says that she will spoil him. Julia says that Toby is ten pounds underweight and has to be encouraged to eat. Winter is coming, and he will spend the cold months in bed unless he has his dinner. Julia goes upstairs. Francis sits down at the table with Helen. Helen is suffering from the dismal feeling of having read too intently on a fine day, and she gives her father and the room a jaded look. She doesn't understand about the plane crash, because there wasn't a drop of rain in Shady Hill.

Julia returns with Toby, and they all sit down and are served. "Do I have to look at that big, fat slob?" Henry says, of Louisa. Everybody but Toby enters into this skirmish, and it rages up and down the table for five minutes. Toward the end, Henry puts his napkin over his head and, trying to eat that way, spills spinach all over his shirt. Francis asks Julia if the children couldn't have their dinner earlier. Julia's guns are loaded for this. She can't cook two dinners and lay two tables. She paints with lightning strokes that panorama of drudgery in which her youth, her beauty, and her wit have been lost. Francis says that he must be understood; he was nearly killed in an airplane crash, and he doesn't like to come home every night to a battlefield. Now Julia is deeply committed. Her voice trembles. He doesn't come home every night to a battlefield. The accusation is stupid and mean. Everything was tranquil until he arrived. She stops speaking, puts down her knife and fork, and looks into her plate as if it is a gulf. She begins to cry. "Poor Mummy!" Toby says, and when Julia gets up from the table, drying her tears with a napkin, Toby goes to her side. "Poor Mummy," he says. "Poor Mummy!" And they climb the stairs together. The other children drift away from the battlefield, and Francis goes into the back garden for a cigarette and some air.

• • •

It was a pleasant garden, with walks and flower beds and places to sit. The sunset had nearly burned out, but there was still plenty of light. Put into a thoughtful mood by the crash and the battle, Francis listened to the evening sounds of Shady Hill. "Varmits! Rascals!" old Mr. Nixon shouted to the squirrels in his bird-feeding station. "Avaunt and quit my sight!" A door slammed. Someone was playing tennis on the Babcocks' court; someone was cutting grass. Then Donald Goslin, who lived at the corner, began to play the *Moonlight* Sonata. He did this nearly every night. He threw the tempo out the window and played it *rubato* from beginning to end, like an outpouring of tearful petulance, lonesomeness, and self-pity—of everything it was Beethoven's greatness not to know. The music rang up and down the street beneath the trees like an appeal for love, for tenderness, aimed at some lonely housemaid—some fresh-faced, homesick girl from Galway, looking at old snapshots in her third-floor room. "Here, Jupiter, here, Jupiter," Francis called to the Mercers' retriever. Jupiter crashed through the tomato vines with the remains of a felt hat in his mouth.

Jupiter was an anomaly. His retrieving instincts and his high spirits were out of place in Shady Hill. He was as black as coal, with a long, alert, intelligent, rakehell face. His eyes gleamed with mischief, and he held his head high. It was the fierce, heavily collared dog's head that appears in heraldry, in tapestry, and that used to appear on umbrella handles and walking sticks. Jupiter went where he pleased, ransacking wastebaskets, clotheslines, garbage pails, and shoe bags. He broke up garden parties and tennis matches, and got mixed up in the processional at Christ's Church on Sunday, barking at the men in red dresses. He crashed through old Mr. Nixon's rose garden two or three times a day, cutting a wide swath through the Condesa de Sastagos, and as soon as Donald Goslin lighted his barbecue fire on Thursday nights, Jupiter would get the scent. Nothing the Goslins did could drive him away. Sticks and stones and rude commands only moved him to the edge of the terrace, where he remained, with his gallant and heraldic muzzle, waiting for Donald Goslin to turn his back and reach for the salt. Then he would spring onto the terrace, lift the steak lightly off the fire, and run away with the Goslins' dinner. Jupiter's days were numbered. The Wrightsons' German gardener or the Farquarsons' cook would soon poison him. Even old Mr. Nixon might put some arsenic in the garbage that Jupiter loved. "Here, Jupiter, Jupiter!" Francis called, but the dog pranced off, shaking the hat in his white teeth. Looking in at the windows of his house, Francis saw that Julia had come down and was blowing out the candles.

• • •

Julia and Francis Weed went out a great deal. Julia was well liked and gregarious, and her love of parties sprang from a most natural dread of chaos and loneliness. She went through her morning mail with real anxiety, looking for invitations, and she usually found some, but she was insatiable, and if she had gone out seven nights a week, it would not have cured her of a reflective look—the look of someone who hears distant music—for she would always suppose that there was a more brilliant party somewhere else. Francis limited her to two week-night parties, putting a flexible interpretation on Friday, and rode through the weekend like a dory in a gale. The day after the airplane crash, the Weeds were to have dinner with the Farquarsons.

Francis got home late from town, and Julia got the sitter while he dressed, and then hurried him out of the house. The party was small and pleasant, and Francis settled down to enjoy himself. A new maid passed the drinks. Her hair was dark, and her face was round and pale and seemed familiar to Francis. He had not developed his memory as a sentimental faculty. Wood smoke, lilac, and other such perfumes did not stir him, and his memory was something like his appendix—a vestigial repository. It was not his limitation at all to be unable to escape the past; it was perhaps his limitation that he had escaped it so successfully. He might have seen the maid at other parties, he might have seen her taking a walk on Sunday afternoons, but in either case he would not be searching his memory now. Her face was, in a wonderful way, a moon face—

Norman or Irish—but it was not beautiful enough to account for his feeling that he had seen her before, in circumstances that he ought to be able to remember. He asked Nellie Farquarson who she was. Nellie said that the maid had come through an agency, and that her home was Trénon, in Normandy—a small place with a church and a restaurant that Nellie had once visited. While Nellie talked on about her travels abroad, Francis realized where he had seen the woman before. It had been at the end of the war. He had left a replacement depot with some other men and taken a three-day pass in Trénon. On their second day, they had walked out to a crossroads to see the public chastisement of a young woman who had lived with the German commandant during the Occupation.

It was a cool morning in the fall. The sky was overcast, and poured down onto the dirt crossroads a very discouraging light. They were on high land and could see how like one another the shapes of the clouds and the hills were as they stretched off toward the sea. The prisoner arrived sitting on a three-legged stool in a farm cart. She stood by the cart while the mayor read the accusation and the sentence. Her head was bent and her face was set in that empty half smile behind which the whipped soul is suspended. When the mayor was finished, she undid her hair and let it fall across her back. A little man with a gray mustache cut off her hair with shears and dropped it on the ground. Then, with a bowl of soapy water and a straight razor, he shaved her skull clean. A woman approached and began to undo the fastenings of her clothes, but the prisoner pushed her aside and undressed herself. When she pulled her chemise over her head and threw it on the ground, she was naked. The women jeered; the men were still. There was no change in the falseness or the plaintiveness of the prisoner's smile. The cold wind made her white skin rough and hardened the nipples of her breasts. The jeering ended gradually, put down by the recognition of their common humanity. One woman spat on her, but some inviolable grandeur in her nakedness lasted through the ordeal. When the crowd was quiet, she turned—she had begun to cry—and, with nothing on but a pair of worn black shoes and stockings, walked down the dirt road alone away from the village. The round white face had aged a little, but there was no question but that the maid who passed his cocktails and later served Francis his dinner was the woman who had been punished at the crossroads.

The war seemed now so distant and that world where the cost of partisanship had been death or torture so long ago. Francis had lost track of the men who had been with him in Vésey. He could not count on Julia's discretion. He could not tell anyone. And if he had told the story now, at the dinner table, it would have been a social as well as a human error. The people in the Farquarsons' living room seemed united in their tacit claim that there had been no past, no war—that there was no danger or trouble in the world. In the recorded history of human arrangements, this extraordinary meeting would have fallen into place, but the atmosphere of Shady Hill made the memory unseemly and impolite. The prisoner withdrew after passing the coffee, but the encounter left Francis feeling languid; it had opened his memory and his senses, and left them dilated. He and Julia drove home when the party ended, and Julia went into the house. Francis stayed in the car to take the sitter home.

Expecting to see Mrs. Henlein, the old lady who usually stayed with the children, he was surprised when a young girl opened the door and came out onto the lighted stoop. She stayed in the light to count her textbooks. She was frowning and beautiful. Now, the world is full of beautiful young girls, but Francis saw here the difference between beauty and perfection. All those endearing flaws, moles, birthmarks, and healed wounds were missing, and he experienced in his consciousness that moment when music breaks glass, and felt a pang of recognition as strange, deep, and wonderful as anything in his life. It hung from her frown, from an impalpable darkness in her face—a look that impressed him as a direct appeal for love. When she had counted her books, she came down the steps and opened the car door. In the light, he saw that her cheeks were wet. She got in and shut the door.

"You're new," Francis said.

"Yes. Mrs. Henlein is sick. I'm Anne Murchison."

"Did the children give you any trouble?"

"Oh, no, no." She turned and smiled at him unhappily in the dim dashboard light. Her light hair caught on the collar of her jacket, and she shook her head to set it loose.

"You've been crying."

"Yes."

"I hope it was nothing that happened in our house."

"No, no, it was nothing that happened in your house." Her voice was bleak. "It's no secret. Everybody in the village knows. Daddy's an alcoholic, and he just called me from some saloon and gave me a piece of his mind. He thinks I'm immoral. He called just before Mrs. Weed came back."

"I'm sorry."

"Oh, *Lord*!" She gasped and began to cry. She turned toward Francis, and he took her in his arms and let her cry on his shoulder. She shook in his embrace, and this movement accentuated his sense of the fineness of her flesh and bone. The layers of their clothing felt thin, and when her shuddering began to diminish, it was so much like a paroxysm of love that Francis lost his head and pulled her roughly against him. She drew away. "I live on Belleview Avenue," she said. "You go down Lansing Street to the railroad bridge."

"All right." He started the car.

"You turn left at that traffic light. . . . Now you turn right here and go straight on toward the tracks."

The road Francis took brought him out of his own neighborhood, across the tracks, and toward the river, to a street where the near-poor lived, in houses whose peaked gables and trimmings of wooden lace conveyed the purest feelings of pride and romance, although the houses themselves could not have offered much privacy or comfort, they were all so small. The street was dark, and, stirred by the grace and beauty of the troubled girl, he seemed, in turning in to it, to have come into the deepest part of some submerged memory. In the distance, he saw a porch light burning. It was the only one, and she said that the house with the light was where she lived. When he stopped the car, he could see beyond the porch light into a dimly-lighted hallway with an old-fashioned clothes tree. "Well, here we are," he said, conscious that a young man would have said something different.

She did not move her hands from the books, where they were folded, and she turned and faced him. There were tears of lust in his eyes. Determinedly—not sadly—he opened the door on his side and walked around to open hers. He took her free hand, letting his fingers in between hers, climbed at her side the two concrete steps, and went up a narrow walk through a front garden where dahlias, marigolds, and roses—things that had withstood the light frosts—still bloomed, and made a bittersweet smell in the night air. At the steps, she freed her hand and then turned and kissed him swiftly. Then she crossed the porch and shut the door. The porch light went out, then the light in the hall. A second later, a light went on upstairs at the side of the house, shining into a tree that was still covered with leaves. It took her only a few minutes to undress and get into bed, and then the house was dark.

Julia was asleep when Francis got home. He opened a second window and got into bed to shut his eyes on that night, but as soon as they were shut—as soon as he had dropped off to sleep—the girl entered his mind, moving with perfect freedom through its shut doors and filling chamber after chamber with her light, her perfume, and the music of her voice. He was crossing the Atlantic with her on the old Mauretania and, later, living with her in Paris. When he woke from this dream, he got up and smoked a cigarette at the open window. Getting back into bed, he cast around in his mind for something he desired to do that would injure no one, and he thought of skiing. Up through the dimness in his mind rose the image of a mountain deep in snow. It was late in the day. Wherever his eyes looked, he saw broad and heartening things. Over his shoulder, there was a snow-filled valley, rising into wooded hills where the trees dimmed the whiteness like a sparse coat of hair. The cold deadened all sound but the loud, iron clanking of the lift machinery. The light on the trails was blue, and it was harder than it had been a minute or two earlier to pick the turns, harder to judge—now that the snow was all deep blue—the crust, the ice, the bare spots, and the deep piles of dry powder. Down the mountain he swung, matching his speed against the contours of a slope that had been formed in the first ice age, seeking with ardor some simplicity of feeling and circumstance. Night fell then, and he drank a Martini with some old friend in a dirty country bar.

In the morning, Francis's snow-covered mountain was gone, and he was left with his vivid memories of Paris and the Mauretania. He had been bitten gravely. He washed his body, shaved his jaws, drank his coffee, and missed the seven-thirty-one. The train pulled out just as he brought his car to the station, and the longing he felt for the coaches as they drew stubbornly away from him reminded him of the humors of love. He waited for the eight-two, on what was now an empty platform. It was a clear morning; the morning seemed thrown like a gleaming bridge of light over his mixed affairs. His spirits were feverish and high. The image of the girl seemed to put him into a relationship to the world that was mysterious and enthralling. Cars were beginning to fill up the parking lot, and he noticed that those that had driven down from the high land above Shady Hill were white with hoarfrost. This first clear sign of autumn thrilled him. An express train—a night train from Buffalo or Albany—came down the tracks between the platforms, and he saw that the roofs of the foremost cars were covered with a skin of ice. Struck by the miraculous physicalness of everything, he smiled at the passengers in the dining car, who could be seen eating eggs and wiping their mouths with napkins as they travelled. The sleeping-car compartments, with their soiled bed linen, trailed through the fresh morning like a string of rooming-house windows. Then he saw an extraordinary thing; at one of the bedroom windows sat an unclothed woman of exceptional beauty, combing her golden hair. She passed like an apparition through Shady Hill, combing and combing her hair, and Francis followed her with his eyes until she was out of sight. Then old Mrs. Wrightson joined him on the platform and began to talk.

"Well, I guess you must be surprised to see me here the third morning in a row," she said, "but because of my window curtains I'm becoming a regular commuter. The curtains I bought on Monday I returned on Tuesday, and the curtains I bought Tuesday I'm returning today. On Monday, I got exactly what I wanted—it's a wool tapestry with roses and birds—but when I got them home, I found they were the wrong length. Well, I exchanged them yesterday, and when I got them home, I found they were still the wrong length. Now I'm praying to high Heaven that the decorator will have them in the right length, because you know my house, you *know* my living-room windows, and you can imagine what a problem they present. I don't know what to do with them."

"I know what to do with them," Francis said.

"What?"

"Paint them black on the inside, and shut up."

There was a gasp from Mrs. Wrightson, and Francis looked down at her to be sure that she knew he meant to be rude. She turned and walked away from him, so damaged in spirit that she limped. A wonderful feeling enveloped him, as if light were being shaken about him, and he thought again of Venus combing and combing her hair as she drifted through the Bronx. The realization of how many years had passed since he had enjoyed being deliberately impolite sobered him. Among his friends and neighbors, there were brilliant and gifted people—he saw that—but many of them, also, were bores and fools, and he had made the mistake of listening to them all with equal attention. He had confused a lack of discrimination with Christian love, and the confusion seemed general and destructive. He was grateful to the girl for this bracing sensation of independence. Birds were singing—cardinals and the last of the robins. The sky shone like enamel. Even the smell of ink from his morning paper honed his appetite for life, and the world that was spread out around him was plainly a paradise.

If Francis had believed in some hierarchy of love—in spirits armed with hunting bows, in the capriciousness of Venus and Eros—or even in magical potions, philtres, and stews, in scapulae and quarters of the moon, it might have explained his susceptibility and his feverish high spirits. The autumnal loves of middle age are well publicized, and he guessed that he was face to face with one of these, but there was not a trace of autumn in what he felt. He wanted to sport in the green woods, scratch where he itched, and drink from the same cup.

His secretary, Miss Rainey, was late that morning—she went to a psychiatrist three mornings a week—and when she came in, Francis wondered what advice a psychiatrist would have for him. But the girl promised to bring back into his life something like the sound of music. The realization that this music might lead him straight to a trial for statutory rape at the county courthouse collapsed his happiness. The photograph of his four children laughing into the camera on the beach at Gay Head reproached him. On the letterhead of his firm there was a drawing of the Laocoön, and the figure of the priest and his sons in the coils of the snake appeared to him to have the deepest meaning.

He had lunch with Pinky Trabert, who told him a couple of dirty stories. At a conversational level, the mores of his friends were robust and elastic, but he knew that the moral card house would come down on them all—on Julia and the children as well—if he got caught taking advantage of a baby-sitter. Looking back over the recent history of Shady Hill for some precedent, he found there was none. There was no turpitude; there had not been a divorce since he lived there; there had not even been a breath of scandal. Things seemed arranged with more propriety even than in the Kingdom of Heaven. After leaving Pinky, Francis went to a jeweller's and bought the girl a bracelet. How happy this clandestine purchase made him, how stuffy and comical the jeweller's clerks seemed, how sweet the women who passed at his back smelled! On Fifth Avenue, passing Atlas with his shoulders bent under the weight of the world, Francis thought of the strenuousness of containing his physicalness within the patterns he had chosen.

He did not know when he would see the girl next. He had the bracelet in his inside pocket when he got home. Opening the door of his house, he found her in the hall. Her back was to him, and she turned when she heard the door close. Her smile was open and loving. Her perfection stunned him like a fine day—a day after a thunderstorm. He seized her and covered her lips with his, and she struggled but she did not have to struggle for long, because just then little Gertrude Flannery appeared from somewhere and said, "Oh, Mr. Weed . . ."

Gertrude was a stray. She had been born with a taste for exploration, and she did not have it in her to center her life with her affectionate parents. People who did not know the Flannerys concluded from Gertrude's behavior that she was the child of a bitterly divided family, where drunken quarrels were the rule. This was not true. The fact that little Gertrude's clothing was ragged and thin was her own triumph over her mother's struggle to dress her warmly and neatly. Garrulous, skinny, and unwashed, she drifted from house to house around the Blenhollow neighborhood, forming and breaking alliances based on an attachment to babies, animals, children her own age, adolescents, and sometimes adults. Opening your front door in the morning, you would find Gertrude sitting on your stoop. Going into the bathroom to shave, you would find Gertrude using the toilet. Looking into your son's crib, you would find it empty, and, looking further, you would find that Gertrude had pushed him in his baby carriage into the next village. She was helpful, pervasive, honest, hungry, and loyal. She never went home of her own choice. When the time to go arrived, she was indifferent to all its signs. "Go home, Gertrude," people could be heard saying in one house or another, night after night. "Go home, Gertrude." "It's time for you to go home now, Gertrude." "You had better go home and get your supper, Gertrude." "I told you to go home twenty minutes ago, Gertrude." "Your mother will be worrying about you, Gertrude." "Go home, Gertrude, go home."

There are times when the lines around the human eye seem like shelves of eroded stone and when the staring eye itself strikes us with such a wilderness of animal feeling that we are at a loss. The look Francis gave the little girl was ugly and queer, and it frightened her. He reached into his pocket—his hands were shaking—and took out a quarter. "Go home, Gertrude, go home, and don't tell anyone, Gertrude. Don't—" He choked and ran into the living room as Julia called down to him from upstairs to hurry and dress.

The thought that he would drive Anne Murchison home later that night ran like a golden thread through the events of the party that Francis and Julia went to, and he laughed uproariously at dull jokes, dried a tear when Mabel Mercer told him about the death of her kitten, and stretched, yawned, sighed, and grunted like any other man with a rendezvous at the back of his mind. The bracelet was in his pocket. As he sat talking, the smell of grass was in his nose, and he was wondering where he would park the car. Nobody lived in the old Parker mansion, and the driveway was used as a lovers' lane. Townsend Street was a dead end, and he could park there, beyond the last house. The old lane that used to connect Elm Street to the riverbanks was overgrown, but he had walked there with his children, and he could drive his car deep enough into the brushwoods to be concealed.

The Weeds were the last to leave the party, and their host and hostess spoke of their own married happiness while they all four stood in the hallway saying good night. "She's my girl," their host said, squeezing his wife. "She's my blue sky. After sixteen years, I still bite her shoulders. She makes me feel like Hannibal crossing the Alps."

The Weeds drove home in silence. Francis brought the car up the driveway and sat still, with the motor running. "You can put the car in the garage," Julia said as she got out. "I told the Murchison girl she could leave at eleven. Someone drove her home." She shut the door, and Francis sat in the dark. He would be spared nothing then, it seemed, that a fool was not spared: ravening lewdness, jealousy, this hurt to his feelings that put tears in his eyes, even scorn—for he could see clearly the image he now presented, his arms spread over the steering wheel and his head buried in them for love.

• • •

Francis had been a dedicated Boy Scout when he was young, and, remembering the precepts of his youth, he left his office early the next afternoon and played some round-robin squash, but, with his body toned up by exercise and a shower, he realized that he might better have stayed at his desk. It was a frosty night when he got home. The air smelled sharply of change. When he stepped into the house, he sensed an unusual stir. The children were in their best clothes, and when Julia came down, she was wearing a lavender dress and her diamond sunburst. She explained the stir: Mr. Hubber was coming at seven to take their photograph for the Christmas card. She had put out Francis' blue suit and a tie with some color in it, because the picture was going to be in color this year. Julia was lighthearted at the thought of being photographed for Christmas. It was the kind of ceremony she enjoyed.

Francis went upstairs to change his clothes. He was tired from the day's work and tired with longing, and sitting on the edge of the bed had the effect of deepening his weariness. He thought of Anne Murchison, and the physical need to express himself, instead of being restrained by the pink lamps on Julia's dressing table, engulfed him. He went to Julia's desk, took a piece of writing paper and began to write on it. "Dear Anne, I love you, I love you, I love you . . ." No one would see the letter, and he used no restraint. He used phrases like "heavenly bliss," and "love nest." He salivated, sighed, and trembled. When Julia called him to come down, the abyss between his fantasy and the practical world opened so wide that he felt it affect the muscles of his heart.

Julia and the children were on the stoop, and the photographer and his assistant had set up a double battery of floodlights to show the family and the architectural beauty of the entrance to their house. People who had come home on a late train slowed their cars to see the Weeds being photographed for their Christmas card. A few waved and called to the family. It took half an hour of smiling and wetting their lips before Mr. Hubber was satisfied. The heat of the lights made an unfresh smell in the frosty air, and when they were turned off, they lingered on the retina of Francis' eyes.

Later that night, while Francis and Julia were drinking their coffee in the living room, the doorbell rang. Julia answered the door and let in Clayton Thomas. He had come to pay her for some theatre tickets that she had given his mother some time ago, and that Helen Thomas had scrupulously insisted on paying for, though Julia had asked her not to. Julia invited him in to have a cup of coffee. "I won't have any coffee," Clayton said, "but I will come in for a minute." He followed her into the living room, said good evening to Francis, and sat awkwardly in a chair.

Clayton's father had been killed in the war, and the young man's fatherlessness surrounded him like an element. This may have been conspicuous in Shady Hill because the Thomases were the only family that lacked a piece; all the other marriages were intact and productive. Clayton was in his second or third year of college, and he and his mother lived alone in a large house, which she hoped to sell. Clayton had once made some trouble. Years ago, he had stolen some money and run away; he had got to California before they caught up with him. He was tall and homely, wore horn-rimmed glasses, and spoke in a deep voice.

"When do you go back to college, Clayton?" Francis asked.

"I'm not going back," Clayton said. "Mother doesn't have the money, and there's no sense in all this pretense. I'm going to get a job, and if we sell the house, we'll take an apartment in New York."

"Won't you miss Shady Hill?" Julia asked.

"No," Clayton said. "I don't like it."

"Why not?" Francis asked.

"Well, there's a lot here I don't approve of," Clayton said gravely. "Things like the club dances. Last Saturday night, I looked in toward the end and saw Mr. Granner trying to put Mrs. Minot into the trophy case. They were both drunk. I disapprove of so much drinking."

"It was Saturday night," Francis said.

"And all the dovecotes are phony," Clayton said. "And the way people clutter up their lives. I've thought about it a lot, and what seems to me to be really wrong with Shady Hill is that it doesn't have any future. So much energy is spent in perpetuating the place—in keeping out undesirables, and so forth—that the only idea of the future anyone has is just more and more commuting trains and more parties. I don't think that's healthy. I think people ought to be able to dream big dreams about the future. I think people ought to be able to dream great dreams."

"It's too bad you couldn't continue with college," Julia said.

"I wanted to go to divinity school," Clayton said.

"What's your church?" Francis asked.

"Unitarian, Theosophist, Transcendentalist, Humanist," Clayton said.

"Wasn't Emerson a transcendentalist?" Julia asked.

"I mean the English transcendentalists," Clayton said. "All the American transcendentalists were goops."

"What kind of a job do you expect to get?" Francis asked.

"Well, I'd like to work for a publisher," Clayton said, "but everyone tells me there's nothing doing. But it's the kind of thing I'm interested in. I'm writing a long verse play about good and evil. Uncle Charlie might get me into a bank, and that would be good for me. I need the discipline. I have a long way to go in forming my character. I have some terrible habits. I talk too much. I think I ought to take vows of silence. I ought to try not to speak for a week, and discipline myself. I've thought of making a retreat at one of the Episcopalian monasteries, but I don't like Trinitarianism."

"Do you have any girl friends?" Francis asked.

"I'm engaged to be married," Clayton said. "Of course, I'm not old enough or rich enough to have my engagement observed or respected or anything, but I bought a simulated emerald for Anne Murchison with the money I made cutting lawns this summer. We're going to be married as soon as she finishes school."

Francis recoiled at the mention of the girl's name. Then a dingy light seemed to emanate from his spirit, showing everything—Julia, the boy, the chairs—in their true colorlessness. It was like a bitter turn of the weather.

"We're going to have a large family," Clayton said. "Her father's a terrible rummy, and I've had my hard times, and we want to have lots of children. Oh, she's wonderful, Mr. and Mrs. Weed, and we have so much in common. We like all the same things. We sent out the same Christmas card last year without planning it, and we both have an allergy to tomatoes, and our eyebrows grow together in the middle. Well, good night."

Julia went to the door with him. When she returned, Francis said that Clayton was lazy, irresponsible, affected, and smelly. Julia said that Francis seemed to be getting intolerant; the Thomas boy was young and should be given a chance. Julia had noticed other cases where Francis had been short-tempered. "Mrs. Wrightson has asked everyone in Shady Hill to her anniversary party but us," she said.

"I'm sorry, Julia."

"Do you know why they didn't ask us?"

"Why?"

"Because you insulted Mrs. Wrightson."

"Then you know about it?"

"June Masterson told me. She was standing behind you."

Julia walked in front of the sofa with a small step that expressed, Francis knew, a feeling of anger.

"I did insult Mrs. Wrightson, Julia, and I meant to. I've never liked her parties, and I'm glad she's dropped us."

"What about Helen?"

"How does Helen come into this?"

"Mrs. Wrightson's the one who decides who goes to the assemblies."

"You mean she can keep Helen from going to the dances?"

"Yes."

"I hadn't thought of that."

"Oh, I knew you hadn't thought of it," Julia cried, thrusting hilt-deep into this chink of his armor. "And it makes me furious to see this kind of stupid thoughtlessness wreck everyone's happiness."

"I don't think I've wrecked anyone's happiness."

"Mrs. Wrightson runs Shady Hill and has run it for the last forty years. I don't know what makes you think that in a community like this you can indulge every impulse you have to be insulting, vulgar, and offensive."

"I have very good manners," Francis said, trying to give the evening a turn toward the light.

"Damn you, Francis Weed!" Julia cried, and the spit of her words struck him in the face. "I've worked hard for the social position we enjoy in this place, and I won't stand by and see you wreck it. You must have understood when you settled here that you couldn't expect to live like a bear in a cave."

"I've got to express my likes and dislikes."

"You can conceal your dislikes. You don't have to meet everything head-on, like a child. Unless you're anxious to be a social leper. It's no accident that we get asked out a great deal. It's no accident that Helen has so many friends. How would you like to spend your Saturday nights at the movies? How would you like to spend your Sundays raking up dead leaves? How would you like it if your daughter spent the assembly nights sitting at her window, listening to the music from the club? How would you like it—" He did something then that was, after all, not so unaccountable, since her words seemed to raise up between them a wall so deadening that he gagged: He struck her full in the face. She staggered and then, a moment later, seemed composed. She went up the stairs to their room. She didn't slam the door. When Francis followed, a few minutes later, he found her packing a suitcase.

"Julia, I'm very sorry."

"It doesn't matter," she said. She was crying.

"Where do you think you're going?"

"I don't know. I just looked at a timetable. There's an eleven-sixteen into New York. I'll take that."

"You can't go, Julia."

"I can't stay. I know that."

"I'm sorry about Mrs. Wrightson, Julia, and I'm—"

"It doesn't matter about Mrs. Wrightson. That isn't the trouble."

"What is the trouble?"

"You don't love me."

"I do love you, Julia."

"No, you don't."

"Julia, I do love you, and I would like to be as we were—sweet and bawdy and dark—but now there are so many people."

"You hate me."

"I don't hate you, Julia."

"You have no idea of how much you hate me. I think it's subconscious. You don't realize the cruel things you've done."

"What cruel things, Julia?"

"The cruel acts your subconscious drives you to in order to express your hatred of me."

"What, Julia?"

"I've never complained."

"Tell me."

"You don't know what you're doing."

"Tell me."

"Your clothes."

"What do you mean?"

"I mean the way you leave your dirty clothes around in order to express your subconscious hatred of me."

"I don't understand."

"I mean your dirty socks and your dirty pajamas and your dirty underwear and your dirty shirts!" She rose from kneeling by the suitcase and faced him, her eyes blazing and her voice ringing with emotion. "I'm talking about the fact that you've never learned to hang up anything. You just leave your clothes all over the floor where they drop, in order to humiliate me. You do it on purpose!" She fell on the bed, sobbing.

"Julia, darling!" he said, but when she felt his hand on her shoulder she got up.

"Leave me alone," she said. "I have to go." She brushed past him to the closet and came back with a dress. "I'm not taking any of the things you've given me," she said. "I'm leaving my pearls and the fur jacket."

"Oh, Julia!" Her figure, so helpless in its self-deceptions, bent over the suitcase made him nearly sick with pity. She did not understand how desolate her life would be without him. She didn't understand the hours that working women have to keep. She didn't understand that most of her friendships existed within the framework of their marriage, and that without this she would find herself alone. She didn't understand about travel, about hotels, about money. "Julia, I can't let you go! What you don't understand, Julia, is that you've come to be dependent on me."

She tossed her head back and covered her face with her hands. "Did you say that *I* was dependent on *you*?" she asked. "Is that what you said? And who is it that tells you what time to get up in the morning and when to go to bed at night? Who is it that prepares your meals and picks up your dirty closet and invites your friends to dinner? If it weren't for me, your neckties would be greasy and your clothing would be full of moth holes. You were alone when I met you, Francis Weed, and you'll be alone when I leave. When Mother asked you for a list to send out invitations to our wedding, how many names did you have to give her? Fourteen!"

"Cleveland wasn't my home, Julia."

"And how many of your friends came to the church? Two!"

"Cleveland wasn't my home, Julia."

"Since I'm not taking the fur jacket," she said quietly, "you'd better put it back into storage. There's an insurance policy on the pearls that comes due in January. The name of the laundry and the maid's telephone number—all those things are in my desk. I hope you won't drink too much, Francis. I hope that nothing bad will happen to you. If you do get into serious trouble, you can call me."

"Oh my darling, I can't let you go!" Francis said. "I can't let you go, Julia!" He took her in his arms.

"I guess I'd better stay and take care of you for a little while longer," she said.

• • •

Riding to work in the morning, Francis saw the girl walk down the aisle of the coach. He was surprised; he hadn't realized that the school she went to was in the city, but she was carrying books, she seemed to be going to school. His surprise delayed his reaction, but then he got up clumsily and stepped into the aisle. Several people had come between them, but he could see her ahead of him, waiting for someone to open the car door, and then, as the train swerved, putting out her hand to support herself as she crossed the platform into the next car. He followed her through that car and halfway through another before calling her name—"Anne! Anne!"—but she didn't turn. He followed her into still another car, and she sat down in an aisle seat. Coming up to her, all his feelings warm and bent in her direction, he put his hand on the back of her seat—even this touch warmed him—and, leaning down to speak to her, he saw that it was not Anne. It was an older woman wearing glasses. He went on deliberately into another car, his face red with embarrassment and the much deeper feeling of having his good sense challenged;

for if he couldn't tell one person from another, what evidence was there that his life with Julia and the children had as much reality as his dreams of iniquity in Paris or the litter, the grass smell, and the cave-shaped trees in Lovers' Lane.

Late that afternoon, Julia called to remind Francis that they were going out for dinner. A few minutes later, Trace Bearden called. "Look, fellar," Trace said. "I'm calling for Mrs. Thomas. You know? Clayton, that boy of hers, doesn't seem able to get a job, and I wondered if you could help. If you'd call Charlie Bell—I know he's indebted to you—and say a good word for the kid, I think Charlie would—"

"Trace, I hate to say this," Francis said, "but I don't feel that I can do anything for that boy. The kid's worthless. I know it's a harsh thing to say, but it's a fact. Any kindness done for him would backfire in everybody's face. He's just a worthless kid, Trace, and there's nothing to be done about it. Even if we got him a job, he wouldn't be able to keep it for a week. I know that to be a fact. It's an awful thing, Trace, and I know it is, but instead of recommending that kid, I'd feel obliged to warn people against him—people who knew his father and would naturally want to step in and do something. I'd feel obliged to warn them. He's a thief . . ."

The moment this conversation was finished, Miss Rainey came in and stood by his desk. "I'm not going to be able to work for you any more, Mr. Weed," she said. "I can stay until the seventeenth if you need me, but I've been offered a whirlwind of a job, and I'd like to leave as soon as possible."

She went out, leaving him to face alone the wickedness of what he had done to the Thomas boy. His children in their photograph laughed and laughed, glazed with all the bright colors of summer, and he remembered that they had met a bagpiper on the beach that day and he had paid the piper a dollar to play them a battle song of the Black Watch. The girl would be at the house when he got home. He would spend another evening among his kind neighbors, picking and choosing dead-end streets, cart tracks, and the driveways of abandoned houses. There was nothing to mitigate his feeling—nothing that laughter or a game of softball with the children would change—and, thinking back over the plane crash, the Farquarsons' new maid, and Anne Murchison's difficulties with her drunken father, he wondered how he could have avoided arriving at just where he was. He was in trouble. He had been lost once in his life, coming back from a trout stream in the north woods, and he had now the same bleak realization that no amount of cheerfulness or hopefulness or valor or perseverance could help him find, in the gathering dark, the path that he'd lost. He smelled the forest. The feeling of bleakness was intolerable, and he saw clearly that he had reached the point where he would have to make a choice.

He could go to a psychiatrist, like Miss Rainey; he could go to church and confess his lusts; he could go to a Danish massage parlor in the West Seventies that had been recommended by a salesman; he could rape the girl or trust that he would somehow be prevented from doing this; or he could get drunk. It was his life, his boat, and, like every other man, he was made to be the father of thousands, and what harm could there be in a tryst that would make them both feel more kindly toward the world? This was the wrong train of thought, and he came back to the first, the psychiatrist. He had the telephone number of Miss Rainey's doctor, and he called and asked for an immediate appointment. He was insistent with the doctor's secretary—it was his manner in business—and when she said that the doctor's schedule was full for the next few weeks, Francis demanded an appointment that day and was told to come at five.

The psychiatrist's office was in a building that was used mostly by doctors and dentists, and the hallways were filled with the candy smell of mouthwash and memories of pain. Francis' character had been formed upon a series of private resolves—resolves about cleanliness, about going off the high diving board or repeating any other feat that challenged his courage, about punctuality, honesty, and virtue. To abdicate the perfect loneliness in which he had made his most vital decisions shattered his concept of character and left him now in a condition that felt like shock. He was stupefied. The scene for his *miserere mei Deus* was, like the waiting room of so many doctors' offices, a crude token gesture toward the sweets of domestic bliss: a place arranged with antiques, coffee tables, potted plants, and etchings of snow-covered bridges and geese in flight, although there were no children, no marriage bed, no stove, even, in this travesty of a house, where no one had ever spent the night and where the curtained windows looked straight onto a dark air shaft. Francis gave his name and address to a secretary and then saw, at the side of the room, a policeman moving toward him. "Hold it, hold it," the policeman said. "Don't move. Keep your hands where they are."

"I think it's all right, Officer," the secretary began. "I think it will be—"

"Let's make sure," the policeman said, and he began to slap Francis' clothes, looking for what—pistols, knives, an icepick? Finding nothing, he went off, and the secretary began a nervous apology: "When you called on the telephone, Mr. Weed, you seemed very excited, and one of the doctor's patients has been threatening his life, and we have to be careful. If you want to go in now?" Francis pushed open a door connected to an electrical chime, and in the doctor's lair sat down heavily, blew his nose into a handkerchief, searched in his pockets for cigarettes, for matches, for something, and said hoarsely, with tears in his eyes, "I'm in love, Dr. Herzog."

. . .

It is a week or ten days later in Shady Hill. The seven-fourteen has come and gone, and here and there dinner is finished and the dishes are in the dishwashing machine. The village hangs, morally and economically, from a thread; but it hangs by its thread in the evening light. Donald Goslin has begun to worry the *Moonlight* Sonata again. *Marcato ma sempre pianissimo!* He seems to be wringing out a wet bath towel, but the housemaid does not heed him. She is writing a letter to Arthur Godfrey. In the cellar of his house, Francis Weed is building a coffee table. Dr. Herzog recommended woodwork as a therapy, and Francis finds some true consolation in the simple arithmetic involved and in the holy smell of new wood. Francis is happy. Upstairs, little Toby is crying, because he is tired. He puts off his cowboy hat, gloves, and fringed jacket, unbuckles the belt studded with gold and rubies, the silver bullets and holsters, slips off his suspenders, his checked shirt, and Levis, and sits on the edge of his bed to pull off his high boots. Leaving this equipment in a heap, he goes to the closet and takes his space suit off a nail. It is a struggle for him to get into the long tights, but he succeeds. He loops the magic cape over his shoulders and, climbing onto the footboard of his bed, he spreads his arms and flies the short distance to the floor, landing with a thump that is audible to everyone in the house but himself.

"Go home, Gertrude, go home," Mrs. Masterson says. "I told you to go home an hour ago, Gertrude. It's way past your suppertime, and your mother will be worried. Go home!" A door on the Babcocks' terrace flies open, and out comes Mrs. Babcock without any clothes on, pursued by her naked husband. (Their children are away at boarding school, and their terrace is screened by a hedge.) Over the terrace they go and in at the kitchen door, as passionate and handsome a nymph and satyr as you will find on any wall in Venice. Cutting the last of the roses in her garden, Julia hears old Mr. Nixon shouting at the squirrels in his bird-feeding station. "Rapscallions! Varmits! Avaunt and quit my sight!" A miserable cat wanders into the garden, sunk in spiritual and physical discomfort. Tied to its head is a small straw hat—a doll's hat—and it is securely buttoned into a doll's dress, from the skirts of which protrudes its long, hairy tail. As it walks, it shakes its feet, as if it had fallen into water.

"Here, pussy, pussy, pussy!" Julia calls.

"Here, pussy, here, poor pussy!" But the cat gives her a skeptical look and stumbles away in its skirts. The last to come is Jupiter. He prances through the tomato vines, holding in his generous mouth the remains of an evening slipper. Then it is dark; it is a night where kings in golden suits ride elephants over the mountains.

November 20, 1954

THE HAPPIEST I'VE BEEN

John Updike

Neil Hovey came for me wearing a good suit. He parked his father's blue Chrysler on the dirt ramp by our barn and got out and stood by the open car door in a double-breasted tan gabardine suit, his hands in his pockets and his hair combed with water, squinting up at a lightning rod an old hurricane had knocked crooked. We were driving to Chicago, so I had packed my good clothes and dressed in worn-out slacks and an outgrown corduroy shirt. But Neil, though not my closest friend, was the one I had always been most relaxed with, so I wasn't very disturbed. My parents and I walked out from the house, across the low stretch of lawn that was mostly mud after the thaw that had come on Christmas Day, and my grandmother, though I had kissed her goodbye inside the house, came out onto the porch, stooped and rather angry-looking, her head haloed by wild old woman's white hair and the hand more severely afflicted by arthritis waggling at her breast in a worried way. It was growing dark, and my grandfather had gone to bed. "Nev-er trust the man who wears the red necktie and parts his hair in the middle" had been his final advice to me.

We had expected Neil since the middle of the afternoon. Nineteen almost twenty, I was a college sophomore home on vacation; that fall I had met in a fine-arts course a girl I had decided I loved, and she had invited me to the New Year's party her parents always gave and to stay at her house a few days. She lived in Chicago and so did Neil now, though he had gone to our high school. His father did something—sold steel was my impression, a huge man opening a briefcase and saying "The I-beams are very good this year"—that required him to be always on the move, so that at about thirteen Neil had been left with Mrs. Hovey's parents. They had lived in Olinger since the town was incorporated;

indeed, old Jesse Lancaster, whose sick larynx whistled when he breathed to us boys his shocking and uproarious thoughts on the girls that walked by his porch all day long, had twice been burgess. Meanwhile Neil's father got a stationary job, in Chicago, but he let Neil stay in Olinger until he finished high school. From Chicago to this part of Pennsylvania was a drive of seventeen hours. In the twenty months Neil had been gone, he had come east fairly often; he loved driving, and Olinger was the one thing he had that was close to a childhood home. In Chicago he was working in a garage and getting his teeth straightened by the Army so they could draft him. The Korean War was on. He had to go back, and I wanted to go to Chicago, so it was a happy arrangement. "You're all dressed up," I accused him immediately.

"I've been saying goodbye."

The knot of his necktie was low and the corners of his mouth were rubbed with pink. Years later my mother recalled how that evening his breath stank so strongly of beer she was frightened to let me go with him. "*Your* grandfather always thought *his* grandfather was a very dubious character," she said.

My father and Neil put my suitcases into the trunk; they contained all the clothes I had brought with me from school, for the girl and I were going back to college on the train together, and I would not see my home again until spring.

"Well, goodbye, boys," my mother said. "I think you're both very brave." In regard to me she meant the girl as much as the roads.

"Don't you worry, Mrs. Nordholm," Neil told her quickly. "He'll be safer than in his own bed. I bet he sleeps from here to Indiana." He looked at me with an irritating imitation of her own fond gaze. When they shook hands goodbye it was with an equality established on the base of my helplessness. His being so slick startled me, but you can have a friend for years and never see how he operates with adults.

I embraced my mother and over her shoulder with the camera of my head tried to take a snapshot I could keep of the house, the woods behind it and the sunset behind them, the bench beneath the walnut tree where my grandfather cut apples into skinless bits and fed them to himself, and the ruts the bakery truck had made in the soft lawn that morning.

We started down the half mile of dirt road to the highway that, one way, went through Olinger to the city of Alton and, the other way, led through farmland to the Turnpike. It was luxurious after the stress of farewell to finger a cigarette out of the pack squaring my shirt pocket. My family knew I smoked but I didn't do it in front of them; we were all too sensitive to bear the awkwardness. I lit mine and held the match for Hovey. It was a relaxed friendship. We were about the same height and had the same degree of athletic incompetence and the same curious lack of whatever force it was that aroused loyalty and compliance in beautiful girls. There was his bad teeth and my skin allergy; these were being remedied now, when they mattered less. But it seemed to me that the most important thing—about both our friendship and our failures to become, for all the love we felt for women, actual lovers—was that he and I lived with grandparents. This improved both our backward and forward vistas; we knew about the midnight coughing fits and bedside commodes that awaited most men, and we had a sense of childhoods before 1900, when the farmer ruled the land and America faced west. We had gained a humane dimension that made us gentle and humorous among peers but diffident at dances and hesitant in cars. Girls hate boys' doubts; they amount to insults. Gentleness is for married women to appreciate. (This is my thinking then.) A girl who has received out of nowhere a gift worth all Africa's ivory and Asia's gold wants more than just humanity to bestow it on.

When he came to the highway Neil turned right, toward Olinger, instead of left, toward the Turnpike. My reaction was to twist and assure myself through the rear window that, though a pink triangle of sandstone stared through the bare treetops, nobody at my house could possibly see.

When he was again in third gear, Neil asked, "Are you in a hurry?"

"No. Not especially."

"Schuman's having his New Year's party two days early so we can go. I thought we'd go for a couple hours and miss the Friday-night stuff on the Pike." His mouth moved and closed carefully over the dull, silver, painful braces.

"Sure," I said. "I don't care." In everything that followed there was this sensation of my being picked up and carried somewhere.

• • •

It was four miles from the farm to Olinger; we entered by Buchanan Road, driving past the tall white brick house I had lived in until I was fifteen. My grandfather had bought it before I was born and his stocks went bad, which had happened in the same year. The new owners had strung colored bulbs all along the front doorframe and the edges of the porch roof. Downtown the cardboard Santa Claus still nodded in the drugstore window, but the loudspeaker on the undertaker's lawn had stopped broadcasting carols. It was quite dark now, so the arches of red and green lights above Grand Avenue seemed miracles of lift; in daylight you saw the bulbs were just hung from a straight cable by cords of different lengths. Larry Schuman lived on the other side of town, the newer side. Lights ran all the way up the front edges of his house and across the rain gutter. The next-door neighbor had a plywood reindeer-and-sleigh floodlit on his front lawn and a snowman of papier-mâché leaning tipsily (his eyes were x's) against the corner of the house. No real snow had fallen yet that winter. The air this evening, though, hinted that harder weather was coming.

The Schumans' living room felt warm. In one corner a blue spruce drenched with tinsel reached to the ceiling; around its pot surged a drift of wrapping paper and ribbon and boxes, a few still containing presents—gloves and diaries and other small properties that hadn't yet been absorbed into the main stream of affluence. The ornamental balls were big as baseballs and all either crimson or indigo; the tree was so well dressed I felt self-conscious in the same room with it, without a coat or tie and wearing an old green shirt too short in the sleeves. Everyone else was dressed for a party. Then Mr. Schuman stamped in comfortingly, crushing us all into one underneath his welcome—Neil and me and the three other boys who had shown up so far. He was dressed to go out on the town, in a vanilla topcoat and silvery silk muffler, and smoking a cigar with the band still on. You could see, in Mr. Schuman, where Larry got the red hair and pale eyelashes and the self-confidence, but what in the son was smirking and pushy was in the father shrewd and masterful. What the one used to make you nervous the other used to put you at ease. While Mr. was jollying us, Zoe Loessner, Larry's probable fiancée and the only girl at the party so far, was talking nicely to Mrs., nodding with her entire neck and fingering her Kresge pearls and blowing cigarette smoke through the corners of her mouth, to keep it away from the middle-aged woman's face. Each time Zoe spat out a plume, the shelf of blond hair overhanging her temple lifted slightly, so emphatic was her politeness. Mrs. Schuman beamed serenely above her fur coat and rhinestone pocketbook. It was odd to see her dressed in the trappings of the prosperity which usually supported her good nature invisibly, like a firm mattress under a homely bright quilt. She was a prime product of the country, a Pennsylvania Dutch woman, who loved feeding her sons, and imagined that the entire world, like her life, was going well. I never saw her not smile, except at her husband. At last she moved him into the outdoors. He turned at the threshold and did a trick with his knees and called in to us, "Be good and if you can't be good, be careful."

With them out of the way, the next item was getting liquor. It was a familiar business. Did anybody have a forged driver's license? If not, who would dare to make one? Larry could provide India ink. Then again, Larry's older brother Dale might be home and would go if it didn't take too much time. However, on weekends he often went straight from work to his fiancée's apartment and stayed until Sunday. If worst came to worst, Larry knew an illegal place in Alton, but they really soaked you. The problem was solved strangely. More people were arriving all the time, and one of them, Cookie Behn, who had been held back one year and hence was deposited in our grade, announced that last November he had become in honest fact twenty-one. I, at least, gave Cookie my share of the money feeling a little queasy, vice had become so handy.

The party was the party I had been going to all my life, beginning with Ann Mahlon's first Halloween party, that I attended as a hot, lumbering, breathless, and blind Donald Duck. My mother had made the costume, and the eyes kept slipping, and were farther apart than my eyes, so that even when the clouds of gauze parted, it was to reveal the frustrating depthless world seen with one eye. Ann, who because her mother loved her so much as a child had remained somewhat childish, and I and another boy and girl who were not involved in any romantic crisis went down into the Schumans' basement to play circular ping-pong. Armed with paddles, we stood each at a side of the table and when the ball was stroked ran around it counterclockwise, slapping the ball and laughing. To run better the girls took off their high-heeled shoes and ruined their stockings on the cement floor. Their faces and arms and shoulder sections became flushed, and when either of the girls lunged forward toward the net the stiff neckline of her semi-formal dress dropped away and the white cups of her brassière could be glimpsed holding in fat, and when one of them reached high her shaved armpit gleamed like a bit of chicken skin. An earring of Ann's flew off and the two connected rhinestones skidded to lie near the wall, among the Schumans' power mower and badminton poles and empty bronze motor-oil cans twice punctured by triangles. All these images were immediately lost in the whirl of our running; we were dizzy before we stopped. Ann leaned on me getting back into her shoes.

When we pushed the cellar door open it banged against the newel post of the carpeted stairs going to the second floor; a third of the way up, a couple sat discussing. The girl, Jacky Iselin, cried without emotion—the tears and nothing else, like water flowing over wood. Some people were in the kitchen, mixing drinks and making noise. In the living room others danced to records: 78s then—stiff discs stacked in a ponderous leaning cylinder on the spindle of the Schumans' console. Every three minutes, with a click and a crash, another dropped and the mood abruptly changed. One moment it would be "Stay As Sweet As You Are": Clarence Lang with the absolute expression of an idiot standing and rocking monotonously with June Kaufmann's boneless sad brown hand trapped in his and their faces, staring in the same direction, pasted together like the facets of an idol. The music stopped; when they parted, a big squarish dark patch stained the cheek of each. Then the next moment it would be Goodman's "Loch Lomond" or "Cherokee" and nobody but Margaret Lento wanted to jitterbug. Mad, she danced by herself, swinging her head recklessly and snapping her backside; a corner of her skirt flipped a Christmas ball onto the rug, where it collapsed into a hundred convex reflectors. Female shoes were scattered in innocent pairs about the room. Some were flats, resting under the sofa shyly toed in; others were high heels lying askew, the spike of one thrust into its mate. Sitting alone and ignored in a great armchair, I experienced within a warm keen dishevelment, as if there were real tears in my eyes. Had things been less unchanged, they would have seemed less tragic. But the girls who had stepped out of these shoes were, with few exceptions, the ones who had attended my life's party. The alterations were so small: a haircut, an engagement ring, a tendency toward plumpness more frankly confessed. While they wheeled above me I sometimes caught from their faces an unfamiliar glint, off of a hardness I did not remember, as if beneath their skins these girls were growing more dense. The brutality added to the features of the boys I knew seemed a more willed effect, more desired and so less grievous. Considering that there was a war, surprisingly many were present—4-F or at college or simply waiting to be called. Shortly before midnight the door rattled, and there, under the porch light, looking forlorn and chilled in their brief athletic jackets, stood three members of the class ahead of ours who in the old days always tried to crash

Schuman's parties. At Olinger High they had been sports stars, and they still stood with that well-coordinated looseness, a look of dangling from strings. The three of them had enrolled together at Melanchthon, a small Lutheran college on the edge of Alton, and in this season played on the Melanchthon basketball team. That is, two did; the third hadn't been good enough. Schuman, out of cowardice more than mercy, let them in, and they hid immediately in the basement, and didn't bother us, having brought their own bottle.

There was one novel awkwardness. Darryl Bechtel had married Emmy Johnson, and the couple came. Darryl had worked in his father's greenhouse and had been considered dull; it was Emmy that we knew. At first no one danced with her, and Darryl didn't know how, but then Schuman, perhaps as host, dared. Others followed, but Schuman had her in his arms most often, and at midnight, when we were pretending the new year began, he kissed her; a wave of kissing swept the room now, and everyone struggled to kiss Emmy. Even I did. There was something about her being married that made it extraordinary. Her cheeks burning, she kept glancing around for rescue, but Darryl, embarrassed to see his wife dance, had gone into old man Schuman's den, where Neil sat brooding, sunk in mysterious sorrow.

When the kissing subsided and Darryl emerged, I went in to see Neil. He was holding his face in his hands and tapping his foot to a record playing on Mr. Schuman's private phonograph: Krupa's "Dark Eyes." The arrangement was droning and circular and Neil had kept the record going for hours. He loved saxophones; most of us children of that depression vintage did. I asked him, "Do you think the traffic on the Turnpike has died down by now?"

He took down the tall glass on the cabinet beside him and took a studied swallow. From the side, his face seemed lean and somewhat blue. "Maybe," he said, staring at the ice cubes submerged in the ochre liquid. "The girl in Chicago's expecting you?"

"Well, yeah, but we can call and let her know, once *we* know."

"You think she'll spoil?"

"How do you mean?"

"I mean, won't you be seeing her all the time after we get there? Aren't you going to marry her?"

"I have no idea. I might."

"Well then you'll have the rest of Kingdom Come to see her." He looked directly at me, and it was plain in the blur of his eyes that he was sick-drunk. "The trouble with you guys that have all the luck," he said slowly, "is that you don't give a damn about us that don't have any." Such melodramatic rudeness, coming from Neil, surprised me, as had his blarney with my mother hours before. In trying to evade his steady, wounded stare, I discovered there was another person in the room: a girl sitting with her shoes on, reading *Holiday*. Though she held the magazine in front of her face, I knew from the gaudy air of her clothes and from her unfamiliar legs that she was the girl friend Margaret Lento had brought.

Margaret didn't come from Olinger but from Riverside, a section of Alton. She had met Larry Schuman at a summer job in a restaurant, and for the rest of high school they had more or less gone together. Since then, though, it had dawned on Mr. and Mrs. Schuman that even in a democracy distinctions exist: probably welcome news to Larry. In the cruelest and most prolonged way he could manage, he had been breaking off with her throughout the year now nearly ended. I had been surprised to find her at this party. Obviously she had felt shaky about attending and had brought the friend as the only kind of protection she could afford. The other girl was acting just like a guard.

There being no answer to Neil, I went into the living room, where Margaret, insanely drunk, was throwing herself around as if wanting to break a bone. Somewhat in time to the music she would run a few steps, then snap her body like a whip, her chin striking her chest and her hands flying backward, fingers fanned, as her shoulders pitched forward. In her state her body was childishly plastic; unharmed, she would bounce back from this jolt and begin to clap and kick and hum. Schuman stayed away from her. Margaret was small, not more than five three, with the smallness ripeness comes to early. She had bleached a section of her black hair platinum, cropped her head all over, and trained the stubble into short hyacinthine curls like those on antique statues of boys. Her face seemed quite coarse from the front, so her profile was classical unexpectedly. She might have been Portia. When she was not putting on her savage, pointless dance, she was in the bathroom being sick. The pity and the vulgarity of her exhibition made everyone who was sober uncomfortable; our common guilt in witnessing this girl's rites brought us so close together in that room that it seemed never, not in all time, could we be parted. I myself was perfectly sober. I had the impression people only drank to stop being unhappy and I nearly always felt at least fairly happy.

Luckily, Margaret was in a sick phase around one o'clock, when the elder Schumans came home. They looked in at us briefly. It was a pleasant joke to see in their smiles that, however corrupt and unwinking we felt, to them we looked young and sleepy: Larry's friends. Things quieted after they went up the stairs. In half an hour, people began coming out of the kitchen balancing cups of coffee. By two o'clock, four girls stood in aprons at Mrs. Schuman's sink, and others were padding back and forth carrying glasses and ashtrays. Another blameless racket pierced the clatter in the kitchen. Out on the cold grass the three Melanchthon athletes had set up the badminton net and in the faint glow given off by the house were playing. The bird, ascending and descending through uneven bars of light, glimmered like a firefly. Now that the party was dying, Neil's apathy seemed deliberately exasperating, even vindictive. For at least another hour, he persisted in hearing "Dark Eyes" over and over again, holding his head and tapping his foot. The entire scene in the den had developed a fixity that was uncanny; the girl remained in the chair and read magazines, *Holiday* and *Esquire,* one after another. In the meantime, cars came and went and raced their motors out front; Schuman took Ann Mahlon home and didn't come back; and the athletes carried the neighbor's artificial snowman into the center of the street and disappeared. Somehow in the arrangements shuffled together at the end, Neil had agreed to take Margaret and the other girl home. Margaret convalesced in the downstairs bathroom for most of that hour. I unlocked a little glass bookcase ornamenting a desk in the dark dining room and removed a volume of Thackeray's Works. It turned out to be Volume II of *Henry Esmond.* I began it, rather than break another book out of the set, which had been squeezed in there so long the bindings had sort of interpenetrated.

Esmond was going off to war again when Neil appeared in the archway and said, "O.K., Norseman. Let's go to Chicago." "Norseman" was a variant of my name he used only when he was feeling special affection.

We turned off all the lamps and left the hall bulb burning against Larry's return. Margaret Lento seemed chastened. Neil gave her his arm and helped her into the back seat of his father's car; I stood aside to let the other girl get in with her, but Neil indicated that I should. I supposed he realized this left only the mute den-girl to go up front with him. She sat well over on her side, was all I noticed. Neil backed into the street and with unusual care steered past the snowman. Our headlights made vivid the fact that the snowman's back was a hollow right-angled gash; he had been built up against the corner of the house.

• • •

From Olinger, Riverside was diagonally across Alton. The city was sleeping as we drove through it. Most of the stop lights were blinking green. Among cities Alton had a bad reputation; its graft and gambling and easy juries and bawdyhouses were supposedly notorious throughout the Middle Atlantic states. But to me it always presented an innocent face: row after row of houses built of a local dusty-red brick, the color of flowerpots, each house fortified with a tiny, intimate, balustraded porch, and nothing but the wealth of movie houses and beer signs along its main street to suggest that its citizens loved pleasure more than the run of mankind. Indeed, as we moved at moderate speed down these hushed streets bordered with parked cars, a limestone church bulking at every corner and the hooded street lamps keeping watch from above, Alton seemed less the ultimate center of an urban region than itself a suburb of some vast mythical metropolis, like Pandemonium or Paradise. I was conscious of evergreen wreaths on door after door and of fanlights of stained glass in which the house number was embedded. I was also conscious that every block was one block farther from the Turnpike.

Riverside, fitted into the bends of the Schuylkill, was not so regularly laid out. Margaret's house was one of a short row, composition-shingled, which we approached from the rear, down a tiny cement alley speckled with drains. The porches were a few inches higher than the narrow pavement. Margaret asked us if we wanted to come in for a cup of coffee, since we were going to Chicago; Neil accepted by getting out of the car and slamming his door. The noise filled the alley, alarming me. I wondered at the easy social life that evidently existed among my friends at three-thirty in the morning. Margaret did, however, lead us in stealthily, and she turned on only the kitchen switch. The kitchen was divided from the living room by a large sofa, which faced into littered gloom where distant light from beyond the alley spilled over a window sill and across the spines of a radiator. In one corner the glass of a television set showed; the screen would seem absurdly small now, but then it seemed disproportionately elegant. The shabbiness everywhere would not have struck me so much if I hadn't just come from Schuman's place. Neil and the other girl sat on the sofa; Margaret held a match to a gas burner and, as the blue flame licked an old kettle, doled instant coffee into four flowered cups.

By the kitchen's solitary window, overlooking a drab Alton street, someone who had once lived in this house had built a breakfast nook like a luncheonette booth, a yellow table between two high-backed benches. I sat in it and read all the words I could see: "Salt," "Pepper," "Have Some LUMPS," "December," "Mohn's Milk Inc.—A Very Merry Christmas and Joyous New Year—Mohn's Milk is *Safe* Milk—'Mommy, Make It Mohn's!,'" "Matches," "Hotpoint," "PRESS," "Magee Stove FEDERAL & Furnace Corp.," "God Is in This House," "Ave Maria Gratia Plena," "SHREDDED WHEAT Benefits—Exciting New Pattern KUNGSHOLM." After serving the two on the sofa, Margaret came to me with coffee and sat down opposite me in the booth. Fatigue had raised two blue welts beneath her eyes.

"Well," I asked her, "did you have a good time?"

She smiled and glanced down and made the small sound "Ch," vestigial of "Jesus." With absent-minded delicacy she stirred her coffee, lifting and replacing the spoon without a ripple.

"Rather odd at the end," I said. "Not even the host there."

"He took Ann Mahlon home."

"I know." I was surprised that she did, having been sick in the bathroom for that hour.

"You sound jealous," she added.

"Who does? I do? I don't."

"You like her, John, don't you?" Her using my first name and the quality of the question did not, though we had really—not counting parties—just met, seem forward, considering the hour and that she had brought me coffee. There is little further to go with a girl who has brought you coffee.

"Oh, I like everybody," I told her, "and the longer I've known them the more I like them, because the more they're me. The only people I like better are ones I've just met. Now Ann Mahlon I've known since kindergarten. Every day her mother used to bring her to the edge of the schoolyard for months after all the other mothers had stopped." I wanted to cut a figure in Margaret's eyes, but they were too dark. Stoically she had got on top of her weariness, but it was growing bigger under her.

"Did you like her then?"

"I felt sorry for her being embarrassed by her mother."

She asked me, "What was Larry like when he was little?"

"Oh, bright. Kind of mean."

"Was he mean?"

"I'd say so. Yes. In some grade or other he and I began to play chess together. I always won until secretly he took lessons from a man his parents knew and read strategy books."

Margaret laughed, genuinely pleased. "Then did he win?"

"Once. After that I really tried, and after *that* he decided chess was kid stuff. Besides, he'd used me up. He'd have these runs on people where you'd be down at his house every afternoon, then in a couple months he'd get a new pet and that'd be that."

"He's funny," she said. "He has a kind of cold mind. He decides on what he wants, then he does what he has to do, you know, and nothing anybody says can change him."

"He does tend to get what he wants," I told her guardedly, realizing that to her this meant her. Poor bruised little girl, in her mind he was all the time cleaving with rare cunning through his parents' objections straight to her.

My coffee was nearly gone, so I glanced toward the sofa in the other room. Neil and the girl had sunk out of sight behind its back. Before this it had honestly not occurred to me that they had a relationship, but now that I saw, it seemed plausible, and, at this time of night, good news, though it meant we would not be going to Chicago quite yet.

So I talked to Margaret about Larry, and she responded, showing really quite an acute sense of him. To me, considering the personality of a childhood friend so seriously, as if overnight he had become a factor in the world, seemed absurd; I couldn't even deeply believe that in her world he mattered much. Larry Schuman, in little more than a year, had become nothing to me. The important thing, rather than the subject, was the conversation itself, the quick agreements, the slow nods, the weave of different memories; it was like one of those Panama baskets shaped underwater around a worthless stone.

She offered me more coffee. When she returned with it, she sat down not opposite but beside me, lifting me to such a pitch of gratitude and affection that the only way I could think to express it was by *not* kissing her, as if a kiss were another piece of abuse women suffered. She said, "Cold. Cheap bastard turns the thermostat down to sixty," meaning her father. She drew my arm around her shoulders and folded my hand about her bare forearm, to warm it. The back of my thumb fitted against the curve of one breast. Her head went into the hollow where my arm and chest joined; she was terribly small, measured against your own body. Perhaps she weighed a hundred pounds. Her lids lowered and I kissed her two beautiful eyebrows and then the spaces of skin between the rough curls, some black and some bleached, that fringed her forehead. Other than this I tried to keep as still as a bed would be. It *had* grown cold. A shiver starting on the side away from her would twitch my shoulders when I tried to repress it; she would frown and unconsciously draw my arm tighter. No one had switched the kitchen light off. On Margaret's foreshortened upper lip there seemed to be two pencil marks; the length of wrist my badly fitting sleeve exposed looked pale and naked against the spiralling down of the smaller arm held beneath it.

Outside on the street the house faced there was no motion. Only once did a car go by—around five o'clock, with twin mufflers, the radio on, and a boy yelling. Neil and the girl murmured together incessantly; some of what they said I could overhear.

"No. Which?" she asked.

"I don't care."

"Wouldn't you want a boy?"

"I'd be happy whatever I got."

"I know, but which would you *rather* have? Don't men want boys?"

"I don't care. You."

Somewhat later, Mohn's truck passed on the other side of the street. The milkman, well bundled, sat behind headlights in a warm orange volume the size of a phone booth, steering one-handed and smoking a cigar that he set on the edge of the dashboard when, his wire carrier vibrant, he ran out of the truck with bottles. His passing led Neil to decide the time had come. Margaret woke up frightened of her father; we hissed our farewells and thanks to her quickly. Neil dropped the other girl off at her house a few blocks away; he knew where it was. Sometime during that night I must have seen this girl's face, but I have no memory of it. She is always behind a magazine or in the dark or with her back turned. Neil married her years later, I know, but after we arrived in Chicago I never saw him again, either.

• • •

Red dawn light touched the clouds above the black slate roofs as, with a few other cars, we drove through Alton. The moon-sized clock of a beer billboard said ten after six. Olinger was deathly still. The air brightened as we moved along the highway; the glowing wall of my home hung above the woods as we rounded the long curve by the Mennonite dairy. With a .22 I could have had a pane of my parents' bedroom window, and they were dreaming I was in Indiana. My grandfather would be up, stamping around in the kitchen for my grandmother to make him breakfast, or outside walking to see if any ice had formed on the brook. For an instant I genuinely feared he might hail me from the peak of the barn roof. Then trees interceded and we were safe in a landscape where no one cared.

At the entrance to the Turnpike Neil did a strange thing; he stopped the car and had me take the wheel. He had never trusted me to drive his father's car before; he had believed my not knowing where the crankshaft or fuel pump was handicapped my competence to steer. But now he was quite complacent. He hunched under an old mackinaw and leaned his head against the metal of the window frame and soon was asleep. We crossed the Susquehanna on a long smooth bridge below Harrisburg, then began climbing toward the Alleghenies. In the mountains there was snow, a dry dusting like sand that waved back and forth on the road surface. Farther along, there had been a fresh fall that night, about two inches, and the plows had not yet cleared all the lanes. I was passing a Sunoco truck on a high curve when without warning the scraped section gave out and I realized I might skid into the fence, if not over the edge. The radio was singing "Carpets of clover, I'll lay right at your feet," and the speedometer said 81. Nothing happened; the car stayed firm in the snow, and Neil slept through the danger, his face turned skyward and his breath struggling in his nose. It was the first time I heard a contemporary of mine snore.

When we came into tunnel country, the flicker and hollow amplification stirred Neil awake. He sat up, the mackinaw dropping to his lap, and lit a cigarette. A second after the scratch of his match the moment occurred of which each following moment was a slight diminution, as we made the long irregular descent toward Pittsburgh. There were many reasons for my feeling so happy. We were on our way. I had seen a dawn. This far, Neil could appreciate, I had brought us safely. Ahead, a girl waited who, if I asked, would marry me, but first there was a long trip; many hours and towns interceded between me and that encounter. There was the quality of the 10 A.M. sunlight as it existed in the air ahead of the windshield, filtered by the thin overcast, blessing irresponsibility—you felt you could slice forever through such a cool pure element—and springing, by implying how high these hills had become, a widespreading pride: Pennsylvania, your state—as if you had made your life. And there was knowing that twice since midnight a person had trusted me enough to fall asleep beside me.

January 3, 1959

DEFENDER OF THE FAITH

Philip Roth

In May of 1945, only a few weeks after the fighting had ended in Europe, I was rotated back to the States, where I spent the remainder of the war with a training company at Camp Crowder, Missouri. Along with the rest of the Ninth Army, I had been racing across Germany so swiftly during the late winter and spring that when I boarded the plane, I couldn't believe its destination lay to the west. My mind might inform me otherwise, but there was an inertia of the spirit that told me we were flying to a new front, where we would disembark and continue our push eastward—eastward until we'd circled the globe, marching through villages along whose twisting, cobbled streets crowds of the enemy would watch us take possession of what, up till then, they'd considered their own. I had changed enough in two years not to mind the trembling of the old people, the crying of the very young, the uncertainty and fear in the eyes of the once arrogant. I had been fortunate enough to develop an infantryman's heart, which, like his feet, at first aches and swells but finally grows horny enough for him to travel the weirdest paths without feeling a thing.

Captain Paul Barrett was my C.O. in Camp Crowder. The day I reported for duty, he came out of his office to shake my hand. He was short, gruff, and fiery, and—indoors or out—he wore his polished helmet liner pulled down to his little eyes. In Europe, he had received a battlefield commission and a serious chest wound, and he'd been returned to the States only a few months before. He spoke easily to me, and at the evening formation he introduced me to the troops. "Gentlemen," he said, "Sergeant Thurston, as you know, is no longer with this company. Your new first sergeant is Sergeant Nathan Marx, here. He is a veteran of the European theatre, and consequently will expect to find a company of soldiers here, and not a company of *boys*."

I sat up late in the orderly room that evening, trying halfheartedly to solve the riddle of duty rosters, personnel forms, and morning reports. The Charge of Quarters slept with his mouth open on a mattress on the floor. A trainee stood reading the next day's duty roster, which was posted on the bulletin board just inside the screen door. It was a warm evening, and I could hear radios playing dance music over in the barracks. The trainee, who had been staring at me whenever he thought I wouldn't notice, finally took a step in my direction.

"Hey, Sarge—we having a G.I. party tomorrow night?" he asked. A G.I. party is a barracks cleaning.

"You usually have them on Friday nights?" I asked him.

"Yes," he said, and then he added, mysteriously, "That's the whole thing."

"Then you'll have a G.I. party."

He turned away, and I heard him mumbling. His shoulders were moving, and I wondered if he was crying.

"What's your name, soldier?" I asked.

He turned, not crying at all. Instead, his green-speckled eyes, long and narrow, flashed like fish in the sun. He walked over to me and sat on the edge of my desk. He reached out a hand. "Sheldon," he said.

"Stand on your feet, Sheldon."

Getting off the desk, he said, "Sheldon Grossbart." He smiled at the familiarity into which he'd led me.

"You against cleaning the barracks Friday night, Grossbart?" I said. "Maybe we shouldn't have G.I. parties. Maybe we should get a maid." My tone startled me. I felt I sounded like every top sergeant I had ever known.

"No, Sergeant." He grew serious, but with a seriousness that seemed to be only the stifling of a smile. "It's just— G.I. parties on Friday night, of all nights."

He slipped up onto the corner of the desk again—not quite sitting, but not quite standing, either. He looked at me with those speckled eyes flashing, and then made a gesture with his hand. It was very slight—no more than a movement back and forth of the wrist—and yet it managed to exclude from our affairs everything else in the orderly room, to make the two of us the center of the world. It seemed, in fact, to exclude everything even about the two of us except our hearts.

"Sergeant Thurston was one thing," he whispered, glancing at the sleeping C.Q., "but we thought that with you here things might be a little different."

"We?"

"The Jewish personnel."

"Why?" I asked, harshly. "What's on your mind?" Whether I was still angry at the "Sheldon" business, or now at something else, I hadn't time to tell, but clearly I was angry.

"We thought you— Marx, you know, like Karl Marx. The Marx Brothers. Those guys are all— M-a-r-x. Isn't that how *you* spell it, Sergeant?"

"M-a-r-x."

"Fishbein said—" He stopped. "What I mean to say, Sergeant—" His face and neck were red, and his mouth moved but no words came out. In a moment, he raised himself to attention, gazing down at me. It was as though he had suddenly decided he could expect no more sympathy from me than from Thurston, the reason being that I was of Thurston's faith, and not his. The young man had managed to confuse himself as to what my faith really was, but I felt no desire to straighten him out. Very simply, I didn't like him.

When I did nothing but return his gaze, he spoke, in an altered tone. "You see, Sergeant," he explained to me, "Friday nights, Jews are supposed to go to services."

"Did Sergeant Thurston tell you you couldn't go to them when there was a G.I. party?"

"No."

"Did he say you had to stay and scrub the floors?"

"No, Sergeant."

"Did the Captain say you had to stay and scrub the floors?"

"That isn't it, Sergeant. It's the other guys in the barracks." He leaned toward me. "They think we're goofing off. But we're not. That's when Jews go to services, Friday night. We have to."

"Then go."

"But the other guys make accusations. They have no right."

"That's not the Army's problem, Grossbart. It's a personal problem you'll have to work out yourself."

"But it's un*fair*."

I got up to leave. "There's nothing I can do about it," I said.

Grossbart stiffened and stood in front of me. "But this is a matter of *religion*, sir."

"Sergeant," I said.

"I mean 'Sergeant,'" he said, almost snarling.

"Look, go see the chaplain. You want to see Captain Barrett, I'll arrange an appointment."

"No, no. I don't want to make trouble, Sergeant. That's the first thing they throw up to you. I just want my rights!"

"Damn it, Grossbart, stop whining. You have your rights. You can stay and scrub floors or you can go to shul—"

The smile swam in again. Spittle gleamed at the corners of his mouth. "You mean church, Sergeant."

"I mean shul, Grossbart!"

I walked past him and went outside. Near me, I heard the scrunching of a guard's boots on gravel. Beyond the lighted windows of the barracks, young men in T shirts and fatigue pants were sitting on their bunks, polishing their rifles. Suddenly there was a light rustling behind me. I turned and saw Grossbart's dark frame fleeing back to the barracks, racing to tell his Jewish friends that they were right—that, like Karl and Harpo, I was one of them.

• • •

The next morning, while chatting with Captain Barrett, I recounted the incident of the previous evening. Somehow, in the telling, it must have seemed to the Captain that I was not so much explaining Grossbart's position as defending it. "Marx, I'd fight side by side with a nigger if the fella proved to me he was a man. I pride myself," he said, looking out the window, "that I've got an open mind. Consequently, Sergeant, nobody gets special treatment here, for the good *or* the bad. All a man's got to do is prove himself. A man fires well on the range, I give him a weekend pass. He scores high in P.T., he gets a weekend pass. He *earns* it." He turned from the window and pointed a finger at me. "You're a Jewish fella, am I right, Marx?"

"Yes, sir."

"And I admire you. I admire you because of the ribbons on your chest. I judge a man by what he shows me on the field of battle, Sergeant. It's what he's got *here*," he said, and then, though I expected he would point to his heart, he jerked a thumb toward the buttons straining to hold his blouse across his belly. "Guts," he said.

"O.K., sir. I only wanted to pass on to you how the men felt."

"Mr. Marx, you're going to be old before your time if you worry about how the men feel. Leave that stuff to the chaplain—that's his business, not yours. Let's us train these fellas to shoot straight. If the Jewish personnel feels the other men are accusing them of goldbricking—well, I just don't know. Seems awful funny that suddenly the Lord is calling so loud in Private Grossman's ear he's just got to run to church."

"Synagogue," I said.

"Synagogue is right, Sergeant. I'll write that down for handy reference. Thank you for stopping by."

That evening, a few minutes before the company gathered outside the orderly room for the chow formation, I called the C.Q., Corporal Robert LaHill, in to see me. LaHill was a dark, burly fellow whose hair curled out of his clothes wherever it could. He had a glaze in his eyes that made one think of caves and dinosaurs. "LaHill," I said, "when you take the formation, remind the men that they're free to attend church services *whenever* they are held, provided they report to the orderly room before they leave the area."

LaHill scratched his wrist, but gave no indication that he'd heard or understood.

"LaHill," I said, "*church*. You remember? Church, priest, Mass, confession."

He curled one lip into a kind of smile; I took it for a signal that for a second he had flickered back up into the human race.

"Jewish personnel who want to attend services this evening are to fall out in front of the orderly room at 1900," I said. Then, as an afterthought, I added, "By order of Captain Barrett."

A little while later, as the day's last light—softer than any I had seen that year—began to drop over Camp Crowder, I heard LaHill's thick, inflectionless voice outside my window: "Give me your ears, troopers. Toppie says for me to tell you that at 1900 hours all Jewish personnel is to fall out in front, here, if they want to attend the Jewish Mass."

. . .

At seven o'clock, I looked out the orderly-room window and saw three soldiers in starched khakis standing on the dusty quadrangle. They looked at their watches and fidgeted while they whispered back and forth. It was getting dimmer, and, alone on the otherwise deserted field, they looked tiny. When I opened the door, I heard the noises of the G.I. party coming from the surrounding barracks—bunks being pushed to the walls, faucets pounding water into buckets, brooms whisking at the wooden floors, cleaning the dirt away for Saturday's inspection. Big puffs of cloth moved round and round on the windowpanes. I walked outside, and the moment my foot hit the ground I thought I heard Grossbart call to the others, "'Ten-*hut*!" Or maybe, when they all three jumped to attention, I imagined I heard the command.

Grossbart stepped forward. "Thank you, sir," he said.

"'Sergeant,' Grossbart," I reminded him. "You call officers 'sir.' I'm not an officer. You've been in the Army three weeks—you know that."

He turned his palms out at his sides to indicate that, in truth, he and I lived beyond convention. "Thank you, anyway," he said.

"Yes," a tall boy behind him said. "Thanks a lot."

And the third boy whispered, "Thank you," but his mouth barely fluttered, so that he did not alter by more than a lip's movement his posture of attention.

"For what?" I asked.

Grossbart snorted happily. "For the announcement. The Corporal's announcement. It helped. It made it—"

"Fancier." The tall boy finished Grossbart's sentence.

Grossbart smiled. "He means formal, sir. Public," he said to me. "Now it won't seem as though we're just taking off—goldbricking because the work has begun."

"It was by order of Captain Barrett," I said.

"Aaah, but you pull a little weight," Grossbart said. "So we thank you." Then he turned to his companions. "Sergeant Marx, I want you to meet Larry Fishbein."

The tall boy stepped forward and extended his hand. I shook it. "You from New York?" he asked.

"Yes."

"Me, too." He had a cadaverous face that collapsed inward from his cheekbone to his jaw, and when he smiled—as he did at the news of our communal attachment—revealed a mouthful of bad teeth. He was blinking his eyes a good deal, as though he were fighting back tears. "What borough?" he asked.

I turned to Grossbart. "It's five after seven. What time are services?"

"Shul," he said, smiling, "is in ten minutes. I want you to meet Mickey Halpern. This is Nathan Marx, our sergeant."

The third boy hopped forward. "Private Michael Halpern." He saluted.

"Salute officers, Halpern," I said. The boy dropped his hand, and, on its way down, in his nervousness, checked to see if his shirt pockets were buttoned.

"Shall I march them over, sir?" Grossbart asked. "Or are you coming along?"

From behind Grossbart, Fishbein piped up. "Afterward, they're having refreshments. A ladies' auxiliary from St. Louis, the rabbi told us last week."

"The chaplain," Halpern whispered.

"You're welcome to come along," Grossbart said.

To avoid his plea, I looked away, and saw, in the windows of the barracks, a cloud of faces staring out at the four of us. "Hurry along, Grossbart," I said.

"O.K., then," he said. He turned to the others. "Double time, *march*!"

They started off, but ten feet away Grossbart spun around and, running backward, called to me, "Good *shabbus,* sir!" And then the three of them were swallowed into the alien Missouri dusk.

Even after they had disappeared over the parade ground, whose green was now a deep blue, I could hear Grossbart singing the double-time cadence, and as it grew dimmer and dimmer, it suddenly touched a deep memory—as did the slant of the light—and I was remembering the shrill sounds of a Bronx playground where, years ago, beside the Grand Concourse, I had played on long spring evenings such as this. It was a pleasant memory for a young man so far from peace and home, and it brought so many recollections with it that I began to grow exceedingly tender about myself. In fact, I indulged myself in a reverie so strong that I felt as though a hand were reaching down inside me. It had to reach so very far to touch me! It had to reach past those days in the forests of Belgium, and past the dying I'd refused to weep over; past the nights in German farmhouses whose books we'd burned to warm us; past endless stretches when I had shut off all softness I might feel for my fellows, and had managed even to deny myself the posture of a conqueror—the swagger that I, as a Jew, might well have worn as my boots whacked against the rubble of Wesel, Münster, and Braunschweig.

But now one night noise, one rumor of home and time past, and memory plunged down through all I had anesthetized, and came to what I suddenly remembered was myself. So it was not altogether curious that, in search of more of me, I found myself following Grossbart's tracks to Chapel No. 3, where the Jewish services were being held.

I took a seat in the last row, which was empty. Two rows in front of me sat Grossbart, Fishbein, and Halpern, holding little white Dixie cups. Each row of seats was raised higher than the one in front of it, and I could see clearly what was going on. Fishbein was pouring the contents of his cup into Grossbart's, and Grossbart looked mirthful as the liquid made a purple arc between Fishbein's hand and his. In the glaring yellow light, I saw the chaplain standing on the platform at the front; he was chanting the first line of the responsive reading. Grossbart's prayer book remained closed on his lap; he was swishing the cup around. Only Halpern responded to the chant by praying. The fingers of his right hand were spread wide across the cover of his open book. His cap was pulled down low onto his brow, which made it round, like a yarmulke. From time to time, Grossbart wet his lips at the cup's edge; Fishbein, his long yellow face a dying light bulb, looked from here to there, craning forward to catch sight of the faces down the row, then of those in front of him, then behind. He saw me, and his eyelids beat a tattoo. His elbow slid into Grossbart's side, his neck inclined toward his friend, he whispered something, and then, when the congregation next responded to the chant, Grossbart's voice was among the others. Fishbein looked into his book now, too; his lips, however, didn't move.

Finally, it was time to drink the wine. The chaplain smiled down at them as Grossbart swigged his in one long gulp, Halpern sipped, meditating, and Fishbein faked devotion with an empty cup. "As I look down amongst the congregation"—the chaplain grinned at the word—"this night, I see many new faces, and I want to welcome you to Friday-night services here at Camp Crowder. I am Major Leo Ben Ezra, your chaplain." Though an American, the chaplain spoke deliberately—syllable by syllable, almost—as though to communicate, above all, with the lip readers in his audience. "I have only a few words to say before we adjourn to the refreshment room, where the kind ladies of the Temple Sinai, St. Louis, Missouri, have a nice setting for you."

Applause and whistling broke out. After another momentary grin, the chaplain raised his hands, palms out, his eyes flicking upward a moment, as if to remind the troops where they were and Who Else might be in attendance. In the sudden silence that followed, I thought I heard Grossbart cackle, "Let the goyim clean the floors!" Were those the words? I wasn't sure, but Fishbein, grinning, nudged Halpern. Halpern looked dumbly at him, then went back to his prayer book, which had been occupying him all through the rabbi's talk. One hand tugged at the black kinky hair that stuck out under his cap. His lips moved.

The rabbi continued. "It is about the food that I want to speak to you for a moment. I know, I know, I know," he intoned, wearily, "how in the mouths of most of you the *trafe* food tastes like ashes. I know how you gag, some of you, and how your parents suffer to think of their children eating foods unclean and offensive to the palate. What can I tell you? I can only say, close your eyes and swallow as best you can. Eat what you must to live, and throw away the rest. I wish I could help more. For those of you who find this impossible, may I ask that you try and try, but then come to see me in private. If your revulsion is so great, we will have to seek aid from those higher up."

A round of chatter rose and subsided. Then everyone sang "Ain Kelohainu"; after all those years, I discovered, I still knew the words. Then, suddenly, the service over, Grossbart was upon me. "Higher up? He means the General?"

"Hey, Shelly," Fishbein said, "he means God." He smacked his face and looked at Halpern. "How high can you go!"

"Sh-h-h!" Grossbart said. "What do you think, Sergeant?"

"I don't know," I said. "You better ask the chaplain."

"I'm going to. I'm making an appointment to see him in private. So is Mickey."

Halpern shook his head. "No, no, Sheldon—"

"You have rights, Mickey," Grossbart said. "They can't push us around."

"It's O.K.," said Halpern. "It bothers my mother, not me."

Grossbart looked at me. "Yesterday he threw up. From the hash. It was all ham and God knows what else."

"I have a cold—that was why," Halpern said. He pushed his yarmulke back into a cap.

"What about you, Fishbein?" I asked. "You kosher, too?"

He flushed. "A little. But I'll let it ride. I have a very strong stomach, and I don't eat a lot anyway." I continued to look at him, and he held up his wrist to reinforce what he'd just said; his watch strap was tightened to the last hole, and he pointed that out to me.

"But services are important to you?" I asked him.

He looked at Grossbart. "Sure, sir."

"'Sergeant.'"

"Not so much at home," said Grossbart, stepping between us, "but away from home it gives one a sense of his Jewishness."

"We have to stick together," Fishbein said.

I started to walk toward the door; Halpern stepped back to make way for me.

"That's what happened in Germany," Grossbart was saying, loud enough for me to hear. "They didn't stick together. They let themselves get pushed around."

I turned. "Look, Grossbart. This is the Army, not summer camp."

He smiled. "So?"

Halpern tried to sneak off, but Grossbart held his arm.

"Grossbart, how old are you?" I asked.

"Nineteen."

"And you?" I said to Fishbein.

"The same. The same month, even."

"And what about him?" I pointed to Halpern, who had by now made it safely to the door.

"Eighteen," Grossbart whispered. "But like he can't tie his shoes or brush his teeth himself. I feel sorry for him."

"I feel sorry for all of us, Grossbart," I said, "but just act like a man. Just don't overdo it."

"Overdo what, sir?"

"The 'sir' business, for one thing. Don't overdo that," I said.

I left him standing there. I passed by Halpern, but he did not look at me. Then I was outside, but, behind, I heard Grossbart call, "Hey, Mickey, my *leben,* come on back. Refreshments!"

"Leben!" My grandmother's word for me!

• • •

One morning a week later, while I was working at my desk, Captain Barrett shouted for me to come into his office. When I entered, he had his helmet liner squashed down so far on his head that I couldn't even see his eyes. He was on the phone, and when he spoke to me, he cupped one hand over the mouthpiece. "Who the hell is Grossbart?"

"Third platoon, Captain," I said. "A trainee."

"What's all this stink about food? His mother called a goddam congressman about the food." He uncovered the mouthpiece and slid his helmet up until I could see his bottom eyelashes. "Yes, sir," he said into the phone. "Yes, sir. I'm still here, sir. I'm asking Marx, here, right now—"

He covered the mouthpiece again and turned his head back toward me. "Lightfoot Harry's on the phone," he said, between his teeth. "This congressman calls General Lyman, who calls Colonel Sousa, who calls the Major, who calls me. They're just dying to stick this thing on me. Whatsa matter?" He shook the phone at me. "I don't feed the troops? What the hell is this?"

"Sir, Grossbart is strange—" Barrett greeted that with a mockingly indulgent smile. I altered my approach. "Captain, he's a very orthodox Jew, and so he's only allowed to eat certain foods."

"He throws up, the congressman said. Every time he eats something, his mother says, he throws up!"

"He's accustomed to observing the dietary laws, Captain."

"So why's his old lady have to call the White House?"

"Jewish parents, sir—they're apt to be more protective than you expect. I mean, Jews have a very close family life. A boy goes away from home, sometimes the mother is liable to get very upset. Probably the boy mentioned something in a letter, and his mother misinterpreted."

"I'd like to punch him one right in the mouth," the Captain said. "There's a goddam war on, and he wants a silver platter!"

"I don't think the boy's to blame, sir. I'm sure we can straighten it out by just asking him. Jewish parents worry—"

"*All* parents worry, for Christ's sake. But they don't get on their high horse and start pulling strings—"

I interrupted, my voice higher, tighter than before. "The home life, Captain, is very important—but you're right, it may sometimes get out of hand. It's a very wonderful thing, Captain, but because it's so close, this kind of thing . . ."

He didn't listen any longer to my attempt to present both myself and Lightfoot Harry with an explanation for the letter. He turned back to the phone. "Sir?" he said. "Sir—Marx, here, tells me Jews have a tendency to be pushy. He says he thinks we can settle it right here in the company. . . . Yes, sir. . . . I *will* call back, sir, soon as I can." He hung up. "Where are the men, Sergeant?"

"On the range."

With a whack on the top of his helmet, he crushed it down over his eyes again, and charged out of his chair. "We're going for a ride," he said.

• • •

The Captain drove, and I sat beside him. It was a hot spring day, and under my newly starched fatigues I felt as though my armpits were melting down onto my sides and chest. The roads were dry, and by the time we reached the firing range, my teeth felt gritty with dust, though my mouth had been shut the whole trip. The Captain slammed the brakes on and told me to get the hell out and find Grossbart.

I found him on his belly, firing wildly at the five-hundred-feet target. Waiting their turns behind him were Halpern and Fishbein. Fishbein, wearing a pair of rimless G.I. glasses I hadn't seen on him before, had the appearance of an old peddler who would gladly have sold you his rifle and the cartridges that were slung all over him. I stood back by the ammo boxes, waiting for Grossbart to finish spraying the distant targets. Fishbein straggled back to stand near me.

"Hello, Sergeant Marx," he said.

"How are you?" I mumbled.

"Fine, thank you. Sheldon's really a good shot."

"I didn't notice."

"I'm not so good, but I think I'm getting the hang of it now. Sergeant, I don't mean to, you know, ask what I shouldn't—" The boy stopped. He was trying to speak intimately, but the noise of the shooting forced him to shout at me.

"What is it?" I asked. Down the range, I saw Captain Barrett standing up in the jeep, scanning the line for me and Grossbart.

"My parents keep asking and asking where we're going," Fishbein said. "Everybody says the Pacific. I don't care, but my parents— If I could relieve their minds, I think I could concentrate more on my shooting."

"I don't know where, Fishbein. Try to concentrate anyway."

"Sheldon says you might be able to find out."

"I don't know a thing, Fishbein. You just take it easy, and don't let Sheldon—"

"*I'm* taking it easy, Sergeant. It's at home—"

Grossbart had finished on the line, and was dusting his fatigues with one hand. I called to him. "Grossbart, the Captain wants to see you."

He came toward us. His eyes blazed and twinkled. "Hi!"

"Don't point that goddam rifle!" I said.

"I wouldn't shoot you, Sarge." He gave me a smile as wide as a pumpkin, and turned the barrel aside.

"Damn you, Grossbart, this is no joke! Follow me."

I walked ahead of him, and had the awful suspicion that, behind me, Grossbart was *marching*, his rifle on his shoulder, as though he were a one-man detachment. At the jeep, he gave the Captain a rifle salute. "Private Sheldon Grossbart, sir."

"At ease, Grossman." The Captain sat down, slid over into the empty seat, and, crooking a finger, invited Grossbart closer.

"Bart, sir. Sheldon Gross*bart*. It's a common error." Grossbart nodded at me; *I* understood, he indicated. I looked away just as the mess truck pulled up to the range, disgorging a half-dozen K.P.s with rolled-up sleeves. The mess sergeant screamed at them while they set up the chow-line equipment.

"Grossbart, your mama wrote some congressman that we don't feed you right. Do you know that?" the Captain said.

"It was my father, sir. He wrote to Representative Franconi that my religion forbids me to eat certain foods."

"What religion is that, Grossbart?"

"Jewish."

"'Jewish, *sir*,'" I said to Grossbart.

"Excuse me, sir. Jewish, sir."

"What have you been living on?" the Captain asked. "You've been in the Army a month already. You don't look to me like you're falling to pieces."

"I eat because I have to, sir. But Sergeant Marx will testify to the fact that I don't eat one mouthful more than I need to in order to survive."

"Is that so, Marx?" Barrett asked.

"I've never seen Grossbart eat, sir," I said.

"But you heard the rabbi," Grossbart said. "He told us what to do, and I listened."

The Captain looked at me. "Well, Marx?"

"I still don't know what he eats and doesn't eat, sir."

Grossbart raised his arms to plead with me, and it looked for a moment as though he were going to hand me his weapon to hold. "But, Sergeant—"

"Look, Grossbart, just answer the Captain's questions," I said sharply.

Barrett smiled at me, and I resented it. "All right, Grossbart," he said. "What is it you want? The little piece of paper? You want out?"

"No, sir. Only to be allowed to live as a Jew. And for the others, too."

"What others?"

"Fishbein, sir, and Halpern."

"They don't like the way we serve, either?"

"Halpern throws up, sir. I've seen it."

"I thought *you* throw up."

"Just once, sir. I didn't know the sausage was sausage."

"We'll give menus, Grossbart. We'll show training films about the food, so you can identify when we're trying to poison you."

Grossbart did not answer. The men had been organized into two long chow lines. At the tail end of one, I spotted Fishbein—or, rather, his glasses spotted me. They winked sunlight back at me. Halpern stood next to him, patting the inside of his collar with a khaki handkerchief. They moved with the line as it began to edge up toward the food. The mess sergeant was still screaming at the K.P.s. For a moment, I was actually terrified by the thought that somehow the mess sergeant was going to become involved in Grossbart's problem.

"Marx," the Captain said, "you're a Jewish fella—am I right?"

I played straight man. "Yes, sir."

"How long you been in the Army? Tell this boy."

"Three years and two months."

"A year in combat, Grossbart. Twelve goddam months in combat all through Europe. I admire this man." The Captain snapped a wrist against my chest. "Do you hear him peeping about the food? Do you? I want an answer, Grossbart. Yes or no."

"No, sir."

"And why not? He's a Jewish fella."

"Some things are more important to some Jews than other things to other Jews."

Barrett blew up. "Look, Grossbart. Marx, here, is a good man—a goddam hero. When you were in high school, Sergeant Marx was killing Germans. Who does more for the Jews—you, by throwing up over a lousy piece of sausage, a piece of first-cut meat, or Marx, by killing those Nazi bastards? If I was a Jew, Grossbart, I'd kiss this man's feet. He's a goddam hero, and *he* eats what we give him. Why do you have to cause trouble is what I want to know! What is it you're buckin' for—a discharge?"

"No, sir."

"I'm talking to a wall! Sergeant, get him out of my way." Barrett swung himself back into the driver's seat. "I'm going to see the chaplain." The engine roared, the jeep spun around in a whirl of dust, and the Captain was headed back to camp.

For a moment, Grossbart and I stood side by side, watching the jeep.

Then he looked at me and said, "I don't want to start trouble. That's the first thing they toss up to us."

When he spoke, I saw that his teeth were white and straight, and the sight of them suddenly made me understand that Grossbart actually did have parents—that once upon a time someone had taken little Sheldon to the dentist. He was their son. Despite all the talk about his parents, it was hard to believe in Grossbart as a child, an heir—as related by blood to anyone, mother, father, or, above all, to me. This realization led me to another.

"What does your father do, Grossbart?" I asked as we started to walk back toward the chow line.

"He's a tailor."

"An American?"

"Now, yes. A son in the Army," he said, jokingly.

"And your mother?" I asked.

He winked. "A *ballabusta*. She practically sleeps with a dustcloth in her hand."

"She's also an immigrant?"

"All she talks is Yiddish, still."

"And your father, too?"

"A little English. 'Clean,' 'Press,' 'Take the pants in.' That's the extent of it. But they're good to me."

"Then, Grossbart—" I reached out and stopped him. He turned toward me, and when our eyes met, his seemed to jump back, to shiver in their sockets. "Grossbart—you were the one who wrote that letter, weren't you?"

It took only a second or two for his eyes to flash happy again. "Yes." He walked on, and I kept pace. "It's what my father *would* have written if he had known how. It was his name, though. *He* signed it. He even mailed it. I sent it home. For the New York postmark."

I was astonished, and he saw it. With complete seriousness, he thrust his right arm in front of me. "Blood is blood, Sergeant," he said, pinching the blue vein in his wrist.

"What the hell *are* you trying to do, Grossbart?" I asked. "I've seen you eat. Do you know that? I told the Captain I don't know what you eat, but I've seen you eat like a hound at chow."

"We work hard, Sergeant. We're in training. For a furnace to work, you've got to feed it coal."

"Why did you say in the letter that you threw up all the time?"

"I was really talking about Mickey there. I was talking *for* him. He would never write, Sergeant, though I pleaded with him. He'll waste away to nothing if I don't help. Sergeant, I used my name—my father's name—but it's Mickey, and Fishbein, too, I'm watching out for."

"You're a regular Messiah, aren't you?"

We were at the chow line now.

"That's a good one, Sergeant," he said, smiling. "But who knows? Who can tell? Maybe you're the Messiah—a little bit. What Mickey says is the Messiah is a collective idea. He went to Yeshiva, Mickey, for a while. He says *together* we're the Messiah. Me a little bit, you a little bit. You should hear that kid talk, Sergeant, when he gets going."

"Me a little bit, you a little bit," I said. "You'd like to believe that, wouldn't you, Grossbart? That would make everything so clean for you."

"It doesn't seem too bad a thing to believe, Sergeant. It only means we should all *give* a little, is all."

I walked off to eat my rations with the other noncoms.

• • •

Two days later, a letter addressed to Captain Barrett passed over my desk. It had come through the chain of command—from the office of Congressman Franconi, where it had been received, to General Lyman, to Colonel Sousa, to Major Lamont, now to Captain Barrett. I read it over twice. It was dated May 14th, the day Barrett had spoken with Grossbart on the rifle range.

Dear Congressman:

First let me thank you for your interest in behalf of my son, Private Sheldon Grossbart. Fortunately, I was able to speak with Sheldon on the phone the other night, and I think I've been able to solve our problem. He is, as I mentioned in my last letter, a very religious boy, and it was only with the greatest difficulty that I could persuade him that the religious thing to do—what God Himself would want Sheldon to do—would be to suffer the pangs of religious remorse for the good of his country and all mankind. It took some doing, Congressman, but finally he saw the light. In fact, what he said (and I wrote down the words on a scratch pad so as never to forget), what he said was "I guess you're right, Dad.

So many millions of my fellow-Jews gave up their lives to the enemy, the least I can do is live for a while minus a bit of my heritage so as to help end this struggle and regain for all the children of God dignity and humanity." That, Congressman, would make any father proud.

By the way, Sheldon wanted me to know—and to pass on to you—the name of a soldier who helped him reach this decision: SERGEANT NATHAN MARX. Sergeant Marx is a combat veteran who is Sheldon's first sergeant. This man has helped Sheldon over some of the first hurdles he's had to face in the Army, and is in part responsible for Sheldon's changing his mind about the dietary laws. I know Sheldon would appreciate any recognition Marx could receive.

Thank you and good luck. I look forward to seeing your name on the next election ballot.

Respectfully,
Samuel E. Grossbart

Attached to the Grossbart communiqué was another, addressed to General Marshall Lyman, the post commander, and signed by Representative Charles E. Franconi, of the House of Representatives. The communiqué informed General Lyman that Sergeant Nathan Marx was a credit to the U.S. Army and the Jewish people.

What was Grossbart's motive in recanting? Did he feel he'd gone too far? Was the letter a strategic retreat—a crafty attempt to strengthen what he considered our alliance? Or had he actually changed his mind, via an imaginary dialogue between Grossbart *père* and Grossbart *fils*? I was puzzled, but only for a few days—that is, only until I realized that, whatever his reasons, he had actually decided to disappear from my life; he was going to allow himself to become just another trainee. I saw him at inspection, but he never winked; at chow formations, but he never flashed me a sign. On Sundays, with the other trainees, he would sit around watching the noncoms' softball team, for which I pitched, but not once did he speak an unnecessary word to me. Fishbein and Halpern retreated, too—at Grossbart's command, I was sure. Apparently he had seen that wisdom lay in turning back before he plunged over into the ugliness of privilege undeserved. Our separation allowed me to forgive him our past encounters, and, finally, to admire him for his good sense.

. . .

Meanwhile, free of Grossbart, I grew used to my job and my administrative tasks. I stepped on a scale one day, and discovered I had truly become a noncombatant; I had gained seven pounds. I found patience to get past the first three pages of a book. I thought about the future more and more, and wrote letters to girls I'd known before the war. I even got a few answers. I sent away to Columbia for a Law School catalogue. I continued to follow the war in the Pacific, but it was not my war. I thought I could see the end, and sometimes, at night, I dreamed that I was walking on the streets of Manhattan—Broadway, Third Avenue, 116th Street, where I had lived the three years I attended Columbia. I curled myself around these dreams and I began to be happy.

And then, one Saturday, when everybody was away and I was alone in the orderly room reading a month-old copy of the *Sporting News,* Grossbart reappeared.

"You a baseball fan, Sergeant?"

I looked up. "How are you?"

"Fine," Grossbart said. "They're making a soldier out of me."

"How are Fishbein and Halpern?"

"Coming along," he said. "We've got no training this afternoon. They're at the movies."

"How come you're not with them?"

"I wanted to come over and say hello."

He smiled—a shy, regular-guy smile, as though he and I well knew that our friendship drew its sustenance from unexpected visits, remembered birthdays, and borrowed lawnmowers. At first it offended me, and then the feeling was swallowed by the general uneasiness I felt at the thought that everyone on the post was locked away in a dark movie theatre and I was here alone with Grossbart. I folded up my paper.

"Sergeant," he said, "I'd like to ask a favor. It is a favor, and I'm making no bones about it."

He stopped, allowing me to refuse him a hearing—which, of course, forced me into a courtesy I did not intend. "Go ahead."

"Well, actually it's two favors."

I said nothing.

"The first one's about these rumors. Everybody says we're going to the Pacific."

"As I told your friend Fishbein, I don't know," I said. "You'll just have to wait to find out. Like everybody else."

"You think there's a chance of any of us going East?"

"Germany?" I said. "Maybe."

"I meant New York."

"I don't think so, Grossbart. Offhand."

"Thanks for the information, Sergeant," he said.

"It's not information, Grossbart. Just what I surmise."

"It certainly would be good to be near home. My parents—you know." He took a step toward the door and then turned back. "Oh, the other thing. May I ask the other?"

"What is it?"

"The other thing is—I've got relatives in St. Louis, and they say they'll give me a whole Passover dinner if I can get down there. God, Sergeant, that'd mean an awful lot to me."

I stood up. "No passes during basic, Grossbart."

"But we're off from now till Monday morning, Sergeant. I could leave the post and no one would even know."

"I'd know. You'd know."

"But that's all. Just the two of us. Last night, I called my aunt, and you should have heard her. 'Come—come,' she said. 'I got gefilte fish, *chrain*—the works!' Just a day, Sergeant. I'd take the blame if anything happened."

"The Captain isn't here to sign a pass."

"You could sign."

"Look, Grossbart—"

"Sergeant, for two months, practically, I've been eating *trafe* till I want to die."

"I thought you'd made up your mind to live with it. To be minus a little bit of heritage."

He pointed a finger at me. "You!" he said. "That wasn't for you to read."

"I read it. So what?"

"That letter was addressed to a congressman."

"Grossbart, don't feed me any baloney. You *wanted* me to read it."

"Why are you persecuting me, Sergeant?"

"Are you kidding!"

"I've run into this before," he said, "but never from my own!"

"Get out of here, Grossbart! Get the hell out of my sight!"

He did not move. "Ashamed, that's what you are," he said. "So you take it out on the rest of us. They say Hitler himself was half a Jew. Hearing you, I wouldn't doubt it."

"What are you trying to do with me, Grossbart?" I asked him. "What are you after? You want me to give you special privileges, to change the food, to find out about your orders, to give you weekend passes."

"You even talk like a goy!" Grossbart shook his fist. "Is this just a weekend pass I'm asking for? Is a Seder sacred, or not?"

Seder! It suddenly occurred to me that Passover had been celebrated weeks before. I said so.

"That's right," he replied. "Who says no? A month ago—and I was in the field eating hash! And now all I ask is a simple favor. A Jewish boy I thought would understand. My aunt's willing to go out of her way—to make a Seder a month later. . . ." He turned to go, mumbling.

"Come back here!" I called. He stopped and looked at me. "Grossbart, why can't you be like the rest? Why do you have to stick out like a sore thumb?"

"Because I'm a Jew, Sergeant. I *am* different. Better, maybe not. But different."

"This is a war, Grossbart. For the time being *be* the same."

"I refuse."

"What?"

"I refuse. I can't stop being me, that's all there is to it." Tears came to his eyes. "It's a hard thing to be a Jew. But now I understand what Mickey says—it's a harder thing to stay one." He raised a hand sadly toward me. "Look at *you*."

"Stop crying!"

"Stop this, stop that, stop the other thing! *You* stop, Sergeant. Stop closing your heart to your own!" And, wiping his face with his sleeve, he ran out the door. "The least we can do for one another—the least . . ."

An hour later, looking out of the window, I saw Grossbart headed across the field. He wore a pair of starched khakis and carried a little leather ditty bag. I went out into the heat of the day. It was quiet; not a soul was in sight except, over by the mess hall, four K.P.s sitting around a pan, sloped forward from their waists, gabbing and peeling potatoes in the sun.

"Grossbart!" I called.

He looked toward me and continued walking.

"Grossbart, get over here!"

He turned and came across the field. Finally, he stood before me.

"Where are you going?" I asked.

"St. Louis. I don't care."

"You'll get caught without a pass."

"So I'll get caught without a pass."

"You'll go to the stockade."

"I'm *in* the stockade." He made an about-face and headed off.

I let him go only a step or two. "Come back here," I said, and he followed me into the office, where I typed out a pass and signed the Captain's name, and my own initials after it.

He took the pass and then, a moment later, reached out and grabbed my hand. "Sergeant, you don't know how much this means to me."

"O.K.," I said. "Don't get in any trouble."

"I wish I could show you how much this means to me."

"Don't do me any favors. Don't write any more congressmen for citations."

He smiled. "You're right. I won't. But let me do something."

"Bring me a piece of that gefilte fish. Just get out of here."

"I will!" he said. "With a slice of carrot and a little horseradish. I won't forget."

"All right. Just show your pass at the gate. And don't tell *anybody*."

"I won't. It's a month late, but a good Yom Tov to you."

"Good Yom Tov, Grossbart," I said.

"You're a good Jew, Sergeant. You like to think you have a hard heart, but underneath you're a fine, decent man. I mean that."

Those last three words touched me more than any words from Grossbart's mouth had the right to. "All right, Grossbart," I said. "Now call me 'sir,' and get the hell out of here."

He ran out the door and was gone. I felt very pleased with myself; it was a great relief to stop fighting Grossbart, and it had cost me nothing. Barrett would never find out, and if he did, I could manage to invent some excuse. For a while, I sat at my desk, comfortable in my decision. Then the screen door flew back and Grossbart burst in again. "Sergeant!" he said. Behind him I saw Fishbein and Halpern, both in starched khakis, both carrying ditty bags like Grossbart's.

"Sergeant, I caught Mickey and Larry coming out of the movies. I almost missed them."

"Grossbart—did I say tell no one?" I said.

"But my aunt said I could bring friends. That I should, in fact."

"*I'm* the Sergeant, Grossbart—not your aunt!"

Grossbart looked at me in disbelief. He pulled Halpern up by his sleeve. "Mickey, tell the Sergeant what this would mean to you."

Halpern looked at me and, shrugging, said, "A lot."

Fishbein stepped forward without prompting. "This would mean a great deal to me and my parents, Sergeant Marx."

"No!" I shouted.

Grossbart was shaking his head. "Sergeant, I could see you denying me, but how you can deny Mickey, a Yeshiva boy—that's beyond me."

"I'm not denying Mickey anything," I said. "You just pushed a little too hard, Grossbart. *You* denied him."

"I'll give him my pass, then," Grossbart said. "I'll give him my aunt's address and a little note. At least let him go."

In a second, he had crammed the pass into Halpern's pants pocket. Halpern looked at me, and so did Fishbein. Grossbart was at the door, pushing it open. "Mickey, bring me a piece of gefilte fish, at least," he said, and then he was outside again.

The three of us looked at one another, and then I said, "Halpern, hand that pass over."

He took it from his pocket and gave it to me. Fishbein had now moved to the doorway, where he lingered. He stood there for a moment with his mouth slightly open, and then he pointed to himself. "And me?" he asked.

His utter ridiculousness exhausted me. I slumped down in my seat and felt pulses knocking at the back of my eyes. "Fishbein," I said, "you understand I'm not trying to deny you anything, don't you? If it was my Army, I'd serve gefilte fish in the mess hall. I'd sell *kugel* in the PX, honest to God."

Halpern smiled.

"You understand, don't you, Halpern?"

"Yes, Sergeant."

"And you, Fishbein? I don't want enemies. I'm just like you—I want to serve my time and go home. I miss the same things you miss."

"Then, Sergeant," Fishbein said, "why don't you come, too?"

"Where?"

"To St. Louis. To Shelly's aunt. We'll have a regular Seder. Play hide-the-matzo." He gave me a broad, black-toothed smile.

I saw Grossbart again, on the other side of the screen.

"Pst!" He waved a piece of paper. "Mickey, here's the address. Tell her I couldn't get away."

Halpern did not move. He looked at me, and I saw the shrug moving up his arms into his shoulders again. I took the cover off my typewriter and made out passes for him and Fishbein. "Go," I said. "The three of you."

I thought Halpern was going to kiss my hand.

• • •

That afternoon, in a bar in Joplin, I drank beer and listened with half an ear to the Cardinal game. I tried to look squarely at what I'd become involved in, and began to wonder if perhaps the struggle with Grossbart wasn't as much my fault as his. What was I that I had to *muster* generous feelings? Who was I to have been feeling so grudging, so tight-hearted? After all, I wasn't being asked to move the world. Had I a right, then, or a reason, to clamp down on Grossbart, when that meant clamping down on Halpern, too? And Fishbein—that ugly, agreeable soul? Out of the many recollections of my childhood that had tumbled over me these past few days, I heard my grandmother's voice: "What are you making a *tsimmes*?" It was what she would ask my mother when, say, I had cut myself while doing something I shouldn't have done, and her daughter was busy bawling me out. I needed a hug and a kiss, and my mother would moralize. But my grandmother knew—mercy overrides justice. I should have known it, too. Who was Nathan Marx to be such a penny pincher with kindness? Surely, I thought, the Messiah himself—if He should ever come—won't niggle over nickels and dimes. God willing, he'll hug and kiss.

The next day, while I was playing softball over on the parade ground, I decided to ask Bob Wright, who was noncom in charge of Classification and Assignment, where he thought our trainees would be sent when their cycle ended, in two weeks. I asked casually, between innings, and he said, "They're pushing them all into the Pacific. Shulman cut the orders on your boys the other day."

The news shocked me, as though I were the father of Halpern, Fishbein, and Grossbart.

That night, I was just sliding into sleep when someone tapped on my door. "Who is it?" I asked.

"Sheldon."

He opened the door and came in. For a moment, I felt his presence without being able to see him. "How was it?" I asked.

He popped into sight in the near-darkness before me. "Great, Sergeant." Then he was sitting on the edge of the bed. I sat up.

"How about you?" he asked. "Have a nice weekend?"

"Yes."

"The others went to sleep." He took a deep, paternal breath. We sat silent for a while, and a homey feeling invaded my ugly little cubicle; the door was locked, the cat was out, the children were safely in bed.

"Sergeant, can I tell you something? Personal?"

I did not answer, and he seemed to know why. "Not about me. About Mickey. Sergeant, I never felt for anybody like I feel for him. Last night I heard Mickey in the bed next to me. He was crying so, it could have broken your heart. Real sobs."

"I'm sorry to hear that."

"I had to talk to him to stop him. He held my hand, Sergeant—he wouldn't let it go. He was almost hysterical. He kept saying if he only knew where we were going. Even if he knew it *was* the Pacific, that would be better than nothing. Just to know."

Long ago, someone had taught Grossbart the sad rule that only lies can get the truth. Not that I couldn't believe in the fact of Halpern's crying; his eyes *always* seemed red-rimmed. But, fact or not, it became a lie when Grossbart uttered it. He was entirely strategic. But then—it came with the force of indictment—so was I! There are strategies of aggression, but there are strategies of retreat as well. And so, recognizing that I myself had not been without craft and guile, I told him what I knew. "It is the Pacific."

He let out a small gasp, which was not a lie. "I'll tell him. I wish it was otherwise."

"So do I."

He jumped on my words. "You mean you think you could do something? A change, maybe?"

"No, I couldn't do a thing."

"Don't you know anybody over at C. and A.?"

"Grossbart, there's nothing I can do," I said. "If your orders are for the Pacific, then it's the Pacific."

"But Mickey—"

"Mickey, you, me—everybody, Grossbart. There's nothing to be done. Maybe the war'll end before you go. Pray for a miracle."

"But—"

"Good night, Grossbart." I settled back, and was relieved to feel the springs unbend as Grossbart rose to leave. I could see him clearly now; his jaw had dropped, and he looked like a dazed prizefighter. I noticed for the first time a little paper bag in his hand.

"Grossbart." I smiled. "My gift?"

"Oh, yes, Sergeant. Here—from all of us." He handed me the bag. "It's egg roll."

"Egg roll?" I accepted the bag and felt a damp grease spot on the bottom. I opened it, sure that Grossbart was joking.

"We thought you'd probably like it. You know—Chinese egg roll. We thought you'd probably have a taste for—"

"Your aunt served egg roll?"

"She wasn't home."

"Grossbart, she invited you. You told me she invited you and your friends."

"I know," he said. "I just reread the letter. *Next* week."

I got out of bed and walked to the window. "Grossbart," I said. But I was not calling to him.

"What?"

"What are you, Grossbart? Honest to God, what are you?"

I think it was the first time I'd asked him a question for which he didn't have an immediate answer.

"How can you do this to people?" I went on.

"Sergeant, the day away did us all a world of good. Fishbein, you should see him, he *loves* Chinese food."

"But the Seder," I said.

"We took second best, Sergeant."

Rage came charging at me. I didn't sidestep. "Grossbart, you're a liar!" I said. "You're a schemer and a crook. You've got no respect for anything. Nothing at all. Not for me, for the truth—not even for poor Halpern! You use us all—"

"Sergeant, Sergeant, I feel for Mickey. Honest to God, I do. I *love* Mickey. I try—"

"You try! You feel!" I lurched toward him and grabbed his shirt front. I shook him furiously. "Grossbart, get out! Get out and stay the hell away from me. Because if I see you, I'll make your life miserable. *You understand that?*"

"Yes."

I let him free, and when he walked from the room, I wanted to spit on the floor where he had stood. I couldn't stop the fury. It engulfed me, owned me, till it seemed I could only rid myself of it with tears or an act of violence. I snatched from the bed the bag Grossbart had given me and, with all my strength, threw it out the window. And the next morning, as the men policed the area around the barracks, I heard a great cry go up from one of the trainees, who had been anticipating only his morning handful of cigarette butts and candy wrappers. "Egg roll!" he shouted. "Holy Christ, Chinese goddam egg roll!"

. . .

A week later, when I read the orders that had come down from C. and A., I couldn't believe my eyes. Every single trainee was to be shipped to Camp Stoneman, California, and from there to the Pacific—every trainee but one. Private Sheldon Grossbart. He was to be sent to Fort Monmouth, New Jersey. I read the mimeographed sheet several times. Dee, Farrell, Fishbein, Fuselli, Fylypowycz, Glinicki, Gromke, Gucwa, Halpern, Hardy, Helebrandt, right down to Anton Zygadlo—all were to be headed West before the month was out. All except Grossbart. He had pulled a string, and I wasn't it.

I lifted the phone and called C. and A.

The voice on the other end said smartly, "Corporal Shulman, sir."

"Let me speak to Sergeant Wright."

"Who is this calling, sir?"

"Sergeant Marx."

And, to my surprise, the voice said, *"Oh!"* Then, "Just a minute, Sergeant."

Shulman's *"Oh!"* stayed with me while I waited for Wright to come to the phone. Why *"Oh!"*? Who was Shulman? And then, so simply, I knew I'd discovered the string that Grossbart had pulled. In fact, I could hear Grossbart the day he'd discovered Shulman in the PX, or in the bowling alley, or maybe even at services. "Glad to meet you. Where you from? Bronx? Me, too. Do you know So-and-So? And So-and-So? Me, too! You work at C. and A.? Really? Hey, how's chances of getting East? Could you do something? Change something? Swindle, cheat, lie? We gotta help each other, you know. If the Jews in Germany . . ."

Bob Wright answered the phone. "How are you, Nate? How's the pitching arm?"

"Good. Bob, I wonder if you could do me a favor." I heard clearly my own words, and they so reminded me of Grossbart that I dropped more easily than I could have imagined into what I had planned. "This may sound crazy, Bob, but I got a kid here on orders to Monmouth who wants them changed. He had a brother killed in Europe, and he's hot to go to the Pacific. Says he'd feel like a coward if he wound up Stateside. I don't know, Bob—can anything be done? Put somebody else in the Monmouth slot?"

"Who?" he asked cagily.

"Anybody. First guy in the alphabet. I don't care. The kid just asked if something could be done."

"What's his name?"

"Grossbart, Sheldon."

Wright didn't answer.

"Yeah," I said. "He's a Jewish kid, so he thought I could help him out. You know."

"I guess I can do something," he finally said. "The Major hasn't been around here for weeks. Temporary duty to the golf course. I'll try, Nate, that's all I can say."

"I'd appreciate it, Bob. See you Sunday." And I hung up, perspiring.

The following day, the corrected orders appeared: Fishbein, Fuselli, Fylypowycz, Glinicki, Gromke, Grossbart, Gucwa, Halpern, Hardy . . . Lucky Private Harley Alton was to go to Fort Monmouth, New Jersey, where, for some reason or other, they wanted an enlisted man with infantry training.

After chow that night, I stopped back at the orderly room to straighten out the guard-duty roster. Grossbart was waiting for me. He spoke first.

"You son of a bitch!"

I sat down at my desk, and while he glared at me, I began to make the necessary alterations in the duty roster.

"What do you have against me?" he cried. "Against my family? Would it kill you for me to be near my father, God knows how many months he has left to him?"

"Why so?"

"His heart," Grossbart said. "He hasn't had enough troubles in a lifetime, you've got to add to them. I curse the day I ever met you, Marx! Shulman told me what happened over there. There's no limit to your anti-Semitism, is there? The damage you've done here isn't enough. You have to make a special phone call! You really want me dead!"

I made the last few notations in the duty roster and got up to leave. "Good night, Grossbart."

"You owe me an explanation!" He stood in my path.

"Sheldon, you're the one who owes explanations."

He scowled. "To *you*?"

"To me, I think so—yes. Mostly to Fishbein and Halpern."

"That's right, twist things around. I owe nobody nothing, I've done all I could do for them. Now I think I've got the right to watch out for myself."

"For each other we have to learn to watch out, Sheldon. You told me yourself."

"You call this watching out for me—what you did?"

"No. For all of us."

I pushed him aside and started for the door. I heard his furious breathing behind me, and it sounded like steam rushing from an engine of terrible strength.

"You'll be all right," I said from the door. And, I thought, so would Fishbein and Halpern be all right, even in the Pacific, if only Grossbart continued to see—in the obsequiousness of the one, the soft spirituality of the other—some profit for himself.

I stood outside the orderly room, and I heard Grossbart weeping behind me. Over in the barracks, in the lighted windows, I could see the boys in their T shirts sitting on their bunks talking about their orders, as they'd been doing for the past two days. With a kind of quiet nervousness, they polished shoes, shined belt buckles, squared away underwear, trying as best they could to accept their fate. Behind me, Grossbart swallowed hard, accepting his. And then, resisting with all my will an impulse to turn and seek pardon for my vindictiveness, I accepted my own.

March 14, 1959

ACKNOWLEDGMENTS

A magazine entering its tenth decade is a ship of Theseus: Every plank having been replaced over time, the galley, never drydocked, is both completely changed and somehow the same. (The barnacles, we like to think, add to its character.) Many oars were in the water to propel this expedition. We're grateful to Rachel Ake, Roger Angell, Madeleine Baverstam, John Bennet, Fabio Bertoni, Andrew Boynton, Chris Curry, Sameen Gauhar, Ann Goldstein, Adam Gopnik, Emily Greenhouse, Mary Hawthorne, Jillian Kosminoff, Risa Leibowitz, Pam McCarthy, Caitlin McKenna, Lev Mendes, Wyatt Mitchell, Erin Overbey, Beth Pearson, Eric Simonoff, and Simon M. Sullivan. Special thanks are due Joshua Rothman, who manned the trawl nets heroically; Alexandra Schwartz, always generous with her editorial skills, who helped reduce bycatch; Noah Eaker, in the crow's nest of Random House, who guided us away from sandbars; and, of course, our marvelous contributors.

CONTRIBUTORS

W. H. AUDEN (1907–1973) was born in York, England, was educated at Oxford University, and achieved fame as a poet in the 1930s. In 1939 he immigrated to the United States and published his first poem in *The New Yorker.* He won a Pulitzer Prize in 1948 for *The Age of Anxiety* and a National Book Award in 1956 for *The Shield of Achilles.*

JOHN BAINBRIDGE (1913–1992) joined the editorial staff of *The New Yorker* in 1938 and started writing for the magazine the next year. His Profile "Toots's World," excerpted in this collection, was the basis of his book *The Wonderful World of Toots Shor* (1951).

WHITNEY BALLIETT (1926–2007) began writing for *The New Yorker* in 1952 and was the magazine's jazz critic from 1957 to 2001. He is the author of *Such Sweet Thunder* (1966), *Improvising* (1977), *American Musicians* (1986), and *Collected Works: A Journal of Jazz 1954–2000* (2000), among other books.

S. N. BEHRMAN (1893–1973), a playwright, screenwriter, and biographer, first appeared in *The New Yorker* in 1929 and continued to contribute to the magazine for nearly half a century.

HARRIET BEN EZRA worked as a researcher at *Time* before joining *The New Yorker* as a Talk of the Town reporter in 1958.

WALTER BERNSTEIN contributed articles to *The New Yorker* from 1939 to 1957, and has written the screenplays of many films, including *Fail Safe, The Front,* and *The House on Carroll Street.* He is the author of *Inside Out: A Memoir of the Blacklist* (1996).

ELIZABETH BISHOP (1911–1979) published her first poem in *The New Yorker* in 1940. She won a Pulitzer Prize in 1956 for *Poems: North &*

South—A Cold Spring and was elected to the American Academy of Arts and Letters in 1976.

HAROLD BRODKEY (1930–1996) published his first short story in *The New Yorker,* included in this collection, in 1954. He contributed fiction, poetry, criticism, and memoir to the magazine throughout his life. He is the author of nine books, among them the short-story collection *First Love and Other Sorrows* (1958) and the novel *The Runaway Soul* (1991).

JOHN BROOKS (1920–1993) began contributing to *The New Yorker* in 1949, and wrote the Annals of Finance column from 1957 until he retired, in 1985. His books include *Once in Golconda* (1969), *Business Adventures* (1969), *The Go-Go Years* (1973), and *The Takeover Game* (1987).

TRUMAN CAPOTE (1924–1984) published his first article for *The New Yorker,* a Talk of the Town piece, in 1944. His books include *Breakfast at Tiffany's* (1958) and *In Cold Blood* (1966), which originated as a series of *New Yorker* articles published the previous year.

HAYDEN CARRUTH (1921–2008) was a poet and a critic. His collection of poems *Scrambled Eggs & Whiskey* (1996) won a National Book Award.

JOHN CHEEVER (1912–1982) sold his first story to *The New Yorker* in 1935 and was a regular contributor of fiction to the magazine until his death. His books include *The Wapshot Chronicle* (1957), *The Wapshot Scandal* (1964), and *Falconer* (1977).

ROBERT M. COATES (1897–1973) joined the staff of *The New Yorker* in 1929. He coined the term "Abstract Expressionism," in a piece for the magazine in 1946. His books include *The Eater of Darkness* (1926) and *The Outlaw Years* (1930).

ROALD DAHL (1916–1990) was a British novelist, memoirist, and short-story writer. He published ten short stories in *The New Yorker* between 1949 and 1959. His books include *Lamb to the Slaughter* (1953), *Boy* (1984), and the celebrated children's books *James and the Giant Peach* (1961), *Charlie and the Chocolate Factory* (1964), and *Matilda* (1988).

JANET FLANNER (1892–1978) became *The New Yorker*'s Paris correspondent in 1925 and wrote the Letter from Paris column until she retired, in 1975. Her books include *The Cubical City* (1926), *Conversation Pieces* (1942), and *Paris Was Yesterday* (1972).

LOUIS P. FORSTER (1910–2004) joined *The New Yorker* as a fact-checker in 1937 and went on to work as assistant to the editor for both Harold Ross and William Shawn, and as an associate editor. Beginning in 1932, he contributed regularly to The Talk of the Town for forty years.

JONATHAN FRANZEN is the author of five novels, among them *The Corrections* (2001), *Freedom* (2010), and *Purity* (2015). Since 1994, he has contributed fiction, criticism, and reportage to *The New Yorker.*

MAVIS GALLANT (1922–2014) was a Canadian-born writer. Between 1951 and 1996, she published 116 stories in *The New Yorker.* Her books include *Green Water, Green Sky* (1959), *The End of the World and Other Stories* (1974), and *Paris Stories* (2002).

WOLCOTT GIBBS (1902–1958) joined *The New Yorker* in 1927 as a writer and editor. In 1940, he became the magazine's drama critic, and in 1950 his play *Season in the Sun* (adapted from his earlier book about Fire Island bohemianism) became a Broadway hit.

BRENDAN GILL (1914–1997) joined *The New Yorker* in 1936 and wrote more than 1,200 pieces for the magazine. He was the magazine's theatre critic from 1968 to 1987, and the main architecture critic from 1987 to 1996. His books include *Tallulah* (1972), *Here at The New Yorker* (1975), and *Late Bloomers* (1996).

MALCOLM GLADWELL has been a staff writer at *The New Yorker* since 1996. In 2001, he was awarded the National Magazine Award for profiles. He is the author of *The Tipping Point* (2000), *Blink* (2005), *Outliers* (2008), *What the Dog Saw* (2009), and *David and Goliath* (2013).

ADAM GOPNIK began writing for *The New Yorker* in 1986. He is the recipient of three National Magazine Awards, for essays and for criticism, and the George Polk Award for magazine reporting. His books include *Paris to the Moon* (2000), *The King in the Window* (2005), *Through the Children's Gate* (2006), and *Angels and Ages* (2009).

NADINE GORDIMER (1923–2014) was a South African writer. She published her first short story in *The New Yorker* in 1951, and contributed fiction, essays, and memoir to the magazine throughout her life. Her books include *Burger's Daughter* (1979), *July's People* (1981), and *No Time Like the Present* (2012). She won the Nobel Prize in Literature in 1991.

JOHN GRAHAM contributed Talk of the Town pieces to the magazine between 1936 and 1952.

EMILY HAHN (1905–1997) began writing for *The New Yorker* in 1928 and became the magazine's China correspondent in 1935. She contributed reportage, poems, and numerous short stories to the magazine until her death. Her more than fifty books include *Chiang Kai-shek* (1955) and *Romantic Rebels* (1967).

PHILIP HAMBURGER (1914–2004) was a staff writer at *The New Yorker* from 1939 until his death. He published eight collections of his work, including *Friends Talking in the Night* (1999) and *Matters of State* (2000), and was one of the few staff writers to have worked for all five of the magazine's editors.

GEOFFREY T. HELLMAN (1907–1977) began reporting for The Talk of the Town in 1929. His books include *How to Disappear for an Hour* (1947), *Mrs. De Peyster's Parties* (1963), *The Smithsonian: Octopus on the Mall* (1966), and *Bankers, Bones and Beetles* (1969).

E. J. KAHN, JR. (1916–1994), became a staff writer at *The New Yorker* in 1937 and remained at the magazine for five decades. He wrote twenty-seven books, including *The Separated People* (1968), *The American People* (1974), and *About The New Yorker and Me* (1979).

ELIZABETH KOLBERT became a staff writer at *The New Yorker* in 1999. She is the author of *The Prophet of Love* (2004), *Field Notes from a Catastrophe* (2006), and *The Sixth Extinction* (2014).

DANIEL LANG (1913–1981) was a war correspondent at *The New Yorker* and a contributor from 1941 until his death. His books include *Early Tales of the Atomic Age* (1948) and *Casualties of War* (1969), about the Incident on Hill 192, which began as a Critic at Large piece for *The New Yorker* and was adapted for film by Brian de Palma.

JOHN LARDNER (1912–1960) wrote *The New Yorker*'s television-and-radio column, The Air, for many years.

REX LARDNER (1918–1998), John Lardner's cousin, was a humorist who began contributing Talk of the Town stories to the magazine in 1946.

JILL LEPORE is the David Woods Kemper '41 Professor of American History at Harvard University and a staff writer at *The New Yorker*, where she has contributed reviews and essays since 2005. Her books include *The Name of War* (1998), *New York Burning* (2005), *The Story of America* (2012), *Book of Ages* (2013), and *The Secret History of Wonder Woman* (2014).

NORMAN LEWIS (1908–2003), an English journalist celebrated for his travel writing, contributed ten pieces to *The New Yorker* between 1955 and 1995. His books include *The Changing Sky* (1959), *The Missionaries* (1988), and *The Tomb in Seville* (2003).

A. J. LIEBLING (1904–1963) joined the staff of *The New Yorker* in 1935 and wrote the magazine's Wayward Press column for many years. His books include *The Sweet Science* (1956), *The Earl of Louisiana* (1961), and *Between Meals* (1962).

DWIGHT MACDONALD (1906–1982) began writing for *The New Yorker* in 1933, and contributed Profiles, essays, and book reviews. His books include *The Memoirs of a Revolutionist* (1957), *Against the American Grain* (1962), and *Discriminations* (1974).

HARDING MASON (1903–1978) was a business manager at *The New Yorker*. He reported more than sixty Talk of the Town stories between 1932 and 1964.

JOHN MCCARTEN (1911–1974) joined the staff of *The New Yorker* in 1934 and began reviewing films for the magazine in 1945.

JOHN MCNULTY (1895–1956) joined *The New Yorker* in 1937 and contributed to the magazine until his death. His books include *Third Avenue New York* (1946), *A Man Gets Around* (1951), and *The World of John McNulty* (1957).

REBECCA MEAD joined *The New Yorker* as a staff writer in 1997. She is the author of *One Perfect Day* (2007) and *My Life in Middlemarch* (2014).

JAMES MERRILL (1926–1995) published his first poem in *The New Yorker*, included in this collection, in 1957. Among his collections are *Divine Comedies* (1976), which won a Pulitzer Prize, and *The Changing Light at Sandover* (1982).

JOSEPH MITCHELL (1908–1996) began writing for the magazine in 1933. His books include *McSorley's Wonderful Saloon* (1943), *Joe Gould's Secret* (1965), and *Up in the Old Hotel and Other Stories* (1992).

MARIANNE MOORE (1887–1972) was a poet, critic, and translator. Her *Collected Poems* (1951) won both a Pulitzer Prize and a National Book Award. She began publishing poems in *The New Yorker* in 1953.

PAUL MULDOON is the Howard G. B. Clark '21 Professor at Princeton University and the poetry editor of *The New Yorker.* His collections of poetry include *New Weather* (1973), *Hay* (1998), and *Moy Sand and Gravel* (2002), which won a Pulitzer Prize. His most recent book is *One Thousand Things Worth Knowing* (2015).

LEWIS MUMFORD (1895–1990), a social theorist, cultural critic, and historian, wrote *The New Yorker*'s architecture column, The Sky Line, from 1931 to 1963. He wrote numerous books, including *The City in History* (1961), which won a National Book Award.

VLADIMIR NABOKOV (1899–1977) was a Russian-born writer who immigrated to the United States in 1940. He began contributing to *The New Yorker* in 1942, and his fiction, poetry, and memoirs appeared in the magazine throughout the rest of his life. His novels include *Lolita* (1955), *Pnin* (1957), and *Pale Fire* (1962).

OGDEN NASH (1902–1971) was a poet renowned for his light verse. He began contributing to *The New Yorker* in 1930, and he spent three months working on the magazine's editorial staff the following year. His books include *I'm a Stranger Here Myself* (1938), *Good Intentions* (1942), and *Bed Riddance* (1969).

EVAN OSNOS became a staff writer at *The New Yorker* in 2008 and began reporting from China for the magazine the same year. His book, *Age of Ambition* (2014), won a National Book Award.

SYLVIA PLATH (1932–1963) published one collection of poetry, *The Colossus* (1960), and a novel, *The Bell Jar* (1963), during her lifetime. Her renown grew after the posthumous publication of her book *Ariel* (1965). Her first poem for *The New Yorker* is included here.

V. S. PRITCHETT (1900–1997), best known for his short stories, was a book critic for *The New Yorker* for many years. His books include *The Complete Short Stories* (1990) and *Complete Collected Essays* (1991).

DAVID REMNICK has been the editor of *The New Yorker* since 1998. He joined the magazine as a staff writer in 1992 and has written more than a hundred pieces. He is the author of *Lenin's Tomb* (1993), for which he won a Pulitzer Prize, *The Devil Problem* (1996), *Resurrection* (1997), *King of the World* (1998), *Reporting* (2006), and *The Bridge* (2010).

ROBERT RICE (1916–1998) was a contributor to *The New Yorker* between 1947 and 1965. He wrote more than a dozen Profiles, on subjects including Mort Sahl, Mike Nichols and Elaine May, and Dave Brubeck.

ADRIENNE CECILE RICH (1929–2012) began publishing poems in *The New Yorker* in 1953. She is the author of twenty-five collections of poems, including *Diving into the Wreck* (1973), which won a National Book Award.

THEODORE ROETHKE (1908–1963) was a poet whose books include *Words for the Wind* (1957) and *The Far Field* (1964), both of which won a National Book Award. He began contributing to *The New Yorker* in 1937.

LILLIAN ROSS became a staff writer at *The New Yorker* in 1945. She is the author of several books, including *Picture* (1952), *Portrait of Hemingway* (1961), and *Here but Not Here* (1998).

PHILIP ROTH sold his first story to *The New Yorker* in 1958. The next year, he published his first book of fiction, *Goodbye, Columbus,* which won a National Book Award. His many novels include *Sabbath's Theater* (1995), which also won a National Book Award, and *American Pastoral* (1997), which received a Pulitzer Prize.

BERTON ROUECHÉ (1910–1994) began contributing to *The New Yorker* in 1944. Two years later, the Annals of Medicine rubric was created for him, and he went on to write for the magazine for nearly five decades. His many books include *Annals of Medical Detection* (1954) and *The Medical Detectives* (1980).

RICHARD H. ROVERE (1915–1979) joined *The New Yorker* in 1944 and wrote the magazine's Letter from Washington from 1948 until his death. His books include *The American Establishment and Other Reports, Opinions, and Speculations* (1962) and *Waist Deep in the Big Muddy* (1968).

WINTHROP SARGEANT (1903–1986) was a writer, critic, and violinist. In 1930, after stints playing with the New York Symphony and the New York Philharmonic, he abandoned his musical career to become a writer. From 1949 to 1972, he wrote the Musical Events column for *The New Yorker,* and he continued to contribute to the magazine until his death.

ANNE SEXTON (1928–1974) began publishing poems in *The New Yorker* in 1959. Her books include *To Bedlam and Part Way Back* (1960), *The Starry Night* (1961), and *The Book of Folly* (1972).

KARL SHAPIRO (1913–2000) contributed poems to *The New Yorker* for more than forty years and from 1946 to 1947 served as Poetry Consultant at the Library of Congress, a position now called the Poet Laureate. He won a Pulitzer Prize for his book *V-Letter and Other Poems* (1944).

LOUIS SIMPSON (1923–2012) was a poet, editor, translator, and critic. His collection of poems *At the End of the Open Road* (1963) won a Pulitzer Prize.

W. D. SNODGRASS (1926–2009) published nine poems in *The New Yorker* between 1954 and 2007. His first collection of poetry, *Heart's Needle* (1959), won a Pulitzer Prize and helped to launch the "confessional" poetry movement.

BERNARD TAPER served, after the Second World War, as one of the U.S. military government's "Monuments men," working to recover art stolen by the Nazis. He began writing for *The New Yorker* in 1942 and continued to contribute to the magazine for the next five decades. He is the author of four books, among them the biography *Balanchine* (1963).

JAMES THURBER (1894–1961) joined *The New Yorker* in 1927 as an editor and a writer; his idiosyncratic cartoons began appearing in the magazine four years later. His books include two children's classics—*The 13 Clocks* (1950) and *The Wonderful O* (1957)—and a memoir of his time at the magazine, *The Years with Ross*. He also co-wrote a successful play, *The Male Animal* (1940), and appeared in *A Thurber Carnival* (1960), a miscellany of his works adapted for the stage.

KENNETH TYNAN (1927–1980) was born in London and made his name as a theatre critic at the London *Observer*. He began writing for *The New Yorker* in 1958, contributing theatre reviews and Profiles on subjects such as Johnny Carson, Tom Stoppard, and Mel Brooks. His books include *Curtains* (1961), *The Sound of Two Hands Clapping* (1975), and *Show People* (1979).

JOHN UPDIKE (1932–2009) contributed fiction, poetry, essays, and criticism to *The New Yorker* for a half century. He is the author of twenty-two novels, including *Rabbit Is Rich* (1981) and *Rabbit at Rest* (1990), both of which won a Pulitzer Prize, as well as fifteen books of short stories, seven collections of poetry, five children's books, a memoir, and a play. His sixth collection of nonfiction, *Due Considerations* (2007), contains more than seventy book reviews and essays that first appeared in the magazine.

JOSEPH WECHSBERG (1907–1983) was born in Czechoslovakia and immigrated to the United States in 1939. He began writing for *The New Yorker* in 1943, and from 1958 to 1973 wrote the magazine's Letter from Berlin. He is the author of *Homecoming* (1946), *The Best Things in Life* (1951), and *Trifles Make Perfection* (1998), among other books.

EUDORA WELTY (1909–2001) was a novelist and short-story writer. She contributed eight short stories to *The New Yorker* between 1951 and 1969. Her books include *Delta Wedding* (1946) and *The Optimist's Daughter* (1972), which won a Pulitzer Prize.

ANTHONY WEST (1914–1987), the son of Rebecca West and H. G. Wells, contributed book reviews, fiction, and reportage to *The New Yorker* from 1951 until 1973. His books include *Heritage* (1955), *Mortal Wounds* (1973), and *H. G. Wells: Aspects of a Life* (1984).

E. B. WHITE (1899–1985) joined the staff of *The New Yorker* in 1927. He contributed humor pieces, poems, short stories, newsbreak captions, and even one cover illustration, but he was most associated with his Notes and Comment essays, which he wrote for thirty years. His books include the children's classics *Stuart Little* (1945), *Charlotte's Web* (1952), and *The Trumpet of the Swan* (1970). He received the Presidential Medal of Freedom in 1963 and an honorary Pulitzer Prize in 1978 for his body of work.

THOMAS WHITESIDE (1918–1997) wrote for *The New Yorker* between 1950 and 1991. His 1970 article "Defoliation," about Agent Orange, led to the curtailment of the herbicide's use. His books include *The Withering Rain* (1971), *Selling Death* (1971), and *The Blockbuster Complex* (1981).

RICHARD WILBUR is a poet and translator. He was the United States Poet Laureate from 1987 to 1988. His books include *Things of This World* (1956), which won a Pulitzer Prize and a National Book Award, and *New and Collected Poems* (1988), which also won a Pulitzer Prize.

WILLIAM CARLOS WILLIAMS (1883–1963) was a poet and a doctor. His books include *Spring and All* (1923), *The Desert Music and Other Poems*

(1954), *Pictures from Brueghel and Other Poems* (1962), which won a Pulitzer Prize, and *Paterson* (1963).

EDMUND WILSON (1895–1972) was a critic, novelist, and poet. He became *The New Yorker*'s book critic in 1944, a position he held for many years. His numerous books include *Axel's Castle* (1931), *To the Finland Station* (1940), and *The Shores of Light* (1952).

ABOUT THE TYPE

This book was set in Caslon, a typeface first designed in 1722 by William Caslon. Its widespread use by most English printers in the early eighteenth century soon supplanted the Dutch typeface that had formerly prevailed. The roman is considered a "workhorse" typeface due to its pleasant, open appearance, while the italic is exceedingly decorative.

ASTOR
THE QUEEN OF SHEBA
GUYS & DOLLS
THE MAN
AUTOWAT
Admiral